SIR ALAN DUNCAN was the Deputy Foreign Secretary, of Parliament for Rutland and Melton until stepping down in 2019. For the past thirty years, he has been at the centre of British political life. He has been at the heart of every Conservative Party leadership race since John Major succeeded Margaret Thatcher in 1990, spearheading William Hague's 1997 leadership campaign, and has held senior positions such as Shadow Secretary of State for Trade and Industry, and Shadow Minister for Justice. He was the first ever openly gay Conservative MP, coming out in 2002.

One of UK politics' most forthright and engaging personalities, Alan is recognised as one of the best-connected and well-informed experts on the Middle East and, as Boris Johnson's deputy in the Foreign Office, sat in the very midst of everything in government that took place between the EU referendum and the UK's eventual exit from the EU in January 2020.

The *Sunday Times* bestseller
Picked as a Waterstones Best Political Book of the Year 2021

'*In the Thick of It* initially grabbed the headlines thanks to the sheer gleeful bitchiness of the insults littered throughout. But there's a more serious message at the heart of this book. What saves it from descending into bitterness and pomposity is the feeling that Duncan frankly has a point; that after four years of purging remain supporters from the Tory ranks, what's left is hardly a government of titans. And as he notes in the foreword, winning a majority has not solved the fundamental problem of reconciling their promises with reality. We may be in the thick of it for a while yet'

GABY HINSLIFF, *Guardian*

'A compelling compendium of high gossip and low intrigue, full of withering put-downs and waspish observations ... Diminutive and dapper, the former oil trader has always been good company and remains ferociously well connected' RACHEL SYLVESTER, *The Times*

'Sensational … Johnson's Cabinet [has been] rocked … It is unprecedented for a politician to lift the lid on feuding in the corridors of power so soon after leaving office … One of the most explosive political diaries ever to be published … Candid, caustic and colourful … In the style of great political diaries like those by Clark or Chips Channon that capture the spirit of the age. The political memoir of the year' *Daily Mail*

'More than merely bracingly readable … [Alan Duncan's diaries] serve the historical function of describing the vortex of vehemence that infected our elite from mid-2016. Insults fly like shot at a pheasant shoot. Actually, make that bullets from a machine gun. This cheerful rudeness will be familiar. Although his acidic quotations were usually "non-attributable, old boy", most people in the business recognised the source. Innocents may be shocked, but such briefings are a valuable part of the truth-telling process. Duncan, for most of his years as an MP, was alive to the absurdity of political life. Duncan chronicles the despair, bafflement, plotting and rising acrimony. Daily entries become black with insults about Brexiteers. Amid this shameless ordure come deft vignettes … Alan Duncan's bark was always worse than his bite' QUENTIN LETTS, *The Times*

'Thoughtful and nuanced … Alan's insights into the role of a foreign office minister provide many of the highlights of the book. I am enjoying it immensely' IAIN DALE

'One of the most sensational, no-holds-barred political diaries of the decade' *Tatler*

'I've thoroughly enjoyed Alan Duncan's incendiary diaries, in which he buries more bodies than a Mafia undertaker'
PIERS MORGAN, *Daily Mail*

'Hugely entertaining' JOHN HUMPHRYS, *Daily Mail*

IN THE THICK OF IT

THE PRIVATE DIARIES
OF A MINISTER

ALAN DUNCAN

WILLIAM
COLLINS

William Collins
An imprint of HarperCollins*Publishers*
1 London Bridge Street
London SE1 9GF

WilliamCollinsBooks.com

HarperCollins*Publishers*
1st Floor, Watermarque Building, Ringsend Road
Dublin 4, Ireland

First published in Great Britain in 2021 by William Collins
This William Collins paperback edition published in 2022

1

A catalogue record for this book is
available from the British Library

ISBN 978-0-00-842229-5

Typeset in Adobe Garamond Pro
Printed and bound in the UK using 100%
renewable electricity at CPI Group (UK) Ltd

MIX
Paper from
responsible sources
FSC
www.fsc.org   FSC™ C007454

This book is produced from independently certified FSC™ paper
to ensure responsible forest management.

For more information visit: www.harpercollins.co.uk/green

For James

CONTENTS

BIOGRAPHICAL NOTE

Sir Alan Duncan, as a Conservative MP and government minister, was at the centre of British politics for nearly thirty years. Born in 1957, Alan is the second of three brothers, and was educated at Beechwood Park School and then Merchant Taylors' School, becoming head boy at both.

His mother Anne was a teacher, and his father was an RAF officer whose job took the family around the world to postings including Gibraltar, Italy and Norway. The family's politics were Liberal, and Alan's first foray into elected politics was at the age of thirteen in a school mock election in 1970 in which he stood unsuccessfully as a Liberal. Two years later he joined the Young Conservatives, and went up to Oxford where he read PPE at St John's College. As a fresher he struck up a friendship with Benazir Bhutto, the future prime minister of Pakistan, and helped to run her successful campaign for the presidency of the Oxford Union.

Other contemporaries included future Cabinet ministers Dominic Grieve and Damian Green, as well as Theresa May (then Theresa Brasier) and her soon-to-be husband Philip May, who was then the more political of the pair. Alan ran successfully for the presidency of the Union himself in 1979, defeating Philip, who later followed him in the role.

After Oxford, Alan began a career in the oil industry, working first for Shell, and then (after a year at Harvard as a Kennedy Scholar) for the legendary and colourful trader Marc Rich, whose company later became Glencore. These years during the 1980s were a period of pioneering change in the industry, which saw the creation of the free market in oil after the price shocks of the 1970s. Duncan helped open up new oil-trading markets in Asia, and was based for a time in Singapore. His business experience during this period afforded him a deep personal understanding of international relations and of the Middle East, which developed into an abiding political interest in the region. He also gained friends and contacts who would remain significant throughout his later life.

Towards the end of the decade he formed his own consultancy to advise foreign governments on oil supplies, establishing his reputation in the industry and giving himself the financial security to embark on a political career. He fought his first unsuccessful parliamentary election in 1987 in the Labour stronghold of Barnsley West and Penistone, and bought a house in Westminster, which was used as the HQ for John Major's leadership campaign in 1990.

Duncan was selected as the Conservative candidate for Rutland and Melton ahead of the 1992 general election, and once in the Commons developed a reputation as a Thatcherite Eurosceptic, carefully navigating a path between these political instincts and personal ambition as a new MP during the turmoil of the government's increasingly bitter civil war over Europe. In 1995 he was appointed as parliamentary private secretary to the Conservative Party chairman, Brian Mawhinney, before the 1997 general election consigned the Conservatives to opposition.

Following the landslide defeat, Duncan championed the leadership campaign of his young friend and former flatmate, William Hague. After this success, he became Hague's parliamentary political secretary and vice-chairman of the Conservative Party. He was then made a junior shadow minister, firstly for health, and then trade and industry.

As part of the generation that held the Conservative Party together during these long years in opposition from 1997–2010, Alan Duncan was a fixture of the Opposition front bench throughout. He served under each of Hague's three successors: Iain Duncan Smith (2001–3), Michael Howard (2003–5) and David Cameron (2005–10), holding six shadow Cabinet posts.

When the Conservatives entered government again after the 2010 election, Alan was appointed as a Minister of State at the Department for International Development, where he served for four years, covering the period of the Arab Spring uprisings, during which he was closely involved in the political transitions in Yemen and Libya.

In 2014 he chose to step down and return to the backbenches, with the award of a knighthood seeming to mark the conclusion of his front-bench career after seventeen years. He was then nominated by the prime minister to join the Intelligence and Security Committee (ISC), and remained in that position as this volume of the diaries begins.

As an MP and since, his domestic life alternates between his London home near Parliament and his constituency home in a small rural village in Rutland, where he lives with his husband James and their cockapoo, Noodle. Having become the first openly gay Conservative MP when he came out in 2002, Alan entered a civil partnership with James Dunseath in 2008. Four years earlier, he had taken a leading role in supporting the passage of the Civil Partnership Act from the Conservative front bench.

Since stepping down from government and leaving Parliament in 2019, he has returned to the private sector and his roots in the oil industry, taking up a position as an executive with a top commodity trader.

PREFACE TO THE PAPERBACK EDITION

The diary entries in this volume conclude just as the UK's first cases of COVID-19 were being reported in early 2020. The pandemic has transformed the world since then, and of course it has transformed our politics, eclipsing Brexit as the primary preoccupation of government and the defining issue of our time. Boris Johnson came to power as 'Mr Brexit', only to find himself having to navigate an unexpected and unprecedented public health crisis, becoming 'Mr Covid' instead.

In such a national and international challenge, we have seen the best and worst of people. For Boris, I think it only fair to record that I gave him favourable billing for his early handling of the pandemic. We now know that his initial hesitancy in imposing a lockdown was a reflection of the scientific advice being received by the government and, knowing nothing of this unique phenomenon, the instruction manual was blank. When the time came to act, I think the nation benefited from the Prime Minister's force of character, which helped sell the draconian restrictions to the public. We saw a leader use his natural charisma to implore us to do what was required, despite the fact that such heavy use of the power of the state clearly went against his liberal instincts.

Within a few weeks, we faced the real prospect that the pandemic could decapitate the government, with Boris fighting for his life in intensive care. It was a sobering moment of reflection, and, like many, I was hugely relieved when he recovered. At that time, he stood as so dominant a figure in his Cabinet that it seemed hard to imagine who might have replaced him. The lack of talent in government is a theme of these diaries, and I think it has become more acute since.

After an initial period of positive reviews, the first major crisis for public confidence in the handling of COVID-19 came with the episode of Dominic Cummings and his infamous trip to Barnard Castle, trading London for leafy Durham – while his family were experiencing Covid symptoms – when all but essential travel was forbidden and infected persons were required to self-isolate. Here we saw both the best and worst of Boris. His backing of his chief adviser showed a level of instinctive personal loyalty that would otherwise be commendable. While the press and public cried for Cummings's head, the Prime Minister ordered the government to close ranks and defend him. It is an instinct we have seen from Boris at other times – when Priti Patel was under fire for bullying officials, he ordered his MPs to 'form a square around the Pritster' and blocked publication of the standards report into her conduct. More recently, he was stupidly advised to do the same for Owen Paterson, seeking to excuse his wrongdoing by applying a three-line whip to negate a damning standards report. This backfired spectacularly, leading to Paterson's resignation as an MP and a crushing by-election defeat.

In all these instances, Boris's behaviour stemmed from a desire to stand by colleagues and not let them be hounded from office by political and media criticism. All well and good. But it also betrayed a cavalier disregard for due process and a frequent tolerance of the intolerable. In the case of Cummings and his sojourn to County Durham, the obvious and necessary political response would have been a severe prime ministerial reprimand, accompanied by a grovelling public apology from the culprit. Any adviser with the Prime Minister's best interests at heart would have accepted this, or even quit entirely to avoid further damage to the government and its vital public health messaging. That Boris failed to compel even an apology from his appointee was a serious and worrying failure of leadership. We can now speculate that he did not dare banish Cummings for fear of being implicated himself.

One of the themes of this diary is my firm disdain for overmighty apparatchiks, who have recently come to blight the body politic.

Bright and gifted advisers, who might have much to offer to public service, are spoiled by being raised above their proper station and given too much power and authority. Without fail, it goes to their head and causes no end of problems for their bosses, who are left to clear up the mess they leave behind.

Dominic Cummings will be viewed by history as the evil genius behind the Vote Leave campaign, who turned anti-establishment disinformation into an art form with which to win the EU referendum, and can thus be credited or blamed for much of what followed with Brexit. He clearly had some campaigning skills, but placing him at the epicentre of power in Downing Street with unquestioned authority over the conduct of government was utter folly. Anyone with any experience of Cummings and his way of working could have predicted it was never going to end well, and indeed it did not. As Boris endures repeated withering broadsides from his sacked guru, he must rue the day he helped create this monster.

If the lesson were not clear enough with Cummings, another obvious error of judgement was the raising up of David Frost as the Prime Minister's all-powerful Brexit negotiator. Another special adviser who got too big for his boots, Frost has shown himself to be unduly infected by his own self-importance, and politically simplistic. Boris created him, indulged him and put him in the House of Lords. As a fairly undistinguished former diplomat, he was never of the calibre needed to conclude such a high-profile negotiation, which should in any case have been led by ministers. The idea that he should be nominated to become the UK's National Security Adviser was absurd, and insulting to our security services. While that appointment rightly ran into the sand, Frost's baffling rise continued with his appointment to the Cabinet to oversee the aftermath of Brexit. Now that the deal he negotiated has begun to unravel and the going has got tough, he's flounced off, keeping the ermine and a seat in our legislature for life, and laughably appointing himself the guardian of Conservative philosophy.

Given that the whole basis for the Johnson premiership was to 'Get Brexit Done', the departures of first Cummings and then Frost are significant. Having steered Boris to win the Brexit referendum on a set of crude and unrealistic platitudes, they repeated the trick to help him win the Tory crown, and then a general election, while holding reality at bay long enough to sign up to a deal with the EU and declare Brexit 'done'.

Inevitably the fundamental dilemma of the Brexit negotiation would always re-emerge: that you cannot diverge from the EU's customs arrangements without creating a border somewhere – either on the island of Ireland or in the Irish Sea. The first option creates problems with the Good Friday Agreement (an international treaty), while the second creates problems for the Union of the United Kingdom itself. It was on that basic truth that the entire Theresa May government was broken, as a woman of innate intellectual honesty struggled in vain to agree a compromise to square the circle while satisfying the demands of the Brexit truthers. She thought it impossible, and refused to yield to magical thinking. Boris and his cohorts destroyed her and felt unconstrained by such considerations. They simply denied the dilemma existed and continued to do so until it became unavoidable. At which point the cheerleaders of his confidence trick jumped ship.

Were it not for COVID-19 blowing all else from the headlines, it would be the exposure of Brexit's implications that would by now be driving the political agenda. There would be no way of disguising the impact on trade, investment and our economy. As it is, the pandemic has confused the picture, with issues such as price rises, shortages of labour and interruptions of supply chains being attributed to coronavirus. Disentangling the effects is not easy, so many commentators and voters have been prepared to give the government the benefit of the doubt. But they won't do so indefinitely.

More worryingly for the government, its new voter coalition in the 'Red Wall' will also not suspend their disbelief forever. Indeed, recent polling evidence has suggested that they too are beginning to suspect they were sold a false prospectus. Talk of 'levelling up' has been aimed squarely at convincing those deprived Leave-voting parts of the country that Boris Johnson's Tories care about them and can offer them all manner of goodies now the UK has thrown off the shackles of the EU, which was somehow to blame for their plight. The emptiness of that promise was then compounded by the fact that coronavirus emptied the Treasury's coffers. Even if the Johnson government of December 2019 had believed in the promises it was making, the Johnson government of 2022 had no funds with which to honour the cheques. The only things many will see being levelled up in the near future will be taxes, interest rates and prices.

Just two years on from his resounding victory in the 2019 general election, Boris suffered an extraordinary nosedive in late 2021, with one crisis after another raising questions about his leadership. While it does appear to be an extraordinary turnaround in the Prime Minister's fortunes, no one can honestly say there was no warning. Indeed, some might say that his whole career to date has been one long warning of what to expect from him. Certainly, my time working alongside Boris in the Foreign Office, charted in these pages, has proved a remarkably accurate indicator of his likely performance in power. As readers will see, there were flashes of brilliance and glimpses of the impressive statesman he could be, were he only able to exert the self-discipline required to take the job seriously and resist the urge to play it for laughs. Once in Number 10, that familiar frustrating pattern was again seen all too often. There has been no discipline, with everything being short-term and media-focused.

Voters may be persuaded to give some leeway for the economic impact of the pandemic, and to excuse the consequences of Brexit as worthwhile, or temporary. But they will not excuse incompetence, arrogance and apparent corruption. Here we see parallels with the 1992–97 Conservative government, which rotted and decayed before our very eyes until it collapsed amid acrimony and was firmly put out of its misery by the voters. But the difference is that at no point in the Major government was the Prime Minister's personal integrity challenged: in the Johnson administration it has become the central charge. This telling contrast was underlined by an excoriating attack on Boris by his predecessor Sir John Major, who used a lecture in February 2022 to decry the damage being done to our democracy by the Prime Minister's cavalier attitude to truthfulness and the rule of law.

The lesson that should be taken from this is what I call the 'dripping ceiling' effect. The 'drip, drip' of numerous scandals and failings has a cumulative effect: you can do your best to put out enough buckets to catch the drips and convince yourself it'll all be OK – but at some point the whole bloody ceiling will come crashing down around you. What is needed is to locate the source of the problems, get a grip and turn the tap off. That means instilling some order and competence, and giving the government a sense of direction. That would be a tall order for even the most accomplished of conviction politicians, or the most talented of Cabinets. I don't think it controversial to suggest that under Boris we have neither.

It may be the case that every generation looks at the current crop of politicians and judges them inferior to the giants of the past. But having been notably rude about several members of the Johnson Cabinet in these diaries, I must claim a degree of retrospective vindication in my assessment of a number of them.

First, we see Dominic Raab, whose woeful performance at the Foreign Office left that institution diminished and directionless. Placed there purely as a Brexit believer rather than for any notable skills he seemed to possess, he lived down to all expectations. His final failure of leadership in going AWOL during the evacuation of Kabul may have been what did for him in the end, but it merely capped an inglorious tenure in which he was unable to direct the wrong-headed amalgamation of the Department for International Development and the Foreign Office.

This merger has been nothing short of disastrous and betrays a fundamental lack of understanding of the objectives of the UK's international development principles. Alongside the underhand cut in our aid budget, it has maintained less effective projects that are bound by three- or four-year contracts, while cutting funds for essential food and medicine in areas facing famine and conflict, such as Yemen. It has harmed our authority and reputation overseas and reduced the influence of international affairs within government by half. In committees and in Cabinet, where previously there were two ministers and two departments speaking up for our global objectives, now there is just one. Since he left the Diplomatic Service in August

2020, Sir Simon (now Lord) McDonald's legacy has become one of wholesale diplomatic collapse.

In yet another parallel with the troubles of a previous Conservative government, Raab's graceless reaction to his demotion from the Foreign Office led to him demanding the empty title of Deputy Prime Minister, while haggling to try to cling onto the use of Chevening House as a weekend retreat. It was a sorry saga, echoing the demotion of Geoffrey Howe in 1989 that signalled the beginning of the end for Margaret Thatcher.

Then there is the embarrassment of Priti Patel's stewardship of the Home Office. As covered in these diaries, her conduct in her previous ministerial role ended in her being sacked in disgrace for conducting an unauthorised foreign policy behind the back of the Foreign Office, and deceiving the Prime Minister about it. This alone should have barred her from ever holding office again, at least in any respectable government. Still worse, we now have evidence of her bullying of officials, in a clear breach of the Ministerial Code that should have seen her ignominiously sacked for a second time. Instead, it was the Permanent Secretary of the Home Office and the Prime Minister's ethics adviser who resigned in disgust at the way Patel was allowed to get away with her behaviour.

Johnson's misguided loyalty towards his home secretary might be more understandable had she been doing a good job, but she transparently has not. She has failed to get a grip of the migrant crisis, while making herself and the government look ridiculous due to the endless empty posturing against her French counterparts in the hope of some cheap tabloid headlines.

Finally in my trio of hopeless ministers we come to the perpetually scheming Gavin Williamson. Thanks to the memoirs of Gavin Barwell (Theresa May's chief of staff at Number 10), we have confirmation of what we all suspected – that Williamson shamelessly used his position as chief whip to force the removal of the defence secretary and award himself the job instead. His slippery and untrustworthy nature was confirmed for all to see when he was himself sacked in disgrace after being found to have leaked from the National Security Council. Like Patel, this should have ruled him out of any return to high office, but apparently not in Johnson's shabby Cabinet of toadies.

Plotting and leaking appear to have been Williamson's only skill-set, and he made such an embarrassing mess of his tenure at the Department for Education that even Boris couldn't miss it, and fired him in 2021's reshuffle. It was a rare example of an incompetent minister being held to account, and welcome though his departure was, there needed to have been a much more thorough clear-out. Patel remains an embarrassment to her office, and it perhaps won't be long before Raab does to the justice system what he did to Britain's international standing.

Believe it or not, I don't relish having my scathing assessments of these ministers vindicated. It is a sad indictment of the state of our politics when such people can rise to the top, and even return after being found guilty of what would in any other walk of life be classed as gross misconduct.

My frustration at the rise of overly ambitions, ruthless and pushy ministers during my time in government can too easily be dismissed as sour grapes, and indeed that was the charge made by my critics as they sought to discredit these diaries. Readers must decide for themselves, but I would far rather look back on my two terms as a Minister of State with a clear conscience than have had to live with the consequences of the undignified jostling and backstabbing required to elbow your way to the top table. This culture is what deters many of the people who might otherwise seek a career in Parliament, and it is an increasing problem. The pool of talent from which our ministers are chosen is becoming smaller, and this inevitably undermines the way we are governed.

Any objective analysis can only conclude that government and Parliament have become debased by the cumulative effects of the last few decades of political fashion. First we had a culture of spin from New Labour that prized style over substance and focused leading politicians on campaigning and pandering rather than governing. Tony Blair's success led my own party to adopt this approach as a formula for success, and it has become the default mode of politics. The culture of overmighty advisers, short-termism and opportunism continued through the Coalition years, before we hit the jackpot of political dysfunction in the Brexit years, when cynicism and outright dishonesty progressively defeated the last vestiges of honest debate.

This has been a progressive degradation, and the current government is not by any means solely responsible for where we find ourselves. For years we have had far too much government by press release, ministers throwing money at problems without proper consideration, and a lack of robust policy-making. But after the last few years, these structural defects have been compounded by a government that seems content to disregard inconvenient facts, stoke crude 'culture war' divisions and indulge the worst excesses of Conservative backbench mindlessness while tolerating standards of conduct that fall well below acceptable levels.

It might seem that I paint an unrelentingly bleak picture of the state of the country. But it need not be a depressing outlook, and one of my great frustrations looking at 2022 is that the foundations are there for the UK to take a proper leading role in the world, and for our politics and institutions to be revitalised for the future. Clear-sighted determination and political leadership are required to 'build back better' after the pandemic and deliver the promised benefits following Brexit. I believe it can be done. So here, from this armchair general, is the broad sweep of what that might look like.

Britain's main challenges are economic and social. The fantastic, perhaps accidental, achievement of Boris Johnson's 2019 election triumph was to parachute into working-class areas that Labour had taken for granted for so long. On the back of Brexit, the real challenge is Disraelian: to improve the condition of the working class. This requires deep thought about deprived areas, educational attainment, split families and the simple ability of poorer people to pay their bills. The 'levelling up' slogan could contain so much to address these challenges, but perhaps the greatest tragedy of this government is that no adequate thought has yet been injected into this slogan of hope.

We also need to establish what the UK's role should be in the post-Brexit era. This should of course have been established by mature debate during and after the 2016 referendum, but instead we had mindless sloganising and nationalistic tubthumping, and sadly haven't progressed much beyond that. Endless soundbites are no replacement for a hard-headed assessment of the UK's strategic interests and the development of suitable diplomatic objectives to fulfil our ambitions on the world stage.

The UK has arguably lacked a cogent foreign policy for well over a decade, possibly two. Since the invasion of Iraq in 2003 and the debacle that followed, a clear statement of the UK's long-term foreign policy has been long overdue, but has never quite emerged. The most we've had recently are two slogans – 'Global Britain' and the 'Rules-based international order' – but little flesh has been put on even these bare bones. The attempt since Brexit to promote trade agreements as a replacement for foreign policy is flimsy and unconvincing – and is no substitute for difficult decisions. It also begs the question whether our foreign policy is mercantilist more than moral.

Devising and pursuing a coherent British foreign policy will and should require Britain occasionally to have gritty opinions which might diverge from those of the United States. The common view is that we are entirely supine to the US and that this is fundamentally what our foreign policy amounts to. Without contriving a moment of confrontation, we should be unafraid to make our own choices and stand by them, even when they differ from those of our American partners. If we believe in a 'rules-based international order', we should make a firm stand for the equitable application of those rules. For example, no British Prime Minister or foreign secretary in recent years has been able to explain convincingly how they can attack the Russians' activities in Ukraine yet not condemn the Israelis' state-backed settler violence in Palestine. By making firm and consistent interventions on issues of principle and decency, Britain can retain a leading and important role as an independent diplomatic actor in the years ahead.

Central to achieving this role in practice, however, has to be the restoration of the Foreign Office as a major Department of State. The wrong-headed merger with DFID, as I have noted, is an experiment that will harm our aid programme. But an associated danger is that this flurry of activity in Whitehall, with the new letterheads and brass plaques, is seen as a strengthening of the Foreign Office, when it is in fact the opposite. An increased headcount from displaced DFID staff and the inclusion of the overseas aid budget in the Foreign Office's accounts are no compensation for the hollowing out of our Diplomatic Service and the continued shrinking of our global footprint.

Recent reports have suggested the Treasury is seeking a 20 per cent cut in Foreign Office spending. Their budget is already half what it should be. Penny-pinching on the £2.4 billion cost of our entire Diplomatic Service around the world is a harmful false economy for 'Global Britain'. If Chancellor Rishi Sunak thinks this is an easy hit, he should realise that in future it will become an easy hit against him.

We have already seen the short-sighted flogging off of many historic and irreplaceable embassies around the world, and cuts upon cuts to the staffing and funding of our diplomatic missions. The result is a diminished presence on the world stage and demoralised diplomats doing the best they can on a shoestring from tatty buildings with not enough staff. An increasing number of those staff are local nationals employed at cheaper rates, which has meant there is often no realistic career path for junior diplomats from the UK.

In all this, Boris has made the right noises about flying the Union flag – and indeed his decision to paint it on the tailfin of the government's modest RAF Voyager plane gained a lot of headlines. But the real question is what happens when ministers step off that plane in foreign capitals? How well-equipped are the Ambassadors who meet them on the tarmac? Who is doing the work of keeping that flag flying, oiling the wheels of diplomacy and promoting the UK's strategic national interests?

A proper commitment to Global Britain means putting some money where our mouth is – investing in recruitment and training of the best and brightest diplomats, and giving them the resources in-country to do the job we send them to do. And yes, to do it with a bit of style! The British Ambassador in an important foreign capital should be seen flying the Union flag from their official Rolls-Royce, and entertaining government officials and local business leaders with excellent food and wine beneath the chandeliers of the palatial British embassy. You can't have soft power without at least some hard cash.

Alongside an increase in resources for the FCO itself and the restoration of DFID, there is a need for greater assertiveness by the Foreign Office within government. Too often in recent years it has been pushed about by the whims of Number 10, by prime ministers who have tried to be their own foreign secretaries and not taken sufficient account of professional diplomats and analysts with long experience who know what they're talking about. We also need more careful selection of ministers, promoting those with an affinity for the complexities of diplomacy, and leaving them in post long enough to acquire experience and establish valuable relationships. In the last decade we've had half a dozen ministers for the Middle East and nine ministers for Africa. That constant churn makes it impossible for them to gain expertise even if they are up to the job.

At a time when Russian belligerence threatens a crisis in Ukraine, it exposes serious doubts about the effectiveness, or perhaps even the existence, of our foreign policy. And when I look at the Gulf, the withering of our relationships there was symbolised for me by the death in January this year of Sir Erik Bennett at the age of ninety-three. Erik had for decades been a close adviser to Sultan Qaboos of Oman, acting as a vital link between our two countries. With the Sultan himself having died in 2020, these diaries chart the end of an era in that long-standing diplomatic relationship. My fear is that not enough is being done to cultivate similar bilateral friendships around the world.

Britain taking a leading role abroad would help restore some much-needed national self-confidence, but we also need to put our own house in order. The depressing diminution of our political institutions need not be irreversible, and if the Brexiteers' simplistic talk of the need to 'take back control' means anything, it should be put into practice through the revitalisation of our democratic structures.

To address the quality of MPs, we need to look again at the way we select candidates. Well-meaning efforts have been made to bring more diversity to the House, but too much of this has been rather superficial, with people of real quality still finding the prospect of public life unappealing, for understandable reasons. The system puts the power of selection in the hands of an increasingly unrepresentative and shrinking clique of party members who barely represent their party's voters, let alone the public at large. That has to be addressed somehow if we are ever to have a truly representative and sensible Parliament.

It is also well past time to reform the House of Lords, which has become something of a dustbin for failed candidates, cronies and advisers, rather than a dignified repository of the great and the good of the realm. The reform plan under the Coalition that provided for a mostly elected house ran into the sand, but was a sensible measure which should be revived.

I have already hinted at the reforms I would welcome inside government itself. These would include better long-term thinking, less pandering to the populist media agenda and less power in the hands of unelected political advisers. Some might wince at the paradox of having left the EU to be shot of the domination of unelected officials, only to be governed by the same ilk back home. Ministers must reassert their own importance, both within their departments and in relation to Number 10. This assumes of course that the quality of ministers should also increase, with expertise and experience, rather than media profile and slavish loyalty, being rewarded. The initiative for that must come from the top.

All of this prompts some fundamental questions about whether the Victorian model of our parliamentary democracy is shot through and irreparable. If that is the case, would we not be better to acknowledge reality and devise a new settlement? For decades it has been said that we have a presidential system in all but name, so perhaps we should make that official. We could elect the Prime Minister separately, and allow them to draw their Cabinet and ministers from outside Parliament, as happens in the United States. This might seem a leap too far, but we should at least be open to some more radical thinking about how we improve our politics.

The question is whether Boris has the ability or inclination to pursue such an ambitious agenda. Or if he does, whether he will be permitted to remain in office long enough to see it through. Readers of the future will have the answer, but I am constrained in this preface by a lack of clairvoyancy. All I can say is that despite the harsh words I have often thrown his way, I would genuinely like Boris to seize the opportunity. He is a compelling character, and has the ability to shape how this story ends for him.

If he fails, the seeds of his failure will have been long sown. Tragic characters in literature are fated to be brought low by an innate flaw that tortures their soul and prevents them from achieving their destiny of greatness. In the case of Boris, the only thing stopping him from currently assuming the role of a doomed Shakespearian king is the fact that he seems determined instead to cast himself as Falstaff, or one of the other comic characters: a blustering rogue whose principal role in proceedings is to provide temporary light relief from the serious events of the play. He might reflect on the irony if he suddenly finds himself with time to complete his promised biography of Shakespeare.

I began my parliamentary career in the 1990s, and I believe there are some lessons we can take from that time. A Conservative Party that comes to be seen as incompetent and arrogant after years in office is destined to lose to a Labour Party that appears more mainstream and capable, or at least more trustworthy. The only way to avoid this fate is for the Conservatives to be the ones projecting energy, determination and optimism. In the 1990s we were the victims of our own success. Having turned the country around and shaped a new political consensus, we were unable to offer a convincing answer to the question 'What do we do for an encore?'. The challenge for today's Conservatives is to give a better sense of what they want to do with power.

There are also striking parallels with the 1990s for readers of these diaries. In the pages that follow we have the sad story of a fundamentally decent Prime Minister struggling gamely on amid the mounting chaos of a parliamentary party that seems collectively to have lost its mind over the vexed issue of Europe. There are leadership challenges, votes of no confidence and the gradual loss of authority as the government's majority melts away. Theresa May's experience in this regard echoes that of John Major before her.

Thirty years ago, that story ended with a landslide defeat for the Conservatives. By contrast, the years of Brexit turmoil covered in these pages ended in a landslide victory in the 2019 general election.

But just over two years later, the government was once again beset by crises and challenges to the Prime Minister's leadership. Normally when a Prime Minister becomes so unpopular it's because the government has taken difficult decisions and has hit the mid-term blues. In 2022, however, the issue hung entirely on the personal integrity of the Prime Minister himself. The fate of Boris Johnson, as he has perhaps always wanted, is all about Boris Johnson. Some concluded that his electoral appeal had been irreparably damaged, with many of his previous strengths turned into liabilities.

The public reacted with understandable fury at the revelation in January that while the rest of the country was banned from social contact by force of law, those who imposed the rules seemed to think they didn't apply in Downing Street. The 'partygate' saga veered between high drama and farce. But the picture it has painted is a perfect illustration of the flaws in Boris's character: the chaotic lack of organisation, the cavalier attitude to rules of proper conduct and his brazen disregard for the truth when he gets caught. These are familiar patterns of behaviour, which have too often been overlooked by his colleagues because he was seen as a winner. Now, as nervous Conservative MPs looked at the dire opinion polls, they suddenly saw the Emperor had no clothes. As Andrew Mitchell vividly said, his behaviour 'like battery acid, is corroding the fabric of the Conservative Party'.

Watching from afar, I felt a personal connection to several of the elements of the scandal. First, there is the formidable character of Sue Gray emerging as the much-vaunted arbiter of ethics in Whitehall. As readers will discover in these diaries, I had my own experience of this infamous civil servant's methods and was less than satisfied with the outcome. But whatever one thinks of her approach, her interim report into the Downing Street parties during lockdown contained ferocious condemnation of the failure of leadership in Number 10. Equally striking was her utterly damning conclusion that the actions of those who worked there, from the Prime Minister down, 'represent a serious failure to observe not just the high standards expected of those working at the heart of government but also of the standards expected of the entire British population at the time'.

These diaries begin with the downfall of David Cameron and the contest to succeed him, in which Theresa May emerged victorious. At the end she herself falls, and we see the triumphant rise of Boris Johnson. Between those events, my misgivings about Boris hardened into a conviction that he was fundamentally unsuited to high office. This volume is the story of how I came to that opinion. As others reach that sad conclusion for themselves, I suspect it might now receive a rather more sympathetic hearing.

When a leader is politically wounded, the attacks on them increase as their enemies smell blood. Rivals start to plot, and supporters melt away. In the bunker itself, things become ever more desperate and chaotic. February 2022 saw an exodus of key Downing Street personnel, with the departure of the communications director, chief of staff and the Prime Minister's principal private secretary. This was unconvincingly spun as being part of a planned shake-up of Number 10 in the wake of the Gray report, but the fightback was sabotaged by Boris himself in the House of Commons with a crass attack on Labour leader Sir Keir Starmer over the past decision of the Crown Prosecution Service not to prosecute Jimmy Savile. The Prime Minister's refusal to apologise for this unedifying performance led one of his closest policy advisers to quit Downing Street in disgust, and sparked a new round of criticism from MPs. One step forward, two steps back. He then contrived a ministerial reshuffle which among other things put a Cabinet minister into the role of chief of staff in the new 'Office of the Prime Minister' and moved the other deckchairs around in order to appoint a new chief whip.

As I was writing this, it was still not clear how the story would end for Boris. The Metropolitan Police had yet to conclude its investigation, the outcome of which might prove decisive. The humiliation of a Prime Minister being fined for breaking his own lockdown laws might prompt Conservative MPs to act swiftly. It has so far seemed like a slow puncture rather than a burst tyre on the Boris bus. But it remains to be seen whether he will be able to repair it and continue, or if the passengers are now set on replacing the driver.

Alan Duncan, February 2022

Brexit: the withdrawal by the United Kingdom from its membership of the European Union. The portmanteau word from 'Britain's'/'British' and 'exit' arose in common parlance in advance of the 2016 referendum on UK membership of the EU, and soon became the accepted term for the process, widely used across the world.

INTRODUCTION

As soon as I became a minister in 2010, I knew that more would happen in my daily life than I would ever be able to remember. I wanted total recall, and the only way of achieving it was to write it down. Every day I kept my appointments diary in my pocket, and would scribble notes and prompts on it as the day unfolded. Then every night or the next morning I'd tap it all into my laptop. I was never far from the all-important memory stick. So one of the motivations was recollection – protection against the brain-fade of age.

But the greater driver was catharsis. Political life can be suffocating. The pettiness of poor decision-making and the strutting of tiresome egos are a constant frustration. I could see that the only way to keep calm and carry on was to write it all down. Use the pen and the page to emote, to download and to vent my feelings. These were often as warm as they were venomous. So much that happened was worth recording but could not be said. Temper was invariably better kept than expressed. It was better to put gossip and fury into a diary than tell a journalist. So instead of briefing the press, I wrote it down. Some might see it as a form of therapy.

Journalism is often called the first draft of history, but a diary is a primary source. Whereas our newspapers express the nation's prejudices, a diary can provide an unfiltered account of events. Assuming it is written up at the time, unvarnished and in the moment, it can capture the hardest thing for any historian to reconstruct – the feeling of the time, with all its uncertainties and lack of hindsight. That is what I hope these diaries can offer to the reader today, and to

historians in the years to come. Much has already been written about
the turbulent period of Brexit, the twists and turns of events, the
personalities and the dramas. Many of the events recorded here are
familiar, but perhaps my perspective can offer some additional
insight and flavour.

The volume begins at the start of 2016, as the weeks tick by to the
calling of the EU referendum. It ends four years later as the UK
finally leaves the European Union. In the interim, two prime ministers fall, there are two general elections, two Conservative leadership
elections and a no-confidence vote. Looking back, it seems an
extraordinarily eventful and even chaotic period in our history. At
least until the next one …

For me, I begin as a backbencher, my ministerial career seemingly
behind me. In the aftermath of the referendum I return to government as a Foreign Office minister, serving as de facto deputy to two
foreign secretaries, Boris Johnson and Jeremy Hunt. These two very
different men then go on to campaign against one another for the
premiership, while I stand down from government and then from
Parliament. For my own life and career, therefore, it was scarcely less
of a rollercoaster.

Since being elected in 1992 as the Member of Parliament for
Rutland and Melton, I had always considered myself to be an instinctive Eurosceptic. I voted 'No' in the 1975 referendum, and
maintained my belief in the following decades that the EU was
undemocratic, inflexible and in need of fundamental reform. As
2016 came around, I still expected to join the Leave campaign, and
began discussions to do so. But, as will be seen, I eventually decided
against it. With age and experience comes, if not wisdom, greater
perspective. Politics cannot always be about indulging one's natural
inclinations.

Like many, I received my share of abuse for backing Remain, but
I do not regret it. If anything, events have reinforced me in my belief
that I was right to pull back from the brink. Nor do I think I have
fundamentally changed my position on Europe. Somewhere along
the line from the early 1990s the cause of honest and thoughtful
Euroscepticism mutated into a form of simplistic nationalism that

strikes me as ugly and demeaning. Rather than devoting their energies to campaigning for the reform of outdated EU institutions and seeking a better deal for the UK, too many Eurosceptics retreated instead to crude sloganeering. There was a rational and pragmatic case to be made for leaving the EU, but few bothered to make it. Instead, we faced a wave of populist nonsense, emotive platitudes and downright lies: a barrage of Farage.

That sort of politics was to be expected from a fringe party like UKIP, but it should never have entered the mainstream of the Conservative Party. It is unworthy of a serious party of government to suggest that highly complex questions have easy answers, or that there are no trade-offs between national sovereignty and economic well-being. Yet during and after the 2016 referendum the increasingly swivel-eyed Brexiteer ultras in the Conservative Party mounted a determined effort to resist the encroachment of reality into their worldview. Inconvenient facts were dismissed as scaremongering, and necessary compromises condemned as betrayals. Brexit was seen as an article of faith instead of a diplomatic and public policy challenge, leaving no room for reasonable solutions. Toxic stalemate was the inevitable result, until finally those who clung to reason were purged and the high priests of the new religion took their place. Having won an election on another simplistic slogan, they finally managed to 'Get Brexit Done'. But the day of reconciling a false prospectus with hard truths seems further away than ever.

My despair as I watched this play out is evident from the text. I was in the peculiar position of being (among other things) the Minister for Europe, but having no direct role in negotiations over the most significant change to the UK's relationship with the continent for forty years. I was more than a bystander, but only a supporting actor in that drama. I loyally supported the government's position and backed the Prime Minister, while avoiding conflict with my immediate boss, whose own position was less straightforward. For my time as a foreign minister, diplomacy began at home.

Serving both Theresa May and Boris Johnson simultaneously for much of this time allowed me to form a clearer view of both of them as politicians. Theresa I had known for forty years since we were at

Oxford together, but I cannot claim to have ever become close to her. I was more friendly with her husband Philip, who was and remains a thoroughly decent man. Having enthusiastically backed her leadership campaign and seen her as the only serious figure in the contest, I earnestly hoped she would be a success in Number 10. As time went on, my disappointment and frustration at her manifest shortcomings as a politician spill out into the diary, sometimes harshly. It was not a happy premiership, and she made some serious errors of judgement. But in retrospect I still think she was a serious grown-up doing her best in an impossible situation. She deserves credit for at least trying to reconcile the possible with the unpersuadable.

Boris is a rather different matter. I suspect that much of the attention these diaries receive in the immediate future will focus on the unsparing criticism I often levelled at him in its pages. This will come as little surprise to those who have read accounts of my supposed hostility towards him, and they will assume that this book is designed as another salvo in an ongoing personal vendetta. The truth is that my relationship with Boris was always perfectly friendly, and while in the Foreign Office together we generally got on well. I also came to respect his unique qualities as a politician. I despaired at his lack of seriousness and refusal to apply himself properly, but he is no fool, and when he focusses on an issue he can be genuinely impressive. I was angered by his nakedly ambitious manoeuvrings for the leadership, but it is undeniable that he brings a rare energy and spark to politics. The problem for me was that the spark too often lit a fuse that ignited an unplanned media explosion.

What frustrated me most of all, and still does, is that he has the makings of an exceptionally good politician – one with moderate, liberal instincts and a gift for rallying an audience. If he could channel his energies into devising a compelling and optimistic vision of the future direction of the country, and use it to consign the unpleasant divisiveness of Brexit to the past, he would be a formidable prime minister. I still hold out hope.

Boris is not the only person who receives a degree of harsh criticism or sharp invective in these pages. Many of those I have been rude about, at length or in passing, will be annoyed, and some with good reason. But, as I wrote at the outset, it is in the nature of a diary that flashes of anger or wicked thoughts are committed to the page as a form of safety valve in the moment. In cool hindsight, some of these comments are unfair or ungenerous, and many don't properly reflect my feelings. I can only apologise where that is the case. But, for this diary to be authentic, there has to be a degree of 'warts and all' about it. These were my thoughts at the time, whether or not I am particularly proud of them now.

Aside from waspish comment on people and events, there are a number of other themes which I hope readers will find interesting. One which might require some explanation is my long-standing association with the Middle East and the Sultanate of Oman in particular. Over many years, since my time in the oil industry before entering Parliament, I have built up extensive contacts and friendships with senior figures across the Middle East and become a committed champion of Palestinian rights.

One of the key figures I got to know well over thirty years was Sultan Qaboos of Oman, who had ruled the country since 1970 and was by 2016 in advanced years and declining health. As will be seen, I was often called upon to use my personal connections to help advance British diplomatic and defence interests in the region, and Oman was a country where I was particularly glad to do so. The Sultan's death in January 2020 was the end of a chapter in his country's history, and a poignant one in my own life.

Despite my first-hand experience and knowledge of the Middle East, the region was excluded from my ministerial portfolio while I was in the Foreign Office. I will allow the story of how this happened to speak for itself, but it remains a general frustration to me that ministers can be blocked from being appointed to jobs for which they are eminently suited by overzealous officials viewing their personal expertise and contacts as *dis*qualifications. It is a completely counter-productive attitude.

Nevertheless, my portfolio in government was extensive. I was Minister for Europe and the Americas, and therefore covered a huge number of countries and diplomatic issues. There is a world outside of Brexit. There were the negotiations on a potential Cyprus settlement; our efforts to establish better relations with Argentina and open a direct airlink with the Falklands; and many other problems.

Reviewing the full diary was a dizzying world tour as I shuttled between ministerial visits, international conferences and meetings. Some flavour of this remains in the finished text, but there is much that had to be cut out for reasons of space. The same is true of the daily schedule of meetings when I was in London – a succession of ambassadors, delegations and meetings with officials, as well as video calls with our diplomats abroad and other foreign ministers (some of us were used to video calls well before the COVID-19 lockdown). We have retained the most noteworthy of these and tried to give an occasional flavour of the sheer variety of meetings on a typical day. But it was a constant backdrop to the other events recorded.

At this point I should pay a heartfelt tribute to our Diplomatic Service and the civil servants I was fortunate to work with during these years. My private office staff were heroic and brilliant, and on visits to our overseas missions I was constantly impressed by the quality of our diplomatic staff there. On the rare occasions someone displeased me, I have removed the disobliging references or anonymised them, so those whose names are recorded can be assured of my admiration and gratitude for the work they did.

Political diaries have such a distinguished pedigree as a literary genre that it is with some trepidation that I offer mine up to join them. Whether they compare favourably for historical significance with those of previous generations is for others to judge, but if nothing else I hope they will prove an entertaining read, with some surprises for the reader along the way.

I just wish I'd started them in 1990.

2016

Rather shambolic start to the new year in Parliament. Instead of a quiet day, Speaker Bercow ran four statements – each for over an hour – so, stupidly, a short day's business has turned into a late sitting. All very silly. But then he is.

Meanwhile [Jeremy] Corbyn is in the midst of an elongated shuffle farce, in which much heralded revenge sackings have not so far amounted to very much. He has sacked Michael Dugher as Shadow Culture Secretary, but seems to be dithering about whether to boot out Hilary Benn, something which would provoke a mass walk-out from others. Less a night of the long knives, more a week of the blunt hammer and sickle.

Wednesday 6 January – London
Road Signs Task Force meeting [I was chairing a government/Department for Transport review group to reduce the number of road signs, one of my passions]. The UK is littered with useless metal poles such as a picture of a traffic light ahead when you can already see the bloomin' traffic light. It meant that I missed [Labour MP] Sarah Champion's Westminster Hall debate on child prisoners in Israel. The Conservative Friends of Israel stooges have been out in force: Guto Bebb, Andrew Percy and the deeply unimpressive John Howell. Afterwards I saw Percy and the CFI ringmaster Stuart Polak in the cloisters corridor smirking and gloating. I learn later that they had positively revelled in defending Israel's incarceration of children. It is repugnant.

To Millbank to do the [BBC] *Daily Politics*. Corbyn's shuffle farce continues, as Stephen Doughty resigned live on air from Labour's front-bench defence team, and then Kevan Jones was reported to have gone too.

When asked about the EU I said I was a non-frothing Leaver, and that if I were to be persuaded otherwise the PM would have to pull an enormous rabbit out of the hat. I leave the studio in a huff for having had so little chance to say anything, but call and then bump into BBC producer Robbie Gibb later and say sorry.

Sam Kiley of Sky called. We sometimes speak of Yemen, in which I have had a thirty-year interest. It seems the UK has half a dozen military personnel assisting the Saudis with their targeting in Yemen. It's fine by me, and a good insurance policy against accusations that we are not paying attention to their adherence to international law: but it works both ways and could equally make us appear complicit. Sam says Andrew Mitchell is gearing up to be ultra-critical. Mitch knows the square root of diddly-squat about Yemen, and is just jumping on a human rights bandwagon. [I was his number two in DfID, the Department for International Development, until he became Chief Whip and then bit the dust after his altercation with the police at the gates of Downing Street.]

Friday 8 January – Rutland
To Rutland [my real, and expanding, home for twenty-five years]. As I walk in, [husband] James greets me with a glass of wine. Yippee! He has recorded the first two episodes of the new series of *Hawaii Five-0*!

Saturday 9 January – Rutland
Jamie Hedgecutter, as we call him, completes the fencing around the three oak trees and the new lime in the paddock. It looks really good, and will make them all cattle- and sheep-proof.

Visit our friend and neighbour Anne Boulton. Her husband Sir Clifford died last week. He had been Chief Clerk of the Commons. She is coping well, but feeling a lot of grief. She says she has ten bags of Clifford's clothes in bin liners in the kitchen and finds it upsetting to keep on looking at them. 'They are haunting me,' she says. So I load them up in the boot and take them to Age Concern in Uppingham.

Mike and Anne Eley from next door come for dinner. Slow-cooked shin of beef. Rather tasty.

Sunday 10 January – Rutland

My mobile pinged with a text alert at about 8am. I looked at it a few minutes later. Oh … it was from [Prime Minister] David Cameron. He asked, 'Can we pull you back from the brink on Europe? Many of the new MPs will be looking to you and other senior colleagues … Happy to talk any time. DC'.

Very interesting. Someone will have told him what I said on the *Daily Politics*, and he will be alarmed that I might take a prominent role in the Leave campaign. What side I come down on worries them, because I am not in any way 'one of the usual suspects'.

I replied that I was being approached by the Leave campaign, but was always open to reason, and had only made mild teasing statements so far. I suggest that we should have a sensible face-to-face discussion about it soon. He pinged back asking me not to commit to any side until we've spoken, which is fair enough, I suppose.

Monday 11 January – London

Meeting with Stephen Parkinson, who has finished as a SpAd [Special Adviser] to Theresa May at the Home Office and has joined the Leave campaign. He is urging me to play a senior role. They really want me, which is interesting. Alongside the PM's message yesterday, it seems I am in demand.

Lunch with the Egyptian Ambassador Nasser Kamel ahead of my visit at the end of the week.

MoD Gulf Advisory Committee with ministers Philip Dunne and Tobias Ellwood. Lord Guthrie, Sir Richard Paniguian, Geoffrey Tantum, Oliver McTernan, Baronesses Symons and Trish Morris. The PM has postponed his January Gulf-visit, and will now only go after the expected June EU referendum. [Chancellor] George Osborne might visit Saudi Arabia in March or April. Quite a lot of senior Arab figures might be in London for the Syria Donors Conference on 4 February. A bit of discussion in particular on Saudi Arabia and the significance of low oil prices. Brent is \$36 this week, and falling, lower in real terms than thirty years ago.

Roger Begy [Rutland Council Leader], sadly, is now thought to be terminally ill with cancer.

A couple of hours in the Chamber for Graham Stewart's debate on fairer funding for rural areas.

Tuesday 12 January – London

Text Rosso, who called yesterday, to say that he should definitely go for the New Schools Network chairmanship. It's a government-supported charity which helps set up new free schools and academies. [David Ross was one of the highly successful founders of Carphone Warehouse. As well as endowing the David Ross Education Trust, and serving on boards supporting the Olympic and Commonwealth Games, he has been Chairman of the National Portrait Gallery and now the Royal Opera House. He is a close constituency neighbour.]

David T. C. Davies MP comes to chat about CMEC [the Conservative Middle East Council, which I chair]. He wants to take a deeper interest in Middle East issues.

Speak to Erik in Oman. He has the Queen's Private Secretary Sir Christopher Geidt staying with him in Oman. We have a good cheerful chat. [Sir Erik Bennett (born 1928) was an RAF officer in the 1960s when he was picked out by Minister Julian Amery to become the pilot of King Hussein of Jordan and then, later, his Equerry. He set up the Sultan of Oman's Air Force in 1972, and became a principal adviser to him from 1992. He has been described as my 'not-quite' godfather.]

Bumped into Norman Lamont in Boots. He says he is not a definite Leaver and is worried about the implications for the City. We will speak soon to discuss it further.

Dinner with James in Shepherd's.

Wednesday 13 January – London

To my doctor. I am determined to get my neck sorted. It is giving me minor dizzy spells and symptoms like the early stages of a migraine.

ISC [Intelligence and Security Committee] reading ahead of our grilling of Theresa May. As a rather specialist select committee it's right up my street. [DC intended me to be its Chairman, but Dominic Grieve staged a coup.]

PMQs [Prime Minister's Questions]. I had primed the Speaker yesterday that I'd quite like to ask a question on oil prices. Brent is nearly down to $30, which is about where it was thirty-five years ago. I just wanted to flag up that this is a mixed blessing which we need to understand. In short, although it is good news for petrol prices, what about regimes under pressure; corporate collapse and default; enormous financial transfers to pay for other countries' deficits; a possible collapse in share prices and pensions dividends; and a liquidity problem in the banking sector? Will the PM assess the problem and also work out how to prevent the destruction of the North Sea oil industry?

Lunch at Roux with David Webster, Chairman of InterContinental Hotels. David thinks I have absolutely nothing to lose by playing a leading role in the Leave campaign.

Guardian blog and Twitter follow-up on the oil PMQ, with Robert Peston, who has just started as ITV political editor, tweeting that it was a serious question on a serious issue.

Media bids from 5 Live, *PM* and *Newsnight*.

David Mundell MP comes out as gay. Beautifully crafted blog announcement, which will attract nothing but generous reaction. On the *PM* prog they put me on with a self-righteous lesbian whose sole purpose in life seems to be to parade her victimhood and preach that all gays are oppressed. She is the worst possible advert for putting everyone at ease about being gay.

Did *Newsnight* on oil along with the quirky Gillian Tett of the *FT*.

Thursday 14 January – London

Oil markets are falling, and hovering just above $30.

ISC. Two hours quizzing our witness on the Draft Regulation of Investigatory Powers Bill. Some in the Commons such as David Davis consider it a grave attack on our privacy and liberty, which it is not.

Hook up with Nick Beech, the clerk of the Foreign Affairs Committee [FAC] about my witness session next Tuesday.

Acupuncture – I've been having it for forty years to help my neck.

To the airport with Leo Docherty and Charlotte Leslie [of CMEC]. Also on the trip: Richard Risby, Sir Gerald Howarth, Kwasi Kwarteng and David Morris. Five-hour flight … I sleep for three hours on the floor in front of some empty seats.

Friday 15 January – Cairo

Another couple of hours' sleep at the Zemalek Marriott.

Lunch with HMA [HM Ambassador] John Casson at the splendid Lutyens residence. Renewed my acquaintance with his wife Kathryn who worked for me in DfID and now has a job with Coca-Cola.

To the Khalili Soukh, a good ancient warren of hustle and bustle.

Dinner with all the senior hotel owners being hurt by the suspension of flights to Sharm el Sheikh following the November crash of the Russian airliner, which is thought to have been downed by a bomb.

Monday 18 January – Rutland/London

Gave the eulogy at the funeral of Sir Clifford Boulton. A large turnout from the worlds of both Parliament and Rutland. He was the only Clerk to have been awarded a GCB, when others have received an ordinary knighthood. I quipped that it obviously stood for the Great Clifford Boulton.

To London. Work on road signs and preparing for my select committee appearance on Libya.

Oddly petulant Mitchell text complaining that I should have told him, as he was my former boss, about my being asked to give evidence to the FAC. It is bizarre. Just because four years ago he was number one in International Development and I was number two is irrelevant to this select committee inquiry. He just thinks that it's all about him, when in fact they want to talk to me about the oil cell, stabilisation plans and the realities of introducing liberal political systems into a country like Libya.

Bumped into Oliver Letwin [brainbox policy-wonk MP] as I was walking home. He did not know that Gulf oil-producing countries need $80–$90 oil in order to meet their spending commitments. And he is supposed to be the font of all policy wisdom!

Tuesday 19 January – London

Head to the Albert Embankment to see Matthew Elliott and Stephen Parkinson at the offices of Vote Leave. Stephen as always was charming and sensible, but as I entered into deeper conversations with Matthew Elliott and observed the others they had assembled in the campaign HQ, I got the feeling that they were pandering to the worst kind of UKIP zealotry. Far from this being a 'Global Britain' internationalist vision, it all appeared rather backward-looking. I thought to myself 'this doesn't quite feel right'. I'm still an instinctive Leaver for all sorts of reasons, but at that moment the only EU organisation I wanted to escape from was theirs.

Appeared before the Foreign Affairs Committee to give evidence to their inquiry into the Libyan intervention and its aftermath. [Cameron avidly supported the toppling of President Muammar Gaddafi in 2011, and I ran a secret UK cell to block Libya's oil flows.] I was on after General Lord Richards, the former Chief of the Defence Staff (CDS). Gave them my frank view that the post-conflict stabilisation plans I'd seen as a DfID minister were completely unrealistic, and that I'd written 'fanciful rot' on them when asked for comment. I also gave a detailed description of the oil cell which I coordinated to stop the baddies selling oil while allowing the opposition to do so, which they seemed to find useful.

Swiss embassy for dinner for the sixtieth anniversary of the Parliamentary Ski Week.

Saturday 23 January – London

DC has chosen Air Chief Marshal Sir Stuart Peach as the next CDS, ahead of my former school contemporary General Sir Richard Barrons. Either would have been an excellent choice.

Google have agreed to pay the UK £134 million in back tax.

East coast of US in worst snow for a century.

Sunday 24 January – London

Agonising over how strongly – and indeed whether – I should campaign in favour of leaving the EU. Am thinking it through, but am increasingly uncomfortable with their whole attitude. The more I think about it, the more my gut feeling tells me the whole idea is impractical and out of date.

Bump into Eric Pickles (hard not to!), and Sam Coates of *The Times*.

Lunch at the Poule au Pot with my brother Kevin and wife Sarah. *Hawaii Five-O*.

Monday 25 January – London

Cecil Parkinson has died, so do appreciation interviews on *BBC News* and 5 Live. After I ran William Hague's successful leadership campaign in 1997, I persuaded him to appoint Cecil as Party Chairman. I thought with a young leader an elder statesman who'd been Chairman before would give some reassurance and make for a good double act. Hence I got to know him quite well and was rather fond of him.

Wednesday 27 January – London

An hour with Sir Simon McDonald, PUS [Permanent Under-Secretary] at the FCO [Foreign and Commonwealth Office]. Oman, the Middle East Peace Process, Yemen, etc.

Lancaster House for the fortieth anniversary of the Anglo-Omani Society with the Prince of Wales and Sayd Shihab, cousin of the Sultan and a former head of the Omani Navy [Sayd, or Sayyid, is an Arabic honorific denoting nobility and descent from the Prophet Muhammad].

Friday 29 January – Rutland
My twenty-fifth annual Melton Ladies lunch. I buy them all a glass of champagne.

Saturday 30 January – Malvern
DC struggling re EU deal [He was trying to renegotiate improved terms for our membership]. He should have just promised an in/out referendum, and not a renegotiation. He could have sprung all that later as a bonus.

Sunday 31 January – Malvern
Terry Wogan has died aged seventy-seven. My Council Leader Roger Begy is being moved into a hospice which sadly suggests he will not live for much longer.

After a lovely weekend, leave after lunch, with James taking my car to Rutland, while I get a lift to London with Hugo Gibbs who seems incapable of driving at less than 100mph.

Donald Tusk, President of the European Council, is in Number 10, but emerges saying 'no deal'.

Monday 1 February – London
Roger Begy has died.

MoD briefing on ISIS, or Daesh as we are now all calling it. Adam Holloway makes a presentation on his idea to build a video database of ISIS atrocities which can be used for future prosecutions.

CMEC 'Musar Monday', my regular soirées with lashings of Lebanese Château Musar, and then a quick dive into Sheryll Murray's sixtieth. Delicious real Cornish pasties.

Tuesday 2 February – London
First of what are intended to be weekly meetings of the CMEC management team in Tufton Street.

DC draft deal with Tusk is announced, but it's pretty useless. One part of the deal is that EU law can be blocked if a majority of national parliaments say so, but this will never happen, and is not what people thought was meant by the promise to reassert the sovereignty of

Parliament. The so-called 'emergency brake' which will permit the UK to pay lower or delayed benefits to migrant workers is similarly messy.

In the Iowa caucuses, Donald Trump is second to Ted Cruz; and Hillary Clinton is a bat squeak ahead of the socialist Bernie Sanders. What a crapshoot.

Seeing Stuart Polak in PCH [Portcullis House], I challenge him following his repulsive intervention in Baroness Tonge's motion in the Lords yesterday on Palestinian recognition, in which he went on about how the Palestinians deliberately stir up anti-Israeli hatred in their schools. I said that I thought his incitement line was wearing a bit thin. After a couple of ping-pong comments he as good as said that all the West Bank belonged to Israel. And this is the man Cameron has put in the Lords!

Impromptu drink with neighbour Henry Wickham, an ex-chorister who went to Christ Church, was headmaster at Lockers Park (the great rival of my old school Beechwood Park). Now managing his wife Maddie's affairs, as she is a successful writer.

Wednesday 3 February – London

I am wrestling with how to react to the draft EU deal. It is a non-deal and deserves to be slammed. I find myself shouting at the radio.

I put my prayer card in at 8am, which reserves my Commons seat for the day, and chat for about five minutes to Gavin Williamson [Parliamentary Private Secretary to the Prime Minister], making it clear that I am having to exercise quite saintly self-control over the EU, which he needs to appreciate and get me in to see the PM asap.

A delegation from Jordan gave a briefing to the ISC, on ISIS etc. We learn more from them than we ever do from the intelligence briefings we get.

Back in the Chamber I get a DfID question in at the last minute on Yemen, which Desmond Swayne handles brilliantly, praising my work as the Envoy.

PMQs, then an EU statement by the PM on his deal: I keep quiet.

Saturday 6 February – Rutland/London

My old friend Ian Taylor's sixtieth at the Dorchester. His adorable Scottish father, who must be nearly ninety, had the entire ballroom crying with laughter after opening his speech with the unexpected line 'Let me just say that, at my age, you're simply grateful that your bowels still work.' If he'd said nothing else it would have still gone down as the best speech of the evening.

Monday 8 February – London

Stuart Polak has fired a letter off to me – it is the usual tirade of anti-Palestinian extremism. I reply politely, but it's hardly worth the bother.

PM makes good speech on prisons, then is drawn into the EU under questioning, in which he makes an unwise comment that we would lose the right to put Border Force people in France who help control our borders. David Davis and Liam Fox both on the warpath.

Wednesday 10 February – London

In New Hampshire, Donald Trump wins for the Republicans with John Kasich coming in a strong second, and Bernie Sanders trounces Hillary Clinton.

Thursday 11 February – London

Went to Number 10 for my 10.45 meeting with the PM. Asked the guy at the door if Jonny Hall, my former Private Secretary in DfID, was around. He soon popped down. He's loving Number 10 but is furiously busy and has just been full tilt on the Syria Donors Conference, which is right up his street. Walked into the PM's outer office, where he was pacing up and down in shirtsleeves in a very jaunty way. We walked through to his study, alone except for Larry the Number 10 cat. At which point DC said, 'Sofa's all yours – next to the pussy. First time for everything!'

'Right,' he said, 'what do we need to cover?' So I said, 'You texted me a couple of weeks ago asking if you could haul me back from the brink and I promised not to join the Leave campaign or say anything irreversible in public until I'd seen you.'

We then had a very animated and sparky twenty minutes with him arguing along the lines of (I paraphrase): 'I know you're a Eurosceptic. So am I. But if you were to come out for Leave it would be enormously damaging for me, for you and the party. You're in a very unusual position where you are a senior and respected figure who a lot of the younger ones respect and will listen to. There are bits of the EU we all hate but I've got a good deal which guarantees the UK can't be forced to do a lot of things they might otherwise ask us to do.

'Just look at what's going on with Russia, the Middle East, North Africa. What would all your friends in the Middle East think if we pull out? We'd be cutting ourselves off from influence at a time when the world is in a very dangerous situation. How can we stand up to ISIS or Putin if we're not working as one?'

I moved the conversation on to handling. I said he's overplaying his hand and needs more people around him instead of doing it all himself, and the mood – fair or unfair – is that people feel they are being taken for a sucker and are being stage-managed. I told him I'd agreed to do something with the *Sun on Sunday* on homegrown gold-plating, i.e. people blaming the EU for rules we've made ourselves – which I thought would be helpful, but they pulled it yesterday saying they wanted a big spread dumping on the PM. 'I know, I know,' said DC. 'I've tried with *Mail* editor Paul Dacre but the tabloids are in full cry and there's not much we can do about it.'

It just shows that if I am for Leave and feed into that media frenzy it really would be doubly difficult. The whole tone of our exchange was very quick-fire, robust and lively. He was very impassioned with occasional moments of exasperation. The truth is because he was genuine and impassioned he was also rather persuasive, and I thought that if only he could just do in the House and on TV what he did in front of me, people would stop and think.

He was also very good at pointing out the dangers of a Leave vote. We both agreed that Scotland and trade supply lines were a deep worry to which he said, 'And also no one would know what a UK outside the EU would look like, because there is no clear model for that.' He said we would just have three years of total 'Euro-wank' and it risks being a catastrophe. When he asked me again how someone as sensible as me could be in favour of leaving, I said it had bugged me for forty years and I thought our membership had sapped our self-confidence and rendered Parliament and our process of government pretty puny, and that I thought it was all going to collapse because there is no way twenty-eight countries could ever hold together as a common government. 'Yes,' he countered, 'but we're outside all the bits that don't suit us and have guarantees that we'll remain so.'

I said I could quite easily do nothing and keep my head down but if I'm actually to change my mind to back Remain and say so in public, it would need a very clever way of plotting a course to being able to do that. I'd be viciously labelled as a quisling turncoat … although I'm sure I could cope with the inevitable attacks from some in my local party such as the (Dowager) Duchess of Rutland and her ilk.

I then told him that the leadership speculation prompted by his pledge not to fight another election was getting silly. There is zero appetite for leadership games at the moment. Most of those who are on manoeuvres are hopelessly ill-equipped, especially Boris, who hardly has any support in the House. DC only made the pledge in an off-the-cuff comment during the [2015] general election campaign, anyway. I tell him, 'Sod it – why can't you just stay?' He laughed.

As I was leaving, he said the best thing I'd ever done for him was to recommend Jonny Hall, who he rates very highly in Number 10. He was 'great for the Syria Conference' and is clearly seen by DC as a top-flight guy.

Sunday 14 February – Rutland

A story in the *Independent on Sunday* about leadership speculation, featuring my comments that DC should stay on, as I told him last week. They also quote Ken Clarke, who says: 'The public loves Boris, but he has to answer the question, "What would you do if you were Prime Minister?"' Well, quite.

Very bright and warm day. Cut the lawns, and then had a lovely walk with [our cockapoo] Noodle down by the river, which is still flowing very strongly after the rain.

Monday 15 February – Rutland
Roger Begy's funeral in Greetham. I delivered the address. He was a large, dishevelled figure – I raised a laugh by saying that anyone talking to him lived in fear of being at the receiving end of a fast-flying shirt button pinging off his ample tummy.

Wednesday 17 February – London
Full day in the office working on the Road Signs Task Force report.

Boris has gone in to see Cameron in Number 10, but has emerged saying they haven't agreed anything, and the briefing that emerges later sounds as though he's not convinced. Tomorrow's Brussels summit, which is intended to agree a deal for the UK within the EU, looks as though it is teetering.

Thursday 18 February – London
See George Osborne at Number 11 for a private chat. All very friendly, but I tell him bluntly that the whole EU issue is being too tightly held by him and DC. Unless it is a broader, more inclusive political effort, it'll be a verdict on the government more than the EU, and it risks going horribly wrong. It has to embrace all parties and interest groups.

Dinner with Stuart Rose and Anna Hartropp, Martha Lane-Fox and boyfriend, Mervyn Davies and wife, Sir Ben Ainslie and wife, James and me.

DC and the other twenty-seven EU leaders are in Brussels hammering out the renegotiation deal.

Friday 19 February – Rutland
Head up to Rutland.

EU leaders have been up all night. No deal yet. Greece blocking on migration, and French and Belgians saying both that this is the last deal for the UK that can be agreed, and that there can be no second referendum – by which they mean that if we leave there is no return.

The timing of the final session for all the leaders to sign off the deal keeps slipping – first it is billed as an 'English breakfast', then it's lunch, then dinner. At this rate it could end up as Sunday lunch. The Cabinet meeting DC had planned for today on his return is postponed until tomorrow. Then it is done – a deal is reported at 9.30pm. But just before the official announcement, [Michael] Gove briefs that he will campaign to Leave. All done in order to get the headlines and stymie DC's announcement. As Justice Secretary his decision carries weight in itself, but the real significance is that he's been such an ally and friend of the PM.

DC gives a good press conference in Brussels, despite clearly having had almost no sleep since getting there yesterday. He makes his pitch for the Remain side in the referendum, and for Britain staying in a reformed EU. The Cabinet will meet tomorrow.

Saturday 20 February – Rutland
Osborne on Radio 4 *Today*. Good interview, but his style is a specialist taste.

10am Cabinet. Gove, [Iain] Duncan Smith, [John] Whittingdale, [Theresa] Villiers, [Chris] Grayling and [Priti] Patel are all to campaign for Leave.

DC makes a statement on the steps of Number 10 formally confirming the referendum is on, with polling day on 23 June.

I can't decide whether this is the beginning of a completely disastrous period in our politics or the only way to end forty years of strain and division. Sadly I fear it's more likely to be the former.

Spend the day writing Road Signs Task Force report.

Sunday 21 February – Rutland
The papers are all the EU. PM on *Marr*. Dolled-up Priti Patel on Sky. She really is a nothing person.

Lunch with neighbour Peter Cox.

Boris is expected to announce in his column tomorrow in the *Telegraph* that he will campaign to leave. At 5pm he makes a statement in front of his house amid an extraordinary media scrum, which he milks to the full. He will campaign to leave. We learn later that he texted DC to tell him just twelve minutes before.

George [Osborne] returns my call. We agree there will be an initial sensation, and then a backwash against Boris, whose leadership intentions are brazen.

It's typical of him – creating a media circus around himself, fuelling speculation while keeping others in the dark and then coming out on the populist side, despite it being perfectly clear he doesn't believe any of this guff. The long-term Eurosceptics don't trust him, and his self-serving ambition is blatant. But it will play well with the Tory base, which is all he cares about.

Monday 22 February – London

One of my regular calls from Erik Bennett. Chat about the end of empire – we both think that the motivation of Leave campaigners is a perverse reaction to Britain's post-imperial decline. On the referendum, he agrees I am wise to play it long, and then support the PM.

I call my Chairman, Mary Anne Donovan, to suggest that the [constituency] Association has a fully prepared press-handling script so that she, Anne and Valerie [who work in the office] won't be caught off guard by journalists calling to conduct a survey.

My old Merchant Taylors' headmaster, Brian Rees, has died. He was housemaster at Eton and then headmaster of Merchant Taylors', Charterhouse and Rugby. A figure in the Cambridge Footlights, he wrote an accomplished biography of the composer Saint-Saëns.

Post-EU summit statement from the PM, which Speaker Hobbit kept going for two hours forty minutes, with 103 MPs asking basically the same questions. It was so over the top. Bercow thinks that maximising the number of questions amounts to effective scrutiny. It doesn't.

The best moment was DC cleverly belittling the idea, floated by some Leavers, that we could have a second referendum after getting a better deal, while also having a sly dig at Boris' private life. As he put it: 'I've known a number of couples who have begun divorce proceedings, but I don't know any who have begun divorce proceedings in order to renew their marriage vows!'

CMEC drinks.

On the way home, saw Andrew Robathan on his bike. I said I thought Boris was rather overdoing it, and he responded by petulantly criticising DC for his jibe earlier. When I said that perhaps Andrew might remember who put him in the Lords, he said, 'Funny that. When I saw Cameron he told me how much he owed me.' Utterly, totally delusional.

Thursday 25 February – London

ISC witness session with senior MI5 officials, part of our inquiry into the rendition and detention of suspects in Afghanistan.

DfID drinks in the Silver Cross pub to mark the release of the Treasury Guarantee to Turks & Caicos Islands. When I was DfID Minister I completely refinanced the islands, which were nearly bankrupt. It required ruthless discipline and ingenuity, but now, four years later, they're completely back on track. If I hadn't driven the issue so hard they would still be in a mess.

Drink at home with Paddy McGuinness, Deputy NSA [National Security Adviser].

Sunday 28 February – Rutland

DC is under fire for dissing Boris in the Commons last week. There are reports of leadership challenges even if he wins the referendum, if he doesn't rein in his 'Blue on Blue' attacks. Nothing could be more absurd when he is the one who is perpetually under attack.

Attack the mice in the attic.

Monday 29 February – London

Saudi Ambassador Prince Sultan will help plan my trip to Riyadh.

Home Sec wants to see me. Chief Whip wants to see me. Both for help on the RIP [Regulation of Investigatory Powers] Bill, I guess.

Hoo-ha about whether ministers who are Leavers will be allowed to see government documents relating to the EU ahead of the referendum. Unfortunately this is being handled by the Teacher's Pet (Matt Hancock) which just makes matters worse.

CMEC drinks in my office. Too much Château Musar. I'm going to stop drinking.

Tuesday 1 March – London
Place an article on ConHome website, jointly with Stephen Kinnock, saying Yuli Edelstein (the Speaker of the Knesset) should be challenged when he comes to address MPs tomorrow on the issue of illegal settlers (of which he is one!).

No booze. Feeling much better.

Wednesday 2 March – London
Trump and Clinton have triumphed in the Super Tuesday primaries.

The EU is to spend hundreds of millions within the EU, especially in Greece, to cope with the humanitarian consequences of the migrant influx.

My ConHome article on Yuli Edelstein appears.

[Foreign Secretary] Philip Hammond makes a speech on what Brexit Britain might look like. Whenever a senior minister does this, it just polarises the debate. This overactivity is 'fuelling the duelling'.

PMQs. Chat with David Davis on RIP Bill. The system is nervous about opposition to the Bill from the likes of DD. Theresa May has never asked him in for a chat. She is so insular. If she would just pick up the phone once in a while, the tingle of a call from the Home Secretary might even work with DD.

Speak to Egyptian Ambassador Nasser Kamel about the flight ban on Sharm el Sheikh. President Sisi and DC are not on speaking terms over it. It rankles very deeply with the Egyptians.

Weekly meeting of the 1922 [All Conservative backbench MPs]. Oddly, despite high emotions, only twenty-five MPs there. As soon as there's no vote in the Commons they all just go home.

Saturday 5 March – Rutland
Uppingham.

Nice walk.

Watch the film *Kingsman*. The main characters are called Harry Hart and Chester King – both named after our friends who are mates of the film director Matthew Vaughn.

Sunday 6 March – Rutland
Papers. Gove interview in the *Sunday Times* in which he claims that the EU has fuelled terrorism and a surge in fascism. For someone so clever, this is both sick and warped.

Rupert Murdoch wedding to Jerry Hall. So – tell me, Miss Hall, what first attracted you to the 84-year-old billionaire Rupert Murdoch?

Johnson on *Marr*. Lamont on Sky.

Nancy Reagan has died aged ninety-four.

Monday 7 March – Nottingham/London
A week without touching a drop. I feel so much better, am sleeping more deeply and wake up rested. James is also on a fitness mission: no alcohol, no ciggies and a daily workout. Fortunately, two weeks into giving up smoking, his forecast grumpiness has not materialised.

To Nottingham for the Citizens UK Commission on Islam. I've agreed to be part of an investigative project to analyse and assess what it's like to be a Muslim in the UK.

Tuesday 8 March – London
CMEC management meeting.

See Theresa May re ISC and RIP Act. She is completely misjudging the extent to which the passage of the Bill is threatened. She is of course going to get some stick from the civil liberties extremists like DD, but the ISC is not really a problem in that regard. We'll quiz her on it robustly, but we're not going to cause her grief in the House.

CMEC energy dinner.

Wednesday 9 March – London
Sun headline 'Queen Backs Brexit' causes a massive row.

This reeks of the worst habits of British journalism. Based on what is probably a sneaky off-the-record comment, no doubt from a

Leave-supporting minister, they splash this about the Queen on the front page. It is despicable on everyone's part, except of course the Queen's. It's almost impossible for the Palace to react in a way that doesn't make things worse. They can't say 'No she didn't say that' or 'No she doesn't support Brexit' – indeed, they can't really say anything. Whoever was the source of this in the first place is a complete and utter shit. But that could be quite a long list.

Friday 11 March – Rutland
To Rutland on the train. Think think think about the EU.

Saturday 12 March – Rutland/London
Michael Ashcroft's seventieth birthday party. Michael Gove is there, having briefed earlier in the day that the leak about the Queen's view on the EU 'did not all come from him'. It looks like a completely artificial denial. Utter sophistry. It was clearly him. It now seems to be the accepted view. The pressure on him is mounting.

Sunday 13 March – London
Lovely sunny day. James goes back to Rutland. I wire in the new Sky TV cable, and keep thinking about the EU, and my AGM next Friday. I'll have to declare my hand, and I now know what I'm going to say.

I've thought about it so much and now I've decided. Wanting to leave the EU pretends to be a route to simple solutions and a supposedly better world. Like all multilateral organisations the EU is not perfect. We're all much more interdependent and the cooperation and free trade of the EU is of massive benefit to us. Being shot of it would not make our life either easier or better.

So that's it – I've made my mind up. For forty years I've always lamented the sacrifice of so-called self-government, but I think our interests are served best by remaining part of the EU. The danger is that the referendum won't solve the problem, it will just create a bigger one. Quite how we extricate ourselves and still expect to trade freely is quite beyond me. The anti-EU lot talk as though it's easy and simple and obvious, but if we vote to leave we'd be heading for a mess.

Tuesday 15 March – London

Meeting at Number 10 to discuss my EU announcement. Speak to DC's Director of Strategy Ameet Gill and SpAd Mats Persson. Had a useful chat – we went over my planned op-ed which they will now try and place. I suggest they put a bit of work into squeezing as much juice out of it as they can – an article on its own will count for little unless they generate wider comment around it as being a significant intervention.

Second reading of the Investigatory Powers Bill. It passes easily, as we all knew it would.

Wednesday 16 March – Berlin

Budget Day, but I'm not there as I'm off on a trip with the ISC to Berlin. I travel to Heathrow with Keith Simpson.

Main headlines out of the Budget itself include a sugar tax and CGT reduction. It also includes funding for a 'Shakespeare of the North' project that's been pushed by George Howarth, who is with us here. I text Osborne to pass on Howarth's profound thanks, telling him the latter 'owes you a big (non-sugary) drink'.

We have dinner with our German counterparts. There is a mad Green Party MP at the table who thinks Julian Assange, holed up in the Ecuadorian embassy, is a good thing. Fiona Mactaggart gives him grief through a bemused translator, calling Assange a 'fucking monster'.

Walk back to the hotel past the Führer bunker, now a car park.

Friday 18 March – Rutland

I open the extension to Brooke Hill Primary School.

Constituency AGM. In my speech I made my position on the referendum clear. I laid out all the arguments – we can't hark back to a bygone age, and pretend that everything used to be perfect and therefore would be again. The world has moved on and the argument has to as well. Some of the nice sensible ones came up afterwards and said they'd never heard the arguments put so clearly, but the unpersuadables were predictably grumpy.

IDS [Iain Duncan Smith] resigns at 9pm, citing disagreements over welfare cuts. This is a major attack on Osborne – who knows?

Might it do for him? Text DC saying perhaps David Gauke would be a good replacement at DWP [Department for Work and Pensions].

Saturday 19 March – Rutland

Buy a new TV in Kettering.

Stephen Crabb replaces IDS. Alun Cairns replaces Crabb at Wales.

See Anne Boulton in Lyddington – two months on from Clifford's death she is struggling rather.

Sunday 20 March – Rutland

IDS on *Marr*. Very impassioned interview complaining about welfare reforms, but it doesn't add up. Text George [Osborne], who says at no point has IDS ever protested about the implementation of welfare changes, and there's IDS now resigning over the policy for which he was responsible. Seems like he was just looking for a way out.

Speak to Michael Savage of *The Times*, defending George.

Good chat with William [Hague]. Told him to use his column in the *Daily Telegraph* to ridicule the list of aspirant leaders who have nothing to commend them – Priti Patel, Penny Mordaunt, Andrea Leadsom.

Ed Argar calls to say that Heidi Allen has used an interview on *Channel 4 News* to slate George, and say that it was her role to 'talk some sense into this government'. She is supposed to be on our side. I like my calls with Ed. Steady Eddie used to work for me when I was a shadow foreign minister, and is now the MP in the Leicestershire constituency next door as well as a good friend.

Monday 21 March – London

Speaker grants a UQ [Urgent Question] on 'Budget Changes', and then two statements: PM on the European Council, and Stephen Crabb on the welfare payments backdown. Day one of the job and he has to navigate a U-turn but does it OK.

See William [Hague] in Smith Square on the way home after dinner. His *DT* column will say that IDS got it wrong, and that his was an illogical and unnecessary resignation.

Tuesday 22 March – London

Bombs in Brussels. One at the airport, one at the station. Thirty-six killed.

Rebuke Paul Goodman of ConHome for saying that Gove should become Deputy Prime Minister.

Osborne opens final day of the debate on the Budget. Acquits himself well.

Number 10 say the *Telegraph* has accepted my article on the EU. No turning back now – my cards will be clearly on the table.

Budget votes.

Wednesday 23 March – London

Sultan Qaboos [of Oman] is undergoing cancer treatment in Germany, which is provoking some anxiety.

PMQs. DC brilliant, having found the Corbyn list of Labour MPs, graded by their relative support for him (few) and hostility (many).

Thursday 24 March – London/Rutland

My article appears in the *Daily Telegraph*, saying we should remain. They've headlined it 'Why this lifelong Eurosceptic is now voting to stay in'. I set out how I had voted 'No' in 1975, had expected to be campaigning to leave and had gone as far as meeting the Leave campaign to discuss it (as they will inevitably leak that anyway). My case for Remain is nuanced and pragmatic – based on the fact I believe leaving would damage our influence internationally and fail to solve the problems its proponents claim it would.

No immediate take-up. But Sir Richard Dearlove, a former 'C' [Chief of SIS/MI6], has written in *Prospect* that withdrawing from the EU would not impede our intelligence capability, and that Europol is pretty useless anyway. This is rebutted by Sir David Omand, who was Director General of GCHQ in the 1990s, which is when I met him at a Jonathan Aitken lunch for the Sultan of Oman.

I do Sky, ITV, BBC News Channel.

Friday 25 March – Rutland

Good Friday. Emails of upset from David Webster and son Mike re my EU article, but many more from others who are equally serious, and very supportive.

The odious Matthew Elliott tweets that I only changed my mind when they refused me a position on the Leave board. Total crap.

Uppingham. The return of Noodle cheers me.

Lovely bright spring day.

Saturday 26 March – Rutland

Noodle limping, and reluctant to chase the ball as usual, so take her to the vet. Probably a thorn in her back right paw, but they can't see it, even though she squeals loudly when a particular spot is touched. On with the poultice bandage, and she is happy.

James is having fun in Mustique. Drinking but not smoking.

The Leave campaign have published a list of 250 biz leaders (so called) who support Brexit. It includes Rosso, who actually never gave his approval, although it's probably where his sympathies lie. Usual Brexit campaign cock-up, and most of the other names are utterly insignificant.

I compose a long detailed reply to David Webster.

Matthew Parris has written an excoriating piece in *The Times* about Boris. He lays into his irresponsible personal behaviour and dishonesty, and says the party needs to 'end our affair with this dangerous charmer'. Very powerful and convincing.

Sunday 27 March – Rutland

Clocks go forward an hour. I suppose it makes sense, but it's high time we changed to European time in general and stopped this nonsense just because of the Scots.

Noodle much better. Mary next door has her family there, along with the gorgeous Labradoodle, Digger, who is blonde to Noodle's black, and three times her size. They love each other.

James has spent weeks, if not months, preparing for today's Easter lunch on the beach in Mustique. Eighty to a hundred guests, and a million carnival feathers. I'm so sorry not to be there.

Monday 28 March – Rutland/Dubai

Stormy. Drive to Heathrow.

Phone Matthew Parris to commend him on his Saturday article. Tim Montgomerie in *The Times* writes the same as Paul Goodman two days ago that Michael Gove should become Deputy PM. I text him: 'Now that you have left the Conservative Party, I can see how you intend to destroy it.'

Flight to Dubai. Ritz Carlton.

Tuesday 29 March – Dubai/Fujairah

Dubai and Fujairah wearing my Fujairah refinery Chairman's hat. In Fujairah I see the ruler, who I've met before. Cheerful chat in which I remind him that his son worked as an intern in my office. I didn't tell him the nickname we gave him, as it was none too flattering about his weight.

Dinner at Zuma. If, as I nearly did, I'd joined Vitol in 1988 when I left pioneering oil trader Marc Rich I'd have many tens of millions in the bank, as they've become the world's top oil traders. But who cares? Politics beckoned.

George Osborne has postponed his trip to Saudi. I am going there myself on Thursday, via Muscat.

Thursday 31 March – Muscat

My fifty-ninth birthday. Breakfast at the residence with Ambassador Jon Wilks and his houseguest David Bull, former Private Secretary to Ted Heath.

I was halfway to the Ministry of Foreign Affairs before I remembered it was my birthday.

Interesting approach from BP on Kurdistan: they want to increase their production of Kirkuk crude, but the only way to market it is through the Kurds themselves, as BP do not want to alienate Baghdad. They are asking me to help them place it with a third party, through whom they could market as much as an extra 200,000–250,000 barrels a day within a year.

Sunday 3 April – Muscat/Riyadh

Am well received by my usual counterparts in the Omani government. Interesting discussion with the head of the Royal Office, who
are vaguely similar to our MI6. Free-ranging discussion about political developments in Saudi Arabia, and about a possible
post-referendum reshuffle in the UK.

Lunch with Sheikh Ahmed Farid of Yemen, who as good as ran a
private army at the end of the 1960s and relocated to Oman when
the pro-Saudi Imamate rulers lost control of the country.

Fly to Riyadh. Connect with the visiting CMEC team, who had
landed half an hour before. Sir Edward Garnier, David Jones, Ed
Argar, Kwasi Kwarteng, Helen Whateley and CMEC Director Leo
Docherty. To the guest palace, dinner and collapse into bed.

Monday 4 April – Riyadh

Breakfast with Ambassador Simon Collis. Our schedule includes
very senior access, which I am combining with a raft of meetings on
Yemen in my role as UK government Envoy. First call is on King
Salman. He is now quite old and has handed executive power to
others, but in Saudi Arabia the King is the revered head of state,
whatever the condition of his faculties.

Afterwards, I peel off from the others to see the Secretary General
of the GCC [Gulf Cooperation Council], Abdullatif al Zayani, and
then the new Vice-President of Yemen, Ali Mohsen al Ahmar.

Tuesday 5 April – Riyadh

Our Saudi Odyssey continues with CMEC meetings with Minister
of Finance Ibrahim al Attaf, Foreign Minister Adel al Jubair and
HRH Prince Turki al Faisal, who is former head of intelligence and
until recently Ambassador to the UK.

While at the Prince Mohammed bin Nayef Centre for Counselling
and Care – which is their deradicalisation centre – we were suddenly
summoned to a meeting with HRH Prince Mohammed bin Salman.
He is only about thirty and as Deputy Crown Prince is being seriously viewed as the rising power in the land. I sat next to him as
CMEC Chairman and tried to include every member of our delega-

tion in the meeting's conversation. MbS (as he is known) is a great bull of a man with a very forceful character. He was amazingly enthusiastic in his sweeping plans for economic reform and privatising companies such as the massive Aramco. To this end, he will be throwing money around no end of advisers in the belief that radical changes can be made overnight. Whereas the world isn't like that. His radiant enthusiasm left a profound impression. We sparked off in a very friendly, animated way, during which he asked why the Ambassador was not taking notes. I said, 'Don't worry, sir, he is recording everything with a tape recorder up his trouser leg!' Amid the laughter, I quipped that it's much better than relying on his brain. An easy gag, which made for a friendly encounter.

Wednesday 6 April – Riyadh

Amusing *Arab News* caption to a photo of me with Deputy Crown Prince Mohammed bin Salman: he 'holds talks with Leader of the Conservative Party, Alan Duncan'. Er … they had missed out the word 'delegation'!

News in the UK is of a detailed leak about Panama offshore trusts. Unfortunately for DC, the press are screaming – stupidly and unfairly – that it was wrong for one ever to have been used by DC's father. To anyone who has even half a financial brain, the use of such a trust, especially for pensions, is a sensible and legitimate method for not having to pay tax twice.

Do the full round of Yemen meetings from the President downwards, as they are all in Riyadh for negotiations. I know more of these people than the UK government, but have never so much as had a meeting with Philip Hammond about this poor dilapidated country, because quite frankly he's not bothered. As Foreign Secretary, he's only interested in the rich ones.

Thursday 7 April – Rutland

Land 5.30am. Drive to Rutland.

HMG is to spend £9 million distributing a pro-Remain leaflet 'giving the facts'. It's a propaganda gift to the other side – plays into their 'establishment' narrative. It's really not clever, because it makes the whole Remain campaign look as though it's only a government-backed position. Big, big mistake.

Dinner in the pub.

Friday 8 April – Rutland

Sort the flower beds with Amanda, our gardener.

DC is under intense fire for having benefited from the proceeds of an offshore savings trust set up by his father before he died. I can see no problem with the trust, and matters have raced out of control. But the problem I suspect will turn out to be whether he registered it or not back in 2010. It's just the sort of nitpicking detail the British press love to gnaw at. As Erik is prone to saying, 'It's just picking fly crap out of pepper.'

Saturday 9 April – Rutland

Extraordinary piece of modern journalism. Charles Moore in the *Daily Telegraph*, through a process of laudable and decent research, handled elegantly, has established that Gavin Welby was not the father of the Archbishop of Canterbury, Justin Welby. His father in fact was Sir Anthony Montague Browne, a former Private Secretary to Winston Churchill. Unmentioned in the papers is the recent claim of the Board of Deputies of British Jews that our Archbishop had extensive Jewish blood in him. As of today, that is proven not to be true.

Lovely day. Lugged a telegraph pole from Phil Grice's garden to the sheds, where we intend to put up an owl box, at last. A nice gang from the village assisted, looping a rope beneath it, and hooking it over their shoulder. Sinking it upright into the ground will prove rather more challenging. Spent the afternoon removing old brambles, before they start sprouting, and watched a very exciting Grand National, won in a dramatic finish by a nineteen-year-old jockey on a horse called Rule the World.

Sunday 10 April – Rutland

All the papers are covering DC's tax returns. The pass has been sold – private tax affairs have become public property. We're heading for a US-style system where leading politicians will have to disclose them before they hold office.

Monday 11 April – London

First day back after the Easter recess. I had managed two days on the beach during a gruelling tour of the Middle East.

Gave a full debrief on Yemen and Saudi to Nick Perry, the PM's Foreign Affairs adviser in Number 10.

During the PM's statement on the Panama tax leaks, and his personal taxation, I ask a question which slightly backfires. I say:

> Should not the Prime Minister's critics just snap out of their
> synthetic indignation and admit that their real point is that they
> hate anyone who has even a hint of wealth in their life? May I
> support the Prime Minister in fending off those who are
> attacking him, thinking particularly of this place, because if he
> does not, we risk seeing a House of Commons that is stuffed full
> of low achievers who hate enterprise and hate people who look
> after their own family and who know absolutely nothing about
> the outside world?

Basically I goof the question with a clumsy turn of phrase while suffering from symptoms like an early migraine. The point is not an unreasonable one, as so many people in Parliament these days have done absolutely nothing and contribute even less. But it was wrong to insinuate that if you're not earning money you can never be effective. That was not what I meant.

Labour MPs made a big display of their outrage, and the whole thing blew up on Twitter. I issued a clarification to try and calm the mob.

Tuesday 12 April – London

My inbox contains about fifty items of highly abusive hate mail about my question yesterday. They are all fuelled by hard-left class war and are simply revolting. There are some pretty ghastly people in this country.

Coffee with Ron Simpson of Uppingham Town Council. As he left he picked up my glasses by mistake, but I tracked him down and swapped them back.

Lunch with Erik Bennett at his usual table in Wilton's. The Sultan is flying home to Oman today from Germany, which I hope means his treatment has been successful.

Brief officials at the FCO about my recent Middle East journeys.

Fabi, my osteopath, administers a proper click to the top of my neck which immediately felt as though it had released all my blurry tension of the last month.

Lovely James, back in Rutland, comforting and supportive over the PMQ 'low achiever' fallout.

[Culture Secretary] John Whittingdale has admitted having had a one-year relationship with a prostitute. But he didn't know she was. So what?

Thursday 14 April – London

Ten weeks to the referendum.

Tuesday 19 April – London

Absurd Gove speech in Clacton in which he suggests the UK would continue to have free trade with the EU even if we leave the single market. Delusional.

Thursday 21 April – London

The Queen is ninety today. Quite the most remarkable person in the world, and so many just take her for granted.

Breakfast with Mohammed Mahfoudh al Ardhi in George [club]. A former head of the Oman air force, he's now a senior banker and investment manager. When he went to Harvard twenty years ago, I introduced him to some of my close friends there, for which he's always been grateful.

ISC meeting, so annoyingly I miss the tributes to the Queen in the Commons.

Friday 22 April – Rutland
Go to Birmingham for another meeting of the Islam Commission which is studying Muslims in the UK. I'm quite enjoying being part of their inquiry, but who knows what will ever come of it?

President Obama is in the UK and in his press conference with DC has said that if the UK leaves the EU and there's a trade negotiation, we'd be 'at the back of the queue' because they'd start by dealing with big blocs rather than one country. But the big news is an attack on him by Boris Johnson, who is serving out his final weeks as Mayor of London as well as now being MP for Uxbridge. It would have been OK and dignified if he'd just made the point that the EU makes too much of our law and we don't like being lectured on our sovereignty by other countries. But in typical Boris fashion he'd already stirred it up by writing in the *Sun* that Obama is anti-British because he has Kenyan roots. That's pretty near the edge, and pretty illogical given his own Turkish origins!

Monday 25 April – London
Accidentally missed a crucial three-line vote on whether the UK should take in 2,000 unaccompanied Syrian orphans. Fortunately the government won by eighteen, and I voted in the following three divisions.

Tuesday 26 April – London
Bit of a hangover after dinner last night with James and Ollie Blake, my friend from Oman. The Leave campaign is being run by an ever narrower bunch of ministers who are hogging it in order to promote themselves. Amusingly, the cast of Gove, Patel, Grayling and Leadsom is believed now to exclude Steve Baker. In such matters one can always detect the hand of Gove.

Wednesday 27 April – London

Owen Jones comes to interview me on Yemen. He is a shamelessly gobby little thing, who is so certain in his own views. Speaking as he does is so easy when all his opinions fit into a formulaic template of left-wing thinking. Strangely, I quite like him. He's quite right that the conflict in Yemen is hideous and unnecessary, but rather ruins his case by blaming it entirely on British arms sales to Saudi Arabia.

Thursday 28 April – London

Ken Livingstone has created an explosive row by defending Labour MP Naz Shah over her recent dumb comments about 'Zionism'. I never use the word, because it's like pushing a button, which releases everyone's own understanding of what it means – both good and bad. It's better to avoid it and just speak sensibly and decently about all the current and historic issues around it. In fact, her words were worse than dumb; they were pretty damn contemptible, by suggesting that you solve the Arab–Israeli problem by exporting Israelis to the United States, and by likening modern Israel to the Nazis. She should be expelled from the Labour Party.

Lovely dinner at Lincoln's Inn as a guest of my constituent, Judge John Goldring. Fabulous. Some really charming top lawyers – also Dame Nicola Brewer, who was brilliant to deal with when she was our High Commissioner in South Africa and a coachload of Melton students was involved in a serious crash.

Friday 29 April – London/Bahrain

Heathrow. Bump into Met Commissioner Bernard Hogan-Howe in Terminal 5. I remonstrated with him about the way the Met is handling the accusations by a seeming nutter against my constituent Harvey Proctor and other senior figures like Field Marshal Lord Bramall. Talk of orgies in Dolphin Square involving Ted Heath, Proctor and others is clearly, obviously, without doubt utter fabrication and fantasy. It has echoes of the insinuation that appeared in *Private Eye* over thirty or forty years ago. It's so bizarre and unconvincing – it should never have led to any arrests, caution or police investigation. The police have gone completely mad and it makes me worry about their judgement.

Fly to Bahrain for a private visit.

Dinner with Geoffrey Tantum, ex-MI6 and a long-standing adviser to the King of Bahrain.

Monday 2 May – London

Land back in London. Bank Holiday. Stay in London. Lunch in Riccardo's with James.

Wednesday 4 May – London

Westminster Hall debate on the Gulf initiated by Charlotte Leslie. The sneering Andy Slaughter makes an ignorant and ill-informed speech which bandied about loose allegations of torture in Bahrain, and betrayed a total lack of understanding of the region. It is the worst type of armchair judgementalism.

PMQs. Unfortunately, I thought the PM misjudged it and was rather vulgar in attacking Sadiq Khan for associating with 'Muslim extremists'. I don't think there were enough grounds for throwing mud like that at him. Anyway, he is clearly going to thrash Zac Goldsmith in the London Mayoral race, so it all looks a bit desperate.

Thursday 5 May – London

Donald Trump has all but won the Republican nomination, and Ted Cruz and John Kasich have pulled out.

Meanwhile back here it's polling day for the London Mayoralty, plus the Scottish Parliament, Welsh Assembly and some local councils.

Friday 6 May – Rutland

A mixed bag of election results – Labour has a pretty dismal night, actually managing to lose council seats, which is quite something for an Opposition. In Scotland the SNP win again but the big story is the success of Ruth Davidson's Scottish Conservatives, who double their number of seats and push Labour into third place. The only good news for Labour is Sadiq Khan predictably winning the London

Mayoralty after Zac Goldsmith's dreadful campaign, or rather non-campaign.

Sunday 8 May – Rutland

The *Mail on Sunday* carry my article saying that the EU debate must not be allowed to become a surrogate leadership race. I attack Boris and Gove for their blatant positioning in the referendum for personal advantage, and the level of attention being given to their self-promotion. We need a sensible debate about the EU, not all this game-playing by those at the top of the Leave campaign.

Oakham Branch lunch at Normanton Park, whose half-submerged church on the edge of Rutland Water is an iconic image of the county.

Back to London.

Monday 9 May – London

DC and BoJo both make speeches on the EU, and DC rather overstates the risk of war in Europe should we leave.

Lunch in the Adjournment restaurant with Ed Argar.

Statement by [Education Secretary] Nicky Morgan, backing down on compulsory academisation. The Speaker calls me, referring to me as the Conservative Party's *éminence grise*, to which I reply 'Very *grise*, Mr Speaker.'

DC addresses the Remain campaign for MPs in 1 Great George Street. The plans and attitude are hopelessly complacent and lack any sort of fizz. See Stanley Johnson, BoJo's father near the entrance. Amusingly a Remainer, as is all of the Johnson family except Boris, it seems.

Rather pissy CMEC drinks. Former UK Ambassador to Israel, Saudi Arabia and Afghanistan Sir Sherard Cowper-Coles, Egyptian Ambassador Nasser Kamel.

Both Boris and Gove come up to me in the voting lobby, Boris claiming not to have seen my *MoS* article, and Gove amusingly mock indignant about it.

The Whip Simon Kirby is unsubtly critical of what he believes to be Dominic Grieve (ISC Chairman) and the committee's plans to table unhelpful amendments at the report stage to the Regulation of Investigatory Powers Bill. I tell him he is completely misreading the risks, as they are not going to disrupt anything.

Tuesday 10 May – London
The *Telegraph* has become the *Daily Boris*, with about five life-size photos of him in today's edition.

Attend a cross-Whitehall Yemen video conference at DfID. Receive an ecstatic welcome from all the reception and security staff, who say they miss me as the minister, which was rather nice.

Chris White to my room at PCH for a good few glasses of wine and a tutorial on Yemen, to assist him as Chair of the Committee on Arms Export Controls.

Friday 13 May – Windsor/Rutland
To the Windsor Horse Show as a guest of the King of Bahrain. Bahrain is so often maligned by pro-Iranian extremists, yet the government there is taking massive steps to extend prosperity to its Shia population. The accusations of torture and oppression are just accepted without question by gullible members of the press. I've built up good relations with the government since I was DfID Minister. A fixture of the calendar is the annual Windsor Horse Show. It was started to raise money for making Spitfires in the war and has been going ever since. The Queen loves it, and the King generously supports it. Lovely lunch in the marquee with King Hamad, senior Bahrainis and associated Brits. The King's son, Sheikh Nasser, is a very athletic horseman and is always in the running to win the cross-country endurance ride. Very touchingly, HM the Queen joins us for tea. The King adores her and would do anything for her. The chemistry between them is a delight to watch. As always, there is nothing that can trump our Queen.

Saturday 14 May – Rutland
To Uppingham School for my first meeting as a Trustee.

Road signs filming with Tony Roe of BBC Midlands. We film two mini-roundabouts near Market Harborough where there are over twenty-five cycle-path and other warning signs, which illustrates the sort of idiocy my task force is trying to eliminate.

I mused at the contrast within my last forty-eight hours, switching from a lovely encounter with two crowned heads to railing in front of a camera about rusting metal poles.

Sunday 15 May – Rutland/London

Brunch. London. BA to Saudi Arabia for a visit as Yemen Envoy.

Tuesday 17 May – Riyadh

At last a practical encounter with our own Foreign Secretary, Philip Hammond. Until now he has never engaged with me on Yemen. He calls me ahead of my meeting with Yemen's President Hadi to ask me to intervene with him, having learnt that the President was threatening to pull his people from the peace talks in Kuwait, and wanted me to put pressure on him to hang on in there. A couple of hours later I faithfully delivered that message, and Hadi confirmed that he would not pull the plug. But otherwise I have no relationship with Hammond on this crucial issue.

Wednesday 18 May – Abu Dhabi

Michael Heseltine has savaged Boris for his whacky and intemperate conduct of the Leave campaign, saying he has made 'preposterous, obscene political remarks' and that 'his judgement is going'. Hezza, now in his eighties, is still a force to be reckoned with.

Friday 20 May – Erbil

Up early for the start of a four-day visit to Kurdistan.

Tuesday 24 May – London

FCO questions. One of the nastiest people in Parliament is the SNP's Tasmina Sheikh – I just can't find any redeeming qualities whatsoever. Her insensitive forthright barracking adds nothing to our politics. She has no hint of politeness or sensitivity and is devoid of any generosity of spirit or clarity of thought. If Parliament is to have any useful function, she is exactly what we do not need. For once she actually asked a perfectly cogent question, but her rasping tone and manner ruins it.

Tuesday 7 June–Wednesday 15 June

The referendum campaign rolls on, getting ever more nasty and silly. We could have had a serious debate about the UK's future with riveting arguments on each side. Instead we have a pantomime driven by the personalities and self-interest of Boris, [Nigel] Farage and the like. It is all profoundly depressing.

Thursday 16 June – Rutland

Drive to Rutland. Lots of issues around finances, pupil numbers and safeguarding. More safeguarding, and so on. I can see this trustee work is going to consume a lot of paper.

When I get home just after lunch the Sky ribbon says an MP has been attacked in Yorkshire, and it turns out to be Labour MP Jo Cox. Within hours it goes from bad to worse to sheer awful – she was shot and stabbed, and has died. I didn't know her really, but that makes it none the less appalling. I think back to Airey Neave and Ian Gow [two MPs murdered by the IRA], but thought in the modern age we face verbal and Twitter abuse but never something so physical. From all the tributes she seemed a lovely person. The attacker appears to have been some nationalistic nutter. What is this referendum doing to the country? It has divided us, and this may have been one of the consequences.

Monday 20 June – London

The House has been recalled for tributes to Jo Cox and a service in St Margaret's. The mood is very sombre, not surprisingly, although as always when there are eulogies in the Chamber they start off well and then peter out rather. What a miserable day, and so hard on her young family.

Thursday 23 June – Rutland/London

Referendum Day.

Do a clip with Claire Kavanagh for the BBC documentary on Brexit I've been contributing to.

Mood is that Remain will just squeak it. Even Nigel Farage says so. Nick Herbert MP insensitively self-important at the results party at the Blue Boar. Also there Dominic Grieve, Party donor Michael Wade. Go home at about 11.30. Rather tired.

Friday 24 June – London/Rutland

Woke up at 6am to hear the result. Shit! 52 per cent Leave, 48 per cent Remain.

The markets immediately dive 10 per cent.

And then – bang! At 8.15am David Cameron emerges from Number 10 and announces his intention to resign. It's almost before anyone's got up, and the government has been decapitated. Not only is the UK split from top to bottom – it's split country to country, family to family, everything to everything. What the hell happens now? I just know the rest of the world will be looking at the UK and thinking, 'What on earth have they just done to themselves? Why do they think this will do them any good?' It's obviously not a good start to lose your Prime Minister within a nanosecond of the result.

I'm due to speak at the annual meeting of Le Cercle – a long-standing, slightly crazy security conference which I've been going to for years. So I pick my way through the ruins of our international standing to the St James's Court Hotel in Buckingham Gate. In my address I present an apocalyptic picture, opening with 'This may be the day on which the Conservative Party destroys its fortunes for the next twenty years.'

After waking them all up with this stark forecast, I settled into a more measured analysis of what I thought it all means. I said people have voted for a concept, not a contract, so all the details of our departure have yet to be agreed. The people have made a choice between the current arrangements, which have been so demonised for so long, and a bright and sunny future of perfect sovereignty and prosperity – the path to which has not been mapped out in any detailed way. However hard we try, this is going to prove far more difficult and disrupting than any of the Leavers have ever admitted.

Almost unnoticed in this maelstrom of shock, Margaret Hodge launched a Commons motion of no confidence against Labour's farce of a Leader Jeremy Corbyn, who had been all but invisible during the referendum, and is known to have been personally sympathetic to Leave.

Saturday 25 June – Rutland

With no time for post-referendum grief, the papers have today moved straight on to leadership speculation, suggesting Theresa May is emerging as the 'Stop Boris' candidate, which seems about right to me. Her problem is that she's a Remainer, though she characteristically managed to keep her head down during the campaign.

I do the *Today* programme playing down the idea Boris is the natural choice. I tell them we need to ensure the whole thing isn't just seen through the prism of the referendum. The pitch has to be unity, sense and competence. The young have deserted Boris, as the scenes of people booing him outside his house yesterday demonstrate. Brexit will not convert into enhanced popularity for Conservatism. In a few months' time will Boris be an electoral asset or not?

The Brexit gang are clearly shocked and have no plan for the reality of exit – meanwhile Whitehall is understaffed and overstretched. Boris has no parliamentary base – he's made no friends, so this is absolutely wide open.

It's also stupid to say it must be a Brexiteer – just because the referendum went for Leave, it doesn't mean you can just take over the Party and Number 10. It's not just about media notoriety – we need the best person for the job and dignity on the world stage. I drop in a decent soundbite – that MPs should think twice about whether they want a non-stop ride on the big dipper. Also mention this is something like my sixth or seventh leadership election!

Sunday 26 June – London

I rush down to London – and discover the basement has a few inches of water covering the floor. The overnight biblical deluge may have been telling us something! Remove wet carpets and underlay from the TV room, which is a pretty miserable task. Quite a few houses nearby have suffered the same fate. It's as if the water came up from beneath.

IDS says on *Marr* that the Vote Leave promises were only possibilities. Oh … so no extra funding for the NHS after all? It is utterly shameless. They thought they would lose, so just said whatever they liked and promised the non-existent earth.

Speak to Ben Gummer, George Osborne, Theresa, then the PM. All disconsolate at the result and aghast at the thought of Boris succeeding as Prime Minister.

Speak to Damian Green, who is supposed to be pulling together Team TM [Theresa May]. Trouble is he rather lacks gumption, and having done so many of these campaigns myself I know the only way to win is to be hungry and hard, and drive the cause with frenzied determination.

Meanwhile in downtown Islington, twelve members of Corbyn's Shadow Cabinet have resigned, after he sacked Hilary Benn overnight for daring to tell him he wasn't up to the job. It's a classic case of shooting the messenger. But if it goes on like this it looks like we could have two leadership contests under way at once.

Pictures on TV of Boris plotting at his home with Jake Berry and Ben Wallace.

See Francis Elliott of *The Times* in Smith Sq. He says Hancock has texted Boris to say that he'll join him, and also that Osborne will endorse Boris. Ugh!

Monday 27 June – London

More Labour frontbenchers have resigned, and Tom Watson has told Corbyn to expect a challenge.

Lunch with Ed Argar at the Beefsteak.

At 3.30pm the PM makes a statement in the House on the referendum result. He cracks a good joke about the chaos on the

Labour side, saying the new MP for Tooting, who had just been sworn in, could be in the Shadow Cabinet by the end of the day.

At 6pm I went to see Theresa in her office in the House. I told her, 'I've only got one thing to say – you must stand. I'm right behind you, go for it!' She was pretty wooden, as she always is. You never quite know what's churning away beneath her undemonstrative demeanour.

I call Damian Green, the invisible leader of her campaign. He says, 'Oh – there's no need for her to declare in public – she'll just give a policy speech in three days.' Hopeless!

I call Stephen Parkinson and Nick Timothy [former SpAds to TM, who are running her campaign] to try to inject some urgency, then speak to George Hollingbery [her Parliamentary Private Secretary] – he says Fiona [Hill, another former SpAd] is doing decisions on declaration, and she's 'not available to speak to'. I follow up with a text to impress on him the need to mount a professional campaign with a 24-hour comms operation. At the moment no phones are being answered – it looks a shambles.

There's a tiny bit of me that thinks I might yet stand myself! Mark Menzies and Ian Liddell-Grainger have been encouraging me, and when I last spoke to Tony Blair he told me, 'You're one of the ones our side fears.' The old flatterer. All very nice, but it's not an option, and I've zero intention of actually doing so.

Vote of no confidence in Corbyn has been called for tomorrow. Crowds of far-left nutters mounted a demo in Parliament Square in support of him. The world has gone mad.

Tuesday 28 June – London

May Campaign meeting at 9am in Portcullis House. Really good YouGov poll this morning – 31 per cent of Conservative voters back her, against 24 per cent for Boris. Osborne has ruled himself out.

Later I speak to the elusive Fiona Hill, and we arrange to meet at Pret on Marsham St – just opposite the Home Office. It was clear she was working from there [Pret], which wasn't ideal – so I told her she should use my house as a base instead, given it is just round the corner. We went back there and I gave her a key so she could come and go.

Wednesday 29 June – London

May Campaign meeting first thing. Numbers are looking good. Danny Finkelstein has a good column in *The Times* today saying Boris is not a certainty. Very true.

Team BoJo certainly seem to be making some errors of judgement – he cancelled an appearance at a hustings for Remain-supporting MPs at short notice this morning, which caused huge irritation among colleagues. It looked rude and arrogant.

I put a note in to the Speaker asking if he might call me at PMQs:

Dear Mr Speaker,

I know this is a long shot, but should you be able to squeeze me in for a short pithy contribution at PMQs, I should be forever in your debt. I appreciate I am not on the Order Paper but in these extraordinary times there are some things which can usefully be said and which matter, for which in the great tide of history there is but one single opportunity!

He duly called me, and I launch my little 'Borisconi' barb.

[*The Times*'s sketchwriter, Patrick Kidd, described the scene the next day: 'Sir Alan Duncan (C, Rutland and Melton), that playful sprite, could not resist a dig at the absent Boris Johnson. He asked Mr Cameron "if he would compare the undemonstrative competence and dignity of Angela Merkel (for which read Theresa May, whom Sir Alan favours) with the theatrical and comical antics of Silvio Borisconi?" Mr Cameron smirked and pretended he had not heard this deliberate slip of the tongue; Mrs May and her supporters chuckled.']

It went down very well in the Chamber and has attracted a lot of attention. And hopefully, beneath the laughter, colleagues will consider the serious point.

TM's stock is rising – tonight she spoke to the same group Boris snubbed and by all accounts stormed it. Some decent jokes, and she appeared a proper grown-up. Her campaign launches properly tomorrow with an article in *The Times* and a speech at RUSI [Royal United Services Institute].

Thursday 30 June – London

Amazing drama.

Team May morning meeting at PCH with lots to discuss – a good poll for TM shows her with a 17-point lead over Boris among Party members. Intel on the Johnson campaign – Matt Hancock has gone over to them, Amber Rudd might introduce BoJo at his launch, Patel and Leadsom have been frozen out of the inner core. Aussie campaign strategist Lynton Crosby is controlling him, and will go heavily on immigration. But didn't Boris suggest an amnesty on illegal immigration? An email to Gove from his wife, the *Mail* columnist Sarah Vine, has been leaked and not only reveals doubts about Boris' suitability as Leader but suggests that Gove has been pressing him to be more hardline.

We'd barely begun the meeting when the news broke that Gove was ditching Boris and standing himself. What an utter shit! Shortly followed by Leadsom also announcing she's standing, all amid stories of utter chaos and a crisis of confidence in the Boris camp.

Against this backdrop, I went up to RUSI for the TM launch, where I was sitting in the front row. She gave a great speech, showing all the right qualities – a serious woman for serious times while the others fight like rats in a sack. There was even a good dig at Boris negotiating the purchase of useless water cannon when he was Mayor. During questions there was a funny one about others throwing their hats in the ring and someone shouted, 'It's not too late, Sir Alan!' Don't tempt me!

Boris then turned up at his launch, made a truncated speech, then abruptly announced he wasn't going to stand. Extraordinary. One whiff of grapeshot from Michael Gove and he has completely buckled. It just doesn't look as if he needed to, when above all others he is clearly the only serious contender other than Theresa.

I bumped into half his team walking back dejected from the St Ermin's Hotel, and invited a handful of them home for drinks, including Nigel Adams and Alec Shelbrooke.

This all makes TM the undeniable favourite, and I suppose we could now be facing Gove in the run-off, as he's clearly taken a good chunk of Boris's supporters with him. But the fury at his treachery has completely trashed his reputation.

Friday 1 July – London
Gove gets a total mauling in the press – it seems he stabbed Boris in the back with calculated intent, giving him only a few minutes' warning that he was going to ditch him and stand himself.

Paradoxically, this tees up nicely my planned meeting with the editor of the *Daily Telegraph*, Chris Evans. I'd set it up thanks to the intervention of Guy Black [formerly of Conservative Campaign Headquarters], with the clear purpose of seeking the paper's endorsement of Theresa. I'd leapt at the obvious opportunity within minutes of Boris withdrawing, thinking 'Where would the *Daily Boris* now plant its flag?'

Chris Evans was charming and welcoming in the corner of their large open-plan office in Buckingham Palace Road. With all the screens and fizzing activity it could equally have been a City trading floor. I put my case for Theresa, saying with a smile about Boris vs Gove: 'Now that your man is out – surely you don't want to endorse a *Times* man!'

He took the pitch and said he'd give TM a call. I think it's a done deal that the *DT* will now endorse her. Job done.

Then there was the Gove campaign launch, which I watched on TV. There's something so socially unaware about him: it lies somewhere between shameless and synthetic. He has often said of himself that he's unsuitable to be Prime Minister, which must go down as one of the strangest advertising pitches ever: 'I'd be no good at it, so vote for me!'

Saturday 2 July – London
The contest is now a very public fight for headlines, and Gove is losing. Those this morning include his old employers at *The Times* splashing with 'Gove fights to stay in race', which must surely be a personal blow to him, but it's true. As well as a veritable stampede

of MPs coming over to Theresa, many of the Brexiteers he thought he could count on are lining up behind the vacuous Andrea Leadsom, who now has more declared supporters than him. This can't have been how he imagined it when he plotted his midnight coup.

There are now even suggestions that TM should take over without a contest, Michael Howard-style. Nice as it would be, a coronation for a Prime Minister might provoke accusations that there was no adequate democratic process.

Popped into fortieth-birthday drinks for Peter Wilson – a Tory researcher turned civil service press officer – at the Jugged Hare pub. The usual crowd of fun researchers and public affairs types. Full of giggles and gossip.

Sunday 3 July – London
Head into TM4PM HQ in Greycoat Place for a meeting with Theresa and the top team. We are under pressure for her to release her tax returns because Michael Gove will. More importantly, it is putting pressure on Leadsom, who has said that she won't unless she gets into the final two, and then only one year's worth.

I'm totally against all this disclosure of private financial affairs, but the pressure has been mounting on Leadsom, so we can't miss the opportunity to paint her into a corner, given that Theresa's tax affairs are utterly uncomplicated, which they're bound to be as she's been in the Cabinet for six years.

By happy coincidence, husband Philip and I share the same bank manager and so can easily cooperate to gather the information for her. We exchange texts and calls. Critically we are preparing to release three years' worth in contrast to Leadsom's offer of just one.

Monday 4 July – London
TM campaign team meeting in the morning, then spend the day sorting the press release on tax returns and getting clear explanatory statements from the bank, who at one point I text, 'The future of the world depends on it and we need it sort of now!'

Once it's all done, have a nice exchange of emails with Philip – I tell him we're on a mission we must win. Ever the cool head, he replies that there's 'still quite a long way to go'.

Tuesday 5 July – London

Boris has endorsed Andrea Leadsom – yet more evidence of his fundamental unseriousness.

TM campaign meeting ahead of the first ballot. [MPs vote in multiple ballots to narrow the candidates down to two, who are put to the wider Conservative Party membership.] Spend the day corralling votes and shoring up our numbers. My prediction is: May 175, Leadsom 50 (poss higher), Crabb 48, Gove 44 (poss lower), Fox 9.

Head to the campaign HQ in Greycoat Place for the result. There is quite a buzz as we wait, and I sit with her and Philip in the open-plan office. Ken Clarke has been caught on camera before a *Sky News* interview referring to Theresa as a 'bloody difficult woman', and there is a slightly awkward moment as they replayed the clip. Everyone was looking over to see her reaction – but she smiled gamely. Philip hadn't seen it, and when it came on the screen his response was 'Well, I think that's rather good, isn't it?'

The results come through: TM's total a bit down on my forecast, Leadsom a bit higher, and Crabb down quite a bit: May 165, Leadsom 66, Gove 48, Crabb 34, Fox 16.

A very strong result for Theresa – half of all our MPs. Fox is eliminated, and Crabb also pulls out. Later on, I text TM with some thoughts:

Theresa. A good day. I think tmrw is the most crucial day in your political life, so forgive me for just telling it straight. The danger is colleagues sink into a frenzy of tactical voting and we end up with peculiar numbers. Your instructions – and I agree – are that all should just play it straight. But we need a ferociously robust process tmrw for ensuring that colleagues do just that. This needs intensive coordination and real-time shared info within the team. Might I suggest you command Gav

[Williamson], Michael [Ellis], George [Hollingbery], Julian [Smith], me and someone from the Crabb team to meet on the hour every hour putting all their cards on the table to cover every conceivable trick.

It is entirely about MPs. This needs phoning, Tea Room trawling, rumour checking, rebuttal tactics, schmoozing before and after PMQs etc. We cannot just go at a medium pace and hope for the best. In Parliamentary terms this will be the last day of the big push, and it needs more than just a morning meeting. End of brain dump. Alan

Wednesday 6 July – London

TM team meeting. Some people have been suggesting that we boost Gove so he beats Leadsom, because he'd be easier to beat in the final. The message passed down from TM at the start was absolutely not to play those games – and that remains the case. But Leadsom's people are still calling foul and saying we lent votes yesterday because we are afraid of facing her.

Later on, Nick Boles sends a silly text to colleagues urging them to vote for Gove to stop Leadsom reaching the run-off: 'Michael doesn't mind spending two months taking a good thrashing from Theresa if that's what it takes but in the party's interest and the national interest surely we must work together to stop AL.'

Inevitably this is leaked, and is hugely damaging for Michael when it's brought up at the 1922 Committee [the parliamentary Conservative Party] hustings later on. The meeting in Committee Room 14 is packed. I stand by the door, texting updates back to Fi Hill on how it's going. TM absolutely aces it – I teed up Richard Graham to ask her a question about Ken Clarke's comment. Her answer is perfect: 'Ken Clarke says I'm a bloody difficult woman. The next man to find that out will be Jean-Claude Juncker!' It brought the house down. Game, set and match.

Thursday 7 July – London

Morning team mtg, then vote in the second ballot, before going into an ISC meeting.

Went to TM's room for the result of the second ballot. She was rather nervous waiting for it – and I got a picture of her looking up at the screen. Our canvassing showed we had over 200 pledged, but there was the nagging doubt about people playing games, and Williamson can be a law unto himself. He can't be trusted an inch.

The actual result was 199 – a couple short of my forecast, and one short of hers, but an overwhelming margin: May 199, Leadsom 84, Gove 46.

The campaign was quick to brief that this was the largest ever vote for any leadership candidate in a final ballot with no incumbent standing. It beats the 185 that John Major got in the final ballot of the 1990 contest. Fittingly, immediately after the result I go with James for a drink with Major at his flat – all very jolly. He loves a good mischievous gossip, and he still has all the right opinions. Funny to think it's twenty-six years since his own leadership campaign was based in my house, and I'm now in the thick of yet another one.

Friday 8 July – London/Rutland

Morning papers very good for Theresa – she's seen as almost unbeatable, but some are hedging their bets given Boris is strongly backing Leadsom, and stranger things have happened lately. Beware complacency.

Various press requests for contributions to profile pieces they're preparing on TM – I message Philip to check he's happy with some lines I'm proposing to give about him.

For some time I have been quietly talking to [Cabinet Secretary] Jeremy Heywood about what a May team might look like, and what the policy emphasis might be from those around her. This is perfectly proper informal contact, which is not for a second pretending to be in any way official, but the civil service being what they are, the idea that I might actually go and see him has been put about the system and filtered to Fi Hill. She has completely erupted, shouting at me, 'Not a good idea … not a good idea!' It seemed sensible to me to open the lines of communication informally and let the machine know some of what to expect and how the voting was going. But of course Fi is insecure and wants everything run through her and Nick. I can see qualities in her all of a sudden which are pretty unsettling.

At 10pm *The Times* front page comes out featuring an interview with Leadsom who says she is better equipped to be PM because she has children! All of my dinner guests are aghast and appalled by it.

I text Philip May: 'Leadsom is like Trump – hoping that horrid news gives her notoriety and success. Keep your cool and your dignity, and make sure Theresa is not hurt by it. Leadsom is despicable – Sarah Palin [former US Vice-Presidential candidate] on crack. Give T a hug from the whole team.'

I then put out a tweet: 'I'm gay and in a civil partnership. No children, but ten nieces and nephews. Do I not have a stake in the future of the country? Vile.' A Twitter storm follows … ramped up perhaps by my own spiky comment. Leadsom has never been through the mincer before – she has risen fast from nowhere, and this will test her mettle.

Saturday 9 July – Rutland
Leadsom story rages all day. She denied that she'd said it, but *The Times* has now produced the transcript, Leadsom having not had any press officer with her to record it. Completely amateurish. My sense is that she must be seriously rattled.

Take Noodle to the vet to remove a seed stuck in her ear.

Monday 11 July – London
Wow, what a dramatic day! It was notionally the first day of the extensive leadership campaign in the country to woo Party members. Hyper-speed rubber-chicken circuit!

TM was in Birmingham for her official launch. The pre-briefed headlines were some mindless Nick Timothy crap about cutting executive pay and putting employees on company boards, but the rest of the speech was strong – unify the country, deliver Brexit and create 'a country that works for everyone'.

Then at 11.30am there's a newsflash – Leadsom is to make a statement at noon, with the immediate speculation that she's going to drop out soon confirmed by various sources. I text Philip to let him know, as I assumed he was at work and wasn't sure anyone in the team would have done so.

Speak to '22 Committee Chairman Graham Brady to check there's no way under the rules that Gove can re-enter by taking Leadsom's place on the ballot, and he confirms categorically that there is not. So that's it – TM is about to become PM in waiting!

I text TM: 'In anticipation … Yippee x 1000!!!!! I am on the edge of joyful tears. Enjoy your journey back from Brum. Savour every minute. Alan'.

Leadsom finally makes her statement and, at 12.15, pulls out. Says she doesn't have enough support in the parliamentary Party and we need to get on with Brexit. Frankly she simply wasn't up to it.

TM races back from Birmingham to claim her crown, as colleagues fall over themselves to declare their loyalty. Brady makes a statement outside St Stephen's Entrance confirming there will be no reopening of the ballot – I rush there with colleagues and stand behind Grayling as he pays tribute to Leadsom on behalf of Team May.

Cameron speaks outside Number 10 to confirm he'll hand over after PMQs on Wednesday. When TM returns there is a packed meeting of the 1922 at which Brady says she is now Leader with immediate effect. We then pile out to St Stephen's for her victorious statement to the waiting press. I get the kiss!

We head over to the campaign office at Greycoat Place where an impromptu victory party is held – cans of lager, and champagne out of plastic cups. Stephen Parkinson hands round 'Theresa May' campaign badges, produced for a national campaign that began only hours before but finished minutes later! TM arrives to huge cheers and gives a little speech standing by the photocopier, a beaming Philip by her side. We all pose for a group photo taken by Andrew Parsons, the nearest thing we have to a modern court painter. She already has the aura of power.

The speed of it all has been extraordinary. First thing this morning all eyes were on Labour's leadership crisis as Angela Eagle announced she was challenging Corbyn, while we were gearing up for a gruelling nine-week campaign around the country. Now it's all done and dusted. That's politics.

Tuesday 12 July – London
Labour's NEC [National Executive Committee] says Corbyn can stand as Leader without fresh nominations – so he doesn't need his MPs' support. Death knell for the Party, as he'll win again with support from leftie grassroots members, isolating Labour further in the eyes of most people.

Much speculation and jostling on TM appointments in her new government. One of my failures as a politician is that unlike all the others I don't ask for a top position when my candidate wins. I never did with William and the next thing I know Osborne and Cameron are coming up on the inside track before they're even in the Commons. I didn't either with Cameron, and some of those who made it to the Cabinet were pretty hopeless. Even now I'm not going to do it – I'm past trying to grub my way to the top. It would be nice to think that after seven shadow Cabinet positions in opposition and four years in DfID something might be looming. I have no illusions, but it would be nice to be offered Leader of the House or Deputy Foreign Secretary.

Wednesday 13 July – London
DC does his last PMQs, where he has some good jokes and really seems to be enjoying himself. He jibes at Corbyn that we've managed to have our entire leadership contest before Labour has even sorted out the rules for theirs, and when it comes to female prime ministers it will soon be two–nil to us. Theresa, on the bench next to him, smiled broadly. He signed off with a poignant 'I was the future once,' referencing his first PMQs line to Blair in 2005, and left to a standing ovation from our side.

And then seamlessly, in the time-honoured British manner, where one Prime Minister passes the baton to the next, the uninterrupted continuity of British government smoothly transfers. Almost as soon as David Cameron leaves Number 10, Theresa May leaves for the Palace to succeed him.

The TV helicopters hover above to track her car up the Mall and back, and a pool camera records her and Philip arriving through the archway of the inner courtyard of the Palace to be met at the steps. The photographs of Theresa May being invited by the Queen to form a government show Theresa making a deep and respectful curtsey – a good start, worthy of Margaret Thatcher at her best.

As CMEC Chair I host their annual reception at the Savoy, which is buzzing with speculation about who will be appointed to her first Cabinet. It's one of those odd things in political life where despite holding seven Shadow Cabinet jobs and hovering near the top of the Party for two decades – not to say having driven some important elements of her leadership campaign – I just know that I will not be summoned.

And then there is astonishment and total disbelief at the reception when the news hits the room that she has appointed Boris to be Foreign Secretary. They are all rather dumbstruck by the choice. All of the CMEC people are by definition internationally minded, and they just don't see him as serious. But it's clearly a big step to have drawn the forces of Brexit inside her tent. Whether the ploy will hold good over time remains to be seen.

Tobias Ellwood asked if I'm staying on afterwards to dine with some of the guests, to which I say no. Then, forty-five minutes later as I'm leaving, he bounds up and berates me, saying that he went back to the Commons only to discover that he was due to stay on for dinner himself. I said, 'Don't have a go at me. It's not my fault – I don't run your diary!'

Thursday 14 July – London
Further Cabinet appointments unfold during the morning. Last night she unceremoniously ditched George Osborne and appointed her top layer: as well as Johnson at FCO, she appointed Fox to Trade, Davis to the new Department for Exiting the European Union (DExEU).

It all felt as if she was teeing things up for a Gove exit, and so it turned out. Around mid-morning he was sacked! It's hardly surprising – he always pushed his luck to the limit, and what he did during the leadership campaign has made him impossible to work with. The news came while the ISC was gathering ahead of a witness session, and we all watched the TV to see the other comings and goings.

More snakes and ladders during the day. Out go Nicky Morgan, John Whittingdale and Oliver Letwin. Not sure yet where Jeremy Hunt will end up, but Patrick McLoughlin was appointed Party Chairman, which is great because everyone loves PatMac. But Gavin Williamson as Chief Whip feels ill-judged. It's too far, too fast. You want someone loyal there, and you won't get that from GW, who is an inexperienced schemer, only in it for himself.

Justine Greening to Education – which might turn out OK. But I'm not sure the legal profession will be too enamoured to have Liz Truss at Justice!

Friday 15 July – Rutland
Was having a coffee in Uppingham with Nick Grindley (of the antique shop) at the Falcon Hotel, where it turned out the Biz Club, which is a business lunch club loosely linked to local Conservatives, had been having its monthly gathering. The speakers were Philip Hollobone MP (who had not let me know he was coming to my patch) and the ex-Tory MEP Roger Helmer. I only realised they were there when they all came pouring out of the dining room around 3pm.

I went over to my Association President Frances, Duchess of Rutland who has been virulently and nastily pro-Leave, and said, 'Well, I guess we are both happy: you have the EU result you want, and I have the PM I want.' To which she erupted and shouted, 'Oh you are so disgusting!' and walked off in a huff. A few minutes later I tried again and asked if there was something she wanted to discuss, and she stormed off saying she didn't want to talk to me. The trouble is, she thinks she's in charge of everything, and that anyone who doesn't share her opinion is beyond the pale. She really is such a haughty old boot.

Back home, the Number 10 switchboard rang at about 6pm asking me to take a call from the PM. She offered me Minister of State at the new Department for International Trade, putting perfectly nice arguments that I was internationally minded and had been the Trade Envoy to Yemen. I had to think quickly as I had no wish to be number two to Liam Fox, despite her obvious plan to put loyalists in beneath strongly Brexit secretaries of state. I demurred in a friendly, chirrupy way, pointing out I was never Trade Envoy to Yemen as it was an entirely political and diplomatic post, and suggested that the Trade job would be insufficiently stretching, and that with all my Middle East experience and knowledge from my DfID days, would she consider the Foreign Office for me instead?

It doesn't often pay to negotiate during a reshuffle, and it's almost impossible to do so in a way that keeps the boss happy, but I somehow managed, while leaving the clear impression that I might even say no to Trade. It was an absolutely critical five-minute call. She said she would come back to me, and did so half an hour later and said yes to the FCO, implicitly as Minister for the Middle East.

Conducted a charity auction for Bringhurst Primary School, where James is Chairman of Governors – generous supplies of alcohol made the bidders suitably generous in return.

After dinner at the pub with James, the main item on the news was coverage of an apparent coup in Turkey, which I guess is now my problem!

Saturday 16 July – London/Rutland

Go to London very early. The Turkish coup seems to have failed, and President Erdoğan appears to have regained control. But there's been a lot of shooting, both from stolen fighter aircraft and tanks. Reports suggest seventy people are dead and 1,000 injured. It looks like a faction within the army carried it out, but the facts are still murky.

My appointment has not yet been announced. Gavin Williamson said at 9am when I called him that he was just going into Number 10 and would try to let me know when it would be public.

At 5.30pm I go to the Foreign Office. All seems clear and agreed that I will be Minister for the Middle East, as expected. Permanent

Under-Secretary Simon McDonald called to say it's all been agreed, and he would recommend it to the Foreign Secretary. But when I see Boris at 6pm it seems a massive problem has arisen, which is nothing short of contemptible. Boris says the Conservative Friends of Israel are going ballistic, and Eric Pickles and Stuart Polak have both called him incessantly saying I must not be appointed. Stuart Polak has been running CFI for thirty years, and now in the Lords promotes a strong Netanyahu/Likud version of Israeli history and ambitions. Pickles, now Sir Eric, and President of CFI, seems even more ardent than Polak. Nobody understands where Pickles' venom has come from – he's no internationalist, but maybe some of it is driven by his experience when he was leader of Bradford Council. Polak's vendetta is palpable. If I'd ever so much as sided with anti-Semitic people, or said anything near it, they'd be fully entitled to have a go at me, but that's not me and I never have. As I see it, it is for no other reason than that I believe in the rights of Palestinians and whereas they pretend to believe in two parallel states, it's quite clear that they don't, and so set out to destroy all genuine advocates for Palestine. They just want to belittle and subjugate the Palestinians.

This had started despite my appointment not having yet been announced. Now Number 10 are telling Boris I cannot have the Middle East. This it seems has come from Nick Timothy, who has also been got at by P & P. For all anyone knows the PM is completely unaware of this inappropriate lobbying. Boris is somewhat indignant at this pressure and its propriety (or lack of it). I offer a compromise – saying I will do the Middle East but not Israel/Palestine. Boris likes the idea and says he will support it. But on any level it is appalling that a PM's appointments can be subject to such lobbying. Our own national interest is being taken for a sucker.

Apparently Tobias Ellwood (Parliamentary Under-Secretary of State or PUSS) wants to keep the Middle East.

In any other country the conduct of Eric Pickles and Stuart Polak would in my view be seen as entrenched espionage that should prompt an inquiry into their conduct.

Sunday 17 July – Rutland/London

Jeffrey Archer party in Grantchester. Hilarious cabaret song by Kit and the Widow. Sinatra's 'I did it my way' became 'I said it "Why May?"'

Ellwood was there and was in animated discussion with Nadhim Zahawi MP while looking at me across the lawn, as if to say 'I hope he's out of earshot.' Unfortunately someone told me they heard him use the words 'He mustn't get the Middle East.'

On the way there, Boris calls. He says keeping the Middle East but giving Israel/Palestine to someone else should be OK, but says they have introduced the 'sniff test', which is little more than making up a rule to say that if it might read badly in the *Daily Mail*, you can't do it – even if the rules say you can. My only recent connection with the Middle East is my appointment as Chairman of the Fujairah refinery, which I have to cancel anyway on becoming a minister. On this basis, if you've ever been a banker you could never be a Treasury minister.

Lots of calls to and from Sue Gray, who is in charge of ethics and propriety at the Cabinet Office. She puts it to me that I can't really have the Middle East because I used to be in the oil business. I cannot see, under the rules as they stand, if properly applied, how anything in my past should disqualify me. I just know that what is behind this is not an issue of propriety at all, but Nick Timothy being in cahoots with CFI lobbying. This whole issue of Israel is utterly out of proportion, but, worse, is permitted to empower interested parties in Number 10 to decide what a minister's responsibilities should be. This is improper. It's wrong. I actually think it's corrupt, but the whole system buys into it without realising how wrong it is. I agree to meet her at 9.30am tomorrow.

While the Turkey coup seems quashed, the Board of Deputies of British Jews have had an open webcast with their Chairman Jonathan Arkush, in which Labour MP Louise Ellman says I must not be an FCO minister. My appointment isn't even public yet. How did they know? Clearly Pickles and Polak have been actively lobbying against me, linking CFI, Labour Friends of Israel and the Board of Deputies. This is the most disgusting interference in our public life. I find it astonishing the system allows it to happen, all the more so as anything I have ever said has been wholly in tune with government policy. The difference seems to be that I believe in that policy, whereas CFI and the government itself do not!

Disturbingly, on Boris's first flight as Foreign Secretary on an RAF plane, it has to make an emergency diversion to Luton.

Monday 18 July – London

I see Sue Gray at 70 Whitehall at 9.30am. She offers what I see as some very flimsy arguments for blocking my Middle East role, which I feel are artificial – I suspect it is not what the Prime Minister wants, but what the PM's Chief of Staff is telling her. This is so wrong on all levels. I see Sir Simon McDonald at 10.30 and say I'll simply not take up the job if I am forced out by the CFI.

I install myself in my new office at the FCO and have further calls to Sue Gray. To be fair to McDonald, he is rather perturbed by what is going on, but is understandably nervous about sticking his neck out with a new PM and a new Foreign Secretary. But he agrees to go and see the Cabinet Secretary Jeremy Heywood and the PM's Principal Private Secretary, Simon Case.

Meanwhile I meet my own Private Secretary and new office, who all seem great. I ask them to delay all my briefings and first put me straight through to our Ambassador in Ankara, Richard Moore, so I can speak to him directly about the failed coup, but also ask after the welfare of embassy staff.

I am told all roads lead to oil interests, and so they cannot sanction me having responsibility for the Gulf. There isn't even a perception that I could be facing a conflict of interests – there is just an illogical insinuation that I might break the Ministerial Code, which I have never done and never would. Ironically, Liam Fox did break it and is now a secretary of state – so why should I be treated harshly for something I've never done? The only people who are acting improperly are CFI and those who accept their browbeating lobbying. Rather galling to read reports of my appointment which are strongly approving, and which all assume I am to be Minister for the Middle East.

I confide in my new Private Secretary, Lance Domm, to tell him what's going on. There is serious argy-bargy all day. I am then offered what they insist is the most serious portfolio beneath the Foreign Secretary: EU, Americas, Central Asia, NATO and European security including Iran.

Everyone is very concerned that I might immediately resign and cause a massive stink about this outside interference. McDonald comes in at about 5.30 anxiously seeking reassurance I am not going to walk. He pleads with me. I mull it over for a few minutes and tell him 'OK', but that he should never forget what it is the FCO has just submitted to.

Trident debate in Commons. Dinner in Members' [Dining Room].

Tuesday 19 July – London

My first (re)appearance at the dispatch box, answering an Urgent Question on the coup in Turkey. A triumph. Lots of nice comments about my 'resurrection' to office. Emily Thornberry, Labour's Shadow Foreign Secretary, made a barbed comment welcoming me and the 'all-male ministerial team'. This allowed me to correct her by pointing out that our Lords Minister, Joyce Anelay, was, the last time I spoke to her, a woman. Alex Salmond noted the 'spectacular late flowering' of my ministerial career, to which I retorted that I had never quite seen myself as a hardy perennial. All good fun.

On the substance, I was able to give a read-out of the PM's phone call with Erdoğan, and announce my visit to Ankara tomorrow.

Small dinner at Lancaster House with US Secretary of State John Kerry. The main agenda item was Yemen, which is probably my *Mastermind* specialist subject. It's early days for Boris, and the complexities of Yemen had clearly not yet dawned on him. If he wants to make a name for himself, this is exactly the sort of issue he should get his head around quickly.

Wednesday 20 July – Ankara
Fly to Ankara via Istanbul. Go immediately to the Turkish Parliament building, which took a direct hit from a fighter flown by the coup perpetrators. There was quite a commotion around me as I viewed the rubble and shattered windows while on my way to meet the Speaker. It was immediately apparent that everyone's emotions were running very high, and that the event had been a deeply searing experience for them.

Dinner with MPs from all four parties, including the former head of the OIC (the Organisation of Islamic Cooperation), Ekmeleddin İhsanoğlu, who I knew from my DfID days.

Our Ambassador's residence is one of the most beautiful. It's a great FCO team. Richard Moore is a brilliant Ambassador. His amazingly charming wife Maggie, who is blind, is pioneering the introduction of guide dogs to Turkey, which is not easy in a Muslim country.

Further details have emerged of Boris' baptism of fire – an emergency landing in Luton on his RAF flight which seems to have been quite dramatic. Hydraulic fluid and smoke in the cabin, oxygen masks deployed and an emergency exit on landing.

Thursday 21 July – Ankara/London
Nice breakfast at the residence. My first FCO intelligence briefing. When I was at DfID I teasingly referred to them all as 'Simon Pook' – 'S.Pook' for short.

All-staff meeting at the embassy – linked into our Istanbul consulate via video – to offer appreciation and reassurance after what they've been through. Some of them were closely in among the fighter jets and explosions of the failed coup.

My visit was not just a diplomatic statement to Turkey in support of their democracy, it was also about exercising a duty of care to our own people.

Arrive to meet Prime Minister Binali Yıldırım just as he suddenly has to leave to go to Parliament, where they were debating the introduction of a three-month state of emergency. Richard Moore and I go back to the residence, assuming we won't now see him before I have to fly out. So we head for the airport, only to be suddenly summoned to see the PM after all at the Parliament. A good meeting after again seeing the rubble in the courtyards of the bombed building.

Just miss our flight, but manage to connect back to London via Istanbul.

A nice email following my visit reports:

[The] visit buys us significant credit … He was the first Minister from any country to visit since last weekend's failed coup … All Turkish interlocutors greeted the Minister with exceptional warmth.

Friday 22 July – London/Rutland

A full day in the office.

Dinner at Mossiman's with Sayd Haitham bin Tarik, one of two who might be the next Sultan, hosted by Oman Ambassador Abdulaziz al Hinai.

David Davis calls on my mobile to say that relations between FCO and DExEU need to work well. I said I'd be happy to meet him soon to discuss how. I suspect there will be territorial boundary disputes fairly soon between FCO, DExEU and the Department of International Trade … to say nothing of Number 10.

Sunday 24 July–Friday 29 July – Scotland

Lovely week's holiday at Invermark with Bim and Tas Hart.

Saturday 30 July – Scotland/Rutland

Drive back to Rutland. Ian Taylor, my friend of nearly forty years since my Oxford and Shell days, runs ginormous oil trader Vitol and is Chairman of the Royal Opera House. He calls to seek my advice because he's learnt the Honours Committee is trying to block him from receiving a knighthood in David Cameron's resignation honours. For inexplicable reasons, the committee are objecting. There is hardly a top businessman in the world who has not been involved in a court case somewhere, and the high-rolling world of oil trading in no exception. But it is intolerable that civil servants, who know all too little about business, can make judgements based on a Google search which would deprive someone like Ian of the recognition he so deserves.

Sunday 31 July – Rutland
Speak to Laurence Mann [David Cameron's former Downing Street Political Secretary, who has stayed on with him to run his office]. Explain the Ian situation and say I hope DC will put his foot down and simply insist.

Monday 1 August – London
Get through to Michael Spicer, who as Lord Spicer now chairs the Political Honours Sub-Committee, to ask what the hell is going on. He says there is a limit to what he can do if a nomination has been obstructed before it reaches him. Meanwhile Ian is in an impossible position. He is a highly worthy nominee, but is so decent he doesn't want to cause embarrassment to anybody.

Tuesday 2 August – London
Email Ian to say that he might be wiser to withdraw from the honours recommendations and save it for later.

A despicable day for the decency of British politics. There is nothing worse than civil servants thinking that they are more important than elected and accountable politicians. An entire report should be written about those in the Cabinet Office who sit in judgement about these matters of propriety in our politics. They stopped me becoming Minister for the Middle East on the grounds that my former links with the region would not pass the 'sniff test', which is nothing more than an arbitrary judgement, rather than something explicitly in the rules.

Ian will issue the statement he discussed with me, which will say he would rather not be considered for an honour. It runs as the main ribbon on Sky at 10pm, within twenty minutes of him announcing it. It's so unjust, but he has emerged from the episode with his dignity intact.

Thursday 4 August – London

As I'm responsible for arms control policy, the FCO has become edgy about a court case in which Saudi Arabia is accused of using cluster munitions in Yemen. I brief Defence Secretary Michael Fallon on our contingency plans for any court judgment criticising us.

Receive various reports of two bad days out for our top ministers – Fox was a disaster at the Arab Chamber of Commerce, and BoJo made a bog of his speech in NY.

Tuesday 16 August – Rutland/Norfolk

To Norfolk with James. A walk and then dinner in the pub with James's old City friend Lisa Mulley, husband Miles and their two daughters. She says her Volvo is the first car in the world to be built entirely by women. I said, 'Does it crash a lot?' She scolds me by sweeping my drink away.

Sunday 21 August – Rutland/London/Sardinia

Leave Noodle with Mary Fairbairn, who lives in the barn next door and loves looking after her. Head for London, and then fly off to Olbia in Sardinia.

Monday 22 August–Wednesday 31 August – Sardinia/Corsica on Talitha

Join the fun gang on the boat with David Ross, his mother Lin and son Carl.

Up the coast of Sardinia to Corsica. Bonifacio, Calvi, then up to Genoa. Occasional FCO updates …

Horrid earthquake in Amatrice, mid-Italy. The President of Uzbekistan is seriously ill. António Guterres is leading the pack to become the next UN Secretary General. The TTIP (US–EU trade agreement) negotiations are thought to have collapsed after three years: which offers an indication of the scale of the challenge facing the UK, post-EU.

The papers keep on reporting that BoJo, Fox and Davis are all at odds. After a joint meeting to clear the air, apparently Boris came back into his office and, when asked for a read-out, said, 'They just don't have a bloody clue!'

We celebrate James's forty-eighth birthday on Tuesday 30th.

Tobias Ellwood is being a childish twit, sending texts of complaint to Boris that I had seen the Bahrain Ambassador when he is the person in charge of the Middle East. He has cancelled three meetings with me now and is basically refusing to talk to me. His stock could not be lower, but I don't want to get sucked into his vortex of awkwardness and end up looking partially to blame for his stupid and unnecessary turf war.

Sunday 4 September – Rutland

The *Sunday Mirror* has the full works on Keith Vaz. Tape, texts and video of him meeting two Romanian rent boys, including talk of poppers and paying for cocaine, all in a shag-pad near his family home. Meanwhile the Home Affairs Committee which he chairs is conducting an inquiry into prostitution. Oh dear: every single tabloid ingredient is there. All it needs is a vicar in drag.

Monday 5 September – London

Ferociously busy day of back-to-back meetings at the FCO.

Interview three people to take over in November from Richard Yates as an Assistant Private Secretary. I choose Harry Dadswell.

Have a friendly meeting with BoJo's Private Secretary Martin Reynolds.

In the Commons, DD's statement on the planned process for leaving the EU is rather mocked as waffly and, so far, ill-defined. It feels like the beginning of a long period of uncertainty, where UK attitudes and expectations just don't match those of the EU.

See Rory Stewart in Portcullis House about his DfID portfolio, which is largely the one I used to have. He has just been to Nepal, where he says I am still a hero for the earthquake planning I did.

Home for a bit to see James. Later in the Smoking Room – BoJo, Ed Argar, new FCO junior minister Alok Sharma, Rory Stewart. Final vote on the Finance Bill at 11.30pm.

Tuesday 6 September – London/Cyprus

PM returns from the G20 summit in China, at which point Tom Newton Dunn of the *Sun* immediately tweets that Number 10 briefed on the plane that she rebuked DD for deviating from the (rather rudimentary) line on the single market during his statement yesterday. This will have come from Fiona Hill and represents all that is wrong with modern government. The press operation briefing against a fellow Cabinet minister is never good, but public slapdowns are divisive and don't establish the authority they pretend to express. The PM and DD will not have spoken to each other; the PM has been on the other side of the world and will be tired; poison will have been poured into her ear. They should have just left it alone and said nothing. It is altogether a wholly counter-productive exercise.

The front pages are rather grim for Keith Vaz. They could be even worse. Apparently he persistently makes solo trips abroad as Chair of the Home Affairs Select Committee and pesters ambassadors to treat him as a minister by offering accommodation and staff assistance. He also uses the position to do things for his diabetes charity … whatever that might involve. In Copenhagen he did all of that, and demanded that the embassy arrange for him to meet prostitutes as part of his committee research work. Er …

BA flight to Cyprus, along with Richard Yates, Lizzie McKinnell (Chief Press Officer, Europe) and Amy Clemitshaw (Head Eastern Med Dept). The restarting of reunification talks is at a critical and encouraging stage, over forty years since civil unrest caused the island's division.

On arrival, the news has just broken that Keith Vaz has resigned as Chair of the Home Affairs Select Committee: there is no way he could possibly have stayed on.

Wednesday 7 September – Cyprus

Dinner last night at the residence with High Commissioner Matthew Kidd and the immediate team.

Cyprus is one of my main responsibilities – its northern part is Turkish occupied, whereas the rest are Greek Cypriots. The EU should never have let Cyprus join before resolving this long-standing dispute. The UN is now having another go at convening talks to see if some agreement can be signed. The UK is pivotal to the outcome, as we remain a guarantor power, so I have to know the personalities first.

We own and use the sovereign defence bases on the island. After a brief on them, I view the north–south buffer zone from our embassy roof and spend the day seeing pretty much everyone who matters in Cypriot politics. When I visit President Nicos Anastasiades at the Presidential Palace, its British past stares out in the form of a massive stone lion and unicorn Royal Crest over the main entrance. What was ours is now theirs.

On the Turkish side, our satellite embassy building, called 'Shakespeare House', is a magnificent but hardly used residence. But it is essential we keep it, both for balance and for impact.

Lance has worked his magic with Martin Reynolds in Boris' office – or possibly via Simon McDonald's office. At the ministerial team meeting (which of course I could not attend) Boris looked pointedly at Tobias and told the meeting that 'we all have to be happy birds in the same nest' and that on all questions and statements on the Middle East I am to back up Ellwood and stand in for him when he cannot be there.

I asked Lance to ping a message to Martin to say that his Minister says 'he is a very happy little fledgling'!

Friday 9 September – London/Rutland

Train to Kettering. Meeting at the Melton Con Club with Conservative councillors concerned about the local plan under which the government will compel them to build a certain number of houses over the next ten years. Their original proposals, which would have put 80 per cent of them in and around Melton, and 20 per cent in the surrounding villages, was thrown out by the planning inspector, thus destroying local judgement and more valid democratic accountability. Their new plan is for 65 per cent in Melton, and 35 per cent in the villages. But quite how they find the space without ruining the character of the Vale of Belvoir is beyond me.

Back for James to have an early night before he leaves at 3am for Croatia.

Saturday 10 September – Rutland

James to Croatia with the Warmans. They had pretty well arrived in Dubrovnik before I got up, but nearly hadn't made the flight as the A14 was closed and the flight had shut by the time they got to East Midlands Airport. But I have Noodle to myself for the day!

Liam Fox has been recorded addressing Conservative Way Forward saying British businessmen are fat and lazy, and would rather play golf than export. Not a very good pitch for his new job.

Fabulous Last Night of the Proms, with a spectacular Peruvian tenor, who sang 'Rule Britannia' dressed as an Inca god.

Sunday 11 September – Rutland/London

British Airways flight to Buenos Aires – BA to BA, as it were. Speak to Boris from the airport lounge. He was very appreciative of my handling of the CFI issue, as was I for his follow-up instructions. If Cyprus is a challenge, Argentina and the Falklands is even more so. We need direct relationships with Argentina in order to secure concessions on trade and air access for the Falklands.

Monday 12 September – Buenos Aires

BoJo has signed up to a new party ginger group called Strong Britain or something. Odd thing for a Foreign Secretary to do, and strikes me as rather impermissible for a minister.

Excellent new Ambassador Mark Kent, who I met in Vietnam while in DfID. Beneath the embassy residence is a fabulous wine cellar, nicely lit, the walls lined with bottles of Merlot. The setting is nice enough for a meeting and we gather there with Carlos Foradori, the Deputy Foreign Minister. It was a good diplomatic backdrop to some delicate negotiations about securing extra flights into the Falklands – for millions of reasons it requires the cooperation of Argentina for any connections that go via the mainland.

As one bottle after another somehow moved from the cellar wall to the table, the negotiations improved. At about 2 in the morning we shook hands on an outline deal.

David Cameron quits Parliament. On one level I don't blame him, but Parliament is so in decline and is made weaker by senior personalities preferring to leave than stay. Part of this is the sheer drudge of the parliamentary timetable, but it is more the vacuous cry about being a 'part-time MP' and having to declare in a register whenever you blow your nose. He's not even fifty, and he's come in, become Prime Minister and gone. He has remarkable qualities of confidence and clear communication, but was prone to being glib. He gambled with the constitution on two referendums, and drew his appointments from too narrow a bunch of close associates. For all his faults he was decent, reasonable and genuine.

I divide politicians into those who do or don't pass the 'holiday test': would you want to go on holiday with them? Blair – yes. Brown – no. Boris – yes. May – no. Cameron passes with flying colours.

Tuesday 13 September – Buenos Aires
Mark Kent says Foradori had just phoned to say he was so pissed last night he couldn't remember all the details. Like a proper Brit, Mark reminded him what he had agreed, faithfully and without embellishment. So I think we're still on track.

We're on the edge of getting the agreement with Argentina for extra flights to the Falklands. At the Argentina Investment Forum I have a brief encounter with President Macri, who gave his blessing to our efforts. We move up a notch from last night to conduct further (sober) negotiations with Foreign Minister Susana Malcorra which go right down to the wire. At times it looked like we wouldn't be able to agree, but we emerge with the first positive joint statement since 1999, on trade, security and opening new airlinks to the Falklands. A real landmark deal.

Flight to Washington via Miami.

Wednesday 14 September – Washington

Brief stopover in Miami first thing for a meeting with HM Consul General, Dave Prodger, then on to DC. Land at Reagan National Airport and on to the residence for a briefing lunch with HMA Kim Darroch. It turns out that Tobias turned up at the US embassy last week. Odd he should be so shirty about me just seeing the Bahrain Ambassador when there he is demanding accommodation in our Washington embassy and seeing people in the US without telling me, even though it is my brief.

Meeting in the afternoon with Senator Jeff Sessions (Republican – Arizona), who is advising Trump on foreign policy. One would imagine that must be quite a challenge. His accent is distinctive, and he was very perky and engaging, although I was left rather puzzled by his lack of foreign policy insight. Then on to the State Dept for meetings with assistant secretaries of state, before my speech at the Brookings Institution in the evening, where I was introduced by the formidable Fiona Hill (not *that* one!). She's originally from the UK and was previously an intelligence analyst at the White House under Bush and Obama. My remarks focussed mainly on Brexit, as did the questions, many of which seemed to be from commendably precocious high school students in the audience. My key line was that the UK would not be 'pulling up the drawbridge'.

Dinner with Kim Darroch and his wife at a nice French bistro. I am a total Darroch fan, having known him on and off for thirty years. A mutual friend introduced us soon after he joined the Foreign Office. He has no airs and graces, and is completely down-to-earth. The opposite of pompous formality.

Thursday 15 September – Washington

Breakfast at the residence, then off to the State Dept for the 'Our Ocean' conference hosted by John Kerry. President Obama dropped in to give a keynote speech, to a rapturous reception. It was interesting to watch him so close up – when he speaks every word has value, and his intonation and expression are theatrical joy.

Lunch back at the residence with Frank Luntz, the Republican strategist, then an all-staff meeting at the embassy.

Call with the Chilean Foreign Minister to get him on board over flights to the Falklands, then a round-table discussion at the think tank Inter-American Dialogue. Back to the residence for a British–American business association reception before heading to the airport.

Friday 16 September – London/Norfolk
Land. Train to Norwich. Met by James. Head to a holiday cottage ahead of the wedding of James' nephew tomorrow.

Saturday 17 September – Norfolk
It seems that Chancellor Philip Hammond has had a run-in with Fiona Hill, and possibly Nick Timothy too. It looks to me like the first of many skirmishes with these two advisers. They are throwing their weight around as if they have complete licence to tell anybody what to do in the name of the Prime Minister. Fiona is the worse of the two, and is abrasive and hectoring. I don't quite know what she's done to Philip, but she will have issued some kind of facile uncompromising diktat on which he's put his foot down and said 'bugger off'. He's one of the few in the government who can do so, but none of this is going to end well. No government can work satisfactorily when special advisers around the PM are so up themselves.

Sunday 18 September – Norfolk/London
Back from Norfolk. Try for the umpteenth time to call Tobias Ellwood, but still no return call after nearly a month.

Monday 19 September – London
Parliament in recess, so wall-to-wall FCO meetings.

Took my PS [Private Secretary] Lance Domm and Denzil Davidson from Number 10 to lunch at the Beefsteak. It's a nice touch to be able to give an occasional lunch to those who work so hard in my private office, and going to the Beefsteak gives them a treat. Denzil knows all things European, having been the Party's main adviser on it for years, and together they were very good company.

Dinner with Trade Minister Lord Price. Trade ministers are put in the Lords from the private sector and then come and go within a year. He could not be more hard-working, but no sooner have they built up good relations than they move on.

Tuesday 20 September – London

Meeting with the Permanent Secretary at the Department for International Trade, Sir Martin Donnelly. He's totally on top of all the issues, but I sense that his ministers have little wish to take honest advantage of his expertise.

A lot of people are pressing the PM to trigger Article 50, which would fire the starting gun on our formal departure from the EU, but as soon as we hit next year we will be in the run-up to the French election, which would be toxic. There is all manner of concern in the City that, if there is no 'passporting', banks will lose their licence to trade in the EU. True or not, it shows what a muddle we're in.

Wednesday 21 September – London

One-to-one with David Lidington, Leader of the House. My top-rate parliamentary assistant Fraser Raleigh is applying to be his SpAd. As my predecessor as Minister for Europe, Lidders says he's always happy to see people when I cannot. He thinks the West is at risk of imploding and says DD wants a bill in the Queen's speech to repeal the European Communities Act, embrace EU law and have it all commence on our departure date. Equally, Liam Fox wants exclusions from the total transfer of EU law.

Thursday 22 September – London

Meeting with Falklands MLA [Member of the Legislative Assembly] Mrs Jan Cheek and their London rep Sukey Cameron.

Association patrons lunch at the RAF club, which is a group of the great and the good (or at least the more generous) of the constituency. The guest speaker was Patrick McLoughlin, who is just supremely sensible and down-to-earth. I was able to introduce him with genuine warmth and affection and he returned the compliment in full.

Boris overdoes it on the EU in a loose interview with Sky in New York, where he has been at the UN. He controversially answers the question the PM herself has dodged and says Article 50 will be triggered early next year, setting the clock ticking for the two-year negotiation period. He says he won't need the full two years and might do it sooner – fat chance!

Later on it's the broadcast of the BBC's documentary *Brexit: A Very British Coup?* I was perfectly nice throughout about Boris, albeit with a strong hint of exasperation. My teasing mimic of him prompted some Twitter reaction.

Sunday 25 September – London/Bahrain
DC's former communications head Craig Oliver and Tim Shipman of the *Sunday Times* both have their Brexit books serialised. Shipman's by far the better of the two – he has excellent contacts and has kept a broadly sourced account of the whole debacle. The fact that Craig Oliver was able to keep a fairly detailed daily account tells me that perhaps it would have been better if he'd been focussing only on his job. He wasn't the right man for a sectarian national campaign, and all of his insights are very 'Number 10 bunker'-minded. You can just see why the Remain efforts failed to reach out and connect.

Trump says if he is elected he will recognise a united and indivisible Jerusalem as the capital of Israel. This would be an outrageous and illegal act of modern colonialism.

Fly to Bahrain for their annual defence and security dialogue.

Monday 26 September – Manama
Very friendly audience with King Hamad, who welcomed me very warmly and was still waxing lyrical about the Windsor Horse Show and how fabulous the Queen is. Such personal approval led immediately into my being able to see all his senior ministers, who I now know quite well. I bridle at those who so unthinkingly attack Bahrain when they are in fact taking commendable steps to keep law and order in a proper way while uniting their own potentially fractious population.

Wednesday 28 September – London

Shimon Peres has died aged ninety-three. Twice Prime Minister and then President of Israel, he was a good influence on Israeli politics for nearly seventy years. He was a wonderful man. I met him a few times and greatly admired him. Israel – and peace – would be in a far better state if his views had held sway.

Friday 30 September – London/Rutland

Catch-up day at home, with everyone coming to me. The admirable Fraser Raleigh brings me up to date with all the constituency stuff. Richard Yates from my private office delivers my red box, while on TV the Prince of Wales, Boris, Cameron and Blair are all at the Peres funeral.

Apparently Ellwood's visit to Uganda this week has been a disaster, and nobody in government ever wants him to go back. He ignored his brief, despite insistent rehearsals with our embassy about what he should say, and raised a series of whacky personal notions, which were said to 'set back UK relations by at least two years'. First he told the President of Uganda that he ought to re-route an oil pipeline, and then he told him how he could bring about extensive reforestation by dropping trees from aeroplanes.

Drive to Rutland.

James arrives at 8.30pm. Nice comfort supper in front of the TV, watching a documentary in appreciation of the late Terry Wogan.

Saturday 1 October – Rutland

Dinner in the Marquess pub. Lance texts at about 8pm to say there's an important email on my FCO Blackberry. At 10pm Number 10 will brief the press that TM will announce tomorrow, the first day of [the Tory Party] Conference, that we will repeal the European Communities Act of 1972 and adopt the entire body of EU law into UK law, allowing us then to repeal any element of it when we so choose, once we have formally left the EU. The need to take anything to Parliament is fraught with danger, but this does no more than entrench the decision of the referendum irreversibly, but it will of course leave open the danger of Parliament never agreeing to step back from the EU in many areas. But the body of law will be fossil-ised: I'm not sure there will be any scope for keeping up with any changes to EU law once we have left, so over time the UK would become increasingly non-compliant, even if a majority of the Commons wanted to remain in alignment.

It's a good plan, and we will submit the issue to a vote in Parliament earlier rather than later, and will do so on the basis of the simple principle of withdrawal as instructed by the voters in a referendum. But if it doesn't get through the Commons we will almost certainly be forced into an election, despite the hurdles of the Fixed-Term Parliaments Act under which two-thirds of MPs have to vote for one; and if it is blocked by the Lords then the government should be able to invoke the Parliament Act and force it through, because the referendum was in the manifesto and the people voted to leave.

Sunday 2 October – Birmingham
News of the Great Repeal Bill (Act) has been well received. TM excellent on BBC's *Marr*. I texted Philip May to say the announce-ment and the interview were both the tops. Nice reply saying he hoped to see me at Conference.

To Birmingham. Straight to Boris' hotel room and along with his SpAds Ben Gascoigne, Liam Parker and Will Walden, and Tom Swarbrick of Number 10 broadcasting, go through his speech. Boris bats about some ideas and alterations, but we only make some small changes.

I sit next to Boris in the Conference hall for TM's speech on Brexit. She was wearing a black outfit and what looked like a yellow judo belt. I tease Boris – 'Would you ever want to put her in a judo hold?'

Later on he delivers his own speech, which is a typical bravura performance. His chatty lark-about style is popular and engaging and suits the audience.

Monday 3 October – London/Athens
To Athens. Ambassador John Kittmer and his civil partner Dave have a new Jack Russell called Annie who is ten weeks old and arrived

today. It has a beautiful temperament and has been drawn from a carefully nurtured pedigree originating in Australia.

Dinner with the rotund Evangelos Venizelos (former Deputy PM and Foreign Minister for centre-left PASOK party) and George Koumoutsakos, spokesman of Cabinet rank for the centre-right New Democracy party. Venizolos blethered on a bit in a rather abstract philosophical stream of consciousness.

Back at the Conference, Philip Hammond has abandoned the timetable set by Osborne when he was Chancellor for deficit reduction, which is probably a good decision. But he also says he 'won't abandon austerity', which is a stupidly missed opportunity to change the public's perception of us as needlessly cruel. We should just ban the word – it only gives Labour the script they want.

Sajid Javid announces a plan to build 25,000 homes. Puny crap which amounts to nothing.

Tuesday 4 October – Athens

Conference time is a good moment to take stock. As Conservatives, we are politically dominant and in pretty good shape; UKIP is in animated suspension, but could revive if there is no certainty to our EU departure; the Lib Dems have eight seats, an invisible leader believed to be Tim Farron and no platform, yet could revive as the 'stop Brexit' party; Labour has re-elected Jeremy Corbyn as leader and, despite a massive increase in its grassroots membership, is now an intense yet narrow protest group because ardent left-wingers have captured the Party but rendered it unappealing to any broader sections of the electorate. So we are riding high – but with a small majority in the Commons, a minority in the Lords and many bumps in the road ahead on the process of Brexit.

Boris wants a hard Brexit on trade, but is pro-immigration; Hammond wants a softer Brexit for fear of economic pain; and my own view is that all that matters is how we reach an agreement with the EU itself about our future relationship. It might mean that we regain total sovereignty over our law-making but have to agree many things on trade and people which replicate much of our current arrangements with the EU.

Hurricane Matthew is heading for the Caribbean: Haiti, Cuba and Jamaica all at risk.

The press summary carries reaction to Boris saying we are unfair to Australians and should have more of them in the UK. It's another of his notions. Extraordinary – he'd been holed up in GCHQ all day and still hits the headlines. Maybe he just reached forward and pressed 'send'.

Meeting with Kyriakos Mitsotakis, Leader of the Greek New Democracy party. His father was PM, and he himself became Leader quite surprisingly. Good-looking and articulate, he is a right-of-centre liberal technocrat, who stands an odds-on chance of becoming the next PM. In trying to guess when the next election will be, he says it's like bankruptcy: 'It all unfolds very slowly, until suddenly it happens.' We meet in his newly built party HQ, a functional three-floor box in the industrial part of town.

Nikolaos (Nikos) Kotzias, Foreign Minister for the Syriza government. A nice roly-poly seventy-year-old, who has family in the UK and is very pro-British. Prone to speaking at length, he is nonetheless forthcoming and sweetly genuine. Also saw Evan Kalpadakis, foreign policy adviser to PM Alexis Tsipras.

With all of them the two main topics are Brexit and Cyprus. They don't want us to leave, but have now come to terms with the fact that we will. They will work with us to explore the best options for a workable EU–UK arrangement. On Cyprus, it is clear that the Greek Cypriots are unlikely to support a unification deal in a referendum unless all Turkish troops (currently over 30,000) are committed to leaving the island.

A long chat with a senior FCO official about the pros and cons of the UK staying in the customs union. If we stay in – it is not an EU institution, but includes the EU – then our supply chains would be protected without impediment. But if we remain in it, we would not be free to negotiate trade deals etc. The FCO is actually being denied information about Brexit and is being told to keep out of the process. Everything is being channelled through DExEU and Number 10. It is totally absurd, and removes from the process the one organisation which has the network and contacts to engage and persuade many in the twenty-seven remaining countries. Boris has already had a set-to with Philip Hammond about the customs union, yet technically neither the Foreign Office nor the Treasury are formally involved in the wider process. It is all being so tightly held, it risks excluding the knowledge and wisdom needed to make it work for the best.

Am confined to row 20 of a packed BA flight home, surrounded by sneezing and spluttering passengers, with no plug for the laptop. Such is the humiliating life of a modern UK foreign minister. And it's late.

Wednesday 5 October – London

FCO catch-up day. Called the Colombian Ambassador to sympathise that their referendum had rejected the FARC guerrilla peace deal by a margin of 0.2 per cent. We agreed that referendums were not always a good thing. The state visit of President Santos will still go ahead in a few days' time.

Theresa May's Conference speech in Birmingham pleased the faithful. But I see little chance of a clean Brexit in time for the next election.

EU brainstorm with excellent officials. It is just so, so complicated, with no easy solutions. We batted about all the big issues: the process of legislation and negotiation, the economic effects and the movement of people.

António Guterres is as good as picked as the next Secretary General of the UN, as none of the P5 [the five permanent members of the Security Council] have vetoed him. I'm a fan of his, having enjoyed working closely with him when I was DfID Minister and he was in Geneva as the UN High Commissioner for Refugees.

Reception in the FCO Locarno Room with all our departmental Permanent Secretaries meeting their Irish equivalents.

Back home, George Robertson drops in for a drink. He's such a wise old bird. Perceptive and engaging, he was Defence Secretary under Blair and then NATO Secretary General. He now advises BP, and is Chancellor of the St Michael and St George order of knighthood, which includes my own. So I teasingly call him my boss. He forecasts no end of trouble in the Lords over Brexit – he doesn't quite know what the determining issue will be, but is sure there will be one.

Monday 10 October – London
House returns after the conference recess. Like last week, it's non-stop FCO-based meetings. There is never any problem with filling any gap in the diary.

Friday 14 October – London/Rutland
Take Noodle into the FCO, where everyone loves her – but have to be careful to keep her apart from Palmerston, aka 'Diplomog', the FCO mouser.

Meeting in the FCO map room with our EU-based ambassadors. The PM addresses them – although technically proficient, there's a feeling of unreality in the air. She was fine as far as it went, but the ambassadors are not at all convinced about the practicality of our being able to leave and strike a workable deal for the future with the EU. Politically, she is caught between the newspapers and the truth. Leaving is impossible without incurring enormous economic costs: but the *Daily Hate* and co say she must because the people have spoken.

Simon McDonald hogs the PM during her visit, meeting her at the entrance, chairing the meeting while I am made to sit at the back. It is clear who he thinks is the most important person in the Foreign Office.

To Rutland.

Saturday 15 October – Rutland
The marrow-weighing is the highlight of the village year in the vicious contest between us and our neighbours Jamie and Clare Warman: great drama with the scales. It's a dead heat! We will each have to buy the other the promised victory dinner.

We watch the latest BBC Brexit documentary with them later.

Sunday 16 October – Rutland/London

To London for dinner with Jonathan Aitken. He has an American friend there who thinks and hopes that Trump is in freefall, but thinks that if he wins he'd make that old walrus John Bolton his Secretary of State. Crikey. Although I'm not convinced by either opinion.

Monday 17 October – London

The inPERU investment conference at the Guildhall. The Peruvian Trade and Tourism Minister, Eduardo Ferreyros, is a Thatcher fan. I promised to try and find him a photo of her. Our chemistry improved even further when I praised the Peruvian tenor Juan Diego Flórez for his performance at the Last Night of the Proms.

Drink in my room with my PPS [Parliamentary Private Secretary] Pauline Latham, who is always genuine and diligent. Tobias Ellwood joins us, but seems utterly blind to the impression he has created by his idiotic behaviour. There is no point making an issue of it.

By coincidence, the Croatian villa James has just stayed in is the same one Boris recently rented, so the owners gave James a bottle of wine to take back for Boris. I delivered it when we gathered for our team prep for Oral Questions.

He conducts the meeting on his feet in front of his chair at the large table in his office until I say, 'Are you like Gladstone, who always liked to hold meetings standing up?' He huffs and puffs, then sits.

Then, referring to a tabled question about Russia Boris says: 'The trouble with Putin is that he expects everyone to come and kiss his ring.' He looks bemused when the entire table collapses in giggles.

I say, 'Foreign Secretary – 10 per cent will think pope; 90 per cent will think anus.'

'Oh, oh, oh!' Hair ruffle. The trouble is: the more a naughty thought gets into his head, the more likely he is to take the risk and say it.

Utter hilarity!

Tuesday 18 October – London

Bump into Martin Donnelly, Permanent Secretary at the Department for International Trade, at the entrance to King Charles Street. He will leave the civil service in February, and has agreed to stay on and set up the new department. He is professionally discreet, but it is clear that he is in despair and thinks that Fox and co haven't a clue. I suggest we quietly go off and have dinner one evening. He went in towards the little side door on the corner of the FCO, which is the way into his department. 'Oh,' I said, 'is that your entrance?' He reacted with a rictus grin.

Senator Safaev of Uzbekistan, Chair of their Foreign Relations Committee. A senior, serious and interesting link.

Oral Questions. Great!! It was BoJo's first ever appearance at the government dispatch box, as he had never before answered questions. In opposition under Cameron, before he resigned as the MP for Henley and became Mayor of London, he had briefly asked questions from the front bench, I think as a DCMS (Culture Dept) spokesman, but that was over eight years ago.

It all went very smoothly. I was on Boris' right, Alok Sharma then Tobias Ellwood on his left. The sequence went well, and I was in a good position to steer and prompt him sotto voce. A question on Turkey came in from Maria Miller, unexpectedly, and I was able to rip a page out of my folder on the topic, which Richard Yates had given me at the last minute after gathering good backbench intelligence, and said to Boris, 'Just read this out word for word.' It was the perfect answer.

There were no fireworks, and a comical exchange on Italy in which Boris flashed some Italian. There was assertive opinion on Russia, especially in respect of their interference in Ukraine and Syria, but without saying anything excessive or offensive.

Ellwood was OK, but only just. Despite tutoring him a million times, he still fails to pronounce names properly – Yaymen, President Haydi, Saudi FM [Foreign Minister] Al Jubrair. Squirmworthy. But he has settled down a bit. I tried to be a supporter and tutor, but he put up barriers. I won't be anti-him. But I'm now neutral and will do nothing special to help him.

Straight to Heathrow. Speak to the fabulous Fraser from the airport. David Lidington, Leader of the Commons, has offered him the job as his Special Adviser. It's very good news, and will not only be good for Lidders but will allow Fraser to broaden his horizons massively, especially as it oversees the government's legislative programme.

Flight to Turkey, Ankara via Istanbul. Great chat with Lance. Throw open the bedroom windows in the residence. Lovely cool air. Good night's sleep.

Wednesday 19 October – Ankara/London

Residence breakfast.

Five-car bumper shunt in the underpass caused entirely by the Ambassador's driver dipping and weaving erratically through the rush-hour traffic for no good reason, and then suddenly jamming on his brakes behind the police escort vehicle. Lance and co had to hail a taxi in order to catch up with us for the meeting.

Visit the Atatürk Mausoleum only to be told a bit later that the security forces had detained a suicide bomber nearby only an hour or so earlier.

See Kemal Kılıçdaroğlu, Leader of the opposition party CHP, and Sebahattin Öztürk, Deputy Minister of the Interior.

Meeting with President Recep Tayyip Erdoğan. Grand palatial setting. He spoke for an hour. He wished to help on Cyprus, but his attitude is locked in a bit of a 2004 time warp when it all collapsed last time. He is the benign face of a pretty vicious power play, but you can't ignore the strong leadership Turkey needs to overcome internal and external threats. I gave him a velvet Commons cushion, whispering quietly to him at the end, 'It's like democracy: you can sit on it, but not for too long.'

PM Binali Yıldırım. He says there is a lack of 'ownership' in the world at the moment, which is a gap for the UK to fill.

EU Minister Ömer Çelik. On Syria he says that Turkish sensitivities and advice should be taken on board; that Syria needs a no-fly zone, and camps for internally displaced persons within the country; and that the Iraq army is pro-Iran Shiites. Press conference. Oddly for a Turk, he has a rather foppish manner.

Airport. Back via Istanbul. My new Assistant Private Secretary Harry Dadswell is on the same plane. Very bright and sparky.

Home by midnight. Much love on arrival from James and Noodle.

Thursday 20 October – London

The Foreign Affairs Select Committee has just been to Ukraine. Reports come back that their lack of diplomatic good manners was rather disgraceful. Apparently Crispin Blunt, their Chairman, valiantly tried to keep them in good order, but Adam Holloway and SNP MP Stephen Gethins had a public spat in front of their Ukrainian counterparts. Adam is never one not to want an adventure, and he complained that the FCO was failing to help them go to forbidden conflict areas. Well, obviously. But overall their behaviour caused considerable upset.

Phone call with Home Office Minister Robert Goodwill on the French clearance of the 'Jungle' refugee camp in Calais, and our process of taking in a few hundred children. There has been a huge amount of vulgar and unmerited criticism of the government, suggesting we wanted to verify their age by testing their teeth. This was a Labour policy from a decade ago, long since dropped. Robert is one of those ministers from whom you get calm good sense.

Briefing from the consular team, headed by Philippa Makepeace. A robust discussion about where the line should be drawn between people expecting our help and us having to give it. Murder, abduction, accidents like a coach crash – all should be assisted by our consular capability. But we are not an international rescue service, or a substitute for prudential travel insurance. There is one person who was in the Bataclan theatre in Paris when the terrorists struck and killed people but was not herself hurt. She is now complaining that the FCO didn't call her back or help her. I understand the issue of trauma, but what was the FCO supposed to do for her when others were shot and injured?

Confirm Alex Hennessy as my new diary secretary. She used to work in Clarence House and seems fabulous.

Another eulogistic DipTel comes in from Ankara: Alan Duncan 'feted' on his trip and 'welcomed with open arms by an appreciative President Erdoğan'. That'll do ...

Impromptu drinks in my office. I gave Richard Yates the tie that Erdoğan gave to me. Bright purple, but actually quite smart.

Political Director Tim Barrow came in. Nearly an hour with him and Lance over a drink. We discussed Yemen, Russia, Cyprus and various internal personalities. I suggested a couple of names for the Queen's Birthday Honours.

Friday 21 October – London
Breakfast at the Travellers with Ben Bridge of BAE.

To the HofC for the usual 9.30am sitting Friday procedural vote, which didn't happen because they moved straight on to the 'Turing Bill' which is moved by John Nicolson of the SNP, and is intended to exonerate/pardon all those who were in the past convicted of gay sex crimes which are no longer illegal.

Sam Gyimah talks it out, supposedly because it would exonerate some people convicted of paedophilic crimes which remain illegal today, and also because we have proposed an amendment to other legislation in the Lords which would achieve the Bill's aims straightaway. But the handling by the government has been hopeless, and has handed the SNP a PR gift on a plate, unchallenged by any robust press management on our part. Poor Sam gets it in the neck from the SNP, and it's not even his ministerial responsibility. He is standing in for someone else.

Robert Goodwill makes his Calais statement. A surprisingly nice text exchange with Fiona Hill. She is with the PM in Brussels and says they are all talking about my Turkey fame.

Lance says that a message has come down from the Foreign Secretary's office that Boris wants me to do more media. I say that's fine – I will navigate a path which is loyal to Boris and loyal to the PM, and doesn't seek publicity for myself. I'd rather play safe and back the government when asked.

The Brexit news is less encouraging. It is thought that some DExEU officials might resign, and the PM has just been heard in total silence at the EU summit, which is a bit of a disaster and is blamed on Juncker. As an indication of how complex the process is, the Canadian–EU trade deal has been vetoed by Paul Magnette, the President of Wallonia. 'The moon's a Walloon,' quipped one wag. It's like the Mayor of Manchester having a veto on our Parliament.

Daniel Korski, who used to work as a staffer in Number 10, has written a long piece for Politico on why we lost the referendum. It is self-focussed nonsense, prompting a recently retired civil servant to send a wonderful email into my private office, recalling that Korski's advice to him had always been 'total crap'.

James has a Stanbridge Earls reunion drinks, his old school, which closed in 2013. I have a night in with a bottle of claret and Noodle.

Saturday 22 October – Rutland

Drive up first thing. James is a touch hung-over …

Send the Chief Whip a text expressing support for Sam Gyimah over the Turing Bill and the unfair SNP vitriol levelled against him. I said I thought the system had let him down, and should have seen that this was an issue that needed rebuttal. Poor Sam – he was standing in for Phillip Lee, who had done a bunk. But Liz Truss is mainly to blame: no grip, no awareness of the toxic campaign against him, no adequate media handling. The SNP Twitter shite is vile. But then that's the SNP for you!

Sunday 23 October – Rutland/Dominican Republic

8am pick-up from Rutland. Good run to Terminal 5 to meet up with Louise Nicol and Kara Owen, the new head of the Americas Dept in the FCO. Rather large and obnoxious woman at the BA executive lounge who wanted to confiscate my old BA Gold Card, when all it does is prove your name and club number. Louise deftly retrieved it from her. I've just become Gold again anyway. The joys of having a private office to solve such problems.

On the first hop to Madrid, they then tried to compel me to put my second small bag in the hold. I had to capitulate. Once again

Louise rescued me. She asked the Captain if she could go back to collect it from the top of the ramp. Result! There was no lack of space in the biz class cabin racks. It was sheer incompetence to make no distinction between spacious club class and congested economy. No Andrew Mitchell Downing Street moment: I remained polite and cool.

It's the first time I've used wi-fi on a commercial flight. Met by HMA Chris Campbell, whose wife is the Ambassador to Haiti.

Santo Domingo for a massive EU–Caribbean–Latin American conference. Dom Rep is the eastern half of Hispaniola, the other being Haiti. The contrast is staggering. Dom Rep is growing fast: Haiti a crime-ridden hellhole.

Monday 24 October – Santo Domingo

Another peculiar text exchange with Ellwood. I say that I gather he wants to meet the Ripon Group of US congressmen. I say of course he can, and we'll help get him a speaking slot etc, but please pick up the phone and talk to me about these things. He then flips and remonstrates that he told his office to tell me, which they did. He just seems frightened to walk in the door and discuss things directly in a normal human way.

He is also refusing to send anyone to Doha to pay condolences following the death of Sheikh Khalifa at the age of eighty-four. He might have been deposed by his son in 1998, but he was the Ruler for twenty-five years. The FCO no longer understands proper diplomatic good manners: especially in the Arabian Gulf.

The PM is stopping BoJo from going to the Gibraltar Day annual lunch. She thinks he will goof and overdo it, just when she has struck up a bit of a relationship with the re-elected Spanish PM, Rajoy, and they have agreed to keep Gibraltar off the radar. But he is the Foreign Secretary, and over-controlling him in this way will only sour their relations.

Call with our embassy in Caracas. Venezuela is falling to pieces, with 500 per cent inflation, and the idiot President Maduro refusing to stand down. They are almost the last bastion of catastrophic Latin American leftism.

To the embassy to write a note for BoJo on the ISC, on which I used to sit. It is to familiarise him ahead of his evidence session in front of them. He won't know what to expect, as there aren't that many officials who would know.

Tuesday 25 October – Santo Domingo

At last, an announcement on airport expansion. It will be Heathrow rather than Gatwick. BoJo and Justine Greening, as historic opponents, have been given some leeway to express their view. Zac Goldsmith pledged he would resign and cause a by-election if they chose Heathrow. This may turn out to have been unwise to the point of being suicidal. The Lib Dems could win back Richmond on a referendum re-run. Vote Lib Dem to be anti-Heathrow and pro-EU. He's anti-Heathrow, but also anti-EU. Richmond voted over 75 per cent Remain. He's toast if he risks it.

BoJo texts gratefully about my note on the ISC.

Wednesday 26 October – Santo Domingo/London

Zac Goldsmith has resigned to fight a by-election. Having so discredited himself as our London Mayoral candidate, I think this might prove terminal for him. Voluntary political euthanasia?

Breakfast with US Ambassador Wally Brewster and his husband Bob Satawake. Wally is something of a rock star in Dom Rep, always on TV, for standing up to the Catholic Church and the government in support of gay rights. The Papal Nuncio in Dom Rep ostracised him in a vicious campaign, so much so that Vice-President Joe Biden flew in to defend him with a public show of support.

Bilateral with Ecuadorian FM Guillaume Long. He has the looks of a polo player, but preens himself unsmilingly, and defends the supposed human rights of Julian Assange, who has been holed up in their London embassy for four years to escape arrest. He calls him a personal friend. He is high-handed and disdainful – a rather unappealing swank.

As if it were not obvious why Venezuela is in such chaos, my meeting with their foreign minister, Rodríguez, illustrates the reasons. He is a delusional Marxist academic who seems content to see his country slide into economic collapse rather than depart from adherence to his manic philosophy.

Back to London via Miami.

Thursday 27 October – London

Meeting with our Ambassador to Colombia, Peter Tibber, ahead of the country's State Visit next week. I'm trying with Protocol to have Hugo Swire invited to the state dinner. When he was an FCO minister he struck up good relationships in Latin America and there is more reason to have him there than many of the other invitees. Trouble is it's not my party, and there is concern about the precedent it would set: which former ministers should or should not be invited? Anyway, I've tried my very best, but I think it's 50–50 whether I succeed.

Sign the book of condolence for Sheikh Khalifa at the Qatar embassy. The Ambassador was deeply appreciative.

Reception at Lancaster House for the fiftieth anniversary of Barbados' independence. Their PM and I both made well-received speeches. His was all about cricket (of which I know sub-zero), and I wished the West Indies every success in the looming Test matches in the UK, 'until we win!'

Monday 31 October – London

To Chatham House [Royal Institute of International Affairs] for the presentation of their annual prize to Secretary John Kerry. Philip Hammond, Tobias Ellwood, US Ambassador Matthew Barzun, Norman Lamont and a useless photographer who missed every interesting shot.

Amusing quip from John Kerry on Philip Hammond: 'You have moved to crunching numbers instead of words. But I know you are happy where you are'!!

View on Boris from the person beside me at lunch: he's intelligent, mercurial, a writer, for whom the production is the output. Limited concentration/retention span. Likes to be liked. Takes the path of least resistance. Trust him? No … because he is not reliably constant.

One on one with Permanent Secretary at DExEU Olly Robbins. He may be in DExEU, but he is in practice Number 10's man for all things Brexit. He is ferociously intelligent and hard-working, but rather than shaping some brilliant strategic plan, he is having to use all his skills to find ingenious solutions to near-insoluble problems. He is confident and likeable, but now so immersed in the trials and tribulations of Brexit that if it all goes wrong, he will go down with the ship.

Dinner with Tony Gallagher, editor of the *Sun*, and political editor Tom Newton Dunn. They are still giving Theresa the benefit of the doubt, but those doubts are growing.

Tuesday 1 November – London

Meeting with BoJo – the chemistry between us is working very well at the moment. I'm studiously keeping out of Brexit and getting on with the diplomacy I enjoy. I will tell him directly if he's ever doing anything which I think does him or our diplomacy harm, but I will say it to his face. My mantra is simple: loyal to Theresa, loyal to Boris, stay out of the news.

It's a big Colombia day – the arrival of President Santos at a ceremony on Horse Guards marks a lovely start to the State Visit. You can just see he loves being in the carriage and beams at his family, who I am sitting with on the side dais. As always, the Palace and Protocol have everything planned in detail to the nanosecond, although they couldn't stop the President's address to both Houses in the Royal Gallery being interrupted by a Commons division. But nobody minded, and he cheerfully made light of it.

The State Banquet at Buckingham Palace was a triumph, except infuriatingly my efforts to include Hugo had failed. Apparently by the time I was prompted to intervene the invitations had gone out and the seating plan had been put together and printed. Our Royals just add a massive wow factor to the event. I sat next to the President's openly gay Chief of Staff who was brimming with excitement and enjoyment. What finally blows them away is the grand finale which signifies the end of dinner when the noisiest Scottish pipers on earth process into the ballroom, down the side, behind the top table and out the other side. Unique or what?

Thursday 3 November – London

Call Frances, Duchess of Rutland, to fix a time for our promised meeting on Saturday.

'Have you received my letter?' she demanded charmlessly.

'No,' I replied, 'where did you send it?'

'Rutland.'

'Parliament is sitting so obviously I'm in London.'

'Well, you had better read it before you come on Saturday.'

When I asked why she had written me a letter when I had said I would come and see her, she sourly said that she thought I'd never come. Senior Association figure Ken Bool says that it's probably a half-apology for her rudeness after the Biz Club lunch. I doubt it: not from such an imperious old bag.

The court verdict on Article 50 is declared. Remain activist Gina Miller has brought a case against the government challenging its right to start the legal process of leaving the EU without a vote or legislation in Parliament. In a very decisive judgment, the High Court has declared that the PM does not have the right under the Royal Prerogative to instigate Article 50 of the Lisbon Treaty, which would trigger our inevitable departure from the EU. Because leaving the EU would repeal, annul or reverse legislation that has been passed or endorsed by Parliament, their verdict states, it can therefore only be undone by Parliament, and there must therefore be a parliamentary vote on it. If this were to go before Parliament now, it would get through easily, as all it does is validate the referendum result but, rather stupidly, the government says it will appeal.

Friday 4 November – Rutland

Appalling *Mail*, *Express* and *Telegraph* headlines slating the judges. The *Mail* puts all their photos on the front page under the headline 'Enemies of the People'. So maybe the *Mail* doesn't believe in the rule of law after all.

When I get to Rutland, there is a highly offensive letter from Her (lack of) Grace, Frances Rutland, copied to a random list of senior local Conservatives.

It seems she has been fuming for six months since I explained to the AGM in March that I would support Remain. What she doesn't realise is that her view is not at all shared by about half of the Association and, whatever they think about Brexit, a large majority know that they don't like her. I long for the day when we can have a local Conservative Party function which doesn't begin with the words 'Your Grace …'.

Her late husband Charles, who as Duke of Rutland was the Association President for fifty years, was loved by everybody. He started with the ructions of the Suez crisis, when the Melton MP and Foreign Minister Sir Anthony Nutting resigned. Now, her attitude is slightly less dignified.

I call Ken Bool, who is Mr Sensible, Mr Decent, Mr Reliable – all of those and more – and suggest she is such an offensive old boot I should perhaps call her and say so and just cancel our meeting. Jocular exchange with him. He says I should still go, and of course I intend to.

Saturday 5 November – Rutland

To her house below Belvoir Castle to see the scowling Duchess. Quite the most insulting meeting I have ever attended in my life. I should really have just annihilated her with withering abuse, but I didn't. I was firm but fair, and far too gentle.

I am greeted charmingly by Petchey, her loyal and long-suffering butler. I said with a smile, 'I've been summoned by the Headmistress.' He looked a little bemused.

The Duchess began, 'Why has it taken four months for you to come and explain yourself?'

'I don't consider I have anything to explain. What is it that I am expected to explain to you?'

'You know. If you don't then you should. I put it in the letter.'

'It is a highly offensive letter. Why did you write it when we had agreed to meet this weekend?'

'I didn't believe you would come.'

'But I said I would call you, and I did, and I am here. It is deeply rude, and also wholly irrational. Language such as "climbing the greasy pole", or furthering my career, is totally unacceptable. I spoke at the AGM about the pros and cons of Brexit, and many afterwards thanked me. At the time the main comment on the street was that they didn't feel they knew enough about the arguments and weren't sure which way to vote, and they all said my speech was the first time they began to understand the issues.'

'But it was a disgusting stunt.'

'That too is offensive. What about it was a stunt?'

'You spent twenty minutes talking about your diary, said almost nothing about the EU and closed down the debate. You filibustered.'

'It was an AGM. I did what was required of me, starting with a report of my year's work as the MP. I then spoke at length about the EU and answered everyone's questions. There was nothing in the meeting which in any way requires me to explain myself to you. It is you who have been insufferably rude since. Your outburst at the Falcon appalled people, but I made light of it and have always been cordial, as I am being now. I spoke to you at Martin Stubbs' patrons' reception, I did so too at the Association lunch, but you have erupted again. You seem to have spent months working yourself into a lather, and your insulting behaviour then and now is quite simply unacceptable.'

'If you don't understand what everyone thinks then there is nothing else to say.'

'Actually there is. Your letter is the rudest and most insulting letter I have ever received from a fellow Conservative. You seem to think that the only opinion that matters is your own. Well, it isn't. You go to political meetings with UKIP, which I consider unbecoming for an Association President, and your attitude is both offensive and unjustified. I am not prepared to sit here being treated by you in this manner, and many others feel the same way about the way you treat them. I say again, very politely, despite my best efforts to rise above your impossible behaviour, that your conduct is unjustified and unacceptable and I am not prepared to sit here and be addressed by you in this way. Enjoy the rest of your weekend.'

The whole encounter lasted less than fifteen minutes. I said to Petchey on the way out that she has gone completely mad, won't listen to reason and has become rather horrid and irrational. 'I'm so sorry, but as soon as you go back into the room you'll get the full replay from her. I'm sorry to inflict that on you.'

When I get back I report to Ken Bool and Mary Anne Donovan to let them know. They will no doubt both get calls soon from the Dippy Dowager. We all know that the Association is split down the middle and that, instead of being a unifying President, her superior attitude is proving deeply divisive.

Monday 7 November – London

The two key people in BoJo's office are probably his Private Secretary Martin Reynolds and one of his SpAds, David Frost. Frost is a mild-mannered former ambassador to Denmark who left the FCO for a time to run the Scotch Whisky Association. His role is not entirely clear, but seems to be that of a policy brain, drawn ever more into the issues of Brexit. Both are likeable and important for securing my working relationship with Boris. So I poke my head round the office door frequently, and, as with this morning, try to get a regular meeting in the diary. It's mostly me downloading to them about what I am doing. Sit on the front bench for the statement about the court judgment about Article 50. DD a bit over-combative at the dispatch box. Sir Clearly Startled [Keir Starmer] responds for Labour and is rather effective in highlighting the lack of detail on what happens next: 'I was going to say it is all process and no substance, but I realised I said that last time and that I am in danger of repeating myself – there are only so many times I can say, "Is that it?"'

Tuesday 8 November – London

Answer an Urgent Question in the House on LGBT rights. I love Sarah Champion – she is a really lovely person and one of Labour's nicest MPs.

Insurance mogul Christopher Moran owns the amazingly restored Crosby Hall on Chelsea Embankment. He runs Cooperation Ireland, which works to build peaceful relations between north and south. He does do things in style – I attend a stunningly elegant reception tonight graced by HM the Queen. Thinking back thirty years, it would have been unthinkable to have HM and Martin McGuinness in the same room, and for the latter to be charmed and delighted to meet her. She is such a unifier: even the IRA melt at her feet.

To the US embassy in Grosvenor Square for their election-night party. I don't stay long, but the unquestioned assumption is that Hillary Clinton will win, and the crush of guests has a distinctly liberal feel to it. It was a strange atmosphere – people don't really like her, but they certainly don't want Trump. And the party food was good – mini-hamburgers and hotdogs.

Wednesday 9 November – London

Wake up to the nightmare of a Trump victory. To everyone's astonishment, the vulgar insurgent has won! There's no knowing what sort of a Presidency this is going to be, other than one that is quirky and unpredictable. He is probably as astonished to have become President as Johnson and Gove were to have won the referendum. And similarly, it may well turn out that none of them has a clue what to do next.

After a day of non-stop FCO meetings, Kim Darroch and his Washington team dial in on video to give me their take on the result. As Kim wisely put it, 'All I can confidently predict is that everything will be unpredictable.' Unlike any previous incoming president there seems to be almost no clear transition plan, and it's very difficult to know who to call about anything.

Friday 11 November – London

Speak to the Ripon Group in Lancaster House, which is a conference of US congressional representatives. They were still rather shellshocked by the Trump result and were clearly deeply polarised in their reaction.

I did the full works at the Polish embassy for their Independence Day ceremonies, making a speech, meeting veterans and laying a wreath at the statue of General Sikorski in Portland Place.

Sunday 13 November – London

As the Foreign Minister in charge of protocol, one of my most enjoyable duties is to greet members of the Royal Family as they arrive at the FCO for the annual Remembrance Sunday service at the Cenotaph.

The convoy of vehicles arrives through the arch off King Charles Street at meticulously timed intervals. It really is the whole family, in sequence, up to HRH the Prince of Wales and Her Majesty the Queen herself. To greet them, see them safely up the steps into the hands of a nominated escort, is a real joy. All without exception engage in a quick friendly conversation, and it is a moment of elegance that is all too lacking in so much of our diplomatic activity these days.

James and I have a seat just inside the FCO Sovereign's Entrance, behind a window from which we can see the wreath-laying. It allows me to scoot back to the top of the stairs to escort the Royal Family along the corridor to the reception afterwards. All in the FCO are on tenterhooks as almost any formal footwear is at risk of skidding on the shiny Victorian floor tiles. They are quite perilous. With Crosby Hall on Tuesday and this today, that's two handshakes with the Queen in a week. And it was good to see the FCO Sovereign's Entrance being used by our Sovereign.

Tuesday 15 November – London

Meeting in my office with António Guterres, who is shortly to take over as UN Secretary General. After our five years through DfID and Yemen we now know each other quite well. He is anxious about Trump's disdain for international organisations, and in particular for the UN, so knows he's going to have to handle things adeptly. He wants Cyprus negotiations to be an early priority for his tenure, so we undertake to work very closely together.

Wednesday 16 November – London

Millions of calls on Cyprus, building relationships and preparing the ground for the expected talks next year. It's taking up a lot of time.

Meeting with the admirable Simon Hoare, MP for North Dorset. More than forty years since the scandal broke about how Thalidomide caused deformities in babies, there are still a few thousand survivors. As they get older they need more help, and Simon is championing their cause with his typical gusto. UK survivors are entitled to some money from a trust set up by the German manufacturers, but are not equipped to make the applications in German. It's all a bit of a mess, and I'll do my best with the German embassy to see if I can help.

Thursday 17 November – London

Answer a UQ on the Chagos Islands in the British Indian Ocean Territories from Andrew Rosindell, whose colonial blimpishness ignores any modern facts. He and the left are united in criticising the removal of the inhabitants from the likes of Diego Garcia at the end of the 1960s. Very few Chagossians have any genuine wish to live on the islands, and they'd have no care or supplies. It's bonkers. But it's a day out for the sort of irrational indignation on which Labour's Emily Thornberry thrives.

Monday 21 November – London

Video meeting with Sir Ivan Rogers, our man in the EU. He was at pains to explain the complexity of our process of departure from the EU. I sense he is in despair at the lack of clear direction, and the delusional optimism at the top of government. Not so much in Number 10 with the PM as with BoJo and DD.

Kim Darroch swings by having briefed Number 10 and a meeting of the National Security Council on the consequences of Trump's election. As always he is sharp and perceptive and openly admits that handling the new President-elect will require imagination and flexibility.

Thursday 24 November – Tblisi

Full day in Georgia as a mainstay of the Wardrop Dialogue. It's our annual bilateral get-together, named after Sir Oliver Wardrop, who was the UK's first Chief Commissioner of Transcaucasia in 1920.

They live constantly in fear of the Russian threat, and cementing our relations with them is an important pivotal support for their more Western ambitions.

Saturday 26 November – Rutland
Fidel Castro has died. The system is whirring to decide who goes to the funeral.

Monday 28 November – London/Amsterdam
I attend a reception for the Polish community at Number 10. As I leave towards St James's Park, Philip Hammond swanks in through the back gate, and walks straight past me with his nose in the air. He doesn't even say hello. He has no idea how to extend elementary courtesies in order to appear friendly.

I am to attend the Castro funeral, but my poor private office is in a bit of a flurry about which flights I can take without missing votes. It's all getting rather silly, as there aren't any looming votes that matter. Take KLM to Amsterdam. As I land, the Whips explode that I haven't been formally slipped [given permission to miss the vote], and threaten to bar Boris from going to Cyprus on Wednesday because I have headed off to Havana. It'll all get sorted. I breathe deeply and leave a grovelling voicemail for Mel Stride, the Pairing Whip.

Schiphol Hilton.

Tuesday 29 November – Amsterdam/Havana
The voicemail seems to have done the trick. All is forgiven … just! The trouble, though, is that it is an inexperienced Whips' Office with no wider view of UK interests. FCO ministers used to enjoy a presumed slip, so they could almost always be released for travel without restriction. There is one fewer Commons minister since the creation of DExEU, but the same world needs to be covered. I have seventy-seven countries, and the Foreign Secretary has the whole lot. We all have setpiece commitments which require UK attendance. The Whips are also over-cautious, calling people back to contribute to majorities of fifty or sixty. Their anger at us as we struggle to juggle

our obligations is unbecoming. They should grow up and work out a modus operandi.

KLM to Havana with Lance Domm.

For Cuba this is its momentous *fin de siècle*. Fidel Castro was, with Che Guevara, the inspiration for every leftist romantic zealot who craved an anti-bourgeois (and later an anti-American) revolution. He was the central figure for over six decades of those Latin American firebrands whose egos challenged traditional authority, championed the rights of the poor and then impoverished them further.

We landed at 3pm and headed to our elegant residence. The nameplate at the entrance is handsomely reminiscent of a former age: 'HBM Ambassador Residence'. In those days it was 'Her Britannic Majesty's'. It boasts a Romanesque indoor pool, but the morons from FCO health & safety tried to force the Ambassador to put ugly railings around it.

Labour's Shadow Foreign Secretary, Emily Thornberry, arrived a couple of hours earlier. Opposition frontbenchers are not entitled to any assistance from the FCO, but I offered a modest degree of help, such as being met at the airport, the use of the residence for a couple of hours, and transport to and from the funeral rally. My only condition (not mentioned to her) was that we were not to be on the same public platform. On arrival, I included her in the briefing meeting. Extraordinary – not a word of appreciation or gratitude. Not even a hint of acknowledgement that I had courteously extended her such assistance. It was as if she owned the place, and I was lucky to be allowed to join her. She is a graceless frump.

To the Revolution Square. Wow! The roads were empty (i.e. cleared) and we were dropped off just behind the memorial obelisk. We walked up the steps and over the brow of the hill where in front of us were perhaps 500,000 people, chanting as only the likes of a football crowd can when they know what to shout together. 'The people, united, will never be defeated,' or whatever the Spanish revolutionary original is. 'Viva Fidel, Viva la Revolución.' I suddenly understood in a nanosecond the foundations of all the imported inspiration and attitudes of the left which have conditioned the UK's trade unionists, its regular protesters and politicians such as Jeremy

Corbyn and Ken Livingstone for the last fifty years. The entire play-book has just been simplistically transplanted, but it has given them a cause, a script and unquestioning arguments.

We had to sit for an hour or so, but I was able to speak to a few foreign ministers who were there – Argentina, Colombia, Luxembourg (Jean Asselborn) – and some of the Qatari delegation. I was along to the right with some old lags from 1960s socialism, including a Portuguese bloke who said that Fidel was the inspiration to his generation who had to fight against fascism. Robert Mugabe of Zimbabwe, now ninety-one, was there, but sufficiently far away for me not to have to make any special effort to avoid him. Then at 7pm it kicked off. A whole series of tribute speeches of varying degrees of passion: those not in Spanish took twice as long, as each sentence had to be repeated in translation. It was a relentless wank-fest of international socialism: a unique historic moment.

Wednesday 30 November – Havana
Amusingly, our Ambassador, Antony Stokes, was a year or two below me at school. Fortunately, or perhaps diplomatically, he says he has no incriminating recollections from when I was Head Boy.

He also earned very high marks for arranging a visit to the dance studio of Carlos Acosta, the legendary Royal Ballet dancer. Acosta was charming, and some of his students put on an amazing perfor-mance of contemporary dance for me.

Friday 2 December – London/Seville
The Lib Dems have won the Richmond by-election. Zac's majority of 23,000 has been turned into a Lib Dem majority of 1,800, with Labour losing their deposit. We did not officially contest it because Zac ran as an independent. Normally, such a move would lead to excommunication from the Party.

By-elections, like referendums, are never simply about the straight-forward issue supposed. Zac Goldsmith, multi-millionaire and failed Mayoral candidate, had always campaigned for statutory 'recall', meaning that if (say) 20 per cent of a constituency's voters petitioned for a by-election for a clearly stated reason, then they could call for

one. It could be because the MP had changed party, or was accused
of impropriety, and so on. Zac did it to justify his opposition to the
expansion of Heathrow Airport, much as David Davis did a few
years ago when arguing against privacy laws/ID cards etc.

To Seville with Harry Dadswell for the Tertulias conference, our
annual get-together with the Spanish. The guest list is wider than just
politicians, although the majority are MPs on both sides. Needless to
say it is Brexit, Brexit and more Brexit. Addressing what is a pro-EU
audience requires a gentle touch, but unfortunately David Davis
doesn't really have that in his skill set, and his speech before dinner
caused much grinding of teeth.

Saturday 3 December – Seville/Rutland

Much as I like David Jones, who is DD's deputy, his tone was utterly
uncompromising, and the two of them were subjected to an
onslaught of caustic questions from the attendees. Whereas I
defended government policy on Brexit, it's the tone that matters, and
unfortunately the two Davids caused needless offence by being so
insensitive.

After meetings with Spain's two new foreign ministers (one for
Europe, one for the world), I delivered my own speech about Brexit
and the way forward.

At the airport, poor Harry had one of those private office heart-
attack moments when I asked him for my passport. He thought I
had it, but the hotel had kept it after check-in. But he is brilliant,
and he calmly arranged for someone to bring it to the airport just
in time for us to board. He was charmingly in control, then looked
me in the eye and said, 'Minister, thank you so much for not
exploding.'

Sat next to Freddie Howe on the flight back to Luton. As Earl
Howe and a defence minister, he is one of those priceless gems in the
Lords whose service to the country is so under-appreciated. Back in
1997, we were both Shadow health ministers when the ridiculous
Ann Widdecombe was Shadow Secretary of State, and he went on to
become the lynchpin of our health team in government.

Sunday 4 December – Rutland

Total flop-out day. So nice just to light the fire, walk the dog and be at home.

Monday 5 December – London

Christmas is in the air, and we have a lovely little ceremony in the FCO quad at which the Norwegians give us a Christmas tree, as they also do in Trafalgar Square. Normally it's just the Norwegian Ambassador, but this year their Foreign Minister, Børge Brende, attended. He has not changed much since I first met him at the 1996 Republican National Convention in San Diego, which nominated Bob Dole as their Presidential candidate.

Dinner at Wilton's with George Robertson and Mark Allen (a lord and a knight, both now of BP). I've known Mark for years – former Middle East Director for MI6, he is probably the most accomplished and perceptive they've had for ages. In my view he has been utterly traduced by accusations of complicity in torture, which have gone on for years and years. I was critical of Dominic Grieve for needlessly perpetuating the ISC's inquiry into detention and rendition, which I would have brought to a close had he not beaten me to the chairmanship.

Mark, although of course not an Arab, is one of the world's most accomplished Arabic calligraphers.

George is a complete joy – droll, cleverly analytical and always generous-spirited. He passes the holiday test with stars, stripes, banners and fireworks. I can't remember what on earth we were talking about after the third bottle, but what I do remember is his lovely quip: 'I've never much admired the courage of a lion tamer: after all, inside his cage he is safe from other men.'

Tuesday 6 December – London

A sort of typical day in my life, which illustrates how I have to dart from meeting to meeting and topic to topic. I expect not many people understand what a minister has to do in their daily life, particularly if they are conscientious, as I try to be. It's a classic rat-a-tat day, which although quickly moving is full of stimulation and requires extraordinary punctuality and mental discipline. Today was:

- PM's EU adviser Denzil Davidson at Number 10;
- lunch with Indiana Governor Eric Holcomb, who took over from him who is now Vice-President-elect Mike Pence;
- drop in on the Foreign Affairs Committee in the FCO as they receive a formal briefing on sanctions;
- meeting with the Duke of York at Buckingham Palace – I don't care what they say, he is commendably full of enthusiasm and doing his very best;
- phone call with Espen Eide, the UN adviser on Cyprus, for a negotiations update;
- meet a senior delegation from Kurdistan, led by their Deputy Prime Minister Qubad Talabani;
- and then impromptu drinks with most of Boris' private office, including Liam Parker and Lance.

Wednesday 7 December – London

The government's appeal against the Article 50 ruling is going on in the Supreme Court.

Attend a meeting at DExEU with the government of Gibraltar, chaired by Robin Walker. Chief Minister Fabian Picardo and his team are very professional, and of course risk becoming serious victims of Brexit.

In a continuing Brexit afternoon I join the Joint Ministerial Committee which is held with the devolved assemblies, chaired by David Jones. Ben Gummer slips me a note saying, 'DJ has the style of a country solicitor reading out a (paltry) will to the family.'

Opposition motion on Article 50, demanding that a plan be presented to Parliament before it is triggered. The government moved an amendment which is carried overwhelmingly.

Chris Bryant sidles up to me outside the Smoking Room with a read-out from the Tertulias. He had stayed on with husband Jared to hit the town a bit. 'Davis and Jones were a disaster. It's not what they said so much as how they said it. They did real damage. Some of the

Spaniards thought David Jones racist. The only one they liked was you.' So … bad news and good news.

Back to the Durbar Court in the FCO to celebrate the end of the Latin American Chevening Scholars' first term in the UK. I was mobbed by fluffy Latinos all wanting a photo. Named after the Foreign Secretary's official country residence, the UK-funded scholarship scheme is steadily building an international network of leaders.

Thursday 8 December – Hamburg

Quick flight to Hamburg for a meeting of the OSCE [Organisation for Security and Cooperation in Europe], returning just in time to tog up in white tie for the diplomatic reception at Buckingham Palace. We are carefully kettled into various state rooms, and although it's a bit of a crush it is the highlight of the year for every foreign ambassador. Each can bring their spouse and children – it's all about them seeing the Queen. She painstakingly works her way down the line and speaks to every single one of them, who then radiate pleasure. The Royal stardust is unique in the world.

Sunday 11 December – London

Lots of awkward stuff in the Sundays, including Nicky Morgan having a real go at the PM for her interview profile last week in which the main photo was her wearing a pair of brown leather trousers that apparently cost £995. 'I don't think I've ever spent that much on anything apart from my wedding dress,' said Morgan.

Back to London.

Monday 12 December – London/Brussels

The papers have noticed that Nicky Morgan's Mulberry handbag cost £1,000.

Early Eurostar to Brussels with Lance for the Foreign Affairs Council, the monthly meeting of European foreign ministers. The EU High Representative (i.e. not the EU's foreign minister) is Federica Mogherini, or FedMog as I call her. She doesn't half bang on, and can never keep to time. Our one o'clock lunch rarely starts before 2pm, even when a distinguished guest is kept waiting. I nonetheless maintain good relations with her and, to be fair to her, she always calls me to speak quite early.

Crispin Blunt calls about his wish to have officials come before the Foreign Affairs Committee about arms exports. I explain that the government is in court, facing a judicial review on sales to Saudi Arabia in respect of Yemen, and that it would be improper to expose officials to detailed questioning in the middle of a court case. He assured me they would not be, and that all they had to do was appear and play it with a 'dead bat'. On that basis I gave permission for our arms-export officials to appear tomorrow and explain the process.

Tuesday 13 December – Brussels/London

Still in Brussels, the FAC has morphed into the GAC. The General Affairs Council is European affairs ministers, which sort of overlaps with foreign ministers. Austria's thirty-year-old Foreign Minister Sebastian Kurz blocks the meeting's conclusions because they want a freeze on Turkey-accession talks.

On the train back I had a spat via text with Crispin Blunt. Contrary to our clear agreement, he and committee members had grilled my officials and required them to defend policy and individual decisions. The firm agreement yesterday with him was that they would only be asked about the process.

The Foreign Secretary's pre-Christmas reception for diplomats at Lancaster House. Boris was hilarious about the Prime Minister, in the light of 'trousergate'. Referring to her EU views, he joked, 'She even wears lederhosen!'

Wednesday 14 December – London

Dinner at China Tang with James for the tenth anniversary of our first meeting.

Thursday 15 December – London/Istanbul/Tashkent

Am trying to arrange to be in New York at the UN for the inauguration of António Guterres on 10 January, even though it is FCO questions that day.

Fly to Tashkent via Istanbul. Two hours' sleep, sitting up …

Friday 16 December – Samarkand/Tashkent

Arrive 0730. Straight to the railway station for a two-hour journey to Samarkand with the Uzbek FM Abdulaziz Kamilov.

Visit the grave of the recently deceased President Islam Karimov, who had led Uzbekistan since 1989.

Lance emails to point out that Ivan Rogers is being lambasted in the press – the *Mail* in particular – just so unfairly, for no more than telling ministers the truth. He has been reported as advising the government that Brexit might take a decade. He is right. I send him a supportive herogram email.

Back in Tashkent, after meetings with other ministers, I am granted one with the new President, Shavkat Mirziyoyev. This really is an opportunity to plant the British flag in Central Asia, and encourage them to liberalise and give hope to their young. Mirziyoyev is a genuine reformer, and we are potentially looking at a new chapter in Uzbek history. All of which will be a far cry from that portrayed by the UK's controversial former Ambassador Craig Murray.

At the end of our meeting he gifts me a carpet. Then on to a fun vodka dinner at the InterContinental.

Saturday 17 December – Tashkent/Rutland

Early start. Plane delayed four hours from Istanbul thanks to fog in London.

I'm getting bashed in *The Times* about St Helena Airport. Oliver Wright in *The Times* has written a piece lampooning my support for it. The truth is that while at DfID I delivered government policy and through rigorous oversight built the airport ahead of schedule and under budget. But what is true is that strong crosswinds are causing safety problems.

Andrew Mitchell texts generously to say it's not my fault.

Only land at 7pm. To Rutland at 10pm.

Monday 19 December – London

As I'm walking to the FCO, a motor scooter ploughs into the pedestrians crossing the street at the corner of Parliament Square, sending a poor Chinese-looking woman flying back on to the pavement. The rider is utterly unapologetic, saying the light was green and that he was allowed to go at 30mph. I gave him the most frightful bollocking as others summoned a Commons copper. What a git. He will not forget both the rocket he received and the gradual gathering of people against him. Needless to say all the cyclists sided with him, even though they had not witnessed the incident.

Spoke to Priti Patel ahead of her appearance as Secretary of State before the International Development Committee, to explain the St Helena Airport facts and her need to defend me should it be raised. As it happened, it wasn't. They focused entirely on how her budget is going into the pockets of corrupt dictators.

Briefing on Russia, ahead of my evidence session tomorrow before the Foreign Affairs Select Committee.

To Lancaster House to open the UK–Argentine Dialogue with the new Minister, Pedro Villagra, who was only appointed yesterday.

Private office Christmas lunch at the Osteria. Not many ministers would treat their team so lavishly.

Michael Fallon has finally made a statement to the House about the use of cluster munitions by the Saudis. He has been sitting on it for weeks, and it is miraculous that he has managed to sneak out an admission and a correction to the record without any Opposition calls for his head. If they were not so useless he'd be toast.

I call the Russian Ambassador whose equivalent in Turkey has been shot. Only later is it clear that he is dead.

Bump into Jonny Hall in Whitehall. He, with Nick Timothy and Fi Hill, had just been to New York, but had only seen medium-level functionaries in the Trump transition team. Number 10 is making a total botch of the whole process.

As if today had not seen enough moments, I get home as news breaks of a truck ploughing into shoppers at a Christmas market in Berlin. Maybe ten are dead.

More talks with the Argentines, and a visit to the Lancaster House wine cellar, one of the privileges of being in charge of protocol.

Tuesday 20 December – London

In a landmark moment with Argentina, I reach a firm agreement with their new Foreign Minister to establish additional flights to the Falkland Islands via the mainland. Even a year ago this would have been impossible, but after painstaking diplomacy and some excellent FCO staff work, we have banked the deal. As it turned out, the greatest challenge in the negotiations was to stop the Falkland Islands politicians from sounding off and kiboshing everything.

Friday 23 December – Rutland

Collect Mum from Amersham.

The UN Security Council has passed a resolution emphatically condemning Israel for its expansion of settlements. The US did not exercise its usual veto. It is a seminal moment, albeit during the last gasp of the Obama Presidency.

Saturday 24 December – Rutland

Nevill Holt carol service at Great Easton. Meet the new Uppingham headmaster, Richard Maloney.

Saturday 31 December – Rutland

Take Noodle for a walk. She leaps into the river after spotting a moorhen in the reeds, and then struggles to get out again because the bank is too muddy and slippery. I grab her by the scruff of the neck, but have to put my leg in up to the knee. It is cold … and muddy.

Speak to Erik in Muscat, just before he heads off to the Sultan's New Year party.

Quiet dinner in Rutland with James.

End of the year!

2017

Sunday 1 January – Rutland

The advantage of going to bed before midnight on New Year's Eve is that you start the year without a hangover. We were sensibly restrained, and just enjoyed being on our own, switching off the iPhone so as to avoid the stream of New Year messages that had dribbled in all night.

At least we weren't in Istanbul, where yet another terrorist attack has seen over thirty killed by someone with a machine gun in a popular nightclub. Over 500 have been killed in Turkey in the last year and a half. I am due in Ankara on Tuesday for the third time in six months.

The events of the coming year are going to thump us hard. Donald Trump will become President in three weeks, and is already proving destabilising. His nominated Ambassador to Israel is in favour of settlements and believes the West Bank belongs to Israel. Trump says he will move his embassy to Jerusalem because it is 'the undivided capital of Israel', which it isn't. He clearly wants perpetual conflict, if not a regional war. Or more likely he just knows so little about the issue he doesn't realise what he is unleashing. He is cosying up to Putin, who has cleverly said he will not retaliate against Obama's expulsion last week of thirty-five Russian 'diplomats' accused of involvement in recent cyber-attacks which supposedly were designed to undermine Hillary Clinton and support Trump.

Meanwhile here, we await the judgment of the Supreme Court, who I guess will uphold the decision to refer the declaration of

Article 50 to Parliament, something that would require urgent legislation. Overall, I can see no path to a painless Brexit, nor any scope for a deal between the UK and the EU which offers anything at all on our undeclared shopping list. We either have to accept all the terms of our current membership, while losing actual membership, or we crunch the gears and just leave. We would then face tariffs, a reduction in inward investment and 5,000 lorries stuck at Calais full of rotting tomatoes.

The FTSE Index may have closed the year at an all-time high of over 7,000, but that's partly because companies' sterling values reflect the devaluation of the pound, and UK quoted companies are now more vulnerable to a takeover. The brave new world of Brexit is going to be a nightmare.

We will easily get a bill through to allow the PM to trigger Article 50 by the end of March, but the Great Repeal Bill could be fraught with difficulty, and will possibly face thousands of amendments. The House of Lords might fight back and create obstacles.

Most significantly though, there is no easy prospect of a UK–EU deal. If anything is agreed it then requires the unanimous acceptance of the EU and its institutions. Of the twenty-seven other countries, the EU Commission, the EU Parliament and the prospect of referendums in some of the twenty-seven, one or more of them is bound to say 'no'. So it's over the cliff, or over the cliff! All those who say we buy lots of BMWs and so the EU needs us and will cave in fail to appreciate both that market volumes are asymmetric – they are looking at the whole world, and not just at us – and also the decision-makers are thinking as much about politics as about economics. We are not dealing with people in a straightforward business negotiation. Many feel that if they give us a workable deal it will encourage others to contemplate leaving. So it's up with the shutters.

Tuesday 3 January – London/Ankara
The idiot Michael Gove is claiming through Change Britain, his tame and facile pro-Brexit group, that leaving the customs union would create 400,000 jobs in the UK. It is sheer fiction: a figment of his Martian theoretical fantasy.

I tell Hugo Swire, who has taken over from me as Chairman, that he needs to flex the muscles of CMEC to use the Balfour centenary year to force the issue of Palestinian recognition in Parliament.

To Ankara, the umpteenth time I've been in transit through Istanbul and eaten the same meal on Turkish Airlines. The Istanbul gunman is on the run.

Speak to Lance while in transit. Sir Ivan Rogers has resigned from his position in UKREP [UK Representation to the EU]. As our foremost expert on EU matters he has been under fire from the *Daily Mail*, and it seems from his letter to Jeremy Heywood that they had spoken before Christmas and discussed the possibility of him going somewhere else, but no go. He has clearly been eased out after suggesting that Brexit, or at least trade deals, might take ten years. All this will do is cocoon the PM and Number 10 further, trapping them in a tiny world of delusion, and denuding them of the honest and informed advice which Ivan has been giving them. So ... offer truth unto power, and get sacked. No doubt the *Mail* will gloat tomorrow, but the UK will be the poorer for it. When the truth of Brexit complexity dawns, the consequences will be all the more dire. Only idiots will be pleased by Ivan's departure. He is a good man, traduced by the press and political bigotry.

Oh dear. More tales of how impossible Tobias Ellwood is. He's a funny mixture of being demanding, insecure and insensitive. I just avoid him, and exchange polite banalities whenever forced to speak to him. I could have been the making of him, but he's too dim. I used to think him worth it, but not now.

Ankara is under a blanket of snow. The residence looks lovely. I congratulate Richard Moore on his CMG. We listen to BBC Radio 4's *In Touch*. Presented by the blind and admirable Peter White, the programme came to Turkey and featured Richard's fabulous blind wife Maggie with her introduction to the country of guide dogs. She has a picture on her iPhone of herself, Star the Labrador, Richard and President Erdoğan, which she waves effectively at any shopowner who tries to bar her dog from their premises. A nice Gevrey-Chambertin, and bed.

Wednesday 4 January – Ankara/Athens

Journalist Clayton Swisher calls. His plans for his four-part exposé of Israeli influence in UK politics will be broadcast on Al Jazeera in ten days, but will hit the *Mail on Sunday* this weekend and the *Guardian* on Monday. He has footage of diplomats from the Israeli embassy in London collaborating with MPs from both Labour and Conservatives on Israel, which includes Shai Masot from the embassy calling for them to destroy the 'Deputy Foreign Minister' (i.e. me), so that he never becomes Foreign Secretary. They say that if Boris were to be sacked, I'd take over, and so both such moments have to be stopped. I really have to think about how I handle this.

The press is full of Ivan Rogers, with the *Daily Hate* predictably saying good riddance, and trashing him viciously. The brainless Iain Duncan Smith delights in his departure, and demands his replacement be a firm Eurosceptic. There he is, a former leader of the Party and former Cabinet minister, overriding support for the fundamental principle of our civil service that civil servants are politically neutral and are there to offer honest advice and to carry out the will of their political masters. But, overall, Ivan comes out of the profiles and reports as a talented and dutiful public servant. It is not clear who 'owns' him, the Treasury (where he was for ages) or the FCO or the Cabinet Office. Assuming he leaves the civil service altogether, he will soon be snapped up by the private sector.

Some good briefings from the Ankara embassy team on Erdoğan's plans to convert the prime ministership into an executive presidency; the hoped-for TFX deal, which would create a long-term UK–Turkey joint venture to manufacture a Turkish fighter aircraft; and the Syria conflict in Al Bab just over the Turkish border.

Three really warm and productive meetings in succession. Although not able to see President Erdoğan this time – he is understandably preoccupied with the aftermath of the Reina nightclub massacre, and only ever usually sees PMs and presidents – I see Foreign Minister Mevlüt Çavuşoğlu, Europe Minister Ömer Çelik and PM Binali Yıldırım.

Our talk is mainly about Cyprus. Following civil unrest between the Greek and Turkish Cypriot communities, which prompted

Turkish military intervention, the island has been divided since 1974 between the Turkish north and the Greek south. Reunification talks are reaching their culmination, and a high-level conference is planned for next week in Geneva. A host of issues are floating about – a rotating presidency, property compensation, an enhanced UN presence, etc. But the main sticking point will be whether Turkey removes its soldiers from the north and drops its right to intervene if their community is under threat. A comprehensive settlement is still a long way off, but the plan is still to try to reach one. Boris and I will go next week, but the PM will and should only go if there's going to be a deal. I don't think there will be.

Tim Barrow is in Number 10, and is to be anointed the new Permanent Rep at UKREP. The story of the Rogers exit is becoming clear. He was essentially forced out by the execrable duo, Hill and Timothy. They control the PM and, in their simplistic approach to the meaning of life, considered him anti-Brexit and obstructive. Yet all he was doing was telling the truth.

It'll mean that Tim will not go to the annual Privy Council in Oman, a one-day event at which senior officials from the UK give the Sultan privileged briefing on hot topics around the world. I give Lance phone numbers for Erik and his aide Mohammed bin Sulaiman, so Tim can tell Erik directly.

Ian Cobain of the *Guardian* has phoned and emailed Harriet Baker in my parliamentary office, saying that they would like me to comment on the imminent Al Jazeera broadcast which has filmed the Israeli embassy trying to coordinate MPs to destroy me. I tell Lance I need to speak to both Simon McDonald and Jeremy Heywood.

To Athens. Met by Andrew Staunton, the Chargé d'Affaires. The new Ambassador only arrives tomorrow.

Thursday 5 January – Athens/London
Barrow will definitely not go to Oman, but nor now can Christopher Geidt.

Philip Barton is thought to be in the frame for Political Director. He used to be number two in Washington under Peter Westmacott, and has since been High Commissioner in Pakistan. The papers are reporting that there was a turf war in which Olly Robbins as Permanent Secretary of DExEU tried to have Tim Barrow's job in Brussels downgraded so that he could be in overall command of the entire Brexit process. He lost, and Tim is top equal.

Speak to Tim. He says with a chuckle that he and I were the star clip on *Newsnight*, because when reporting his tussle with Robbins they used footage from the Foreign Affairs Committee session we both attended.

Al Jazeera have put a teaser on YouTube, which trails their breaking story about improper influence-peddling in the British political establishment, and it contains a clip of the journalist Peter Oborne calling for a full investigation by British intelligence services into Israeli interference in our democratic affairs.

I discuss with Lance how he thinks I should handle the issue. We both agree that it has such serious implications that I should alert the government at the highest level so that they can be forewarned. But we have to protect the PM and the Foreign Secretary and not suck them in at this stage.

Greek FM Nikos Kotzias, his usual jolly voluble self. An old leftie, he is nonetheless smart, and says he's trying really hard to find common ground with the Turks on Cyprus. He is off to New York after our meeting, and will see the new Secretary General António Guterres.

Lunch with half a dozen Greek journalists on Cyprus – nitpicking as always and unable to see the bigger picture. Also see George Koumoutsakos, Head of Foreign Policy for Mitsotakis' New Democracy party, along with Costas Alexandris and Ioannis Papadimos; then Evan Kalpadakis, adviser to PM Tsipras. Of all my meetings, he is probably the most directly involved face to face in the detail.

Kate Smith, our new Ambassador to Greece, arrives on the inbound plane, so we overlap for half an hour before I fly off. She is accompanied by her cats. A good effusive DipTel from Ankara suggesting that my recent visit prepares the ground perfectly for the PM's at the end of the month.

Lots of scheduling shenanigans about my itinerary for next week. Oman tomorrow night; back Sunday; New York Monday; back Wednesday; Geneva Thursday. The plan for me to travel with Boris to Geneva won't quite work. All complicated by the Whips insisting we can't all be away at the same time, so I will end up having to vote on Wednesday so that Ellwood can fly off and add nothing to our relations with Iran.

Fly back to sub-zero weather in London. I have faced a lot of climate change this week. Speak from the car to Crispin Blunt, who has just received an email like mine asking for his reaction to the Al Jazeera video evidence. Crispin is appalled, all the more so as he is named and criticised too.

Friday 6 January – London/Muscat

The admirable Lance has secured a 10am landing slot for me with Cabinet Secretary Sir Jeremy Heywood. I show him the emails from the *Guardian* and the similar one they sent to Crispin, and explain what I think is coming down the track. I obviously know more about the broader content of the Al Jazeera reports than I let on, but I present an accurate factual account of the news that is likely to break. Jeremy immediately asks the National Security Adviser, Sir Mark Lyall Grant, to join the meeting.

I keep very cool, and express the wish to be relaxed and grown up about it. We must look at the broader interests of HMG etc. Indeed we must, as the Israel issue has already caused serious friction between us and the incoming Trump team.

Donald Trump, in all his wisdom, takes the simple 'Israel is always right' line; he has nominated a pro-settlements ambassador to Israel; he has said that Jerusalem is the undivided capital of Israel and that he will move the US embassy from Tel Aviv to Jerusalem; the UNSCR [UN Security Council Resolution] condemning settlements went through with the UK voting for and the US abstaining; Israel then went bonkers; Kerry makes his brilliant speech forensically outlining Israeli misconduct; the UK dilutes its principles and criticises the Kerry speech (to suck up to Trump); and Jared Kushner, Trump's son-in-law, gives our Ambassador in the US, Sir Kim

Darroch, the most rude, vulgar and aggressive dressing down for the UK having voted for the UNSCR – 'we expect our friends to behave like friends … this will count against the UK' etc.

So the sensitivities over wanting to slam the Israeli Ambassador or carpet him for what they have done to me and in the UK more generally are tempered by the wider context of how to handle relations with the incoming President. Where's our self-respect and confidence? We could kill two birds with one stone and assert our independent, confident view of the world by telling both Trump and Netanyahu to bugger off and adhere to the rule of law and international justice. But we will instead capitulate and be supine. I of course play the card of being a grown-up. We must protect our wider equities; the UK in general matters much more than me as an individual; I am prepared to do whatever is in our broader national interests. They are both enormously grateful for the advance warning. I show them the email in which Israeli Ambassador Regev has asked for an urgent phone call with me, and explain that he has obviously received a letter from the *Guardian* too and so will be in full crisis-response mode. We agree that I should make the call to him later, and that I should ask him to make a public statement so that HMG won't have to get too sucked into having to comment.

To the FCO. I call Simon McDonald and brief him similarly. I teasingly remind him of what happened and what I said to him on my first day as a minister. 'Simon … didn't I tell you? The CFI and the Israelis think they control the Foreign Office. And they do!'

Simon Walters of the *Mail on Sunday* comes to see me at home. They are going to run with it hard. Clay Swisher has given them the entire transcript of all the undercover filming, and has shown them a screening of their four-part exposé. Simon is an old hand, and can be trusted not to stitch me up. Background will be background, and I will properly uphold my undertaking to Heywood not to make any public comment.

Back to the FCO. I make the planned 12.30 call to Ambassador Regev. We have never before met or spoken. He used to be Netanyahu's media spokesman, so is well versed in press handling.

He is one of those spin-the-line people. He thinks he's so very clever, he's actually rather stupid.

His opening sentence, blurted out deliberately and emphatically, was 'I am calling to apologise to you personally and on behalf of the Israeli embassy.' I responded by saying that I very much appreciated his doing so, but then unsettled him by saying that I think I know what he is apologising for, but I only have an email from the *Guardian* to go on, and so perhaps we might compare notes on what we think has been going on.

He then goes into full super-shit 'not me guv' mode. 'Someone called Shai Masot has been filmed etc. He is a local hire, works in a junior capacity and does not have diplomatic status. What he has been doing does not have the authority of the embassy. It is totally unacceptable. We do not do this sort of thing. You are a minister of the Crown, and it would of course be wholly improper to undermine a government minister. He will be disciplined. He might be dismissed, but we have to go through proper procedures. He is only twenty-seven.'

It's all total bollocks. Masot is a First or Second Secretary, a member of military intelligence, employed specifically as a parliamentary and undercover propagandist. It is of course exactly why the CFI sat Masot next to me at their annual lunch. It is all part of a carefully defined strategy to promote an Israel which will one day take over the West Bank and to destroy anyone who opposes settlement expansion. They are driven by the threat of BDS – boycott, disinvestment (or divestment) and sanctions – a rational cause of the left, but something I have never so much as mentioned. Their scheming is probably about to recruit many more exponents to the call for BDS.

I remain polite, but firm in tone. 'Oh yes. I know Shai. I remember him when he was an IDF [Israel Defence Forces] soldier who I met at the Erez checkpoint when I was going into Gaza a few years ago.' I express appreciation for his apology. I say that I am puzzled by what has been happening, as I am pro-Israel but against settlements. That after all is our government policy, and my understanding was that Israel is also in favour of a two-state solution. Maybe I got that wrong?

I make my disappointment clear, but offer to respond in a grown-up and responsible way, 'in the interests of our broader relationship'. He confirms he will make a statement saying he has called me personally to apologise, and saying it was unauthorised activity by a junior employee with no formal diplomatic status. Disingenuous deceitful mendacious crap. However, I say how much I look forward to meeting him and having lunch in due course. I also suggest that our respective press offices speak to each other immediately so as to coordinate any inquiries. His bloke is called Yiftah Curiel. I tell him that Simon McGee, FCO Head of Press, will call.

Within minutes of the call FCO Protocol have checked out Shai Masot. We know full well he is not a 'local hire' and, contrary to Regev's white lie, he does in fact have diplomatic status. He is on the official diplomatic list, albeit at a low level, but is immune from prosecution and is described as an official 'political officer'. What on earth is the point of Regev stating something that is so blatantly untrue, and about which we both hold the facts? What a muppet.

Put simply, they have been caught red-handed, Regev had started off well by apologising and then screwed himself by lying. Par for the course.

A quick meeting with Jonathan Allen, who has stood in at short notice to replace Tim Barrow as the head of our delegation to the Cyprus talks next week in Geneva. He knows his stuff, and is mucking in well.

Lance and I brief Simon McGee to contact the Israelis.

Catch Boris in his office following his spending an hour and a half with Tim Barrow, who he really likes. I show him the *Guardian* emails, explain what Al Jazeera has been up to and give him a readout of my phone call with Regev. He is both indignant and all over the place. 'They shouldn't behave like this,' he exclaimed, though I'd told him a million times that they do. 'The UNSCR was right, but it achieved nothing, so why did we do it?' The scales dropping from his eyes were scattered all over the floor. The *Guardian* email refers to Shai Masot making 'disparaging comments about Boris'. He stares at the email and is clearly ruminating on quite what might have been said about him. I know that they referred to him as an 'idiot', but don't tell him so. The Al Jazeera tapes essentially say that I run the FCO, BoJo is an idiot, I take the serious decisions, and if anything happens to Boris I will become Foreign Secretary and so I must be destroyed. It's a poor reading of the facts – indeed it's balls – but it gives a useful insight into Israel's mentality. At least as ministers we're legitimate, unlike Israel's settler ministers and settler Knesset members.

Boris is ambivalent, and rather muddled. On the one hand he thinks that Kushner's assault on Kim Darroch is reprehensible and that we should tell them to 'fuck off'; on the other he says the UNSCR should never have happened as it achieved nothing. He's fast learning some important facts of life. But he is finding it rather unsettling. He says Richard Moore is in the frame to be Political Director. That would be good.

Back home to pack for my trip to Oman. Clay Swisher asks to pop by. He gives me a memory stick of their planned broadcasts. He had just been briefing Seumas Milne, Jeremy Corbyn's Wykehamist leftie ex-*Guardian* journo Chief of Staff. I think what happened is that Al Jazeera went undercover because the Labour Party was being accused of institutional anti-Semitism. They also suspected that the issue was to some extent being exploited by the Israeli embassy, and was designed to counter any political view that was either in favour of BDS or against settlements. Once they got going, they hit a goldmine and to their amazement discovered far more besides.

James overlapped for a few minutes as he picked up Noodle and headed on to Rutland ahead of my going to Stansted.

Fly overnight to Oman with Lord King of Lothbury, who as Mervyn King was Governor of the Bank of England. He is charming, engaging and gently amusing.

Saturday 7 January – Muscat

Land at 9am, and straight to the Bait al Baraka, the Royal Palace. No Barrow or Geidt, but a good enough cast to justify the effort of gathering as the Sultan's Privy Council for its annual session. Air Chief Marshal Sir Stuart Peach (Chief of the Defence Staff), Alex

Younger ('C'), Mervyn King (former Governor of the Bank of England), Lord Astor (Johnnie, both Trade and Defence Envoy to Oman) and me. Also attending are two long-standing advisers to the Sultan, Sir Erik Bennett and Dr Omar Zawawi.

We have the morning to ourselves in the sunshine by the pool of the guest palace. By lunchtime all have arrived. Dr Omar can hardly sit down and get up again without help, and is looking older and rather stooped, but then he is about ninety. Erik, at eighty-eight, is rather more spry.

A long chat with Stuart Peach. He is so convivial and very straight-forward. He is very pro-Richard Moore and agrees he'd be a good 'C' to succeed Alex in a couple of years.

In the US, the absurd President-elect Trump is denying that the Russians did anything untoward trying to cyber-influence the US election, even though the CIA et al. have released evidence to the congressional committee that they did so.

A few calls to Peter Oborne, Clay Swisher and Simon Walters. The Al Jazeera exposé is going to run in the *Mail*, and Peter will ramp it up in Middle East Eye. It will all burst at about 2am Oman time, 10pm UK.

We are asked to gather at 7.30pm, but we only start with HM after 11pm. It's the normal routine. So we have the PC meeting from 11pm to 1.30am. A well-planned agenda covering all the regional and global issues you would expect.

The Sultan was skinny and a little stooped, but perfectly with it, and intellectually engaged in all the presentations. We managed to land some important messages on some crucial things he needs to do on cyber-protection and national economic management, so assuming he follows up as he said he would we will have achieved something tangible.

Dinner afterwards finished at 4am, but it meant that I sat next to him for well over two hours. I told him about the Israeli antics in London, and we spoke of Theresa May, Brexit, the Queen and the recent visit of the Prince of Wales. I buttered him up and kept him amused. In return he teasingly force-fed me, demanding with an impish grin that I taste each of the seven lamb recipes on offer, and have at least three puddings from the trolley. Fatoramus maximus!

To my room at midnight UK time, and look at my iPad. The Israeli embassy story is the full front-page *Mail on Sunday* splash, but Sky and the BBC hardly mention it, preferring to cover Corbyn on the NHS and May on some social justice speech that is coming next week. Anyway, at least the story's out in public with a splash and is not a half-hearted dribble.

Texts from Robert Halfon, whose pretty Italian female assistant was one of the people filmed trying to do me over, and, needless to say, a message from Stuart Polak, both no doubt orchestrated. Halfon just asking me to call him, which I don't. It's past midnight UK time anyway. Polak's is rather less subtle: 'I have just come back from dinner and have just seen the news, so have issued a press release on behalf of CFI condemning any such behaviour.' Yeah, right! I will ignore him, but will contact Rob Halfon when appropriate. Let's see how it all runs.

Sunday 8 January – Muscat/London

Four hours' sleep. A massive breakfast is on offer, but I manage two slices of papaya and a cup of tea. Fly back on the Royal Flight with Sir Stuart Peach and Lord Astor. Lots of texts flow in as we are about to leave, which is when the UK is waking up, all reacting to the *Mail on Sunday* headline – Andrew Mitchell, David Jones, Hugo Swire, Crispin Blunt etc. The BBC are itching to interview me, but I just can't and just mustn't. I'd been told we would arrive at Stansted at 13.30, but it's now due at 4.15. Oops. Email Lance to change the time of my car. But at least I am incommunicado for a few hours and can escape media bids.

Stuart Peach is a proper person. We confide in each other. Unstuffy and practical, he is just my sort of CDS. He likes his Secretary of State Michael Fallon, as do I, albeit one day I'd love the job myself.

Speak from the car to Hugo Swire and Sayd Badr bin Hamad, the Deputy FM of Oman who is in London and at the airport on the way home. He is grateful for my read-out from the meeting, and my congratulations on his just becoming a grand-father.

Home soon after 6pm. James already there which is great. Home sweet home. James gorgeous James. Noodle cuddly Noodle.

Calls from and to Crispin Blunt, Hugo Swire and Nicholas Soames. All full of praise and support, which was kind. Hugo and Nicholas have asked to see the PM (wearing their CMEC hats) about the recent UN Security Council Resolution on the illegality of Israel's settlements and the UK reaction, and this latest development today about the Israeli embassy will empower them further. Ben Wallace, also, as the Minister for Security, is in full cry. He thinks the whole government is naive and hence a vulnerable, open, undefended target for foreign influence.

I am so non-enervated by the whole episode today. It is extraordinary how the opposite is true when you are directly under attack, or the object of the story for all the wrong reasons, but as I am but the 'victim' when others are the miscreants, I feel totally relaxed about it all, morally justified and almost on a high of personal contentment. It's extraordinary. I suppose at the root of it is that I feel that I have right and dignity and self-esteem on my side. I must be sure to keep my dignity. Er … and the other two.

Boris has gone to New York and Washington to see the Trump transition team.

Speak to Nick Timothy who, to his credit, returns my earlier call. I felt I ought to explain what had been going on for the last few days on Al Jazeera etc. He was easy-going and the call was an important moment. But there's still something about him which makes him seem untrustworthy.

The Queen has gone to church today at Sandringham – beautiful in blue – and is clearly in good health. It's a real super-charged 'God bless the Queen' moment.

I wanted to turn in at 9pm, but James said we should just have a bit of cosy time together. It's a moment like this when you realise what love means. I show it quite well, but should always show it more. We watched *Hawaii Five-O*, both giggling at the end of it when our usual Sunday heroes were given the George Cross by the

Queen for saving the world from a software programme which would have seen every nuclear reactor overheat and explode – a marked change from zapping some pock-faced criminal in a hail of bullets in downtown Honolulu. It was just so ridiculous it was great. Zzzzz.

Monday 9 January – London/New York

Turkey, Greece and Oman last week, New York and Geneva this week. It's all a bit much, and I am feeling lassitude – a good word, i.e. bloomin' knackered. So I get up at 6.30am and run ten laps around Victoria Gardens, and do some training exercises. It felt so good, I should do it every day. It corrected the effects of the Sultan's culinary taxidermy.

Call Erik in Muscat. He was very happy with the Privy Council meeting. So was the Sultan. He is a phenomenon: both of them are.

To the Commons. To her great credit I unlocked my office at 8.15am to find that Harriet was already there. She is excellent. I photocopied some of the *Mail on Sunday* stuff, to go with a memo from me, and put it on the Commons letter board for Hugo Swire in case there is an Urgent Question as Parliament is back today.

I popped my head into the office of the Speaker's secretary to reconfirm my non-attendance at Oral Questions tomorrow, and left a message with Shadow Foreign Secretary Emily Thornberry's office to say the same.

The papers have enough within the early pages to make the Israel story matter. Alex Salmond from the SNP wants a full inquiry; Halfon's Italian employee has been sacked, from the civil service if not from the (incompatible) part-time parliamentary job with him which she also holds; and there is the prospect of questions, statements and inquiries in the Commons.

While briefly in the FCO I brief Boris's SpAd Ben Gascoigne on the whole Al Jazeera operation, and explain my meeting with Jeremy Heywood.

Quick chat with Emily Thornberry to see if Labour intend to table an Urgent Question on the Al Jazeera allegations. They won't, because it would risk stirring up more anti-Semitism accusations against them.

Text exchange with Chief Whip Gavin Williamson. I say that I'd like to see him when I'm back from NY to explain all the events of the weekend. I add that I have sent an emollient text to Rob Halfon saying 'no hard feelings' but that he might still need a bit of solace from the Chief. Not that he really deserved it. The Chief and I will meet for a drink on my return.

BA flight to New York. Am recognised by the cabin crew. I'm in biz class, and Lance is two rows behind in premium economy. I tickle the crew to send him a glass of proper claret. He comes for a chat and reveals that Jonny Hall had come around unannounced on Friday, ostensibly to see if I was OK on all the Israeli stuff, which could mean he wanted to ask whether I am miserably upset, or angry, or scheming ... or any or all of such. I am confident that Lance will have fairly reflected our genuine view, which is that we learnt it was likely to happen, waited until we had a clear picture and then did all we could to handle it loyally and skilfully.

Al Jazeera are going to bring forward their broadcast of the Israeli embassy files – promising 'the truth about the lobby' – by four days. It will start on Tuesday. The moment has passed for any dramatic further impact it will have, but this episode has rebalanced the argument about settlements and the conduct of the Israeli government away from the propaganda of deceit and – a step – towards lawfulness and truth.

The BA cabin crew are just fantastically charming. They seem to want to get me totally pissed. I think it must be an Israeli plot ...

To the UKMIS [UK Mission to the UN] residence in Beekman Place. Early supper with UKMIS head Matthew Rycroft and Lance. To bed at 8.30 NY time.

Tuesday 10 January – New York

As always when on a US trip I wake at 4am. Boris has seen Kushner, [Steve] Bannon and [Stephen] Miller in Washington, and the top congressional figures in Washington: [Paul] Ryan, [Mitch] McConnell and [Bob] Corker. I'll get a read-out later.

Watch FCO Oral Questions live on the Parliament feed, which is 6.30–7.30am in New York. Neither Ellwood nor BoJo explains my absence, which is rather cack-handed. Ellwood once again talks about the 'Bellfar Declaration'. He is such a muppet. Hugo Swire asks a serious question about the conduct of the Israeli embassy, but receives the expected fob-off answer.

To the UN Security Council for the first session chaired by the new Secretary General António Guterres. The US Permanent Rep, Samantha Power, ignored the five-minute limit and spoke for fifteen. The US can get away with that sort of thing. She was impassioned and really rather good, injecting some principle and fizz into what is usually a stilted process. I tried to do the same a few minutes later, but much more briefly. A good chat with António.

To former ministerial colleague Stephen O'Brien, now of OCHA [UN Office for the Coordination of Humanitarian Affairs]. He is for the chop, but doesn't yet know it. Always a UK nominee, our proposed names to succeed him are crazy, and even include Lib Dem former minister Lynne Featherstone, which is not sufficiently heavyweight. Guterres wants someone better, but we have to be discreet as we have to push an alternative candidate before O'Brien knows he is on the way out.

A thoroughly boring working lunch. Forced discussions around a table of twenty just don't work.

A meeting in the corner later with the new Italian Foreign Minister who used to be Theresa May's Home Office/Interior counterpart, followed by the Kazakh Foreign Minister.

Then my old-time favourite, Filippo Grandi, who used to run the UN Work and Relief Agency (UNWRA), which supports stateless Palestinians. He says the UN is very anxious about US funding, and their attitude to Palestine. UNWRA is nearly out of funds, and the whole Palestinian population is on the edge of erupting.

See former MP Archie Norman at the airport. He is now Chairman of Lazards. He said Labour's wily supremo Peter Mandelson was speaking warmly of me the other day. Oops … worrying?

Wednesday 11 January – London/Geneva
A gruelling day, taking in New York, London and Geneva. Land at 7am. Pop home, then the FCO.

Andrew Mitchell is in Yemen, and will see former President Ali Abdullah Saleh in Sana'a. He doesn't fully understand Yemen, but is trying to reinvent himself as Mr Humanitarian, which has its merits. Nobody from the UK has seen Saleh for years, and his alliance with the anti-Saudi Houthis has given him near-pariah status. But he remains the chirrupy bandit who, for all his many faults, is still a crucial player. Actually, all credit to Andrew for taking an interest and for beating a path to Saleh's door. If it weren't for him, the UK's engagement with Yemen would be near-zero, when history suggests we should still be an influence.

Ministerial team meeting: totally pointless. Liam Parker looks at me with a smirk and raises his eyes to the heavens whenever Ellwood opens his mouth. Speak to BoJo afterwards about UN appointments and the rumoured next US Ambassador to the EU, the oddball Ted Roosevelt Malloch, who I will see next week.

Boris raised Rob Halfon. Why on earth he thinks that Halfon is more deserving of sympathy than me shows his lack of awareness and balance. It is Halfon's mates in CFI who have been attacking me, and it was his assistant who was caught on film slagging me off. But I told Boris I'd made the first magnanimous move and that I'd also told the Chief Whip that Halfon needs reassurance. I feel like a figure out of Kipling who is destined to play the game and always lose.

Read-out on BoJo's meetings in New York and Washington. Liam says the team around Trump are all full of simple certainties, and they believe they have turned the world on its head. What is perhaps most disconcerting is their unflinching belief in their own revolutionary power. They might have it their own way for a few weeks, but sooner or later they are not going to have an easy ride.

FCO Head of Comms Simon McGee has found a photo of Shai Masot in the *Diplomat* magazine. 'Local hire' my arse! He is standing there with other diplomats, and is listed as an equivalent.

The new (good) candidate in the frame to succeed Stephen O'Brien as head of UN OCHA is Sir Mark Lowcock, our DfID Permanent Secretary. I like the idea. But it still needs delicate handling, perhaps all the more so as Stephen will feel deeply miffed to be displaced by his former PUS.

Walk home. Kevin Hollinrake MP says hi on Abingdon Green and expresses total solidarity with me against the Israeli subterfuge. Fellow MP Stephen Metcalfe, he says, had initially gone on a trip with CFI and had been taken in, and then went again with the Council for Arab–British Understanding (CAABU) and completely changed his mind.

To Heathrow. The news is running that there are some leaked intelligence reports about Trump, Russia and prostitutes.

To Geneva.

Thursday 12 January – Geneva

Trump says he would never have let prostitutes urinate on the Russian hotel bed once slept in by President Obama, because he is a 'germophobe'. An ex-SIS officer called Christopher Steele, with his company Orbis, has been named as the author of the dossier on Trump which has been published on BuzzFeed. He has gone into hiding! Was it Tim Barrow he worked with, people are asking, as Tim was our Ambassador to Russia at the time? Intriguingly, was Boris President of the Oxford Union when Steele was President of the Cambridge Union? What would the world look like now if they'd done a job swap?

To the Cyprus settlement conference in the UN building. In the opening session, Cypriot President Anastasiades says, 'This is one of the world's horniest problems.' After the giggles had subsided he said, 'I'm sorry – I meant thorniest.'

Lunch, then up and down the corridors for bilateral meetings with all the differing parties who we and the UN are trying to reconcile. Not so much shuttle diplomacy as shuffle diplomacy. We've only just started and contrary to my earlier view of him Greek Foreign Minister Nikos Kotzias is behaving awkwardly. Boris, at his very best, breaks the ice and speaks well to all the negotiators.

Late steak supper in the hotel bar. Good giggly gas with Liam, while Richard Moore and Julian Braithwaite natter with BoJo. They are probably the final two to succeed Tim Barrow as FCO Political Director.

Boris accepts my £50 bet that Trump will not last his full four years.

Given that alcohol cannot be put on the FCO bill, I end up paying £300! I'm happy to do it – they all deserve it.

Friday 13 January – Geneva/Rutland

While Boris and I are slaving away with the Gordian knot of Cyprus, the Polish Foreign Minister has caused great amusement in the UN by claiming that one of his policies has gained the support of San Escador. Unfortunately there is no such country. After Boris cycles around the CERN Large Hadron Collider, we take the Royal Squadron Flight back to Northolt, during which we have a lovely chat.

I suggest to BoJo we need more thinking time and should live less hand to mouth. He says he'd like that from now until March. We should ask some fundamental questions on issues where we have lost credibility. I suggest they could be: 'Assad must go'; 'we want a two-state solution'; 'we need more smart sanctions', etc.

Lindsay Appleby [FCO Europe Director] confesses that he is also a fan of *Hawaii Five-O*! Great man. There has been snow in the UK, but it has mostly melted. The Earl of Snowdon has died.

Monday 16 January – London

Gove has secured an interview with Donald Trump for *The Times*. On one level it's quite a journalistic coup, but it just feels creepy and arse-licking, keeping him on the map as an ex-minister, and no doubt all set up by Rupert Murdoch.

Reception for the outgoing US Secretary of State, John Kerry, at the Foreign Secretary's residence at 1 Carlton Gardens hosted by Boris. Most of our ministerial team are there. Kerry kindly signs a copy of his recent Middle East speech for me, and I give him a copy of mine. Boris gives him a ministerial red box, inside which he had put a Trump baseball cap. All very entertaining and good-natured.

BoJo has a word with me in the margins and asks, 'How about Hugh Powell as Political Director?'

I raise my eyebrow to express a measure of astonishment at the prospect.

Tuesday 17 January – London
The PM's big Brexit speech at Lancaster House. Although much heralded as a massively important statement of government policy, it doesn't appear to have been shared at all widely among ministers. She sets out, rather *ex cathedra*, her negotiating objectives. Everyone is talking about 'red lines', by which they mean our non-negotiable demands. She lists the main ones as withdrawal from the single market and from 'full membership' of the customs union.

Although the speech was an attempt to be clear, I just feel in my bones that everything that is yet to follow is going to be very untidy and contentious. Although it doesn't bother me in the least, because I'm glad to keep my fingers out of the mangle, it is surely absurd that the Minister for Europe is not even invited to the PM's seminal statement on Europe, let alone given any role in drafting it. It just shows how far the FCO has been side-lined from serious involvement in this historic process.

Long-standing PR friend Andrew Gifford comes in with Ted Roosevelt Malloch, who claims to be Trump's imminent nominee as US Ambassador to the EU. He is pretty whacky. His anti-EU 'Tea Party' Republican views are so simplistic it's embarrassing. Meanwhile one of Trump's team has amusingly called the EU a 'supernatural' organisation, rather than supranational one. It probably more accurately reflects what they think.

However, somewhat more seriously, the new US Ambassador to the UK will be businessman 'Woody' Johnson, a wealthy backer of Trump. His fortune was made in cotton buds and baby oil through Johnson & Johnson.

Drink with Chief Whip Gavin Williamson. Discuss the Brexit speech. Say the PM's gatekeepers are isolating her. She needs to meet ministerial teams directly, or the two SpAds will do for her.

Thursday 19 January – London

BoJo has been getting some stick, as it were, for comparing French President François Hollande to a Second World War prison-camp guard administering punishment beatings. His attempt, while in Delhi, to compare any attempt to punish Britain for leaving the EU to a wartime escape movie is typically Boris. But I wish he would just resist the temptation, as it undermines his authority as Foreign Secretary.

Chat with Gove in the Tea Room about his Trump interview. I told him it was quite a coup, for which he must have pulled all his Murdoch strings. 'Oh [Scottish squeak] ... Oh [over-polite smile]. Oh ... [i.e. yes].'

Friday 20 January – Rutland

Trump inauguration. An odd affair. His address was utterly banal with no oratory or sense of occasion. It will take time to get used to this unconventional President – if ever we do.

Sunday 22 January – Rutland

A heavy frost, and minus 2 degrees.

Over 2 million women across the world demonstrated yesterday against Trump's supposed misogyny and racist views. He has been to see the CIA, who he had recently accused of leaking material against him. He says that, as everyone knows, he is 'at war with the media, and their fake news', but nonetheless values the CIA. His spokesman has vehemently attacked the press for printing photos which suggest that the attendance at his inauguration was low compared to the numbers who attended Obama's. It may well be that the crowd scenes were not filmed at the same time, i.e. both at midday on the Friday when each President swears the oath, but who knows?

The Churchill bust has been returned to the Oval Office, after Obama replaced it with one of Martin Luther King. Obama's red curtains have been replaced with gold ones, and Theresa May will see him in the White House next Friday. Such an early visit augurs well for Anglo-American relations, but not if he mishandles Vladimir Putin and supports the Israelis' subjugation of Palestinians.

And nobody seems able to reconcile his protectionist language with his stated wish to give us an early free-trade agreement. He had within hours of becoming President issued an executive order which rolls back the Obamacare health legislation by rescinding the power of government to fine those who do not take out health insurance.

The *Telegraph* states that our recent test of a Trident missile misfired, and it headed in the wrong direction … towards the US. May, on the *Marr* show, was asked if she knew this before the July debate was held on replacing it. So what if she'd said yes? It would have been the perfect argument for saying it needed to be replaced.

The Israelis have announced that they are going to build 566 settlement units in East Jerusalem: totally illegal, but protected by the new President. Apparently Jared Kushner is a donor to settlement causes in the West Bank. This is catastrophic. It means the major power in the world intends to support the illegal annexation of someone else's land.

The President's new spokesman Sean Spicer has convened a White House press conference, ranted at the assembled journalists and called them liars for stating that the inauguration crowds were smaller than Obama's. The photos are now known definitely to show otherwise. So he has called the press liars, when he is the one who is lying: then he refused to take any questions and walked out. I'm not sure he's ever going to recover from that one!

To London. *Hawaii Five-O* is going downhill.

Monday 23 January – London

Bump into a DfID acquaintance, who was on their way to a fatuous training course. They hate Priti Patel in DfID, mainly because she seems to hate all of them. She is clearly a complete and utter nightmare. When Professor Anthony King, the renowned political analyst, died a couple of weeks ago, it was reported that there is a current senior MP whose thesis at Essex University he considered abysmal beyond measure. The press named John Bercow, but carry an apology today because it was in fact Priti Patel. The Wicked Witch of Witham scores again.

Meeting with officials to discuss the FCO's plans and responsibilities in the event of the Queen's funeral, especially in respect of who precisely needs to greet and handle visiting dignitaries. This is one aspect of the otherwise meticulous preparations that seems to be a bit thin. It needs work, as there will be no other event ever that is likely to attract so many heads of state and dignitaries all at once. It is the greatest logistical, diplomatic and protocol challenge the world has ever seen.

I love our Ambassador in Tashkent and told him I'd be back to Uzbekistan soon, but expressed slight huffiness that he had secured such a ridiculously over-high valuation for the rug I was given (which of course I have to hand over to HM Government rather than keep). It means I won't buy it, which at a more realistic price I would have liked to.

Tuesday 24 January – London
It's the Supreme Court judgment today on whether the PM has the power to trigger Article 50, and at 9.30, by a decision 8–3, they uphold the original verdict of the High Court that only Parliament can undo what it did in the first place. So we will have to enact a short bill authorising the PM to press the Article 50 button. The loser in all this is Attorney General Jeremy Wright, who is putting a brave face on having lost the case. His advocacy was thought not really to have been up to it, which is a shame because everybody likes him.

DD Commons statement on the Article 50 judgment. Briefly sat next to Boris on the front bench. When I asked him to mention to the PM that I should accompany her to Turkey, although he had previously supported the idea enthusiastically, he was evasive. I brushed past the PM and asked the same of her: she said she'd think about it. Not very encouraging, and rather tiresome to have to manoeuvre for it. Erdoğan would never travel abroad without his Foreign Minister.

Sam Coates of *The Times* says that Nick Timothy, to appease the White House, is unilaterally trying to dilute the UK policy of discouraging the purchase of products from illegal Israeli settlements.

Timothy thinks he's the fucking Prime Minister. Also Trump wants us to ban the Muslim Brotherhood. It might please the US, Egypt and the UAE, but we probably won't do it because they do not pass our threshold of illicit conduct.

Wednesday 25 January – London
Ministerial team meeting. Pretty useless gathering. Boris skips over serious issues like a gadfly, and so we never really discuss anything constructively.

They will not let me go to Turkey. It's just all so silly. The UK belittles itself when the PM travels abroad. She, as with others before her, just takes self-important flunkeys and never a minister. Other countries bring the foreign minister with the PM or President, and play the team. But not the UK. Officials think they are more important than ministers: maybe these days they are.

7pm division … in my kilt, greeted with much teasing. Then to the Burns Night reception at Lancaster House.

Thursday 26 January – London
Speak in the street to Black Rod, the Lords equivalent of the Serjeant at Arms. Discussed the proposed Holocaust museum. Most in the Lords are dead against it, as it will annex part of Victoria Tower Gardens at the Lords end which are a Royal Park, notionally preserved in perpetuity, and are part of a UNESCO Heritage Site. In the Commons the likes of Edward Leigh are vociferously against it.

Bump into Beth Rigby of Sky News. She used to be with the *FT* and is sensible and trustworthy. I explained I had some forebodings about Number 10 getting so close to Trump, but it's all the staffers' doing. Slurp slurp. I told her, 'If we suck up, we'll fuck up.' She laughed and said, 'If only I could broadcast that!' I said how about 'If we suck up, we'll muck up.' 'Great … I'll use that.' And off she went with a broad grin.

Lovely text from Trade Minister Lord Price. 'Just leaving Turkey after three day trade visit. They LOVE you here. There is Ataturk then Sir Alan Duncan! You have done a brilliant job in building our joint relationship.' I texted back, 'You are very kind. I'm sure after your visit you are now second equal.'

Trump says he is pro-torture, pro-waterboarding. I text Dominic Grieve, who will just be heading to his Thursday meeting of the ISC: 'I guess that'll liven up your proceedings.' 'Yes – we can arrest all of his officials when they visit.'

Ian and Tina Taylor New Year drinks. Very upsettingly, Ian has to go into hospital on Saturday for another massive throat-cancer operation.

Friday 27 January – Rutland

May is in Washington. The body language with Trump is forced and awkward. She has no easy manner. As they walk down a ramp, Trump holds her hand. Bizarre. We offer him a State Visit.

I call Turkish Foreign Minister Ömer Çelik to ask for a lunch and a press conference for May with Erdoğan when she's there, as there seems to be some uncertainty about the arrangements.

To my annual Ladies' lunch in Melton Mowbray. My tweet, by accident, is rather infelicitous: '50 years of Melton Ladies' lunches. I've done 25 of them.'

Saturday 28 January – Rutland

May in Ankara. A triumph. Good access and optics. Erdoğan treats her well. But Nick Timothy attends meetings open-necked. So damned rude.

Sunday 29 January – Rutland

While the PM was heading for Turkey, Trump signed an executive order banning anyone entering the US from Iraq, Syria, Yemen, Somalia, Sudan, Libya or Iran. It took immediate effect, leaving passengers stranded at airports during their journey. Nadhim Zahawi, our very own MP for Stratford, and also on the Foreign Affairs Committee, believes he is therefore banned from entering the US because he was born in Iraq. He even has two children studying at Princeton. He has hit all the Sunday interviews.

May is now caught up in the storm, as she was asked about it while in Turkey signing the joint-fighter deal. It was sprung on her unfairly: the perils of breaking news when you're travelling. But Number 10 announced overnight her total disagreement with the order, and an online petition via the government website has already attracted 100,000 signatures: all within twelve hours. It has become the story, although I think the overall impression left by her two visits has been broadly positive. The UK is on the world stage; we are significant, and we matter.

The touching pictures of Trump reaching for Theresa's hand as they walked down a gentle slope in the White House was not what it seemed. He has a fear of slopes and steps called bathmophobia. How does that fit with being a germophobe?

Without referring to ministers, the UK system has drawn up revised advice for travel to the US, but it stupidly says almost nothing about the new travel ban, because we simply don't know how it will work. It should anticipate the obvious questions about who it affects, and state that we are seeking urgent clarification.

As if this were not enough, Trump has removed the Chairman of the Joint Chiefs, and the Director of National Intelligence, from the permanent NSC [National Security Council] and has replaced them with Steve Bannon. Dr Strangelove now has a formal security role in the US.

Calls are growing to rescind the State Visit invitation to Trump, and some are now predicting mass marches against him if he doesn't lift the 'Muslim travel ban' – marches in the US, and mass protests when he visits the UK. A gov.uk petition had 100,000 signatures this morning calling for the State Visit invitation to be withdrawn. I said to James that I bet it'll bust through 1 million. By 7.00 this evening it was already halfway there.

The PM has directed Boris and Amber Rudd [Home Secretary] to call their opposite numbers in the US about the travel ban. The FCO was about to change its travel advice without any reference to ministers. Are they really that politically unaware?

What a difference twenty-four hours can make. It's only the end of Trump's first week as President. And he spoke for an hour last night to Putin. God knows where that's heading.

Speak to Richard Moore in Ankara to say well done. Despite the usual last-minute chaotic organisation, the PM's visit went as well as could ever be hoped for. She ended up with nearly four hours with Erdoğan; top officials had good engagement with their counterparts; PM Yıldırım sang my praises both to her and in public; the fighter deal was signed; and they made progress on aviation security. All good except Fi Hill sat next to the PM, and the tieless Nick Timothy had only Richard between himself and the PM. Who the hell do these SpAds think they are?

A wet Rutland. Heavy rain all the way to London.

At 9.30pm a Sky newsflash. 'Britons with dual nationality will be exempt from Trump's travel ban.' The phones must be red hot. The novices in the White House just have no idea what it takes to prepare and implement a policy.

Hawaii Five-O. Much better: a straightforward courtroom siege.

Monday 30 January – London

The anti-Trump petition is now over 1 million. I find it amusing that the very same social media force which arguably got him elected is now the weapon being directed against him. Not that he cares a damn.

FCO all-staff meeting in the Durbar Court, addressed by Boris. He is entertaining as always, but not profound about any issue. As soon as he begins to touch on anything difficult, or is asked a searching question, he bats it away with short sentences and disarming quips. They like him, but don't really respect him. He commands affection, but not authority. They just don't take him seriously. An example is that whenever quizzed about the complexity of securing a deal with the EU, he just lapses into 'Come on. Come on … [clenched fist, punchy arm wave] Be positive! We have to do this. Come on. Let's all just go for it! Come on, guys. Don't be negative. We can do this!' But they all know it's bollocks: after all, they are the ones who understand the complexity of the details.

Meeting with Montenegrin chief EU negotiator Aleksandar Pejović. Bald as a coot, but well informed on the details of their EU accession negotiations.

Boris will do the statement on the Trump ban on US visas, and I go to Boris' office on hearing that the Speaker will also almost certainly grant an SO24 [Standing Order 24] emergency debate on the same thing. I tell Boris that he should skedaddle after his statement, and I'll handle any subsequent debate. He agrees and is grateful, otherwise he'd be stuck in the Chamber all day and would increasingly come under fire. Gumpy Ellwood is fussing around outside the door of Foreign Secretary's office. He is best ignored, but he's up to something. Not sure what.

Statement on US Trump travel ban by BoJo. He had to walk the tightrope of defending President Trump, and the PM's visit, but not his policy. We are pulling our punches tactically. The most we are prepared to say is that it is divisive and wrong. At least he could say that we had received assurances that it won't apply at all to UK passport holders. There were some really sick comparisons from the SNP and some Labour women saying that this was like the first step the Nazis took, and how awful that it should have been announced on National Holocaust Day. There is no logical validity to such a view. It demeans the compelling decency of Holocaust commemoration. But it provoked Boris into becoming more aggressive than he might have wished to be.

Under Standing Order 24 Speaker Hobbit allows Ed Miliband the permitted three minutes to say why he wants an emergency debate on the Trump executive order. I knew the Speaker would grant the three-hour debate, as the Deputy Speaker, Lindsay Hoylè, told me in the Tea Room that Bercow had already decided that morning after Labour's former leader Ed Miliband and former Chief Whip Rosie Winterton had been to see him. So I will have to reply just before 9pm. The debate is powerful and of a high standard. In contrast to Boris, I adopt an emollient tone. 'The House at its best, we have a right to speak up,' etc. Nadhim Zahawi was on the edge of tears as he spoke of how the ban stood to affect him personally.

While all this was going on, there was a sizeable demo in Whitehall.

Nice Chris Doyle of CAABU tweets praising my tone and sensitivity in the wind-up speech, all as the petition hits 1.5 million.

I have a sore knee.

Tuesday 31 January – London

Faff about around the Commons to kill a bit of time before the opening of the debate on the second reading of the Bill which authorises the PM to trigger Article 50. DD handled it well, despite having a croaking voice. Most speakers, though, made appalling speeches which deviated well away from the subject of the Bill into broader points about the referendum and future negotiations, all of which the Speaker should really have ruled out of order.

Witness session before the Foreign Affairs Committee for two hours on Turkey, alongside the FCO Europe Director, Lindsay Appleby. Lots of concern about human rights and democracy in the wake of the coup attempt. On the proposed constitutional referendum there, Ian Murray asked if I would be recommending that Erdoğan hires a big red bus with a slogan on the side. I said I would have to consult the Foreign Secretary on that one …

Dinner in the Dining Room with Ed Argar, Amanda Milling and Chris White who chairs the Committee on Arms Export Control. Chris says he would happily pinch Liz Truss's bottom. I said that's why we need 'arms control'.

It turns out that Ellwood had been angling to do the SO24 debate on the Trump travel ban. If he'd done it he would have been completely monstered.

Andrew Murrison, who is still pro-BoJo, thinks that the PM's health won't be able to take it. So he is clearly on manoeuvres to undermine Theresa.

Gerald Kaufman has been sectioned, so who now is officially Father of the House? The poor guy has lost it and, although disqualified from standing in an election, it is not clear if he is now disqualified from the proceedings of the House. Can Ken Clarke be declared Father of the House? At least if Kaufman dies, I think Ken is ahead of the idiot Labour MP David Winnick.

My thought for the day (although not sure where it came from): 'Diplomacy is about surviving into the next decade; politics is about surviving into the next week; Twitter is about surviving through 140 characters.'

Wednesday 1 February – London

Word has reached me that Ellwood has a nutty proposal that the UK should buy Svalbard, the archipelago between Norway and the North Pole – he wants it to become a UK spaceport. He's bonkers.

Former ExxonMobil CEO Rex Tillerson is confirmed as US Secretary of State.

Meanwhile I am having enormous fun trying to get the system to accept an unbeatable offer we have received to provide our Ambassador in Washington with a Bentley. We do have a standing deal with Jaguar for our top embassy locations, but the Bentley offer is pretty well the same cost. Boris is leery about the likely press reaction. I think it is a good story about UK confidence, and if the numbers add up then why shouldn't we? Kim Darroch would really like it, and when John Kerr was there he famously had a dark green one (or possibly a Rolls-Royce) from which at arm's length he would hang his smoking cigarette out of the window. I will win this one.

Netanyahu is due to visit the UK next week. It will include a meeting and lunch with the PM.

Little demo outside Parliament. Almost touchingly sweet. A small, almost shy, group of teenagers are chanting 'No Trump, no Brexit: no racist EU exit'.

Thursday 2 February – London

Knee quite a bit better, but I can't easily walk down the stairs. And unlike Trump there's no PM to hold my hand.

Apparently Trump put the phone down on Malcolm Turnbull, the PM of Australia, during a call about his immigration announcement.

Ankara have sent a local press digest: I am a total hero in Turkey following my appearance before the FAC on Tuesday. Two front pages with a photo etc. I have a larger fan club in Turkey than in the UK.

Ellwood is still on his Svalbard kick. His idea has never so much as been mentioned before either as a possible Party or government policy. Apparently he tried it before with Hammond, who just bawled him out and never spoke to him again. I have written a personal note to Boris – it is almost comical – to say that the quicker he knocks on the head the idea that we should buy this archipelago the better. The thought of our doing so has reached the Norwegians, who think we've gone totally nuts.

I explained that a cursory investigation has convinced me that none of the supposed advantages stack up. Regardless of who owns the land, it would remain under Norwegian sovereignty; it would not be part of the UK. We could expect Norway strongly to object to any resource exploitation. We do not need an earth observation station as we get the relevant information from the US. The Treaty of Svalbard, to which we are a signatory, prohibits any militarisation of the island – and were we to breach the Treaty, not only would we dismay our Allies, but we would presumably encourage Russia to follow suit. And the less said about his idea to use it as a space shuttle launch site the better.

My strong advice was that we should not take these proposals any further.

To his great credit Boris quickly replies: 'Dear Alan, The matter is in hand! I think it unlikely, to put it mildly, that HMG will be either purchasing or assisting in the purchase of this enigmatic expanse of snowy wilderness. B'.

Friday 3 February – Rutland

PM is at an EU meeting in Valletta. Some of the PMs and presidents there are less important than the Mayor of Birmingham, but they are flexing their muscles by rejecting the concept of her being a bridge between the EU and the US. The trouble is, all these serious strategic moments are being steered by the diplomatically untested Nick Timothy, who thinks he can pull all the levers. Proximity to power does not automatically equip someone with knowledge and wisdom about international affairs. That's what the Foreign Office is for.

Saturday 4 February – Rutland

A federal court in the US has ruled that Trump's travel ban is unconstitutional, and so some airlines are again allowing travellers from the seven countries to board their planes. This will test the verdict.

Both Ukraine and Romania are in turmoil. There is revived conflict in Ukraine with Russian-backed forces, and demonstrations against the government of Romania for their decision to decriminalise political corruption and bribery.

Dinner with Jane Micklethwait, and son John, former editor of the *Economist* and now CEO of Bloomberg in New York. John's co-author Adrian Wooldridge will become 'Bagehot' on the *Economist*. Sadly, Jane's sister Tessa Wheeler, married to the eccentric Stuart Wheeler, died just before Christmas.

Sunday 5 February – Rutland
Trump's legal appeal to overturn the court's rejection of the ban has been initially further rejected by a judge, while demanding that the US government provide more information in defence of their order. Tee-hee. Reality dawns.

Monday 6 February – London
A fun encounter with Liam Parker, Boris' energetic press SpAd who has set up a Facebook account for me. Already the emails are flooding in trying to make me a Facebook friend. The problem is, I don't know how it works. I haven't a clue how to use it.

Netanyahu is being feted in Number 10, meeting the PM, followed by lunch, and then we let him use the FCO media suite to peddle his pro-settlement propaganda. We are supine, lickspittle, insignificant cowards. I am ashamed of my own government. Instead of sucking up to him we should have taken offence and called him out.

To the Commons for the PM's statement on Friday's summit in Valletta. Corbyn was utterly hopeless, as usual, but the petulant Emily Thornberry kept on chuntering away and heckling Theresa, who then fired at ET, using her married name 'Lady Nugee'. Speaker Hobbit was distracted and didn't hear, which made Lady Nugee-Thornberry frump and fulminate, and then go up to the Chair to complain.

Later, on a point of order at the end of the statement, the PM elegantly apologised, but won the day by saying, 'I'm sorry she doesn't like being called Lady Nugee, but on my part for the last thirty-six years I've been happy to use my husband's name.' Slam-dunk, push off, Lady N.

Not a good day for Speaker Hobbit. First he tells the House that from after the recess the Clerks will no longer wear their traditional wigs. He uses the announcement as a vehicle for promoting his own personal modernisation agenda. After bumping into Sir Paul Beresford, who sits on the HofC Commission responsible for administering the House, it transpires that the reason is that a greater number of clerks are sitting at the table, and that wigs are not considered hygienic, which means that each would need their own. They are expensive, so their use is actually being discontinued on the grounds of cost.

Then, when asked in a planted point of order about whether President Trump will or should present an address to 'both Houses of Parliament', Bercow launches into a vicious attack on the President, saying we would never invite someone who is sexist or racist. Bang goes the neutrality of the speakership. He is there to uphold the will of the House, not to express his own opinions.

Dinner with Sir Kim Darroch in the Churchill Room. What fun. Such a good man. Slightly croaky from the regular throat bugs from the germ centre which is Washington. Swamp climate or what?

The unfortunate truth is the PM did not do very well in Washington. She should have done media, but didn't. The decisions of the silly gatekeepers, Hill and Timothy, were beyond useless on their first foray to Washington. They were incapable of conversing, and even when asked what the main objective of the May prime ministership was, they had nothing to say.

I said, 'How do you find Tobias Ellwood?' Kim replies, 'It's funny – whenever he wants to stay we are always full, and I'm somehow not in Washington.'

My friend John Kasich, Governor of Ohio, who was a serious challenger for the Presidential nomination, is coming over. Kim remained grateful for my introduction to him a few months ago.

Tuesday 7 February – London

The recent scan on my knee shows I have a torn cartilage. And today it is even more painful.

The Lord Speaker, Lord Fowler, makes a statement from the Woolsack making it clear that he was not consulted before Bercow's outburst about Trump, and declaring that he would never do such a thing himself, preferring to follow convention and consensus. It just shows that the Bercow move was an indulgent stunt. The contrast in dignity is stark.

The Article 50 Bill continues its committee stage in the Commons. We have defeated amendments which would unrealistically have required the government to go back into (unavailable) renegotiations with the 'EU' should the Commons be unsatisfied with any proposed exit deal. The truth is: 1) there probably is no deal, because someone in the EU will reject anything that dilutes free movement, and 2) at best, as has always been the most likely position, we will face a 'take it or leave it' decision. The trouble is, there might be no deal to take or leave, so the only thing we will leave is the EU itself. We are about to head into two years of supposed negotiations, but with no easy ground for making any progress.

Wednesday 8 February – London

Receive a note from the PM saying she is sorry to hear about my knee injury and hoping that the surgery goes well. It isn't happening for a while yet, but it was a nice thought.

Thursday 9 February – London

Ted Roosevelt Malloch is being slated by the *FT* over claims about various accolades he says he received. *Quelle surprise.*

FCO Supervisory Board meeting. Independent members Julia Bond, Miranda Curtis and Richard Lambert are all very good, but the whole set-up is perfunctory. Boris chairs it, but isn't really interested in the administrative workings of the place, and Simon McDonald would probably prefer there was no ministerial involvement. I am constantly infuriated by the willingness to sell off prime embassy sites and be satisfied with mere functional property. Once they've gone, they've gone for ever. Also, the maintenance standards are slipping. I say that our estates management function should be put in special measures. But I won't get anywhere. They just blame the Treasury.

To the MoD [Ministry of Defence] to speak to an annual gathering of European officers, mainly French. Clever and professional, it's a refreshing change from the usual petty political speaker meeting.

Go to see Oliver Heald MP about prisoner voting rights. We are obliged by an EU ruling to give the vote to prisoners, one of Theresa May's most stubborn sticking points. She is treating the issue as if we are being told to give the vote to all prisoners, but we could satisfy the ruling by extending it only to those who are sentenced to less than a year. It's all a bit artificial anyway, as most of them won't be on the electoral register and many won't even have an address. It wastes so much time: better just to get on with it and move on.

Victory! Sweet victory! I manage to persuade BoJo to approve the Bentley for our Ambassador in Washington. PS Lance Domm has written a genius letter on the costs and the residual value, and all such things, which proves convincingly that it is good value for money. So it would only be political cowardice that stops it. But I've got there. A Bentley it will be. And Kim Darroch will owe me a ride, with the cocktail cabinet suitably stocked.

Drink with Boris SpAd David Frost, who as it turns out is conducting a 'policy review', which I guess is intended to define our diplomatic objectives. Irrelevant ministers, it seems, are not to be included in this process, even though it's our job.

Friday 10 February – Rutland
Drive to Rutland. Karen Pierce is to be FCO Political Director. She is quite a phenomenon. It's a great appointment. I send her a bottle.

Monday 13 February – Rutland/London
Chat with James Duddridge who wants to table a vote of no confidence in Speaker Hobbit. Bercow is a law unto himself, increasingly undignified, and is changing the nature of the speakership for the worse, but any attempt to clip his wings will fail because the Labour Party tribally back him.

Tuesday 14 February – London
General Michael Flynn has resigned as President Trump's National Security Advisor. He's only been there three weeks, but accusations were flying around about his previous phone contacts with the US Ambassador to Russia, in which he is said to have hinted at a relaxation of sanctions against them. He denied it vehemently but then intercepts proved otherwise, which meant he had misled the Vice-President, so he's gone.

How ironic that after so comprehensively slamming the security services, Trump has now taken their evidence in his first month and lost a member of his Cabinet. The farce concluded with Kellyanne Conway, Trump's senior counsellor, saying the President had full confidence in him, and within fifteen minutes his spokesman Sean Spicer saying the President was 'evaluating' him.

Valentine dinner with James and Noodle in Franco's. It's nine years since I proposed to him.

Wednesday 15 February – London
Nice note from Karen Pierce saying, 'Thanks for the champagne, but we need to plot on FCO funding.'

Thursday 16 February – London
Yesterday, in a press conference with Netanyahu, Trump said that Judaea is Israel's. Now, combined with his comments at a Netanyahu press conference saying 'Maybe one state, maybe two states, whatever they can agree on', it is being taken as him having abandoned the two-state solution. And Trump's nominee for Labour Secretary has stood down, as she used to employ an illegal immigrant.

Plan for next week's e-petition debate on whether Trump should be afforded a State Visit.

Meeting with Police Gold Commander about Assange. Julian Assange has been self-imprisoned in the Ecuador embassy for years, and we need to get him out but also ensure that he doesn't escape unnoticed. I am gradually taking control of the situation to be 100 per cent sure that the police surveillance is adequate and that we are not caught napping. Although it would be a Home Office problem primarily, the diplomatic aspects are important.

The wonderful financier and former Party Treasurer Michael Spencer comes to my office for a drink, kindly bringing a rather splendid bottle. His generosity has held the Party together for years, but he keeps getting knocked off the honours list, even though he's far more worthy than many who get through.

Saturday 18 February – Munich

To Munich for the annual Security Conference. Millions of meetings and encounters. It's upstairs, downstairs, upstairs, downstairs. And my knee is really hurting. The place is just too crowded to use the lifts, and as soon as one of them is free it's hijacked by someone's mob of security goons.

Nice chat with my friend John Kasich. His close backer is Wilber James, my close friend of thirty-five years since I was at Harvard. He says Wilber is his most uncompromising critic. 'He says I wear awful shoes, and can't hold a knife and fork properly. He tells me no US President can be allowed to get these things wrong.' It's really nice when someone can be so teasing about themselves.

Trump rally for a better America. Yet another diatribe against 'fake news'.

Sunday 19 February – Munich

Sunday Telegraph front page is about Whitehall sources saying there was a Russian plot last October to kill the PM of Montenegro. I'll need to have some answers ready when I go there next week.

Panel with Senators Sam Graham and Christopher Murphy. Murphy much the more thoughtful, in contrast to Graham's simplistic diatribe against Iran and evident ignorance about Yemen. Murphy is someone to watch.

Then a further panel of successive statements from Israeli Defence Minister Avigdor Lieberman, Turkish FM Mevlüt Çavuşoğlu, and Saudi Deputy FM Adel al Jubair. Lieberman nothing short of a hideous unreconstructed Russian settler; Mevlüt composed and forceful; and Adel tough on Iran, but far more cogent than Sam

Graham. Introduce myself to Tzipi Livni, altogether a more reasonable Israeli.

Bilats with Mevlüt, and then with UN envoy Espen Eide on Cyprus.

Really friendly lunch with John Kasich. He thinks there is something odd about VP Mike Pence: 'When I spoke to him he stared at me close and never took his eyes off mine. It was odd. Odd.'

There was a very moving moment when John leant forward across the table and said, 'The thing about you, Alan, which is why I so admire you, is that you quietly do it for your country out of duty. You could have earned millions and you were one of the main backers of Theresa May, but you ask for nothing and just get on with it. To me that's really something.' It was straight out of the blue, and I was genuinely touched. Even if he was just being kind, it was a nice thing to say.

No time, unfortunately, to go to Dachau with John.

Monday 20 February – London

Breakfast with Nicholas Soames at the Goring. Always a pleasure, as we hold the same opinions on almost everything. He thinks the Speaker is a frightful little man.

Westminster Hall e-petition debate this afternoon about the possible State Visit for Trump. Number10 are nervous about it, but even though they trust me to handle it without goofing, the SpAds want to go over the debate speech. So we do, and they calm down.

Pre-Oral Questions meeting with Boris. As usual there are very few questions listed on the Order Paper covering my patch, as all the Europe ones are Brexit-related, so will be taken by Boris.

Tuesday 21 February – London/Vienna

John Kasich is passing through London on his way back to the US and has asked to visit Westminster Abbey. Alex works her magic, and within minutes has arranged for him to have a special tour.

Oral Questions went fine. There have been some press reports about the discovery of the fossilised remains of an enormous woolly mammoth. During one answer I quip that the Foreign Secretary is living proof that the woolly mammoth can return from extinction. Later on the SpAds are a bit jumpy because Boris was not amused. Ridiculous. It was light-hearted and affectionate, so what's the problem? Chill!

John Kasich comes to the FCO and gets a whistle-stop tour including inside the Foreign Secretary's office. He says Wilber is behaving oddly. It's probably because John rather despises Trump, but Wilber is less disparaging.

To Vienna. When I land, Lance has sent a series of texts saying I had better contact Boris about the woolly mammoth. What on earth is all the fuss about? It was fun and harmless, and as the man who composed a limerick about Erdoğan which described him as rhyming with Ankara, he's in no position to take offence. But I text anyway saying I gather he wasn't as amused as everyone else. It's all because he is in a frightful stew about Ellwood who failed to answer a topical question on which he had been extensively briefed, leaving Boris to reply with no understanding of either the question or the answer. I have just been caught up in the slipstream.

Drink with HMA Vienna, Leigh Turner.

Wednesday 22 February – Podgorica

Montenegro has only existed since 2002. My visit is well timed, as they are feeling the heat from Russia.

Record a Facebook film to camera. Our Montenegrin embassy press guy was holding up a flipchart-sized paper script, which suddenly started flapping. 'I'm so sorry, Minister, I have a problem with wind.' I said, 'I'm sorry to hear that.' After a pause he twigged, and said, 'Oh no. Oh no!' and we all got the giggles. Seconds away, take two.

When asked about Russia, my standard line has become 'Russia's principal aim is always to cause problems: ours is always to solve them.'

Thursday 23 February – Belgrade/Skopje

Naftali Bennett, the pro-settlement party leader in Israel, has said that all Judaea and Samaria belongs to Israel. Where is the British reaction? There is none.

Fly to Belgrade. Senior staff briefing, then I address all staff and have a group photo. There are some fabulous black and white photos on the wall of Churchill with Marshal Tito, and one of Thatcher at Tito's funeral. And an amazing one of a young Mark Allen in Belgrade with Wilfred Thesiger. I take a pic, and send it with a teasing message to Mark.

Fly to Skopje. Greeted by HMA Charles Garrett. Address all the embassy staff.

Meeting with Nikola Gruevski, President of the ethnic Macedonian VMRO party. Then Radmila Šekerinska, Deputy President of the other ethnic Macedonian SDSM party. Their Prime Minister Zoran Zaev was detained elsewhere, namely by a court summons on (concocted) corruption charges.

There are 120 seats in the Parliament, and in the December election VMRO won fifty-one seats and SDSM forty-nine. To get the necessary sixty-one or more seats, one of them will have to form a coalition with the ethnic Albanian party, DUI, who have ten seats, plus any other willing ethnic Albanians. It's far from straightforward, as the weak VMRO puppet of a President and the more venal Gruevski will try to bend the rules to stay in power.

Friday 24 February – Skopje/Rutland

Labour have lost the Copeland by-election, with us gaining a seat which had been held by Labour for eighty years. It's the first time a government has won a seat from the Opposition for decades.

Crucial meeting with the current President of Macedonia, Gjorge Ivanov. Almost surprising myself, I was very forceful and indignant about his refusal to accept the verdict of the recent election. Adopting a very uncompromising tone, I was vigorously robust with him about how unacceptable it was to hang on to power when he had lost the election.

Am taken to visit the Salvation Monastery, which is a stunning sixteenth-century Orthodox church. Although small, it packs quite a punch. It includes an amazing carved icon screen, which makes Grinling Gibbons look like an amateur.

Airport. Wizz Air to Luton. Absurd giggles with my entertaining official for the Balkans, Peter Bainbridge. We recall the apocryphal tale of a minister writing 'Round objects' in the margins of a submission as a polite version of 'balls', and wonder what would be the modern equivalent for text-message emojis? If responding to something with 'Bollocks!', what is the correct symbol?

Saturday 25 February – Rutland
Corbyn just has no credibility. He has done a series of cringeworthy interviews denying he is responsible for Labour's disaster in Copeland, while calls for him to resign are all over the papers today. Even the unions are giving him a 'final warning'.

Sunday 26 February – Rutland
A quiet day at home.

Monday 27 February – London
At the Oscars, they read the wrong card and awarded the Best Movie to *La La Land* instead of *Moonlight*. Oops.

Sir Gerald Kaufman has died at the age of eighty-six after forty-seven years in Parliament. His problems of the last few months have been sad and cruel for such a consistently distinguished figure. Ken Clarke becomes Father of the House.

Exercise my right as a Privy Counsellor to sit on the steps of the throne in the Lords for a while to watch the Article 50 debate. Good Paddy Ashdown speech.

John Major has made a speech at Chatham House saying the government must be careful not to overpromise on what it can deliver on Brexit and must manage expectations. Quite right.

Tuesday 28 February – London
Mark Sedwill is appointed National Security Adviser. He replaces the dutiful Mark Lyall Grant, who has been so disgustingly driven out by the gruesome twosome, Hill and Timothy.

Meeting with officials to discuss the supposed foreign policy 'review', which it now appears is being overseen by Number 10. It's potentially interesting, but I suspect it has become an exercise in making Boris explain what he thinks our foreign policy actually is, and then getting him to stick to a clear position.

Have a drink with Sayeeda Warsi in the Lords. Her book *The Enemy Within* will be published next month. She is a very plucky defender of just causes and has taken extensive unfair stick from sniping critics. She understands UK Muslims and rightly resents those who dismiss them collectively as a threat to Britain. Why isn't there a good word for anti-Muslim – better than Islamophobic – which has the equivalent oomph of anti-Semitic?

Meeting with the ever amusing Patrick Forbes. He wants me to figure on behalf of the government in his documentary on Brexit. On BoJo, he says his reference points, such as calling Brexit 'liberation', just don't work, and all his gags are too England-focussed. His life is a carapace, born of his eccentric father, his UK education and his exploding marriage. Everything he does is designed 'to hide the inner Boris'. It's not entirely accurate, but nobody fails to have a view of some sort about Boris.

Wednesday 1 March – London

Just after lunch a couple of officials come into my office. I could tell something was wrong. There has been a potentially explosive incident in Gibraltar. The Chief of Police has arrested the UK base Commander and blocked an RAF plane from taking off. He has also arrested the Provost Marshal. It is all because the Chief of Police is mightily pissed off as he thinks he was lied to about the whereabouts of a naval rating suspected of having images of children on his laptop, after which military officers obstructed justice by trying to fly him off the Rock. Quite who has power over what, as between the armed forces there and the civilian law, is very unclear.

I know that Gibraltar's Chief Minister Fabian Picardo is in town, so ask to see him pronto. Defence Minister Mike Penning has dived for cover. But in a quick face-to-face meeting with Fabian, he and I rapidly solve the problem. Service officers will grovel. We will say that the suspect is subject to Gibraltar judicial processes and not UK military ones. And I will arrange for the MoD and the government of Gib to meet urgently to address the absence of adequate jurisdiction protocols. This has all arisen because nobody in the MoD has paid adequate attention to the modern workings of the Armed Forces Act.

Video conference with Kim Darroch. Much Bentley humour. He is effusively grateful, and admires the artistry of my manoeuvring to persuade both the Permanent Under-Secretary and Boris to agree to it.

Thursday 2 March – London/Rutland

Catch-up meeting with our lovely Protocol officials about honours. I try to recommend a couple of people but despite their good sense on such things, too many good names get weeded out by the tiresome committees and the judgement of Simon McDonald. The private sector hardly gets a look-in, and even the rations for ambassadors are now very paltry.

Address the Economic Diplomacy Conference – ambassadors and the like – in the Locarno Room.

New US Attorney General Jeff Sessions is under pressure for not saying while under oath that he had met the Russian Ambassador during the campaign – twice. As some wag said, 'The Russian Ambassador must be the most insignificant person in Washington – nobody can ever remember having met him.'

Friday 3 March – Rutland

A house full of tradesmen: boiler service, gardener, burglar-alarm survey and house-insurance valuation. Good to get it all done at once. It's chucking it down.

My knee is just so painful.

Sinn Féin and the DUP [Democratic Unionist Party] are almost neck and neck in the Northern Ireland election, following the recent collapse of the power-sharing government.

Banksy has secretly set up and decorated a hotel in Bethlehem right next to the separation barrier, and called it the Walled Off Hotel. I phone Palestinian diplomat Husam Zomlot, who had appeared on the *Channel 4 News* bulletin about it. A close adviser to

President Mahmoud Abbas, he is about to become the Palestinian Rep in Washington, and is charged with the task of revamping their missions abroad. Rather a tall order.

Monday 6 March – London

Just when I thought I had solved the problem, the Commanding Officer in Gibraltar, a navy commodore, has made a total bog of things and has reignited the whole issue. He failed to follow his orders to be contrite and completely screwed it all up by sending a long email explaining why he had been right all along, adding only a tiny one-line apology at the end. The Police Chief has hit the roof and has now demanded an admission of guilt before he will let the three officers off the hook. So I have to leap into action again. I speak to Rear Admiral Radakin, who had just arrived on the Rock. He was very sensible and without him everything would have deteriorated completely. But the hopeless MoD, not helped by Penning, have no grip. They wouldn't win a war behaving like this.

Tuesday 7 March – London

To the HofC. Chance encounters in the Tea Room/lobby with each of Michael Fallon, Mike Penning and Oliver Letwin. Fallon totally laid-back about Gibraltar; Penning not really on top of it and content to leave it to me; and Letwin passing on gratitude from his wife Isabel, who is the MoD's top lawyer. Also there, the admirable Kris Hopkins, who hates Eric Pickles from their days in South Yorkshire local government.

Read a DipTel which is totally alarming. The Israelis are intending to evict 500 Bedouin from the E1 area on the edge of Jerusalem and turn it into settlements. It's not just the end of the two-state solution: it is the end of any principled stand on the issue by the UK given that this has always been a red line for us, yet once again we intend to do nothing.

And the Israelis intend to ban entry to anybody who might have called for BDS (boycott, disinvestment, sanctions), thus creating the ultimate paradox that those who might advocate a ban on certain supposedly Israeli things are to be subject to a ban by Israel. This potentially includes Jeremy Corbyn, and Roger Waters of Pink Floyd, who I met in Mustique.

Geoffrey Tantum came in for a cup of tea. He wants to suggest to King Hamad that I gradually step into Geoffrey's shoes as a long-term adviser to HM in Bahrain, along with General Tom Beckett. He says he has just had lunch at Harry's Bar with David Cameron and Mohammed Mahfoudh al Ardhi, at which the prospect of DC joining Investcorp's advisory board was discussed. It's just great: William [Hague] gets the chairmanship of ICE derivatives exchange, and DC might hitch up with Investcorp, thus pinching my two main possible job prospects.

Ed says six Tory MPs are under police investigation for overspending on their 2015 election campaign. They include Amanda Milling and Alex Chalk. If anyone is to blame it is 100 per cent CCHQ [Conservative Campaign Headquarters]. But most exposed is Craig Mackinlay in Thanet, who saw off Nigel Farage of UKIP. We do not want any by-elections. [In the event, most were not charged and none was convicted.]

It transpires that the Westminster flood from the underground water table also affected George Hollingbery in Storey's Gate. He is still not back in his house. It means that the rise in the water level must have affected something like a square mile of residences from the river inwards to the other side of Westminster Abbey.

I'm told that Matt Hancock, when he was retained as a minister by Theresa in July, demanded a chauffeur-driven Jaguar as Minister of State at DCMS. It seems his boss Karen Bradley is not a fan.

The Lords have passed another amendment to the Article 50 Bill, by a majority of nearly 100, calling for a 'meaningful' parliamentary vote on the final exit deal. In practical legislative terms this is in fact quite 'meaningless', but it is seen as a serious government defeat, and will be reversed next week. The PM has sacked Michael Heseltine from his advisory positions to the government (investment in the North; inner-city infrastructure, etc) as he spoke and voted for the amendment, all of which is stupidly petty and won't bother him in the least. After all, he is over eighty, worth £300 million, and probably regards most of the government as a load of children. He's not wholly wrong.

We will get the Bill through after a bit of ping-pong with the Lords, and after their two amendments have been overturned the PM will trigger Article 50 in a couple of weeks.

But what then? I am seeing more and more internal papers which call on government departments to make contingency plans for what they term a 'non-negotiated outcome', i.e. no deal. That would mean the hardest of all exits, maximum uncertainty and no end of unresolved consequences. It would prove a costly disaster.

It is also the opposite of ministers' rosy rhetoric. Boris says, 'Come on – what are we waiting for? Let's get on with it. We can have a jumbo trade deal. It'll all be fine.' But it's bollocks. It won't be fine.

He, Davis and Fox all are oblivious to the pain of a hard departure, and still maintain that a good deal with the EU can yet be secured. I don't share their view. There is insufficient common ground for them and us to enter into serious discussions. What worries me above all is that, whatever our best intentions, EU–UK negotiations will fail to gain enough traction to be conclusive. They will speak one language: we will speak another. Already the fissures are emerging, with growing talk of the EU only being prepared to venture into broader issues once we have accepted the principle of paying billions (£60 billion?) as the price for leaving. Fat chance, so where's the deal?

Wednesday 8 March – London/Warsaw

Budget Day. My knee is just so much better. All praise to Fabi, my wonderful physio of over ten years.

Flight to Warsaw. Fat lump Pickles is in biz class, along with Sir Malcolm Rifkind, former Foreign Secretary, Chairman of the Belvedere Forum dialogue with the Poles, all paid for by our embassy in Poland, while I fly in economy. I suppose that whereas FLP might just fit into an economy seat, he would probably never get out of it again.

The Turkish Ambassador has (annoyingly) written to Fiona Hill in Number 10 to express (inflated) concern that PACE, the

Parliamentary Assembly of the Council of Europe, will vote this week to extend election monitoring to Turkey, which will require intensive scrutiny of their democratic conduct just as they head for a referendum on having an executive presidency. They are threatening to pull out of the Parliamentary Assembly, which would be stupidly isolationist. Sir Roger Gale leads our delegation, and he will argue against the monitoring idea. HMG cannot direct our MPs on PACE, but it helps that I have explained that the government are nonetheless onside. Ankara will be angered by any adverse decision, but at least the UK will not get the blame.

To the Bristol Hotel, and the Belvedere Forum, our annual bilateral meeting with the Poles. Foreign Minister Witold Waszczykowski and I each made a speech. Standard stuff from me about loving the Poles, and the UK leaving the EU but not leaving Europe. Witold has just been to Ukraine with Boris. He likes Boris, but after a while confided that although he thinks he is learning, he doesn't really know very much and is simply incapable of presenting himself as a serious minister. I'm afraid it is becoming the common view, and is all rather worrying.

The PM will attend the European Council in Brussels tomorrow at which former Polish PM Donald Tusk is due to be reappointed as President. The Polish government are vehemently opposed to him for domestic political reasons and want us to oppose him too, which we won't, because he's going to win anyway. So I have to duck all mention of 'the Tusk' while in Warsaw.

Back home the Budget has been broadly cautious and uneventful, and Hammond even made a few gags, which managed to raise a snigger. Our annual deficit borrowing is soon to fall below £50 billion a year, but he seems to have made a classic error, just as I always thought he might. He has no feeling whatsoever for people on low incomes, and is a Spock-like trampler over anyone else's sensitivities. In our manifesto for the 2015 general election, it explicitly stated that for the full duration of the Parliament we would not increase the rates of income tax, VAT, or national insurance contributions. But he has increased NICs for the self-employed from 8 per cent to 10. This is an undeniable breach of faith, and clearly a broken promise.

Thursday 9 March – Warsaw

On the *Today* programme, Nick Robinson (of course a slip of the tongue … oh yeah!) referred to Hammond as 'Spreadshit Phil'. He could just have ploughed on and later claimed he said 'Spreadsheet' but by correcting himself immediately, he validated the error. Hammond is under intensive fire, almost entirely from our own side. By saying that £240 a year is not very much he sounds like someone who is aloof from other people's finances; and if it's not very much then why has he done it? For me, it's breaking our word on a manifesto pledge that bothers me. It will backfire badly on the PM and will damage her reputation for straight-dealing. The *Mail* has hit the roof, and our long honeymoon with them is now over for sure. Hammond's attempt at humour yesterday does not seem so funny today.

It's the Rutland Council by-election today. I think we will win, but in a small local contest you just never know.

To the Belvedere Palace, to be greeted by the Polish Ambassador to the UK, Professor Arkady Rzegocki. Malcolm Rifkind very smoothly opened the formal session of the Forum, after which I did three newspaper and TV interviews, and then headed for the airport.

On return, there's a letter on my desk from the PUS which I am once again being asked to sign. It is the result of some stupid bollocks promise by the PM about austerity. While she has been on a Cabinet salary for eight years, we others are being asked to accept a 5 per cent reduction in our permitted salary, both ministerial and parliamentary. We farm these salary judgements out to independent evaluation, and then second-guess it all by cutting them. It is cheap spineless gesture-politics which gains nothing. Fortunately for me, I'm not too bothered, but it is extortion. Others, especially those with a family, are struggling financially. I had been delaying for weeks just to make the point. I drew a cartoon on the letter of a sad scowling face, signed it and sent it back to the PUS. I could have drawn something far worse …

Speak at an LGBT event in someone's enormous house in Wimpole Street.

Friday 10 March – London/Rutland

Car and Noodle to King Charles Street. Breakfast at the Goring with Russian Deputy FM Titov, then meeting with him in the FCO. I am the nominated first stage in developing more workmanlike relations with Russia. There is no relationship at the top with Putin, and their FM Sergei Lavrov is so haughty as to be almost impossible to deal with. So it falls to me to start some sort of sensible dialogue with them, and my counterpart for the purpose is their Deputy FM Vladimir Titov.

He is ex-KGB, of course, and, with a minor stammer, he is undemonstrative and methodical. In our meeting I have to start with the obvious 'health warning': that we find Russian intervention in Ukraine, and their interference in other countries' politics, wholly unacceptable. We cannot go straight into 'business as usual' until they behave more responsibly. I smile and say, 'We'd like to treat you with the respect your history deserves, but can't do so while you continue to do silly things.'

We meet for a couple of hours. It's a start. But they work within a completely different value system.

One strange request at the end was that he wanted their eighty-year-old former astronaut Valentina Tereshkova – who I later learnt is a member of the Duma – to meet Princess Anne.

Saturday 11 March – Rutland

Tim Shipman tells me Numbers 10 and 11 are viciously at loggerheads in the post-Budget fallout, with one source close to Hammond labelling the PM 'economically innumerate'.

Dinner with local friend Mark Laycock, aka Louis, in his cleverly restored town house in Uppingham, during which it seems all is going wrong in Holland. Their own elections are already controversial enough. The odious quasi-fascist Geert Wilders (who, although married, looks like a repressed gay weirdo) is ahead in the polls, though unlikely to figure in any governing coalition. In the midst of this, Turkish ministers want to fly in and campaign among their expat community in support of the referendum which would give more powers to Erdoğan. So we have a racist Dutch leader stirring up

James at home in London with Noodle.

Campaigning in Rutland for Remain (eventually), June 2016.

Colleagues in the Commons Chamber during the security lockdown: Nicholas Soames, Andrew Mitchell, Michael Gove and David Lidington. 22 March 2017.

Boris gets down to work as Foreign Secretary.

At work in my office at the FCO, watched over by Mrs Thatcher.

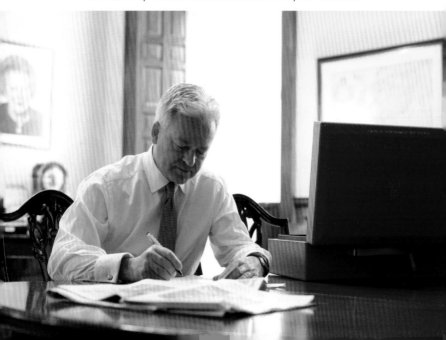

'I get the kiss!' Theresa May wins the Conservative Leadership, 11 July 2016.

Theres-air: on the plane with the PM, 2017.

'We will help each other!' Sharing a joke with Angela Merkel at the Western Balkans Summit, 10 July 2018.

EU Council meeting with President Donald Tusk,
Theresa May and Tim Barrow, 24 November 2017.

In discussion with 'FedMog' (EU High Representative Federica Mogherini).

With James and other guests at Blenheim Palace,
awaiting the arrival of President Trump, 12 July 2018.

At Buckingham Palace for the Trump State Dinner, 3 June 2019.

With HM The Queen and HM the King of Bahrain at the Windsor Horse Show.

Signing of the UK/Oman Comprehensive Agreement by Jeremy Hunt and Omani Foreign Minister Yousef bin Alawi, 22 May 2019.

Addressing the crowd at the Gibraltar National Day rally in Casemates Square, 10 September 2018.

On the steps of Number 10 as it prepares to welcome
President Erdoğan, 15 May 2018.

Being highly amused by His Royal Highness; with the
Prince of Wales in Germany, May 2019.

hate against immigrants, and members of the Turkish government want to come in person to woo hundreds of thousands of Turks in the country to vote in a referendum back home. It is a toxic cocktail. During dinner I texted Mevlüt Çavuşoğlu, having learnt that his flight had just been banned from landing in Holland and that the Turkish Culture Minister who was already in the country had been prevented from entering the Turkish consulate. None of this is helped by Erdoğan describing the Dutch as 'Nazi remnants'. During dinner Mevlüt called me to let me know what was happening. I called Lance so that he could warn the system that a spat was brewing.

Sunday 12 March – Rutland

The Dutch have expelled the female Turkish Families Minister from the country, and PM Binali Yıldırım has threatened to respond 'with maximum force'. This is getting mucky.

Boris cleverly asked Mevlüt to Chevening for lunch, but in the end it didn't happen.

To Wimbledon to see Ian Taylor. He is up and about, and doing remarkably well. They have rebuilt the entire right side of his jaw and neck. They think they have cut out all the cancer, but he is having to learn how to swallow again. He is amazingly cheerful and bouncy.

Hawaii Five-0.

Monday 13 March – London

All morning at MI6 HQ in Vauxhall Cross.

All afternoon from 3pm in the Commons. The two Lords amendments to the Article 50 Bill, which gives authority to the PM to trigger Brexit, were debated for two hours and then returned to the Lords with a Commons majority of about fifty. The Lords later back off, and so the starting gun will be fired in the last week of March.

Boris then opens the second day's debate on the Budget. He was his usual blustering self, which when analysed was flippant and shallow. He deliberately allowed himself to support the purchase of a new Royal Yacht, and claimed a free-trade deal would once again allow the Scots to export haggis to the US. Beneath all the wealth of character, he just isn't serious enough. If only he were. I do try, I do plead, but I get nowhere.

True to form, now that Article 50 will be triggered, the execrable Nicola Sturgeon has immediately called for a second referendum on Scottish independence, but it seems that the EU has made it crystal clear that if they were to leave the UK, they would have to apply afresh for membership of the EU, which would take years, and anyway the Spanish would block it lest it encourage Catalonia to do the same. Perhaps Sturgeon has overstepped the mark and can be gradually discredited on the back of it.

Tuesday 14 March – London

Catch-up meeting with Caroline Wilson, our EU Director. She is one of the FCO's best.

Sit in the Chamber for Nus Ghani's ridiculous but amusing Ten-Minute Rule Bill which would compel our embassies to serve English wine and bubbly. Whatever the merits, I don't see that we need be compelled to do so by force of law.

The PM has decided not to allow my plan for a written ministerial statement on Argentina until such time as there is more substantive progress on the Falklands in the form of clearer steps taken by Buenos Aires to deliver on their side of the understanding. I am a little irked, as it means we lose the moral advantage over them.

The Syrian war has now been going on for six years.

Amazing Hockney exhibition at the Tate, followed by dinner there with Rosso, David Snowdon, Lord Crathorne and forty other guests. The collection is so extensive, the full scope and development of his brilliance is striking.

Wednesday 15 March – London

Just before PMQs we announce a full climbdown on Hammond's unpopular Budget tax rise. It does nothing for his reputation, but at least it's decisive and closes it down.

Head for lunch with Oman Ambassador, Abdulaziz al Hinai, and bump into Simon Walters of the *Mail on Sunday* outside Harry's Bar. He says Blair is pitching to Jared Kushner to offer advice on the

Middle East, and (bizarre and not true) that Trump demanded the dismissal of Robert Hannigan from GCHQ, blaming him for trying to stitch him up over Russia.

Initial briefing on the Sanctions Bill, which I am leading on. The White Paper is abysmally written and is a truly shoddy piece of work. Any sanctions regime needs precision, a process under which anyone affected can appeal and seek redress, and a proper sense of justice for those wrongly caught up in it. None of this is in the White Paper, despite my previous instructions.

CCHQ is under fire for what are now police investigations into Conservative MPs' election expenses, all caused by the misallocation of the costs of the national battlebus.

Thursday 16 March – London

Brief from Stephen Hilton (the FCO official, not the idiot adviser to Cameron) updating me on the ministerial working group on maritime security which I chair.

Deep dive on Venezuela with desk officers and FCO researchers. The country is crumbling, and I want to be on top of unfolding events there and not be caught by surprise. I want to prepare full intellectual arguments to explain how Venezuela has got into such a terrible state.

Good natter at an FCO press reception with Tim Shipman – he says he has ample ammo (on tape) from people about Nick Timothy. It could completely demolish him, but he does not want to burn his bridges with the current regime. As I knew already, he says Fiona Hill had a blazing row with Philip Hammond, who just told her to get knotted. She thinks she can just tell any Cabinet minister what to do – she's mental.

Friday 17 March – Rutland

To Peterborough on the train to collect my new car! After years of arguing that diesel is more environmentally friendly, the government has completely changed its tune and is suddenly planning to penalise diesel vehicles with excise duty, higher congestion charges and more expensive parking fees. So I have bought a new petrol car before some of these higher costs kick in on 1 April. Its technology package is amazing, but it will take me a bit of time to work out all the bells and whistles. It is made in Mexico!

While in Peterborough, I accept a call as planned from Argentine FM Susana Malcorra. She speaks very frankly and explains that they just cannot take any further steps to help the Falklands until after the October mid-term elections, because they cannot risk the political consequences. So, within forty-eight hours of my being annoyed at Theresa's blocking of the written statement I wanted, she has been proved right.

I drive the twenty miles home, and am totally aghast at the news that George Osborne is to become editor of the *Evening Standard*, as well as remaining an adviser to BlackRock and an MP. It just won't wash.

My AGM in Oakham. The usual tedious procedural bollocks, before I give my speech. I bang the drum for the government like the loyal little trooper I am – which isn't so difficult when we have a nineteen-point lead in the polls. I tell them the PM has brought authority and popularity – then end with a melodramatic declaration that 'this age is ours for the taking', which whips them up into a frenzy of indifference.

Saturday 18 March – Rutland
Uppingham School Trustees meeting. Former Health Secretary Stephen Dorrell will soon hand over to a new Chairman. It is a fabulous school, but I'd feel better equipped to make an adequate contribution if I'd been a pupil there.

Monday 20 March – London
We will trigger Article 50 on the 29th.

Meet the new FCO Director of Estates and Security. I gave her my full nine yards about Estates and said that I wanted to put them into special measures but had all the wind taken out of my sails by her turning out to be so charming and lovely.

PUS catch-up. I just don't know what he does all day. I find him so supercilious.

Reports are emerging that explosives can be concealed in iPads and small laptops, and in a way that may be undetectable at airport security. So it is proposed to ban anything other than phones from the cabin: everything else will have to go in the hold, but only on certain flights, and not from the same origin countries as the US list. This is inconvenient, but also illogical. If you want to blow up a plane, then just try to do it on another route.

Drink with Leo Docherty, CEO of CMEC, and the gorgeous Emirati Sarah bin Ashoor, who wanted to wish me happy birthday for next week.

Tuesday 21 March – London
Martin McGuinness has died. He must have been very ill when I saw him at the reception with the Queen last November. The tributes reflect his reconciliation and even respectability at the end far more than his activities in the IRA in the decades before.

The aviation security laptop ban has suddenly been announced.

Hopeless meeting with David Jones in DExEU. He'd asked to see me, and he just read a stream of things from his brief which made no sense to me. After a while I said, 'You seem to be talking to me as if we have an agreed agenda and know what the topics are. Nobody has given me any such thing, and I am puzzled to know what you are on about and what the purpose of this meeting is.' He was astonished and embarrassed. His Private Secretary, who had failed to tee up the meeting properly, just squirmed. It slightly proves my adage that ministers must drive their diary, not let their diary drive them.

Wednesday 22 March – London
Meeting with MPs Oliver Letwin and Jane Ellison about a consular case in which a student in Moscow was drugged and dumped at the edge of a wood in freezing conditions, and was found dead the next day. Then Lilian Greenwood MP on another consular case. All such cases leave me wishing we could do more, when the truth is we simply can't.

Head over to the Commons to be ready to vote, and then just at the start of a division at 2.40pm the air is suddenly filled with the sense that something has happened. Colleagues coming into the Chamber as we are filing into the lobbies say there has been an incident in New Palace Yard. Grant Shapps and Mark Prisk, both looking slightly agitated, say they are sure there were shots fired at someone. From the Chamber I'd heard sharp cracks of sound, perhaps two or three. It is Twitter which feeds the stream of emerging facts: a car has driven through people on Westminster Bridge; attack of some sort at the Parliament Square gates; four shots fired, etc.

I noticed that the PM was hurried by her detectives out of the lobby entrance behind the Speaker's Chair back towards her Commons office. Something serious was unfolding. Deputy Speaker Lindsay Hoyle (fortunately) was in the Chair and maintained throughout an air of calm authority.

Within a few minutes Hoyle said that we must all stay within the immediate vicinity of the Chamber itself and the lobbies and their entrance areas. Twitter furnished the facts, which although unverified seem to paint a fairly clear picture of what had unfolded. After an hour or so David Lidington, striking just the right tone, made an impromptu statement to keep us as officially informed as possible. The entire Palace of Westminster was under lockdown. The facts so far gathered were that a car had mown people down on Westminster Bridge, a cyclist and perhaps others had been killed, the car had rammed the gates on New Palace Yard and an intruder with a knife had been shot by police. It was some time later that to a stunned House he rose again to say that a policeman had been killed. Word somehow also gradually seeped into the Chamber that Tobias Ellwood had been in the thick of it and had dramatically attempted to save the life of the stabbed policeman, who was bleeding to death on the cobbles near the doors of Westminster Hall.

I was asked to attend a COBRA meeting in place of the Foreign Secretary, and was escorted by police out of the Commons. [COBRA is short for Cabinet Office Briefing Room A, and refers to the Civil Contingencies Committee.] Originally scheduled for 6pm, it was deferred to 7.30pm. While waiting in the FCO, my private office tell me that Tobias Ellwood had returned to the FCO at about 3.30pm with blood all over his hands and in quite a state of shock. He had really been pretty heroic, and with his soldier's training had just waded in to help as the policeman lay horribly stabbed.

At COBRA I relayed in as much detail as I was able the actions of Tobias and suggested to the Prime Minister that she should call him. Her deadpan, inexpressive manner conveyed no commitment one way or the other.

Condolences start pouring into the FCO from around the world. It is clear that there was a party of French schoolchildren on the bridge at the time, and it was at first feared that there might have been deaths among them. At the very least, three of them have been injured. Immediately, without consulting our system, I pick up the phone on my desk and directly call the French Ambassador and just tell him that we will offer any assistance we can possibly give.

Impromptu dinner at home with Vicki Atkins MP and her husband Paul, and Ed Argar, all of whom I met in the street as they were released from their five-hour parliamentary lockdown and I was walking back home from COBRA.

Thursday 23 March – London

I went in the ministerial car early to meet the French Foreign Minister Jean-Marc Ayrault at the Marriott County Hall hotel. He had flown instantly from Paris to see the group of students whose trip to London had turned into such a nightmare. There were twenty or more fifteen-year-olds, who were amazingly composed and polite. Jean-Marc sat on a sofa with the kids assembled informally around him telling their story. It was highly emotional to watch. Quiet, moving, sensitive.

We then drove over Lambeth Bridge to the Commons, through the police roadblocks around Parliament and in via Black Rod's Entrance, through which I'd left yesterday evening. I put Jean-Marc in the Special Gallery, and at Questions – for once he got something right – Speaker Bercow made a generous reference to him in the gallery, at which the Commons burst into applause while looking up at him. Moving, touching and a special moment of brilliant diplomacy and decency.

Lunchtime reception by TRH the Prince of Wales and the Duchess of Cornwall at Clarence House. Inevitably a little subdued, but good that it went ahead.

Nigel Dodds MP and other DUP types there. We speak a little of Martin McGuinness. And HRH says we will see the Pope when I am due to accompany him in Italy in a few weeks.

The government is keen to deliver an important message to Oman about the conflict in Yemen, and I have offered, and have since been asked, to secure an audience with the Sultan to do so. Later see Colonel John Clark at Number 10. He says there is now some doubt about whether I am after all to be permitted to deliver the message to Oman – but I've already got the audience, so I can't back out. I ask Colonel Clark to 'crunch the gears and de-fuck it up'.

Sir Martin Donnelly's farewell as Permanent Secretary at International Trade. I think he's relieved to be out of it.

Dinner at Peter Mandelson's house off Regent's Park with a bunch of people from Lazard. Time with Mandelson is never dull.

Friday 24 March – Antalya, Turkey

Up at 4.45 for the car to Gatwick. Flea-fugged the house on departure, an occasional protection against doggy things, although Noodle is always perfect! Thomas Cook flight to Antalya for the Tatlı Dil (sweet talk) Anglo-Turkish annual dialogue.

Nice text from Peter Mandelson as I boarded the plane, to thank me for coming to dinner last night. All the papers are full of the stabbing aftermath. It seems that the assailant was shot by one of Michael Fallon's protection officers, and not by one of the many policemen with machine guns who are based there for just that sort of eventuality.

Crispin Blunt gave me an early copy of his committee's report on Turkey. As far as I'm concerned it is balanced and sensible, but I doubt the Turks will see it that way, and I'm not sure it is appropriate for him to drop it into the dialogue meeting without prior notice. It is almost the Alan Duncan report on Turkey, as it draws heavily on my oral witness session to the committee. An amusing misprint on page 41 calls on the FCO to 'dully' implement their recommendations.

The Tatlı Dil is chaired by former Foreign Secretary Jack Straw and former Vodafone executive Sir Julian Horn-Smith. The Duke of York is the Patron/President, something he does very well. Also there Crispin Blunt (with his FAC report), ex-Ambassador Sir Peter Westmacott, Lieutenant General Sir Simon Mayall, Trade Envoy Lord Janvrin and our Ambassador Richard Moore.

My trip to Oman is definitely on. The PM has agreed to it. Speak to Oman Deputy Foreign Minister Sayd Badr.

Reception. Dinner. Unfortunately BoJo's speech was just embarrassing. It was all about him and his Turkish ancestors. A bit of that would have been OK, but he discarded his official speech and just waffled. He made incomprehensible public school quips which cannot be translated, and banged on about being a supportive buttress, assisting the EU from outside it, which came over to the Turks in translation as 'a supportive bucket'.

Nice drink with Peter Westmacott, who thought the BoJo speech a disgrace: simply inappropriate, ramshackle and sloppy.

Saturday 25 March – Antalya, Turkey
Tobias Ellwood and Ben Wallace are to be made Privy Counsellors.

BoJo makes a much better speech in the morning plenary. When he is good, he is very good, but too often he slips into shallow jollity and lets himself down.

Just in time for the dinner, Erdoğan returns from a campaign rally wearing his signature blue-checked jacket, but first has a bilateral meeting with HRH the Duke of York, which I am asked to join.

Big dinner. Speeches from HRH and Erdoğan. I receive a special mention in Erdoğan's speech, which was being broadcast live on Turkish TV. Although speaking in Turkish, it was translated simultaneously. He said that he would never forget what Britain did after the coup attempt. 'They were the only country to understand what we went through. I will always be grateful for the visit of Sir Alan Duncan, and will never forget it. I feel bound to him as if within a hoop of steel.'

A cheeky official texted me across the table: 'That's a new bondage experience for you, Minister!'

Lord (Hugh) Dykes was charming afterwards about the panel I'd been on earlier. 'You should be Foreign Secretary: you were magisterial today.'

Sunday 26 March – Antalya/Muscat

It's been an exhausting week and, although I didn't witness the shooting itself, the effect has been emotionally draining. The French schoolchildren and James's flashbacks to him being stabbed in 2000, combined with cumulative tiredness, have slightly choked me up. James was starting a skiing holiday with the family and was taking some cash out of an ATM at the Gare du Nord when a drug-crazed immigrant slit his neck from behind him. Had an ambulance not been there on the spot, he'd have died.

I've had to switch in the course of any one day between so many issues and countries, it has been rather sapping.

So here I am, approaching sixty, on the way to Oman to try to help resolve a knotty issue; flying from Antalya where I've been named in a televised speech by the President; four days after a policeman was killed two minutes after I'd walked past him; and three days before we trigger our departure from the EU. Meanwhile President Trump is turning out to be a complete lunatic and has just binned his abolition of Obamacare because it has been blocked by Republicans of all people. So much in the world has gone totally mad.

It'll be just Monday in Muscat, and then back to London just in time for Oral Questions. Then NATO, my birthday, Italy with the Prince of Wales and Duchess of Cornwall, then off to Mustique. At least my knee is feeling better.

To Muscat via a five-hour stopover in Istanbul – again – where I link up with Lance. The good news is that we have been told to be ready in Muscat to leave the hotel for the Palace at 1.10pm tomorrow. Check into the Grand Hyatt just after 1am.

Monday 27 March – Muscat

A leisurely start with breakfast outside and time to put my thoughts in order ahead of the audience. An hour in the embassy first with Ambassador Jon Wilks. They all agree with my game plan for the meeting. Meanwhile Badr has left a message for me to call him. He suggests that I go into the audience alone, and then we all have lunch afterwards. Fine by me.

We head for Bait al Baraka as planned but, as we approach the Palace at 2.30pm, we are asked only to be there at 3pm, so we overshoot the entrance road, and fill in time going up to and around neighbouring Barka, then back for 3pm. We receive a friendly greeting from all the staff and are treated to the usual pleasure of Puligny-Montrachet while waiting for a further hour, sadly declining the temptation of Pétrus for fear of losing mental clarity.

I am conscious that my audience with Sultan Qaboos might be my last. There is no knowing whether he will survive another five years or five weeks. He is skinny, but fully alert. Our meeting lasts a full hour, and I manage to land the government's message exactly as we'd planned.

Sumptuous lunch, at which as usual the Sultan force-fed me with puddings for which I had no easy space. Others there were Jon Wilks, Lance Domm, head of the Diwan (Royal Court) Sayd Khaled and Deputy FM Sayd Badr bin Hamad.

Midnight flight home.

Tuesday 28 March – London

Straight home, then into FCO Oral Questions. BoJo is assailed on the issue of Israel imposing a ban on people who have advocated a boycott of settlement produce. When replying it seems his bluff-and-bluster routine has run out of road.

Lunch at the Reform with Adrian Wooldridge, the new 'Bagehot' in the *Economist*. Encounter my old Oxford contemporary, the eccentric Professor Nicholas O'Shaughnessy in the bar there. He hasn't changed in forty years, and speaks like nobody else, with accentuated vowel sounds which are something between a Pathé News voiceover and a Regency fop. His book *Selling Hitler* is a classic analysis of the power of propaganda through imagery.

Neil Parish MP comes to see me on a consular case. His constituent's son was run over and killed a few years ago in Ukraine, and it looks like murder. Once again we all feel rather helpless.

See Sir Mark Sedwill, soon to be the new NSA. Meeting with David Gauke, Chief Secretary to the Treasury, to discuss FCO funding. Please sir, can I have some more?

Wednesday 29 March – London
It's Article 50 day.

Bumped into Kwasi Kwarteng MP in New Palace Yard. He says Boris doesn't appreciate that diplomacy is not about having nice conversations with your friends: it's about how you engage with those who are awkward.

Ministerial team meeting: as usual a complete waste of time.

To Westminster Hall to join Italian FM Angelino Alfano in laying a wreath and signing the condolence book for the victims of last week (when two Italians were injured).

Receive lovely notes from both Jack Straw and Richard Moore passing on their effusive gratitude for the way I handled the meetings in Turkey.

Thursday 30 March – London
Lunch with Erik. My friend Sheikh Ahmed Farid, who Erik describes as 'Prince of Yemen', is dying and is at home in London, hardly conscious and receiving constant care.

Friday 31 March – London
My sixtieth birthday.

Radio Leicester interview on tomorrow's twentieth anniversary of Rutland's restoration as a county. I secured it in 1996, and it formally took place in 1997.

Birthday dinner at Franco's with James, Kevin and Sarah. Noodle too, and they have arranged for a lovely cake.

Saturday 1 April – Rutland
Up early. Straight to Oakham Castle for the celebration of Rutland's twentieth. Lovely ceremony and speeches, particularly by Lord Lieutenant Laurence Howard, who is one of the most charming people in the world.

Sunday 2 April – Rutland/London

Gibraltar has flared up. It was not specifically mentioned in the PM's letter triggering Article 50, starting the formal process of our leaving the EU, but the leaked draft negotiating guidelines from Brussels include a sentence that gives Spain the right to approve or reject anything in the agreement in respect of Gibraltar. Understandably, the government of Gibraltar are incandescent. In an interview [former Conservative Leader] Michael Howard stupidly linked it to the thirty-fifth anniversary of the invasion of the Falklands, thus introducing the language of war into the Gibraltar issue. Not helpful: indeed crass and irresponsible. Think, m'lud, in future, please.

Plough, seed and roll the wildflower paddock.

Monday 3 April – London/Florence

I am due to join the Prince of Wales and Duchess of Cornwall on their tour of Italy, but am delayed for two hours at City Airport by fog. I eventually join Their Royal Highnesses at the British Council exhibition in Florence. Later at a rather splendid dinner at the Palazzo Strozzi, the Prince is awarded 'Renaissance Man of 2016'.

Tuesday 4 April – Florence/Rome

We have to drive to Pisa to fly to Rome because the clumsy Voyager aircraft is too big for the Florence runway. Drab and grey on the outside, the industrial configuration of the seats on the inside – a sort of spartan business class – make it wholly unsuitable for Royal travel.

When in Rome, as it were, amid a radiant array of cardinals, we have a tour of the Vatican Library and an audience with the Pope. All in a day's work! I give my Papal medallion to Lance for his daughter.

Wednesday 5 April – Rome/London

TRH's visit shifts from the religious to the political, seeing the President and Prime Minister of Italy. HRH kindly asks me to sit in the car with him for the journey between the two, after which I take my leave and head back to London.

Friday 7 April – Rutland
The US have carried out a missile strike on the Syrian airfield that launched the chemical/gas attack forty-eight hours ago. Good! Trump has done something right.

Call the Romanian Ambassador about the woman who was thrown off Westminster Bridge by the BMW-driving terrorist sixteen days ago. She has died. The decision was taken to switch off her machine. So I express condolences.

Sunday 9 April – Rutland
Everyone is in a tizzy about who should go to the EU summit next week in Lucca. Speak to Boris and say I'm quite happy to make an early return to Tuscany. He can't decide whether to go or not, and one moment I am to go, the next moment he's not so sure. At moments like this you just have to go with the flow.

Monday 10 April – London
Farewell drinks for Mark Lyall Grant – a good man, forced out by the gruesome twosome, Fi and Nick.

Tuesday 11 April – London
Boris has made a complete Horlicks of the G7. His plan to get everyone to agree to tougher sanctions on Russia at the foreign ministers' meeting in Lucca has been publicly rebuffed by other leaders. Meanwhile, Tom Newton Dunn says that Fi Hill has been shouting and screaming at Boris. I don't know why he just sits there and takes it. Fi Hill is a total nutcase and is not fit to be in the Prime Minister's office. Her recent tantrums have been directed recently at both the Chancellor and the Foreign Secretary. These SpAds are poison in government and are to be blamed for creating dysfunction.

Wednesday 12 April – London/Mustique
To Gatwick, slightly hung-over. To St Lucia/Mustique for ten days in the sun.

Newspapers rather excoriating about Boris, describing his handling of the Russians and the G7 in Lucca as 'humiliating'. This is a classic case of governing by press release rather than policy – you should never go for the headline unless you have thoroughly prepared the policy ground in advance.

Friday 14 April – Mustique
It's Good Friday: while others go up the St Vincent volcano, I stay back at base.

The PM has taken the Passing-Out Parade at Sandhurst, wearing an unusual red hat and a dress that looks like a long loose frock coat. It's a bit early for her to dress like a Chelsea Pensioner.

Saturday 15 April – Mustique
The sabre-rattling between the US and North Korea is getting scary. There is no doubt that North Korea is the last totally closed Orwellian state, with a despotic nutter ruling over brainwashed serfs. But, squeezed as they are between South Korea and China, releasing them from the grip of Kim Jong-un is no easy matter and risks apocalyptic consequences. The Chinese have been content to keep them in misery for decades in order to maintain stability on the Korean peninsula, but it has come at a high human price, and presents a growing risk from Kim's developing nuclear threat.

Lunch with Bryan Adams. What a wonderful man. In addition to his amazing musical success he is a great photographer. He has published a compendium of black and white photographs of limbless soldiers. It is so incredibly poignant and powerful – each and every one of them looks like a hero. As a tease, we gave him an Easter Bunny costume. He later sent pictures of himself wearing it with his kids chasing him down the beach.

Sunday 16 April – Mustique
Easter Sunday. Adam Boulton in the *Sunday Times* has written a caustic piece on Boris, with the headline 'May is happy for Boris to bumble and gurn around the globe – for now'. He states that EU leaders know Boris well and cordially detest him; that officials avoid referring issues to him, because they rarely get clear answers; that most colleagues have turned their backs on this Cavalier in a

Roundhead government; that we will need a coherent foreign policy again, but Johnson is showing he is not the Foreign Secretary for that job. Ouch!

Tuesday 18 April – Mustique
I could hear the message and email sounds pinging on my iPhone and laptop from an early hour. So at about 5.30am I take a look. The news is extraordinary. Theresa May, it seems, will make a surprise announcement at 11am on the steps of Number 10, and the raging speculation is that she will announce a sudden general election. And indeed she does! For 8 June, i.e. in seven weeks. The Commons will vote on it tomorrow, and then probably rise on 3 May which is the day of the county council elections.

My first task is to rebook my flight home, and after a bit of scrabbling around manage to advance by two days and book the only remaining seat for tonight, which is first class for an extra £750. As all I'll get is better catering on the same flight, it'll be the most expensive glass of wine I've ever bought … or two, or three, suggested James.

Speak to Lance, who is as astonished as I am. We agree on the rationale. He learnt this morning that it was the PM who recently stopped Boris from going to Moscow, although it is not entirely clear why. It was probably because she did not trust him not to mess up. He can't see that it was a deliberate attempt to humiliate him. What I don't understand is why Boris just allows himself to be trampled over. He is looking seriously belittled and discredited. If he were to project himself as more serious, he'd be in a better position to stand his ground.

I have to say, I neither thought she'd do it nor did I really think it possible. But it may be that she will win her first two gambles – first that she will be able to secure the election, and second that she will then win it. To trigger an election you need to secure the support of two-thirds of the Commons, and it looks as though it will be doable. Conservatives (330) plus SNP (54) plus Lib Dems (9) takes you to 393. Two-thirds is 434, and it looks as though Corbyn is dumb enough to whip his party to vote in favour – an act of national suicidal sacrifice.

The 20 per cent lead measures the binary choice between May and Corbyn. It is very wide, and will reduce somewhat as the campaign develops, but it seems inconceivable that we will not gain seats and demolish the Labour Party. The Lib Dems will probably pick up a few, and the SNP will have peaked, I suspect. And progress in Scotland might yet be the pleasant surprise. Importantly, though, a good result would give TM robust authority in the Party, and allow her to see off the extreme Brexiteer nutters, even to the point where she sacks or demotes Boris. And it buys time, thus avoiding the collision of a 2020 election just as exit negotiations reach their climax. So it takes the pressure off. If it works – which I think it should – she will have played a blinder. It is a gamble, but a bold and rational one. Just by being so audacious she has added to her reputation. But if it goes wrong and we perform badly, we will end up in stasis. It is all to play for, but entirely ours to screw up.

Should I stand again? Of course. It will be my seventh general election. But I had a moment of doubt.

Wednesday 19 April – London

Gatwick 9am. Home 11am. Good chat with Erik. He is in Oman.

HofC. PMQs. Debate for ninety minutes on whether to hold a general election. Am on the front bench for the result, sitting between Theresa May and BoJo. I say to her, 'You have played a blinder. You have gained a two-year breather, which avoids the horrors of a collision between a 2020 election and the conclusion of the exit negotiations.' She said that once you work that out, it's an obvious decision. I said that it had always been my view, but that I had never seen how we might get two-thirds of the Commons to vote for it. She said, 'We'll know in five minutes.' We won 522–13.

George Osborne is to leave the Commons. The general view is that he should.

Thursday 20 April – London

Urgent Question on the persecution of LGBT people in Chechnya. I took it at short notice. It's much more about style than content – assemble a few facts, but on a topic like this you just need to get the tone right, which I did, and so managed to draw the House together as one. Let's be honest, it's not an issue they can easily bash me about personally.

US Speaker Paul Ryan and a congressional delegation to the FCO. Boris is waffly and all over the place. He just wings these things and never prepares.

Friday 21 April – London
To Melton for general election planning. We will do the minimum. We are not exactly a battleground seat.

Saturday 22 April – Rutland
There has been much speculation about whether we will maintain the commitment and legislation to spend 0.7 per cent of GDP on international development. We have now said we will, it is thought in order to retain our appeal in Lib Dem challenge seats in the South-West.

Sunday 23 April – Rutland/London
Ken Bool called me on his daughter Sarah's phone. I saw her name and said 'Hello, Darling'. Oops. It was him. There was a period of silence and then raucous joint laughter.

In the French election Emmanuel Macron has come top of the poll, with Marine Le Pen second. It is the first time since 1958 that neither of the two main parties has reached the final. So it's a 39-year-old former banker, who was a minister under the unpopular François Hollande, versus the hard-right nationalist.

Monday 24 April – London
See Mounir Bouaziz, Vice-President of Shell, and our Ambassador, about Venezuela. The country is falling to bits, all thanks to Maduro's idiotic left-wing government. Meet the UK delegation to the NATO Parliamentary Assembly. Czech Deputy Foreign Minister Jakub Dürr, and then a large congressional delegation from their defence committee.

Photo with the PM. I said that if she wanted a safe pair of hands to do back-up interviews during the campaign, I'd be more than willing. All I got in return was a dead stare. Her social skills are sub-zero.

It is odd that, after I did so much to galvanise her leadership campaign, and asked for nothing in return, she has never once even said thank you, or even had a substantial conversation of any sort. Instead she has put Brexiteers into strong positions when they were against her, and then added a series of rather puny sycophants. There are no serious figures, with the exception of Hammond (who is rather soulless) and Fallon (who is rather moody).

CCHQ briefing in the Boothroyd Room for MPs about the election campaign. It was all about process, and rather familiar old hat to most of us. Lots of what they say must happen simply won't. They speak of resources which don't exist, and people on the ground who aren't there. There is a lot of fantasy floating around.

Tuesday 25 April – London

Sit with Martin Reynolds to give him my appraisal of Lance Domm as my PS. I do so in glowing terms. He is exceptional, with a calm intelligent nature and top-flight initiative and confidence. He is totally trustworthy. It has prompted a private office joke: 'Why is the minister like King Arthur?' 'Because he likes Lance a lot!'

To Windsor Castle, sharing a car with Joyce Anelay, for the Privy Council meeting to dissolve Parliament and approve the general election (strictly speaking, since the utterly stupid Fixed-Term Parliaments Act, the dissolution is automatic, but HM still needs to issue the Proclamation to summon the new Parliament). Four of us as serving ministers, and David Lidington as Lord President of the Council, attend on Her Majesty and so authorise (or rather witness) the Order in Council.

The Council meeting took place (we of course remain standing) in HM's private quarters. She was relaxed and unadorned, in a tartan skirt and cardigan. The rooms have a commanding view over the rose garden and its fountain, but are affected by the nuisance of Heathrow. She is a legend beyond all others.

Thursday 27 April – London/Malta
Eddie Powell, a successful Cambridge businessman with strong views in support of Palestinian justice, contributes £10,000 to my re-election campaign. That's as much as it will cost in total. He is a decent, principled bloke.

Speak to Governor Ed Davis in Gibraltar. Evening flight to Valletta.

Friday 28 April – Malta/London
The Gymnich is an informal meeting of EU foreign ministers. I stand in for Boris. Federica Mogherini is a former Italian FM and now the EU's High Representative for foreign affairs and security. Only forty-four, and perfectly nice as a person, FedMog doesn't really carry enough weight, and has the capacity when chairing a meeting to kill the room stone dead. It's a bit of a yawn. Back to Gatwick.

Saturday 29 April – Rutland
Adoption meeting in Oakham to get the election started. The Association members are in good enough heart, and are united in thinking so little of Jeremy Corbyn, but nothing in politics is ever straightforward.

Monday 1 May – Rutland
Bank Holiday. Really shocking news. My old schoolfriend Guy Hedger has been shot dead by intruders at his home in Dorset. It would seem from the BBC report that he and his husband were woken up and threatened by burglars on Saturday night, one of whom then panicked and shot him. It's unimaginably awful. When I first saw the news I couldn't believe it was actually him, but it was.

Wednesday 3 May – London
Dissolution of Parliament. While in the FCO I watched the TV choppers zooming in over my office, which overlooks Number 10. I could see everything both from my window and on the TV. Theresa goes to Buck Palace to see HMTQ. She is greeted obsequi-

ously by the Queen's Equerry, Wing Commander Sam Fletcher. On return to Number 10 she makes a clever statement in front of the door all but telling the EU to shove off, but expressed rather more politely as telling them not to interfere in our election. All political competition collapses when she simply does what you wish to see done! But she so rarely does. When she is not robotic, there is something there.

I manage to lift online the perfect shot of Sam Fletcher and the PM at the steps of Buckingham Palace, and text it to him with the caption 'Bloody swank.' He responded, most amused.

Thursday 4 May – Rutland
The Duke of Edinburgh is to retire. He is amazing to have stuck with so many Royal duties for so long.

To Melton for more election planning. We have local elections today, but for us only at the county level.

Friday 5 May – Rutland
Good local election results for us, and all the more so given that two weeks ago the PM announced a general election for 8 June. We won 61 per cent of seats fought, and Labour only 18 per cent. Admittedly the counties are historically more fruitful for us, but the Con vs Lab contrast is stark and heartening. It augurs well for the general.

Saturday 6 May – Rutland
Uppingham School Trustees Meeting. There was a discussion about compulsory rugby. I said I thought all that went out ages ago along with cold showers and caning.

Sunday 7 May – Rutland
The Sunday papers are strongly supportive of us, and miss no opportunity to deride Jeremy Corbyn and his team, especially Diane Abbott. And John McDonnell on *Marr* fails to deny he is a Marxist, which offers us a welcome lift.

Speak to Neil O'Brien, who is understandably thrilled to have been picked for Harborough.

Our neighbours Peter Cox and Mary Fairbairn come for lunch. CCHQ's website has crashed, and nobody has been able to file their election leaflets for printing.

Emmanuel Macron has swept to victory in the second and final round of the French Presidential election, beating Marine Le Pen by 30 per cent. Their presidential system is different from our parliamentary one, and there is no tide in France which offers an easy guide to the mood in the UK.

Monday 8 May – Rutland

Finally manage to send my leaflet proofs to the absurdly centralised, micromanaged system which is now modern politics. So much for individualism: if you don't comply with Party Newspeak, you're out.

Ellwood just doesn't get it. It has been made perfectly clear to him that although he is the Middle East Minister (albeit only at Parliamentary Under-Secretary level) I'm the one with the personal relationships with the Sultan of Oman and the King of Bahrain. I will not tread on his toes, but he must grow up and allow what is in the best interests of the country overall.

Out of courtesy I have told Ellwood that when I see the King on Friday I will carry a letter to him from the PM. He is now trying to muscle in on what the letter should say, and is demanding to see the King himself. NFI, mate. Shut up.

Wednesday 10 May – Rutland

Trump has sacked FBI Director James Comey.

Call with Simon-Pierre Hedger-Cooper, who is understandably still in a state of utter distress after his husband Guy's murder.

To Nottingham for a rather uninspiring campaign rally with the PM. It was an artificial gathering of about fifty people with no excitement or pizzazz – the press were bored already and so were all the supporters.

What is it with Ellwood? He has now gone behind my back to Number 10 about the Bahrain letter and has hacked off the PM's office, Sheikh Fawaz, the King's adviser Geoffrey Tantum ... and me.

And now he has demanded that he displace me on a RUSI election hustings panel to which I have been invited because it's me they want. What do you do?

Thursday 11 May – London
Labour's manifesto has been leaked. It is worthy of Cuba, and contains wholesale nationalisation and all sorts of bonkers economics.

I have been asked by Number 10 to greet the dignitaries arriving at Lancaster House for the Somalia Conference. I don't do Africa, but am responsible for protocol and know most of the non-African attendees. I welcome Binali Yıldırım, PM of Turkey, Anwar Gargash, FM of United Arab Emirates, etc, and then suddenly Ellwood barges in, and in an extraordinary outburst demands to know why I am greeting guests and not him. He's nuts.

Saturday 13 May – Rutland
Lunch at Barnsdale Lodge, generously put on by the Association to celebrate my twenty-five years in Parliament. Many of the faces were there when it all started. Very friendly and touching. They give me a lovely old map of Rutland.

I reflected in my speech on having seen five PMs come and go and seven leadership contests, and here I am now contesting my seventh general election. I'd like to think that I've done all that without yet becoming a boring old fart.

Dinner at Nevill Holt. While sitting in the cloisters beforehand having a nice drink in the lovely evening sun, James spots a rabbit on the lawn. On closer study it's a young hare. He points it out to Noodle, and all hell breaks loose. She sprints for it at full tilt, and after a couple of racing traverses across the entire garden there is a terrible squealing noise behind the bushes. Noodle got it. She has a determined instinct once it's sparked. There's no stopping her.

Sunday 14 May – Rutland
Emily Thornberry catastrophic on *Marr*. She's becoming our secret weapon.

Noodle to the vet. Minor op to remove a detached dewclaw, which she'd ripped off during the leveret chase in a way that left it hanging like a loose tooth.

Text apology from Ellwood about his conduct outside Lancaster House, but it contains a gripe about territory and responsibilities, so I ignore it. He's behaving very oddly.

President Macron is sworn in. Beautiful Rutland evening.

Monday 15 May – Rutland/London

To London by train. At the FCO, the feedback from the system about my hard message to the Sultan has come back as positive, and the read-out of the Chief of the Defence Staff seeing him two weeks later is fine.

Erik says my March visit was appreciated, and that I am totally trusted. Given that Trump is due to go to Saudi Arabia, it is as well that the Sultan has been made to stop and think what an axis between Saudi Arabia, the Emirates, Netanyahu and Trump might stir up against Oman. It also means I owe the German Ambassador £10, as I bet him £10 to 10 euros that Trump's first visit abroad would be to see Putin.

Someone has jumped on the line north of Kettering, stopping the train, but I manage to get a taxi there from Wellingborough to reconnect with my car.

Mary says Noodle has been a little subdued. Poor thing. I think she remains slightly shocked by the pain of the ripped claw and yesterday's sedation.

The election campaign rumbles on. May rather lacklustre: Corbyn hopeless and hapless. Our slogan is that we offer a government which is 'strong and stable' but it's beginning to feel a little rickety. There's not much more to be said.

Tuesday 16 May – Rutland

To Oxford for the opening by the Prince of Wales of the new Centre for Islamic Studies building. It has all the hallmarks of an elegant Oxford college and has been the lifelong project of Dr Farhan Nizami. The Prince is an enthusiast, and every major Islamic country sent a senior dignitary to the event. I have spoken at some of their lectures in the past and was glad I could make it. Because there's an election on I had to keep apart from the Prince and avoid any photographs, but it was a special occasion.

Thursday 18 May – Rutland/London

Our manifesto launch. Another stupid pledge on net migration. May's obsession with this facile statistic so belittles our policy-making. You can reduce net migration by chucking out all the good people you want to keep, while still receiving those you don't. The target is simplistic bollocks. Anyway, the greater problem is asylum.

Monday 22 May – Rutland

It's just so difficult to get activity going on the ground. The Whips keep texting candidates demanding to know what canvassing they've been doing; which seats they've visited to give mutual aid; how many Party members they've taken with them, etc. It's all complete fantasy, reminiscent of the last days of the Reich, where those close to the top protect and promote themselves by telling their seniors that it's all going brilliantly, but when they pull a lever there's nothing at the other end. MPs just don't have local armies any more which they can direct and deploy. The election is fought and won on TV and Facebook, so why pretend otherwise? So I'm just going to spend a day at home catching up with lots of things.

It has become wobbly Monday. Our manifesto policy on old-age care has exploded. We have basically announced that people will have to pay for themselves, be they in their own home or in a care home, and that the costs of provision will be docked off the value of their house until they have £100,000 left. In principle it is wholly right, but nobody has thought it through. Never put a figure on such a policy when it is sprung on people from nowhere, and never put numbers in a manifesto. The cap on a person's total payments has been removed. It is always wrong to introduce welfare changes of such magnitude with no phase-in, and in a way which destroys people's existing plans. And anyway (although nobody has yet pointed this out) how do you value the house? How do you price the care? Can people buy it more cheaply than the state, but still ask the state to pay? How do you stop people just stripping themselves of their own assets in their final years? It is supposedly the brainchild of Nick Timothy, who along with Fi Hill is increasingly hated. In fact, they are poisonous, arrogant shits.

The PM in Wales announces that there will be a cap, but no figure is given, and is being castigated for making a U-turn. It is messy. Her strong and stable image is deflating somewhat, and voices are targeting her coterie. The press are mocking her for being weak and wobbly.

Trump is in Tel Aviv, and gives a speech on the tarmac which was better than one might have feared.

James has had a sudden OFSTED inspection imposed on his school tomorrow, so comes up after work. As we turn in soon after 10.30pm I see a Sky TV alert on my iPhone saying there are reports of an explosion in Manchester, but I didn't turn on the TV.

Tuesday 23 May – Rutland

The explosion is a major atrocity. A suicide bomber has killed twenty-two in the foyer of the Manchester Arena at the end of a concert by Ariana Grande. Her audience are children, who were there with their parents or other adults. It is as bad as it can get.

COBRA. Campaign suspension. PM statement. She goes to Manchester. Also there of course is Andy Burnham, the Mayor of Greater Manchester. She's done absolutely the right thing, but somehow she just cannot project empathy. On one level it would be wholly wrong to exploit this for electoral purposes, but on the other it's very important to display the right measure of human emotion. But she just can't.

Sunny day in the garden. Condolences calls and messages pour into the FCO.

Bringhurst School's OFSTED inspection is 'Good'.

The US have unhelpfully released the name of the Manchester culprit, who was a 22-year-old UK-born person of Libyan origin called Salman Abedi. Someone must have helped him make the bomb, which is thought to have had nuts and bolts in it. Trump has been so irresponsible. By releasing the name when our police might still be tracing Abedi's connections and links, he undermines our investigations.

A genius podcast about the Manchester bomb from Matt Chorley of the *Times*' Red Box, which reduced me to tears. Matt Chorley is a seriously talented comic and commentator: a really genuine person, and a contrast to many of his soulless fellow journalists. From that unusual background, he is morphing into one of our most acute and astute journalists. He is a Matthew Parris for a new generation.

James decides to stay, and go down on the train in the morning.

Wednesday 24 May – Rutland

The day after the day before. All campaigning is suspended, and it is just wall-to-wall news coverage on Manchester. There's something in me which says we are overdoing it, and it's all going to be so saturated that it risks losing its dignity.

The threat level has gone up to critical, which is the highest, and means that a further incident is expected. Supposedly at the behest of JTAC [the Joint Terrorism Analysis Committee] it smacks too of political angst on the part of the PM. And now we are putting 1,000 troops on the streets. Good pictures, but perhaps a tad OTT. They've arrested Abedi's brother. It was a sophisticated bomb, so there must be a whole network behind it. The US leaked Abedi's name, just when we were trying to keep it quiet while preparing further steps. It is totally irresponsible of them.

A nice chat with Ben Gummer. Unfortunately, once he was sucked into the inner circle to write much of the manifesto it rather went to his head. He is being fingered for the social care fiasco – I like him a lot, and these accusations are probably unfair.

As there's no campaigning, the garden beckons. It's a lovely sunny day, so it's on with the shorts and tee-shirt.

Thursday 25 May – Rutland

US intelligence have leaked lots of post-explosion photos to the *New York Times*, which has infuriated us here. It includes a close-up of the detonator, and nuts and bolts which were packed around the explosives. Just imagine if we were to do the same to them.

The PM has NATO in Brussels and then the G7 in Sicily, so it's both a diversion from the election trail and a Trumpfest.

I call someone who has sent a very articulate email resigning from the Party (he won't …) because of the collapse of collective Cabinet government and the unacceptable dominance of May's SpAds. Her stock, though, has been seriously diminished. The social care policy in the manifesto is backfiring massively, especially among our own supporters.

Sunday 28 May – Rutland
Papers not good for May. Her standing is seriously dented. Matt Chorley has as good as said that the Empress has no clothes. Her advisers, especially Nick Timothy, are now not just disliked by ministers, but are seriously despised by Conservatives who do not like government by a clique. Someone is quoted in the *Sunday Times* saying, 'Timothy will go down in history as the person who cost us the landslide.' As of today, that's exactly how it feels.

Monday 29 May – Rutland
My Whip David Evennett calls for a stocktake chat, and I make it clear that I think we are on the skids.

Wednesday 31 May – Rutland
TV debate meant for the seven party leaders, but with the PM and Sturgeon sending substitutes, the line-up was: Amber Rudd (Conservative), Angus Robertson (SNP), Jeremy Corbyn (Labour), Tim Farron (Lib Dem), Leanne Wood (Plaid Cymru), Caroline Lucas (Green), Paul 'Nutty' Nuttall (UKIP).

May facing massive criticism for not participating, but she didn't miss much. With so many participants it was a scrappy affair, and added very little in the way of edifying national debate. My PPS Pauline Latham texts to say she is pessimistic about how things are going overall – I rather agree with her.

Thursday 1 June – Rutland

To Oakham with Noodle to meet a BBC TV camera. *East Midlands Today* are profiling Noodle as the most attractive political asset in the region. So true!

Theresa is in Derby for an early-evening rally, but there's a complete lack of excitement around her and the campaign. The trouble is that everything has curdled. The mood has turned against her personally, and Corbyn looks human and authentic. It's the political equivalent of Tories looking the other way when they see her in the street.

Friday 2 June – Rutland

I call Philip Hammond and leave a message saying that I was just calling to convey a dose of solidarity, and that I'm appalled that he is being briefed against by Number 10 as if heading for the sack. He texts back: 'Thanks for the call. Lots of undercurrents and not a little media boredom at work here. As you say, it will all come out in the wash! Meanwhile, five more days of visits to target seats in England and Scotland. See you back at the funny-farm in due course. Philip'.

For Fi Hill to be putting it about that there is a Chancellor short-list of Amber Rudd and Michael Fallon is inexcusable. Sky/BBC *Question Time* with May followed by Corbyn, just the two of them grilled separately. The two together would have been better, but she has refused any head-to-head encounter.

Saturday 3 June – Rutland

Houston, we have a problem. We started this election with a supposed lead of nearly 20 per cent. Anyone with a brain would expect this to be at worst halved, and for there to be wobbly moments, but it has been the most disastrous campaign imaginable.

Perhaps at the root of it is that we had it fixed in our mind that the simple message or context of 'May vs Corbyn, under the umbrella of Brexit' would prevail, and that nobody could contemplate Corbyn as PM. We have had an hermetically sealed campaign (with the emphasis on 'her') with only Fallon and Rudd allowed out. The trouble is, Corbyn has nothing to lose, and so he has opened up with seeming confidence and good rent-a-crowd photo ops. She has looked wooden and defensive, like a frightened rabbit, declining interviews and TV debates. We have engaged in the politics of personality – without any personality.

Candidates cannot so much as publish a 'Hello, it's me!' card without central approval, and the Stalinist control is backfiring badly. The public can see, and don't like, the presidential supremacy of it, and after the old-age care manifesto announcement, they can also see the malign influence of Fiona Hill and Nick Timothy, and don't like that at all. The most furious are Conservative supporters and activists, who despise the erosion of collective responsibility and Cabinet government.

Even worse, no doubt inspired by the poisonous Hill, is that before we have even won – or lost – the briefings are focussing on a pre-shuffle. In other words, Hammond is being briefed against, and is excluded from the campaign. It's all the more stupid, as the result is increasingly hanging on economic issues rather than Brexit. The latest report touts David Davis as Foreign Secretary to replace Boris. This is indulgent folly: if we don't win, and win well, all such talk is fantasy.

It is the worst campaign ever. Stupid idiots at the centre thinking they know it all, and telling those who are standing for election what to do. It is the wrong way round. It is the end of proper democratic politics.

Matthew Parris has a brilliant article in *The Times*, in which he says, 'This has been a stupid election and the British do not like stupid elections.' He concluded that he and millions of others would grit their teeth and vote Conservative because the alternative is unthinkable, but suggests that the collapse in confidence could fuel demands to rethink Brexit. I text him to say he is spot on. Theresa's stock is falling sharply while Corbyn's is rising. It is perilous that our own people have become so sulky about her ill-judged presidential pitch – they have too little to be enthusiastic about. It is the worst campaign I have ever known.

David Cameron texts me. He asks whether I think it's all still going to be OK. His guess is we'll end up with a majority of fifty-plus, but says it's been a 'very strange campaign – and very strange not to be in it!' I reply with my analysis – that it's all gone very sour, and that UKIP voters going back to Labour will deny us blue-collar marginals. I share with him my frustrations about the campaign and about the contemptible briefings from the PM's team about a post-election reshuffle. He says he bets Boris won't be moved, as 'she's scared of him'. He suggests we have a drink when it's all over.

I spend a couple of hours in Oakham with my rosette on. A nice response, but I sense there is a high degree of uncertainty and bewilderment.

Afternoon in the sunshine in the garden, popping inside to watch the Derby. The Queen is quite amazing in yellow, and loving every moment of it, at one point tapping one of her entourage on the wrist as if to say, 'Oh, don't be so cheeky.' Wings of Eagles won with the most amazing final sprint to the finish.

James is having a lovely time in Scotland, has been to Mull and Skye and is now sailing off Stornoway. He said the fish restaurant on Skye is stunningly good.

At 9.30pm the various polls give us a lead ranging across 1, 4, 6, 9 and 12 points. That looks pretty grim news to me. Average is 7, but there is no guarantee of consistency in the final results. It's going to be quite a results night with uneven patterns. But the broad prediction is that we stand only to have inched forward at best. It could be worse than that on the night. We might even lose some seats. Shit.

May's ploy, cooked up in isolation, looks as though it might turn out to be a catastrophe. We are chuntering on about Brexit, the IRA and Trident. Corbyn is promising the earth to carefully selected interest groups. We are rehashing old issues. It's the fucking economy, stupid, and we are talking a foreign language. Could it really be that her ill-prepared gamble will lead to the election of Jeremy Corbyn as Prime Minister? He's our Fidel Castro, and we'll end up like Venezuela.

Just watching the final of *Britain's Got Talent* when Sky report there's a serious incident on London Bridge, with all emergency services racing there in force. It looks as though a vehicle might have mown people down. Not again! The station has been closed, but that suggests something else. The reports of the last half an hour have talked about the incident, but nobody has yet said quite what the incident is.

Ed calls. He is also watching the news. Tweets suggest multiple injuries, and perhaps stabbings, but we just don't know.

Switch to the BBC, who are way ahead of Sky, and reporting an eyewitness who said that a white van had driven into five or six people, and that the police response took a mere three minutes. Police Twitter saying they have armed police at London Bridge and Borough Market. All will become clear soon.

Sunday 4 June – Rutland

Switch on the TV at 6am. Three men had driven a white van through pedestrians on London Bridge, then drove to Borough Market round the corner and started stabbing people. Six are dead. The police were indeed on the scene within three minutes, and shot the three attackers dead within eight. Heavily masked police squads are now trawling through Borough Market carrying enough kit to win a small war. The death toll is now that seven have died, plus the culprits, and forty-eight are in hospital.

To the Rutland County Show. The new showground is brilliant, and the show itself now quite sizeable, with lots of stalls, a wonderful display of livestock and thousands of people. I follow the spirit of this morning's announcement to suspend campaigning, and so do not wear a rosette, unlike my Lib Dem opponent – surprise, surprise. All the Rutland county set were at lunch, so just being there was sufficient.

William Hague phoned to ask how I thought it was going. I said I thought the PM was having an awful campaign, and that her stock has plummeted. We both agreed that Thursday's results will prove uneven and full of shocks and surprises. I said I thought we were more likely to face losses than gains.

Back home, of the thirty-eight still in hospital, twenty-eight are in a critical condition. The eight police had fired fifty rounds, and it looks as though they hit a member of the public. But outside Number 10 the PM has made a statement which feels very ill-judged: 'There is far too much tolerance of extremism in our country.' She is emotionally incompetent. Zero empathy.

It opens up the question of further legislation against extremism – a fatuous gesture at this juncture – and her whole demeanour is wooden and robotic. She is incapable of pathos and has no elementary acting skills, a contrast to Corbyn's folksy authenticity. She has unwittingly politicised the issue of security, and opened up her own record as Home Secretary to deeper scrutiny. The Sunday papers (first editions before the incident) are doing their level best to demonise Corbyn and promote her strongly, but why have we left it to them to present the argument for a Conservative government?

If she had confidence in herself, she would have invited Corbyn to share a platform with her after the shootings. Fat chance.

Ariana Grande and others give a most emotional benefit concert in Manchester – Justin Bieber, Coldplay, Liam Gallagher. Chris Martin of Coldplay is quite a hunk. Why have I never noticed him before? Fantastic event. Proud to be British. And I'm a bit pissed.

Monday 5 June – Rutland

The papers are wall-to-wall terrorism, countering extremism, arming the police, the PM's record as Home Secretary, etc. Corbyn says she should resign for having cut police numbers. It's all a tad undignified, and also stupid because policing is not just about numbers. I could double the number of armed police in five minutes by giving all coppers a holster and a pistol, but that wouldn't make our policing any better. Karen Bradley was weak on *Today*, but Met Commissioner Cressida Dick was superb. She is a highly intelligent-sounding police officer – a unique phenomenon.

A wet and windy day. Trump has stupidly, and then again for a second time despite the evidence, attacked Sadiq Khan on Twitter for saying that 'London should not be alarmed.' What Sadiq as Mayor in fact had said was that London should not be alarmed by an enhanced police presence on the streets. So to hell with Trump. Former DC adviser Steve Hilton has echoed Corbyn by saying that May should resign as PM. He is such a tosser. Oh, and what a surprise – he is about to start a new show on Fox TV. What a total wanker. Total, total, total.

Tuesday 6 June – Rutland

Unseasonal gales, which have taken half a tree down. Sadly it's the most beautifully shaped specimen tree with a circular bench beneath, which has fabulous copper leaves in the early autumn. Half of it has split off. The fork had an ancient crack down most of it, so the main centre had been hanging on by a thread for ages. Arboreal Darwinism.

To Melton market. In the manager's office I met my transgender Labour opponent and a fine array of farmers in tweed. I have been punctiliously cordial towards the Labour candidate and am pleased there have been no murmurs about her being transgender.

Diane Abbott, who is having a worse election than Theresa May, has been pulled off *Woman's Hour* at a few minutes' notice for being ill, and has been replaced by the patronising Emily Thornberry. I think she might be ill, as her last interview was punctuated with long pauses. In which case all should back off and leave her alone.

I remonstrate with Sam Coates who in *The Times* has promoted the need for Gove as a stabilising influence following the election. Gove is an unctuous freak who generates his own publicity, but he has a coterie and extensive support in the press, especially Rupert Murdoch personally. And his brazen wife works for the *Mail*. So we'd risk reverting to the politics of media cronyism, which will bring trouble for May, not salvation. Gove is a whacky weirdo who is both unappealing and untrustworthy. God help us if he is thought to be the answer to our woes. I can't imagine it would please Boris.

I mention to Sam that one of his lobby colleagues says that Fi Hill is a psychotic weirdo, but he can't write it because his stories would dry up. He knew immediately that I was talking about Tim Shipman. Very revealing, because Tim had previously told me about someone around Theresa resenting me getting so involved in the leadership campaign; so now it's clear it came from Hill. She's just the pits.

Wednesday 7 June – London

Train to London with Kurtis Christoforides, who's helping me during the campaign. As we arrived at St Pancras I stuck the *Daily Mail* into my bag and said, 'They've done a much better job for us than we have.' The dick sitting opposite me, a Nottingham leftie, then tweeted it.

Interview with Patrick Forbes for his BBC follow-up documentary.

Late birthday dinner at the Beefsteak, as a generous present from David Ross. Among the guests were Ian Burnett (High Court judge) and his wife, former staffers Andrew Smith and Salma Shah (now married), Wafic and Rosemary Saïd, Danny Dougramachi, James Perkins and my godson Ed Perkins, and needless to say William [Hague] – who gave an hilarious speech taking the piss out of me mercilessly, which I then tried to do in return, putting on a baseball cap and doing the usual impersonation. James and I thought it was one of the nicest dinners ever. It was lovely of Rosso to host it as he did.

Thursday 8 June – Rutland

General election day! Visit a few polling stations in the Vale of Belvoir, but as always on polling day there's nothing more to be done except wait for the verdict.

At 10pm the night starts with a shock. Totally disastrous exit poll suggests we will lose our working majority and only be the largest party. Although the SNP will go backwards in Scotland, we will do poorly in London and we stand to lose seventeen seats, while Labour will gain thirty-four.

If that's right, our credibility is shot. TM is toast. But it risks leaving an insoluble vacuum. It's down to the curse of Brexit and the failure on our part to advance a well-crafted narrative on the economy. This is a colossal disaster which will have thrown away three years of majority government. We might yet do better than the exit poll …

To my count. 4am declaration, announces my biggest majority and share of the vote ever. Con 36,169 (62.8 per cent), Lab 13,065

(22.7 per cent), Lib Dem 4,711 (8.2 per cent), UKIP 1,869 (3.2 per cent), Green 1,755 (3.0 per cent). Turnout 73.4 per cent. Increased share by 7.2 per cent. Majority 23,104.

In the course of the night the grim news continues: Amber Rudd might lose in Hastings. Ben Gummer loses in Ipswich. Other casualties could be Simon Kirby and Brandon Lewis. But, oddly, some swings in the north, Sunderland/Newcastle, are a few from Lab to Con, and Scotland look as though it has shifted a little from the SNP.

But overall it feels like a total disaster. We're heading for a hung Parliament!

Friday 9 June – Rutland

We have gone seriously backwards, losing thirty-three seats, but gaining well in Scotland, which compensates a little. We are the largest party and, when combined with the DUP, will just have a technical majority in the Commons.

Despite my initial enthusiasm for her decision to call the election, it soon became clear that the PM has zero campaigning zeal, and wasn't going to fight it. She hid. And by the last fortnight anyone with good antennae could sense that we were losing it. We were going backwards and had forfeited our potential advantage. It was all to play for: but she failed to play.

Final seat tally: Con 317, Labour 262, SNP 35, Lib Dem 12, DUP 10, Sinn Fein 7, Plaid 4, Green 1. We're nearly ten short of an overall majority, and so can only cling on to govern with the help of the DUP, God help us.

Despite all the snide briefing, the top layer of the Cabinet is reappointed: Johnson, Hammond, Rudd, Davis, Fallon. We'll soon see if there's any churn among junior ministers.

PM's statement outside Number 10 was awful – utterly tone deaf, and sounding like she had just won a convincing majority, rather than been humiliated by losing one!

Saturday 10 June – Rutland

Spoke to Tom Tugendhat. Told him to button it. He'd been pontificating against any cooperation with the DUP because they don't support equal marriage etc. Well, I've got views on equal marriage, but I've also got views on the need to form a government for the greater good of the country. He's been in Parliament for two minutes and he thinks his judgement carries importance and weight.

Oh dear. There are rumours that Gove might come back in.

Rather better news is that Hill and Timothy are under massive pressure to go, and … yippee! Finally they do. Their high-handed tyrannical self-importance has destroyed the government's majority and may well destroy her too. It seems that donor pressure has been ferocious, blaming the SpAds much more than the PM for the Party going backwards.

Mail on Sunday splashes that Boris is going to challenge the PM. I text his SpAd Liam Parker to give a ferocious rocket. The Boris coverage totally backfires, although apparently TM had to be persuaded not to resign.

Sunday 11 June – Rutland

Osborne sticks the knife in on *Marr*, saying, 'Theresa May is a dead woman walking, it's just [a matter of] how long she's going to remain on death row.'

The papers are uniformly dreadful – Boris being urged to topple May; 'May's premiership in peril'; and perhaps most damningly, in the *Sunday Telegraph*, 'In office, but not in power'.

While driving down to London, have a long chat with Hammond: and a short one with David Davis.

Hammond and I totally agree on the dangers of a hard exit. His account of dealing with the PM through the ghastly Fiona Hill is damning. The PM was told nothing beyond what she and Nick Timothy let her see. We have to stick with her, but she is a cardboard cut-out. Philip and I will talk regularly. He thinks that a soft Brexit could be concluded within a year, and if we face down the extremists in our own Party we could get it through the Commons, or at least in theory we could, but Labour will be playing hard politics by then and the country will come second.

It is also clear that such is the level of distrust between Boris and Number 10 that he is being excluded from things he has a right to know. It all stems from how he is perceived politically in the UK. He is seen to be in it for himself and has no real understanding of the details of Brexit. Philip says the manifesto should never have been eighty pages of detail: it should have been eight pages of broad direction, and nothing more. I so agree.

Boris posts a seven-point defence of the PM on the Conservative MPs' WhatsApp group, and then releases it to the press:

Folks we need to calm down and get behind the prime minister.

1. She won more votes than anyone since Margaret Thatcher
2. I can't remember us having anything like 43 per cent of the vote
3. We have got to stop the narrative that Corbyn somehow won this thing – he barely did better than Gordon useless Brown when we beat him in 2010
4. We must get on and deliver for the people of this country – including a great Brexit deal
5. We must not allow the media to spread mischief not least because the public are fed up to the back teeth of politics and politicians and they certainly DO NOT want another election
6. Yes of course we need to think about the lessons of this election but not in the papers
7. The PM is a woman of extraordinary qualities and frankly the public are looking to us to get behind her with discipline and determination
8. On with the job!

This is so disingenuous. The Party will never have him if he behaves like this.

Journalist Ian Birrell tweets that EU diplomats have told him that Article 50 can be rescinded as the UK only leaves the EU when it signs an exit deal. Hmm. Not so sure. She can't just do it through the Royal Prerogative now that it has been activated through legislation.

Reshuffle frenzy. I follow the news ribbons as rumours and facts unfold. James Brokenshire is thought to be staying in Northern Ireland, as it is known he is about to fly to Dublin. Damian Green is First Secretary of State and Minister at the Cabinet Office. Greg Clark to stay at Biz, Energy & Industrial Strategy. David Gauke to Work and Pensions. Liz Truss Chief Secretary to the Treasury, an absurdly weak and useless appointment. Liam Fox stays at Trade. Justine Greening stays at Education, and also Women and Equality. Sajid Javid stays at Communities & Local Government. David Lidington to be Justice Secretary and Lord Chancellor. Alun Cairns Wales. Jeremy Hunt stays at Health. Gavin Williamson stays as Chief Whip. Chris Grayling stays at Transport. Priti Patel stays at DfID. Karen Bradley DCMS.

Brandon Lewis possibly Chairman? Which would be good on organisation, but no good on political presentation or donors. And Gove is coming to Number 10. So totally ghastly. I want to puke. But still no Leadsom announcement.

Later:

Very odd. Andrea Leadsom is to be Leader of the House. Mad. So surely not Gove as Chairman … in charge of donors, and candidates??? Please, please, please no. Phew! Gove is Environment Secretary, and PatMac to remain as Chairman. Brandon Minister of State in the Home Office, attending Cabinet. Jeremy Wright still Attorney General.

So the simple outcome is that nobody has been sacked, there has been a minor redistribution, and the unctuous Gove comes in as Gummer goes out. It is quite the most unimpressive Cabinet imaginable. They are all just there: but what are they actually going to do? The trouble is, it looks as though we are on the run.

This is the shuffle that wasn't. It's like a crowd of zombies, aimlessly circling.

Monday 12 June – London

Day one of the Government of the Walking Dead. It is just a depressing picture of drift. May has lost all authority and control. A Cabinet with too many weirdos in it now enjoys more dominance. War is simmering over the nature of Brexit, reinforcing, thank goodness, the power of the softer option. The manifesto has all but been ripped up. We are dependent on the DUP, and will face massive difficulty getting any EU legislation at all through the Commons. Pygmies in Lilliput now govern us.

As I wanted, I am to remain in the FCO. But I'm told Ellwood is out. There might be other ministers, maybe with responsibilities linked with DfID. Boris has invited the cameras into the FCO tomorrow.

Take Matt Hancock to lunch at the Beefsteak. Good natter. I tell him just how awful Fi Hill was during the leadership election, especially when she flared up at me for speaking to Jeremy Heywood. Big burly journalist Bruce Anderson there. Also Andrew Gifford, who said I should be caretaker PM for two years. An enticing fantasy option!

The Cabinet meeting takes more than two hours. Then at 5pm the PM addresses the 1922 Committee meeting, somehow rising above the underlying mood, which has turned understandably sullen as the plight of lost colleagues and the bigger lost opportunity begin to sink in. She made a half-hearted apology for the election result.

The Chief [Whip] calls at 9.30pm to confirm my reappointment as FCO Minister. He knows Ellwood has been a catastrophe, but would not let on quite what else might happen in the FCO line-up.

Tuesday 13 June – London

All-staff meeting in the Durbar Court, with its awful acoustics. It's a critical moment, and BoJo offers little more than a rambling stream of consciousness, devoid of any foreign policy. It's rather embarrassing.

As Ellwood departs (we now know), we are to be joined by Alistair Burt and Rory Stewart, both of whom will be double-hatted with DfID. It's the wrong answer to the right question: how do you better align the focus of the two departments, only one of which has the money? I guess Burt will do the Middle East and Rory Africa. But the geographical allocation between FCO and DfID won't be contiguous.

Re-election of Speaker Hobbit. See the surgeon about my knee, and agree just to get it done next Tuesday. Reception for the Falkland Islands at Middle Temple. Then 1922 drinks at 1 Great George St.

Wednesday 14 June – London

Fire has engulfed a high-rise block of flats in Kensington. We awoke to TV footage of smoke and flames billowing throughout all the floors. It's an utterly horrific inferno, with the entire outer shell aflame. I hope people managed to get out, otherwise the death toll will be enormous.

Swearing-in of Members. Tim Farron resigns as Leader of the Lib Dems.

A day of non-stop FCO meetings, allocating portfolios and priorities. Tobias Ellwood is to become the Minister for Veterans at the MoD.

During all the goings-on Graham Brady as Chairman of the '22 has behaved very well and calmed things down rather than stirred them up. He will matter more now we've lost our majority. I write a supportive letter to Gavin Barwell, who lost his Croydon seat and is now the PM's new Chief of Staff. I include in it a suggestion that she should make Brady a Privy Counsellor.

Thursday 15 June – London

Hopeless visit by May to Grenfell Tower. The day after so many people died, most of them immigrants, she just stood there expressionless, and avoided any human interaction with anybody affected. It was painful to watch such a characterless display of robotic lack of emotion.

The Fire Service had told residents to stay put, expecting the fire to be contained in perhaps a few flats on one floor, yet the cladding on the outside of the building rapidly engulfed the entire building in smoke and flames.

Lunch at Wilton's with Erik. Further Brexit discussion in the FCO. I say to David Frost, Boris' SpAd for Europe, 'We beat them all on the battlefield, now they'll trounce us in the conference room.' Though he is likeable, I'm not sure he has the clout to fight our corner.

Call with John Sullivan, my counterpart in the State Department. He doesn't seem to travel anywhere.

Friday 16 June – Rutland

Fire anger mounts. Theresa May goes back to Grenfell Tower. The government response is lame. Protesters take over Kensington & Chelsea Town Hall.

Association drinks at Goadby Hall to celebrate my twenty-five years as the local MP. Hosted by Harry and Vicki Westropp. Harry is one of my local Association stars – amusing, unflappable and elegant, he was at Lazard's with Andrew Mitchell and he often entertains me with accounts of Mitch as a young banker. As a senior figure in the constituency Association, he is a welcome contrast to the dastardly Duchess.

Sunday 18 June – Rutland

Non-stop reaction and fury about the Grenfell Tower fire. The Sunday press is writing her off. I speak to Damian Green about our plight – he is supposed to be her number two but is rather ineffectual.

Monday 19 June – London

Someone has driven into a group of Muslims leaving the Finsbury Park Mosque. Please – not another one.

Brexit talks start today. I'm not brimming with optimism. We start from a worrying position of weakness and disarray. As I enter through the back gate of Number 10, Hammond walks straight past me without even saying hello. Again. His problem is that he's just not very user-friendly.

Speak to Mitch who, as his erstwhile leadership campaign manager, insists DD is not on manoeuvres. BoJo calls from Brussels, saying 'we must speak regularly'. So that must mean that he is on manoeuvres. But at least he called.

A colleague says Andrea Leadsom is blatantly revving up her putative leadership team, and went to the Grenfell Tower for no other reason than to promote herself.

Tuesday 20 June – London
Knee operation King Edward VII Hospital. Arrived at 8am. They knocked me out at 11am, and I was awake again and sprightly by about 12.30. All very slick, and James picked me up at 6.30pm. Quite amazing really. Just hope it does the trick.

Wednesday 21 June – London
King Salman of Saudi Arabia has sacked his nephew Mohammed bin Nayef as Crown Prince, and replaced him with his own younger son, the 31-year-old raging bull Mohammed bin Salman. Although an energetic moderniser, he is also bombing Yemen to bits and is massively controversial. It could all go horribly wrong.

The *Telegraph* has run a pre-documentary piece which takes a quote by me rather out of context suggesting I have publicly told Boris Johnson to 'stop playing games' in respect of any future leadership race. It is of course semantic exaggeration, but he phones at 8am to suggest I pen a letter to the *Daily Telegraph* to correct the record. It is an absurd suggestion, as it will only give the issue more legs. It is only on page 7, at the bottom, and is so obviously a teaser for tonight's documentary. He loves double-page spreads puffing him up, but is over-sensitive and loses all perspective when he faces an inch of adverse comment.

I was due to be announced by him in the FCO as the 'Senior Minister of State', but he has binned the idea following the *Telegraph* story. So petty. A poor reflection on him, and not a clever way of handling me. He is an egotistical showman who just doesn't understand Parliament, or how to run and motivate a team around him.

I dial into his first ministerial meeting with the new team, preferring to stay at home the day after my knee surgery. It is perfectly good-natured, albeit just a rather shallow *tour d'horizon*.

I watch on TV as HM arrives by car for the State Opening. I'd love to be at the Commons, but remain at home to recover. As Trooping the Colour was only last Saturday, and today's Opening was at short notice, the ceremony has been much reduced. HM is accompanied by the Prince of Wales, as it turns out that the Duke of Edinburgh arrived at King Edward VII Hospital soon after I left it yesterday. We all hope he's OK. The last sentence of the Queen's Speech is always about the wisdom of God resting on our counsels – or some such – to which she might amusingly have added 'and on the 2.40 at Ascot'.

Richard Benyon and Kwasi Kwarteng move and second the Loyal Address, Richard rather better than Kwasi. The speeches are marked by a minute's silence to remember the four recent tragedies: the Manchester suicide bomb, the London Bridge stabbings, the Grenfell Tower inferno and the mowing down of Ramadan worshippers outside the Finsbury Park Mosque.

Oman Ambassador Abdulaziz comes to see me. General chat about FCO moves and responsibilities. He and I both lament the fall in the UK's overall reputation internationally, compounded now by having a weak government. The Saudis, Emiratis and Bahrainis have for two weeks now boycotted and nearly blockaded Qatar for their supposed support for extremists. The Turks have committed troops to Qatar and signed a defence pact, and the Iranians and the Russians are aligning with them. This presents a potentially cataclysmic stand-off within and around the GCC with us not even beginning to think about where we would stand on it all.

Brexit documentary on BBC2. Too much Andrew Bridgen, and less good than the first one.

Monday 26 June – London

Breakfast with Boris at the Travellers. It's a nice gesture, but we've been working together for a year, and although we get on well it takes a lot of effort to get him to focus on FCO stuff rather than Brexit.

To have him pinned down for an hour allowed us a rare opportunity to cover a lot of ground.

I say I'm longing to get the Party off its Brexit-only diet and return to the politics of left vs right. It would be a much better dividing line for him personally. We speculate on whether the Party can get through anything very much when the parliamentary arithmetic is now so perilous. He says we can make a great success of Brexit, but it's going to be difficult when we can't even get our bills through Parliament. But we do both agree that TM has no charisma.

Boris says Fi Hill had exploded about my proposal to honour our contract to deliver the Argentina cogwheel, an issue she knows nothing about. They paid years ago for a spare part for a non-armed ship, which we have never since supplied, even though it's packed and ready in a warehouse. As part of the diplomatic reset I am carefully negotiating with them, I want now to authorise the delivery of the part in order to win benefits for the Falklands. But Fi Hill is deranged and, just because it's Argentina, insists we should not. If she has some reasons for it, fine – give me a call, but don't just blow up and shout and scream.

We both speculated – will Hammond and David Davis form an alliance? We both agreed not, and could DD ever hack it anyway? No. I say a leadership contest would risk total meltdown. We briefly covered Middle East issues. Having first gone to Yemen thirty years ago, and with experience of business, DfID and being an envoy there, I told Boris that the expertise in the Foreign Office is so thin the UK is seriously underperforming in using its historic influence. I explain why double-hatting DfID/FCO ministers is the wrong answer to the right question. At its simplest, if you don't change the law on our 0.7 per cent spending commitment, there is no way you can divert development money into broader FCO spending.

I say he should think more about social policy – the EU immigration issue has allowed us to blame it for everything, and ignore deep social decay in the UK – skills, family breakdown, urban poverty, unequal education and economic prospects, all issues on which he could be a distinctive and effective champion.

Sit on the front bench for much of the evening for the Queen's Speech debate.

Tuesday 27 June – Geneva

To Geneva with Boris for the beginning of the UN-sponsored talks on Cyprus. Parliamentary votes permitting, we are due to be holed up in the Crans Montana mountain resort for as long as it takes to try and solve the decades-long split on the island of Cyprus between the majority Greek Cypriots and the Turks in the north. All the participants are due to be there from Cyprus itself, Greece and Turkey, along with the UN and the UK.

Hammond has made a speech in Germany in which he mocks Boris. In a caustic reference to Boris having said we can 'have our cake and eat it' in relation to Brexit, he says he wants to discourage colleagues from talking about cake. Ha ha.

Wednesday 28 June – Geneva/London

As always with international talks, they start slowly with participants setting out their stall. After two days of everyone doing this … at length, I chopper to Geneva with Boris and fly back to London, where in our first main test of parliamentary arithmetic we win the vote on the Queen's Speech by fourteen.

Thursday 29 June – London

Meeting for ministers of state at Number 10 with Gavin Barwell. These group movements are always pretty pointless. We sit there and listen to platitudinous homilies and all sorts of nonsense about how a streamlined Downing Street will work better with ministers. It's all total guff.

Ministerial team meeting at the FCO. Boris says that as we won by fourteen votes last night we can get Brexit through, no problem. I point out that a vote on the Queen's Speech is much easier than a million amendments on Brexit, which will drag on for two years. His optimism is delusional.

I try to steer the meeting towards proper FCO business. I say we need to form a view on the Qatar crisis, where they're being ostracised by the rest of the Gulf (except Oman). I say Saudi and the Emirates are behaving like two bullies smashing up an errant schoolboy in the playground. Boris says he'll try to get there for a visit.

Friday 30 June – London/Geneva
Back to Geneva. Millions of meetings, but insufficient progress.

António Guterres has arrived and gives a brilliant *tour d'horizon* to all the principals over dinner. It contains all of the history of the Cyprus dispute and the sticking points, along with possible solutions. It was the perfect foundation for a proper grown-up discussion, but sadly it deteriorated into petty nitpicking.

Tuesday 4 July – London/Geneva
Having nipped back to London for votes, I've spent the last two days trying to get the Whips' permission to return to Geneva. Eventually Chris Pincher, the Pairing Whip, phones and most helpfully confirms I can, so the office leaps into action and books me and Lance on to the 3pm flight.

The Grenfell Tower catastrophe drags on and on. There is a horrible mood of recrimination, with talk of a judge-led inquiry, possible prosecutions, and shambles over rehousing of the survivors. It just keeps on going, has all but destroyed the reputation of Kensington and Chelsea Council, and probably also much Conservative support in London.

May's popularity has plummeted and Parliament is increasingly jittery. Some Cabinet ministers have been mouthing off about spending and the need to end 'austerity'. Their panicky calls are balanced by a sensible article by William Hague in the *Daily Telegraph* about taxing the young less, but without mimicking Corbyn on spending.

Wednesday 5 July – Geneva
Lovely day. Breakfast on the Guarda Golf Hotel terrace in glorious sunshine with a view of the snow-capped mountains, during which Bob Wigley, Chairman of UK Finance, calls asking me to help secure his attendance at the planned David Davis meeting at Chevening on

the economic consequences of Brexit. What could be more ridiculous than not inviting the principal representative of the UK financial sector to a meeting like that?

The Cyprus talks go on intensively, but without a breakthrough. We discuss with Number 10 whether parachuting the PM into them would successfully force the progress we need. Understandably, she wants to help, but only if it's to bank success, not to walk into failure.

It turns out that Boris has been taking calls from Kotzias, and so effectively making Kotzias think he has a backchannel. Very unhelpful. It means anything we say is immediately second-guessed and played by the Greeks. All the more so as Kotzias' backchannel doesn't feed anything back to us! With Boris in London and us unaware of the calls, it's a troubling complication.

Thursday 6 July – Geneva

António Guterres arrives fresh (or possibly not so fresh) from New York. He chairs a plenary session at 11am with the main players, each plus one official. So it's the UN, EU as observers, Greek Cypriots, Turkish Cypriots, Greeks, Turks and the UK. António proposes that they all treat him as a trusted recipient of their full proposals and flexibility, and that he will see all four in sequence in the course of the morning. We see him just before lunch, and he lets us know in confidence that he thinks the Turks might offer to annul their Treaty right to intervene militarily to protect the Turkish Cypriots in the north. This would be a massive concession, and would deliver the Greek Cypriots' main demand. The Greeks also want the removal of all Turkish troops, albeit 650 are legally permitted to be there under the Treaty of Alliance, as distinct from the Treaty of Guarantee.

After five hours, over dinner and subsequent exchanges, including Vice-President Pence calling the two Cypriot leaders, it all disintegrates into a childish shouting match and the talks collapse – a tragic missed opportunity to resolve the long-running dispute. Our hard-working, professional team are disconsolate, most of all our High Commissioner to Cyprus, Matthew Kidd.

Monday 10 July – London

Drink with Kim Darroch. Always a joy to get his Washington download.

To Lancaster House to host a reception for the new batch of Kennedy Scholars ahead of their departure to the US. Set up after the assassination of J. F. Kennedy, it is like a reverse Rhodes Scholarship which funds a few UK students each year to go to Harvard. One of them, Dr Adam Hunt, was particularly impressive. Also there was Richard Moore, who like me is himself a former scholar. In my speech I urge them to use their time to travel across the US as much as possible. Among the guests is a DfID humanitarian figure who absolutely hates Priti Patel and insists the feeling is widely shared.

We have to hang around the Commons for a vote that never happens. For the first time ever in my experience, the PM appears in the Smoking Room to socialise and have a drink. But as usual she says almost nothing.

Tuesday 11 July – London

FCO Orals. Boris taunted Emily Thornberry by suggesting that Corbyn agrees with the thrust of our Brexit position, which he probably does. I used a question on Venezuela to highlight Corbyn's support for the regime there, and compared him to Fidel Castro, which was rather satisfying.

Wednesday 12 July – London

Ceremonial arrival on Horse Guards of the King and Queen of Spain for their State Visit.

I then attend the King's address to Parliament, after which I spoke to Corbyn. I've always got on rather well with him, and he's perfectly cordial and approachable, but there's no oomph of any sort. He uses an out-of-date leftie script that just goes round in a loop.

Most of the Royals were at the State Banquet tonight at Buckingham Palace. As is customary for a State Visit, each side confers their orders and decorations on the other, so there were proud Spaniards wearing CMGs and KCMGs, and UK officials in some very bright Spanish ribbons. The Duke of York was hilarious in his account of an error that was once made when Prince Philip stepped out in Belgium with the wrong sash across his waistcoat – it wasn't Belgium, it was the Belgian Congo! True or not, it was an entertaining yarn.

Friday 14 July – Sofia/Rutland

In Sofia. While visiting Bulgarian government figures, I just miss, so once again fail to connect with, HMS *Duncan*, the Type 45 frigate named after my not quite ancestor Admiral Duncan. I'm longing to go on board and leave behind some tartan or some memento. The MoD would be delighted, but my schedule never quite fits theirs. I will keep on trying.

My good friend and Oxford contemporary Ian Burnett is announced as the next Lord Chief Justice. At Oxford we always called him 'the Judge' and they always called me 'Prime Minister', but Ian's the one who's got there.

Sunday 16 July – Rutland/London

Awful press attacks on Hammond for his reported comments in Cabinet about public sector workers being overpaid compared with the private sector. Predictable backlash, but he's not exactly wrong.

Monday 17 July – London

JMC(GEN), the committee for general matters relating to Brexit, in this case the Joint Ministerial Committee on Gibraltar. DExEU minister Robin Walker, an all-round good bloke, chairs it very well albeit just reading from the script in his folder. Fabian Picardo is a highly capable Chief Minister of Gibraltar and heads a very thorough team. They seem far better versed in the complexities of Brexit than the government. Meet afterwards with Fabian and Mark Lancaster, so they can converse properly and discuss the application of the Armed Forces Act to MoD personnel in Gib.

Get briefed by two excellent officials on FCO finances. The undeniable problem is that the FCO is being asked to do too much with too little, and we just can't go on like this.

A formal letter from Boris arrives confirming my new ministerial responsibilities. Of course it's written entirely by the PUS. But it ends with a list of priority areas for the next two years and the expectation that 'In most of these areas I expect I will take the lead but that the outcomes will be delivered collaboratively between me and you in your areas of responsibility.' This last sentence, as with all ministers and their Secretary of State, roughly translates as 'You do the work, and I take the credit.'

Wednesday 19 July – London
Breakfast with Mohammed Mahfoudh al Ardhi of Investcorp. He's having coffee with David Cameron later, and lunch with Shaukat Aziz, the former Prime Minister of Pakistan who was my banker when I was supplying oil there twenty-five years ago.

Lunch at Le Gavroche with Sir Christopher Geidt, the Queen's Private Secretary. Should he ever move on from his current role, I would like to think we would make him a senior ambassador somewhere. After all, he came from the FCO in the first place.

Attend the PM's reception in the garden of Number 10 to celebrate the LGBT+ community, and give an interview to Mike Cowan for the *Victoria Derbyshire* show on what it meant to be the first Tory MP to come out.

Debate in the House to give an update on preparations for the Sanctions Bill. Robin Walker opens; I wind up. Various complaints about 'Where is the Bill?', but with the election intervening, it simply isn't ready yet. Awkward slip-up when I said Kemi Badenoch's constituents had 'rabidly' taken her to their hearts rather than 'rapidly'. Much amusement. I also noted that I was disappointed that with the retirement of her predecessor, Sir Alan Haselhurst, the population of Sir Alans in the House has reduced.

Thursday 20 July – London
Meeting with Gavin Barwell first thing.

Phone call with Edward Lister, the other non-exec on the FCO board.

To the Surrey home of General Sultan al Numani, head of the

Omani Royal Office. He is recovering from an operation on his back. We get on extremely well and are able to cover a lot of ground. The PM's call to the Sultan took precedence over Trump's, who had twenty-eight minutes on the phone two days ago.

Monday 25 July – Majorca

Having a week in Majorca with James. Dinner with Ian Taylor, who by chance is also on the island. Tomorrow we're all having lunch with James and Beatrice Lupton at La Fortaleza, Pollensa, their amazing fortress house which was used as the film set for *The Night Manager*.

Tuesday 15 August – London/Istanbul

DD has published a paper on a post-Brexit, or transition, customs regime. It is fanciful. The whole Brexit case rests on so many falsities and unjustifiable assumptions. Go ahead and do it – fine. But don't be dishonest about its detrimental consequences.

To Istanbul on the worst imaginable flight, with crying babies and squeaking computer games. Ugh!

Stay in the Pera Hotel, which smacks of past grandeur, and rests its reputation on being where Agatha Christie used to stay. Judith Slater is the Consul General and, as we attempt a nightcap on the terrace, the heavens open and we are soaked.

Saturday 26 August – Wales

To William and Ffion in Wales. The Hague property is being turned into a beautiful estate – they are showing extraordinary creativity in restoring and landscaping the grounds, while tastefully remodelling the house itself. The library he has built deserves a design award, and would dignify any Oxford college.

Sunday 27 August – Wales

Over the summer I've pieced together the outline of two or three speeches or articles, encapsulating my thinking on where we are with Brexit and a number of other issues. It's a useful intellectual exercise and an outlet for my frustrations, despite the fact I wouldn't actually be able to publish them. At least not while I'm a minister.

Brexit

In trying to resolve Brexit, we risk retreating into a world of make-believe. In an effort to soothe our nation's post-imperial hurt pride, we are trying to return to a world that no longer exists. There is no such option as a pain-free exit, so we should either admit that pain, or abandon Brexit altogether.

There may have been a referendum, but the simplicity of the question does not mean that all the details have been decided, or indeed that it is an easy matter. It is very complicated.

The origin of all this was an attempt to buy off UKIP – an unforgivably short-term ploy that turned out to be David Cameron's huge mistake. The campaign was then conducted disgracefully – with the lies about the NHS on the side of the bus and the whole thing framed by Leave as about taking back control of Parliament and immigration. The arguments and the politics were far from enlightened, and in the eyes of many were deceitful and vulgar.

The referendum has now given an instruction, but it was for a concept, not a detailed contract. It's like buying a house – you might be attracted by the pictures, but you still need to go and view it and get a survey done before you sign on the dotted line. It was not a conclusive result, and the divisions unleashed have compounded the problems we face, not solved them.

As the issues become more clear and the tidiness of the outcome less so, it is quite possible that now, a year later, a majority of voters wish that we had not voted to leave, and might now wish to remain. Therefore, those advocating 'just get on with it' are in a land of fantasy, given the binary division in the country. They need to appreciate its tectonic characteristics and admit the full implications. The Leavers deceived people to win the referendum, and continue to delude themselves now.

The economic cost is becoming more obvious: most international businesses with an interest in Britain are crunching their gears into reverse. Meanwhile the political cost is undeniable. We are consumed by Brexit and will be for years to come. Government is paralysed, while at home and abroad we are increasingly despised and written off. It is becoming a slowly-unfolding catastrophe.

Negotiations are not going well, and while the vision outlined by some has been of a Global Britain trading freely, the reality of securing free-trade agreements is that there will be huge obstacles and further pain to come. And after our exit we will not be around the political table – something not to be dismissed lightly. While we focus on a self-indulgent internal debate, all that matters ultimately is the negotiation with the EU. And what about Gibraltar, Northern Ireland, fishing? And Scotland? These real-world issues cannot be solved by appealing to nationalistic sentiment and by shouting louder. We are diminishing ourselves to satisfy an indulgent fantasy.

The Conservative Party has been infected by 'Marxism of the Right', a neo-con delusion which misunderstands the state of the world. Across the EU in modern times, Spain and Portugal emerged from fascism, while other countries have emerged from communism. International politics and economics are more co-operative and interdependent. History moves on. *Tempora mutantur, nos et mutamur in illis* – 'Times change, and we change with them.' But so many of the Brexiteers have not and don't.

They are backward-looking, and we are now betraying future generations in order to indulge the blimpish grumps of the old who voted Leave. MPs are there to lead, not to follow; 500 of us voted to remain, yet we are told we cannot question the wisdom of the course we are now following. We face a choice: we can be united and join with our fellow lemmings in leaping off the white cliffs of Dover, or we can shout (to mix a metaphor) that the Brexit Emperor has no clothes.

Changing course would unleash fresh horrors – we can't abandon Brexit without imperilling the government and our party. But if we don't abandon Brexit, we imperil the country. The Conservative Party I joined was not one that tried to save itself at the expense of our country.

I've no wish to harm my own Party, the Government or especially the PM, and I know that the first casualty of this cri de

coeur will be my career. But a dutiful politician should never risk
destroying their country in order to save themselves. The
country must come first.

That's what I really think – if only I could persuade, but I can't. Oh,
shitty shitty bang bang!

Tuesday 29 August – London/Astana

Our house in London is looking rather bare. The great post-flood
building project has begun!

There is a Rachel Sylvester article in *The Times* tagging Boris as an
'international joke' and citing civil servants and 'one well-travelled
Tory MP' who is quoted as saying, 'He is undermining our ability to
negotiate internationally and degrading our position abroad. The
foreign secretary is supposed to enhance Britain's reputation but all
over the world Boris is making matters worse.'

It also reports that 'civil servants in the Foreign Office are horrified
by their boss's lack of discipline and have taken to slipping in to see
his deputy Sir Alan Duncan, the Europe minister, when they need a
decision'.

Boris calls. He wants to see me.

We discuss the article, and Brexit. For the first time ever, we have
something of a stand-up confrontation. He has completely popped
and accuses me of briefing it, which I hadn't. He says, 'Why do you
say they don't take me seriously?' I shake my head and say, 'Just look
in the fucking mirror!'

While I was not the source – it could have been any number
of people, and was probably an amalgamation of lots of comments
– it was pretty accurate. He's always larking about and loves
the publicity, but as soon as it turns on him he's amazingly thin-
skinned.

Lunch at Wilton's with Woody Johnson, the new US Ambassador.
He'd love the Queen to open their new embassy, probably early next
year.

Wednesday 30 August – Astana

Overnight flight to Kazakhstan, where I'm greeted by our eccentric but splendid Ambassador Carolyn Browne. I go around Astana on the top of a London bus, posing for photos at the main landmarks, and following a couple of interviews address all the embassy staff.

After lunch with the Foreign Minister, Kairat Abdrakhmanov, I have an extensive tour of the Expo pavilions. Charles Hendry, former MP colleague and the best Energy Minister we ever had, has been nothing short of genius in assisting the UK's efforts and our own contribution to the Expo, and has won widespread praise and recognition. It has planted our flag firmly in all Central Asian markets.

After phoning James to wish him happy birthday, I attended a reception with civil society figures at the residence. It was a perfectly nice occasion, though a little disconcerting to have someone faint in the middle of my speech and crash with a thud on to the wooden floor.

Steven Swinford of the *Telegraph* calls. The PM is in Japan, but they have an embargoed statement in which she says that she will stay and fight the next election. All such comments are double-edged; they are trying to establish certainty but are a response to vulnerability. The Davis camp had been putting it about that she had marked the summer of 2019 for her departure, and this was becoming the accepted wisdom. But by saying she will stay, it acknowledges the pressure and will also prompt accusations that a longer tenure and her fighting the next election are simply not credible.

Friday 1 September – Rutland

Lunch and meeting at Belvoir Lodge, home of the haughty and tiresome Frances, Duchess of Rutland (the Dowager). She is of a world which thinks that because you have a title you can boss someone around. And worse, that her snotty nasty opinions are the only ones that matter. Why am I so tolerant of her unmerited superiority?

Hurricane Irma is beginning to thrash the Caribbean, and the forecasts for its growing ferocity are rather startling. The threat to thousands of poor people in the Caribbean matters much more to me than lunch with this perverse matron.

Saturday 2 September – Rutland

Dinner at Belvoir Castle. Emma, the current Duchess, is better than fabulous, and the polar opposite of her mother-in-law. So yesterday it was the Dowager's house at the bottom gate, tonight it's the Castle, and the better part of the family. The top of the hill is markedly better than its bottom.

Monday 4 September – London

Call Erik to brief him on the lunch I have set up between him and Mark Sedwill.

Meeting with officials on the three cross-departmental funds: the CSSF (Conflict, Stability and Security Fund), the Prosperity Fund and the Empowerment Fund. These are massive pots of money, but the trouble is nobody fully owns or controls quite how the money is allocated and disbursed – a lot of it comes out of the DfID 0.7 per cent pot and therefore can only be spent on causes that count as Official Development Assistance (ODA). Some of the post-conflict spending probably makes sense, but some of the other thematic projects such as trying to make a country's markets work better or its women more powerful just do not deliver convincing outcomes. If the government don't like the way DfID spends its money, and hence the criteria for its spending priorities, then they need to change the law and properly define an alternative policy. Likewise, if the FCO is underfunded, then increase its funding and stop pretending that you can make up the shortfall for what is really needed by raiding these useless funds. All these funds together well exceed £1 billion a year – a quarter of that would transform the Foreign Office for the better.

Tuesday 5 September – London

House returns for the silly September sitting. We used to break from the last week of July for all of August and September, until the early October conference season was over. Cameron introduced this idiotic ten days in September, which achieves nothing. It was a jack-ass gesture. Instead of cutting the cost of politics, it adds to costs by mucking up all the building's maintenance schedules.

The Caribbean hurricane has hit land. It is very destructive.

I respond to a Westminster Hall debate on Venezuela. Rather annoyingly, Graham Jones, who tabled the motion, focussed on the malign influence of the illegal cocaine trade in his speech, when his letter to the FCO had been about the political situation, which is what my prepared response concentrated on.

Private office team meeting. See Julia Longbottom, Consular Director, to discuss the issue of citizens' rights when we leave the EU. Will Poles who have lived in the UK be allowed to stay, and use the NHS, and educate their kids, for instance? The HMG system is just beginning to realise that this is a massive issue, which affects the lives of millions.

Wednesday 6 September – London

On *Good Morning Britain*, Jacob Rees-Mogg has made some uncompromising comments about his opposition to abortion. He is against it, even if the woman is raped. So – abortion and rape – that's a double whammy. It is his Catholic view. But his lack of sensitivity to modern opinion is provocative, and casts him as an anachronism – which he is. I often reflect on Bruce Anderson's encapsulation of the abortion issue: 'It's murder, but we're stuck with it.'

Rather odd ministerial team meeting. BoJo says he has a strong ministerial team. We have great experience. We need to avoid crappy pieces in the papers. We need a diet of triumphs. We need to be more proactive. We need more than tweets. In other words, he is hurt by the Rachel Sylvester piece in *The Times*.

I visit the Crisis Centre in the basement of the FCO, which is whirring away at full tilt in response to Hurricane Irma which has belted into the Caribbean, and in particular the British Virgin Islands (BVI).

Thursday 7 September – London

A pretty full hurricane day. I make a statement in the Commons on it, then attend a COBRA meeting. I'm spending all my time helping to coordinate DfID, the MoD and the FCO.

Friday 8 September – London

Telecon call from the FCO Crisis Centre with US Acting Assistant Secretary Elisabeth Millard, in which we offer to help each other wherever we can.

The Governor of BVI is very worried about the collapse of law and order on the islands, and fears looting and unrest. RFA [Royal Fleet Auxiliary] *Mounts Bay*, with supplies and Marines on board, is due there now, and the Governor has asked for some soldiers to reinforce his small police force.

I'm in the Crisis Centre at about 10pm when a call comes in from the BVI Governor to say that there has been a prison breakout and 100 fugitives are now roaming about. He is on *Mounts Bay* and is asking for help. My senior officials, Kara Owen and Ben Merrick, look at me (albeit the exceptional Ben is registered blind) and hand me the phone. I just go for it: 'Governor, this is Alan Duncan, the Minister. I authorise you to take twelve Marines off *Mounts Bay*, and use them as you see fit.' It was quite literally a 'Send in the Marines' moment. The response, both in BVI and in the Crisis Centre, was extraordinary. They almost whooped and cheered.

Slightly concerning for me, though, is that the Marines are not really my assets to deploy. I call Mark Lancaster, Minister for the Armed Forces, to say what I have done. He is just such a superstar cool good guy. He immediately confirms that the instructions are valid, authorised, and should be followed. Within ninety seconds he sends me a text saying, 'To confirm in writing I authorise a contingent to stay on the island. I've informed the MoD.' How about that for decisiveness?

Saturday 9 September – Gibraltar

Fly to Gibraltar for their National Day celebrations. To the Convent (the Governor's house). Visit my childhood home at Four Corners, part of RAF Gibraltar, or North Front, where we lived 1960–2 when my father was Commanding Officer of 224 Squadron, and used to fly Shackletons up and down the Mediterranean.

Drinks reception on HMS *Diamond*. MPs Ian Paisley, Nigel Evans, Alec Shelbrooke, Bob Neill and others also there, then a Royal

Philharmonic Concert in the caves, rather like the Last Night of the Proms.

Sunday 10 September – Gibraltar/London

Gibraltar National Day. Walk up Main Street with Chief Minister Fabian Picardo and his family. Everyone is dressed in red and white. In Casemates Square I address over 10,000 people and wow them by saying, 'I lived in Gib, my father was CO with the RAF, my brother was born here, my husband was born here, and you will forever remain a part of the UK family.' I made no mention of Brexit, which some idiot did last year and was loudly booed. Fly back.

Tuesday 12 September – London

Friendly meeting with Macedonian Foreign Minister Nikola Dimitrov. A good ally, he's such a smart guy and is doing everything he can to secure an acceptable resolution to the name Macedonia, which causes continuous dispute with their Greek neighbours. We are being as helpful as we can, and I think we'll succeed.

In a meeting about the hurricane and the use of RAF aircraft to help rescue people, I quite seriously suggested using the Royal/PM's Voyager plane. It would be a bit like using the *QEII* during the Falklands War in 1982, or the Royal Yacht *Britannia* for the evacuation of Aden in 1968. It also draws the sting from anyone criticising the PM/Queen having a plane. It would go into folklore. Where's our imagination? Nowhere … so they won't.

Defence Secretary Michael Fallon is annoyed that Tobias Ellwood has bypassed him and written directly to the PM on something. What a surprise.

Wednesday 13 September – London/Baku, Azerbaijan

Lunch with BBC diplomatic correspondent James Landale at Shepherd's Restaurant. Told him that the stupid OECD rules which define Overseas Development Assistance, and therefore how it can be used, do not permit us to use ODA for hurricane response in the Overseas Territories because they are not poor enough. Well, they bloody well are now! There is so much stupid comment from ministers about the use of ODA, when they are wilfully ignorant about how it can legally be spent.

James runs the story hard, and it makes the headlines. The PM says she is frustrated by ODA. OK, but then tell your stupid ministers (in particular Priti Patel) not to brag about deploying it after the hurricane when they can't, because it would have to come out of a non-DfID, non-ODA budget, and there isn't one. Meanwhile Boris has hoofed it to BVI to inspect the damage.

Overnight on the BP plane to Baku.

Thursday 14 September – Baku/Kiev

Turn around in the Marriott after only a couple of hours' sleep, then attend the massive BP contract-signing ceremony. Their CEO Bob Dudley is very pleased I am there to represent the British government at this enormous oil production sharing and pipeline venture.

Meeting with President Ilham Aliyev, then FM Elmar Mammadyarov. As always there is constant reference to their historic tension with Armenia. These legacy hatreds never seem to disappear. Natter with Turkish Energy Minister Berat Albayrak, Erdoğan's son-in-law.

To Kiev.

Friday 15 September – Kiev

Boris has written 4,000 words in the *Telegraph*, aka the *Torygraph*, or more accurately these days the *Daily Boris* – 'My vision for a bold, thriving Britain, enabled by Brexit'.

It is a massive splash and is a carefully worded apologia – or manifesto – intended to strain his relations with May to the limit, challenge her to sack him and define him as the outstanding cheerleader of the Brexit cause. It is a passionate explosion of pent-up everything inside him. It has the feeling of him going for broke.

Meanwhile, back in downtown Kiev I arrived and addressed an all-staff meeting at the embassy before lunch at the InterContinental with Crimean human rights activists. In the afternoon I see Anders Fogh Rasmussen (former NATO Secretary General), and do some

TV interviews before my speech at the Yalta European Strategy (YES) conference. I speak immediately after Prime Minister Groysman.

Walking chat outside the conference hall with David Cameron. There is no route to Brexit abandonment, he thinks.

Trouble with the Spanish. It seems there is someone called Lord Duncan (how presumptuous) who I have never heard of before. He is a former MEP called Ian Duncan, who has recently been put in the Lords and made a PUSS in the Scottish Office. He attended a meeting in the Lords with the Speaker of the Catalonia Parliament – they are controversially seeking independence from Spain – and then he tweeted about it. The Spanish are furious and are demanding an apology.

Saturday 16 September – Kiev/Rutland

Having fired a torpedo at HMS Theresa yesterday, the *DT* headline today is 'Boris – I'm still behind Theresa for a "glorious Brexit"'. I think he's only right behind her so as to push her off a cliff.

Bit hung-over. Breakfast with Tony Blair. We cover Brexit, Hamas and the Gulf. He loves having his fingers in Middle Eastern things, but I always feel it's more to make money than to make peace.

I link up with the Ambassador, where we were joined by the Ukrainian Deputy Foreign Minister, all amid a bit of confusion, as I didn't realise it was her. I expressed displeasure to our Ambassador for her not having the basic diplomatic courtesy of informing me who I was being introduced to. I was blindsided.

Sunday 17 September – Rutland

It's all Boris. All the papers are full of it.

Roast chicken lunch. James later heads to Clapham to avoid the building site at home in London. I keep Noodle and stay up in Rutland.

My old friend the historian Jeremy Catto says Boris is like Churchill – but sadly he means Lord Randolph Churchill, who resigned thinking he could bring down Salisbury. But failed.

Monday 18 September – Rutland

More from Boris in the *Telegraph*. After his article last week, the headline today is 'FS to tell PM £30bn "divorce" bill is not acceptable'. His headlines are coming in thick and fast. Boris is clearly on a roll, and the *Daily Boris* is giving him a daily headline.

Another hurricane, Maria, is coming. It's the fourth in a row and is strengthening. It looks as though we face the danger of the recent destruction all happening again. Am summoned to a 3.15pm COBRA, so have to race for a train to London.

In the meeting, I was astonished, even appalled, at the attitude of the Prison Service, who point-blank refused to let prison officers remain on BVI, insisting they went there to secure the prison, not to face the danger of a hurricane. In itself, that's reasonable, but the defiant manner in which their views were expressed was intolerable. So here we go again having to ask how we will secure and protect the BVI prison when Maria hits.

Olly Robbins is to leave DExEU and go to Number 10, following reports that he and DD do not get on. Philip Rycroft will take over as Permanent Secretary at DExEU. BoJo believes Jeremy Heywood was behind the UK Statistics Authority letter on statistical distortion, criticising the famous £350 million per week claim on the bus.

Hammond, BoJo + DD are to go to Florence for the PM's speech on Friday. It also now appears that while BoJo was in BVI last week the PM had a meeting with Hammond, Rudd and Damian Green. Not being there, Boris feared he was about to be stitched up, and so wrote the *Telegraph* article.

Meanwhile former Lib Dem MP David Laws' new book on the coalition government, which is serialised this week, documents TM's obduracy on immigration, especially on visas. Interesting.

Tuesday 19 September – Rutland

A day to myself in Rutland, but with lots of calls diverting me. Hurricane Maria is rolling in.

Boris and the PM are in NY at the UN General Assembly, where Trump is making the main speech. But it's the PM/BoJo who are dominating the news here. And it doesn't exactly look like a love-in. There's talk of him threatening to resign. Nobody thinks Boris comes out of this well.

Thursday 21 September – London

Cabinet meeting ahead of the PM's Brexit speech in Florence tomorrow, in order to square everyone beforehand. The Boris article grenade has made them very jittery. After it, Hammond and Johnson pose for friendly pictures in Downing Street – it's so artificial, you know there's trouble.

My annual constituency lunch at the Carlton Club, with Jacob Rees-Mogg as guest of honour. I introduced him with some amusing references to him living over my garden wall in Westminster and knowing him since he was a teenager. He is an utterly absurd anachronism, but everyone lapped it up and loved it. He lives in a world of his own, but it entertained and made people happy, so what the hell.

Friday 22 September – Rutland

Theresa's speech in Florence. It was OK, but a bit banal. It conceded there would be a transition period after Brexit, but gave little of substance on key issues such as the Irish border or the future trading relationship.

Lunch with Erik Bennett. He says he hopes Christopher Geidt will retain a role at the Palace after he stands down next month, and that Mark Sedwill will speak on Iran at the Oman Privy Council meeting in Muscat in the new year.

The afternoon was spent calling foreign ministers in Malta, Bulgaria and Greece to explain the PM's speech. Or as much as anyone could, anyway …

In among all the high-level diplomacy, I try to take an interest in the FCO building – after all, it is in my remit, but is the kind of thing that the system always tries to steer you away from. As you turn off Whitehall into King Charles Street, and again as you reach the main entrance arch itself, the whole set-up looks shoddy and dilapidated. The guards' uniforms are inconsistent, the 'Stop and be searched' signs are all rusty – there are sandbags and dirty fire extinguishers strewn all over the place – it's a complete shambles. I am determined to improve it so that there are smart guards, tasteful signs, tidiness and some training about handling vehicles and their passengers more politely. It is easier for ministers to declare war than to smarten up the FCO's front door.

Sunday 24 September – Rutland

It just doesn't stop. The *Sunday Telegraph* headline says 'Boris sets red lines on Brexit'. It's impossible to stick your neck out any further.

So, what do we make of the last ten days of Boris? It's like this: six days before the much heralded PM speech in Florence, an event designed to break the deadlock in EU exit talks, Boris issues a 4,000-word essay on his views – indeed his terms and conditions – for any deal. To do so is a total challenge to the PM, and to the concept of collective responsibility. As such it is insubordinate and divisive. Much worse, his reasoning is facile. It is puerile junk – worrying on a number of counts.

That he should believe that what he has written is credible is disturbing enough, but he probably does. Perhaps even worse is that perhaps he knows it is simplistic nonsense, and that it is designed to appeal to Tory activists to serve his own ambition. It is clearly self-serving, but the scary truth is that he might actually believe it.

I think he despises May, and thinks he is the next Churchill. He has a self-deluding mock-romantic passion which is not rooted in realism. He is disloyal. A decade of press attention has gone to his head, and he doesn't appreciate that the gloss has gone. His comedy routine has gone stale; his lack of seriousness in a serious job rankles; and he has little following among MPs. Most activists, even if still amused by his buffoonery, no longer see him as a credible prime minister. He seems to have embarked on a reckless journey into oblivion. I try to be the dutiful number two, and resist any temptation to feed journalists against him, but since his *Daily Telegraph* essay I have lost any respect for him. He is a clown, a self-centred ego, an embarrassing buffoon, with an untidy mind and sub-zero diplomatic judgement. He is an international stain on our reputation. He is a lonely, selfish, ill-disciplined, shambolic, shameless clot. Grrr. Got that out of my system. I feel better now. Smile and press on!

Monday 25 September – Minsk, Belarus

Up at 4am. It is raining heavily, which will helpfully wash the mulched seeds into the wildflower paddock. My theory is that by mowing, mulching and then soaking it, the paddock will be self-perpetuating and should bloom well again next year. Let's see.

Traffic congestion caused by the heavy rain meant I cut it a bit fine for the flight to Amsterdam, and then Minsk, but it worked out OK. The papers are full of the conflict between Hammond and Johnson over the transition period for leaving, which is as close as it can be to open warfare. Hammond is 100 per cent right, but politically unpalatable: Boris is 100 per cent wrong, and although historically attractive is gradually imploding. May is a plain and characterless keel in the middle, keeping it all upright but somewhat beleaguered. She remains the best option, but only because any alternative is bound to be disastrous.

The *Telegraph* has BoJo accused of being too simplistic about Brexit, which is an understatement. The latest Shipman book says Hammond in a text offered on election night in June to back Boris for PM if he would leave him to run the economy. Hammond is not denying it, but it shows him for the first time as someone who is capable of political scheming. He is lessened by it, and doesn't really know how to do it.

Supposedly, the fourth round of Brexit talks will start again in earnest in Brussels. Meanwhile Donald Tusk in Number 10 tells Theresa that her Florence speech has not done enough. It's scrappy.

I am the first ever British minister to visit Belarus, and the likeable Belarus Ambassador to London, Sergei Aleinik, is at Minsk airport to meet me. He is personable and thorough, with no awkward edge or pushiness. I like him. To the embassy, in the incongruously named Karl Marx Street.

I normally dread collective meetings with NGOs and human rights groups, but the gathering I walked into was refreshing. Not so much a series of gripes and whinges, everything they described could be distilled into a perfectly reasonable cause. Their requests were realistic. On domestic violence, what can be wrong with supporting beaten women through judicial fairness, appropriate changes to the law and access to redress through proper police attention? The LGBT guy, and lesbian colleague, simply asked that transgender persons should be allowed to register themselves clearly and not face employment discrimination. The journalists merely wanted to be able to write an article without fear of arrest. Simple objectives are so much better than general buzzword complaints.

Dinner with Foreign Minister Vladimir Makei. Furtive and articulate, he is in Belarus terms very progressive. We dined in a Bavarian beer cellar (albeit upstairs) with tons of food on the table, most of it left uneaten, while we were force-fed a nice salad, potato pancakes, grilled pork with cheese on top, and gateau. Eeks!

Makei is a rapid-talking fastidious former ambassador, engaging and reasonable. We cover Russia, Ukraine, Brexit and the crucial issue of human rights, which I call 'citizens' freedoms' in order to avoid the usual tired finger-wagging script. He was receptive, and we discussed in very frank terms the path Belarus was trying to take. Squeezed as they are between Russia and Poland, they took a massive hammering in the war, and that legacy of casualty and destruction still haunts them. It means that President Alexander Lukashenko has to tread a careful path between asserting a measure of Europe-facing independence and keeping a beady eye on Russia next door on which they are still extensively dependent economically.

Then a reception for Chevening Scholars, John Smith Memorial Trust alumni, Future Leaders Programme, business figures, etc.

Interesting drink afterwards with a banker who was at Eton with Boris. He was no fan, and says Boris took his economics revision notes without permission and then never gave them back.

Tuesday 26 September – Minsk, Belarus

To the Palace of Independence to meet President Lukashenko. It's the ultimate test of diplomacy to meet someone you know to be a bit of a monster yet you know there's no point having a head-on confrontation. After all, he's a brutal ice-hockey player and twice my size! Any bravado I might have wanted to display was squeezed out of me when he greeted me not with a handshake but with a bear hug. The best I could do was to urge him to loosen up on citizens' rights and realise that the best future for Belarus lay with a greater focus on the West rather than Russia.

I've been reflecting on the FCO and its quality of administration. Estates are shameful, with many of our buildings becoming tatty and grotty. FCO Services is the in-house design and maintenance organisation (rather like a 1970s council's direct labour organisation) which is slow, petty and charges too much. Nobody has any commercial nous, and there are poorly performing contracts all over the place. The Berlin embassy, for instance, was built under a private finance initiative under which we pay higher-than-cost maintenance prices, pay a full repayment mortgage equivalent over twenty-five years for its construction, and then have to buy the building at the end at market value, which means we will have paid for it twice!

Briefing packs are now done centrally, which is dumb. If a country desk can't put together a brief, what are they there for? And some embassies have to report into neighbouring ones, rather than into London, something which offends many of the host countries. The Foreign Office has lost its way and is driven by the dominance of process and budgets, not by diplomacy and national interest. It is an organisation living on its past, one without leadership, initiative or confidence. Boris adds nothing to it. Indeed his ego subtracts from what we have, because he has no interest in either strategy or the minutiae of administration. He consumes our reputation: he does not add to it. Amid a long succession of characterful foreign secretaries he is Harold Wilson's George Brown without the alcohol.

To Yerevan, Armenia, via Kiev, arriving well past midnight.

Wednesday 27 September – Yerevan, Armenia
Breakfast with our excellent Ambassador Judith Farnworth. To the Tsitsernakaberd Memorial to lay a wreath. What with Baku and Minsk, this is my third recent ceremony with elegant, goose-stepping

soldiers conducting a display of dignified commemoration. It was immediately followed by a tour of the Armenian Genocide Museum, whose layout and contents are closely reminiscent of the (since modernised) Yad Vashem in Jerusalem. It is deeply moving. About 1.5 million Armenians were systematically killed by the Ottomans a century ago. The parallel with the wholesale murder of Jews is compelling. The Armenians are demanding it be labelled 'genocide', a strict legal definition, a designation opposed by the Turks and the Azeris. We steer a middle course, because we need to work with Turkey and Azerbaijan and not inflame the festering sore which is Nagorno-Karabakh, but it was without doubt wholesale cleansing.

Poor Armenia. Small (population around 3 million) and with a rich Christian history, but squashed by so much, and most of its people are scattered elsewhere across the world. Even today their diaspora have faced further horror in Syria and are being displaced again, with the destruction of ancient monasteries, and tens of thousands fleeing the war.

Angela Merkel is the daughter of a Lutheran pastor; Theresa May is the daughter of a vicar. Neither seems to have any understanding of the plight of the Christian world, be it the Yazidis in Iraq and Syria, the Christians and Palestinians in the Holy Land, and so many Armenians. Both are plain and parochial, with little sense of the wider world or of the complexity, challenges and opportunities of international relations. Theresa May simply has no worldview beyond inherited thought from the Thatcher era. If only she would ask, she might quickly learn and get it. But she has no such intellectual or leadership instinct.

To the National Assembly of the Republic of Armenia. Why does a self-confident nation ever need to put the word Republic into their official title? It just makes them sound young and tacky. 'Armenia' would suffice.

Interestingly, without massive fuss, they are quietly converting from a presidency into something that more closely resembles a parliamentary democracy. I delivered a fifteen-minute speech extolling their journey towards an amended system and comparing it with ours. Inside myself I'm ashamed, as I think our own system of government is seriously deficient. Parliament is dead. Government is bureaucratic. Political leadership hardly exists. We are stagnant and ossified. We are living in post-imperial delusion, with no political vibrancy, and in a climate of political debate which is outdated. It's not just the Conservative side. Jeremy Corbyn is reviving absurd revamped socialist thought, such as wanting to nationalise everything. But our side is arguably even worse.

MPs go through the drudgery of their working day, changing nothing, and the likes of John Redwood, aka Mr Swivel-Eyed Bonkers, advertise our unsuitability for remaining a serious force in national politics. It is his ilk who hold Theresa (through their views and our parliamentary arithmetic) hostage on Brexit and are forcing us ever more tightly into a political straitjacket which will make us unelectable, even to the point at which we cease to be significant.

My speech is fine, but trite. The usual stuff about swords in the Chamber, PMQs and all that frippery. It was also very shallow about the meaning of a representative democracy, in that it hinted at having to replicate the country in terms of gender, ethnicity, sexuality, etc. It's not quite what I said, but when I cited with approval the fact that we had forty-three MPs who were openly gay or lesbian, two wrinkled old crones in the back row scowled to each other in obvious disapproval. If I'd known I was live on YouTube I'd have rounded on them in a vigorous public challenge, which would have become a massively significant moment of public record. But such is the amateurishness of the FCO press office, they don't ever think to alert you to what really matters.

The questions, obviously, were about Armenian genocide, the Azerbaijani slush fund (a *Guardian* story, called in Yerevan the Azeri Laundromat) to buy votes in the Council of Europe, and Brexit.

Meeting with the PM, Karen Karapetyan. Fun and cordial. When the structure of government changes next April the question is whether Karapetyan shifts to the newly constituted PM position, or whether the President, Serzh Sargsyan, currently in the more powerful post but who is less popular, tries to hold on to executive power by moving to be PM, or alternatively moves to the more ceremonial position as a newly constituted President.

Dinner with FM Edward Nalbandian at his official residence. Nicely done, but he rabbited on a bit.

My mind has been whirring about the consistency or otherwise of FCO thinking and UK foreign policy more generally. What are the difficult areas of sovereignty and control, and does the FCO have a consistent philosophy of self-determination? We speak of self-determination in some circumstances, such as Gibraltar and the Falklands, but not in the same way of others such as Scotland and Catalonia. We use simple labels about arguments when it suits us, but duck them when it's awkward. We are intellectually muddled. Where is our intellectual clarity and consistency on: Kashmir, Western Sahara, Palestine, Nagorno-Karabakh, South Ossetia & Abkhazia, Crimea, Cyprus, Gibraltar, Transnistria, Kurdistan, Catalonia, Kosovo, Scotland and lots of conflicted corners of Africa? It has the makings of a substantial PhD thesis: 'Self-determination, disputed sovereignty, independence and breakaway ambition – a moral philosophy'. Get started with that one!

Thursday 28 September – Yerevan, Armenia

Heavy-going breakfast with the lugubrious but intellectual Vache Gabrielyan, Deputy PM with the government's main economic brief. Perfectly nice and thoughtful, but with no understanding about how to host a table. There was a window of bright sunshine behind him, so I spent the entire breakfast blinded and staring into a silhouette. He has theories about trade and sectors, but doesn't appreciate that it's all about business choices not government wishes.

Quite the most amazing visit to the Matenadaran Institute-Museum which contains the largest collection of ancient Armenian manuscripts. Fly back via Kiev. Land 9.30. Rutland at midnight. Zzzz.

Friday 29 September – Rutland

Full constituency day. Office intern George Greville Williams, who is proving highly efficient, arrives by train, and we have a full-speed, multi-tweet day. The CEOs of both Melton and Rutland councils; the police at all levels, Inspector Gavin Drummond as well as Chief

Constable Simon Cole; Macmillan Nurses and Action in Melton; and the opening of Surface Generation's new hi-tech lab in Lyndon, beside Rutland Water. George is making my constituency activity hum along.

Saturday 30 September – Rutland

Boris has done it again with an interview in the *Sun*. Although political editor Tom Newton Dunn considers him a prat, or possibly because of it, he has given him a double pager in which Boris insists on his 'red lines' (i.e. ultimatums) on Brexit. A transition of no more than two years; no changes to regulations which might affect us during that period; and something else and something else. He is seriously chancing his arm. It is one day before Party Conference – how dare he?

Sunday 1 October – London

Start of Party Conference in Manchester. Journos call me non-stop, asking if Boris should be sacked, and judging May's interview on the *Marr* programme this morning as both faltering and weak. I decline to pass comment on either. The *Sunday Times* reports that the Palace were unhappy with her and Gavin Williamson for over-egging the certainty of the post-election DUP deal before it was done, and it says that May was a wreck after the election, often collapsing in tears and having to be consoled. Aside from family tragedy, she has never been hardened by experience of the real world.

It is now openly reported that Monarch Airlines might collapse tomorrow. The government has been preparing for this for months.

The (illegal) Catalan independence referendum is turning sour. We've seen bad clips of the Spanish police ripping away ballot boxes from polling stations, firing rubber bullets and manhandling voters. So very stupid. They should have just humoured the whole process, yet declared it illegal and invalid.

Speak to Mum. Her ankle cast came off on Tuesday, a few weeks after breaking it in a fall, but her foot is still very painful. Nephew Ben's wife Dee has had a baby daughter, Nualla, a sister for three-year-old Hewey.

Flight to Chicago, much enhanced by a very good-looking Northern steward called Benjamin.

Monday 2 October – Chicago

Wake up to news of what may turn out to be the worst mass shooting in US history: over fifty concertgoers mown down and killed by gunfire from a hotel room overlooking the venue. Hideous. Soon after breakfast the number injured has risen to 400.

Meanwhile, back in Manchester, Boris is receiving heavy pounding in the papers for his disloyalty and for causing so much havoc.

Staff meeting at the British consulate with all of the team. Speech at the Chicago Council on Global Affairs, followed by Q&A. I gave my frank assessment of what I thought had driven people to vote as they did in the referendum. At its simplest, people were angry about a lot of things and took it out on the establishment as well as the EU.

Tuesday 3 October – Chicago/Columbus/Indianapolis

The *Guardian* has written up my Brexit remarks from yesterday in an online story by Patrick Wintour. The headline is 'Brexit vote was "tantrum" by British working class, says Alan Duncan', which is a mischievous distortion of what I said. It makes it sound like I was being dismissive, when in fact I spoke about the complex motivations and emotions that drove people in how they voted. It really is a problem with the modern world of politics that you cannot be thoughtful without being traduced.

Dinner with John Kasich at his house, with wife Karen and daughters Emma and Reece. He's a very thoughtful guy, and perhaps too nice to have developed a single-minded killer instinct, unlike the maniac Trump.

Drive to Indianapolis, arriving at midnight, zonked. Thanks to the *Guardian* piece, I am being comprehensively trolled by the filth of UKIP and Breitbart, who in matters like this seem to act as one. Farage has tweeted that I should be sacked (thanks, mate, you're such a charmer!). I then receive a text message that reads: 'Stupid, arrogant comments as usual. Concentrate on your job maybe? Stewart'. The sender wasn't in my contacts so I respond, 'Who is this, please?' The reply reveals it to be the execrable Stewart Jackson, the defeated MP for Peterborough who is now Chief of Staff to David Davis. There he is, a Cabinet minister's SpAd, and he sends that sort of rude text to a minister. I send a sharp reply that he should show better manners. He retorts, 'You're a Minister of the Crown. I suggest you reflect on your unhelpful comments at a sensitive time in our negotiations.'

He is one of life's horrid people. But also so stupid that he can be wound up by a press story that anyone can see was built on an exaggerated and selective version of my comments. If I were as much of a shit as him, I would send this exchange to his Permanent Secretary and mine, asking for him to be rebuked, or even sacked.

Wednesday 4 October – Indianapolis/Washington

Fabulous meeting with Indiana Governor Eric Holcomb and his Commerce Secretary Jim Schellinger. Eric took over from Mike Pence when he became Vice-President. The State House is as grand as any country's.

To South Bend, for a meeting with Mayor Pete Buttigieg (and his unpronounceable Maltese name). Only thirty-five, Harvard, Rhodes Scholar at Oxford, service in Afghanistan, gay, Democrat. Good guy – I really liked him. He's quite mild-mannered, but with a bit of gumption could be really significant.

Speak at Notre Dame University. I am still being e-trolled by global Euroturds.

Fly to Washington DC.

Meanwhile back in Manchester, the PM's conference speech seems to have resembled every politician's stage nightmare, or a piece of performance art on the theme of 'disaster'. First some jerk of a prankster handed her a P45, then she had an appalling coughing fit that wouldn't go away, and to top it all off, the letter O fell off the backdrop. Impossible not to feel sorry for her – it was a pathetic sight. Much sympathy for her predicament, and comment on her bravery in soldiering on to the end of the speech.

The whole thing seemed to symbolise her fall from the new Iron Lady to the 'Maybot' who lost a majority when she should have got a landslide. She's been badly wounded ever since, and today she looked it.

Called Tom Newton Dunn. He says it is Grant Shapps who claims to have thirty or more names of MPs ready to strike to trigger a vote of no confidence, and he is manoeuvring behind the scenes out of self-importance. Tom Tug, when asked if he'd like to be PM, cockily answers that he'd be honoured to serve his country in any capacity, to which Soames tweets in reply, 'And I'm putting in for Pope.'

Monday 9 October – London/Dublin
House returns.

In the *DT*, BoJo allies are saying 'sack Hammond'.

Wednesday 11 October – London
Have a bit of a set-to with PUS Simon McDonald. One of our top industrialists, who I and others have proposed for an honour, has been rejected because a Google search has shown he sacked people while simultaneously increasing his own salary. Bloody hell, what have we come to when a civil servant with zero knowledge of business can condemn someone in this way? On the same basis, no permanent secretary should ever be knighted when we're in a recession and unemployment is rising.

Here we go again. Ellwood has suggested to the PM that as a Reservist with strong links to the US he should be sent to take control of the situation in the British Virgin Islands following last month's hurricane.

Thursday 12 October – London/Budapest
Speak at Panama Invest conference at Skinners' Hall. I tease them that I am a Merchant Taylor. The rivalry between the two livery companies for precedence in the Lord Mayor's Procession is the origin of the phrase 'They are all at sixes and sevens'.

I text TND [Tom Newton Dunn of the *Sun*] to rebuke him ferociously for tweeting that 'it is the duty of the Queen to attend the Cenotaph even if she has to crawl there'. She is due to watch from the FCO balcony while Prince Charles lays her wreath, which he thought insufficient. We speak, and after initially justifying it he calls back an hour later and says, 'You are right. I relent. It was too much. Thank you for making me realise it was wrong. I've deleted it.' TND is a proper person.

BoJo is hosting eight EU foreign ministers next weekend at Chevening. Typical of our system, I know nothing about it and am not included. It won't have been a deliberate snub: it's just that the system never thinks to include other ministers, and Boris certainly doesn't.

Monday 16 October – London
Update from officials on Brexit and Turkey.

Meeting with Leader of the House Andrea Leadsom about the Sanctions and Anti-Money Laundering Bill (I had insisted on the 'Anti-' in its title). She is logical and articulate, but strangely disconnected from normal human interaction. She is superficially personable, but somehow otherwise distant.

Tuesday 17 October – London
FCO Orals. Joanna Cherry asked about policy heavy-handedness in the Catalonia referendum and took great exception when I in reply chided her and her SNP colleagues for claiming to have been 'official election observers' at what was an illegal referendum. She made a pantomime display of outrage and raised a point of order afterwards, saying they had never claimed to be official observers. As I had based my remarks on an email to the FCO from her own Chief of Staff, this was really very silly of her. It was crass to demand an apology for citing her own words. So silly that afterwards I copied the email to the Speaker.

Wednesday 18 October – London
Builders at home for the post-flood redevelopment.

Ministerial team meeting.

Lunch at his enormous house in Cheyne Walk with the Armenian Ambassador Armen Sarkissian.

Parliamentary stuff.

Drink with John Major at his London home, with James. These occasional drinks are a treat – he remains plugged-in and perceptive, but rather despairs of the conduct of so many MPs who should know better.

Friday 20 October – Rutland

Perhaps two or three times a year I pen a private letter to Sultan Qaboos in Oman, giving him my version of what I think is happening in UK politics. It gives him, I hope, a helpful insight and a better explanation than he might pick up from news reports. He is always appreciative, and it keeps our top-level links in working order.

Wednesday 25 October – London

Defence and Security Exports working group. Ben Fender is a real character. He knows his brief inside out, which is just as well because the export process is convoluted spaghetti, and he's about the only FCO official who could ever make it comprehensible.

Saturday 28 October – Rutland

To Ditchley Park for a Chatham House seminar for Britain and Turkey. The ham was delicious, but not the cleverest thing to serve at that particular event!

Sunday 29 October – Rutland

Most amusing *BBC News* broadcast: 'After failing a drugs test, six sailors have been fired by the Royal Navy from a nuclear submarine.'

Monday 30 October – London

Great lunch at Franco's with local grandee Harry Westropp. A good way to start the week: lots of gossip, and non-stop demolition of all the people in the constituency who we both think are nuts.

I am very attentive to a visiting Turkish parliamentary delegation. One of them took me aside at the end, and charmingly said that as soon as they walked into the room they could tell they were in the presence of someone 'friendly and electric'.

There's quite a lot going on. The Catalonian regional government has been dissolved, and its 'President' Carles Puigdemont has fled to Belgium with five of his ministers. In the US, the Mueller inquiry into Trump, funding and Russian influence has led to the indictment of Paul Manafort and Rick Gates, both members of his campaign team. Meanwhile the whole of Westminster is buzzing with talk of a spreadsheet which lists about twenty MPs as sex pests, reportedly describing what they have done wrong. It is supposedly explosive and will lead to resignations. Oh dear. That's all we need.

Yet another three-line whip to stay and vote at 10pm, but then with no division.

Tuesday 31 October – London

The Sexminster, or Pestminster, spreadsheet is running riot, and shows all the signs of getting very messy. It is reported that Mark Garnier asked his staffer, years ago, to buy some sex toys.

Meanwhile it seems that Ellwood had a meeting with Trump foreign policy adviser George Papadopoulos – who is now discredited as a result of the Mueller inquiry in the US and is cooperating with the FBI after pleading guilty to lying about his contact with the Russians.

Meeting with Protocol to discuss the vexed issue of how we protect top embassies in London. It's a real problem, in that any change in how we do it has diplomatic consequences, yet the FCO is at the mercy of others. The Home Office supposedly can set policy, but they wash their hands of the specifics, saying it is 'an operational matter' for the Met Police. It is very frustrating.

To the Durbar Court in the FCO for a thank-you gathering for all those who helped with the hurricane crisis a few weeks ago. All we got were plastic cups and orange juice, which looked rather ungrateful. I thanked them all, and mentioned poor Kara Owen who after my constant visits to the Crisis Centre kept diverting her, had to heat her noodles for a third time. And I recalled the short video I made there, during which an owl appeared in an insurance ad on the big screen behind me, looking in the video as though it was sitting on my head.

Wednesday 1 November – London

The Pestminster scandal claims its biggest scalp, as Michael Fallon resigns as Defence Secretary. He had been accused of putting his hand on the knee of Talkradio's Julia Hartley-Brewer at a dinner fifteen years ago, which even she said shouldn't be a cause for resignation. He is a fundamentally decent man, and has had a distinguished career, so this is a really sad ending.

Thursday 2 November – London

In quite the most extraordinary Cabinet appointment I can think of, Gavin Williamson has been appointed as the new Defence Secretary to replace Michael Fallon. It is absolutely absurd and has been greeted with astonishment by the press. As Chief Whip he must have had a role in telling the PM to give Fallon the boot, and now he seems to have pushed himself forward for this undeserved promotion. It is a brazenly self-serving manoeuvre that will further embed the view of him as a sly schemer, which he undoubtedly is.

He is also ludicrously unqualified for the heavyweight job of Defence Secretary, having never run anything. His experience amounts to having been a fireplace salesman, then bag-carrier for two PMs, then Chief Whip for a year. He has neither the gravitas nor the experience needed for the job – what on earth was the PM thinking? It will damage her among colleagues, most of whom are furious about it. If I were rather more precious, I'd be pretty damned annoyed that I didn't get it myself. As a nice colleague said, it's the third time (following the departures from the MoD of Fox, Hammond and Fallon) that I've been passed over. It's clearly not such an outlandish idea when compared with a nobody like Gavin, and I would have done my late father – who was thirty years in the RAF – proud. But, as ever, scheming triumphs over loyalty and suitability.

Saturday 4 November – Rutland

There are reports of sudden and extensive arrests in Saudi Arabia, ordered by Crown Prince Mohammed bin Salman. It looks as though he is asserting himself very strongly, but there is no knowing whether it will consolidate his authority or backfire.

Monday 6 November – London/Tirana

Go through FCO plans for Remembrance Sunday, then host lunch for Latin American ambassadors at 1 Carlton Gardens.

Priti Horrendous is in a deep mess. Last week, sparked by someone finding a tweet from an Israeli she met in the summer, it now turns out that she went to Israel on what she called a holiday and met some Israeli ministers there without telling the embassy. When first asked about it, she said she had told the FCO – by speaking to Boris – and that it was only a couple of meetings. It is now clear that she lied. She had not told Boris, and in fact had a whole series of meetings, including with PM Netanyahu. All but one of them were also attended by Lord Polak, who for three decades has been the mainstay of the Conservative Friends of Israel. Thus she spent a week there on a programme put together by Polak, without telling the FCO or even her own Department, attending meetings at the highest level, accompanied by the principal pro-Israel donor lobbyist in the UK.

She has been forced to publish a statement. It lists a raft of meetings, and then says that as a result she commissioned policy work in DfID about working with the Israeli Army in Palestine! So by her own admission she has directly linked undeclared meetings to subsequent policy-making. She could not be more compromised. It is yet further evidence of the pernicious influence of Polak and the CFI, something that amounts to embedded outside influence at the heart of our politics. The press will not like having been lied to.

Meanwhile Boris has made a costly gaffe. He said in evidence to the Foreign Affairs Committee that Nazanin Zaghari-Ratcliffe, who is imprisoned by the Iranian Revolutionary Guard, had been training journalists there. She never had. But, as a result, reports suggest she has been sentenced to an extra five years.

To Tirana via Rome. Arrive at midnight, at the residence of Ambassador Duncan Norman, his adorable nurse wife Kerry and Albert the Irish Setter.

Tuesday 7 November – Tirana, Albania

Quite the most extraordinary day back in Westminster. The Priti Patel story looked as though it was fizzling out, overshadowed by Boris' gaffe, but has been reawakened by the press now realising they'd been lied to when she said that the FCO knew about her visit. The catalogue of misdemeanours is endless: full programme organised by CFI; neither DfID nor FCO were told; she says she paid; saw the Israeli PM and other ministers, all accompanied by Lord Polak who is the pinnacle of pro-Israeli lobbying and party donations; lied to the press; was forced to make a statement revealing more than she had previously admitted; says that after the meetings she commissioned policy work; our PM did not know when she saw Netanyahu last week that Priti Outrageous had seen him in Tel Aviv; and she did not know until this morning that Patel had recommended that DfID pay for the Israeli Defence Forces to do 'humanitarian' work in the Golan Heights (which is not Israeli), and which is against the long-standing DfID policy never to use military forces to deliver aid.

So poor Alistair Burt had to answer an Urgent Question in the House on Patel, then Boris made a catastrophic statement on his Nazanin Zaghari-Ratcliffe comments, in which he refused to apologise.

The press and Twitter have gone red hot, not quite knowing whose resignation they should call for first. In my view, Boris' comments were slapdash but with dire consequences, but Priti Patel's are deceitful, morally corrupt and improper. She has engaged offline with a foreign government over issues of policy. It is contemptible. She is quite despicable.

Then things get even hotter with further developments about Patel. Her personal statement was billed as the full record of all the people she saw in Israel, yet she failed to include in her list of meetings the people she subsequently saw in London when she was back. So she lied – to the public and also to the PM. They are all saying she will be sacked tomorrow, but she is somewhere in Africa.

Wednesday 8 November – Pristina, Kosovo

Three-hour drive from Tirana to Pristina, changing cars at the border like Checkpoint Charlie.

Everything to do with Patel is, minute by minute, unfolding on Twitter. The PM has instructed her to return to London; a reporter who is with her and Liam Fox in Nairobi tweets every detail about officials not returning with her, which flight she will take, what she is doing, etc etc. The tracking of the flight itself goes viral, with quip after quip following the plane's progress over each and every city. But she is not due to land until 3.30pm. So-called friends of Patel try to claim that the PM did indeed know about the further meetings in London, but this is then hotly denied by Number 10.

PP is such a brassy monster that on return she has clearly threatened the PM both with a challenge to her version of events – 'Yes, PM, you did know' – and with a threat about Brexit – 'If you mess me around, I'll cause you difficulty.' As a result, she is demanding that she be allowed to resign rather than be dismissed. She should be sacked.

Meanwhile … in downtown Pristina, my itinerary was quite full, seeing the President, the PM, Deputy PM and three other ministers, with a joint press conference and TV interviews.

Priti Appalling's every step is still being followed live on Twitter: in the back door of Number 10 at about 6pm; PM not yet in the building; descriptions of what people imagine to be the scene inside; finally she is dismissed, but it will be called a resignation. Nothing in the exchange of letters even mentions Israel and the deep impropriety of her actions, merely an apology about her lack of transparency. So the whole structure of the questionable influence from Israel and the CFI remains in place, unchallenged and only obliquely mentioned. The Conservative Party and the PM remain in total denial, and once again brush it under the carpet. It reeks; it stinks; it festers; it moulders – all rotten to the core. The rules of propriety, and all the morality and principle that goes with it, are discarded and rewritten to accommodate this exceptional pro-Israel infiltration into the very centre of our public life. What is the point of having a guardian of ethics in Whitehall when they fail to put their foot down on this wickedness?

Was dining with the Kosovan Prime Minister Ramush Haradinaj when the joyous news of Patel's departure came through.

Thursday 9 November – Pristina/Rutland

I email Lance: 'You will think me mad, but I have decided overnight that if I am offered DfID I will decline … Anyway, it probably won't happen, because in order to qualify I'd need to be a Brexiteer and have gone through rapid gender transition.' To the airport. Swissair to Zurich, then BA to London.

So, Fallon last week, Patel this. A beleaguered Prime Minister and a Boris at bay. It feels as though the government is in its death throes, but with no way of anyone predicting how it will end. We limp on, we limp to win. All the overambitious youngsters are jockeying for advancement, a process which so undermines the government there will no government for them to be promoted in. Brexit is poisoning everything such that journalists are analysing who might replace PP at DfID according to whether or not they are a Brexiteer. The issue is dominating and paralysing government. We are doomed, both the government and the country, all because of wretched Brexit.

Boris is in Washington from where he texts me to say they (whoever 'they' are) are blaming me for briefing against Patel. I text back to say she did a pretty comprehensive job of destroying herself without the need for others to assist. None of us knew about her meetings, so we couldn't brief about them. It was proper journalism which flushed out ever more material about undisclosed meetings and her subsequent lies. I said in my reply that she is lucky not to be in the Tower of London.

Sunday 12 November – London

Remembrance Sunday. Once again I have the pleasure of greeting all the Royals as they arrive at the FCO. Love it.

Monday 13 November – London

Meeting with the Chancellor. Perfectly nice catch-up with Philip Hammond in Number 11. It's as if there's a hidden switch somewhere that can change him from his normal rather cold and aloof manner into someone really quite personable and amusing. For once the switch was in the right position, and we had quite a jaunty discussion about where we are. About Brexit he's one of the most logical and sensible, but all our efforts just to protect business and the economy are rather outgunned by the irrepressible nutty brigade who think they own the world. Philip should actually be commended for making a brave stand where so many others have just given up.

Wednesday 15 November – London

Drinks in Speaker's House hosted by Deputy Speaker Lindsay Hoyle, to celebrate (somewhat belatedly) the twenty-fifth anniversary of the 1992 intake of MPs. We are a diminishing band, and it is a salutary reminder that in politics there is no fixed hierarchy, unlike the civil service or the armed forces: you can be a general one day and a corporal the next, as Iain Duncan Smith discovered. Age and experience count for little, and anyone can be rapidly overtaken by more recent arrivals. It is nothing to do with talent or fairness: it is just snakes and ladders, and 90 per cent luck.

Speak at the Investcorp International Advisory Board dinner.

Monday 20 November – London/Rutland

To St James's Church, Gretton [the village I can see across the valley from my home], for the funeral of Sir Michael Latham, who for eighteen years was my predecessor as the local MP. He was well liked, and in the twenty-five years since was very warm in his support for me, which I always appreciated. A well-packed church and a good send-off for a nice and decent man.

Wednesday 22 November – London

Budget Day. Within a gloomy economic outlook, the Budget was relatively uneventful. Hammond has set aside £3 billion for Brexit no-deal preparations, hit diesel car-owners, cut stamp duty for first-time house-buyers and has done nothing on social care, which so destroyed us in the election. It was more of a 'keep things steady' Budget during the uncertainty of Brexit.

Friday 24 November – Rutland

Fly from Northolt to Brussels with the PM for the Eastern Partnership Summit, which joins the EU with six former Soviet states. The whole set-up is designed to be an antidote to the influence of Moscow, and takes place amid growing concern over the Kremlin's use of cyber-interference and disinformation to destabilise wherever it can. It doesn't take any substantive decisions, but is a helpful echo chamber for the likes of Theresa May's warning that Russia is attempting to tear apart our collective strength. And it allows Ukraine to reassert its wish to join the EU.

The PM's staffers are a fun and jocular gang who tease each other mercilessly, much of which is directed towards 'Tricky Dicky' (Richard Jackson). Larger than life in all respects, Tricky is the guy who carries the PM's insulin in a rucksack and is often known to barge through security gates and overzealous officials so as to remain close at hand, as if he were the carrier of the nuclear button.

Nice chat with the PM on the plane back, although she never really lets on what she is really thinking.

Wednesday 29 November – London

To the Cabinet Office in Whitehall for yet another inter-ministerial meeting about leaving the EU. These have become formulaic and purposeless. Each minister has their own little departmental brief, but there is a complete lack of realistic strategic grip. Everyone's going through the motions but not making any difference to anything. We are all navigating our way through unintelligible mush towards an ill-defined and uncertain outcome.

Thursday 30 November – London

Interesting meeting with the FCO's Open Source Unit. A team of enthusiastic young techies has been put together to monitor anything they judge useful in websites, news coverage and social media across the world. By taking such a wide global approach they have identified no end of interference by states in other states, and of course also in us. Being able to hoover up so much out of open-source material is far more valuable than many had realised. It is beginning to offer a degree of reassurance because I have been very suspicious that our system has been extremely naive about the influence of social media and has proved itself gullible. There just seems to be such an overlap between Breitbart, Brexit and Russian tweets that something is going on that we haven't adequately rumbled.

Friday 1 December – Malvern

To Hanslope Park near Milton Keynes, which falls within my ministerial responsibilities. A rambling collection of buildings centred around an old manor house, it is owned by the Foreign Office and houses many of its facilities. It's the HQ of FCO Services, who manage all our embassy maintenance and diplomatic bags, is the principal base for all the FCO's communications and, of great interest to historians, is home to all the FCO's archives. A team of mostly retired diplomats weed and sort the current flow of documentation so it is quickly put in order for future reference. A real treasure trove.

Monday 4 December – London

To the main FCO courtyard for the annual lighting-up of the Christmas tree, which the Norwegians give us every year. London's Norwegian primary school gathers to sing some carols, but the poor little nippers were rather shivering in the cold.

Tuesday 5 December – London

To Buckingham Palace for the Queen's annual reception for the Diplomatic Corps – who just lap it up and love it, as indeed do I.

Wednesday 6 December – London

CMEC reception with John Kerry for the centenary of the Balfour Declaration. The entire issue just brims with the causes of so much contemporary conflict, but also with what could have been, and could still be. If the Balfour Declaration had been or were to be implemented in full, we would even now have a two-state solution with Israel and Palestine living side by side. But we don't. The failure to honour it is costly and dishonourable. John Kerry clearly believes what he says about the illegality of Israelis taking other people's land. It's just such a pity that our own government does not. I am a John Kerry fan.

Friday 8 December – Moscow/London
Arrive in Moscow for a meeting with Deputy Foreign Minister Vladimir Titov – he is my opposite number and I met him in London in March. Our relations with Russia are decidedly frosty, and although Boris occasionally encounters Sergei Lavrov, he (Lavrov) is so haughty and studiously grand that there is little chance of easily breaking the ice with him.

With Vladimir we cover international security and Russia's behaviour in the world, but we need to establish a modus vivendi for cooperation ahead of next year's World Cup in Russia. Mine is the first UK ministerial visit to Russia for over two years and is designed to pave the way for a visit by Boris in a couple of weeks. Along with a visit to the Luzhniki Stadium, where some of the matches will take place, our meetings had the intended effect and passed off satisfactorily.

Monday 11 December – Brussels
Foreign Affairs Council in Brussels, which Benjamin Netanyahu is asked to address for half an hour. The EU has a clear united position that it considers Israeli settlements illegal and looks to a two-state solution with Jerusalem as the shared capital. I manage to contain myself and leave it to Federica Mogherini and the impressive Simon Coveney of Ireland to challenge Netanyahu. He of course smiles sweetly but doesn't give a damn about the EU as all he needs for his ambitions for a wider Israel is the support of the US.

The Eurostar back was late, and so annoyingly I missed Jeffrey and Mary Archer's Christmas party.

Tuesday 12 December – London

Foreign Secretary's diplomatic reception Lancaster House. Intensive, rapid-fire speed dating. I cover over seventy countries, so there are as many ambassadors to charm over the canapés. An attentive private secretary glued to your elbow at such events is crucial for spotting them and not getting them mixed up.

Saturday 16 December – Bucharest/Rutland

In Bucharest with HRH the Prince of Wales for the funeral of King Michael of Romania. Quite an extraordinary day of history and emotion. King Michael was a remarkable figure who stood up against both fascism and communism. FCO brainboxes think he is the only monarch in history to have both preceded and succeeded his own father as head of state. The feeling in the street for him was very special, but also reflected their own disapproval of the current government. The funeral started in the throne room of the old Royal Palace, which is now the National Art Museum, and graduated to a chapel service with a smaller selection of dignitaries. At one point we all had to kneel while holding a lit candle, which gave rise to a startling moment of comedy as my good friend Archduke Karl von Habsburg inadvertently set fire to the long grey hair of the gentleman in front of him. There was much patting and dabbing to extinguish the smoke.

The funeral procession then proceeded through central Bucharest. There was an extraordinary moment when the Prince of Wales left the Royal Palace in full public view to observe the start of the funeral procession to the Romanian Orthodox Cathedral. Unusually for a funeral, the entire crowd, on seeing the Prince, cheered and burst into applause. He is an absolute rock-star hero in Romania, and as a regular visitor has become revered. We were all left with the impression that some of them would like him to be their King.

Back to Brize Norton with HRH, and home to Rutland.

Thursday 21 December – London

I take all my private office out for a Christmas Party, starting with drinks at home, then a fun noisy dinner at the Chinese restaurant nearby, which doubles up as an hilarious karaoke dive. Universal embarrassment for all attending, and a nice conclusion to the working year before Christmas in Rutland and New Year in Mustique.

2018

Monday 1 January – Mustique
Darling Carling [Henry] is a total wreck! I recommend a paracetamol omelette. I sensibly turned in at about 1am, with all the others returning in dribs and drabs until 7am. I am feeling suitably virtuous.

Demonstrations in Iran have broken out in six cities, prompted by rising prices and the biting effect of UN sanctions. Ten people have died. Similar outbursts were suppressed in 2009, but one day things will take off and become a counter-revolution to the theocratic takeover of 1979. There is less chance now that Nazanin Zaghari-Ratcliffe will be released: the IRGC (Iranian Revolutionary Guard Corps) who run the nasty side of the country are surely unlikely to make any concessions in the middle of this. The difference though between these demonstrations and those of 2009 is that last time the protesters were middle-class, but this time it is the much poorer elements of society who are taking to the streets. The main driver seems to have been a sudden increase in the price of eggs. It remains to be seen whether this is a political outburst or a popular rising.

Tuesday 2 January – Mustique
Iranian protests are continuing across the country. There is a lot of silly talk in the UK papers about changing the regime, but a DipTel from our embassy in Teheran offers a much more sensible and measured analysis, explaining that the situation is very difficult to read and its outcome far from certain.

The objectionable Nikki Haley, the US Permanent Rep at the UN, has announced that the US is to cancel its funding of UNWRA, the relief agency for Palestinian refugees, on the specious grounds that the Palestinians have withdrawn from the so-called peace process. This is disgusting and immoral as there *is* no peace process, and apart from taking their land at every opportunity the Israelis have put up insuperable political obstacles to the Palestinians being able to be part of anything. Trump's approach to Israel and Palestine is nothing short of contemptible. But what is more annoying is the pathetically supine attitude of Johnson and May who do nothing to defend the Palestinians properly.

The Ambassador of Kazakhstan has asked me to help secure a police escort for President Nazarbayev when he passes through London on his way to New York. You would think that the Foreign Minister could just flick his fingers and fix this in an instant. He is after all the incoming President of the UN Security Council of which we are a P5 member, and he will be on his way there via the White House. But it all has to go through the Home Office, and some idiot committee will sit in judgement about whether this is a sufficiently official visit to justify offering flashing blue lights. It is yet another issue that makes the UK look so utterly puny, and I despair once again at how hopeless we are at showing dignified diplomatic manners. It makes a mockery of all our language about Global Britain.

I've tried a couple of times to call Julian Smith. Given I launched his political career you'd think he'd take my calls or be sure to reply quickly, but now that he is Chief Whip his attitude does seem to have changed. I think he has been totally sucked into the Gavin Williamson vortex and risks losing the confident perspective which any Chief Whip needs. There will have to be a reshuffle next week to replace Damian Green in the Cabinet Office, after his recent resignation thanks to the weird Pestminister furore, but it is far from clear how extensive any other changes will have to be. The *Sunday Times* listed the vulnerable as McLoughlin, Greening, Clark and Grayling along with the prospect of Boris being moved to a business department with a strong Brexit focus. Rumours therefore abound of Amber Rudd coming to the FCO. A stupid idea. Just when the world is falling to bits we need people in the Foreign Office who at least know something about foreign affairs. It's also totally unfair to say that McLoughlin is in for the sack when we all know that he wants to stand down and even asked to do so immediately after last year's election.

Thursday 4 January – Mustique

It's my fourth session of yoga on the beach. It is proving very beneficial. James and I are thinking of finding someone who can regularly train us in London.

Call Erik. I tell him how I so despair of the lack of initiative in the Cabinet. He said it could be worse. 'It's democracy.' He recalls a moment some years ago in Ireland when someone was elected to their parliament for a constituency near Port Laoise and the first thing they did was to send him to school, because he couldn't read.

Lance is making no progress with the Home Office in securing a police escort for Nazarbayev. They refuse to offer one for a private visit; there are only twenty-five trained police motorcyclists who can do it; they don't do it at weekends, etc. All we need is a black car with some blue strobes to make it look official.

Lance says he has learnt that the intention is to divert the Privy Council team to the embassy for a briefing when they arrive in Muscat. This is unusual. I call our Ambassador Hamish Cowell to check he has told Erik. He hadn't. We don't want Erik upset at having his plans altered.

Fly back to London overnight.

Friday 5 January – London

Back home, there has been some building progress in the house, but not much.

To Stansted. Speak to Julian Smith on the way. I'd been trying to call him and was beginning to think that he was avoiding me. But he answered after one ring while I was in the car and was suitably apologetic for not responding before. His manner is charming, but to think that my rather naive intern of ten years ago is now Chief Whip carries a certain air of absurdity. Parliament's institutional wisdom has been rather dissipated by the cult of youth and gender. Sensibly paced hierarchy now counts for nothing. It will cost them in the end, because they will all misjudge the mood and power of our own MPs.

Am first to arrive at the airport, where the great and the good are gathering to fly to Muscat for the Sultan's annual Privy Council advisory meeting. Good chat with Stuart Peach, then Mark Sedwill, then Christopher (now Lord) Geidt and Mervyn King. All charming and fun.

Flight over in the Sultan's Gulfstream 6. Lovely if you are upright, but it's mile-high camping if you want to sleep. Peach slept on the floor (he said for his back), but nobody was complaining.

Saturday 6 January – Muscat

The headlines are full of the new book out in the US called *Fire and Fury* by Michael Wolff. Its sensational claim is that Trump is not mentally stable. He is evidently an obsessive narcissist, but it's what we don't yet know about him in relation to Russia, money and improper influence that worries me more.

To the HM's Palace, the Bait al Baraka. After settling in, Mark Sedwill and I go to see FM Yousef bin Alawi, along with Hamish Cowell. We cover Iran and Yemen, but I leave it all to Mark. I did so deliberately, because Yousef is often difficult to hear, and therefore to understand. I mischievously asked Mark afterwards, 'Did you understand any of that?' When he looked bewildered I explained how challenging I'd always found him. 'Oh. Thank heavens,' he said. 'I was worried it was just me.'

Lunch beside the pool. Calm and dignified. Erik joins us. On offer is Pétrus, Cheval Blanc, etc.

Trump has tweeted that he is 'a very stable genius' and 'My two greatest assets are mental stability, and being really, like, smart.' Oh dear.

Drinks in the Palace Majlis. The same bottles on offer, but we all hold back, not quite knowing when we will be called to the meeting. We gather at 8pm, and once the clock nears 11 we are suddenly summoned. Our three-hour meeting with the Sultan covers all the topics he has asked for: regional security, the US Presidency and UK politics. As is his wont, we move on to a late and sumptuous dinner. As always HM was inquisitive and perky. His dark brown eyes always alert and energetic, but he was looking skinny, which is hardly surprising. The entire evening is a unique format which reflects the closeness of the UK's relationship with Oman.

Sunday 7 January – Muscat/London

We had finally turned in at 4.30am. After two nights on a plane, five hours' sleep in a bed was quite a luxury. Take off from Muscat at noon.

There seems no doubt the PM will shuffle tomorrow. She might shy away from moving Jeremy Hunt, as the NHS is facing something of a winter crisis, but the poor guy has kept the lid on it for so long he is always being barred from promotion for fear of it crumbling in anyone else's hands. I hope he gets the Cabinet Office job. The *Sunday Times* lists Rishi Sunak, Suella Fernandes, Nusrat Ghani and Seema Kennedy as tips for junior office. All fine, but it's a tad overdriven by gender and ethnicity: symbolism trumping broader meritocratic fairness. It sensibly excludes James Cleverly, who has been far too self-promoting. And Tugendhat should be given a bollocking rather than a step up.

So much for new-year discipline: I ended up having a full claret dinner with Ed [Argar] at the Poule au Pot.

Monday 8 January – London

It's reshuffle day, which is due to start at 11am. I have no expectations beyond staying where I am.

First proper day back in the office. The shuffle turns into a long-drawn-out affair, with little overall change. First, James Brokenshire resigns because he has to have a serious operation on his lungs, and Patrick McLoughlin stands down as planned. James B should just have asked for time off, but things are perhaps too critical in Northern Ireland to take that risk. But then it all goes a bit funny. Chris Grayling is mistakenly announced by CCHQ as the new Chairman, when in fact it is Brandon Lewis. He is lampooned throughout the day as the shortest-serving Chairman in political history – only thirty minutes. James Cleverly is Deputy Chairman, along with nine new Vice-Chairs, Kemi Badenoch, Ben Bradley, Chris Skidmore, Maria Caulfield, Rehman Chishti, Helen Grant. Andrew Jones, Marcus Jones and James Morris. Overload, or what?

The top three, Johnson, Rudd and Hammond, all stay, and David Lidington goes to the Cabinet Office to replace Damian Green, but not as First Secretary of State. Then, at a slow pace, throughout the day, the musical chairs are minor and at times confused. Who knows what really went on, but it seems that Hunt declined Business, and preferred to stay at Health to which is now added Social Care. Most, one by one, remain where they are, but the whole process was like pulling teeth. David Gauke to Justice; Karen Bradley to Northern Ireland; Matt Hancock to DCMS. Then Justine Greening throws a wobbly while staging a sit-in at Number 10 for three hours, refusing Work & Pensions, and so resigning from the government. Damian Hinds goes to Education, and Esther McVey goes to DWP. The only new face who has never before attended Cabinet is Damian Hinds – that's all, after all that. I'm not sure it'll get a good press tomorrow. Indeed the online *Telegraph* front-page headline is 'Night of the blunt stiletto'. Other ranks due tomorrow.

Tuesday 9 January – London

The crazy reshuffle continues at junior ministerial level. After only a few months immersing himself in Africa – albeit while indulging in absurd empire-building with far more private secretaries than he needs across two departments – Rory Stewart is moved to Justice, in charge of prisons, and Harriett Baldwin replaces him in FCO/DfID. It's probably to ensure that every department has a woman in the team. The Chief phones me to confirm that I am to stay put. I'm happy with that, and appreciate the personal call. The shuffle seems rather zero-sum and purposeless. No deliberate senior dismissals, and disruptive change-around elsewhere for no obvious gain. Ejected ministers are Mark Garnier, Philip Dunne, John Hayes, Robert Goodwill. It is especially unfair on the estimable Philip Dunne, who was far more eligible to be SofS for Defence than the pushy Williamson.

FCO Orals at 11.30, just before which Rory is summoned to wait in Downing Street. Slightly awkward choreography for us at the dispatch box as we have to juggle questions at the last minute with one fewer minister.

To the Horseguards Hotel for a drink with Clay Swisher. Who should appear but Corbyn's Svengali Chief of Staff, Seumas Milne, who had been meeting Clay earlier. He was charming, and we rather hit it off. It was one of those extraordinary encounters which bridges the massive political and ideological divide by being entertaining and frank. I rather enjoyed his company. There was almost a sense of trust built on our honest admissions about our own sides.

Wednesday 10 January – London
Ministerial team meeting with Boris in his office. These monthly get-togethers are cheerful but shallow. We just go around the table saying quickly what we've done and what we plan to do, but there is little depth of thought or comment. But at least we all like each other. At this one BoJo went on about saving the elephants; Secretary General Guterres' over-gloomy New Year message; and the importance of girls' education. He seems more comfortably cast as a champion for DfID issues than he is in dealing with those of world conflict and diplomacy.

Meeting with MPs who form the UK's new delegation to the Parliamentary Assembly of the Council of Europe. Led by Sir Roger Gale, who quips that the two Russian representatives are named Tolstoy and Kalashnikov.

Thursday 11 January – London
I suddenly had to respond to a UQ on Yemen, not officially my portfolio, but I was comfortable doing it and knew more than the briefing I was offered. As a sudden day out goes, it was an enjoyable and productive parliamentary occasion. But I feel very uneasy morally about having to defend Saudi excesses. They are bombing the country to bits and will achieve nothing except its miserable destruction.

Boris has a madcap idea of declaring the waters around the South Sandwich Islands a no-fishing zone. Although there is almost no fishing there anyway, there is nonetheless a licensing process and quota, which in its politics is delicately balanced through an organisation called CCAMLR (Commission for the Conservation of Antarctic Marine Living Resources), and the seas are the focus of our Antarctic Survey. Any change in its current administration would risk the reassertion of Argentine sovereignty claims and would prove environmentally damaging by pushing what krill fishing there is to less suitable waters where the fish are younger. It's all to satisfy the idiot Gove's thirst for credibility (or publicity) on green matters. Boris should just tell him to sod off as it's an FCO matter, not DEFRA [Department for Environment, Food and Rural Affairs]. I am ardently opposed to the Gove plan (for indeed it is his), but Boris seems set on indulging him.

Monday 15 January – London

Carillion, the massive construction and outsourcing company, has collapsed. Its plight has been obvious for months. It has a ramshackle mix of business streams, was overextended in the Gulf and faces mounting bad debts and loss-making contracts. It should have closed or been broken up ages ago, and for the government to have awarded it new contracts when its financial weakness was already so apparent is a scandal.

To Lambeth Palace to meet Archbishop Justin Welby. He is just so normal and human. No airs and graces. He is off on his travels, and I offer full cooperation and briefing from the FCO. Defending the Holy Land in its troubled region of today is a delicate challenge. And the woes of the CofE in Africa are dispiriting.

Proper discussion about Oman with Colonel John Clark from Number 10. It's good as far as it goes, in that he agrees with my efforts to shape a renewed UK strategic commitment to Oman, but nobody is getting a grip on it, and it is not yet coming together.

Drink with Amber Rudd in the Smoking Room. Priti Frightful brings Lord Polak in for a drink, which is against the rules, as it is strictly for MPs, and peers who are former MPs. Some colleagues are clearly annoyed, but nobody asks him to leave.

Tuesday 16 January – London

I sit on the bench for a Ten Minute Rule Bill debate on BIOT, the British Indian Overseas Territories, aka the Chagos Islands. We removed the small population from BIOT in the 1960s but won't let them return. We say they can go back when we've stopped using it for defence purposes, but I think another genuine reason is that if it is once again inhabited we would have to spend money under the Overseas Territories Act to 'meet their reasonable needs'. It's all rather artificial anyway as the campaign exaggerates the ex-islanders' real wishes.

Thursday 18 January – London

To the V&A for the reception for President Macron, who has been at Number 10 today. He was so late, I gave up and left as he arrived, so as to attend Ian and Tina Taylor's annual 'New Year' drinks at Eaton Square.

Friday 19 January – London

Boris says we should build a bridge across the Channel, because the tunnel is at full capacity. Well – that should all be quick and easy. Job done!

Sunday 21 January – London/Brussels

UKIP is imploding: what joy. Having binned Nutty Nuttall as their leader last year, they're now trying to remove his successor Henry Bolton. Who cares anyway? They are just a ragbag army of oddballs.

Monday 22 January – Brussels/London

In Brussels for the monthly meeting of EU foreign ministers. Breakfast with the European Investment Bank President Werner Hoyer, who impressed. The EIB is much bigger than the World Bank, which surprised me. It disburses more funds yet is staffed by fewer people.

At the main session EU High Rep Federica Mogherini reports on Iran, the JCPOA [Joint Comprehensive Plan of Action, the Iran nuclear deal], Libya and the EU dialogue on human rights in Cuba.

The trouble is, FedMog witters on monotonously, is a poor chairman and even worse timekeeper. The guest of honour for lunch is President Abbas of Palestine, but she keeps him waiting an hour, and then closes the session by saying, 'We are now due to have lunch with President Assad— er, I mean President Abbas.' Not her best day.

Back to London.

Tuesday 23 January – London

Boris, both annoyingly and disgracefully, refuses to support Palestine attending the UN Conference on Disarmament as an observer. Why the hell not?

Wednesday 24 January – London

See Dr Armen Sarkissian, whose plan to become the next President of Armenia seems to be on course. Speak to Alistair Burt about the Friends of Oman lunch. HMA Brazil Vijay Rangarajan comes in: he wants my support for his pitch for Good Governance/Prosperity Fund spending on some programmes he has designed for Brazil. I am so sceptical about the efficacy and value of these programmes. They have good intentions but poor outcomes.

Lunch with Tom Newton Dunn of the *Sun*. He is a pukka guy, but sometimes he holds slightly simplistic patriotic opinions which verge on the blimpish. But then I suppose that's what *Sun* readers feed on.

Friday 26 January – Rutland

A full constituency schedule, which is rather rare these days. Harriet comes up by train.

A proper catch-up with Leicestershire County Council: Nick Rushton, John Sinnott, Byron Rhodes and David Briscombe. We cover the Melton bypass, their Medium-Term Financial Strategy and the potential closure of children's centres. The Council will face enormous financial pressure in two years' time.

Talk to Rutland Radio. Then my twenty-seventh Melton Ladies' lunch. Usual cheerful gathering of eighty-year-olds. My annual *tour d'horizon*: last June's election farce; Brexit complexity; difficult year coming; Corbyn is dreadful; need to return to real politics; local issues; FCO travels; spare us from President Trump. They were happy.

Saturday 27 January – Rutland
The Party has gone mad. Rees-Mogg has a massive splash double-page interview in the *Daily Telegraph*. He doesn't merit it. He is a character among dullards, but is espousing a point of view which is a total caricature. It is little more than a cartoon picture of Britain's place in the world which, outside the narrow adulation of anti-EU Conservative activists, is subject only to ridicule. Oh, these comical Etonians.

Meanwhile it would seem that Gavin Williamson has seriously overplayed his hand. In his rush to ascend the greasy pole he manoeuvred to get Michael Fallon's job at Defence, only now to be accused of having been sacked from his job as a fireplace salesman ten years ago for having an affair with an employee. He gave the story himself to the *Mail* after the *Guardian* approached him for comment, but I doubt his account is complete. If she squeals, and more salacious facts emerge, then I think he is in difficulty. We will see what the papers look like tomorrow.

But, beneath it all, the Prime Minister's authority is once again on the slide.

Sunday 28 January – Rutland/London
Gavin W is getting off lightly. He destroyed Fallon in the knee-touching frenzy, even though Fallon had done nothing wrong: and now he is under the cosh, it seems for having left his job as MD of a fireplace company owned by Aga, but he will survive because all the focus is on the declining authority of Theresa May. Her inactivity and icy indecisiveness leave an unfilled vacuum. Fallon was Defence Secretary and was forced to leave by the then Chief Whip: that Chief Whip is now Defence Secretary and has done much worse. If he were the Chief sitting in judgement on himself, he'd be toast.

Grant Shapps has written an article in the *Mail* saying Theresa should set a date for her departure. Doubling down or what? He clearly hates her.

When you are in the middle of a political phase of events, it is usually difficult to judge their significance. The government has been paralysed by Brexit for over a year. Following June's election, and given the drabness of May, to say nothing of a sub-standard Cabinet and Party division, the government is in intensive care and might drift haplessly to its end within months.

Monday 29 January – London

A round-table discussion on the South Sandwich Islands, and the fishing issue, in the Entente Cordiale Room with Boris. It was just so embarrassing. He bluffed and blustered with no grip on detail. All he wants to do is suck up to the NGOs, and he refuses to take a stand based on science and the national interest. The trouble is he just likes to be liked.

Wednesday 31 January – London

Meeting with Irish FM Simon Coveney. He is one of the best. Practical, coherent and with clear analysis and opinions, I really like him. I just wonder how many of our ministers and Cabinet ministers can create such a good impression. He has no easy solutions to Brexit, but is the opposite of our delusional ideologues.

Ministerial team meeting. The usual performance from Boris. Cheerful and amusing on one level, totally disengaged on another.

I am given a policy submission on diversity and equality which is probably the most appalling piece of work I have ever received. It is as if written by a fourteen-year-old who has become enthused by gender equality and has all sorts of adolescent ideas about how to enforce their views. The paper recommended that every minister's private office should have an equal gender balance and that, when travelling, at least one official must be female. I actually have a majority female office, who I doubt would want to be thought to have been appointed only because they were women. And as for travelling, I normally only have one official with me anyway. I returned it with the most virulent comments, which amounted to me saying this was the worst piece of work I had ever seen, that its thinking was a disgrace to the FCO, and that it should be shredded.

Boris is just going mad about 'no-fish' for the South Atlantic. We had a serious set-to, with me remonstrating with him that he risks destroying a delicately crafted policy, is ignoring all the scientific advice, is risking a new sovereignty skirmish with Argentina and will incur the wrath of the Falkland Islanders. All for the sake of a press release. Just leave it alone.

Speak at the Higher Command and Staff Course in the Map Room. Lots of rising mid-ranking officers across the services. They like and respect frankness, and their questions are intelligent and precise. I must have done ten of these speeches by now.

Sit down with John Glen, Economic Secretary to the Treasury, to discuss the Sanctions Bill. I'll be steering it through the Commons and the FCO is in the lead, but in addition to establishing an autonomous UK regime for international sanctions so that we can implement UN ones and replace those currently run by the EU, it will contain some anti-money-laundering clauses which come under the Treasury. John's calm and conscientious, a good colleague.

Thursday 1 February – London
To Wilton Park, the stately home conference venue owned, or at least financed, by the Foreign Office. They gather some good people for serious academic and journalistic sessions, but the 'brains trust' wisdom seems to stay in the room and rarely filters down into FCO briefings or policy. I am, as always, a little too candid about what I really think about Brexit, but as they all agree with me I am in safe company.

Sunday 4 February – Rutland/London
So many people now think they can or should take over from Theresa. Housing Minister Dominic Raab is at it again on Sky. Backbenchers Johnny Mercer and Tugendhat have a Faustian pact with the *Sun*, under which they tell Tom Newton Dunn everything in return for being regularly plugged and tipped in his reports. Boris feigns no interest in standing, and then texts back anybody who might intimate that they support him. Meanwhile he plots relentlessly with the scheming Gove, who he should never trust

again. Rees-Mogg is just incessantly over the top, and has accused Treasury officials of being biased against Brexit. There is due to be a two-day Cabinet to thrash out our stand, but the PM is just so trapped. The quiet majority are getting pretty fed up with the noisy hardliners.

Monday 5 February – London
Boris is planning to make a big speech on Brexit, but has postponed it until the 14th. It will no doubt be entirely subversive.

Natter in the corridor with Nicholas Soames, Nick Herbert, Ben Wallace. Johnny Mercer goes past and gets ribbed wholesale. Soames shouts, 'I'll see you in ten minutes for a serious interview.' I add, 'Without much coffee.'

Dinner with Ben Wallace in the Firecracker. He is a gem. Every time I see him he is full of fabulously energetic opinions. He says rumours about Boris resigning are the concoction of Gavin Williamson, who is briefing manically in order to tarnish Boris and knock out all others who might be leader. The man is crazed.

Tuesday 6 February – London
On the way to the FCO I bump into Richard Luce in Abbey Yard. A former FCO minister, he resigned with Lord Carrington over the Falklands, then went to the House of Lords and served in the Royal Household as Lord Chamberlain to the Queen. He is one of my heroes – we so agree on the Middle East and indeed on everything. He is a wonderful man.

It's a century since women earned the vote, so it's a full-on media day for the Suffragettes. But nothing illustrates the weakness of the Prime Minister more than the visual awkwardness with which she joined their photo op. Gangly, looking around as if lost, no poise or presence. Charisma bypass. No personality. She is the only credible game in town, but there's not much there, and I despair.

Wednesday 7 February – London
Meeting with Philip Barton, who runs Consular and Security in the FCO. He has all the demeanour of a deputy headmaster who is head

of the history department, but beneath his quiet, studied manner lies a razor-sharp brain and excellent unemotional judgement.

At the ministers' meeting I pointedly raised Brexit, looking directly at Boris, ahead of a much heralded two-day Cabinet session. I stressed that it is not simple, and that it was not reasonable to fence in the PM by repeatedly stating that all we need is a jumbo trade deal. The simple certainties of the Brexit ideologues are unrelated to the real world: they are just fantasy imaginings which cannot be delivered. By all means advocate just walking away from everything, but be honest about the cost, and stop pretending there's an easy glorious prosperous alternative to some sort of trading relationship with the EU 27. Boris just maintains a jaunty 'come on; let's get on with it' attitude. He is impervious to reason.

Richard Clarke, International Director of the Home Office. He is great. If we succeed in having Julian Assange evicted from the Ecuador embassy, he will be warmly embraced by Inspector Knacker of the Yard.

Tuesday 13 February – Muscat

Overnight flight to Muscat, and then straight to the Royal Office to see General Sultan al Numani and his deputy.

Focussed mostly on Yemen and Iran. In large part rehearsing the same concerns expressed by the Sultan at last month's Privy Council meeting, they want to do their utmost to mediate between their neighbours to the north and Iran, to try and bring an end to the carnage in Yemen.

Wednesday 14 February – Muscat

Valentine's Day, and exactly ten years since I proposed to James on the beach in Muscat walking back after dinner.

Quiet day, then a lovely sumptuous dinner at the Tuscany in the Hyatt. A twelve-course tasting menu with an over-generous different wine with each. The alcohol intake was a tad excessive.

Meanwhile Boris has made his much heralded Brexit speech. There was no way of stopping him, so the PM ensured that four other Cabinet ministers made one as well: David Lidington on the

implications for the devolved assemblies, Greg Clark on UK industry, etc. The Boris speech was vacuous: there was nothing in it except
bluff, bluster and rhetorical optimism. Hot air with zero detail. It
was so intellectually empty I just don't understand how any serious
journalist can do anything other than mock it.

Thursday 15 February – Muscat
Ollie [Blake] and Emily have arrived from London, and will stay
near the Hyatt before checking in on Saturday.

Lunch at Caramel in the Opera House mall with James and Sayd
Badr. He is very reflective about Yemen and Boris.

To the Muttrah soukh where we buy some attractive Omani
Moussa (turban wraps, which are great as scarves) and on to the
Shangri La hotel for a drink with David Cameron and his brother-
in-law, the other Lord Astor, William. They have been on a family
holiday and have loved it: camping in the desert, staying in the
sumptuous Alila hotel on top of the Jebel Akhdar and now enjoying
some time by the beach. DC was due to see Yousef bin Alawi, but
now probably won't as Yousef is flying from Ramallah to the Munich
Security Conference. I nonetheless gave DC a teach-in on Yemen,
but we mostly dwelt on Brexit and speculated on whether it could
ever be stopped by hard-line Remainers in the House. We both
concluded that, although nigh on impossible, blocking it could only
ever happen towards the end of the process on an unforeseen amendment in the Commons which suddenly arose out of a procedural
opportunity. But it won't.

Friday 16 February – Muscat
To Wadi Ash Shab with friends Ollie and Emily. It's a dramatic
two-hour drive on a road cut through the mountains, which rise
above Muscat offering a stunning view of the city. A boat takes us the
twenty yards across the mouth of the wadi, from which we walk,
paddle and swim the mile or so to the inner pools and its caves at the
end. Walking on the pebbles is like painful reflexology: next time I'll
take rock shoes.

Sunday 18 February – Muscat

An hour with former Yemeni FM Abu Bakr al Qirbi. He gave me a comprehensive download on Yemen. He's about the only serious Yemeni anyone in the FCO is actually talking to, while so much of the focus is otherwise on the Saudis. There won't be a Yemen solution without Yemenis.

Monday 19 February – London

Land early, and straight into the FCO to address a US congressional delegation. These group movements are always a little tiresome, but I press the charm button. Every meeting with US politicians seems to be male-dominated, and they are much older than their UK equivalents.

Meeting on honours with Lance. The whole process is wrong. It is too public-sector dominated, and the most deserving are deemed too risky and are relegated. Almost no ambassadors are up for reward. McDonald has far too much say over it. When shaped in his image it becomes ill-judged and grotty.

The BBC are making a documentary on the workings of the Foreign Office, and they have chosen as part of it to follow the passage of the Sanctions Bill, which I am pleased to assist. So they are filming some of my briefing meetings as the Bill takes shape, supplemented by face-to-face interviews afterwards. The second reading is not far off, so they sit in for a briefing meeting on it.

Tuesday 20 February – London

FCO Orals, followed by the second reading of the Sanctions Bill. I did all the work, but as I suppose is customary Boris will do the debate. I have gone to great lengths to ensure that the Bill is in good shape, but they have added some anti-money-laundering clauses to it which will open up scope for amendments about the OTs [Overseas Territories] being tax havens, and issues about Russian oligarchs' money. We have probably created some needless problems for ourselves, which no doubt will be dumped on me to sort out.

Thursday 22 February – London/Washington

BA flight to Washington. Just occasionally it's great to have a daytime flight. Eight hours without interruption to read, write and think.

The Brexit Cabinet have been at Chequers all day trying to thrash out a common position on our Phase 2 negotiations with the EU. But it's only us talking incoherently to ourselves.

Friday 23 February – Washington

Donald Tusk in Brussels has described our pick 'n' mix approach to the negotiations as 'utterly delusional', thus illustrating early on that it's all very well the Brexit Cabinet reaching a common view, but as it is wholly at odds with anything that might be agreed in a deal, it is an irrelevant exercise which bears no relation to reality.

After meetings at the State Department, I address students at the Churchill Center at George Washington University. I am shown Churchill's original diary cards from the war: June 1940 to July 1946. Frequent entries saying 'Lunch with the King'.

In the White House we see Trump adviser and speechwriter Stephen Miller. It was really quite unsettling that someone with such an ardent and simplistic worldview – not to mention opinions on immigration and policing which have a whiff of white supremacy about them – has such direct influence on the President. It's as if he had been injected with the very worst characteristics of UKIP.

Fabulous dinner with Governor John Kasich. I give him a signed copy of William Hague's book on William Wilberforce, which thrills him. He is equivocal about whether he wants to run for President again …

Saturday 24 February – Washington

The *Sun* says that if anyone in the Party threatens to rebel on any decision about leaving the customs union, then May should make it a vote of confidence. That would up the ante and inject an air of desperation into it all. But it would signal that the government is in intensive care. She might win the vote at this stage, but other more critical votes later on might not enjoy the same outcome.

Dinner with Sir Kim Darroch and his wife Vanessa in a local restaurant. I love having a naughty gossip with him. He is such a gas.

Monday 26 February – London

Back in London, and it's snowing. To the EBRD (European Bank for Reconstruction and Development) HQ in the City for their Western Balkans Investment Conference. It is a useful start to a series of Balkans events which will culminate in our summit in July. Today is a good opportunity to meet the players and express, through the EBRD, the UK's serious interest in the region.

Lunch at White's with US Ambassador Woody Johnson. He's a character. Nice and perky, but his comments just dart around like a butterfly hopping from one flower to another. It is impossible to discern any consistent train of thought, or discuss any issue in depth. He starts by asking the waiter if he can have an iced coffee. Not quite the Club's usual beverage.

Sanctions Bill briefing with officials ahead of the committee stage. As I predicted, the Whips are worried about amendments and votes, but just won't engage on any detail. So their SpAds are bossing officials and presenting me with potential problems, but I have no route into resolving them because Julian Smith is impossible to contact.

EBRD reception hosted by the PM at Number 10 for Balkans leaders. I know them all fairly well now, and wheel them in front of the PM, who requires a confident introduction if she is to say anything. Otherwise she just stands there dumbstruck.

Tuesday 27 February – London

Sanctions Bill committee stage in Committee Room 12, the first of at least four days on it. As if I hadn't told them weeks ago, the Whips are now agitated by the prospect of amendments on the financial status of our OTs and of a 'Magnitsky' amendment. Based on the campaigning of US-born British financier Bill Browder, whose anti-corruption lawyer Sergei Magnitsky died in a Russian prison in 2009, such a clause could impose sanctions on those deemed to have committed gross violations of human rights. But we can't be obliged to slap sanctions on someone just because an NGO says they are that bad, nor can we be obliged to slap sanctions on everyone we deem to be in such violation – the list would run into thousands and thousands.

Back to the Bill committee. My opposite number, Helen Goodman, is decidedly batty. She was when I knew her at Oxford. The two contentious issues are Magnitsky, and open registers for the beneficial owners of offshore companies in the OTs. The plan was to defer committee scrutiny of the Magnitsky issue, which is actually Clause 1, until later on. We have rattled on and stand to finish our planned progress pretty well as soon as we've started this afternoon. So Labour are trying to get on to Magnitsky today. We will force an adjournment of the committee, and are planning to breach a pair because we (a) want to win the vote, which we will anyway, and (b) want to retaliate against Labour who agreed to a programme and have now reversed their agreement. [Pairing works on trust and honour, and is crucial to the parliamentary process. If each side agrees that one of their MPs can be absent, then neither should return to vote. Cheating on a pair is a parliamentary crime.]

I don't like us stretching the rules of decency in this way even though we have a reason for it. It's using a nuclear weapon in a minor bunfight.

Wednesday 28 February – London

A letter from Boris to Number 10, or at least its first page, has leaked. I wonder who did that? And now, surprise surprise, in order to clarify its misinterpretation by the media, Boris has said he will publish the full text of the letter. Number 10 are furious, and any deliberate release by Boris would constitute a breach of the ministerial code. So there's another fine mess he's got himself into. Once again, he is undermining the government and playing no end of silly games.

Thursday 1 March – London

Full tilt on the committee stage of the Sanctions Bill for most of the morning and afternoon. We are making good progress, and I am getting the better of Helen Goodman and the Opposition, winning the arguments by smothering them in sweet reason.

Friday 2 March – London

I am trying my utmost to construct a future strategy for our relations with and support for Oman, and have at last managed to convene a high-level group to discuss it. All the bits of the jigsaw are sitting across Whitehall, with no fundamental disagreement anywhere, but there is no top-level direction prepared to take the initiative to put all the pieces together into a finished picture. I will keep trying ... or keep crying.

Interviews for my new private secretary. Heavy snowfalls across the country. We decide to stay put in London rather than drive through the snow. We had no plans for Rutland, so why not have a London weekend?

Theresa makes her much trailed speech on Brexit at Mansion House. It is intended to map out the principles underpinning our negotiating stance. Inevitably it is a bit wooden, and I'm not sure it takes us much further forward, but at least it's something to chew on.

Tuesday 6 March – London

Sanctions Bill committee most of the morning and afternoon. We are getting there without mishap.

Something odd is going on in Salisbury. A Russian dissident who is also a former intelligence officer, Sergei Skripal, and his daughter Yulia have been found slumped on a park bench there, seemingly poisoned. This all looks very sinister and would appear to be another hit in the UK against figures who are enemies of Putin. More to come on this one, I sense.

Thursday 8 March – London

The two poisoned in Salisbury are still in a critical condition, and a policeman has also been affected and is now in hospital.

There's been a stupid decision to delay the report stage of the Sanctions Bill. Just when I have commenced negotiations with Labour which stand a good chance of achieving unity on the two contentious amendments that remain, officials (probably within the offices of the Chief Whip and the Leader of the House) have briefed

Ben Wallace without my permission, concluded that there are problems and so have decided to defer report stage by a month. This far exceeds their remit or authority, and they have completely fouled up the pace and mood of my discussions. I'm supposed to be driving this Bill, and nobody deigns to talk to me.

Overnight flight to Chile.

Friday 9 March – Santiago
180 police are scouring Salisbury in white spacesuits.

After the head of South Korean intelligence visits Washington, Trump says he will meet Kim Jong-un of North Korea, but announces it without consulting or telling anyone else in the administration. He is whacky.

Land 10.30am. At sixteen hours it is the longest flight I have ever taken, but it allows for a proper sleep and a bit of work.

Saturday 10 March – Chile
It looks as though the Salisbury poisoning was caused by a Russian nerve agent. This is serious.

Non-stop ministers and meetings followed by a rather intoxicating wine tasting at top wine shop Concha y Toro consuming, rather than just sipping, twelve Chilean wines. I bought a few bottles of a delicious red called El Incidente.

I also spend a fortune on two large and heavy onyx flamingos. One is about eighteen inches high, the other about twenty-four. The challenge is now to get them into a holdall and on to the plane as extra hand luggage. I went to buy lapis lazuli, but the onyx were more beautiful and a tenth of the price. One more glass and I might have succumbed!

Sunday 11 March – Santiago/Valparaíso
Back in the UK the PM is taking a bit of stick for not reacting firmly to the suspected Russian poisoning of Sergei Skripal and his daughter. Williamson cheaply hawkish: he's becoming a populist menace.

It's Mother's Day. Phoned Mum: the flowers had just arrived. She was very pleased, and sounding very spritely.

To Valparaíso. Visit to the Navy Museum high on the hill over-looking the bay. It is as much a tribute to British influence in Chile as it is to the Chileans themselves. It includes the capsule in which 300 miners were rescued from underground in the amazing incident of 2010. It was an ingenious feat of engineering created by the Chilean Navy. On the way we stopped at a remarkable fire station which contains murals and artefacts of our Royal Family going back to 1901. It's a fascinating time warp. It was all the more pleasing to be greeted spontaneously by a dishy young fireman.

To the airport. I managed to be the first on to the plane – with the flamingos – and all is well. The only pain will be lugging them the first half-mile at Heathrow from the plane to the baggage hall to get a trolley. Same charming BA crew as on the way out.

Monday 12 March – London
Land, home, then FCO.

There is a flurry in the office about Russia and clear vibes that something is about to be announced. I am given a full brief, which matches and confirms all the rumours, and suspicions which have gained currency in the media are confirmed. The government labo-ratory at Porton Down has confirmed beyond doubt that the poison used in Salisbury was a banned military-grade nerve agent called Novichok. It is known to be Russian-made, and as such they were supposed to have destroyed all their stocks years ago. Our approach, though, has to be well crafted so as not to press accusations too far and risk a Russian response which neutralises our honest position. Philip Barton and the team have constructed a well-reasoned state-ment which leaves the Russians no latitude for a convincing fightback.

We state simply: it is Russian-made; its mere existence, let alone its use, is a serious breach of the Chemical Weapons Convention; no such agent has been used on European soil since 1946; it can only be handled by experts who are necessarily part of government; so either the Russian government did it themselves or they have lost control of their (illegal) Novichok stocks. They should tell us which.

We have summoned Russian Ambassador Alexander Yakovenko to the FCO. Whatever anyone might ever think about Boris on so many things, on this occasion he was brilliant. As an interview without coffee goes, this was a masterclass. In his room were just Boris, Philip Barton and me. He had been given a clear script, and he stuck to it faithfully.

Yakovenko and his deputy came in, all jaunty and smiling as if nothing had happened. Boris and I were suitably severe. We all remained standing up, on facing sides of the Foreign Secretary's large office table.

'Ambassador. Two people have been poisoned on UK soil in Salisbury. One is in a critical condition and might die. His daughter and a policeman are in hospital. Our laboratory has established beyond doubt that the poison used was a banned military-grade nerve agent called Novichok. We know that this was made in Russia, and can only have been handled by the Russian state. Either the Russian state did this or it has lost control of its Novichok stocks. You have until midnight tomorrow to let us know which.'

And then he raised his tone and, with fabulous indignation verging on anger, told him in no uncertain terms how unacceptable it was to violate our security, try to murder someone on British soil, breach a highly important international convention, etc. It was a deliciously delivered dressing down, in response to which the dumbstruck Yakovenko couldn't say anything, and just left.

Well done, Boris! I felt genuinely proud of him. Perhaps it worked so well because he was not larking about and playing to the gallery – he spoke from the heart and meant what he said. It was a magic moment, which shows that little can beat Boris at his best.

To the Commons. The PM's statement is a bit late in the making, but she will have been so profoundly cautious about saying anything that isn't incontestably proven. It was emphatic and logical.

I address thirty ambassadors, who have been invited to the FCO for a detailed briefing. I text Boris to point out that it was a rather stupid and inexplicable FCO decision to exclude the Gulfies from it, but the briefing was a good thing to have done.

Watch TV, and learn more about the Salisbury incident from

Newsnight than I've ever been told in the FCO in supposed top secrecy.

Tuesday 13 March – London

Do a few things in the office before attending COBRA on the Salisbury poisoning. Our Ambassador in Moscow, Laurie Bristow, will be going to the Russian MFA [Ministry of Foreign Affairs] at 1pm. We will expel twenty-one or more of their diplomats from London.

I take the chance beforehand, while we are milling around, to make a gentle point to Sajid Javid about the proposed Holocaust centre in Victoria Palace Gardens. It's a good project but in the wrong place. It violates a UNESCO World Heritage Site, and the gardens are specifically preserved in a 1900 Act of Parliament about developing the embankment. My ever so slight objection provokes an extraordinarily tart response: 'I'm in charge of the Holocaust centre, and I'm in charge of planning, so they will get it. And I've already chosen the architect.'

He is the Secretary of State for Communities and Local Government, so he is indeed the ultimate determinant of any planning appeal, should it be turned down by Westminster City Council. But his is a semi-judicial role and process. So if he has already decided the outcome, he would be on the wrong side of the law. The whole project reeks of impropriety and seems to me to be linked to donor influence more than anything else.

Phone call with the admirable ex-Defence Secretary and former NATO Secretary General George Robertson who makes a few points about Russia and our possible response. First, do not block Russian money coming in: it benefits us, and drains them. Second, use our cyber-power to open up and allow internet activity in Russia, i.e. stop them blocking it. It matters more than us blocking what they do to us in social media. He's smart.

Oh well … it's all happening. Rex Tillerson has been replaced as Trump's Secretary of State by Mike Pompeo. He didn't stay long, and Trump's turnover of senior appointees is unprecedented.

Wednesday 14 March – London

Ministerial team meeting. Superficial as always.

PM's statement on Russia immediately following PMQs. I sat in the corner of the Chamber diagonally opposite her, up near the Serjeant at Arms, and close to the door into the No lobby. I wanted to watch as much of her statement as possible before slipping into the Central Lobby to do some TV interviews. I took an illicit iPhone photo.

The statement was cool and logical. Skripal poisoned. It was Novichok. Military-grade nerve agent. No explanation has been given by Moscow. Undeclared chemical weapons programme. Have referred it to the OPCW [Organisation for the Prohibition of Chemical Weapons]. Russian response has been one of sarcasm and disdain. It is part of an established pattern.

We will expel twenty-three intelligence officers who must leave within a week. We will establish new powers to harden our defences. There will be extra UK border controls on Russians and we will freeze Russian assets (oh yeah … whose?). We will retain proper liberal values, and will suspend all high-level contacts, including those in respect of the World Cup in June/July.

Lots of interviews in Central Lobby. I have had so little coverage recently it is good to know I can get back on my bike.

The irrational Russian reaction, full of absurd denials and conspiracy theories, reconfirms that their Ambassador Yakovenko is off his trolley.

Further briefing of diplomats, this time with the Gulfies.

Watched the UN open session. Jonathan Allen, he of the Cyprus talks, is now our interim UN Rep. He made our statement very well, in stark contrast to the Russian, who is a fat thug with a hole for a brain.

Thursday 15 March – London

Helen Goodman and her Whip Nick Smith. Nick is sensible, and I am embarrassed at the way we treat the Opposition. One thing Julian Smith doesn't understand is the importance of trust in the way two opposing parties conduct their procedural hostilities. Even war has rules. Parliament most certainly does. It is wise never to flout them, and inexcusable that we just did.

To Number 10 for a long-awaited face-to-face meeting with the PM, who I was seeing at my request. She is just so remote and disconnected from people. I really don't know who she talks to or confides in. Certainly not me, which is so silly. I told her emphatically when DC resigned as PM that she must stand; I've known her (albeit with no particular friendship) for forty years; I waded enthusiastically into her leadership campaign; I'm holding the line in the FCO; and am able to help shore up her support among older colleagues. However, I made it clear at the start that the meeting was not about me: rather it was to canter through a list of issues quickly to ensure she was aware of what was going on.

My opening was to say that only she can hold it all together. Under anyone else the whole show would disintegrate. And it most certainly would.

I mentioned that Ian has cancer and she should give him a K. Her deadpan reaction was not that she doesn't want it to happen, it's just that she is not prepared to push for something in the way Cameron used to. She will never stick her neck out. The system controls her, not the other way round.

She agrees to write a letter to Jack Swaab, father of James' close friend Richard, for his 100th. I explain that I am getting on perfectly well with Boris, but it takes work. She should see Bob Dudley of BP; it's crazy that he can see Putin but not his own PM. We need a ten-year plan for Oman. Yemen is a catastrophe. I was the one who secured her invitation to address the GCC in Bahrain, which stopped them inviting Putin instead. Updated her on Ecuador and Assange: she might want to butter up President Moreno. We are making progress on flights to the Falklands. Plans for the Balkans Summit are going well – although it will coincide with events celebrating the centenary of the RAF. A few comments on Armen Sarkissian and Armenia, and Aliyev of Azerbaijan. On Brexit, I said I stay out of it, but would object strongly to leaving with no deal. Gavin Williamson's 'shut up and go away' remarks about Russia were antagonistic and puerile. The Sanctions Bill is in good shape and it's better we make progress as fast as possible. Richard Moore would make a good Political Director, now that Karen Pierce is moving on to the UN, and I hope the PM will release him from the NSC even though he's only been there six months.

We covered a lot of ground. She smiled sweetly and took it all in, but she is just so inexpressive you just don't know if it was worth the bother.

Friday 16 March – Sarajevo

Up at 4.30am for a 7.40 flight to Munich, then on to Sarajevo. I'm accompanied by the admirable Lance, who I hope will be confirmed as the next Balkans director once he leaves me.

Straight into lunch with the six Balkans foreign ministers, the Bulgarian Foreign Minister (because they currently hold the EU Presidency) and two senior officials from the EU. They had been meeting during the morning, so asked me to speak as soon as I sat down. I talked them through our plans for the July summit, but then made an impassioned plea for united international condemnation of the nerve-agent attack in Salisbury. The Serbian winced slightly, as they are the closest to the Russians, but all the others were totally onside.

Saturday 17 March – Sarajevo/Rutland

A walk around Sarajevo, seeing the evidence of the 1990s siege such as bullet holes and reconstructed buildings, and was told tales of the episode. To the corner where the Archduke was assassinated in 1914. Had the driver not taken the wrong turning it wouldn't have happened.

Bosnia Herzegovina is a precarious construct, born of the Dayton Peace Accords of twenty years ago, under which there is one state and two entities beneath, the Federation and the more Russia-leaning Republika Srpska. Coffee with the PMs of the two entities Fadil Novalić from the Federation, and Željka Cvijanović from RS.

Laurie Bristow has been summoned to the Russian MFA for 11am Moscow time for the Russian counter-offensive. We soon learn what we face. They will expel twenty-three of our diplomats, but also close the British Council and the consulate in St Petersburg. They have upped the ante with an asymmetric response, doing more to us than our actions did to them. We are due to close our consulate in Ekaterinburg, which of course they knew, which is why they have deliberately caused additional disruption to us by picking St Petersburg.

I suspect they have been riled by Johnson, and by Williamson whose childish conduct may well have added to their planned retaliation. I've been receiving texts with damning criticism of both. Williamson, more so than Boris, has taken a lot of stick. Russian military intelligence has accused him of using the language of a 'market wench' and has used words which seem to translate into calling him 'a silly little pretty boy'. The *Times* cartoon plays on the schoolboy story-book image by portraying him as 'Just Williamson', up a tree holding a catapult.

I speak to Boris from the airport to assure him that I will watch him on *Marr* and will be sure to be aligned with him in what I will then say an hour or so later on the *Sunday Politics* tomorrow.

Fly into Birmingham. Reunite with Noodle.

Monday 19 March – London
Call Ian Blackford MP and Alison Thewliss MP, the Scot Nats I am dealing with on the Sanctions Bill. She is incapable of taking a decision, and says it's all up to someone else. There isn't really any point in talking to her. But we are in supposed negotiations about whether we can agree a joint approach at report stage to the Magnitsky clause and the handling of the OTs' public asset registers. It would seem the answer is no, but they won't be clear about it.

It is said that Davis and the EU's negotiator Michel Barnier might have reached a deal in Brussels on the transition period following our formal departure on 29 March 2019.

Wednesday 21 March – London
Mum is eighty-seven today.

Andriy Kobolyev, CEO of Naftogaz Ukraine. He is a slightly chubby forty-year-old who is full of energy and dynamism. He puts up a robust case against allowing the Russians to build Nordstream II, a massive pipeline which would export gas from Russia to Europe bypassing Ukraine, which currently earns $2 billion a year in transit fees for the existing pipeline route.

The main customer would be Germany, but Ukraine considers the pipeline a strategic threat as it would remove any influence it has over Russia and it would put Germany in a dangerously dependent position. It is of minimal concern to us, and although Shell and BP are shareholders in the project and would earn a regular dividend, we have no sway over the decision. The route is entirely sub-sea, and only Denmark has the practical power to obstruct it. Commercially, it's the obvious route for Gazprom to take.

Karen Pierce's farewell drinks before heading to become our Permanent Rep at the UN.

Friday 23 March – Rutland
General McMaster has been replaced by John Bolton as Trump's NSA. Oh dear, oh dear, oh dear.

Sunday 25 March – Rutland
To Bottesford in the very north of my large patch to launch the 'Friendly Bench', a rather touching community scheme to create a seat within a small planted space on the edge of a council estate. Anyone can go there, and the whole idea is that all social barriers are broken down, and whoever turns up is both allowed and expected to talk to anyone else. It is elementary social courtesy, but in this modern world it needs encouragement.

Rutland is brilliant with its civic services and ceremonial events. Today's is just such an example. The wonderful Lord Lieutenant for the last fourteen years, Sir Laurence Howard, is being thanked on his retirement. Typically, he insists that it is not to be just about him, and so they have combined it with the Centenary of the RAF, in which he is an honorary air vice-marshal. At Oakham Castle afterwards I was asked to propose the toast. It was a pleasure to do so.

Monday 26 March – London

Meeting with Boris on the preparation for CHOGM (the Commonwealth Heads of Government Meeting).

I attend the opening and closing of the Commons debate on Russia, on a day which has seen the widespread sympathetic expulsion of Russian diplomats in other countries such as Germany and France. They are wise to have done so. The attack was on us, but it could have been on them.

Putin has made a serious miscalculation, which one day will return to bite him. But it will take time. It was one murder attempt too many. He was caught out. He just did what he'd done before, but lacks any appreciation of wider perception and opinion. He probably thinks it strengthens him.

A colleague said earlier to me today of Gavin Williamson's 'shut up and go away' comment: 'It said nothing about Putin, but it said everything about the guy who said it.'

Tuesday 27 March – London

Farewell drinks for two exceptional members of my private office, Louise Nicol and Lance Domm. The price you pay for good people is that the turnover is high.

I was reminded about my description of Trump well before he was elected: 'A lone wolf, not a team player. An independent, not a Republican. A businessman, not a politician.'

Friday 30 March – London

Russian tit-for-tat expulsions against all those who have joined us in taking action.

A poll puts Theresa 11 points ahead of Corbyn as the voters' preferred Prime Minister. Corbyn has the enthusiastic support of a narrow, rather nasty, ideological base, but is old, plain and intellectually weak. His party is controlled at the constituency level by the hard left, and their Party rules ensure that even if he were to lose the support of the majority of his parliamentary Party, he would still be re-elected as their leader. His relative success and popularity at last

June's general election has gradually evaporated, and his authority is eroding without totally collapsing.

Saturday 31 March–Friday 6 April – Marrakech
To Marrakech for a week's break.

Over sixteen Palestinians have been killed in the Gaza Strip. Israel rejects calls for an independent inquiry. So Happy Easter from them!

Saturday 7 April – Rutland
Noodle returns from Mary next door, very excited but a little weepy and unsettled for about half an hour, and then normality resumes.

Uppingham for a haircut. Brief shop in Oakham. Walk by the river. Quiet night in.

Ben Wallace texts, concerned that while the US have slapped a range of sanctions on Russian oligarchs we have failed to explain why we have not. There is a good reason. It's because, until we are out of the EU and have our own autonomous sanctions law, we have to do everything collectively with the EU.

The Skripals are recovering, Yulia is OK to be discharged, and Sergei is conscious again after a month. The Russians only had five supporters in a meeting of the OPCW: we should give President Aliyev of Azerbaijan a bollocking when he sees the PM next month, as he was one of them.

Harriett Baldwin WhatsApps our FCO ministers group to suggest a Commons debate in order to highlight Corbyn's equivocation over Russian culpability. I strongly advise against – such debates always deteriorate, there isn't much one can add, it will turn into Russia-bashing, the OPCW has yet to report, and we should rise above doing anything for domestic political gain. Also it might destroy our agreement for the report stage of the Sanctions Bill because our finely negotiated stance on the Magnitsky Amendment might be disturbed. Indeed the Boris attacks on Corbyn might have jeopardised it already.

James and I watch a film, *The Death of Stalin*, a well-reviewed lampoon of Stalin's Russia, with telling parallels to Vladimir Putin today.

Sunday 8 April – Rutland/Yerevan

To Armenia from Gatwick.

Boris has laid into Corbyn in an article in the *Sunday Times*. He is not having a good war. He could have done, but has blown it somewhat. He just cannot maintain a dignified high-minded approach to Putin without lapsing into a publicity-seeking scrap.

It is fifty years since Enoch Powell gave his anti-immigration Rivers of Blood speech. Despite being demonised as a racist, he was a genius on economics and as such was a lone pioneer on government finance. During a period of seemingly insoluble inflation in the 1970s he was a prophet for fiscal and monetary discipline.

His was the first political meeting I ever went to, in Westminster Methodist Central Hall during the 1975 EEC referendum campaign: Enoch Powell, Douglas Jay, Tony Benn. I sat in the front row wearing my school boater and blazer, fully supporting their wish to leave, Ted Heath having made us join two years earlier. I still have the copy of Douglas Jay's signed book *After the Common Market?*.

Prince Charles is in Australia for the Commonwealth Games. His gags have been masterly. Tom Bower has written a rather idiotic book about him, initially accusing him of taking his own sheets and bed to the homes of people he visits, and then saying he even takes his own loo seat. 'Any such suggestion is total crap,' says a spokeswoman ('HRH poo-poos the story'!). Then in a speech HRH says: 'As I approach seventy, things change. Bits of me are starting to fall off. At least they say I have brilliant genes. But the trouble is, I can't get into them any longer.'

HRH 1, Bower 0.

Monday 9 April – Yerevan

Breakfast with First Deputy PM Vache Gabrielyan and Deputy FM Karen Nazaryan. The DPM is a droopy-eyed guy who rather talks in riddles, but is thoughtful and genuine. His main concern was that the ratification of the CEPA, the Comprehensive Enhanced Partnership Agreement, between the EU and Armenia might be derailed by Brexit. It won't be. We plan to pass it through the Commons in June.

While milling around before the inauguration I met the Gladstone Library team from Wales. They receive significant support from Armenia because Gladstone campaigned vigorously against the 'Turkish atrocities' in Armenia. I should use the same basis for seeking a massive donation to the Oxford Union, which was founded by Gladstone.

The inauguration of Armen Sarkissian as the new President of Armenia. Elegantly done with the right balance between ceremony and dignity. A good blast of trumpets and a mixture of goose-stepping and religious blessing. It began with a long solitary walk into the auditorium – shown on screens inside – along a mile of red carpet from the car to the podium. Good warm atmospherics.

At the reception afterwards he scooped me up and told me to come to the front of the receiving line. UK in pole position: indeed I was the only foreign minister attending, albeit there were senior figures present from the old Soviet countries.

Meeting with FM Edward Nalbandian. He is shrewd and experienced. He has been in post for ten years, and was the Ambassador in Lebanon in the 1980s, before the collapse of the Soviet Union. So he has served as a Soviet-era ambassador, and as the Foreign Minister of an independent Armenia. That offers a unique perspective.

Dinner at a good table, the first below the President's own top table. David, Earl of Snowdon on chirrupy form, there as Chairman of Christie's; Dariga Nazarbayeva, daughter of Nursultan Nazarbayev, the President of Kazakhstan; Armenian PM Karen Karapetyan; and Senator Sodiq Safoyev of Uzbekistan who I have come to know well, and seriously like. Dariga is seemingly enlightened and utterly straightforward: not a hint of superiority or grandeur. We bubbled along happily. When she asked if I was married, and I quietly explained that I was, but to a man, she was not in the least bit fazed. We agreed that I would send her a speech her father might consider making in defence of gay rights. It would revolutionise social attitudes within the old Soviet bloc, and transform the world's view of their social intolerance. Gays in Russian Chechnya are viciously persecuted and tortured: an act of radical leadership from such an unexpected quarter as President Nazarbayev could prove fundamentally transformational.

Tuesday 10 April – London
Back to London.

The Syrians have undeniably used nerve gas in Ghouta, probably chlorine but who knows? The trouble is that it is now being whipped up into a frenzy of international outrage. No doubt Trump is being wound up by the Israelis, but the danger is that we will now all do something rash and get sucked into a deeper conflict from which there is no exit. Taking some sort of action against gas use is one thing – it's what Cameron should have done in 2013 when he failed to just get on with it, and instead recalled Parliament and lost the vote. President Obama then backed off from taking action. But rushing into a complex conflict now is quite another matter. Nobody really understands the Syrian war, and most of us are in no position to assess who are the goodies and who are the baddies, let alone design a strategic course of action that is logical and conclusive. We are against the gas … but then what? I'm not sure we'd win a Commons vote for action, except in support of a very limited punitive strike.

Thursday 12 April – London
The news is all about the prospect of a strike on Syria. I speak to Richard Moore, now *in situ* as Political Director. I say we have to be with the US if they do something, but in a minor and finite way, and justified only as a response to the use of chemical weapons, not as forming a coalition to solve the broader conflict.

The OPCW has unequivocally corroborated our assertion that the Salisbury nerve agent was Novichok, stating that it was 'of the highest purity'. Slam-dunk.

Meanwhile the French have stated that gas was used in Syria, and the OPCW is now assessing that one. Although it was probably chlorine and/or sarin, it is nonetheless a breach of the Chemical Weapons Convention. Political opinion on what we should do is influenced by the deceit over the existence of chemical weapons in

Iraq in 2002; the failure to take action in Syria in 2003; the international support we received especially from the US after Salisbury; and the perfectly reasonable questions about what the result would be of military action.

I write a speech for the Gallipoli commemoration I am due to address later this month.

Simon Dodsworth calls from Dubai to say that his father Geoffrey died a few days ago. I worked for Geoffrey Dodsworth for six months in 1976 (between school and going to Oxford) when he was the MP for SW Herts. It was a fascinating period, and allowed me to witness the resignation of Harold Wilson as PM, and Jim Callaghan's selection over Denis Healey and others to succeed him. Three years later, when I was President of the Oxford Union, the Callaghan government was collapsing as he lost the support of the Welsh and Scots Nationalists after the devolution referendums.

Friday 13 April – London/Rutland

Halabja in Iraq 1986, Syria 2013, Salisbury 2018, Syria again 2018 – the use of chemical agents or gas risks escalating. I am very wary of us getting too immersed in Syria. It won't solve the plight of Syria itself, and risks serious conflict with the Russians. Our failure to understand Syria right from the start of its disintegration from 2011 has allowed the Russians to step in and so further complicate the conflict. We adopted a simplistic position from about 2012, demonising Assad and supporting the so-called moderate opposition. This has got us and them absolutely nowhere.

I suspect we will hit some carefully chosen targets over the weekend. But then that should be that.

Saturday 14 April – Rutland

As I hoped, and sort of predicted, there have been strikes on Syria overnight, carried out by the US, France and us. They have supposedly targeted buildings and facilities thought to manufacture chemical weapons. It had to be done. If action isn't taken, the use of gas as a weapon will become normal in conflict, and all of the progress of the last century will be put into reverse.

Sunday 15 April – Rutland/London

Boris very good on the *Marr* show, keeping a serious tone and putting up a cogent defence of our actions in Syria.

To Dorneywood. For the official country home of the Chancellor of the Exchequer, it's a fairly run-down building. George Osborne used it quite a bit, but I don't think Phillip Hammond has ever spent a night there.

Lunch – Philip and Susan Hammond; Alastair Gornall and his wife Fiona (sister of my friend John Antcliffe who died a few years ago); Sir Peter Westmacott and wife Susie; James and me. After lunch Noodle jumped the ha-ha to chase a rabbit, and returned from behind the shrubbery after some serious squealing noises.

Monday 16 April – London

Gavin Williamson has been to Oman and had the full works – an audience and a late dinner. It seems he handled it perfectly well.

Sit next to the PM for the SO24 debate on Syria. She also did three hours on her feet for a statement. It is an absurd and unreasonable call on her time, let alone her bladder. Hours and hours of her time in a Chamber which is thinly attended after the initial burst. Those sitting on the benches aren't even listening. When I first arrived in Parliament over twenty-five years ago, there were a few message pagers, no emails, no mobiles and no iPads – now the majority are just looking down at their devices. It is one respect in which Parliament is increasingly dysfunctional and discourteous.

Tuesday 17 April – London

Brief chat with Gavin Williamson in the lobby. He was bowled over by his encounter with the Sultan, but then kept on mentioning to me some mad notion he has about turning the Maldives into a new UK defence base.

Wednesday 18 April – London

Barbara Bush, matriarch of the family which has produced two Presidents, has died at the age of ninety-two.

The government, and the Home Office in particular, are under massive pressure for supposedly having betrayed the '*Windrush* Generation'. The first Caribbean immigrants arrived on a ship called the *Empire Windrush*, arriving in their overcoats and carrying leather suitcases, looking very formal. But over the last fifty years, despite living here and having family, they have never been issued with formal documents of residence. Some are now being sent 'home'. It is quite staggering incompetence, not just by today's authorities, but on the part of all governments over five decades. I can just imagine the turmoil in the Home Office and the poor ministers who are being given half the story and crap advice.

Commonwealth Heads of Government Meeting in Lancaster House. When Boris was in the chair, the helicopter noise overhead was infuriating. For once it was the police rather than TV. Furious calls were made to Scotland Yard to say move the bloody thing away. And they did, within about twenty minutes.

In the Smoking Room later, I congratulate Mark Francois on his excellent speech in yesterday's debate about the horrors of chlorine gas. Justine Greening was there too – so much nicer than when she was DfID Secretary.

We have been defeated in the Lords on the Withdrawal Bill, with peers voting for two amendments which aim to leave open the option of us staying in the customs union. The majorities against us were sizeable, and with several days left for them to pick over it at report stage, there could be more defeats to come which we'll struggle to overturn in the Commons.

Sunday 22 April – Rutland/London

Lovely sunny day and a walk by the river with Noodle. Leave for London at 3pm.

Dinner with Ed Argar in Poule au Pot. Nice chat at the next table with Sir John Scarlett, former Chief of MI6, who was there with Michael Chertoff, Homeland Security Secretary under George W. Bush.

Ed says that Amber Rudd is feeling the pressure of *Windrush*, which is totally unfair. She has inherited the problem, and then is being made to take the rap for an independent agency under the Home Office taking decisions about deportations. She is not allowed to instruct the agency what to do, and then gets blamed for their crap decisions. So much for the old assertion that advisers advise, ministers decide – if only they did.

It's clear that Gove is bitching against her, lobbing questions into conversations with journos. 'Did the HO know about deportations? How many?' etc. Meanwhile the increasingly odious Dawn Butler from the Labour benches calls it institutional racism, accusing the PM of delighting in having created a hostile climate for migrants. She didn't – only for the illegal ones. Butler is being completely unreasonable and opportunistic.

Apparently Carrie Symonds, head of press in Conservative HQ, is due to become a SpAd in the FCO. It's the first I've heard of it.

Monday 23 April – London
The Duchess of Cambridge has given birth to a boy, the third child to William and Kate. All quick and fine.

Nervousness remains on the Sanctions Bill. Report stage will probably be next Tuesday 1 May, but nobody has told me formally. The arithmetic on the two amendments (Magnitsky Act equivalent on sanctions for human rights abuse, and forcing the OTs to have open registers on beneficial ownership) risks being very tight.

Fly to Turkey with First Sea Lord Admiral Sir Philip Jones for the annual Gallipoli commemoration services.

Tuesday 24 April – Turkey
Two days of intensive services across the Gallipoli peninsula, starting with the main Turkish service. At our own, I read the Rupert Brooke poem ('If I should die, think only this of me: That there's some corner of a foreign field That is for ever England'). The cadences of it are amazing. If you get the expression right, it injects so much meaning and emotion into the poem. If you don't, it's just a plain sequence of words.

Wednesday 25 April – Turkey
Up at 3am for what is always seen as the highlight of the commemorations, the ANZAC dawn service. Timed to remember all those
from Australia and New Zealand who landed and met their deaths
at sunrise, it is very moving, and at the start rather cold.

By the time I leave, I have attended seven services, laid six wreaths,
made one speech and read one poem.

Thursday 26 April – London
The Chief Whip is getting jittery about the risk of losing a vote or
votes on amendments to the Sanctions Bill. We have Magnitsky
under control, although the Chief is still doubtful, and on open
public registers of asset ownership in the OTs he keeps on demanding I negotiate with Andrew Mitchell and Margaret Hodge, who are
leading the charge demanding open registers in the OTs' tax havens.
But I'd be mad to do so without having a clear agreement with the
Chief on when the Bill will come back to the House.

We are dead against compelling the OTs to have open registers
because it would amount to overriding their sovereignty, but the
Mitchell amendment would do just that. It's now blindingly obvious
that I am going to be told that I must concede. So we now have a
'when do we say so?' issue. The press are not mugs, and with numerous Mitchell briefings will want to write it up soon.

I can't get anything out of the Chief.

Friday 27 April – Rutland
North and South Korea are to meet, which is a step forward amid
the tension of North Korea's relations with the US.

Constituency day.

Monday 30 April – London
It's a day of non-stop Sanctions Bill activity. Meetings in the FCO,
and phone lobbying of potential rebels such as Richard Benyon.

Oh. Bugger. Amber Rudd has resigned as Home Secretary.
It's so unfair on her, as she was clearly grossly let down by her
officials.

Sajid Javid is appointed to replace her: as so often in politics, the one crucial promotion that benefits someone's career trajectory comes by sheer fluke. James Brokenshire comes back into the Cabinet in the Local Government slot. And it seems that the over-ambitious Williamson has somehow engaged the help of James Wharton, ex-MP and now in PR, to begin to agitate for a GW leadership bid. They are all so self-serving.

Tuesday 1 May – London

Report stage of the Sanctions Bill. I have spent over five days non-stop drafting and tabling a compromise amendment which should (just) satisfy those campaigning for open asset registers in the Overseas Territories, but which stops short of us compelling them to do so. I am still in the process of canvassing colleagues to support our amendment when I am told that the Speaker says he will not select or call it. It is extraordinary that a government amendment will not be called. It was tabled late in the day, but was not procedurally late, so should have been seen as a sensible compromise that merited debate and being voted on. But our compromise is sunk. Typical Bercow. He is driven by his own opinions. He is not impartial, he is just bloody awkward.

So it's now a straight fight between us holding to the original text of the Bill, and Andrew Mitchell and co on their new clause demanding open registers.

Boris comes to my office. He's had a long call with the Chief Whip, and it has been decided that, subject to the PM's agreement, we will concede to the Mitchell amendment. But we will keep quiet about it, and blame our change of tune on the Speaker's failure to select our compromise. I have to handle the climbdown in the Chamber, but am not happy. The Chief just doesn't want a defeat on anything, so will always capitulate before risking one.

Drinks in Boris' Commons office after third reading. Amber joined us. She is sensible and free of any bitterness.

Wednesday 2 May – London

Drinks for the Sanctions team in my FCO office. Really nice post-legislation gathering. The entire team came, along with those involved from DIT [Department for International Trade], Treasury and Number 10. Ministers John Glen and Andrew Griffiths, plus Joe Moor and Nikki da Costa from Downing Street.

Analysing what had happened, we all concluded that we had been let down by the Chief Whip. He'd gone behind the back of the system to make the Speaker think that the official government amendment was immaterial. In short, he had pulled a fast one.

Joe sent a text later saying, 'What if the amendment appears again in the Lords during ping-pong exactly as we had drafted it?' I said that if Lord Pannick puts it down and wins, it would be a service to our country. Clever boy. But I fear it won't happen.

There was a nasty posting on the highly partial Guido Fawkes website attacking Emily Thornberry. I called her to express solidarity.

Reception in the Locarno Room for the senior echelons of the UN who are in London for their annual staff conference. António Guterres, Pierre Krähenbühl, Filippo Grandi and many other UN mates.

Thursday 3 May – London

Meeting with the FCO's Chief Information Officer. I want him to minimise the email disclaimer on all FCO communications. At the moment, half of an iPhone email is taken up by a large-font double-spaced disclaimer which is not necessary and a total pain.

Tuesday 8 May – London

I have called in the Executive Director of the Financial Conduct Authority, because a number of embassies in London are finding it impossible to open a bank account. The money-laundering rules are being excessively applied and banks' risk aversion makes them turn down many of the applications. I want to agree a protocol with the FCA under which, if the use of an account is for a series of defined and specified purposes, then a bank should have no reason to decline.

Lunch with Erik Bennett. Always at Wilton's and always fun.

There is speculation about Vladimir Putin's health, as the photo of him over the weekend made it look as though his arm was impaired. Might he have suffered a stroke? Probably not, but we will know soon enough.

Drinks with Jesse Norman. He's not quite in the real world. He's cerebral, but is he a good minister? Can he get a grip on anything and take a decision? I just don't know. But I suspect he is one of those who is incapable of wiring a plug.

Bloody Trump has pulled out of the Iran nuclear deal. It is so irresponsible, and also a culpable breach of trust. It was a deal. It might have been Obama's deal, but it was a contract nonetheless and just because he is not Obama shouldn't mean that he thinks it OK for the US to welch on it.

Wednesday 9 May – London

Start the day in the FCO Map Room for the framework launch of our Arctic Policy. It's important stuff, but difficult to get revved up about.

Ministerial team meeting. For once there was a relatively substantive discussion. We analysed and assessed our failure to persuade the US not to bin the Iran deal. To me it's fairly straightforward: Trump, pushed by Kushner, has wholly bought into the Netanyahu playbook which demonises Iran at every turn. Israel, the UAE and now Saudi Arabia are all Iran-obsessed. So Trump simply thinks Iran = bad, so the deal = bad. And so that's that.

He rather fails to consider that it is the US who have been more interventionist than Iran, and by invading Iraq they went some way to re-empowering Iran. And Israel hates Hizbollah, Lebanon's Shiite militants, but were probably responsible for their very creation which stems from the Israeli invasion of Lebanon in the 1980s. So it's one set of rules for the US and Israel, but a completely different set for Iran, Iraq and everybody else.

Statement in the House on Iran.

The Whips are being infuriating. I am due at a dinner in Windsor with HM the Queen and HM King Hamad of Bahrain, ahead of the

Royal Windsor Horse Show. They won't release me, or Burt or Williamson. I intend to get there somehow, and have sought leave from the Palace to be late. We vote at 7pm and I immediately race down the M4 – driven by the admirable John Oakes – to Coworth Park in Sunningdale, arriving as the main course was finishing. The Queen looked radiant, and Prince Philip was there looking amazingly good following his recent operation. Alistair Burt made it a little later, but Williamson baled out altogether – such appalling bad manners. It was a lovely evening, and well worth the effort to get there. I had a nice chat with the King after HMTQ had departed. He was brimming.

Thursday 10 May – London

FCO Supervisory Board. We have an agenda dumped on us with no prior consultation, a raft of useless papers including facile power-point slides, and utterly superficial discussions. The non-execs are very good, but they are being fed a diet of inconsequential rubbish. This Board serves little or no purpose, although it could if Boris were to get a grip on it. At the moment it is just the purposeless poodle of PUS McDonald.

Phone call with new Armenian PM Nikol Pashinyan. He has emerged from the opposition after the transfer of power from the old President to Armen Sarkissian took a strange turn of events, and the former President was unable to hold on as the new PM.

Friday 11 May – Windsor/Reading

Drive down with James and Noodle to the endurance race of the Windsor Horse Show. Lunch with the King of Bahrain. The Queen drops in for tea. Always a nice intimate occasion.

The Iranians have shelled the Golan Heights, which is pushing their luck somewhat … even though it does not belong to Israel who have occupied it for decades.

Saturday 12 May – Reading/Rutland

I do my bit for the Anglo-Turkish Dialogue by attending the opening plenary in a hotel near Reading and performing in a panel with their minister Ömer Çelik on Brexit.

President Erdoğan is coming after all to the lunch tomorrow. In a meeting to discuss arrangements, the Turkish Ambassador seriously oversteps the mark. He wants sixty people to be allowed straight through security at Brize Norton, and then he 'insists' on certain conditions for the meeting with the Queen, such as including Erdoğan's daughter and her husband. I lean across the table and say with calm and menacing fierceness: 'Ambassador – nobody from any country, in any position, never mind how senior they are, ever, *ever* "insists" on anything in respect of Her Majesty the Queen. Have you got it?'

Boris texts. 'Odd chat with your new friend the PM of Armenia.' Wasn't quite sure what he meant, but it seems he spoke to someone else.

Sunday 13 May – London

To Reading again. Erdoğan turns up for lunch in a massive convoy. Those with him have firearms, against all understandings. They just lie and ram things through. They marched into the dining room and displaced all the place names even though we are the hosts, and removed everyone from the top table except the Duke of York and me. We have been completely outgunned – literally. We should have had police at the door and locked the room. So, so rude.

Erdoğan did his bit and left. I oozed diplomatic courtesy, unlike his bullying entourage.

Monday 14 May – London

It's all happening. The Israelis have killed forty-one Palestinians in Gaza (no response from the UK). The US is opening its embassy in Jerusalem. Meghan Markle's father has been set up and photographed ahead of her wedding to Prince Harry (possibly for money) and so may not attend. And it seems that both my and Boris' recent calls with new Armenian PM Nikol Pashinyan were a hoax, and probably the work of a prankster.

Tuesday 15 May – London

To Stansted first thing to see President Shavkat Mirziyoyev of Uzbekistan and FM Abdulaziz Kamilov, who were in transit on their way to Washington. It was well worth the effort. They were highly appreciative, and I am without doubt the main UK contact with the country.

Wednesday 16 May – London/Sofia

Ministerial team meeting. Speak at the Americas Directorate all-staff meeting. Rendezvous at Number 10 to join the PM's party to Northolt to fly to Sofia for the Eastern Partnership Summit. Chat with Theresa on the plane, but I stick to pleasantries. She is rather leaden and has no easy conversation. It's as if she is frightened to express an opinion on anything in case it comes back at her later. Just like she was at Oxford.

Dinner with Nikola Dimitrov, the Macedonian FM. We walk around the residence garden, and he confides in me with the details of the negotiations they are having with the Greeks to change the name of Macedonia to something else, because for twenty-five years the Greeks have baulked at the use of their historic label. It's all a big cultural fight over who owns the legacy of Alexander the Great. The Ilinden Uprising of August 1903 was an organised Macedonian revolt against the Ottoman Empire. It is contained within their national anthem, and is of course anti-Turkish rather than in any way a challenge to the Greeks. So the latest idea is to call themselves Ilinden Macedonia. Solving the name issue is a fundamental diplomatic objective. Theresa will go straight to Macedonia after the Sofia summit.

Saturday 19 May – Rutland/London

Prince Harry's marriage to Meghan Markle. I was glued to the TV. A beautiful ceremony on a beautiful day. Wonderful pageantry, and very touching scenes. It was perfectly done.

Wednesday 23 May – London

Proper meeting with Kim Darroch, following our dinner at home last night. He is annoyed that McDonald will not permit the Washington embassy to rent a decent residence for a couple of years while the Lutyens building is being renovated. If the ambassador lives in the deputy's house, we would have to hire no end of expensive premises for costly and indifferent entertainment for millions of functions. Washington is exorbitantly expensive, and it will all cost so much more than renting a place with adequate space. Lots of insights into the whacky President.

Thursday 24 May – London

It is clear beyond doubt that Lee Cain, Boris' media SpAd, has been briefing against me. Although the Armenia hoax was of little newsworthiness, he has been covering Boris' back by saying to journos that it was all my fault and that I gave Boris the number. It's total nonsense – the pranksters duped my office and the desk officers. I confronted him in front of Boris, and gave him a force 8 blast, which left him in no doubt. He knew, and half admitted by accident in the way he protested, that I was justified in my complaint.

I was due to have a call with John Sullivan in the State Department, but he kept on being detained, and in the end we couldn't speak. But it soon became clear what he was due to tell me, as it appeared a little later on the TV. Trump has cancelled the nuclear summit with North Korea. Who knows why? It's probably him just playing games.

Boris speech at the ambassadors' leadership conference in the Locarno Room. He just doesn't know how to be serious and commanding. It is all too flippant. Superficially amusing, but it doesn't impress.

To Number 10 to help brief the PM ahead of her meeting with the leaders of our Overseas Territories. Her encounter requires delicate handling in the aftermath of the successful Mitchell amendment to the Sanctions Bill which has so pissed them off.

Friday 25 May – Rutland

Sheila Randall is one of my most stalwart Party workers. Her husband Ian has just died and at rather short notice she asked me to give a short eulogy at his funeral at Grantham Crematorium. I did so, but found it emotionally difficult. The golden rule is never to look at the front row of principal mourners, as it's their grief that can set you off. It did … I blubbed, but only afterwards, outside.

Saturday 26 May – Rutland

It's brightened up nicely for Uppingham School Speech Day. They did it brilliantly. A minimum of speeches, a maximum of drama and music. The violin solo was stupendous and prompted a standing ovation from the 1,000 or so in the marquee.

Monday 28 May – Brussels/London

Up at 4am to go to East Midlands Airport for the flight to Brussels for the Foreign Affairs Council. Once again I strike up a good rapport with Irish FM Simon Coveney in the main session. We echo each other strongly on both Iran and Gaza.

Friday 1 June – Rutland

A quiet day in Rutland.

Speak to the leader of the opposition in Macedonia. He was uncompromising and obstructive, both on the name change and in his labelling Prime Minister Zoran Zaev a crook. A touch crazed, he was no help on anything.

We fail to support the UNSCR on Gaza. Usual disgrace.

Lobster supper at home. Yummee.

Sunday 3 June – Rutland

The Singapore summit between US and North Korea is back on again.

To the Rutland County Show in Oakham. It really has become an event of serious stature, all proving that little Rutland is indeed *Multum in parvo* [Rutland's motto]. Fabulous livestock, lots of stalls and many thousands attending. It was wise to get there as early as we did, as there was a mile-long queue to get in when we left at 2pm. Everyone, needless to say, admires and adores Noodle.

Monday 4 June – London
To St Paul's Cathedral for a short wreath-laying ceremony at the Falklands Memorial plaque in the crypt with Marcos Peña, the Chief of Staff to Argentina's President Macri. It is a poignant moment and a further positive diplomatic step towards lasting rapprochement thirty-five years after the Falklands War.

Tuesday 5 June – London
Chat with Robert Buckland, Solicitor General, on the way into the House. He says Gavin Williamson when Chief Whip 'was happy to be detested so long as he was feared', to which I responded, 'Now that he is no longer feared, he is universally detested.'

Give a quick tour of Parliament to Robert Nederlander, the 88-year-old American theatre owner and impresario, who has London's two greatest theatre successes at the moment, *Tina* and *Hamilton*.

Thursday 7 June – London/Berlin/Rutland
To Berlin to deliver a speech at an annual German foreign policy conference. I give them chapter and verse on Brexit, stating clearly that we want a deal that is mutually beneficial, and busting two myths widely believed in Germany – that Brexit might not happen, and that there will be a second referendum. I explain that in theory there could be a second referendum, as some could argue that people voted for a concept and not a contract, and so that once the terms of a deal, or no deal, are known there is a logic behind demanding one. But then I emphatically mapped out why there will not be one – there isn't time, it could only happen if the government passed the legislation, and they have absolutely no intention of doing that. My speech and questions were then followed by Chancellor Merkel's keynote speech.

Back home, David Davis and Theresa May are locked in a dispute over the customs union. There is lots of toing and froing and talk of a possible DD resignation. Twitter is fizzing with speculation and comments. At 3pm there is a compromise statement saying that there might have to be a backstop customs arrangement for Northern Ireland which would keep us in the customs union for longer.

BoJo is determined to do the South Sandwich Islands no-fish announcement, and it seems he has agreed with Simon McDonald that he will himself lead on all oceans matters. Fine if that's what he wants, but the slippery PUS doesn't tell me, nor does BoJo; it just comes in as an email from the PUS's office.

I land at Birmingham, switch on my mobile and find about twenty new text messages. The *Daily Telegraph*'s Chris Hope, who is often prone to trivialising things, has tweeted that I have called for a second referendum. The entire speech was designed to state the precise opposite. Twitter has gone haywire. So I tweet a pretty sharp riposte, linking to the speech and saying that I deplore the state of British journalism when it can wilfully get something so wrong. I text Hope himself saying that this is the day on which I have lost all faith in him, and announcing that I have placed a personal fatwa on him.

Saturday 9 June – Rutland

Quiet day. Trooping the Colour, and a delight to see Geoffrey Tantum's knighthood in the Birthday Honours List.

Monday 11 June – London

PM address to the parliamentary Party in the Attlee Suite at Portcullis House. It's always better to say as little as possible, but as a minister we shouldn't say anything anyway. Those who speak are: Benyon, Goodwill, Villiers, Fabricant, Leigh, Davies P., Graham, Rudd, Evans N., Philp. Robert Goodwill, who finished recently as a minister, was particularly amusing: 'Since the reshuffle I receive a lot more calls from journalists.'

The unpleasant website/blogger Guido Fawkes, run by Paul Staines, asserts that Speaker Bercow's decision to grant an Urgent Question on Hodeidah is 'his most stupid decision'. Hodeidah is the western Yemeni port through which all humanitarian supplies need to be channelled for the entire country and which is about to be the subject of a Saudi assault, and even a siege. There is every justification for raising the issue. Is the Guido comment simply because he is anti-Keith Vaz, who tabled the question, or that humanitarian disaster just doesn't register on his values radar?

Tuesday 12 June – London

Phillip Lee resigns as junior Justice Minister. He is seriously touched in the head. He thinks he's the Messiah, and probably believes that his resignation will prove so seismic that the cause of Brexit will collapse, and he will soon be elevated to the Cabinet. He is genuinely principled, but is deluded about his own relevance. He does have a conscience, but he lacks judgement.

Sajid Javid wants to ban Hizbollah – or at least their political wing – in the UK. Their actions are to be condemned whenever they turn to violence, but the thing about a political wing is that it gives you someone to talk to when trying to solve historic problems. Banning them closes down that option. You'd have thought our IRA experience would give us a clue. It's not as if he knows anything much about international relations, but it is quite clear who has got to him.

Lunch with Steven Swinford, my best contact at the *Daily Telegraph*. I take him to the Strangers' Dining Room, because we are expecting numerous divisions today. I can speak very frankly with him, and he is a well-rooted assessor of the political tea leaves, with no partisan axes to grind. As always, we broadly agree on who the nutters are.

Also in Strangers are Arron Banks and Andy Wigmore, the Leave. EU tearaways, who have just walked out of the DCMS Select Committee. They just love being contrary: but ultimately they are irresponsible. I say hi and have a nice jaunty chat, but there are no two ways about it – they are wrong 'uns.

An amusing scene in New Palace Yard: Ken Clarke in a little red car, one hand on the wheel and the other holding a cigar, chats to some of us out of the open window as he slowly drives along.

Wednesday 13 June – London

It's the day after the day before! After marathon votes yesterday, all of which we won, today feels like an anticlimax. Strangely, there are no Opposition voices trying to exploit the government's precarious condition, which makes life easier than it could be.

More worrying is the Saudi Coalition's launch of an assault in Yemen to take the port town of Hodeidah from the Houthis. This is the only route into the country for all the food and supplies on which most of the country depends. The humanitarian costs risk being very high indeed.

Quip of the day: I was on the front bench, Bercow was on his feet stating which motion we were considering and said of the clause that 'I think it is properly referred to as little 2.' So I said loudly, 'That covers the both of us then.'

Drink at home with Richard Tice. One of the four Bad Boys of Brexit, he wants to be the Conservative Party's candidate for Mayor of London because he knows about housing. Which he does, but there's no way they will ever consider him.

Thursday 14 June – London

Gay rights campaigner Peter Tatchell has been arrested in Moscow for making a mild protest ahead of the World Cup.

Boris is still pushing for the no-fish policy on krill in the South Atlantic. Mention of having a big ego crops up in our chat. I said that I've long since managed to cut mine down to size … with a high degree of help from others.

Excellent news. Ed Argar succeeds Phillip Lee as the junior Minister for Justice.

Saturday 16 June – Rutland

Uppingham School Trustees meeting. An amusing moment when Richard Tice tells them that he is happy to be reappointed to the Board, but should let them know that he would have to step aside if he were to become a candidate to be Mayor of London. I quipped instantaneously, 'My support for Richard to become Mayor should not be misinterpreted by our fellow Trustees.'

Tuesday 19 June – London

In his *Telegraph* column William Hague has called for the legalisation of cannabis. It's twenty-three years since I did so in my book *Saturn's Children* when he was Leader, and he slapped me down. I text him to say he's a slow learner.

Wednesday 20 June – London

My deal with the Moldovan FM has fallen into place. In return for me sorting out something for him in the UN, he agrees to co-sponsor a motion we want in the OPCW.

Westminster Hall debate on Polish War Reparations. Daniel Kawczynski is nuts. He says the Germans should compensate the Poles for the Second World War, and that we should lobby for it.

Thursday 21 June – London

Greg Hands has resigned as Trade Minister. There will be a vote next week in which the government will support the expansion of Heathrow, and Greg's election address was so emphatically opposed to it that he has little choice but to resign on principle – something I immediately label a 'Hands Stand'. George Hollingbery replaces him. Meanwhile, Boris who was equally opposed and is known to have been so for years, decides to stay put. Awkward. He says to me in the corridor outside his office, 'I'd better find somewhere else I need to be.' He really is just so unscrupulous. But, on this one, also highly amusing.

Friday 22 June – Rutland

Boris is getting pilloried about Heathrow. The contrast to Hands is stark. The Commons vote will be on Monday.

Sunday 24 June – Rutland

Gavin Williamson is splashed over the front of the *Mail*, supposedly having threatened to bring down May if she doesn't increase defence spending, saying 'I made her, so I can break her.' He really is a venomous, self-seeking little shit. And Boris is the subject of a double-page account of the FCO Queen's Birthday reception at which, when asked about businesses (Airbus, BMW, etc) who were saying Brexit would stop them investing as much in the UK, he is said to have responded with the words 'Fuck business.'

Last night former FCO PUS Sir Simon Fraser tweeted, 'Is there Cabinet Office guidance on how long former FCO permanent secretaries have to go on biting their tongue about Boris Johnson?'

England play Panama, having beaten Tunisia in the opening match of their World Cup campaign. Amazing – we are 5–0 up at half-time. Panama far too rough and aggressive though.

Monday 25 June – Luxembourg

Receive lots of phone calls asking where Boris will go in order to escape the Heathrow vote, but I don't know and wouldn't say anyway. They all know he's doing a bunk. It'll be Afghanistan or Iraq I expect. Sarah Wollaston MP says he should resign.

Speak to Greek FM Nikos Kotzias at length about Macedonia. There is definitely progress.

Back from Luxembourg in time for the Heathrow vote. But no Boris! As I suspected, he had found a pressing reason to visit Afghanistan.

Tuesday 26 June – London

Liz Truss has made an extraordinarily lame and corny speech attacking Gove and just making herself look bizarre. But then she is.

Prince William is in Israel, and has conducted himself meticulously. By contrast, the Israeli President has breached all protocol and the agreements made prior to the visit by saying in front of the cameras, 'Please convey a message of peace to Mahmoud Abbas when you are in Ramallah.' It is just so phoney, but that's what they do.

Wednesday 27 June – London

Prince William is now in Ramallah, where once again he acquits himself brilliantly.

Speak to Field Marshal Charles Guthrie. He is recovering from falling off his horse during the Queen's Birthday Parade. He has broken quite a few bones and, for the first time in three weeks, will today take some steps outdoors. Not easy when you're about to turn eighty.

Pizza with James and Noodle as we watch the documentary about the new US embassy. I am in it and come out OK, although I am filmed in conversation with the Ambassador who rather oddly keeps talking about a peregrine falcon. I had no idea what he was referring to (and still don't), and when he says it has ferocious talons and can swoop and kill at speed, I just laugh and say that I must learn how to do that. Gavin Williamson comes out of it badly, repeating in his whiney voice that he'd like to visit the embassy on his own one day.

Friday 29 June – London/Rutland
A rare uncrowded Friday in London. I buy a large porcelain ashtray from Asprey for James. Our tenth wedding anniversary will be on the 24th.

Briefing for *Any Questions* from Number 10 by the charming and rather dashing Aidan Corley. Then to Ampthill near Milton Keynes. On the panel too, Gina Miller the Remain campaigner, Liam Halligan of the *Telegraph* and Angela Smith, Labour's leader in the Lords. Gina Miller would be far more persuasive if she didn't always speak as if she considers herself the only person in the world whose opinion matters. It was broadly OK, although at one point I referred to coal-powered fire stations instead of coal-fired power stations, but nobody seemed to notice.

Sunday 1 July – Rutland/London
Amazing sunny day. May says she will defy the hard Brexiteers. Good! But we are heading inexorably for the tectonic crunch.

Monday 2 July – London
I am so infuriated by the disdainful, patronising way in which Rees-Mogg insists on issuing instructions and demands to the PM that at about 8am I tweet, 'Rees-Mogg's insolence @Telegraph in lecturing & threatening the PM is just too much. Risks debasing gov't, party, country and himself. PM must be given maximum latitude & back-

ing. The ideological right are a minority despite their noise and should pipe down. #totalsupportforMay.'

It seems to strike a nerve. Texts start pouring in, and by the end of the day the tweet has reached 250,000 people.

I suddenly have the UQ on the ISC Report on detention and rendition landed on me. As it happens I served on the committee for nearly two years, so know the subject matter. It's all about whether the UK's intelligence agencies were complicit with the Americans in illegally detaining, torturing and imprisoning suspected terrorists and combatants in Afghanistan and Iraq. Ken Clarke, Andrew Mitchell and others want a judge-led inquiry. The committee has just spent four years investigating, taking up an extraordinary amount of Agency time and revealing nothing new of concern about the UK. The thought of having another one is just bonkers. The Number 10 line is that they will announce after sixty days whether we will or not. I trust we will not.

Tuesday 3 July – London

I write to Moggy to explain why I tweeted, half apologising for not alerting him in advance, but outlining uncompromisingly why I think he is not acting in the national interest. Nigel Farage wrote some disparaging comments about me in the *DT*, so I texted him: 'Nigel. Just loved your DT article about me! Always a pleasure to spar with you. If only the solutions were as straightforward as you and Moggy say … But am enjoying your LBC stuff. Alan'. His reply: 'It is all about political will. Thanks for the message. Rule Britannia. Nigel'. If only.

Lunch at the National Portrait Gallery with Robert Shrimsley of the *FT*. We went through all the Brexit permutations, but it was the first time I've heard a journalist muse about what I've been quietly saying for weeks, that the only logical way out to avoid total Brexit chaos and parliamentary collapse is a national government of some sort. But it's too logical to be practical.

Attend the PM's reception in the garden of Number 10 to celebrate Pride. I have a lovely chat with Simon Callow and introduce him to the PM. For once she was chatty.

England beat Colombia 4–3 on penalties and so win a place in the World Cup quarter-finals.

Wednesday 4 July – London

Lunch with George Osborne at the Ivy Kensington. Very convivial. He hates Theresa May, and considers her characterless and robotic. He still maintains a fascination for Boris but there is no love there. He thinks Gove has some worrying aspects running in his favour – he has *The Times* and the *Mail* on his side, he will start where he left off in terms of leadership support, he is staying inside the pack and is trying to appeal to the middle ground. George might be right, but Gove's still a wholesale weirdo. We went through all the possible courses of events over Brexit. If there's no deal we're sunk. I floated the concept of a temporary cross-party alliance to see it through, but we both agreed the chances are infinitesimally slim.

There's now a Novichok victim in Amesbury, not far from Salisbury. This will challenge the detectives.

Thursday 5 July – London/Rutland

Lots of briefing ahead of next week's Western Balkans Summit. A Commons debate on the preparations offers a platform on which to advertise next week's events.

There is due to be a Cabinet meeting at Chequers tomorrow on Brexit, and it turns out that while I was in the Commons Boris was hosting a meeting in his FCO office about it for Brexiteers. It's a reunion of Vote Leave minus Grayling. Fox was in Number 10 for something else, but attendees were Gove, Mordaunt, Leadsom, McVey. Oh dear. Why can't they let up for just a second?

Friday 6 July – Rutland

Cabinet meeting taking place all day at Chequers to thrash out an EU exit consensus. But it's still only us talking to ourselves (or at least the Cabinet doing so): it's a parallel universe, when it's what is agreed between the UK and the EU that matters.

The details of the Trump visit have been released: Blenheim, Windsor, Chequers. It's all clearly designed to keep him away from demonstrators in London. James and I will attend the Blenheim dinner.

Twelve Thai boys are stuck in a cave near Pattaya, and with the waters rising the prospects look bleak. One navy diver has died trying to reach them.

At around 9pm the PM claims she has secured Cabinet agreement. But who the hell are the Cabinet anyway? They are so puny, with others invited too, such as the Minister for Housing. It is logically absurd that a housing minister attends but the Minister for Europe does not. Not that I want to.

The press say that there won't be any resignations. Not yet anyway.

Saturday 7 July – Rutland

The heatwave continues. It's over 30 degrees.

In our quarter-final we beat Sweden 2–0, so England are in the semi-finals and will play Croatia or Russia. Then later in the other match it's 2–2, and Croatia win on penalties.

Sunday 8 July – Rutland/London

Four of the twelve boys have been rescued. They have to make a long dive through flooded tunnels holding on to some amazing divers who have found them. What an ordeal. But it does look as though they might all survive.

The woman contaminated in Amesbury with Novichok has died. So now it's a case of murder, although that it should move from Salisbury to a random victim in Amesbury is bizarre.

Monday 9 July – London

David Davis resigned at midnight last night. So all was agreed at Chequers on Friday, and then Davis bales out as Brexit Secretary forty-eight hours later. This is on one level catastrophic, on another completely immaterial. He has not exactly been a striking success. The little tick Steve Baker, the PUSS at DExEU, has also gone. He has been quite the most useless minister and is just so simplistic he might just as well not have a brain.

To the Crystal building, beside City Airport for the Western Balkans Summit. The driver was late and hopeless at tuning his radio. So I listened to the David Davis *Today* programme interview on my iPhone – twenty minutes of it. He said that his resignation was career-ending, but that he couldn't front up and sell something he didn't believe in. It's logical, and basically honest. He has run out of steam. That's it really.

The ghastly Andrea Jenkyns MP is calling for Theresa to be challenged. She is a brainless nothing.

The issue as soon as I arrive at the summit is 'Will Boris go?' His credibility is shot through, and will not recover by resigning. I text him to ask if he is still hoping to get to it as planned, given that he is due to chair it, but there is no immediate response.

Dominic Raab goes to DExEU to replace DD. He's a self-important humourless bore.

There's all sorts of toing and froing about when and whether Boris will turn up to the summit. He is holed up with his SpAds in the FCO, taking no calls and cancelling all meetings. At 1.46pm he finally responds to my text with: 'Hold fort comrade.'

It feels as though he's going to jump ship. I continue chairing the meeting while keeping a beady eye on my iPhone news feeds. At 3pm, he resigns. I tell the astonished summit, and briefly speak to him twenty minutes later. He asks me to say nice things about him, which I do. Later on I text him with what I said:

I had two amazing years in the Foreign Office working with Boris Johnson. He was and remains a larger-than-life figure, one of politics' great characters. He was probably the best-known politician even before he became Foreign Secretary, and I'm sure he will contribute massively still to British politics … And I think we should really just say to him, 'Thank you for playing your part in public life in the way that you have.' His sheer force of personality was a massive diplomatic asset. A lot of what he did in the Foreign Office was not seen by people outside it. He was a supremely strong character in diplomatic lobbying and persuasion. I really enjoyed working for him.

The summit is electrified, and I explain that the PM will make a Commons statement at 3.30pm, as she was due to do anyway, and has to address the 1922 at 5.30pm. Her statement would certainly last till 5, so nothing would happen on a new Foreign Secretary before 7pm.

I text Julian Smith ... just remember where it all started. Fat chance. I will just enjoy my four hours as acting Foreign Secretary.

After sorting out cars and confirming I would not be required to vote, I managed to join the Balkans lot on the cable car to a boat and dinner on the river up to Westminster.

They were all fantastically supportive ... we want you to be the next Foreign Secretary etc. I praise Boris both at the press conference and in the boat, where I raised a toast to him, and shook hands with everyone as they left on the jetty, just as I learn that the next Foreign Secretary is to be Jeremy Hunt.

Boris texts in reply to my message summarising what I'd said about him to the conference: 'Thanks Alan – massively appreciated. You were a great colleague ... by the end!!! You achieved a massive amount in your areas and showed amazing diplomatic skill in my view. Your view on krill and fish will now, I fear, prevail. Let's keep working together and good luck.'

Richard Moore comes for a drink. I called Jeremy Hunt within minutes of him being announced. At least I like him and don't resent his appointment over me. He sent the quick reflex reply 'Can't talk right now'. Better than nothing.

In the minishuffle, Hancock goes to Health; Attorney Jeremy Wright to DCMS and Geoffrey Cox to Attorney General.

One further silver lining is the departure alongside DD of Stewart Jackson. He is a most repulsive figure and a champion thicko, who was rescued from post-parliamentary unemployment by being made Chief of Staff to Davis. He is incapable of being chief of anything. He is vicious, leaking, etc. Given he once texted me such utter abuse, I am so glad the little turd has gone.

Tuesday 10 July – London

Day two of the Western Balkans Summit, and day one of a new foreign secretary. We start with the signing in the Locarno Rooms of a Western Balkans Agreement on Missing Persons, which enshrines cooperation on identifying those killed in the conflicts twenty years ago.

I'm already in my morning suit as I have to go immediately afterwards to the RAF Centenary Service in Westminster Abbey. All the Royals there. A fitting service, although sadly without anyone reading the poem known as 'An Eighteenth-Century Prophecy', based on a translation of Thomas Gray's 'Luna Habitabilis' of 1837, which I had recommended. It would have been perfect:

> The time will come, when thou shalt lift thine eyes
> To watch a long-drawn battle in the skies,
> While aged peasants, too amazed for words,
> Stare at the flying fleets of wondrous birds.
> England, so long the mistress of the sea,
> Where winds and waves confess her sovereignty,
> Her ancient triumphs yet on high shall bear,
> And reign, the sovereign of the conquered air.

A quick change at home, and a hop to Lancaster House in front of which I greet all the Heads, enjoying a friendly chat with Chancellor Angela Merkel and Alexis Tsipras. I teased Merkel by saying that 'You two Mrs Ms can exchange tips on how to hold a government together.' She was most amused, and said, 'Yes – we will help each other.'

The RAF fly-past was something special. It's far from straightforward, as the different planes, ancient and modern, come in from different airfields and the fast ones at their slowest are still faster than the slow ones at their fastest. So the choreography is quite a logistical challenge. Merkel seemed perfectly happy with it – even when the Spitfires went over.

I joined the Heads lunch, which was a privileged moment. It was all the better for not having Boris, although Theresa was rather wooden and not sufficiently the confident hostess. In truth, it was a rather dire occasion, dwelling mainly on the Balkans economy. The PM of Serbia spoke for far too long. But I was buoyed by being given spontaneous rave reviews for the way I handled the summit yesterday.

The main plenary was fine, and regarded by all as a success. As indeed was HRH the Prince of Wales' reception in the garden of St James's Palace. I was at the door beside HRH as the main dignitaries were presented to him, whispering such details as 'the President of Serbia', 'Chancellor Merkel', 'PM Tsipras of Greece' etc. It all went hummingly.

In the garden I steered HRH from one prearranged group to another. Some of the parents of missing persons had met him before. He gave one plump character in a beret an enormous hug. They adore the Prince. Looking over my shoulder a few minutes later I could see that a couple of them were in tears.

All twelve – eleven little footballers plus their coach – have been rescued from the Thai cave, each of them having had to swim considerable distances underwater accompanied by a navy diver dragging extra oxygen tanks.

Two vice-chairmen of the Party – Maria Caulfield and Ben Bradley – have resigned. Silly buggers.

France is into the World Cup final after beating Belgium 1–0. So it's England or Croatia to face France in the final.

Wednesday 11 July – London

Lunch at White's with Sir John Nutting. I arrived in the front hall with a rather conspicuous parcel wrapped in brown paper. He was absolutely thrilled by its contents: four framed copies, quite as good as the originals, of his father's election results notices for each of his victories in Melton – 1945, 1950, 1951 and 1955. Sir Anthony resigned as Foreign Minister over Suez in 1956. John was clearly very touched.

England lose 2–1 to Croatia after extra time.

Thursday 12 July – London

We are in full-tilt mode for Trump's visit which starts properly today after his arrival last night.

Car to Blenheim Palace. It's a beautiful summer evening and all the guests are gathered on the main steps for the President to arrive by helicopter. The Americans know how to make an entrance, as he was preceded by hovering Osprey aircraft. Melania is absolutely striking in flowing yellow, and the Duke of Marlborough, who knows Trump, handled him brilliantly and gave him a tour of the Churchill memorabilia.

The sumptuous dinner passed without a hitch, until there was a sudden flurry towards the end, caused, we learnt later, by a Trump interview in tomorrow's *Sun*, in which he criticises the PM's handling of Brexit.

Friday 13 July – London

The full details of the Trump interview make for uncomfortable reading: he says the PM ignored his advice on how to handle Brexit and suggests her approach is endangering the prospect of a US trade deal. He also talks up Boris, saying he would make a great PM. Ouch.

It has understandably caused a huge fuss, with many MPs expressing outrage at the President's rudeness to us as his hosts, and to the PM personally. All this when I have been asked to do an extensive media round talking up the positive nature of US–UK relations ahead of their talks at Chequers today.

Inevitably, the furore is all they want to talk about, but I maintain a poker-faced insistence that all is going absolutely swimmingly, and that we're perfectly relaxed about his comments, which were made before he had seen the details of our position on the trade talks. I describe him as a controversialist who brings a bit of colour to the international stage. Yeah, and the rest.

The truth is it is about the most unhelpful thing he could possibly have said at any time, but to do so while on his way to be feted by us on an official visit is utterly crass and offensive. But that's the man.

Sunday 15 July – Rutland

I do LBC, Radio 5 Live, Sky TV. In all of them I am asked if the government can survive and whether May's blueprint for Brexit amounts to anything other than something close to continuing EU membership. I robustly defend the PM and urge all to back her otherwise the Party will face serious danger. Rees-Mogg unhelpfully talks of a possible split, as if he quite likes the idea. He and his ilk are total wreckers.

Steve Bannon, he of the Trump campaign and Breitbart, is reported, off air after a scratchy interview, to have said to the political editor of LBC Theo Usherwood: 'Fuck you. Don't you fucking say you're calling me out. You fucking liberal elite. Tommy Robinson [jailed fascist] is the backbone of this country.' Could he be more vile?!

As I was driving down to London I hear on the 5pm news that my PPS, Robert Courts, has resigned. I stop to text him and express astonishment that I heard it from the BBC rather than from him. He calls back, suitably contrite, and we have a cordial chat. I said I had come to rate him and had appreciated his work, and that I hoped he had found it enriching. It was yes to all that from him, along with a cogent explanation as to why he just couldn't swallow the Chequers deal and the ensuing White Paper. He considers it membership of the EU in all but name, and he just could not live with it.

France beat Croatia 4–2 in the World Cup Final. England's Harry Kane wins the golden boot as the highest goal scorer in the tournament. No sooner have France won than there is a torrential downpour across the stadium, and Macron gets drenched.

Monday 16 July – London

Justine Greening calls for a second referendum because Parliament is 'stalemated'. English is clearly her second language. I call Joe Murphy of the *Standard* to say that she is undermined by her own logic. If Parliament is gridlocked then it won't be able to pass a bill to have a referendum. If the government were so much as to try, it would simply collapse. So there will not be one under this government.

Cornish MP Scott Mann resigns as a PPS in the Treasury, the ninth resignation within little more than a week. It is all being coordinated by the little wanker Steve Baker, whose orchestration of it is the step-by-step destruction of the government, and hence eventually also of the Party and the country. Anne-Marie Trevelyan, a PPS, is whipping for them.

A morning in the FCO mopping up. Jeremy Hunt texts to thank me for taking another hospital pass, after which it becomes clear that he thought I'd gone to the FAC in Brussels to stand in for him at the last minute, but it was too late to get a commercial flight, and no one would authorise me to take his plane, even though it was sitting there ready for him, so … no plane, no trip.

Lunch with Joe Murphy of the *Standard*. He gets it: if anyone other than Theresa becomes Party leader they might not be able to form a government.

The government has accepted four amendments to the Customs Bill about the EU and VAT which has left everyone astonished. They effectively cave in to the Brexiteers' demands and would stop us collecting EU tariffs, rule out a border in the Irish Sea and overall make the Chequers plan unworkable. I think the Chief Whip has (probably needlessly) caved in to avoid the threat of a defeat.

Trump is with Putin in Helsinki: Trump is mad; Putin is sinister. The encounter is surreal. Back in the US, Trump is getting it in the neck from the likes of Senators John McCain and Lindsey Graham.

Tuesday 17 July – London
All-staff meeting: Jeremy Hunt's first outing in front of them all. He was just so much more grown-up than Boris. He said, 'Here's the hard-headed bit: we need our network to put pressure on the EU27 to get a deal. Here's the ethical bit: the rules-based international order is being challenged. We need to understand the power of UK soft diplomacy, and maximise its use.' OK for week one.

Tea with Nigel Fletcher to discuss the LGBT speech I want Dariga Nazarbayeva to persuade her father to give.

Newly elected Independent Rutland councillor Richard Alderman's Facebook page and Twitter account is full of horrid postings such as 'PM May should be assassinated.' He's a nasty 72-year-old ex-UKIP grump. A number of people call my Commons office to register their protest. I complain formally to the police and lodge a statement.

We have votes at 3.30, 5.00, 6.00 and 7.00, losing one division by three votes, but winning the crucial one by six.

Deputy Chief Whip Chris Pincher stupidly threatens a vote of confidence. Idiot. That's how you start the slippery slide.

Wednesday 18 July – London

Anna Soubry MP on the *Today* programme says the government is being run by extremist Brexiteers like Rees-Mogg and she calls for a government of national unity. She is broadly correct, but it's a bit early for any public discussion about some sort of cross-party alliance to prevent an election, or no deal, and to push through some sort of deal. The whole concept only works if we need to prevent an unwanted election and the mood has become electric enough to make it possible. Very long odds on all that.

Boris' resignation statement in the Commons. He's not naturally comfortable speaking in the Chamber. He rehashed the familiar criticisms of the Chequers plan, saying it meant 'economic vassalage' for the UK, but it was fairly weak, and certainly no Geoffrey Howe moment. The parallels were all there to be made – a former foreign secretary clashing with a female PM over Europe and trying to provoke a change in leadership – but unlike Howe's with Thatcher, Boris' statement will not enter the history books as a fatal blow to the PM.

To Buckingham Palace for a Privy Council meeting in which HM the Queen can present Jeremy Hunt with his seal of office. Once we'd taken our leave of HM and withdrawn to the next room, JH was a little gauche in suggesting that we all have a photo. The problem was that we were still in the Queen's private apartments, stepping around the corgis. It is not the place to take photographs.

Councillor Alderman has been arrested by Leicestershire Police and is going to be charged.

Friday 20 July – Rutland

I drive over to Eydon to see Jeremy Catto. He is upstairs in his dressing gown sitting in a chair beside his bed, not able to go down the
stairs. He is dying. I know the look. He is sunken-faced, drifts in and
out of wanting to talk, has to make every effort to concentrate, and
talks of his will and funeral. I don't think he will last the summer. I
stay for about forty minutes, but just know in my heart that it's the
last time I'll see him.

Sunday 22 July – Rutland

John Major, as always, talks good sense on the *Marr* show. He offers
the logic of why the first referendum was flawed, and why there
might be grounds for another one. But twenty-one years after he left
Number 10, you really need to be over thirty to know who he is.

I speak to Labour's Yvette Cooper for half an hour. She broadly
agrees with my thesis that if we default into No Deal then there are
grounds for a unity government and a referendum to choose between
No Deal and Remain. We do not want No Deal, nor an election, but
would not easily peel off to support a unity administration: they
definitely don't want No Deal, would be inclined to pile in to support
a unity government, but are more inclined to have a general election
(because they might win) and so probably won't peel off.

Monday 23 July – London

Sajid Javid has briefed the *Daily Telegraph* that he will not oppose the
death penalty for the two UK-origin terrorists who have been
detained in Syria. They will be extradited to the US. Although they
have already had their UK citizenship removed, it is nonetheless
contemptible that he has played to the right-wing neo-con gallery in
order to promote himself, and has at the same time overturned
decades of principled policy under which we oppose the death
penalty in all circumstances. It never came across my desk in the
FCO, and by mid-morning it turns out that Boris had signed it off.
I despair at both of them.

Wednesday 1 August – Rutland

James to his parents in Westbury. I take the train to London.

Corbyn is facing another massive row over anti-Semitism. The *Mail* reports that he had hosted an event comparing the Israeli government to the Nazis. Such a simplistic attack is utterly sick – and precisely what Labour needs to purge. Their hate-filled sloganising destroys the credibility of many arguments that *are* justified, and the anti-Israeli Marxists in his midst are vile. If they were both reasonable and rational they could defend the rights of Palestinians and attack the wrongs of Israel without spilling into contemptible anti-Semitism.

Sunday 5 August – Sardinia

Off on holiday to Sardinia. Tom Newton Dunn of the *Sun* calls to ask me to support a story he's writing. It's an absolute gift for easy publicity. The World Campaign for Dogs is launching a campaign in the UK to prohibit the killing of dogs and the consumption of dog meat. The practice is creeping in from Asia, but there is no law against it in the UK, only a law about the manner in which a dog is killed.

He wants me to champion the story in association with Noodle, which I willingly agree to, and send him half a dozen photos and a robust quote saying that any civilised country should have laws against the eating of dogs.

A delicious dinner of swordfish and pork loin cutlets.

Monday 6 August – Sardinia

We sail at breakfast time to the islands between Sardinia and Corsica, for a fabulous day of waterskiing and paddleboarding, etc. I gorge myself on prawns at lunch, after which Carl Ross cleverly labelled me a 'champion prawn star'.

The dog story in the *Sun* has come out brilliantly. Noodle is the hero of the cause.

It is Vicente Solera-Deuchar's first day in the office as my new Private Secretary. He is extremely smart, and a really good choice. He can enjoy a few quiet weeks during which to settle in.

Tuesday 7 August – Corsica

An idyllic day. Meanwhile back home, Boris has made a complete tit of himself by writing an article in the *DT* mocking burqas – 'they look like letter boxes' – while saying that he wouldn't ban them as Denmark has this week. Party Chairman Brandon Lewis, aka Mr Mumble, has criticised him, and so has Number 10. All the Brexiteers are backing him: all the Remainers are calling for him to apologise.

A lovely small pod of dolphins escorts the bow of our boat as we move around the corner of south-west Corsica towards Ajaccio.

Wednesday 8 August – Corsica

Boris has once again made himself the centre of press attention. What a surprise. Lord Sheikh is demanding the withdrawal of the whip. Boris has gone to ground and is refusing to apologise. His burqa comments don't strike me as a capital offence, although they will have empowered nasty types to use similar language. It's just that if he's going to fire such cheap shots, he's just going to look cheap himself.

Thursday 9 August – Corsica

The MPs' WhatsApp group has gone mental over the referral of Boris to the Party's disciplinary process. Any complaint goes to it automatically, but can be quickly dismissed as frivolous. CCHQ/Lewis have made a total bog of it. But the problem with Boris' silliness is that, apart from being intellectually sloppy, it has already created incidents in which burqa-wearing women have been abused in the street.

I read the book by sacked FBI Director James Comey, *A Higher Loyalty*. It is rather pious, but convincingly demolishes Trump.

Saturday 11 August – Sardinia/Rutland

Rees-Mogg, now clearly linked up with Boris for a future leadership partnership, has written in the *Telegraph* condemning May et al. for subjecting Boris to a kangaroo court. For all his absurdity on everything else, he has a point on this. Matthew Parris has written a brilliant article in *The Times* defending Boris' right to say insulting silly things. Sam Coates has posted an equally brilliant article despairing at the state of political leadership in the UK.

Mutual friend Simon King texts to say that Jeremy Catto has moved to hospital, and is not responding to treatment. I fear he'll be dead within the week, which will mark the end of over forty years of close and inspiring friendship.

Tuesday 14 August – Rutland

A car has deliberately crashed into the steel barrier outside St Stephen's entrance to the Commons, veering crazily from the corner of Parliament Square, narrowly missing three cyclists and crunching to a halt within a couple of feet of the duty policeman. The police were there within about two minutes, and they have arrested a Sudanese-origin British passport holder. Seemingly a lone nutter. But lucky nobody was critically injured.

Some texts from BoJo saying why on earth is the UK not involved in the Franco-German talks on Syria. I could have answered with my honest thoughts, which are that he left the FCO in such policy disarray that we are adrift. And we screwed up Syria right from the start in 2011.

An extensive span of a high bridge in Genoa has collapsed. Very unpleasant. It's decades old and smacks of cockily smug design which put too much faith in narrow stilts and which fifty years later can't take the weight. It looks as though thirty or forty people have been killed.

Turkey is in a vicious spat with the US. Trump has put high steel tariffs on Turkey as punishment for their detention of an American pastor. The Turkish economy, more for other reasons, is now in freefall. The lira has been hit by a 40 per cent devaluation, Erdoğan refuses to put up interest rates and the stock market has plummeted. It looks like one of those moments when initial defiant pseudo-patriotism might turn into popular discontent and protest.

Friday 17 August – Rutland

John Wolfe calls. Jeremy Catto has died. He had slipped into a coma on Wednesday night, and died in the John Radcliffe at 8.30 this morning. John was in Eydon, and it has not quite hit him yet. They have been together for well over forty years. Jeremy was one of the few great influences in my life. Witty, stimulating, perceptive: just one of those constant underpinnings in everything I have done or thought since I first arrived in Oxford in 1976.

Long phone call with Jeremy Hunt. He's good to work with – very straightforward and thoughtful. What he lacks in experience in foreign affairs he makes up for with a keen intellect and a readiness to listen. His weakness is that his only real sources of influence will be the officials by his side.

Saturday 18 August – Rutland
Chat with Chief Whip Julian Smith for thirty-five minutes. Very friendly. I say the Chequers plan has bombed. So has Boris, but the Party's cack-handed response to Burqagate, thanks to Brandon Lewis' awful judgement, has rescued him. Williamson is a treacherous failure, and Javid is now super-cocky. Hunt is great. Do not get involved in Labour's anti-Semitism arguments and on no account have a Commons debate on it.

Wednesday 22 August – Marbella
A productive day, of sorts, gradually feeling more energetic as the holiday sets in. I think I have overcome my end-of-term exhaustion. Good chat with the admirable Sarah Furness, the new Lord Lieutenant of Rutland. There is a completely anachronistic rule within the Lieutenancy that only men can wear a uniform. Sarah has had a beautiful tunic made, and has been told by the regional Lieutenancy that it is inappropriate. I share her view that this is very offensive. It is not determined by the Palace, but by the informal hierarchy of serving Lieutenants. I suddenly recall a dinner conversation with William while he was Foreign Secretary that when he wanted to reconfirm the existence of proper formal uniform for ambassadors he was told by the FCO lawyers that he could only do so within equalities legislation if he ensured there was an equivalent design for women ambassadors. I told Sarah I'd had a brainwave and would do some homework.

I pick up the *Telegraph* after lunch and find in it a magnificent obituary of Jeremy. Rather nicely I receive a couple of mentions in it, along with William Hague, but perhaps for reasons of dignity and discretion there is no mention of John Wolfe, which there should be.

Trump is in deep doo-doo. His former campaign manager, Paul Manafort, has been convicted on eight counts of tax fraud, and his long-time lawyer, Michael Cohen, has entered into a plea bargain and is spilling the beans on Trump's pay-offs to former flings including the porn star Stormy Daniels. Trump is a liar, plain and simple. But his unflinching defiance just shores up his ugly core base.

Thursday 23 August – Marbella
Gavin Williamson has been monstered in the *Sun*, their front page portraying him as the Minister of Silly Wars in a skit on *Monty Python*'s Ministry of Silly Walks. They have reports of him wanting to mount guns on tractors and missiles on old cruise ships, and to disguise tanks as Coca-Cola trucks. It looks like a comprehensive briefing from a reliable source, or sources, to ridicule and damage him. I speak to Tom Newton Dunn, although the byline for the story is his colleague David Willetts. TND says that even though Williamson pleaded with the editor yesterday for over twenty minutes, they still ran the story unaltered. TND says he has never known a Cabinet minister before who has no friends and allies at all. He has overreached himself. Then Steven Swinford of the *DT* calls me for a reality check. 'I'm writing the leader on him for tomorrow's paper. I mean … he really is a total jerk, isn't he?' When I said yes, he simply said, 'Good. Thought so. That's really all I needed to be sure of. Time we had another good lunch, my friend. Bye.'

Friday 31 August – Rutland
Alex Salmond resigns from the SNP over their treatment of him in connection with an ancient claim of sexual harassment.

Saturday 1 September – Rutland
Trump is such a tosser. He has terminated the US's remaining $200 million annual payment to UNWRA, the UN Works and Relief

Agency. They'd already suspended $300 million in January. All displaced Palestinians have been stateless since 1948 and eke out a difficult existence in Lebanon, Jordan and (even now) Syria. His extreme support for Israeli policy at the profound expense of the Palestinians is nothing short of contemptible. Ignorance, prejudice, who knows? But it is just so callous and unenlightened.

In Uppingham I encounter Sir Kevin Tebbit, former Permanent Secretary at the MoD. He says that Peter Carrington was his great hero, and that he was able to learn of Boris's resignation just a few hours before he died. He wouldn't tell me the great man's precise words, save that it was a mixture of contempt for the Foreign Secretary and pleasure at the turn of events.

Alistair Burt is in Iran, but despite all the better publicity about his and Hunt's handling of the Nazanin Zaghari-Ratcliffe case we are probably no nearer to a solution. Unless they are engaging with the Revolutionary Guard they are talking to the wrong people.

The BBC *News Quiz* is hilarious about Theresa's lame attempt to join in a tribal dance during her visit to Africa this week. But at least she tried. The President of Kenya referred to Boris disparagingly as 'that bicycle chap'. Everyone forgets that the Boris bike was in fact the policy brainchild of leftie Mayor Ken Livingstone.

Sunday 2 September – Rutland/London
The *Sunday Times* reports that Lynton Crosby is helping Boris to undermine Theresa May and even to bring her down.

Dinner with Ed Argar and Jeremy Quin. Jeremy has just become a Whip. He is a good solid decent guy, with no excessive ambition, plenty of money and good judgement. A former President of the Union (like me), he also went to Beechwood Park, although he reminds me that he was never Head Boy there as I was.

Monday 3 September – London
Erik's ninetieth birthday.

Johnson has savaged May on the front page of the *DT*, deriding the Chequers Deal and accusing her of not even trying to get a good agreement. 'Scandal of Brexit is not that we've failed, but that we have not tried: Boris Johnson claims May's Chequers plan means "going into battle with the white flag fluttering", as he says Britain will get "diddly squat" from the EU.' So the *Daily Boris* has put him on the front page once again. He is on manoeuvres, but as always overplays his hand and equates publicity with support. I contemplate penning a ferocious rebuttal, but am simply too busy to do it. Probably just as well. Later on, Number 10 is dismissive in a well-judged way, by just saying that there is nothing new in anything Boris has said.

Berat Albayrak, son-in-law of President Erdoğan, and now Finance Minister, having been Energy Minister, comes in. The Turkish economy has suffered a devaluation of 40 per cent, but Erdoğan refuses to raise interest rates. Berat argues that personal and national debt in Turkey is very low, so they can sustain this assault. They are in a fierce fight with the US who have put massive tariffs on them and are demanding the release of Pastor Brunson, who is accused of espionage by the Turks.

An hour with Jeremy Hunt, plus minister Harriett Baldwin and SpAds, to prepare for Oral Questions tomorrow. Alistair Burt is in Paris, Mark Field in the Far East. Jeremy gets very bogged down about how he handles Brexit questions, but I like his manner. I point out that Labour will simply try to drive a wedge between him and Boris in order to embarrass the government.

Tuesday 4 September – London

The bitter feud between the Jewish community and Corbyn's Labour Party has been seething for over two months. It has culminated today in an agreement to adopt the International Holocaust Remembrance Alliance (IHRA) definition of anti-Semitism, but instead of championing the contemporary Palestinian cause Corbyn continues to attack the manner in which Israel was founded. There are indeed many arguments to be made about Irgun, the bombing of the King David Hotel, etc, but he undermines any argument he might hold about defending Palestinian rights by seeming to challenge the right of Israel to exist at all. Such an unacceptable attitude is a gift to his critics. He is a plonker.

On the *Today* programme, corroborating Kevin Tebbit's hint to me last week, Lord Carrington's biographer Christopher Lee said that his view of Boris was that 'he used the FCO as an adventure playground for his political ambition'. He also said of Theresa, 'I think she is probably a good leader on some occasions, but nobody knows when those occasions are.' Deliciously droll.

William in the *DT* warns of seven months of Tory mayhem. If it is to be mayhem, then we won't last as long as seven months, and the government will have collapsed. Let's hope not. Muddle is better than mayhem. We need a glorious British fudge to see us through Brexit.

To Number 10 for a meeting with Chief of Staff Gavin Barwell with all the Commons and Lords ministers who are not in the Cabinet. I normally hate group movements, but he handled it well. He gave a frank account of likely progress, mapping out the informal meeting of EU ministers in Salzburg at the end of this month, I guess at PM level; the formal such meeting in October, which has always been seen as the crunch point; and a probable additional Council early in November which will focus exclusively on Brexit.

The main message was that they do expect to have a deal, they do expect Parliament to support it and they as good as think it will be all done and dusted by Christmas. I normally say nothing at these meetings, but when Gavin invited comments from us there was a bit of a pause, so I launched in. 'Chequers was designed to be unifying in the face of a warring Cabinet, but the Deal has turned out to be seriously polarising. How do you want to handle the next ten weeks or so? Do you want to focus on what you call "selling Chequers", or do you want to convey a sense of progress? What has been lacking is any sense that the negotiations have established some degree of traction, so it's left a vacuum in which we are just arguing among ourselves about rather fatuous and circular statements of supposed principle. Do we just let that happen, and wait for a deal to appear out of the blue and hope that Parliament will vote for it? Or do we try to outline where there is progress along the way, but risk opening up a new area of contention around where we might have deviated from Chequers? Which is your preferred route?' Gavin answered well, saying what should have been said before but which hasn't been, namely that the Chequers blueprint is a clear offer by the UK, but that we must now negotiate based on it, expect some alterations and reach an agreement. It is not just take it or leave it.

The Chief, Julian Smith, came in at the end, and was short and funny. 'She will get a deal. We will get it through the House. Having predicted that, I invite you to be on the winning team and not join the commentators.' Well delivered. He has grown up rather, and established much greater authority.

Back to the FCO via the steps at the back of Downing Street through the Ambassadors' Entrance. Chat with the admirable FCO official Jane Rumble on Gove's proposal to JH in which he is trying to assume control of the government's entire oceans policy, whereas as DEFRA Secretary he covers the UK only, and we do the rest of the world. He just won't back off. Having pushed for a no-fishing zone in the entire South Atlantic, he just won't listen to all the arguments against, that it is scientifically ill-advised because it would push krill fishing to more destructive areas, and it would reawaken sovereignty claims from Argentina. I spent months stopping Boris from agreeing to the lunatic self-seeking Gove, and no sooner has he gone than Gove tries to bounce Jeremy. Now, even worse, he wants to adopt the campaign of swimmer Lewis Pugh to declare 30 per cent of the world's oceans a no-fishing zone. This is just a blunt campaign target with no logical merit. We don't own all the world's oceans, so it's not in our gift.

I am trying to piece together a strategic package for Oman, to refresh our long-standing commitment to the Sultanate. Talk the Middle East department through my thoughts, but one or two of them are leaving soon, thus weakening the FCO's knowledge base. All this job rotation means that the FCO doesn't know nearly as much as people think it does.

FCO Orals. What a difference in tone. Jeremy was excellent, and although they couldn't bash him politically, I felt that the other side welcomed the change. We covered a lot of ground, and the team were all self-assured and competent, covering skilfully on the hoof for Mark Field who was on a lengthy trip to the Antipodes.

Speak on the phone to Stuart Andrew about the Gulf Advisory Council. Andrew took over from Guto Bebb as PUSS for Defence Procurement after Guto resigned a few weeks ago over Brexit. He is a lovely guy but will be rather out of his depth. The job should be higher ranking anyway, but with no experience himself, and working to an erratic Defence Secretary, it won't be easy. He has convened a meeting of the Gulf Advisory Council which I won't be able to attend, and I just wanted to give him a teach-in. The last one was a catastrophe with someone from the FCO spouting a load of inane platitudes about the Middle East, when the whole purpose of the meeting is for outside experts to say what they know. I suggested he ensure that the officials are told to shut up, and that he provoke a discussion among the wise by tabling two or three exam questions such as: Will Mohammed bin Salman ever become King of Saudi Arabia? Can the schism in the GCC be healed? Are we any longer thought to be relevant, or have we been displaced by the Israelis and the Chinese? That would get them going.

Wednesday 5 September – London

Phew! Quite a day. At 9am, I am confidentially briefed on what will be today's big news. At 11.30am the police will hold a press conference to announce that charges will be brought against two Russians for attempted murder using the Novichok nerve agent in Salisbury, and for the subsequent death in Amesbury. The detective work has been superb. They have CCTV footage and the flight and passport details of two agents of the GRU, the military secret service, travelling under false names to Salisbury and to the road in which the Skripals lived. It was the Russkies wot dunnit! The PM will make a statement at 12.30 after PMQs. They might want me to brief the London Diplomatic Corps tomorrow morning. So it's all systems go.

Our first proper ministerial team meeting with Jeremy. Fantastic discussion on Yemen and Iran.

PM statement on the Salisbury Novichok poisonings, setting out what I'd been told earlier. This was followed by a totally pathetic response from Corbyn, who failed to condemn Russia outright. Boris described that as 'weasely', and he wasn't wrong.

Thursday 6 September – London

Brief diplomats with Ben Wallace in the Locarno Room on the Russian prosecution.

To Wychwood House [residence] for US embassy drinks, with Deputy Lew Lukens.

Woody Johnson was there. I said, 'Woody, I have a confession about your embassy documentary and the clip they used of us. When you were talking about the peregrine falcon, I didn't really have a clue what you were talking about.' He laughed in his jaunty way and said, 'No. Nor did I.' He's a bit dotty.

Friday 7 September – Rutland

'Bonking Boris booted out by wife' splashes the *Sun*. He has sepa-rated, he is divorcing. His eldest daughter has been overheard deriding him and saying Marina will never have anything to do with him again. This, and feeling the financial pinch, will probably have been an influence on his decision to resign as Foreign Secretary. I just think it makes him look even more recklessly irresponsible, although his supporters (fewer than people think) will spin it that it's a personal matter, that people have discounted it already in their view of Boris and that he is deliberately clearing the decks before having a run at the leadership. All crap. He's a shambles. He needs to tidy up his act.

The *Sun* and the *Sun on Sunday* are digging like crazy and will run it hard over the weekend. Now that anti-Brexit Geordie Greig has replaced Paul Dacre as editor of the *Mail*, I can't imagine they will be kind to him.

Mid-year Executive Meeting of the Rutland & Melton Conservatives. Perhaps forty people there. Our Chairman, Byron Rhodes, is a good councillor but can sometimes be a bit socially awkward. After all the usual stuff about membership (we have 457) and the accounts (we have £50,000 in the bank) he rather surprised the Exec Cttee by announcing they intend to sell our second prop-erty, an old office we have owned for sixty years. It's the right thing to do, and the price is fair, all the more so as it is a flying freehold over the estate agents beneath, and it's only of value to the dentist next door. They could have done it by now if they hadn't been so unimaginative about how to handle it.

Then Geoffrey Pointon, the most ugly nasty shit in the Association, tried to move a motion that I be subjected to quarterly appraisal by the members. Although he is a lone voice on the matter and his motion would have been voted down, I whispered to Byron that the motion was not in order as there had been no prior notification of it. Eyes rolled as Pointon tried to explain his reasons for it. It was deferred to the next meeting, by which time the forces of decency will be prepared to round on Pointon and hopefully mash him to pulp.

My speech focusses on the FCO and the welcome change from Boris to Jeremy; the Melton bypass success; the sale and redevelopment of St George's Barracks in Rutland; and then a full analysis of Brexit, saying we will get there, but we must all stick together and never risk the prospect of Jeremy Corbyn as Prime Minister. They were happy. Indeed two of them afterwards said thank you for the best and clearest exposition of Brexit they had heard. Hmm … why am I not on TV more?

Saturday 8 September – Rutland
Rather chilly and overcast compared with the last three months.

George Papadopoulos, the former Trump adviser, is the first person in the Mueller investigation to go to prison, albeit for only fourteen days, for lying about his meeting with Russians ahead of the 2016 Presidential election. More to come methinks. Keep going, guys – work your way up!

Tons of Boris stuff in the papers, of course. But journalists' assessment of his degree of support, be it in Parliament or among activists, just doesn't feel right. I don't think there's much there or anywhere any more. The facts on the ground are different from the noise in the media.

I tweet against Boris at midnight after the first edition of the *Mail on Sunday* has him comparing Theresa May to someone who has put a suicide vest around the country and given the detonator to Michel Barnier. This is just the sort of attention-seeking excess which makes him look like a clown. It so diminishes any reputation that he has left. My tweet is pretty vicious: 'For Boris to say that the PM's view is like that of a suicide bomber is too much. This marks one of the most disgusting moments in modern British politics. I'm sorry, but this is the political end of Boris Johnson. If it isn't now, I will make sure it is later.'

It's rather hyperbolic, but it's the only way to get noticed. He is trying to build himself up in order to land a hammer blow against her at Conference. Given all his divorce and affair stuff he'd have been wise to remain silent. To me it's very simple – the PM must be defended. So I just have to seize the chance to kick him when he's down. I'm one of the few people who can afford to spend some political capital and take the wind out of his sails to help her. If he is intent on destroying her, then I will fight back against him. In all other respects I actually rather like him.

Sunday 9 September – Rutland/Gibraltar

My tweet is leading the news. David Gauke and Sajid Javid echo it on morning TV. Tom Tugendhat and others such as Alistair Burt wade in too. Roger Gale calls to express total support.

The tweet tally says it has been seen by over half a million by the time I land in Gibraltar. All this sort of thing is new to me. I've been tough, but I'm not going to stand idly by while he tries to topple the PM. He is just so unsuitable for further high office, and she needs all the backing anyone can offer her. If he wants to replace her, then make a big principled stand. Don't just play these sniping games.

Fraser Nelson offers an interview in the *Spectator*.

In Gibraltar am greeted by the Governor Lieutenant General Ed Davis at the Convent residence. See Chief Minister Fabian Picardo. The Brexit talks with Spain are using a channel which links directly into new PM Pedro Sánchez, and they have taken a constructive turn. Whether Spain can deliver on being so accommodating to Gibraltar is another matter. Quick dinner at the Waterfront on Queensway Quay with the Deputy Governor Nick Pyle. A really fun reception at the Caleta Hotel, with the great and the good of Gibraltar plus twenty-eight UK parliamentarians including Arlene Foster of the DUP. I make a little speech which amuses them suitably. The MPs such as Bob Neill and David Morris are very approving and supportive both for my Gibraltar efforts and for my stance on Boris.

My new Private Secretary Vicente is proving to be top notch. Another official, Liam McShane, who has spent a month in my private office, has rather blossomed suddenly. He is brilliant at appearing at just the right moment with a glass of beer for me.

Views of the tweet have hit a million.

Monday 10 September – Gibraltar/London

Breakfast with the Commander British Forces Gibraltar. He is very sensible and has clearly revived good relations on the Rock since the runway blocking and the tensions over the Armed Forces Act. He and Mark Lancaster are a million times better than their predecessors.

There is a lovely moment for me, as the son of a former RAF commanding officer in Gibraltar, when the navy prove unable to take me out in their coastal patrol boat because the starboard engine won't start. I teased, 'My father's Shackletons could always start their starboard engines and take off. Sorry about the boat!'

Walk down Main Street among hundreds of Gibraltarians in red and white. I am suitably attired, but not excessively so – red socks, red belt, red tie, but not an absurd pantomime blast of colour. Sir Joe Bossano, whose knighthood I quietly helped along, receives his Freedom of the City in a lovely ceremony at the start of the Gibraltar National Day rally in Casemates Square. I make a speech … Er, basically the same as last year, but with a bit more spice. To the reception at Grand Battery House, do a bit of media, rather enjoy myself, and after a quick tour of the under-utilised airport which is built to connect with Spain, I fly off.

My Twitter views have hit 1.8 million.

Not a bad day.

Tuesday 11 September – London

To Oxford for Jeremy Catto's funeral and Requiem Mass. An hour and a half of music and Latin, and lots of old friends who I hadn't seen for ages, A. N. Wilson among them … just so many interesting people.

Give a lift back to London to Ed Argar and Sir David Manning – our former Ambassador to Israel and Washington, foreign policy adviser to Blair in Number 10, and now mentor and guide to Prince William on all things diplomatic. Such a charming and sensible person, he is wisdom and dignity on stilts.

Bump into Gavin Barwell outside the Red Lion. Good chat for about ten minutes. He gently said that my last few words in the BoJo tweet were a tad over the top. I admitted that they were, but said that you can land a point these days, particularly in contrast to Boris, only if you over-egg it somewhat. I reasoned with him that someone had to defend the PM's back and stop him going into Conference determined to upstage her and even start the process of replacing her. I had to puncture his plan to be the destructive Conference darling. I was in a unique position as an old stager, his former deputy and someone whose rare interventions get noticed, to fire the bazooka. He took the point. He doesn't think the ERG [the backbench Tory Brexiteers' European Research Group] has the numbers, but worries they are a serious danger.

I pen a note to Boris and stick it on the letter board:

> Dear Boris. It's not personal. Or at least it is not born of any animosity. It's just that if you are going to challenge the PM so threateningly I will in return support her vigorously and fight fire with fire. If she goes we all go. Noises off are constantly undermining our negotiating position. In essence I think that she is acting in the national interest and you are not. So it's out with the cannons. Country first … It's as simple as that. Yours ever, Alan.

Lots of colleagues during the two evening divisions prove very supportive, such as Richard Harrington, Michael Fallon, etc.

Jeremy Hunt confides in me that he's about to make a decision I won't like. He will agree to the proposal for the Home Office to proscribe Hizbollah. I think it plays into the Netanyahu/Kushner playbook and will remove essential intelligence for us in Lebanon, but he hints that he has to do it in order to preserve our robust stand on Iran and hence to support the Iran nuclear deal. It's a trade-off designed to protect bigger equities. I see the point and respect his directness with me. The trouble is … we conceded to the US and all they will do is take more and never say thank you. We are being played by nutty mania, and we are compromising our integrity.

A delicious George Young moment in the Lords. The baronet, and now peer, is at the dispatch box in response to a committee report slamming Boris for taking up his job as *Telegraph* columnist without referring it to the committee which approves post-ministerial appointments. Boris is castigated in the report. Asked to pass judgement, George replies, 'I am not an apologist for the former Foreign Secretary. That requires a portfolio of skills which I don't possess.'

Wednesday 12 September – London

The ERG met last night in the Thatcher Room in PCH. Although the main figures such as Johnson, Davis, Rees-Mogg, [Owen] Paterson and Duncan Smith were not there, they claim to have had fifty in the room and reports suggest they spent much of the time discussing how they could get rid of Theresa, and how they would do everything to that end unless she binned the Chequers plan. They are destructive dimwits. If she goes, the whole government would collapse, and we'd be going into a no man's land of potential ungovernability and mayhem. They are all just too blinkered and stupid to grasp the strategic consequences of their folly.

Another really stimulating ministers' meeting with Jeremy, this time covering Brexit, the Boris phenomenon, No Deal consequences and so on. JH said he met DD yesterday, who said that if pure Chequers were presented to the House he would vote against, but that it would get through. JH thinks that if we did indeed get Chequers, then it would be a great deal for the UK, as it contains a mix of arrangements which would suit us well. But the ERG think it is but the first of many compromises and concessions, so they are digging their heels in.

We assessed Boris' future. The consensus was that he is a much reduced figure. We teased Mark Field for his Phileas Fogg circumnavigation of the globe, as he had spent nearly three weeks on the other side of the world.

Interview with Fraser Nelson, editor of the *Spectator*. I injected some choice turns of phrase about Boris and Brexit, such as:

> Publicity is his cocaine … but now it's getting up everyone's nose. He was impossible to dislike: but he was impossible. If he thinks he is the UK's Trump, it simply won't fly. I don't want the Conservative Party to become the mutant child of UKIP. He used to be an electoral asset, but he has squandered his inheritance.

Friday 14 September – Rutland

I'm not in the *Spectator*. Tugendhat is! My interview has been bounced. It explains why there have been some reports in the *DT* about him this week, with him calling for a younger person to assume the crown of the Party when she goes. I wonder who he might have in mind?

All of these people want to run before they can walk. They see politics as a perpetual battle for succession, and not as a journey of duty and obligation which may or may not bring the political promotion they seek. It's only the promotion that matters to them. They don't realise how corrosive it is for so many people to be given high office without any earlier experience of government, and sometimes with no real experience of anything. Tom Tug thinks he should be the next Prime Minister, yet he will only have been the Chairman of a select committee. These types have little concept of what it takes to be a minister, let alone the Prime Minister. So many over the last twenty years have gone straight into the Cabinet without ever being a junior minister. Only a ghastly period on the Opposition front bench begins to help them qualify instead, and the way they are behaving, that might come sooner than they'd wish.

Fraser Nelson says our interview took place after this week's print deadline, so it will appear next week. Their leading article carries a silly load of guff, probably written by that oddball James Forsyth, stating that everyone always knew I loathed Boris and that I was appointed to the FCO as a deliberate act of sabotage. So I have dispatched a letter to the editor.

> Sir: You assert in your editorial 'Divided they fail' three supposed truths – that when appointed as a minister in the Foreign Office I loathed Boris Johnson; that this was a fact known by everyone at Westminster; and that the Prime Minister appointed me as a deliberate act of sabotage against him as Foreign Secretary.
>
> Given that each of these statements has never had any basis in evidence and amounts to mere surmise and concoction dreamt up two years later, I'm afraid that in my view it profoundly discredits the journalist on whom your anonymous opinion relied. Yours etc.

Let's see if they publish it. It would sit amusingly alongside my interview next week.

The number of times people have seen my tweet about Boris now stands at 2,012,408.

Sunday 16 September – Rutland/London

BBC Midlands come to interview me for their *Sunday Politics* programme. They ask me a perfectly fair question about my comments last weekend about Boris. It allowed me to say precisely what I wanted to: that this is not so much about Boris as about the need to give full support to the PM. We are in a crucial moment of history which will determine our fortunes for decades to come. I was concerned that Boris intended to go into Party Conference determined to attack the Chequers Deal, the PM and hence the national interest. I said I urge all colleagues to back the PM, and hence the prospects of securing a good deal for the UK. All pretty straightforward, but it's the antis who are winning all the coverage.

I replay the recording, but the quality of their broadcast was abysmal. It kept on freezing the frame and cutting out the sound. The trouble is, by removing the satellite dish and relying on 4G, they are useless in rural areas. My superfast fibre broadband is there, and would provide a reliable link, but the BBC refuse to use broadband 'for security reasons' … but it's a live broadcast to the general public. Durr!

Monday 17 September – Vienna/Skopje

Early flight. I love Vienna. Elegant grandeur that well exceeds the significance of the capital of such a small country, but it is beautifully intact across the integrity of the city, and pleasingly reflects its imperial past.

It looks as though we might just have got there on krill. In response to Michael Gove's absurd grandstanding on oceans policy, in order to ingratiate himself to campaigning NGOs, the proposed riposte to him at last is adequately robust. In essence: a general nod towards wanting to preserve 30 per cent of the world's oceans to satisfy the campaign is just OK, but it must not imply that the 30 per cent will be no-take (i.e. all fishing is banned). It should allow for more clearly defined categories of marine protection and must be led by science. I think we've cracked it.

I deliver the UK's national statement at the annual plenary session of the IAEA [International Atomic Energy Authority]. Then meet the Chairman of the China Atomic Energy Authority, Zhang Kejian. We covered technical cooperation in the UK, and the influence China might have on North Korea to help reach a deal with Trump on non-proliferation. Then the Chair of India's Atomic Energy Commission, Dr Sekhar Basu. What a bore.

Much more lively and genuinely stimulating was my half-hour with Dr Ali Akbar Salehi, head of Iran's Atomic Energy Organisation, who is also a Vice-President of Iran and a former Foreign Minister. I hit it off with him quickly after dropping mention of my oil-trading days, and the deals I did with Majid Hedeyatzadeh thirty years ago. He was with NIOC [National Iranian Oil Company], and is now its President. I said how much I regretted the way the Saudis, the Emiratis and the Israelis had revved up the US to gang up on Iran. I added that the UK was a firm supporter of the JCPOA and would not flinch from being so in the face of US disagreement.

A drink in the embassy garden and a light supper, then to the Palais Ferstel for the US reception. A short but sparky meeting with US Energy Secretary Rick Perry, a former Governor of Texas. He is highly convivial, and mention of oil and my working for Marc Rich worked wonders for creating a lively exchange.

Late flight to Skopje. To the Aleksandar Palace Hotel. Bed at 1am.

Tuesday 18 September – Skopje/Belgrade
Quick breakfast with HMA Rachel Galloway and her embassy team, then a meeting with Hristijan Mickoski, President and hence leader of VMRO-DPMNE, now the main opposition party. An academic cast in an unconvincing role as a tribal politician, he replaced Nikola Gruevski when Zoran Zaev took over as Prime Minister after the last election, and is now failing to support the name-change referendum, finding lame excuses to criticise it without directly opposing it. The referendum on the 30th, although only consultative, needs to secure a turnout of 50 per cent and then be passed in Parliament. So a boycott is tantamount to voting against. Parliament is more important than the 50 per cent threshold, but anything under 50 per cent would create a legitimacy problem.

A million times more impressive is Prime Minister Zaev. I now know him very well. He is energetic and optimistic. No end of international figures have swung by Skopje recently: Chancellor Merkel, Secretary Mattis, Commissioner Hahn, Chancellor Kurz, etc. The feeling is that they have a massive majority in favour of changing the name to North Macedonia, but that the turnout might, by a whisker, fall short of the necessary 50 per cent.

Back to Skopje to see my mate Nikola Dimitrov, the FM. He is hovering on the verge of pessimism, but will campaign full tilt outside Skopje for the next ten days. I advise him to keep it simple and tell it straight by repeating a basic message.

Air Serbia to Belgrade in time for tea with Quint ambassadors, the five main interested parties in the Balkans: France, Germany, EU, US and UK, plus guest Italy.

The big issue is whether there is about to be a Serbia–Kosovo deal – it's clearly under discussion – between President Hashim Thaçi of

Kosovo and President Aleksandar Vučić of Serbia which might include land swaps and balance up the ethnic content of the two. The Dayton Accords, which resolved the vicious conflict in the Balkans in the early 1990s between Serbs, Kosovans, Bosnians, Albanians and hence Muslims and others, opposed mono-ethnic nations and was based on multi-ethnic countries. Kosovo was only recognised as a country in 2009, something on which we took the lead, and it was also the UK which championed the NATO bombing of Serbia in 1999 in response to their ethnic cleansing of Muslims in Bosnia.

Our fear is that border swaps could ignite new eruptions of discontent and cause more problems than they solve. But if there is a wider package, amounting to a sort of peace treaty in which Serbia recognises Kosovo, and the UN and the EU endorse it, then they might register lasting progress. The trouble is that everyone has an opinion, but it is largely speculative because we don't really know what the two sides' agenda is.

Wednesday 19 September – Belgrade/London

Jeremy's obituary is in *The Times*. Lovely, albeit with some needless errors such as saying he lived in Aston le Walls in Northamptonshire when that was where his nearest Catholic church is. He lived in Eydon. And again saying that William Hague was his pupil, when they barely knew each other at Oxford, and did so only later through me.

An extraordinarily friendly meeting with Serbian FM Ivica Dačić. I gave him a photo of all the Balkans ministers at the party in my garden. The event and the July summit more generally have had a lasting effect. He was very forthcoming about Serbia's discussions with Kosovo, dangling the notion that they are only close to Russia because they offer them a backstop safeguard on Kosovo, backing up as they do their non-recognition. If they square everything with Kosovo, then they would no longer need Russia. It's a good pitch, which echoes the comments yesterday of the US Ambassador. I suggested that there was a lot of speculative opinion about the danger of border swaps, but that nobody really knew quite what Serbia and Kosovo were negotiating. If they were more open about the agenda then they would attract more international support. I invited him to London for a solid day's dialogue. He leapt at the idea. It will put the UK deeply in the loop if he comes.

Serbia's Europe Minister Jadranka Joksimović. She was dressed in vibrant colours and proved lively and engaging. We covered the need for Serbia to improve its track record on issues such as press freedom and the integrity of judicial appointments. All seemed fine until she suddenly slid into a diatribe in favour of undiluted Serbian nationalism. Her mask had dropped.

Prime Minister Ana Brnabić who I now know reasonably well. She too praised the Western Balkans Summit, and was happy when I handed over a photo of her with Theresa May. She is unusual. An open lesbian who dresses like a teenage boy, she cuts a singular figure. More of a technocrat than a politician, she likes her e-government and all things digital.

To the British Council which has the contract to introduce digital skills and computer programming to all 10–14-year-olds across the Balkans under a UK-funded scheme. Some really enthusiastic youngsters proved charmingly impressive.

The DEFRA press office is pushing for Gove to make a statement on oceans policy at the G7 Environmental Conference next week. He just won't give up. Our own press office has received no clear instructions from the Foreign Secretary's office about the acute sensitivities around it, and so the danger is that Gove gets his way by default. I insist on a few conditions – any mention of preserving 30 per cent of the world's oceans is only OK if it is clear that they might be Marine Preservation Areas but not 100 per cent no-fishing zones; a footnote must make it clear that domestic waters are DEFRA, but international seas are FCO; and it must state that the FCO is due soon to publish the government's Oceans Strategy, i.e. we own oceans policy, not DEFRA. After a tough talking to, the press office banks the lot. So good for them after all. Got there!

EU leaders are gathering in Salzburg for their informal Heads of State/Government meeting for the next couple of days.

Thursday 20 September – London

Oh Mike Penning – what a dumbo. He is one of the dimmest MPs on our side. He has been over-promoted at every stage: as an MP, as a minister, as a Rt Hon. and as Sir Mike. Instead of being grateful for his good fortune, he lives in a permanent sulk that he isn't in the Cabinet – God spare us when it's bad enough already – and he has now done an interview in the *Telegraph* attacking the PM and demanding she chuck Chequers. So thank you, Mike, you moronic, ungrateful, self-deluded, treacherous dunce.

The Czech and Maltese PMs in Salzburg have both suggested we should hold a second referendum, which is less than helpful. It's a wish that can have no fulfilment. The informal summit is supposed to be mostly about migration, but Brexit is the underlying issue at every turn.

R&M [Rutland and Melton] lunch at the Carlton with Johnny Mercer MP. He was very good. He only has one speech: I was born in a council house; I joined the army; I wasn't interested in politics until I realised it was the only way I could help veterans; we must appear to be interested in normal issues, not airy-fairy policy, etc. It worked. They really liked him.

I am trying to shape a simple bill to pitch for inclusion in the Queen's Speech which enhances the protection of diplomatic missions in London by clarifying the powers of the police to act against demonstrators on their doorstep. The police only look at domestic public order laws, and so do nothing unless there is a near riot, but the embassies and we in the FCO are in despair that they fail to enforce the clear intent of the Vienna Convention on the inviolability of diplomatic missions – something that is embedded in our law, but which fails to specify what the police should do in practice to uphold it.

One option is to replicate the terms of the Act which protects Parliament Square and Parliament itself. I suggest that the simplest measure would be to establish an exclusion zone that can and should be enforced around every embassy. In other words, the police would have to push protesters to the other side of the road, and remove them from the immediate vicinity of the pavement and the embassy's front door.

A really useful hour with Philip Barton, our senior official who covers Russia, intelligence, counter-terrorism. I will meet him regularly in future.

Meanwhile on Brexit, all reports state that Salzburg has been a disaster. Tusk and others have all dismissed the agreement reached at Chequers as unacceptable. PM seems humiliated. It has clearly gone wrong, but I just don't understand how it could all have gone so badly off track. How can they have made such a mess of it? Surely they would have had clear indications of where the sticking points were? It's not the end – there's still October and November – but it is very worrying.

Friday 21 September – Rutland

My letter is in the *Spectator*, but my interview isn't. So he's holding it over till next week for the day before Conference. That's a bit sneaky. Fraser Nelson has egged me on, then let me down.

The Salzburg fallout is dismal. Quite how we recover the necessary momentum is anyone's guess.

Andrew Bridgen has apparently told our Council Leader David Rushton that Boris has promised him (i.e. Bridgen) a position in his Cabinet if he becomes PM. Bloody hell!!! Australia here I come.

The PM makes a 2pm press statement in Number 10 on the Brexit negotiations … or lack of them. No questions, but actually quite a compelling, logical setting-out of where we are and what needs to happen. She says that we are doing our best and have received no substantive counter-proposal from the EU, and if they force us into having No Deal, then that's what it will be. It's fair and sensible, but can't escape from the looming danger of crashing out with no arrangement. The EU bang on about maintaining the integrity of the single market: for the twenty-seven who remain, the single market will still be there in the same way. If we are outside the EU, then why not a different structure? I suppose in a nutshell what she said was 'Mind your manners.'

Call with Ecuador FM José Valencia to discuss Venezuela, and Assange. We both want Assange out of the embassy, after what is now six years, but the Ecuador government won't quite yet take the necessary final step for fear of the domestic reaction.

Half an hour on the phone with Yvette Cooper. We totally agree on all the ins and outs of No Deal, the chances of a second referendum, the mood against No Deal but also against being pushed around by Brussels, etc. We can see all the scenarios, all the issues, but can't see any way out. The only realistic solution is a deal of any sort which is supported by the Commons … and then we move on. But it is looking less probable than we would both like.

Saturday 22 September – Rutland

The PM has come out of the Salzburg spat with an enhanced reputation. Just. A day is a long time in politics! She woke up yesterday at rock bottom, but salvaged it with her statement in front of two Union Jacks in Number 10. Jeremy Hunt gives a calm, rational interview on *Today*, which was due to focus on his trip to Burma but was mostly on Salzburg. He just quietly repeated that we had made proposals but the EU had not. So they should offer us a counter-proposal in the same spirit of respect in which we had offered them ours. I texted him a 'well done' message. He's only been Foreign Secretary for two months, but has noticeably injected dignity and authority into the role.

In Ahvaz in south-west Iran, at the top of the Arabian Gulf, gunmen have fired on a military parade and killed twenty-four people, including members of the Revolutionary Guard. The parade was marking the beginning of the 1980–8 war against Iraq thirty-eight years ago. But incidents like this need to be watched and analysed very carefully lest they indicate the beginning of the end of the forty years of revolutionary rule in Iran. Oh for a counter-revolution to release them from the IRGC and theocratic dictatorship.

My Google alert has picked up a blog by the broadcaster and publisher Iain Dale from today, in which he says he has fallen upon a diary he kept for a few weeks in 2002 in which he was agonising about declaring himself as gay. It includes a reference to the lunch we had on 25 November that year at Bank in Buckingham Gate. He says I spent all my time ogling the waiters. I text him to say I was only trying to help him on his journey. He texts back, 'I should have kept it up – the diary I mean.'

Liz Truss has completed her visit to the US, but it has been odd, unproductive and purposeless. I sent an official a mock DipTel draft, daring them to issue it: 'Chief Sec Liz Truss visited. Her stay was deemed both timely and useful. But to whom is not wholly clear. She arrived, accompanied by four officials etc. The Consulate met her request to see a game of American football, and go shopping. Our local hosts proved most welcoming, but expressed a degree of bemusement at the purpose of her visit, and indeed at the minister herself.'

Sunday 23 September – Rutland

Labour Party Conference in Liverpool. Corbyn is beginning to make Michael Foot look like a moderate. They said at the time [1983] that Foot's manifesto was the longest suicide note in history. Labour's contemporary suicide note is already being written: renationalise the railways, even without compensation; introduce a basic income for all, and at a level which is economically self-devouring; compulsory quotas for workers on all company boards, although whether public, private, large or small is not clear (and what about women?). No doubt we can add the prohibition of private health, the abolition of all private education (or at the very least the abolition of their charitable status and the imposition of VAT on all fees). Add too, probably, the abolition of the honours system, and swingeing levels of taxation on the so-called higher paid.

The owls are hooting in concert, it seems, from our rooftop to our neighbour's. It is all one can hear on such a still night, and the tu-whit tu-whoo is just pure and beautifully pitched.

Monday 24 September – Rutland

As I was going to bed the Sky News ribbon states that the government is to protect 30 per cent of the world's oceans and 'Sir Alan Duncan says we must protect the oceans against unsustainable activities.' Oh well. At least that came out relatively OK.

Tuesday 25 September – Rutland

Patrick Forbes and Steve the cameraman come at 4pm. He had interviewed Mogg earlier and thinks he is both exhausted and mad. It's all gone to Moggy's head, and he seems to think his great moment in British politics may have come. It may be about to come, but there won't be any British politics left in which he can enjoy the moment.

I contributed what I hope will prove a useful, not to say memorable, part of the documentary, saying that all the wreckers are fantasists and that the only way forward is to support the PM in anything she can get. Any ideas from Mogg et al. are mere theorising. We are looking at the art of the possible. It's not about whether the PM simply accepts an alternative proposal kindly offered by Conservative MPs: it's about whether she can get us an agreement, whatever it is.

Vicky Ford, now an FCO PPS, is a former MEP and widely considered a bit dippy. But despite giving that impression I find her both bright and well informed on Euro-matters. She has just been in Brussels for a couple of days, a timely reality check after Salzburg, and texts me from the Eurostar to say that Barnier is furious about last week, and is convinced we are trying to undermine the single market and undercut EU manufacturers. This is also a concern shared by MEPs, she says:

> Some members of EP Brexit cttee just want to complete the
> withdrawal agreement and get it off their desks. Others
> understand the need to help find a face save for Leo V [Varadkar,
> the Taoiseach] on backstop as well as PM on Chequers.

That is indeed an informed and perceptive reflection of the position. The MEPs might not count for as much as the leaders of the twenty-seven, but they do matter, and the Barnier attitude most certainly does. What a shambles.

Wednesday 26 September – Rutland

Labour's MP for Crewe & Nantwich, Laura Smith, has called for a general strike to bring down the government if there isn't an immediate general election. What a stupid, silly, rancid little idiot.

Unfortunately it's not just her: the Labour benches are now populated by quite a number of rasping nasties – more often women than men – who haven't moved on from their first year in the students' union.

Interview in Rutland with Francis Elliott of *The Times*, who has had enough of the Labour Party Conference. It's their final day in Liverpool. Corbyn's speech was far more dynamic than anyone might have expected. There were many frightening absurdities in it, such as a ridiculous promise to create 400,000 jobs, and a policy to cover the country with wind farms, but one sentence I fully agreed with was his pledge to recognise Palestine immediately he is elected.

One of the Russians who arrived with Novichok was supposedly Rushnan Bashirov. He has now been identified as a decorated GRU officer Anatoly Chepiga. The PM has rammed this home at the UN.

Thursday 27 September – Rutland

Angela Merkel's government is looking very rickety. They think May is in difficulty, but the other Mrs M is fighting to survive. This is potentially disastrous for our Brexit negotiations. Both Merkel and Macron are facing domestic pressure, which will relegate the attention paid to reaching a Brexit deal. The combination of all these elements is exactly what causes wider problems of disintegration and protest.

Rutland Councillor Mr Alderman has pleaded guilty in court in Birmingham to posting illegal hate messages on his Facebook page. He will be sentenced next week, and will probably face a fine, but we all need to pile in and force him to resign as a councillor.

Lots of conversations with Ken Bool and Oliver Hemsley, our main Conservatives on Rutland County Council. The MoD housing project by the villages of North Luffenham and Edith Weston must be curtailed. Maybe 500 houses and long-term quarrying, but not 3,000. I have written to the MoD to request a meeting.

On another issue I despair. Fraser Nelson has not used my interview and has not had the courtesy to let me know one way or the other. Today's edition has an interview with David Lidington conducted by Fraser and James Forsyth. I assume I have been spiked. Unless, that is, he's holding it for a Conference Special, which would be decidedly sneaky.

It's been a lovely sunny day, and the digger has cleared the ditch, made a massive pile of usable compost and reduced a mountain of cut shrubbery to ashes. I love being organised.

Friday 28 September – Rutland

Oh here we go again. The *Daily Boris* is off on one. The *Telegraph* have given him over 4,000 words to argue for a Canada-like deal. It doesn't solve the Northern Ireland problem and it's not on offer. It is polemical deceit. The EU won't agree to it, and the DUP would vote against it, so the government would fall and there'd be no deal of any sort. So it is phantasmagorical bollocks.

Fraser Nelson apologises for not using my interview. He says they were offered David Lidington, and the *Speccie* thought they should play ball with Number 10. But he will put me up online by midday. Jason Groves on the *Mail* will look out for it, and in the meantime I have given him a response to Boris: 'This is him acting in his self-interest, not the national interest. Canada+ is not on offer, and the DUP wouldn't wear it.'

The *Speccie* goes online, and Francis Elliott says he'll have to run my piece straightaway. Because they are doing a profile of Hunt tomorrow, I am posted as a story at the top of their online site at 5pm. It's well written and will get picked up, but I suspect that that's as much as I'll get. It provokes a dozen or so approving texts.

The final day of massive progress in the garden: digging out the ditch, turning the compost heaps, moving the little front hedge to allow for a slight widening of the driveway and scooping and turning the soil in a redefined main flower bed. Oh how satisfying.

Trump's nominee for the Supreme Court, Brett Kavanaugh, has undergone a torrid Senate hearing, accused by a woman who is now a professor of being sexually assaulted by him at high school. He has been approved, but it depends on him first being investigated by the FBI.

Saturday 29 September – Rutland

No full *Times* interview. So an interesting time spent with Francis and a photographer and a good interview come to just a few paragraphs online. Not surprising. They can't do both me and Jeremy on the same day. So understandably he comes first.

For all her rebellious attitude, Heidi Allen gave an excellent interview on *Today*. Broadly the same thesis as mine, that if the wreckers destroy the prospect of a deal, then there is a case for going back to the people for them to choose between No Deal and Remain. Our difference is that whereas she says it will happen, I know that it won't.

Sunday 30 September – Bahrain

Flight to Bahrain.

The Party's Conference app has been hacked because it had no password protection. They took the phone numbers of Cabinet ministers and posted a photo of Eeyore in place of Hammond.

Boris has done an interview in the *Sunday Times*. The front page has a photo of him on one side and Theresa on the other, facing him. It is basically all-out war between the two of them. Tim Shipman of the *ST* refers to the attack from his 'diminutive' former deputy, to which Boris replies that Alan 'should pick on someone his own size'. Cheap – both of them.

I exchange texts with Tim, expressing amusement at the diminutive remark, but explaining clearly that I am only doing what I am doing because I believe it to be in the national interest. I am not playing games: I am deadly serious that even though nobody can say they love Theresa, nobody can do any better. Boris has no credible answers and his destructive antics could bring everything crashing down.

On landing, my lead has been followed by Digby Jones. As Lord Jones, former Director General of the CBI [Confederation of British Industry] and a Biz Minister under Gordon Brown, he enjoys enough profile to matter, and he has a robust no-nonsense style. He speaks in the main hall at the Conference opening attended by the PM, refers to Boris, labels him 'irrelevant and offensive' and receives extensive applause. Perfect. The tone is set: the die is cast. Others will also follow I'm sure.

Monday 1 October – Bahrain

A poll puts Corbyn ahead of Johnson by 6 points. Jeremy Hunt has drawn an unfortunate parallel in his speech likening the EU to a 'Soviet-style prison'. It has backfired, particularly among the EU member states who joined to escape from communism. It was pretty clumsy.

Meanwhile Philip Hammond has attacked Boris, saying that he is incapable of grown-up politics. Indeed, most of the front pages have a 'Tory backlash against Boris' headline. My original tweet and subsequent comments have led the way and given people the confidence to speak out against him. I hope his bubble has been well and truly pricked. He must either be a big boy or fail.

Tuesday 2 October – Bahrain

First meeting of day in Bahrain is with Deputy PM Sheikh Mohammed bin Mubarak. I get a bit of a scrubbing over our failure to protect their London embassy from persistent demonstrators. Their complaint is fully justified.

To Awali, the original 1930s Oil SOCAL compound (Standard Oil of California, now Chevron), to meet the Minister of Oil Sheikh Mohammed bin Khalifa al Khalifa. Young and very smart. He is so on the ball, and especially interesting about the global supply-and-demand picture. Crude today has risen to about $83. When I ask what's driving it, his analysis is very acute. In addition to supply uncertainty around Iran and sanctions, it is also about investment. Oil fields don't last for ever: output can decline and fields expire. So the world's oil production is not a fixed constant (currently about 100 million barrels a day). Each year the world needs to invest successfully in an extra million barrels a day in order to replace the production lost elsewhere. If ever my theory of counter-cyclical investment were to be proved true, this is the moment. Because of low oil prices, investment in exploration and in new fields has declined. So global production is reducing faster than it is being replaced. Always invest when the price is low, i.e. counter-cyclically: don't delay.

Dinner with Tom and Fiona Beckett, and their eldest daughter Anastasia, who are all charming. The IISS Manama Dialogue, which he now runs, is a British invention, but for the first time ever we will have no Cabinet-ranking figure there in three weeks' time.

Back in the UK Boris arrived at Conference in the usual media scrum, having contrived a front-page photo in the *DT* running through a field of wheat as a deliberate piss-take parody of the PM [who once said it was the naughtiest thing she'd ever done]. Ha ha. He has been slagged off non-stop by colleagues and ministers, but the Vote Leave faithful were gathered for him, with the usual MP suspects in the front row: Owen Paterson, Priti Patel, John Redwood, Steve Baker, Zac Goldsmith, Iain Duncan Smith, Conor Burns.

Ed Argar calls. He went to the PM's birthday drinks last night and passed on my good wishes. She said, 'Ah. How is he?' Ed told her that I felt I had done my bit for her ahead of Conference and had enjoyed mixing business with pleasure. She smiled and sort of winked.

Wednesday 3 October – Bahrain/London
Back to London.

Reaction to the PM's Conference speech was streaming in on Twitter when I landed. It seems to have gone well, and started with some self-deprecating dance moves, preceded by a stentorian pro-Brexit warm-up by Attorney General Geoffrey Cox, whose deep booming voice is unique in the modern world.

It's always useful for any Conservative leader, and the Conservatives in general, to have the last word in the annual conference season. All the more so this year when Theresa can round it all off on a high note and confine Boris to the shadows.

To the FCO for a full brief on the joint announcement with the Dutch, planned for tomorrow morning, which will reveal the full extent of Russian cyber-activity in The Hague.

Thursday 4 October – The Hague/Rutland

Up at 5am. To City airport. My flight to Rotterdam is cancelled by fog.

The masterplan had been for me to attend the joint announcement with the Dutch government about the Russians. In April, Dutch intelligence apprehended two GRU agents outside the OPCW in a car stuffed with hacking equipment. The laptop contained links to the hacking into WADA (the World Anti-Doping Agency) and the inquiry in Malaysia into the downing by the Russians of the Malaysian flight MH-17. They gathered evidence of full-scale cyber-attacks, proving beyond doubt that Russian intelligence (or in this case Russian stupidity) was guilty of malign intrusion.

The press conference was due to be with the Head of Defence Intelligence and the Dutch Defence Minister. It was prime-time stuff, broadcast live, and taking the media by surprise. Even when they were alerted under embargo that something was going to be announced they assumed it was another step in the Skripal saga. They had not anticipated the extent of the revelations. In my infuriating absence, Ambassador Peter Wilson reads out my statement with dignity and authority.

Although I had to stay in London, I managed to secure an extensive media round: CNN, Channel 4, ITV, Sky, *BBC News*, LBC – the works.

Friday 5 October – Rutland

BBC Radio 4 *Any Questions* in Birmingham. Diane Abbott, Shadow Home Secretary; Dr Philippa Whitford, SNP Health Spokesman; Saqib Bhatti, President of the Greater Birmingham Chambers of Commerce. Did Theresa May's dancing at Conference put her back in the groove? Will the Brexit Deal be 'bodge it and fix it later'? How will cash-strapped local authorities know that austerity is over? After the Russian revelations, will war be with guns or computers? Then (ugh!) pick a song for your arrival at Conference. It all went fine, but the austerity question was not easy, and the SNP say the answer to austerity is to print money. Crazy!

Jean-Claude Juncker is now saying that he thinks there will be a deal on Brexit, and Taoiseach Leo Varadkar is also making optimistic noises.

Saturday 6 October – Rutland
Good chat with Whip Mike Freer. I say that Conference has gone well, and that we have reduced Boris somewhat. But when ministers wave their willy and ingratiate themselves with the faithful, it always comes back to bite us. Muscular signals on immigration, the end of austerity and so on beg all the questions of detail which then have to be answered later.

Monday 8 October – London
Meeting with our Protocol team. We covered our plan to amend legislation to empower the police to put an exclusion zone around any embassy that might be facing protests. They say that officials in the Home Office are being totally obstructive on the grounds that they don't want to risk legal action against the HO for breaching human rights legislation. It's total bollocks. It is just typical of HO officials that they lack initiative and are spineless.

There are some real defects in our honours system. The nominations for K-level awards are so arbitrary; and the names for honorary ones for non-British citizens should have a system across the FCO network. There isn't one.

Phone call with Sedat Önal, one of Turkey's new Deputy FMs. It was partly to say hello, but also to probe into the strange disappearance in the Saudi consulate in Istanbul of Jamal Khashoggi, a Saudi pundit who is attached as a journalist to the *Washington Post*, and who has become a critic of Mohammed bin Salman. Erdoğan has accused the Saudis of murdering him in the building, and it is now a matter of international focus. There is mention of cars leaving the consulate and heading to a waiting jet. But who knows?

Tuesday 9 October – London

Parliament starts again today. It's going to be bumpy!

See Fabian Picardo and his Gibraltar team. They had spent yesterday in Gibraltar with Olly Robbins and Lindsay Appleby. On most issues, such as differential tobacco pricing and workers' rights, they have the essence of a deal with the Spanish, but they have not yet found the language which expresses it to the satisfaction of both sides. Also Gibraltar is prepared to agree certain things with the UK, which the UK can then agree with Spain, but any direct agreement risks blurring the lines of sovereignty.

Nikki Haley has suddenly resigned as the US Permanent Rep at the UN. Nobody knows why. She has been critical of the UN's supposed anti-Israel bias and was in favour of moving the US embassy to Jerusalem, so where are her moral bearings? It is an odd departure.

Wednesday 10 October – London

Bump into Michael and Susi Ashcroft in Great Peter Street. His book *White Flag?* will come out tomorrow. It's a lament about the state of our defence spending.

The whole world is looking at the disappearance in Istanbul of Khashoggi. All the media reports, with increasing certainty, suggest he was murdered in the consulate, dismembered and his remains taken out of Turkey in a private jet. There are CCTV pictures of a convoy of vehicles travelling to and from the building, accounts of fifteen heavies arriving from Saudi Arabia, and then later on his fiancée offers an account of events from the evidence of his iWatch which she had, even though his own iPhone will have been taken away from him. The heartbeat suddenly disappeared. It seems certain that he is no more. If Saudi Arabia has become no better than Russia, the structure of alliances in the world is now in turmoil.

To the Commons. Say hi briefly to the Chief in the tunnel on the way to Portcullis House. He is grateful for my clear stand against Boris. He's in a bit of a dash, but says, 'Just remember, Boris only needs 106 members to get on to the final ballot.' He's right: it's one-third plus one. Julian has the air of a man with too many crises to manage at once.

FCO ministerial meeting. Jeremy wants a Euro-chat ahead of next week's potentially explosive Cabinet meeting. We quickly cover what we've been up to and what is coming. From me: Venezuela opposition leader has been thrown to his death out of a tenth-floor window while in police custody; quick discussion of Saudi/Turkey/Khashoggi; report on my aborted flight to The Hague; Macedonia name-change challenge. Alistair Burt mentions the legal issues around KSA [Kingdom of Saudi Arabia] targeting in Yemen – I resist the urge to explain that I'd seen all of this in detail, on the spot, when I was Yemen Envoy.

Jeremy gives his take on next week. There will be a Cabinet meeting on Tuesday at which the PM will propose that the whole of the UK stays in the customs union with no defined limit. JH says it's the right thing to do, but it risks Cabinet resignations: Fox, McVey, Mordaunt? He just wonders whether we can ever sell this without having appeared to have exhausted all the possible negotiating stands we could make.

To me, this is the unfolding seismic crunch which right from the start has always been the inevitable endgame.

Meeting with Alistair Burt so I can tell him where we are about Oman. My plan for a strategy has been evolving for five years. Within the FCO it predates him and he has never met the Sultan. He doesn't really have many relationships in the Gulf. He is unnecessarily huffy with me as if he is being kept out of the loop, when the whole point of my seeing him is to put him properly in it.

Ian Copson of Spink comes in to show me a beautifully restored 1940 Garrard KCMG medal set, rather better than my own inasmuch as the enamelling is crisper, the image of St George and the Dragon is superior, and the pendant has a lovely domed finish. It's a ridiculous extravagance, but later on James says he'll give it to me for Christmas.

Yet another meeting with officials on krill. For starters we will announce an enhancement of marine protection around the South Sandwich Islands.

Cherie Blair swings by, dressed as if for the gym, to say she is advising Kosovo on historic war crimes processes. To be fair to her, it's a good thing to be doing.

The Saudi issue is massive. He *was* murdered and sliced up. It's a game-changer. I think we should take an international lead by saying we love KSA but have growing doubts about MbS. Aim for the man, not the country. We should … but we can't afford to … so we won't.

Thursday 11 October – London
There is fervent speculation that the data from Jamal Khashoggi's Apple watch is preserved on an iPhone, or perhaps that it was intercepted by devices nearby. Audio or video evidence would be so damning and undeniable.

Breakfast with Peter Westmacott at the Goring. Soames was there on his own at one table, and former MP Derek Conway with his wife Colette and colourful son Henry were at another, down from Northumberland to celebrate their wedding anniversary. Peter is just a delight: wise, experienced and full of gossip. The most scandalous tale involves a very senior civil servant who seems to have been playing the field across Whitehall, and giving a whole new meaning to joined-up government.

Bump into William Hague while walking back through St James's Park. I tease him that his *Telegraph* columns are nowhere near as radical as he was in his youth.

Meeting with Andrew Mitchell about his constituent whose daughter has been taken to Russia by his ex-wife, and he can't get her back despite Russian court orders in his favour. When the bailiffs go to enforce it in that part of southern Russia, they are repelled by the gun-toting family.

Spain National Day at their embassy in Belgrave Square. I make a speech, as is required, but hopefully one a bit above the usual. The Echeverría parents were there. Their son Ignacio was killed in the London Bridge terrorist attack while defending a woman from the terrorists. They had just received his posthumous George Medal from the Queen at that morning's investiture. It was very touching.

Video link to the Falklands MLAs. They are just so tiresome and locked in their Falklands War time warp that they just cannot see sense and realise the best way to pursue their own interests. We are trying to establish extra regular flights to the Falklands within the terms of the joint communiqué I negotiated two years ago, but they have no guile. Instead they issue press releases asserting their 'red lines' and demands, thus needlessly pissing off the Argies, instead of cleverly wooing them so they can secure what they want. They have at last agreed to go to Buenos Aires – the first time since the 1982 war – but say they will make a statement in advance. I tell them in robust terms that if they do they will forfeit all further cooperation from me and will be on their own. I give them a firm lesson in negotiating tactics, which the sensible ones totally get. In everything they want to achieve with Argentina, they are their own worst enemy.

A proper face-to-face with Jeremy Hunt. His formidable diary secretary Valerie has me booked in for half an hour, and I have since teased her that it needed to be an hour. But at least I have a landing slot.

We cover an extensive list of items. First, on Saudi, he is proper. We all know what we think happened with Khashoggi, and whereas the UK is instinctively cautious about ever being critical of any Gulf state, I said we should really work out what we think is going on in the country. We should at least have a private view about what is right and what is wrong, along with assessing the internal politics of their Royal Family. The FCO's understanding is a bit thin.

We cover Oman and my plan to launch a strategy refresh.

I tell him I despair of the Home Office on diplomatic protection legislation. So does he. On honours, the PUS, the Supervisory Board and HR issues, he agrees with my judgements but admits he has not yet been able to focus on any of it. I tell him that's what they always hope for.

Other issues we cover: oceans policy; Brexit engagement; Russia … we will somehow work out what to do next; the need to gather comprehensive evidence of how our visa regime is so awful; my looming Venezuela speech. He is very good to deal with, and has assumed informed command of his brief at lightning speed.

Friday 12 October – London/Rutland
Harriet Baker in my parliamentary office brings in a letter dated 4 October in reply to mine of 11 September, a postcard actually, from

Boris which says: 'Dear Alan, On the contrary I fear it is the noises off, as you call them, that have been the only thing to stiffen the spine of our negotiations and postpone the day of abject capitulation! Boris'. He does not appreciate that these unique negotiations are not about muscularity. Bolshiness achieves nothing other than disaster for us. We have few cards to play. If we walk away, we are the ones who will suffer most. Threats from us are empty and self-defeating. He and his ilk have screwed us over, and now they are looking for someone else to blame.

The Home Office decline to support our bid for legislation on embassy guarding, sending us the most unhelpful letter which just dwells on a specific embassy rather than the broader problem, and reiterates the offer of three months' police protection for which we would have to pay. But our letter was about legislation, not the (now resolved) problem of one specific embassy. If this is the awareness of both officials and the Home Secretary, then the entire building should be replaced by a fresh set of people who are competent. I'm sadly forced to conclude that Sajid Javid is just not up to it. It's a pity that Jeremy didn't even try properly with him.

The wedding in Windsor of Princess Eugenie to Jack Brooksbank. Watch the whole thing on telly. Windy but beautiful. There are murmurs that the public purse should not pay for a carriage procession and extensive security for someone who fulfils no public engagements, but the crowds have gathered and cheered, and everyone's happy, so what the hell?

Saturday 13 October – Rutland
Further fallout on the Khashoggi murder. The Turks seem to know exactly what did happen. It is gruesome. It shines a sharp light on Mohammed bin Salman.

There is a worrying impasse in the talks about Brexit and Gibraltar. I speak to Fabian Picardo ahead of senior officials flying there tomorrow to thrash out further details.

Sunday 14 October – Rutland/London

At last, a proper downpour. It has been chucking it down since 5am, and is for the first time in months giving everything a decent soaking.

DD in the *Sunday Times* is openly calling for a 'Cabinet rebellion' to firm up our position on Brexit. Well … he couldn't firm anything up himself when he was Secretary of State for DExEU. He couldn't even come up with workable proposals. That's the whole problem: nobody can design a realistic template. Every option has a serious imperfection.

We have three days before the main EU summit, and we are in complete disarray. Theresa is doing her level best, but faces widespread dissatisfaction around the Cabinet table. She will seek support for a phantasmagorical Euro-fudge tomorrow or Tuesday, but it could result in Liam Fox 'being resigned' by our indefinitely remaining in the customs union and hence leaving us unable to reach free-trade agreements with the rest of the world. He'd in practice be out of a job. There's also threatening briefing from the irrelevant Esther McVey, who is facing serious flak on Universal Credit as Work & Pensions Secretary, and the self-inflated Penny Mordaunt in DfID. Who the hell do they think they are?

The Gibraltar negotiations are getting tetchy. If Fabian Picardo concedes a few more technical things in order to get a deal with the Spanish, he risks a disproportionate reaction within Gibraltar, such as a couple of resignations from his own government. There's no point in anyone in Gibraltar resigning until they know the broader UK–EU picture.

Tried to call the Chief Whip while I was driving down to London. He couldn't take the call as 'I'm in deep EU stuff, but will call you back later.' Dominic Raab has headed to Brussels to see Michel Barnier, but there is no sign it amounts to any sort of breakthrough.

Speak to Soames, and we share the mood of despair – more for the idiocy of the ERG lot than for the parlous state of our negotiations. Nadine Dorries, aka Mad Nad, is promoting David Davis as an interim PM. No, no, please, please, NO!

Anna Soubry tweets, 'The uncomfortable truth is that Brexit cannot be delivered. It's time we all faced the reality and were honest with the British people. We owe them a huge apology for a referendum with an option that was undefined and undeliverable.' Spot on. Then, rather nastily, Tim Montgomerie tweets back, 'I kept insisting that Anna Soubry's every action betrayed how she didn't accept the referendum result and she kept insisting that she did. I'm glad the "reality" is now evident to all.' He is not a nice man and seems to have quite a few issues.

The BBC report that Assange's internet connection has been restored in the Ecuador embassy. The embassy have as good as laid a trap for him. If he misuses it, as he probably will, then they will chuck him out. Let's see.

And the UK, Germany and France have issued a joint statement calling for a credible investigation into the disappearance of Jamal Khashoggi. It's something, but it's rather weak, and it's now twelve days after the event. Over time, the indignation and outrage will dissipate, and nothing will be done.

Monday 15 October – London

Dominic Raab has got nowhere on Brexit and has returned to London, while Michel Barnier cites massive obstacles on the Irish backstop, in other words not being able to square the Northern Ireland circle. David Davis swaggering around; other (useless) Cabinet ministers murmuring about resigning; the whole ship taking in water. None of them, whatever they think, holds a workable blueprint for establishing free trade with the EU without treating Northern Ireland differently. Or if we establish free trade with NI, we stay in the customs union with the EU, which is anathema to the Brexiteers. Wednesday's EU summit looms.

Lunch with James Landale, diplomatic correspondent of the BBC. He is thoroughly decent – he will follow any story assiduously, and to his credit always resists the temptation to exaggerate and embellish.

The PM makes a statement on Brexit, saying a deal can be done and people should keep the faith. In other words, a message to the critics to shut up.

Greet Turkish FM Mevlüt Çavuşoğlu at Ambassadors' Entrance. He comes with the usual convoy of flunkies and cameras. Ten minutes with him in the waiting room in a corner with Richard Moore. They have substantive evidence of what happened with Khashoggi, which has gone to the judiciary in Turkey.

Fantastic meeting with Sir Mark Sedwill, along with Vicente. What a joy, and what a stark contrast to some of the obstruction I have faced in the FCO. I start by asking for the 4 December National Security Council meeting to be brought forward to approve the contents of a new agreement with Oman so that I can see the Sultan sooner than the end of the year. No need, he says; it has been agreed that I can go and see HM before the NSC, present the plan, and then the NSC can endorse it afterwards. In other words, go to HM as if to consult him about his opinions ahead of the NSC, and take a revised defence commitment in the form of a May letter as an update to the 1983 Thatcher letter, which offered a defence guarantee. Brilliant.

We also covered Russia, maritime security and KSA/Khashoggi. I told him what Çavuşoğlu had told me. But joy of joys, my master-plan for a refreshed Oman strategy is on the launch pad.

Dinner at Roux with Mohammed bin Badr from the Oman embassy. He is just a gem. I tee up the strategy plan, and lodge a request for an audience with the Sultan in mid-November, subject to the PM approving the plan. He says Alistair Burt annoyed them during the recent Anglo-Omani dialogue talks in Muscat by telling them to sever their links with the Houthis. How stupid. We need the Omanis to be a link into the Houthis and the Iranians. What the hell was Burt up to?

Tuesday 16 October – London

Bump into Tom Strathclyde, our former Leader in the Lords, in Great Peter Street. He agrees we are surrounded by nutters.

I text Jeremy to say that for what it's worth my opinion is that he should attend Cabinet determined to back her 100 per cent. There is no room for movement: we just have to go for broke and bank something.

Go via the FCO to Number 10 for a totally purposeless meeting of junior ministers with Chief of Staff Gavin Barwell. Nicely done in

most respects, but talking us through the PM's Conference speech
was like having a primary school teach-in. The stream of ministers
saying how brilliant the speech was, and then lodging a petty departmental point, was annoyingly childish. There was minimal mention
of Brexit, even though it is the main raging topic. Meanwhile, downstairs the Cabinet is meeting for a crucial Brexit punch-up. It is
rather farcical. There are banks of TV cameras outside for this simul-
taneous gathering. It concludes with a whimper.

Call Ardeshir Zahedi in Geneva to congratulate him on his ninetieth birthday. He was the Shah of Iran's last Foreign Minister, before
the 1979 revolution. I have known him for thirty years, and he is still
lively and alert.

Speaker Bercow is an uppity little man. I am careful to maintain
cordial relations with him – such is my respect for the House and its
conventions – but his so-called reforming agenda is in itself an abuse
of the position he holds. He is supposed to be impartial and should
only hold a view which is set by the Commons. All these historic
assumptions have been obliterated by Labour's capture of the Speaker
in the name of progressive causes … diversity, equality, women and
so on. The fundamental rules of the place now count for nothing. He
has an unbalanced temperament and frequently flies off the handle.
A report today on bullying in Parliament may be the final blow for
him. It is said that he will announce that he will stand down next
summer. But Labour still want him to stay … he is biased, and they
think he will make helpful procedural decisions on Brexit. Supporting
him for his views rather than for his impartial integrity is woeful. It's
a bit like the appointment of a Supreme Court judge in the US.

The Cabinet meeting, although not explosive, is reported to have
made no decision. The bomb remains undetonated.

Wednesday 17 October – London

Bercow will probably go next summer, but rather more disturbing is
the sort of interview we heard on the *Today* programme. I've not yet
read it, but the report by Dame Laura Cox, a former High Court
judge, talks of a general mood of unacceptable bullying in Parliament,
and a girl in her twenties spews out indignation that nothing has

been done. It was all in general terms, and it's totally unclear what precisely she is complaining about. Is she only speaking of MPs as employers, or is she talking of Parliament itself as an employer? Who is said to have been a bullying employer? And to whom? It's all expressed in terms of general accusations about sexual misconduct, none of which I recognise from my own experience of twenty-six years in the place. It is another example of hyperbolic indignation, in this case turning into weird hysteria.

Ministerial team meeting. Once again Jeremy is a million times more interesting than Boris. He is due to give a speech on human rights, and is trying to get his head around what we think and what he should say. He is conscious that we can be pure of thought for easy targets such as Burma, but then we trim and equivocate when it's our friends or where we have interests. I say that where we have neither interests nor responsibility it is easy to talk in absolute terms. It is the current privilege of his opposite number Emily Thornberry, whose sanctimonious judgementalism is rather nauseating. Most moral decisions or attitudes are a varying shade of grey; they are rarely black or white.

Trump now says Saudi has been treated as guilty until proven innocent; Theresa May flies to Brussels this afternoon; Michel Barnier says he would consider extending the transitional period by a year until mid-2021. Oh what a glorious mess in an ever more messy world.

Really sensible and productive meeting on maritime security, focussing on the risk of a terrorist attack on a ferry or cruise ship.

Oh my God. Gruesome details are emerging from Turkey. It looks as though there are audio recordings of Khashoggi being tortured, having his fingers ripped off, being killed and dismembered, and then chopped up. Trump lauds Saudi Arabia as a super ally on the grounds that the US sells them arms worth billions. It is not the best moral calculus.

Then some good news. Greek Foreign Minister Nikos Kotzias has resigned. The blocker of the Cyprus settlement has wobbled off, although his redemption is that at least he was on the right side of the argument over the Macedonian name change.

Oh dear. The vibes coming out of the EU summit tonight are that the November special summit on Brexit will be cancelled. It all has the air of a bitter stalemate.

Thursday 18 October – London
Catch-up meeting with Simon McDonald. For once he wasn't too bad. But I was quite tough on him. I justified my attack on Boris, which after the traditional sucking of teeth and collywobbles he admitted was appreciated in Number 10. The collywobbles were more his than theirs. I asked for more regular information ahead of senior appointments. He then told me of one he had just decided which made me look at him in despair.

Friday 19 October – London/Rutland
The Ecuador Ambassador says they have taken away Assange's cat. After living in their embassy for five years, Assange has today launched a lawsuit against the Ecuador government for violating his human rights, but probably for restricting his internet rather than taking away his cat.

Saturday 20 October – Rutland
The Saudis have now admitted that Khashoggi died inside the consulate after a fight that went sadly wrong. Oh yeah. So there was one of him and fifteen of them; and there's no body; and they just happened to have a saw and a cleaver in their pocket at the time; and … Former 'C' Sir John Sawers has said that it is inconceivable that it was not authorised at the highest level, which is as good as saying it was MbS wot done it.

The Macedonian parliament has voted in favour of the name change. It's the first step in a longer process, but is a good start.

The People's Vote march in London seems to have been attended by over half a million. Farage and co have held a counter-rally in Manchester, a rather pathetic one; they are just so unbendingly cocksure of themselves. The marchers are sensible ordinary, non-manic good people. They all just feel so let down.

We both have a flu jab in Boots in Uppingham. What a simple and efficient system for an important precaution so many people stupidly just don't bother with. It could be the best £20 we've ever spent.

Sunday 21 October – Rutland/London
Johnnie Mercer has slagged off the PM. If he were still in a regiment he'd be taken behind the officers' mess and roughed up.

Trump has announced he is to withdraw unilaterally from a nuclear weapons accord with the Russians dating back to the 1960s. US National Security Advisor John Bolton is due to visit Russia this week. Trump's reckless game-playing is on one level just plain silly, but on another dangerously destabilising.

Dominic Raab has said on TV that he does not find Saudi Arabia's explanation of the Khashoggi death at all convincing. I'm glad he has said so. He is right, and he has lifted the logic of our reaction up a further notch, but he is not quite in the right ministerial role to be able to judge the calculated subtlety of our response.

A fellow MP texts me, 'Andrea Jenkyns is a fucking idiot.' Er yes, mate – what's new?

Dinner with a parliamentary colleague who comes out with a stream of unrestrained gossip: Dan Poulter is in trouble with his constituency Association for having a second job as a doctor which they think takes up too much of his time – rather unfair; one female MP colleague is being knocked off by two uniformed officers, but presumably not at the same time; David Gauke hates Boris; the Chief hates Tom Tugendhat; David Davis was always pissed while SofS DExEU; Gove recently barged into a Thérèse Coffey-chaired Cabinet sub-committee and said he'd just watch from the back, which is very peculiar behaviour; and the bovine potato-trader Andrew Bridgen is known as Spuduhate.

Monday 22 October – London
Breakfast with a senior Gulf businessman. We covered the usual ground – the Gulf, Brexit and of course Saudi Arabia. Despite their shared hatred of Iran, the Emiratis do harbour some concerns about

MbS. He did not just lure President Hariri of Lebanon to Riyadh in 2017 and force him to resign, they also beat him up. [He rescinded his resignation a month later.] But Saudi opinion sees Jamal Khashoggi as having been a friend and sympathiser of Osama bin Laden and the Muslim Brotherhood. And when it comes to the Royal Family it's not just Mohammed bin Nayef who is held in detention. He believes quite a number are.

Coincidentally, later in the day at lunch another Middle Eastern figure gives me a list of half a dozen senior Saudi Royals who are believed to have disappeared over the last two years.

Briefly see the Foreign Secretary when I returned. I told him I'd give him a list of the disappeared so he could look into it.

Tuesday 23 October – London

Buckingham Palace Banquet for the Dutch State Visit. Nice chat with Philip May. Lovely drink afterwards with the two Royal Families – there was a moment that was more amusing than embarrassing when I was talking to the Prince of Wales. The neckstrap of my heavily starched white waistcoat chose to detach itself, allowing my pristine garment to slip down my front. I had a glass in one hand and the guestlist and menu in the other, which left me ill-equipped to grab it quickly enough to halt the slide.

Now Trump says that the Istanbul murder is one of the worst cover-ups in the history of cover-ups.

Wednesday 24 October – London

Mark Sedwill is appointed Cabinet Secretary, while also retaining the position of National Security Adviser.

FCO ministerial team meeting. We discussed what we should do about Saudi and MbS. We will of course do nothing.

Khashoggi's son is pictured in front of King Salman and MbS, supposedly to receive their condolences, which is all very well (up to a point) until you look more closely and see that the policeman in the background is staring intently at Khashoggi junior and has his hand firmly around the handle of a revolver which is half out of its holster.

Thursday 25 October – London

I deliver a speech on Venezuela at Chatham House. As the product of weeks of working with officials, it was designed to be a proper intellectual account of Venezuela's misgovernment and mismanagement over four decades. Instead of spouting the usual diet of critical soundbites, it laid out a cogent thesis to explain why President Maduro was so palpably awful.

Meeting with Cypriot Vice-President Demetris Syllouris, who is also House Speaker. He was unbending and quite unable to converse rationally, and seemed determined only to intone uncompromising Greek Cypriot complaints about the Turks. You just cannot discuss serious issues in a serious way with him, as he is not in the least bit interested in reaching a Cyprus unification deal; he just wants to slag off the Turks.

Saturday 27 October – Malaga/Rutland

In Malaga for the annual Anglo-Spanish dialogue. Breakfast with David Lidington and the Spanish Foreign Minister Josep Borrell and their Europe Minister Jose Ignacio Aguiriano. It gets a bit sticky on Gibraltar, with Borrell complaining that Fabian Picardo 'goes behind his back' after each and every meeting. Most elements of an exit deal are agreed, but the Spanish will not consent to a three-way deal which includes Gibraltar; they will only entertain a bilateral handshake between them and us.

There are still loose ends on how to design a commitment on tobacco pricing in Gibraltar in a way that doesn't undercut Spanish tax revenues; how to overcome Spanish objections to low business taxation in Gib, where they have unfounded fears that Spanish companies will incorporate in Gib and thereby use it as a vehicle for reducing their overall personal tax liability, denying Spain its revenue; and how to bank a commitment by Gib not to press on with land reclamation in a way that doesn't force Fabian to say so publicly and so look as though he has sold out.

I call Fabian. He is in London with his son and, as it happens, is just walking past Gibraltar House. I describe the tone of Borrell's comments at breakfast, especially his irritation at Fabian playing all the layers of Spanish government at once.

Monday 29 October – Istanbul

To the opening of the new airport in Istanbul. It's about as big as an airport can get, and I don't relish the thought of having to walk a mile to catch a connecting flight.

It offered an opportunity to meet eight heads of government in the course of an hour.

Tuesday 30 October – Istanbul/London

Chamber of Commerce.

Consulate staff.

Following my meeting with Demetris Syllouris last week, the Cyprus FM Christodoulides has phoned our High Commissioner Stephen Lillie in a massive rage about me, all because I said that I thought the Turks had tried to make a serious offer at the Crans Montana talks. I know what I'd like to say to him, but won't.

Fly back to London.

JH makes an excellent pre-dinner speech to the Canning reception – the FCO's Canning agenda is designed to revitalise our relationships in Latin America. He did so standing on a chair, which rather pre-empts my own formal one later. He also slightly steals my script, but at the dinner afterwards I have enough to tell them, and make a nice reference to Hugo Swire and Jeremy Browne, who were there as former ministers for the region.

Wednesday 31 October – London

Lo and behold, Secretaries Mattis and Pompeo in the US have called for an end to the Yemen bombing within thirty days. But it looks as though this might have taken us by surprise, and that we had no prior notice. If that's so it's almost culpable, as the phones should have been ringing so much between capitals that it should have been impossible for us not to be in the loop, and indeed part of the call for a ceasefire.

JH speech today will make some sensible comments about the purpose and direction of the FCO, but contains a silly gimmick about making one or two ambassador jobs open to businessmen 'in order to help our trade effort'. It's tosh. He must learn to resist such things.

Sunday 4 November – Rutland/The Hague

Jeremy Heywood has died. He was made Lord Heywood of Whitehall just recently, which was a nice touch. I met him first during the John Major leadership campaign when he was his Private Secretary in the Treasury. It's wretchedly unfair that someone who was only fifty-six and at the peak of their career should be taken away by illness. All Cabinet secretaries are remarkable in their own way, and Jeremy had an easy style and a razor-sharp mind.

The *Sunday Times* says that a Brexit deal is all but there.

Monday 5 November – The Hague/London

More stories in the papers of a likely Brexit deal this month.

US sanctions on Iran start again.

Less appealing is news of the 116th knife murder in London so far this year. Hardly a squeak from the mumbling Mayor Sadiq Khan.

Tuesday 6 November – London

Press reports about today's Cabinet meeting, principally about the Irish backstop. Gove is being a knob by demanding that the PM publish the Attorney General's legal advice on the status of the Northern Ireland border.

Dinner convened by Jeremy Hunt at 1 Carlton Gardens. He has gathered a small array of academics and politicians, including former Foreign Secretary Malcolm Rifkind, to brainstorm about Russia. I like his intellectual curiosity, and the manner in which he teases out people's real opinions. Jeremy launched it well by posing a series of questions such as 'Can Putin change?', 'Need we bother with Russia at all?', 'Have we treated them badly?', 'Can we offer them respect without appearing weak?'

These occasions never provide all the answers, but the stimulus and greater awareness are very valuable.

Wednesday 7 November – London/Tblisi

The US mid-term elections have resulted in the Democrats regaining control of the House, while the Republicans increase their hold on the Senate. So Trump loses his complete grip on Congress, and it sets the stage for what I imagine will be a pretty vicious partisan battle in the second half of his term. The Trump Presidency certainly isn't dull.

Our lovely neighbour Mary Fairbairn is seriously ill and on oxygen. The doctors think she might not pull through.

Friday 9 November – London

FCO. James calls very upset. Mary died early this morning.

Protocol call with a problem. Our charming officials in the Immigration Service are refusing to issue visas for the Queen of Morocco's domestic staff for when she comes to London for the Prince of Wales' seventieth birthday party next week. This is just the sort of idiotic jobsworth prattishness which can turn into a full-blown diplomatic crisis. I leap into action to get it sorted.

Rather unexpectedly, Boris' brother Jo Johnson resigns as a transport minister and calls for a second referendum. That'll make for an interesting game of Happy Families.

Saturday 10 November – London

Quiet morning in London. Walk in St James's Park with Noodle, but it's difficult to keep her from the squirrels.

The PM has been laying commemorative wreaths in France with Macron, before returning for our service at the Cenotaph tomorrow. But there are mucky bust-ups elsewhere there: Macron has called for a European Army to protect Europe from the Russians … and the US. Trump has issued a terse response. And Trump has called off laying a wreath at a major ceremony because of the weather, which has attracted scathing comment, including a cracker from Soames, who tweeted with the hashtag #HeIsNotFitToRepresentHisGreatCountry.

James and I watch the documentary on the Prince of Wales turning seventy. He comes over amazingly well, with William and Harry excelling in their well-established double act.

Sunday 11 November – London

James goes to Rutland with Noodle and will see all of Mary's family. He ends up spending hours with them in a friendly cathartic evening. Stuart, Mary's son, reveals what we never quite appreciated, which is just how much she loved having us next door. Looking after Noodle so much probably added three years to her life.

Remembrance Sunday. Dressed in morning suit, I and DCMS SofS Jeremy Wright greet all the Royal Family in the main courtyard of the Foreign Office.

After the service I chat with the PM over coffee: 'Don't flinch, and let me know if you want me to finish off anyone else.' 'You are a little Exocet missile!' she said, in a rare moment of banter.

I show Gauke, Clark and Brokenshire my office, all of them from the sensible wing of the Cabinet, and a contrast to the nutters like Gove, Leadsom and Mordaunt.

Jeremy Hunt's kids are lovely and lively. I take a photo of them all larking about in front of the door of Number 10.

A pause at home for a few hours, and then the evening service at Westminster Abbey for the final commemoration to mark the end of the First World War. All the ambassadors there: I have the first chat for ages with Russia's Ambassador Yakovenko who still seems oblivious to the malign consequences of Russia's foolhardy conduct.

Monday 12 November – London

The news is full of foreboding: 'Forty-eight hours to get a Brexit deal', 'Government assailed from all sides', etc. Boris has called for the Cabinet to 'mutiny'. He is an egotistical wrecker.

Tuesday 13 November – London

Hilarious meeting to discuss my speech to the Foreign Press Association. I speculated on the likely reaction to a speech in which I said what I really thought instead of one that just spouts bland, boring platitudes based on what we laughingly call our current foreign policy. Rory Bremner is due to chair the proceedings, so I might lob in occasional impressions of William Hague and Boris.

Just after 4pm, reports start circulating that a deal has been reached on the draft Withdrawal Agreement, at negotiator level. The white smoke rises!

There is a flurry of activity and reaction – a Cabinet meeting is to be held to sign it off tomorrow, and in the meantime individual ministers are reported to be going into Number 10 one by one to discuss it with the PM. Such is the paranoia and fear of leaks that they are not being given copies, but are having to go and read it in a secure room in the Cabinet Office.

Meanwhile, Boris, Jacob Rees-Mogg and the rest of their ERG backing singers are all over the media denouncing a text they haven't read on the basis of issues they don't understand. Boris himself is fulminating frothily on TV: 'It's vassal-state stuff as for the first time in 1,000 years this Parliament will not have a say over the laws that govern this country.' Histrionic fantasy, as he offers no practical alternative. He knows what he doesn't want, but has no idea what he does. It's a bit like the House of Lords – you might be against it, but what the hell do you put in its place?

Wednesday 14 November – London
The crisis Brexit Cabinet is scheduled to last from 2 to 4pm, but runs on until 7.30pm.

Sky say those who spoke out strongly were: Fox, Hunt, Williamson, Mordaunt, Javid, Leadsom, Evans, Grayling … but not McVey? The PM has spoken to the DUP's Arlene Foster, called Nicola Sturgeon and is meeting Corbyn in the Commons.

I exchange texts with Jeremy Hunt, opening with 'So … we live to fight another day. Phew!' He replies: 'Indeed. Day by day though.'

Thursday 15 November – London
Crikey. What a tumultuous day! I wake up to the news that Shailesh Vara has resigned as junior Northern Ireland minister. He is nice but insignificant. For some ridiculous reason he thinks it worth making a stand against the Deal. Then at 9am Dominic Raab resigns. He's been the DExEU SofS for four months, and now he buggers off. Then at 10am out goes Esther McVey from Work and Pensions, and

then finally (for the moment) Suella Braverman from her PUSS job in DExEU. So it's four resignations in as many hours. The PM makes a statement in the House at 10.30 and ploughs on. Her calmness under fire is quite remarkable. But the shitty little Speaker Hobbit keeps her at the dispatch box for three hours.

Mogg lets it be known that he has put in a letter calling for a vote of confidence in May as Leader and calls a press conference outside St Stephen's to announce it. The arrogance of the man. He claims that there are now the forty-eight MPs' letters needed to trigger a vote, and stands on the steps pompously condemning her. It's more than I can take, so as soon as he is finished I march in front of his bank of cameras and offer full support for the PM and rail against all the plotters. I then do non-stop interviews for the next two hours, and in a step that makes Mogg appear absurd, Graham Brady then reveals that he has not received forty-eight letters. What a frenzy.

I leave Noodle in the FCO while I briefly go to Number 10 so Theresa can briefly see and thank Fabian Picardo and his Gibraltar team, and then dinner at Franco's with James and Noodle.

Friday 16 November – London

Gove has left his home, looking ghastly in jogging kit, thus acting out the usual tacky publicity stunt. He is milking it as usual with extensive briefings behind the scenes, while feigning loyalty to the PM. It fuels attention-seeking headlines: the 'will he resign or not?' crap.

After her torrid day yesterday, the PM has gone straight on to LBC to kick-start the fightback. Her rational explanation is head and shoulders above anybody else.

There are only twenty-two signatures, and the identities behind them are now public. Steve Baker says in a formal statement that we will see forty-eight today. He does so in a typical press interview of fake reasonableness. He is just a self-centred wrecker, an unflinching zealot.

To Rutland. The post-resignation shuffle details emerge: Steve Barclay goes from being Minister of Health to SofS DExEU, but only with responsibility for domestic arrangements. Amber Rudd is

back as SofS DWP. Kwasi Kwarteng to DExEU. John Penrose to NI.
Steve Hammond to somewhere. We are running out of deckchairs.

Monday 19 November – Brussels

Up at 5am to take the Eurostar to Brussels for the Foreign Affairs
Council.

Speak to the banks of cameras on arrival and deliver a rallying
message for the audience back home, telling the plotters to back the
PM 100 per cent.

Initial plenary meeting on Iran in which I made my intervention.
Bilateral meetings with Slovenia and Cyprus. Then with Spain,
whose Foreign Minister Josep Borrell was in a lather. He was fuming
about a clause in the Withdrawal Agreement which he says removes
Spain from having any say over Gibraltar and makes it only a matter
between the EU and the UK. I'm not sure he's got that right.

We discuss Yemen over lunch. Once again I rather silenced them
with my knowledge of the origins of the war there and its real
elements: the GCC Initiative on Yemen transition removed Saleh, it
created a vacuum, it was filled by the Houthis, the Saudis started
bombing, that sucked in the Iranians, so it turned it into a proxy
conflict, the UK could have stopped the conflict etc.

Both Olly Robbins and David Miliband were at Brussels station,
so we had an impromptu 'three-power conference', as Jeremy Catto
would have described it. The Spanish are kicking off and are threatening to veto the entire exit Deal. The ERG have not yet submitted
forty-eight names and seem to be stuck on thirty-six. If we lose the
vote on the Deal in a couple of weeks, we might need some latitude
to pursue other options. If the PM has fought and won a leadership
challenge, then they can't touch her for another year. So it is perhaps
preferable for her to be challenged now, win and be safe at least as
Leader through the difficult period that would follow.

But the mood is changing – against the ERG and in May's favour.
I speak to Andrew Pierce of the *Mail*, and give him my July letter to
Jacob Rees-Mogg which accuses him of not acting in the national
interest and jeopardising the government, the Party and the country.

Tuesday 20 November – London
The forty-eight letters have not materialised, and the ERG crackpot coup is backfiring on them. Likewise the fatuous five Cabinet ministers have gone all quiet. Theresa will head to Brussels tomorrow, but will fly straight into the Gibraltar problem.

I deliver the eulogy at Mary's funeral, attended by the whole village and more besides. It's as well to raise some smiles and chuckles, even on such a sad occasion, which I did, but wobbled a bit at the end, as I was genuinely upset.

Lovely dinner at St James's Palace hosted by the Prince of Wales and the Duchess of Cornwall for the International Rescue charity, now headed by David Miliband.

Wednesday 21 November – London
Bit of a breakthrough – it looks as though the Gibraltar/Spain protocols are now fixed.

Bump into Daniel Seidemann outside Millbank. He is a remarkable person who has given tours around Jerusalem and Bethlehem to a galaxy of dignitaries. He explains in detail where Palestinian land has been or is likely to be taken by Israel. One such dignitary was David Cameron. Daniel is a man of great integrity and probity, and suffers a lot of abuse from settlers and the like. He tells me that Alistair Burt, our Middle East Minister, has asked him to go and see Stuart Polak and the Conservative Friends of Israel. Quite what Burt thinks is going to be achieved by that, and quite why he has highlighted the role of CFI on this issue, I have no idea, but it is ill-judged and I consider it improper.

Thursday 22 November – The Hague
Up at 5.30. To Amsterdam. OPCW, CWC [Chemical Weapons Convention] Review Conference. An important meeting to keep the international community together so as to hold the line against Russia's use of a chemical weapon.

Speak to Fabian Picardo: he says the Spanish are cutting up rough again.

Friday 23 November – Rutland

Text from Mark Sedwill, who has been a strong supporter of a new agreement with Oman. Succinctly expressed, he says he is fed up with the FCO being so slow and will put a squib up them.

Rather surprisingly, John Hayes has been given a knighthood. Many eyebrows are raised – it's the first time that a pantomime dame has become a knight.

Saturday 24 November – Rutland

I make plaintive calls to Picardo not to reject a deal with the Spanish. The EU Deal is ready to be signed in Brussels tomorrow, and so this is a last-minute fight we really don't need.

Sunday 25 November – Rutland

Chat with Fabian Picardo. Boris has been trying to call him! He has not returned the calls. Fabian will delay asking Lidington to sign the MOUs [Memorandums of Understanding] with the Spanish.

In the event, the EU Council endorses the Brexit Deal with less than an hour's discussion, and it is agreed by 11am.

As James and I were watching TV, my friend in Ukraine WhatsApped me repeatedly with videos of Russian aggression against Ukrainian ships beside the Kersh Bridge at the entrance to the Sea of Asov.

Monday 26 November – London

After yesterday's clear verdict in Brussels, the PM announces that there will be a 'meaningful vote' on the Deal on Tuesday 11 December. For once, talk of a meaningful vote might actually mean something, as the Commons will be asked to back a deal that has been agreed, rather than the principles around it.

The Assange issue is progressing. Our channels into Ecuador are paving the way to a solution.

Compared with my own contact in Ukraine, my FCO officials don't really seem to know what's been going on at the Kersh Bridge. I ended up showing them the WhatsApp videos I had received, in what was as close to real time as you can get when you're trying to gather intelligence.

My speech at the Foreign Press Association dinner went rather well, and it gave me the chance to praise Fabian Picardo, who was the main guest. Rory Bremner is such a genius observer of our politics. He rather outdid my well-received impressions with an hilarious gag: 'Why is it that all the mad Brexiteers have triple-barrelled names? Iain Duncan Smith, Jacob Rees-Mogg, Boris Fucking Johnson?'

Tuesday 27 November – London
At last the Falklands flights are done and dusted. I take some bottles up to the South America Dept to say well done. It's been a long slog of delicate diplomacy, balancing all sorts of interests and egos, but we've got there.

Wednesday 28 November – London
Ministerial team meeting. Long chat on the meaningful vote and its consequences. What will the debate format be? How will the parliamentary arithmetic shape up? Hammond is proving difficult on Iran … On Zimbabwe, if Mugabe dies, do we fly the flag? I say, 'Take down the flagpole for essential repairs.' Linking it to Brexit, Jeremy offers an amusing quote from Barack Obama: 'This would be very interesting shit if I wasn't in the middle of it.'

Entertaining Labour MP Steve Pound drew me aside at the division to say I'm the only one who attracts cross-party trust. He says he has been saying so in interviews but intends to say it more loudly. He is fun and kind, but I'm not sure it'll catch on widely enough!

Michael Fallon tells me that the real issue with Russia and Ukraine is Russia's wish to take over Mariupol, on the north side of the Sea of Asov. We could support it by bolstering the railway to it. An interesting strategic observation, which has no chance of being adopted.

Gavin Williamson in the lobby is very pro-Oman, and has grasped the significance of the need for a broader overarching framework. He at least possesses this one redeeming quality.

To the Kuwait embassy residence in Kensington Palace Gardens for the reception to celebrate Khaled al Duwaisan clocking up twenty-five years as their Ambassador. A lovely man, he is the Dean of the Arab Ambos, and is an absolute legend.

Friday 30 November – Rutland
Sam Gyimah resigns as a minister. I text him to express my dismay. George Freeman replaces him.

Saturday 1 December – Rutland
President George Bush Snr has died. The G20 meeting is going on in Buenos Aires. MbS has attended and is pictured in a warm embrace with Putin.

To Nevill Holt for a fabulous performance of *Messiah*, a pre-Christmas outing by the NH Opera. Dinner afterwards with the estimable David Ross, including Kwasi Kwarteng. Also Northampton MP Michael Ellis. The latter always raises a smile for being so openly referred to as Lady Ellis. It's actually quite affectionate and is little more than a reference to his overmannered, fastidious approach to all things ceremonial.

Sunday 2 December – Rutland/London
A lovely lunch at Chevening, to which Jeremy had invited all ministers and their children. Harriett Baldwin and I also took our adorable little dogs.

The intention is that I should attend the Bush funeral.

The MPs' WhatsApp group has gone mental with a whole stream of exchanges about Brexit. All of them utterly self-indulgent.

Once home, James and I watch the documentary about the FCO. It should have been called 'The Gospel according to Simon McDonald', who featured even more than Boris.

Monday 3 December – London
Am not permitted to go to the Bush funeral: the Whips say I must remain here in case there is a contempt motion in respect of the government's refusal to publish the Attorney General's legal advice on the backstop, despite a Commons motion that it must.

In the first statement to the Commons by an Attorney General in forty years, Geoffrey Cox put in a bravura performance on why he will not publish his advice.

The day's business begins to peter out, and I have the Adjournment Debate which starts at just after 8pm, much earlier than the usual thirty minutes from 10pm, so potentially it could last for two and a half hours. The topic is Scotland's Foreign Policy Footprint (a rather fatuous concept), which turns into an SNP day out, as they enjoy the unexpected opportunity offered by the early collapse of government business. Steve Gethins opens with a forty-minute speech, followed by several of his SNP colleagues. Normally I'd be on my feet within thirty minutes, but an hour and twenty minutes later I'm still waiting to respond.

Then at 9.22pm, the Speaker came into the Chamber to rule that as the government may be in contempt of the House, there will be an emergency debate tomorrow on an Opposition motion. He then immediately called me to respond to the Adjournment Debate.

I was about to speak only briefly in response to the epic SNP debate when the Whip passed me a note: 'Keep it going; we need the House to continue sitting until we have tabled an amendment to Labour's contempt motion.' I have to perform a complete handbrake turn and change gear from wanting to close it down to having to keep it going.

And so began a legendary filibuster – I slowed down the delivery of my response, added little flourishes and embellishments, as a flurry of activity began beside me. The Whips were summoning the cavalry to come in from the Smoking Room to help. Meanwhile I gladly took interventions, talked about my (Scottish) late aunt's work as a medical missionary, my previous work in DfID and anything else I could think of to pad it out.

Gradually, colleagues answered the call to arms and gamely tried to help, but seeing them starting to bob up, Lindsay Hoyle (Deputy Speaker) told them they should wait a bit before seeking to intervene: 'I understand things are at play, but I'm sure Sir Alan will keep it going.' Thanks a bunch!

But keep it going I did. Lengthy rhapsodies of praise to our diplomatic service, philosophical reflections on the nature of soft power, even a review of the recent TV documentary on the FCO. Helpful colleagues intervened asking me to comment on the role of the British Council, the G20 and so on, and I grabbed on to each tenuously linked lifeline to agree how absolutely vital that particular point was to the topic of the debate. It became increasingly comical, as I found myself paying tribute to a succession of great Scottish inventors, discussing the formation of the Chilean Navy by a Scot and (appropriately) Admiral Duncan's victory at the Battle of Camperdown. Eventually, a note from the Whip told me I was clear to conclude and so I did – gratefully. Much cheering in the Smoking Room for me afterwards.

Rees-Mogg compounds his fogey fop image on *Newsnight*. He was sitting in the chair, wired up to be interviewed, while Emily Maitlis stands nearby for the opening headlines. As she then walks over to her chair Moggy half stands. His over-studied politesse looks ridiculous on TV.

Tuesday 4 December – London

Julian Smith says to me, 'You didn't play my game yesterday.' When the Speaker came in to make his statement on the contempt issue, Julian persistently leant along the front bench to speak to me, provoking Bercow to tell him to be quiet. I didn't realise at the time that this was a deliberate ploy by the Chief to provoke him. It's childish on one level, but Bercow deserves it on another.

We lose the contempt motion, as Dominic Grieve's amendment wins.

Into white tie and decorations for the Queen's diplomatic reception. The Prince of Wales leaves after the reception to fly overnight to Washington for the Bush funeral. As the contempt motion debate had finished, I could have gone after all. Sloppy staff work in the FCO not to have worked that out.

Wednesday 5 December – London

Now it's Mark Harper's day out, going on the *Today* programme to say he'll vote against the Deal. You're a former Chief Whip and should know better. Thanks, mate.

A friend with links to the MoD swings by my office. He says Gavin Williamson is bonkers; he has mad notions more appropriate to an imperialist power the size of the US.

A meeting for MPs to meet Fabian Picardo clashed with everything else, so didn't work. So I suggest to the Chief's SpAd that they ask Graham Brady if Fabian can address the 5pm 1922 meeting for a few minutes at the start. Later on in the corridor I bump into Graham and ask if he had agreed. Graham had said no, because the SpAd had been such a bossy little shit: instead of asking politely, he'd as good as instructed him to do it. So it was a no.

The debate on the meaningful vote continues, and today's designated topic is security and immigration. Emily Thornberry gives the most appalling wind-up speech imaginable. She just spewed out a tirade of vitriol, so I heckled her firmly ahead of Jeremy Hunt's wind-up speech.

Leo Docherty and Kwasi Kwarteng come for a nightcap at home.

Thursday 6 December – London

Travel with JH to the US embassy to sign the book of condolence for President George Bush. On the way, Sajid calls him to discuss how we can avoid a crushing defeat on next Tuesday's vote on the Brexit Deal. The way things are going it's looking like 2–1 against but the amendments, should one be chosen and passed, would make it more murky.

The PM could pull the vote, or accept an amendment, or just be defeated and press on. JH is due to see her later. My advice was that she should follow the course of action which 'maximises her control over events' and not die in the ditch. Live to fight another day and soldier on.

In the embassy foyer, as JH and I were talking to US Ambassador Woody Johnson, the new Serbian Ambassador just barged in between us. She ignored us, pushed us both aside and spoke loudly to Woody.

Later on I told the office to call the Serbs to make it clear how offended and displeased we were.

Farewell call on me by Duncan Taylor, former HMA Mexico, who is leaving the FCO after thirty-five years.

German SPD Leader Martin Schulz says he wants to see a federal Europe, which is precisely what pisses off nearly everyone in the UK. Meanwhile Merkel's potential successor as Party leader is chosen.

My thought for the day is that, whereas we all get annoyed by EU actions, the stupidity is that the Brexiteers think that if they isolate themselves from the imperfections of the world then they will no longer be affected by its continuing imperfections. We still will, so it's far better for us to be in the mix than on the sidelines.

Saturday 8 December – Rutland

To Uppingham. My Whip Mike Freer calls to canvass his flock. I am emphatic in my view that we must support the PM to the hilt. In the street, passers-by volunteer their similar opinion. It is increasingly clear that the more the PM is attacked, the more the public support her.

Former EU Commission President Romano Prodi has said, 'Whereas I thought it would be a divided EU facing a united UK, it's turned out to be a united EU facing a divided UK.' Too right, mate: spot on.

Walk by the river with Noodle.

Violin concert in Uppingham church by Freya Goldmark. We stay for the first half then head to the Marquess for dinner with Rosso. We are joined by Melanie Sykes. Charming and fun, I'd never heard of her, but she is a top radio presenter. Carl Ross and Henry Carling there too.

Sunday 9 December – Rutland/London

Two days to go till the meaningful vote. The news is of little else. On Sky there's Hilary Benn, Esther McVey, Dominic Raab and Kwasi Kwarteng. On *Marr* there's Boris Johnson, Steve Barclay and the irritating Rebecca Long-Bailey for Labour.

Boris was so artificial: let's take back control and become champion innovators. He was anti-backstop, disingenuous about his leadership manoeuvring, and affected an unconvincing veneer of seriousness. At heart he and his ilk don't know their exit from their backstop.

While driving down to London I speak to Philip May. I say, 'Tell her to hang on in there.' She must retain the maximum control of events and play it into the new year. She could perhaps accept an amendment and smother defeat in the cloak of reasonableness, avoiding any stark headcount which measures the full scale of opposition.

Monday 10 December – London

On Saturday I'd called Nick Robinson of the *Today* programme to ask if he was due to present it today. He isn't, it's Justin Webb, but he undertook to get me on the programme. I've got the 6.50am slot, bounced somewhat by the ridiculous Theresa Villiers who'll be in the prime slot after the news.

I go to Broadcasting House for it. I say I want to echo Nicholas Soames and inject some sense of realism into colleagues' thinking. Look at the big picture and the risk of chaos. It's crazy to try to replace the PM. A general election would be even worse. Ironic that France and Germany are in disarray, and whereas we could be top dog in Europe we are beating ourselves up. PM has a sense of duty etc. Boris is a spent force.

The bumptious Mark Francois muttered something gratuitously rude to me as I walked into New Palace Yard. Such is the current mood, but he's also a pent-up oddball. Into the Tea Room. Cup of tea with Penny Mordaunt, Guy Opperman and Bim Afolami. Guy has a lovely dry teasing wit. Mordaunt is very angst-ridden.

Have a tough meeting with the Russia team. Labour have accused us of funding a unit which issues disparaging tweets about Jeremy Corbyn. Unknown to me, we indeed pay for activity by the pro-democracy think tank Institute of Statecraft's Integrity Initiative whose purpose is to counter Russian disinformation. They also retweet open-source material about Russia, some of which has mentioned Corbyn. The dividing line is not clear enough. I have been landed in it, having emphatically defended the programme and stated that FCO money does not pay for any such party political activity. It is all being pushed by the odious Chris Williamson, the hard-left Labour MP who is probably the most hated man in Parliament.

At about 11am, it's announced that the PM has convened a conference call for all the Cabinet to discuss tomorrow's meaningful vote. There are rumours it might be pulled. She is due to make a statement at 3.30pm to report, or so it is believed, on her weekend calls across the EU.

To Millbank to do *Politics Live*. I'm on with Layla Moran, pretty but naive Lib Dem, and Richard Burgon for Labour, who's a bit of an ass – a trade union speaking clock. Just as we come on air it looks as though the vote is to be pulled and deferred. Confirmation of this is sprung on me in the first five seconds of the programme. Somewhat aghast, I just smile and say, 'Ah. OK.' It will probably be replayed for years to come as a classic 'Oops' moment. The programme is good-natured and something of a one-off. I defend the PM vigorously, and Moran and Burgon are perfectly tame.

I am asked to see the PM in her room at 2.45pm 'so she can say thank you'. I call JH, who is just taking off from Brussels. I can't believe for a second that she is going to resign, and JH agrees she won't. The meeting is for a largish group of about forty colleagues who gather in the Foreign Secretary's room before going next door to the PM's. Some nice plaudits for my *Today* programme interview this morning.

The PM is relaxed, indeed quite jaunty. She explains that she will formally announce at 3.30pm that she will delay the vote. We tell her to hang on in there. Far from seeming under pressure, she is positively jolly.

In the Tea Room, Soames is on typically ebullient form. When I mention that my office do all my tweeting, and that I don't know how to, he grabs my phone and says, 'It's easy – look,' at which point he tweets 'Bollocks' in reaction to Laura Kuenssberg's latest BBC tweet. He is a naughty boy.

I have to call my office to get them to tweet to say that it wasn't me, and text Laura to explain.

Tuesday 11 December – London
The PM is in Brussels all day for further, no doubt rather fruitless, engagement with the EU Commission.

A day of relative calm, with non-stop FCO business. After months of Boris–Gove buggering about, we finally have clarity on the proposed marine protection area around the South Sandwich Islands. I have seen off all the lunatic representations from the various ill-informed lobbies and am now free to announce what we want. I will use tomorrow's Westminster Hall debate to do so.

Catch-up with Philip Barton on Russia, Ukraine, etc. Meeting with Erdoğan's adviser İbrahim Kalın. See new deputy of the Middle East Dept, Helen Winterton, who I used to work closely with in DfID. Speak at the Kazakh National Day party in Banqueting House.

There are growing rumours that the forty-eight signatures calling for a no-confidence vote in Theresa are now in, but we'll only know when we know.

Wednesday 12 December – London
Leadership challenge …!!!

An extraordinary day of drama. Just before 8am, Graham Brady confirmed he'd received sufficient letters calling for a no-confidence vote in the PM as Leader of the Party and that the ballot would take place this evening between 6pm and 8pm.

Cabinet ministers rush to declare their 100 per cent support, and I put out a tweet: 'For the sake of country, Government and Party I urge all my fellow Conservative MPs to vote for Theresa May this evening. Changing the PM at this critical moment in history would be a massive mistake. Stick with her and let's see it through!'

I then do an interview expressing my dismay at the recklessness of colleagues. The PM gives a strong statement outside Number 10 – calling for support to 'finish the job'. I do *BBC Breakfast* shortly afterwards – they begin by asking me for my thoughts and I tell them some of them are unbroadcastable! They asked if I was embarrassed by the state of British politics, and I said that I was – how could anyone not be?

It is a total act of sabotage, colossal folly and poor judgement. The idea we would get rid of the PM the day before she's due to go to a European summit is absolute madness – we'd be a laughing stock. These people are totally undermining our national interest and don't seem to care. We risk looking ungovernable.

With the worst possible timing, the Speaker grants a UQ from Labour on the Integrity Initiative debacle, which I will have to answer following PMQs. I am already down to respond to the Westminster Hall debate on the South Sandwich Islands at 11am, so I have to prep for both while keeping track of the leadership drama. It leaves me no time to rally colleagues behind the PM.

She puts in a strong performance at PMQs, at the end of which I pass her on my way on to the bench to do the UQ. Emily Thornberry in indignant-outrage mode – I rather lose it with her in my reply as she seemed to be accusing me of lying, and Speaker Hobbit pops up to call for calm.

PM addresses the 1922 at 5pm, before the vote opens. When it closes, I stand on the desk to take a photo of the assembled hacks who have been allowed into Committee Room 14 for the result.

She wins convincingly – 200 votes to 117 – pleasingly, this is one vote *more* than she got in the final MPs' leadership ballot in 2016. She makes another strong statement outside Number 10. Quite a day.

Monday 17 December – London

The PM makes a statement on the EU Council and sets a new date for the meaningful vote, which will now take place in the week beginning 14 January. Unless it doesn't, I guess.

Christmas drinks including officials from other ministerial offices.

At about 6pm Corbyn makes a bog of proposing a motion of no confidence in the government. He stands on a point of order after the day's statements saying he wanted to move a motion of no confidence in the Prime Minister, rather than against the government. The logic is perhaps that he wanted to single out the PM in the hope

Walking down Whitehall with Boris on the day Theresa May
triggered Article 50, 29 March 2017.

With Boris and President of the EU Commission Jean-Claude Juncker.

With US Secretary of State Mike Pompeo at
the UN Security Council, 26 January 2019.

Delivering 'quite a humdinger' denouncing
President Maduro of Venezuela to the
Security Council, 26 January 2019.

Arriving at the OSCE summit in Hamburg,
8 December 2016.

Going over Boris's first party conference speech as Foreign Secretary, Birmingham, 2 October 2016.

Sir Nicholas Soames in the Smoking Room on our last evening in Parliament, 4 November 2019.

'Priti Awful' (Priti Patel).

'Speaker Hobbit' (Mr John Bercow).

Listening to news coverage of the leadership contest with Team TM, July 2016.

Theresa and Philip May in her room at the House of Commons awaiting the result of the second ballot, 7 July 2016.

A rare visit to the Smoking Room by the PM, July 2017.

With Boris and UN Secretary General António Guterres
at the Cyprus talks in Geneva, 12 January 2017.

At the presentation of a dispatch box to outgoing
US Secretary of State John Kerry, 16 January 2017.

With HM Sultan Qaboos of Oman.

The great and the good in Oman for the Sultan's Privy Council.

With James at Royal Ascot, June 2017.

'Never mind wars and pestilence: this will be my lasting legacy!' – smartening up the FCO signage (see entry for 24 June 2019).

that the DUP would join him in going for her, whereas they would not if it might destroy the government overall.

The problem for Corbyn is that procedurally his motion is not compliant. If it complied with the precise words of the Fixed-Term Parliaments Act, then it would automatically take precedence over all other business, whereas a motion of no confidence in anything else does not.

Monday 31 December – Muscat
In Oman for the Sultan's New Year dinner.

Sajid Javid has cut short his (expensive) safari holiday to face pressure over Iranians and others crossing the Channel to Dover in small inflatables. So far a mere thirty-three have been spotted. It hardly compares with the 1.33 million Syrian refugees who have fled to Jordan.

I'm really thinking of quitting politics next year. I am finding it so suffocating and small-minded. It is stultifying.

And my end-of-year thought on us leaving the EU is: 'I am not in the business of betraying the young who are looking to the future in order to please the old who are looking to the past.'

That … is my considered verdict on Brexit. So there! Good night, and goodbye 2018.

2019

Tuesday 1 January – Muscat

The Sultan's dinner at the Bait al Baraka started at the same time as the new year. He arrived at five minutes past midnight, after we'd been waiting at the tables since 10.45pm. We could have mingled usefully for another hour with all his ministers, and it also meant that we missed out on copious rations of Montrachet and Cheval Blanc as we had to switch to pomegranate juice. But we're spoilt, so let's not be churlish.

I was at the same seat I've occupied for the last twenty years, in the middle of the right side of the gentle horseshoe top table. HM is obviously in the middle, with five on either side. To his left Sir David Manning, to his right Field Marshal Lord Guthrie, Baroness [Patricia] Rawlings, me, Darwish al Balushi the Finance Minister and HMA Hamish Cowell.

General Sultan had fully briefed HM on our lunch, and choreographed it so that when HM rose to walk to each of the three stages of the buffet dinner I was asked to accompany him. This gave me over half an hour of face-to-face conversation.

It is not so much a buffet as a sumptuous feast with two lines of tables, each perhaps fifteen yards long, groaning with massive platters of lobster, prawns, chicken, etc. That's just for starters. We come back again for all the main courses beneath domed silver lids. Then puddings and the New Year cake, which is eight feet high. A gold sovereign, as usual, was in my slice, albeit only a modern reproduction.

I manage to cover a lot of ground with the Sultan. He likes the idea of a forward-looking strategic plan for UK–Oman engagement, and likes the concept of it being comprehensive and not just a commitment based on defence and security. So I landed that one.

He was very open about the Netanyahu visit. He felt that the Middle East Peace Process has gone stale and that he could broker some renewed activity. He found Netanyahu 'flexible' and prepared to allow Gaza gas to go to Gaza as well as to the West Bank. 'Netanyahu's prepared to talk to Abu Mazen [Mahmoud Abbas] about a two-state outcome, but will not compromise on security.' I remonstrate politely, suggesting that he will always say such things but in practice considers all the West Bank to be his and he will always continue to annex it with illegal settlements until eventually he controls and owns the whole lot.

US Secretary of State Pompeo will visit on the 14th. HM knows him from when he was head of the CIA.

I said I had briefed General Sultan on Iran, and the prospect of Oman helping us with the IRGC and the detention of Nazanin Zaghari-Ratcliffe. He likes the idea of trying to help.

Dinner finished at about 2am, and then we had the concert till 4.30am. It was a lively one. The *William Tell* Overture and the Radetzky March are both good for not falling asleep.

Thursday 3 January – Muscat/Jebel Akhdar

To the Jebel Akhdar, arriving in time for lunch. The Anantara hotel is fabulous, situated on the top of all the craggy peaks, and built where Princess Diana was iconically photographed staring wistfully across the ravine.

Walk from the hotel, but not quite as far as the village of Al Aqur.

Dramatic sunset as we gather for drinks on the glass-edged platform which now constitutes Diana Point, all exquisite but for the property in the distance owned by Sheikh Tamim, the ruler of Qatar. It's under construction but offends the natural view by being too much of a tall tower. It is out of keeping. The hotel sets up dinner for us on Diana Point surrounded by gas-heater obelisks as the temperature drops dramatically, and with blankets on our knees.

Two amusing stories about the Sultan from Patricia. First, he was once given a bullet-proof Range Rover as a gift, which had all the latest bells and whistles on it. HM ordered the Royal Guard to take it out into the desert and fire at it. They did so, upon which it promptly exploded in a massive fireball. Hmm!

Second, during the Arab Spring in 2011 there were noisy protests all over the Arab world. Demonstrations in Oman were rather more tame and genteel, although those at the Sur roundabout continued for some weeks. The students at Sultan Qaboos University wanted to organise a protest march and cordially asked the Sultan for permission. He said, 'Of course you can demonstrate. Where?' They said where, and he said yes. 'On which day?' They named the date and he said yes. He then said all of that is fine, and you will start your demonstration march at midday. They did so, and wilted after less than an hour!

Friday 4 January – Jebel Akhdar/Muscat
Our room is lovely. It sits on the corner with a staggering view across the ravine and catches both sunrise and sunset.

Over lunch, go through with David Manning his dinner conversation with the Sultan. Our notes compare well.

Two-hour drive back to the Kempinski Hotel in Muscat.

Dinner at the Chedi with William and Ffion who are holidaying there. As a guess at who might eventually succeed May, he punted for Sajid and I punted for Gove. His father's funeral last week went as he would have wished – no religion. They are having a few days' rest, adhering to their strict rule of no meetings that resemble public life or duty.

Saturday 5 January – Muscat
Bronzage. Leave at 12 for the Bait al Baraka. Lunch around the pool with Erik Bennett, Brigadier Mohammed bin Sulaiman, Field Marshal Lord [Charles] Guthrie, CDS General Sir Nick Carter, Sir David Manning, Sir Richard Dearlove, Marshal of the Royal Air Force Lord [Jock] Stirrup, Christopher Geidt and Richard Moore. Quite the top team.

After a relaxing afternoon we gather in the Majlis at 8pm. Puligny-Montrachet, Cheval Blanc and Pétrus on offer. You never quite know when the wait will end, so it's not easy to judge how to pace the slurping. Somehow we managed.

Christopher was called in for an audience at 10.30pm. We then walked down the corridor flanked by diamond-encrusted artefacts in exquisite display cases to have the Privy Council from 11pm to 1am. It hummed along perfectly, exactly as planned, which is a first.

Over dinner with the Sultan, I likened Leave/Remain to Sunni/Shia, describing Theresa May as the sensible Ibadi in the middle. (Whereas most of the Arab world divides starkly into Sunni or Shia, the Omanis are Ibadi – mild-mannered religious centrists akin to the Methodists.) The Sultan smiled appreciatively. But I was frank in admitting that we had no clue how it would unfold, and there was a danger that the government might collapse within weeks.

Our feast took place in a magnificent new receiving hall, lasting until 4.30am, during which Charles Guthrie struggled to stay awake.

Monday 7 January – Muscat/London
Returning to London, the Commons debate on the Brexit Deal has started again. We'll have a week of it. But I just cannot see how we can possibly win the vote on the 15th. It'll be 2–1 against. So what then? Heaven knows. It's going to be a mess of pottage.

Tuesday 8 January – London
The Commons yesterday was non-stop Urgent Questions, courtesy of Speaker Hobbit. The EU debate will start on Thursday. Nicky Morgan and Yvette Cooper have tabled an amendment for today to the Finance Bill which ingeniously would prevent the government from spending anything on preparing for a No Deal exit without the permission of the Commons. More generally positions are so deeply entrenched there just seems no way that we can win support for the Deal in time for next Tuesday's vote on it. Down down the slippery slope we steadily slide.

Jane Holl Lute, UN envoy to Cyprus. There's clearly no prospect of unification talks resuming. For the moment they remain doomed.

Senior official Nigel Baker re Ecuador. Annoyingly Assange's forcible exit from the Ecuadorian embassy has been delayed. Ecuador's government lawyers are now saying that it requires a Presidential decree which will take at least a week or two.

To HofC. Meet the new Ecuador Ambassador Jaime Marchán-Romero. His principal mission is to get Assange out of the embassy – it has been six years – and although he had been aiming for tomorrow, as I'd just learnt it's going to take longer. A tad frustrating, but we'll get there.

One-on-one meeting with Jeremy H. He was thoughtful, as ever, about Brexit, but openly exasperated. He had been against concluding the negotiations so early, he had been against putting the meaningful vote so early and he had then been against pulling the meaningful vote. She had not taken his advice on any of them, and it has cost us. But his view was that we must 'hammer on'.

I talked him through my Oman visit. I can't quite get him to engage and realise that I'm the only one who can deliver a deal with the Omanis. He keeps on fretting that Burt might get annoyed. Alistair knows nothing about Oman and doesn't know any of the people who matter. It is just absurd that our deeper interests are frustrated by the pettiness of ministerial turf. Had I been given responsibility for the Gulf from the start, our entire set of relationships would be in a stronger state.

I updated him on Ecuador/Assange, Turkey (suggesting he meet Erdoğan, possibly by us going together to Ankara), Russia (how do we get going again with them?).

Government defeated by seven on the No Deal amendment on the Finance Bill.

Watch the Channel 4 docudrama *Brexit: The Uncivil War*. It exaggerates the persona and importance of Dominic Cummings, but some of the characterisations aren't bad, especially those of irrepressible Leaver Bernard Jenkin and Leave.EU bruiser Arron Banks. The portrayal of Bernard is more convincing than the real thing.

Wednesday 9 January – London

Chat about the programme with Stephen Parkinson at the back gates of Number 10. Was it really like that in the Leave campaign? He says Cummings was a dominant figure, but the drama did rather over-state it.

Phone call with my old school friend Michael Morley. He is rather dejected by our leaving the EU. He advocates Remain, Reform, Redistribute, and thought the scene in the docudrama when a woman in a focus group burst into tears in a cry of despair was eerily accurate. Many Leavers were expressing anger and frustration at their economic powerlessness, hence his 'redistribute' call.

The Speaker will accept the Dominic Grieve amendment to the programme motion for the renewed debate on the postponed deci-sion on the exit Deal. A programme motion is designed to determine the timetable of a debate or bill, i.e. it will take place on specified days for a precise number of hours. But Dominic has dreamt up a clever amendment which says that if the Deal at the end of the debate is voted down, then the PM must return to the House after three days to outline her Plan B. The amendment bears no relation to the subject matter of the motion to which it has been attached. Deeming the amendment to be in order is unprecedented; it has probably been accepted contrary to the Clerks' advice; and doing so is undoubtedly an act of Bercow bias.

Ministerial team meeting. JH as always is astute in his analysis and shares it freely with us. His view is stimulating. Tusk and Macron stupidly think we might yet be forced into holding a second referen-dum; the Commission want the Deal to go through and so have become allies of a sort; the Irish think No Deal would deliver a united Ireland; the EU think the Deal will eventually go through, but that it will require an extension to the Article 50 deadline of 29 March. But a government defeat has weakened the government; Bernard Jenkin doesn't think that Parliament could stop No Deal; Dominic Grieve and Nicky Morgan think that parliamentary proce-dure can stop No Deal, whereas the ERG think it cannot; in the Cabinet, those who are Brexiteers (Fox, Gove, Leadsom) are commit-ted to the Deal; but the 'out and out' Brexiteers on the backbenches

(Johnson, Rees-Mogg, Davis, Duncan Smith, Baker) are increasingly for No Deal … 'out and out' is indeed what they are.

In terms of how we might successfully stop No Deal, Jeremy's hunch is that the government would be threatened by a vote of confidence if we were heading for it. We might find ourselves on the cliff edge facing either No Deal or No Brexit. Either would destroy the Conservative Party, so we *must* have a deal.

A furious row breaks out in the Commons, with over an hour of points of order. The Speaker behaves abominably. He has clearly defied the Clerks' advice by allowing Dominic's amendment to the programme motion, but his manner of behaving in the Chair is ghastly. The points of order should have been wrapped up after a few minutes, but he lets it run and run. It is humiliating for the Commons. Towards the end, he is accused of bias and of displaying a 'Bollocks to Brexit' sticker in his car. He says the car belongs to his wife and not even someone on the Tory benches should regard their wife as a chattel. He has no decorum. It is grandstanding partiality.

We later lose the Business Motion vote by nine.

Download on Oman with diligent officials Julie Scott and Helen Winterton. Amazingly, there is massive progress. Julie actually has a draft text for a comprehensive agreement with them. Oh joy!

Give Burt a full Oman debrief. Instead of being appreciative, he behaves rather chippily, showing no understanding of how significant this step is, yet demands I keep him informed. I really am doing my best not to go behind his back, but his territorial snippiness is disappointing. But I keep my cool.

Attend the PM's reception in Number 10 with James. The rather loveable Andrew Bowie has become the PM's new PPS. I say to Theresa it's a very good appointment … 'he's just the right height'. She laughs. Result … a laugh from Theresa!

Thursday 10 January – London
Chat with Hamish Cowell in Muscat. I express surprised pleasure at the state of the draft agreement.

Ministerial meeting to discuss preparations for No Deal. Steve Barclay in the chair. It's all rather perfunctory, but is lightened by some texts from Mark Lancaster. 'So boring. I can see you are distracting yourself by staring at Steve Barclay.' Bloody Lancaster – typical tease – because, looking around the room, I couldn't see him. Then I realise that whenever I looked towards where he was, up towards the windows behind someone, he swerved sideways so as to obscure my line of sight. I text back: 'I couldn't bloomin' see you.' ML: 'He probably used to be good eye candy.' Me: 'Less so these days.' ML: 'I was enjoying hiding from you.' Me: 'SB is a sort of "not quite George Clooney".' ML: 'It's the voice – lacks a degree of sophistication.' Me: 'Precisely!'

Dearlove and Guthrie have published a joint letter criticising the Deal on the grounds that it compromises intelligence and security. It's total crap. I text Richard Dearlove, 'Nice to see you in Muscat. I avert my gaze for half a second, and out pops your letter on Sky!'

Dinner with Abdulaziz [al Hinai] in Harry's Bar. No alcohol for me. I give him the Privy Council read-out, which he appreciates. John Scarlett is at the next table. He is angry with Dearlove for dragging SIS into politics. I doubt Dearlove has any fans left in Vauxhall.

Friday 11 January – London/Rutland

An hour on the front bench for the EU debate, opened by Sajid and due to be closed by Jeremy. Usual sectarian nonsense on Europe.

To Rutland Council to see Councillors Oliver Hemsley and Gordon Brown to thrash out some of the facts about St George's Barracks. I am adamant that they need some early work on what the design criteria are going to be. Stone and slate? Higgledy-piggledy streets? Some thatch? We need to build local confidence in the project. At the moment it faces ferocious opposition, and threatens to destroy our control of the Council in next May's local elections.

Briefly home, then to Melton for the R&M Executive Meeting. Unfortunately Brexit has brought out some nasty qualities in some of our members.

The unpleasant Geoffrey Pointon – fat, ugly and eighty – has tabled two resolutions, one to call for an annual public meeting to meet the MP, something that can happen anyway were they ever to ask, and another to set up a sub-committee to 'propose the processes to select a candidate to succeed the current Member of Parliament'. He pretends loyalty and argues that it is just for the future, but in practice he is a deceitful toad. The first motion is what the Association itself should be doing: it's what they're there for. The second is an attack on me, but expressed very clumsily.

Motion 1 is passed 16–14. Motion 2 is defeated 8–25.

I am then readopted as the candidate for the next election by 24–12. The voting numbers were supposed to be secret, but I was sitting next to the Chairman, and could easily see the bit of paper recording the result. The twelve are the usual horrid lot, who are all the more venomous because of Brexit. The snide and distasteful Christine Emmett revived the old attack that I'd said the Leave campaign was a working-class tantrum, and then later on fired the Dearlove–Guthrie letter at me to ask how on earth I could support the Deal when such distinguished people say it is a danger to national security. And of course the band of malcontents would not be complete without Frances, Duchess of Rutland weighing in. She asked me how I intended to vote on Tuesday, as if to insist I should vote against the Deal. I reply, 'It's a bit of a paradox that some in this meeting, which is the Executive of a political association dedicated to the election of a Conservative government, only seem prepared to support the reselection of their MP if he is prepared to vote against the very government of which he is a part. I fully intend to vote with the government, and I *will* do so.'

I won, despite robustly dealing with the disloyal questions. In any other circumstances my readoption would have been almost unanimous. But 2–1 is fine, so the numbers don't matter. I have the option I wanted – I can decide if I want to stand or not. For a moment I was half hoping I'd lose and be deselected. I'd be so happy to be shot of them.

The Macedonian parliament has passed the country's name change, so now it's up to the Greeks to seal the final deal, then it formally becomes North Macedonia. But it's going to be tricky for Tsipras in Greece. I texted congratulations to Macedonia FM Nikola Dimitrov.

I am trying to place an op-ed in the *Telegraph* for Monday rebutting the Dearlove–Guthrie attack. I will then send a signed copy to Christine Emmett.

Saturday 12 January – Rutland

Meeting on St George's Barracks at North Luffenham Primary School with ten parish councillors from all the villages affected by the proposed development. The issue is getting very contentious, as they just won't accept that without the Council's deal with the MoD they'd get 4,000 houses instead of 2,000. Nor would they have the planning and design control which they've just been granted.

Nice afternoon in Rutland. Take down the Christmas tree and go for a nice walk along the river.

Hawaii Five-O, series 9 has begun, but the story line has deteriorated.

Sunday 13 January – Rutland/London

The papers are all trying to find a new angle on the obvious – Tuesday's vote. The issue that has taken off a bit is Bercow's claim to be returning power to the Commons against the Executive. It's exaggerated and has massive constitutional implications, but it is logical inasmuch as it might appear to offer a route out of the Brexit impasse. Precisely how is a different matter.

Nicholas Soames calls. 'Hunk, you're one of the big boys, and we really need you. You must work to help find a solution. We've all got to try to find some way out of this mess.' He bounced around the idea of replacing May with Lidington, but I said there's nothing to be gained as he'd still have all the same Brexit problems. Soames wanted to get rid of all the idiots in the Cabinet, and have a new government of grown-ups. I repeated that we'd have the same unresolved Brexit crisis and it would mean more nutters outside government causing it grief. So we'd have gained nothing.

I write my thoughts about how to handle a vote of no confidence. If we lose it, we should avoid having a general election and just let Corbyn govern for a few weeks so as to flush him out and discredit him.

Monday 14 January – London

Not such a great start to the week: my article about Dearlove–Guthrie has not appeared in the *Telegraph*, but one by Ben Wallace has. Mine was cleared in detail with both the Home Office and Number 10, but I doubt the Wallace one was cleared with anyone.

I also learn that JH held a meeting last week with all the EU ambassadors in London to discuss Brexit. I knew nothing of it and was not included. He rebuked a couple of them for being slow to agree to protect UK citizens' rights in the event of No Deal, but targeted some of the wrong countries. Oops.

Labour MP Laura Pidcock came in to discuss a consular case involving child abduction. She was actually OK, despite being best known for saying that she could never be friends with a Tory. My enormous portrait photo of Margaret Thatcher discomfited her somewhat. Just what it's there for!

Meeting of the Sensible Brexit front-bench group in the Chancellor's office. Gauke and Rudd among others.

Gareth Johnson has resigned as a Whip. So silly and pointless.

Party meeting with the PM in the Boothroyd Room. Her speech solid and rational. In essence: 'Without the Deal, respect for politics would go. The backstop is not a threat to the Union; crashing out without a deal most certainly is.'

[Hertsmere MP] Oli Dowden says we are splitting before our very eyes into two: ideologues and pragmatists. Burt's intervention was funny and effective. 'I've been here for thirty-two years [cries of 'Nooo!']. Oh. I started on a youth opportunity scheme. But I'd like to be able to be here for another thirty-two, so let's all stick together,' etc. He did it very well.

Mark Sedwill texts to say that Putin has suggested we resume relations of a sort, starting with me meeting Deputy FM Titov again. Apparently Putin mentioned me by name via his intelligence chief. Interesting.

Tuesday 15 January – London

Today's the day of the big meaningful vote. Hilary Benn has pulled his amendment, which would have prevented a No Deal Brexit, but would have also stopped the main vote on the Deal and masked the scale of opposition to it. His withdrawing it therefore makes our plight more stark.

My security article has appeared in the Times Online and is rather better than Ben Wallace's of yesterday.

Chat with DUP MP Gavin Robinson while on the way into my office. He is big and friendly, and a good measure of DUP opinion.

Harold Elletson comes in to brief me on the Integrity Initiative. We were both first elected in 1992, but he was defeated in 1997. An Etonian with good security links, both his sons learnt Arabic at SOAS [School of Oriental and Africa Studies]. He knows exactly what has been going on in the Institute for Statecraft. They are good people doing good things, but the repulsive Chris Williamson MP is a stooge of *Russia Today* TV, if not of the Russians themselves, and is determined to make mischief.

Chat with Tom Newton Dunn of the *Sun* in the committee corridor, and give him a quote saying that the wreckers will destroy the Party.

Evidence session before the Defence Select Committee about Trump's termination of the Intermediate Nuclear Forces Treaty. It was a success in 1986 between Reagan and Gorbachev, and has lasted thirty years. But the Russians have been cheating. I suspect that the US wants to develop the sort of missiles which the INF Treaty forbids so as to arm themselves against the rise of China. Fortunately, my office had anticipated most of the questions, so I came out of it well.

Soames in the Tea Room, very anxious about the way Brexit is going.

Serena Stone, Jeremy's PS, meets in my office to discuss my letter to Simon McDonald concerning senior appointments. She is fine, and the outcome is too. They will provide me with regular info about the various comings and goings, so as to allow me to express a view on people before any decision is taken.

Europe Director Caroline Wilson drops by. She is fab.

Drop by the FCO Crisis Centre, which is now permanently staffed as a focal point for the handling of Brexit.

The meaningful vote looms. Labour, the SNP and Edward Leigh all pull their amendments, but John Baron insists on moving his. He is obsessive and has zero judgement. I have never known so many MPs file through one lobby, and I found it very claustrophobic. I stood just inside the door nervously guarding what little space I had. It was defeated 24–600.

For the main meaningful vote, the Deal was defeated 202–432.

The PM made an immediate statement, anticipating and hence challenging Corbyn to table a motion of no confidence, which he then does.

Some of us hold an immediate meeting of what soon becomes known as the 'Jan 15th Group' in the Chancellor's office: Rudd, Gauke, indeed all the moderate sensible colleagues who are not mentally certifiable.

Wednesday 16 January – London

Speak to Erik in Muscat. Neither of us can work out what on earth will happen next.

Ministerial team meeting. We all brainstorm energetically. Lots of thinking … We are trapped between the ERG and the EU. The Deal is dead. Tinkering with it will not deliver a result. The basis for an outcome has always been about Parliament and the EU, not just about what it is we want. What is also dead are collective responsibility and certainty about parliamentary procedure. After today we will be in office but not in power. The ERG is a party within a party, so the only route out is cross-party, so we can't just shun Corbyn, we need to go back to first principles. We shouldn't give a damn about trade deals, but the common market matters. Work and deal with Labour, not with the ERG. If we could be shot of Momentum on the Labour side and Moggmentum on ours, sensible people could sort this out. Anyone can blackmail so far, but then think of the future. JH: it'll be a difficult Cabinet tomorrow. Either we are very tough with Brussels, or we need big compromises to attract others in Parliament. AD: one problem is that anything that might unite Parliament would divide the Conservative Party.

So there we are … that's all fine then.

Meeting of the Jan 15th Group in Chex [Chancellor of the Exchequer] office. Inconclusive ramblings, although someone whose comments are becoming ever more cogent and assertive is Richard Harrington.

The no confidence in HMG motion came at 7pm. The result was a comfortable majority of nineteen: Ayes 306, Noes 325. Michael Gove hammed it up in the winding-up speech and was excoriating about Corbyn. It was popular with colleagues, but I am increasingly disturbed by the way he has wormed his way back into favour. Anyway, we won, as we were bound to do. It was almost an anticlimax.

In her statement afterwards, the PM invited other party leaders to come in for consultations. It should have happened months ago, but it won't achieve anything now.

Dinner with Matthew Parris and Julian Glover. I hadn't seen them for ages. Nice catch-up. But depressing on Brexit.

Thursday 17 January – London

Sir Richard Dearlove comes in for a correctional tutorial on his idiotic letter. But he won't be budged despite all the evidence offered by officials.

There have been comings and goings all day at Number 10, as the PM sees party leaders other than Corbyn. Various groups have been traipsing in and out.

The Jan 15th WhatsApp group has been pinging away all day, but to no avail.

Friday 18 January – Rutland

The news was trailing a speech that Boris is due to give this morning at the JCB factory in Staffordshire, a place that has become a rather hackneyed location for such events. The Boris speech is a pitch on the UK's great future, free-market capitalism, inequality, etc, but zilch on how to end the current Brexit impasse. It looks like he's just mentioning a litany of grievances which he will miraculously put right. Ahead of the speech, I tweeted: 'Boris – You are not equipped to unite the Party which you have so recklessly divided. Please think less about yourself and instead focus only on solving the historic crisis we now face which you have done so much to create … #backthePMtheclockisticking.'

Yesterday's meetings, and the vibes today, suggest that thinking is narrowing towards the ultimate dilemma – endorse a/the customs union so as to win support across all parties for a deal, but risk alienating the ERG and splitting the Party; or placate the ERG and head for No Deal, but risk the eruption of Party moderates and Parliament. It must be the former, otherwise they will take us over for ever and destroy both Party and country. Again, if by endorsing a customs union we get the DUP on board for a deal, then we will have regained command of the argument and might be in with a chance.

The customs union possibility has focussed media attention on the readiness of any future free-trade agreement. But not a single one is oven-ready. Liam Fox's great claims have amounted to nothing, and if we stay in the customs union he and his entire department are redundant. The Dept for International Trade should anyway have been part of the FCO from the outset.

The Times carries a report saying that we will deny Bercow a peerage when he steps down as Speaker. What a stupid thing to say, especially at this critical moment in the Brexit process. It smacks of Gove, who lacks any judgement when it comes to briefing such things. The language feels as if it can only be him. The Buckingham constituency Association is also reported to be selecting a new candidate, which means that Bercow will once again be contested, something we should have done in the surprise 2017 general election. He is now a cornered rat and will behave accordingly, which is not in our interests.

Phone calls to the foreign ministers of Romania and Luxembourg. They both seem better informed about the issues and the workings of Parliament than most of us. Speak to George Ciamba of Romania, which holds the EU Presidency until July, and Jean Asselborn of Luxembourg, who is my favourite counterpart. I talk them through the events of the week, and try to analyse what will follow, which amounts to me saying that I haven't a clue.

Speak to Laura Kuenssberg of the BBC, Henry Mance of the *FT* and my bright and witty Whip Mike Freer. I say that we cannot limp on to failure and oblivion; if the only way to secure a deal is to take on the ERG and risk a Party split, then we must. If we can freeze them out fully, so much the better. But if all we do is kowtow to them then both Party and country will go down the plughole.

Henry Mance was hilarious: 'Boris once said he would lie in front of the bulldozer: but today he was caught lying in front of forty of them!'

Sunday 20 January – Rutland/London

Air Vice-Marshal (Retd) Nigel Sudborough phoned. Really nice call. He just wanted to express support for the way I am handling things on Brexit, and to reassure me that there are many sensible people in Rutland who agree with me, especially on Boris. He despairs at the state of British politics, as do we all.

The papers are full of Brexit turmoil ahead of tomorrow's Commons statement by the PM. Heaven knows what she can say.

Monday 21 January – London

Excellent interview on *Today* by Richard Harrington explaining why No Deal would be such a disaster. When pitted against Peter Lilley, now in the Lords, Richard nailed him. If WTO [World Trade Organisation] rules were to apply, they would add tariffs and there would be friction.

Phone call with Lord (David) Triesman. He's a former FCO minister under Blair, and now runs the Cuba initiative. He is concerned by America's extraterritorial sanctions against all who do business in Cuba. I think the US just wants to discourage investment there, and won't actually prosecute UK companies which do. He said in passing that under Corbyn no Jew could feel comfortable in the Labour Party. I said Corbyn was too stupid to make the distinction between Jews in general and the actions of Israel in Palestine.

Meeting in Committee Room 16 with the PM for junior ministers in the Lords and Commons. She was very relaxed ahead of her 3.30pm statement. But there was nothing new. It was round and round the houses on Brexit, but at least the questions and analysis were better than her encounters with backbenchers.

In the Chamber she said she would go to Brussels and ask for more on the backstop, but it didn't amount to much change. Once again the wretched Speaker made her answer questions for over two and a half hours.

Dinner with Ed in Quirinale. Oil entrepreneur and neighbour Algy Cluff chatted on his way out, telling us that Hugo Swire is Dominic Raab's leadership campaign manager. Wow! News indeed, but rather bonkers. He also says that Rory Stewart is doing well, but 'although he used to look quite pretty, as he grows older he looks more and more like a horse'.

Tuesday 22 January – London
I'm told James Cleverly really thinks that he is a credible candidate to take over from Theresa May, and that he would definitely make it to the last two in any contest. It lifts absurdity to a new level as he's been in the House for two minutes, has never been a minister and seems to think that his clandestine briefing of the press and his being a mere vice-chairman of the Party (which doesn't mean much these days) all somehow equip him. The place has gone mad.

Every single social conversation wherever I go is about Brexit. I just cannot escape. My latest take is that it's all about the DUP. If we get them back on board for a deal of any sort, then we have a chance. If we can't, then we remain in our dark room with no exits. A couple of tweets suggest that Leo Varadkar in Ireland might seek a bilateral agreement with the UK on the backstop if it's the only way to overcome the problem. I doubt it, but if he would then we'd be in with a chance.

Wednesday 23 January – London
Bump into the feisty Anna Soubry on my way into the Commons. She is fervent and outspoken in favour of remaining. She has many detractors, but I think she's both courageous and articulate.

Ministerial team meeting. Usual Brexit stocktake. We all agree with each other, but can't see the way out. I say that the biggest mistake we made with the EU referendum was to allow the results to be disaggregated from one single national outcome. They are known by constituency, by council area, by region and by nation/province. As a consequence, we have over 650 separate results and obligations, and hence multiplied division.

The edgy Mark Harper comes in about one of his constituents who was gang-raped in Turkey. A ghastly incident, but MPs do tend to have an unrealistic understanding of what we can and cannot do in another country. We don't run the world any more. Should I send a gunboat?

A series of Brexit-related meetings. The stuff on Northern Ireland makes grim reading. In short, the threats to the Union should there be No Deal are colossal.

No Deal ministerial meeting with Chris Heaton-Harris chairing. Ministers were irritable and unhappy. It was supposed to be about the problems with data handling if there's No Deal, as any electronic transfer between the UK and the EU would become unlawful. But nobody knew if they were there to talk about their department's ability to operate or about the national activities for which their department was responsible. An utterly dysfunctional meeting.

Jan 15th Group in the Macmillan Room with David Lidington. Alistair Burt was very agitated and is contemplating resignation.

My school contemporary John Randall, now in the Lords, has taken delivery of his coat of arms. Amusingly, as he is a bearded twitcher, illustrated on the top of the crest is a bearded tit.

President Maduro is under pressure in Venezuela. The President of the National Assembly which, unlike Maduro, has been properly elected has declared himself 'interim President'. I insist on tweeting something supportive, but speak to Andrew Soper, our Ambassador first, as we don't want him to be chucked out. So we are one step away from saying we recognise Juan Guaidó as the legitimate interim President, but choosing only to say for the time being that we consider Maduro illegitimate.

Thursday 24 January – London/Rutland

On Venezuela, we got it right. Jeremy is in Washington today and will have a mid-morning meeting with SofS Mike Pompeo, and then Vice-Pres Mike Pence. He then takes us a little by surprise and ramps it up by suddenly saying that we will consider recognising Guaidó. It throws us somewhat, but we will adjust accordingly.

Speak to the Spanish Ambassador about Gibraltar. The Spanish are introducing the language of 'colonisation' into the exchange of documents preparing for the eventuality of No Deal. This is provocative, but they are not stupid. They can sense our weakness over Brexit and will not miss the chance. They say they will stick to our existing language on sovereignty while we remain in the EU, but if we leave with no agreement then the relationship will have changed, and so their language will change too. Idiot Brexiteers just have no appreciation of the damage they are inflicting on UK interests in so many areas.

Alex Salmond, former Leader of the SNP, has been arrested and charged with a number of counts of sexual assault and attempted rape. Last week it looked as though a Party inquiry had cleared him of any wrongdoing, and Nicola Sturgeon was under fire for having interfered in the process. This week he is in the most serious position imaginable, but I just don't know where that leaves Nicola Sturgeon. Still up to her neck in it, I hope. [After a trial in March 2020, Salmond was acquitted on all charges.]

Friday 25 January – Rutland/New York

To Melton with Noodle. Meet the County Council. Quick photo op with the Melton police, then later on do a Radio Leicester interview. There has been a recent spike in burglary in Melton, and some drug-related car-smashing. A few loud and vulgar women are blaming the police, and me, for failing to act on it. There was a public meeting last night at which I was universally slagged off. I'd heard the meeting was due to happen, so sent a statement to be read out to them, despite which I was openly accused of not replying to 150 emails. I have not been sent even one. They've tweeted that the police are fatarses, and called them fucking useless. If they think they can boss me about, they've judged it wrong. Bad manners don't win.

Phone call with Mark Carney, Governor of the Bank of England, about Venezuela's gold. They hold bullion which is now worth about $2 billion. Maduro has asked for it back, but the Bank are hesitating, quite sensibly. They want to be quite sure they are doing so on firm legal grounds – even though Venezuela has proposed it is returned via the Bank of International Settlements, rather than directly to Caracas. I tell Carney that I fully appreciate that, although it's a decision for the Bank, he needs a measure of political air cover from us. I tell him I will write him the most robust letter I can get through the FCO lawyers, and it will outline the growing doubts over Maduro's legitimacy and explain that many countries no longer consider him to be the country's President. A Marc Rich oil trader knows how to do business with a Goldman Sachs banker.

Speak to Jeremy, who is back from Washington. I have been asked to drop everything to go to the UN. He confides that we need to use Venezuela as an issue on which we can be as fully in line with the US as possible, because he is out of line on a number of other issues such as Syria. It's one of those trade-off moments which we need if we are to handle the Trump administration cleverly. 'Venezuela is in their back yard, and it's probably the only foreign adventure they might just pursue. If we end up resolving our own Brexit problems by staying in a customs union it would prevent a US–UK trade deal. A trade deal is something the US wants, if only to prove they can do such things outside any multilateral system.' It is a fundamental difference between us that, Brexit apart, we remain multilateralists whereas the US does not.

Take the evening flight to New York, during which I rewrite my draft UN statement from scratch, turning it into quite a fiery condemnation of President Maduro. It is now a cut above the drab bland inconsequential rot I was given to start with by the FCO.

Saturday 26 January – New York
Breakfast with the team. My draft speech is approved, and has passed the fact-check tests. I call Jeremy to agree our precise line on the

recognition on Juan Guaidó. We are not yet going so far as to say we will definitely recognise him as the legitimate interim President.

To the UN building. Glad-hand all the Permanent Reps. I'm the only European minister there, and as usual the UK sits next to the US, so I'm alongside US Secretary Mike Pompeo. He reads his speech rather lamely, and I deliver quite a humdinger denouncing Maduro.

Russian Permanent Rep Vasily Nebenzya, who of course supports Maduro, manages to lampoon me by saying my reference to stuffing ballot boxes was invalid because Venezuela has electronic voting. I passed him a note saying, 'Enjoyed the joke. But as a modern progressive Conservative government we appreciate the concept of electronic stuffing.'

The Venezuelan FM tried the old line against US interventionism and colonialism, but was unconvincing and appeared frightened. He only had South Africa, Russia and Nicaragua on his side. One of the good guys uttered the memorable line: 'Democracy cannot happen without elections: and elections cannot happen without democracy.'

Lunch at a nearby Greek restaurant called Ethos with Jonathan Allen and the team. When packing to leave at the residence my phone is subject to odd texts requesting a secure call with Sir Kim Darroch by downloading the Viber app. Before opening it up to my contacts I rumbled that it was an attempted hack.

Sunday 27 January – Rutland/London

Back at home in time for breakfast. Windy walk by the river. All the papers are full of Brexit uncertainty, plus a bit of Venezuela.

Chat to Robert Buckland for half an hour. He is such a sharp and sensible guy. With his keen analysis and perky trustworthy manner, we go over all the possible positions and outcomes for Tuesday's votes. I'm not sure we're any the wiser, but he is due to talk to the Chief at 5pm, and will make it clear that moderate loyal figures are becoming exasperated, and are anxious that we may be at the point of no return for preventing No Deal. Richard Harrington in particular is very exercised – quite rightly – about the anger and exodus of business. The Jan 15th WhatsApp group has been chattering away incessantly.

Conference call for the Jan 15th Group at 6pm. The conversation, as ever, was circular, and finished with anxiety rather than action.

It's leaked to Steve Swinford of the *Telegraph* within an hour, who tweets about it.

Monday 28 January – London

To the Commons to respond to Mike Gapes' Venezuela UQ. He is onside on the issue, as are all the sensible Labour MPs, many of whom have a special interest in Colombia next door. I loved it, and was able to sock it to the obnoxious Chris Williamson, who is hated by us and even more so by his own side. An unreconstructed leftie, whose beliefs are those of Castro, Chávez and Maduro, not to say Marx, Lenin, Trotsky and Mao, he is a Momentum nasty who is working to have many moderate Labour MPs deselected. They hate him with a passion, so I laid into him and relished every moment of it. Nice plaudits afterwards from both sides, especially Labour.

Dinner in the Dining Room with Nicholas Soames, joined later by Philip Dunne, Nick Boles and Oliver Letwin. The conversation on one level was hilarious, but once we discussed Brexit it became depressing. The PM had just addressed the Party and said she would whip in support of the Graham Brady amendment tomorrow, which calls for the EU to do something on the backstop, following which the House should support the PM's Deal. It's declaratory, but at least it expresses a view. Some in the ERG just won't row in behind it. At the meeting, Boris aggressively relived his morning's article in the *DT* and demanded she say what her solution is. To think that six months ago he was her Foreign Secretary and today he is like the slovenly teenager at the back of the classroom being insolent to his teacher. She raised her voice and made it clear to the tiresome Boris that her solution was for everyone to vote for her Deal.

In the corridor before the ten o'clock division were Hugo Swire, Richard Benyon and Dominic Grieve. They are not happy. Across the whole Commons sits a cloud of despondency. The mood is very glum and pessimistic.

I was cheered up in the lobby by Matt Hancock who had just had dinner with Mark Carney. 'My God, he loves you. He was effusive.

He said he'd been trying to get through to the FCO for ages about the Venezuelan gold, and one quick phone call with Alan Duncan fixed it in a trice.'

At 11pm there is an extensive flurry of activity on the MPs' WhatsApp group as the moderates and the ERG have reached some sort of understanding around which they can coalesce. It's all fantasy and offers unity around an undeliverable option. Started by Kit Malthouse, it has brought together Jacob Rees-Mogg and Steve Baker with Robert Buckland and Nicky Morgan. But it's all just people talking to themselves. It's not a solution.

Tuesday 29 January – London
Sixty days till Brexit.

To 1 Carlton Gardens for breakfast with Henry Kissinger. He is now ninety-five, and it's over forty years since he was Secretary of State under President Nixon. He was there for the Vietnam War and its end, the opening up of relations with China in the final years of Chairman Mao and the Watergate scandal.

His faculties are amazing. His gravelly voice delivers insights and wisdom, always with a thoughtful pause before he says anything. He was between me and Jeremy, who had kindly invited all his ministers. Harriett Baldwin, Tariq Ahmad and I were able to attend, along with Mark Sedwill and Jeremy's wife Lucia. Kissinger's walking stick wouldn't stay leant against the round table, and kept on slipping over my lap.

His recollections and observations were fascinating: he first went to China in July 1971, but had to avoid meeting Mao Tse-tung so as to save it up for Richard Nixon. Kissinger's policy had been to get closer to China and Russia than they were to each other. Today Trump wants better relations with the Russians, but political types have turned them into an outcast. Some EU speeches sound like prayers to an ancient religion. Trump is not a strategist: he is a decision-maker who wants to be seen as the dominant figure. He hates process. Condescension does not bring out the best in Russia: they are a weak country conducting a major foreign policy. No one can stop the rise of China: it probably wants to be rich rather than dominate via imperial expansion. When analysing how China conducts its foreign policy do not assume it does it on a European model. Don't label it as an aggressor because the Chinese don't look at foreign policy as we do. Toughness on trade by Trump will lead to Chinese concessions rather than confrontation. When they confront each other, the key is how each side interprets the other. They don't need speeches every week explaining their evil intent. US policy should be one of soft containment rather than one of threatening challenges.

Meet John Glen, Economic Secretary to the Treasury, to brief him on the FCO advice being offered to the Bank of England about Venezuela's gold. He is just a straight-down-the-line sensible decent guy. I'm full tilt on Venezuela, and now have an hour's debate in Westminster Hall moved by the Labour MP for Hyndburn, Graham Jones. All the MPs are well informed and genuinely concerned about the country. They all despise Nicolás Maduro, except for one – the odious Chris Williamson, who brazenly claims that Maduro's elections were above reproach. The whole room is aghast. I lay into him, saying 'he seems to want to make himself the most hated man in Venezuela, but is perhaps in a race between that and becoming the most hated man in the Commons'. Philip Hollobone in the Chair has to call for order in the gallery as they burst into collective coughing when Williamson speaks.

Encounter Justin Welby, the Archbishop of Canterbury, in New Palace Yard. He is always jocular. I say I haven't a clue what will happen this evening, but that given the lunacy of colleagues it requires a serious dose of divine intervention.

Seven divisions over nearly two hours on EU exit. Two amendments were added to the main government motion, one by Caroline Spelman which rejects the UK leaving without a Withdrawal Agreement, and one by Graham Brady which was endorsed by the government and commits to supporting a deal so long as the backstop is renegotiated.

At most it is part mandate, part instruction, for the PM to renegotiate the backstop with Brussels following which the House will have to back her Deal. But in truth it doesn't really amount to much, and doesn't take things forward with any certainty.

Nice chat in the Lobby with Iain Duncan Smith. We agree that Brexit is a million times worse than the battles over ratifying the Maastricht Treaty which we went through in our first Parliament of 1992–7. We said we'd have a drink some time. He was very pleasant, and initiated the chat.

The front pages for tomorrow offer a degree of respite for Theresa, saying she has regained control. But I fear she will just be rebuffed by Brussels and hit a brick wall. But we are momentarily cheered up.

Wednesday 30 January – London

The better headlines have created a slight mood of calm, but underlying doubts about whether it actually represents progress are steadily simmering away. There are growing fears that we have united behind a doomed objective. The EU's instant reaction has been obstinately negative.

Witness session before the Lords Constitution Committee on the future treatment of treaties. Do we scrutinise them enough? Should Parliament determine the scope of treaties being negotiated by the government? Should the process be totally transparent? etc. I was joined by David Lidington, who has a Rolls-Royce brain but is so fidgety he is enervating to watch, let alone sit next to. His arms jab out in random jerky gesticulations, reaching upwards, in front and sideways like a windmill with broken sails. It was one of those moments when their Lordships parade their cleverness. Or pernicketiness.

Talk to Fabian Picardo. The system is worried that he is in a frenzy, fearing that if the Withdrawal Agreement is to be revisited it will open up scope for the Spanish to reintroduce the whole Gibraltar sovereignty issue. When we speak he is actually perfectly relaxed and is sensible enough to understand that there is no way the whole Deal will be reopened, and that any step forward will be through an addendum or codicil which explains the backstop and perhaps agrees a legally binding interpretative codicil.

Nice chat with the PM during the 4pm division. She asked me if I might speak to Fabian. I said I'd already done so and that he was not as exercised as Number 10 thought. As we were chatting, Mark

Field said, 'Ah. Just the two I was looking for.' He'd just had lunch with John Patten, now in the Lords and a geography tutor at Oxford when she and I were there. She lit up and recalled that he had declined to be her tutor (he was at Hertford College, she was at St Hugh's) for a course on political geography because he, the future MP and Cabinet Minister, considered politics to be only his hobby. I said, 'And so it remained!' It's the most I've seen her laugh ever.

Ed says I was mentioned affectionately by the PM at lunch in the Dining Room after PMQs. There was a comment about ministers feeling they had to look old and serious. 'Alan wouldn't like that,' said someone. 'No indeed,' she said. 'For him it's all about still looking young.'

Thursday 31 January – London

PM has had talks with Corbyn, not that they will lead to very much.

Memorial service for Lord Carrington in Westminster Abbey. This is what Henry Kissinger had come over for. Fantastically well attended, and one just felt that a measure of greatness was passing. He was perhaps the last of those who fought in the war who went on to such distinguished public service. There are none like him left any more.

Monday 4 February – Ottawa

Am in Ottawa for an international meeting on Venezuela. It is for the Peruvian-led Lima Group of Latin American countries concerned about Venezuela. A few hours earlier than planned, JH has tweeted that we now recognise Juan Guaidó as its interim President, as Maduro had not called elections by the end of the eight days we all gave him, so he's on his own. We are in good company – Spain, France, Germany, Austria, the Netherlands.

Have a very friendly phone call with DfID Secretary Penny Mordaunt, which I'd been trying to achieve for a week. My pitch was clear – when we lift the lid, Venezuela will be seen as the most pressing country of need in the western hemisphere; it affects its neighbours too, who are hosting 3 million migrants; our current activity comprising two humanitarian advisers and aid through multilateral organisations looks too flimsy; this is a Global Britain moment; it needs to be part of our broader policy in the continent; it allies us with all the Lima Group countries, along with the US and Canada; we need to gear up now in anticipation; we need to brand it clearly as UK Aid, but be cautious about partnering with US Aid, because of America's rather tainted reputation in the region; in short, it's a moment we must not miss.

The Lima Group meeting is opened by PM Justin Trudeau and chaired by Peruvian FM Néstor Popolizio and Canadian FM Chrystia Freeland.

I can't make out whether Trudeau is really handsome, or just nicely so. But he is genuinely likeable and free of any pomposity. His speech set the tone perfectly. The translation of Popolizio's words went slightly wonky, stating that 'we'd like to thank Canada for the excellent hospitalisation given to all the delegates'.

There were video messages from Juan Guaidó and opposition leader Leopoldo López, who is under house arrest. Then Mike Pompeo.

I then do my bit, very freestyle, saying how we must work out how the momentum that has built up can be translated into effective pressure on Maduro. I pointedly say we must speak with one voice 'without diversion, duplication or delay', which was designed to echo the Group's anger with FedMog for pressing ahead with her plans for an EU-driven international contact group, which they all feel would lead to a false dialogue.

Good encounter with Brazil FM Ernesto Araújo. How nice for him that he arrived in a private jet. It seems you have to be a developing country to warrant such luxury travel.

Air Canada to Heathrow overnight.

Tuesday 5 February – London
Commons Committee to adopt the Kimberley Process, which regulates the trade in rough diamonds. At the end I tease the committee chair Nigel Evans, saying: 'It has the added advantage, Mr Evans, of making me a greater expert in rough trade than even you, sir. I commend the regulations to the committee.'

I tell Nick Boles, who is facing deselection in Grantham, that if he wants some local support I'm there to help. He smiles with a hint of resignation. 'I rather want them to deselect me …' I quietly empathise.

Wednesday 6 February – London
Another pre-Brexit day: fifty-one to go.

JH's latest take on the Brexit talks is that he is more optimistic that the EU27 generally might be becoming more flexible; the Irish are taking a hard line but have no solution and think we might crumble; the next EU Council is on 21 March, which might possibly mean we will face a vote on the 24th … just when I'm due to be in Cuba with the Prince of Wales. He thinks Angela Merkel will intervene to stop No Deal – German FM Heiko Maas said as much to JH last week at the Gymnich in Bucharest.

If the PM gets a deal in Brussels this week there will be a vote on it next Wednesday; if not then there will be an amendable motion next Thursday.

The PM is in Northern Ireland and will be in Brussels tomorrow, but there is just no suggestion of any sort that she is set to make any progress on anything. And she certainly looks less likely to do so after Donald Tusk says at a podium, 'I've been wondering what the special place looks like in hell for those who promoted Brexit without even a sketch of a plan on how to carry it out safely.' Good for Tusk. He is spot on, but his comments are the perfect gift to those who wish to express anti-EU outrage.

At the No Deal ministerial meeting chaired by Chris Heaton-Harris, Kit Malthouse and Richard Harrington became the naughty corner by chuntering constantly that the meeting was a waste of time and should be between officials, not ministers.

Nice gathering in the Reform to celebrate fifty years of MORI – research not polling is their preferred term – now Ipsos MORI. Sir Bob Worcester founded it and has been the lynchpin ever since. A good mix of media types, politicians of all colours and all sorts of other grandees.

Another day. Continuing Brexit mayhem. We are no further forward. Gloom. Gloom. Gloom.

Sunday 10 February – Rutland/London

Adam Boulton's article in the *Sunday Times* begins with an anonymous reference to our encounter at the MORI party. 'It's a measure of the state of politics that a senior minister at a party in the heart of London's clubland said that he hates half his party, and that any of them who think we can hold on to those 20 or so seats we currently hold by less than 1000 must need their head examined.'

Monday 11 February – London

Gavin Williamson has made a bizarre speech at RUSI saying defence must be more lethal. As a contribution to our public debate, it seems to lack any intellectual content.

Tuesday 12 February – London

Worrying text from Fabian Picardo. He says the main betting company in Gibraltar, because of Brexit, is threatening to move to Malta, partly because it is being offered inducements which are illegal under EU law. It would remove 40 per cent of the Rock's tax revenue, all the more so as others would follow.

To the Parliamentary Education Centre to speak to twenty students from Uppingham School. The first question was designed to be a bit of a trick question for me as the local MP, but backfired hilariously. 'So … have you ever been to Uppingham?' 'Yes – I live there and am a Trustee of your school.'

Thursday 14 February – London

Valentine's Day. It's eleven years since I proposed to James!

To the Home Office for what turned out to be an inexcusably unacceptable meeting about visas. Hardly a day goes by when we don't get representations from ambassadors and foreign ministers about the expense and offensiveness of the UK visa system. A few simple changes could overcome so many problems, and all it needs from the Home Office is the willingness to engage. Even before I could put my case and offer some ideas, Caroline Nokes was extremely aggressive, and had clearly been worked into a lather ahead of my arrival. It was a classic example of how such needless territorial defensiveness can make government completely dysfunctional.

More EU votes. The government loses 258–303. Rumours of big breaking news due at 8pm. It turns out only to be a *House* magazine interview with Richard Harrington ...

Friday 15 February – Munich

Last night's vote was not binding and didn't really decide anything substantive, but it determines the fundamental backdrop against which the PM is negotiating and so determines the basis on which she will be able to deliver anything she might finally agree with the Commission. What this fanatical ERG lot refuse to acknowledge is that across Europe, and sadly much more widely, we are seen as fools. It looks as though our political system is in meltdown – which it is – and our international standing is in freefall. Last night sixty-seven of them abstained, and five of them voted against the government. That's a fifth of the parliamentary Party against her. After the series of votes a week or so ago, it seemed we had a truce of sorts, but that has now been dynamited by the fuckwits in the ERG.

The real crunch point is coming at the end of the month. The vote on the 27th is probably the whopper. The vacuous little upstart Steve Baker shamelessly tells *Today* how fair-minded he's been, but his constant use of the word 'we' to describe how reasonable 'we' have been and how 'we' are allowing the PM to do this and that is the language of a party within a party deigning to give her permission to do anything. In an ideal world we would expel the lot of them and make them join Nigel Farage's newly constituted Brexit Party, which is where they belong.

Munich Security Conference. Breakfast with Richard Moore and staff.

Opening session with Gavin Williamson and German Defence Minister Ursula von der Leyen. GW makes some unduly aggressive comments about Russia. He possesses no diplomatic subtlety. His comments about sending our new aircraft carrier HMS *Queen Elizabeth* to the South China Sea has led to the Chinese cancelling

Philip Hammond's planned visit. It wasn't even contained in the speech, and appeared as a story in the papers after some over-zealous spinning. Williamson is blaming it on his SpAd, yet he always tends to ingratiate himself with journalists by spinning personally. He is a liability.

Join him later for bilateral with Senator Lindsey Graham and US congressional delegation. GW goes on about when he was Chief Whip, which doesn't work with them because they simply don't understand what he's talking about. Bizarre.

Saturday 16 February – Munich/Rutland

My planned bilateral meeting with Deputy Russian Foreign Minister Vladimir Titov has satisfactorily landed on the neutral ground of the Munich Security Conference. A large room has been set up with nothing but a large table at one end with the Russian flag facing the Union Jack, with accompanying officials kept to two each; we have a two-hour meeting. On one level it is straightforward and predictable, and contains a firm reprise of our rebukes over the Salisbury poisoning and their interference in Ukraine and Georgia. He is a perfectly cordial interlocutor, but unfortunately he is the representative of a president whose conduct is way outside anything that is decent and proper. There is no other political setting in which any similar exchange has taken place for years.

Bump into George Osborne in the foyer. As soon as 'Private Pike' Williamson spots him, he immediately drops all his bilateral meetings, to the fury of his private office staff, both civil and military, choosing instead the opportunity to suck up to George.

Speaking myself to George later, he still thinks Boris can or will win the leadership. He says it'll be a quick three-part sequence: a ConHome poll putting Boris at the top; then good survey numbers among MPs; then building up his coalition with opportunists like Hancock backing him in return for the promise of a job. I say Boris doesn't have as much support as he thinks, and reiterate my oft-made point that even if he were to win, he might not be able to retain a governing majority in the Commons.

Brief encounter with Jared Kushner. There is something unusually baby-faced and attractive about him, which is very annoying as I'd expected and wanted to find him inherently dislikeable.

Sunday 17 February – Rutland/London
Seeing Boris in the corridor last week, I noticed he'd taken off more than half his hair. The tousled blond mop had been turned into a scraggy layer resembling the lunar surface. It means he's on manoeuvres. It's therefore no surprise to hear this morning that he intends to make a speech casting himself as the champion of social justice and business enterprise. It's so naked, so brazen. He is gradually splitting the Party.

Walk Noodle by the river.

Then the fun starts … My chairman Byron Rhodes sends me a short email saying that there is a plot afoot for the 15 March constituency AGM to put Brexiteers in all my Association committee positions (such as they are). His reason for saying so is that Frances Rutland has been quizzing him about the rules for the meeting (which as President she will chair), especially in respect of the tabling of motions. The poisonous Christine Emmett has also been fishing around, asking about no-confidence rules. So it's the same old nasty gang at play, the same cast of characters who caused trouble at the Executive Meeting in January.

Just as I'm about to call Byron back, Chris Hope of the *Telegraph* calls. 'Apparently there is to be a motion of no confidence in you at your AGM in March.' Good old Chris – he's no slouch on these things. I laughed and said, 'It'll be one of three people who will have phoned you – Frances Duchess of Rutland, Geoffrey Pointon or Christine Emmett.' I explained to him that because I've already been readopted, there's no provision in the rules for a motion of no confidence to have any effect. He thinks this sort of thing is happening in a lot of constituencies.

I then speak to Byron and tell him that someone has already phoned the *DT* to say there will be a motion of confidence against me. He is aghast. But I'm rather pleased, as should the *DT* print something tomorrow it will usefully put the issue out into the open. Byron will assist in every possible way.

I feel totally relaxed about the danger. Given that I've just been reselected as the candidate only a few weeks ago, and given that they have no grounds for any complaint, such as having defied the whip or having said that I'll quit the Party for any reason, they don't have a leg to stand on. They have no cogent arguments: they are just hideous people. But quite who is the source of the call to the *DT* is a bit of a mystery.

Monday 18 February – London

The *Daily Telegraph* carries little bits about deselection. It notes that I have already been readopted, and focusses more on a similar threat to Sarah Wollaston in her constituency. As a story, it is utterly groundless beyond one malicious phone call to Chris Hope.

Rather touchingly, John Major calls to express outrage at the story and offering to help. It is typical of the man that he should do so. I was able to reassure him that it was all nonsense and wouldn't go anywhere, but is sadly reflective of the state of the Party. Meanwhile, seven Labour MPs have quit theirs to form their own anti-Corbyn breakaway group. It could be a big moment, or it might come to nothing.

Tuesday 19 February – London

Meeting with senior official Caroline Wilson on how we should or should not engage with extremist MPs and parties across Europe.

Fruitful meeting with Mark Sedwill in his office, primarily on banking the comprehensive agreement with Oman.

Dinner with James and Noodle in the nearby Italian. At the next table is Howard Leigh, now in the Lords. A charming financier and fundraiser for the Party, he sits at the sensible end of CFI – he is invariably polite and mild-mannered, and has no angular qualities. His only weakness is that he is seemingly oblivious to the counter-productive manoeuvrings of Polak and Pickles.

Wednesday 20 February – London

After the seven from Labour yesterday, three of our MPs resign from the Party today – Heidi Allen, Anna Soubry and Sarah Wollaston. They join what is now called the Independent Group.

Friday 22 February – Rutland

My local papers are fine about the supposed deselection story. They know enough not to take it seriously.

Rudd, Gauke and Clark have made it clear they will walk unless No Deal is ruled out, while Ian Austin has now also left the Labour Party, but will not join the Independent Group.

Sunday 24 February – Rutland/London

As I am driving back to London, it is announced that the PM, who is in Sharm el Sheikh for an EU–Arab summit, has said that the vote on Wednesday will not be a meaningful vote after all and that it has been deferred to 12 March. Bloody hell!

Monday 25 February – London

St George's Barracks letter exchange with Gavin Williamson. He has actually been very helpful in confirming that when redeveloping the barracks they are content to see a maximum of about 2,000 houses over the twenty years, which is far better than the 4,000–5,000 that would probably result from unrestrained development by a series of housebuilders.

With echoes of his speech before Christmas, comparing the EU to the Soviet Union, JH has made a gaffe in Slovenia, calling it a former slave of the USSR, which it never was.

Summit of EU leaders and the League of Arab States at Sharm el Sheikh; it's co-chaired by Donald Tusk and President Sisi of Egypt. As always in our media it is entirely Brexit-focussed. There are some pretty creepy scenes of the PM playing snooker with the Italian PM Giuseppe Conte. I'm not sure she'd ever played before.

Meanwhile Dutch PM Rutte was scathing about the UK's approach: he says the UK looks awful, and we are sleepwalking into

No Deal, but nobody knows what the UK view is. It's a bit rich when the EU just says no to any view we ever do express.

Meeting of like-minded frontbenchers in Room W2. Letwin makes a pitch for the amendment, tabled by him and Yvette Cooper, which would rule out a No Deal exit.

I called Steve Swinford of the *DT* to say that there is a head of steam building up, and that ministers intend to support the Letwin amendment. The WhatsApp group was looking more and more determined.

Tuesday 26 February – London

Richard Harrington, Claire Perry and Margot James have written a joint article in the *Mail* calling on the PM to rule out No Deal. Meanwhile Labour have moved to supporting a second referendum, but without saying what the question would be. Everything is in turmoil.

Alistair Burt has just returned from Egypt on the plane with the PM and all the journalists. He has picked up what will probably happen when the PM makes her statement to the House today. She will say that if there is No Deal by 12 March she will test and then follow the will of the House. Let's see.

See one of Germany's largest fund managers. He is quite well informed about Brexit, but as with most Germans cannot grasp that Brexit is definitely going to happen.

The FCO legal team brief me on the ICJ [International Court of Justice] judgment on the Chagos Islands, which isn't a judgment at all, despite the campaigners' wishes and claims – it's an opinion which requires us to do nothing different.

FCO Orals. They go fine, although some colleagues ask a different supplementary from the one they said they would. But I was able to answer firmly and crisply on Ukraine, Venezuela and marine protected areas.

I was next to the PM for the last few minutes of questions before her statement. The Cabinet had been meeting for nearly three hours beforehand, and it soon became clear that it was a tense one. The saintly three – Clark, Gauke and Rudd – had held the line against salvoes from Leadsom, Truss, Williamson and Javid.

The PM agreed that if the Commons fails to back her Deal on or by 12 March, she will bring forward a motion that allows the House to choose to leave with a Deal or No Deal, or delay. It amounts to a guarantee that we can vote to block a No Deal exit on 29 March if her Deal fails to get through on the 12th. There will be a vote on the 13th to agree to or reject No Deal: No Deal will be decisively rejected. Then on the 14th we will be able to vote for a delay: the House would vote in favour of delay. That's something the EU then would have to agree to. But then they would.

Meeting with our Ambassador to Argentina, Mark Kent. We are in good nick with them. The new flights are being negotiated; about 110 of the 120 Argentine soldier corpses in Darwin Cemetery have been DNA-identified. All of which is good news, but the looming problems are their autumn elections and any Falklands attempt to drill for oil.

Internal meeting on Ecuador, who have gone quiet on pushing Assange out of the embassy despite saying that it was going to happen on 9 January. It looks as though their Foreign Minister had said it would happen without explicitly telling the President. Assange is not mentally stable; he has been defecating in wastepaper bins; he has taken delivery of a number of oxygen tanks (for reasons nobody can discern, but they can't make a bomb); and the Ambassador is concerned he might turn violent. It is a disgusting situation. I insist we lay a clear paper trail tracking our constant demands that he be evicted, and that we are increasingly anxious about his health and mental state.

Bump into Greg Clark and Claire Perry. They say the PM is furious with them both for the forthright views they expressed at Cabinet (Claire attends as a minister of state, God knows why). TM doesn't like being told what to do. Tough. She has been pandering to the ERG for too long.

The key thing for the PM to realise is that she is not negotiating with the EU nearly as much as she is negotiating with the ERG. So ruling out No Deal shoots the ERG fox and is far more important a negotiating step than anything we might do with the Commission.

But she doesn't get it. This has been a good day, and Clark, Gauke and Rudd deserve high praise. So do Perry, Harrington and James. The disappointing aspect of it is the PM's reluctance to face down the ERG, despite their constant undermining of her efforts. She has only ended up doing so by accident, because she has at last been forced into a corner by the rational members of her Cabinet. David Mundell is also one of the good guys.

Sajid Javid bans Hizbollah. They are 'terrists'. Their 'terrist' activity is deplorable. He is inarticulate and just sucking up to the CFI, who are out in force behind him reading out their scripted interventions. He is always trying too hard and lacks any poise or dignity. Meanwhile Polak and Pickles are in the Peers' Gallery gloating from above about having deployed their Commons troops in Israel's cause. We are supposed to be Great Britain, but I fear we are too willing to let others pull our strings.

Supper in the Tea Room with Bob Neill and Greg Clark. I congratulate Greg on his courage and adept politics.

Today has marked a new record winter temperature, in excess of 20 degrees.

The *Daily Telegraph* headline illustrates just how stupid the paper has become: 'Delaying Brexit is a plot to stop it'. No it isn't. Any risk that might ever exist of Brexit not happening at all will be entirely down to the antics of the ERG. Rees-Mogg says it's a deliberate attempt by May to block Brexit. He is bonkers.

Wednesday 27 February – London

Danny Finkelstein's article in *The Times* exactly echoes my thoughts, even finding similar language. He says he explained to a hard-Leaver, 'The Government isn't just negotiating with the EU; it's also negotiating with you.' Precisely. Then Moggy sounds ridiculous on *Today*. Apart from his pompous, overmannered 'Good morning, Mr Robinson', he was in a fantasy land of nitpicking nonsense and proved himself incapable of seeing the big picture and admitting that it is he and the ERG who are the wreckers and blockers, not the Remainers who are trying to bank the PM's exit Deal. He thinks he's clever: he is not.

Patrick Forbes and the Channel 4 Brexit documentary team came to do some more filming. I praise the Cabinet three, and say we are in a better position today thanks to them. Noodle features in the filming, so they are bound to use it.

Mike Freer advises that the Cooper–Boles amendment to avoid No Deal is still on the Order Paper. It will probably be withdrawn. Alberto Costa, although a PPS (to Mundell in the Scottish Office), has tabled an amendment which would recognise the enduring rights of all EU citizens in the UK, and has secured Corbyn in support. He will be sacked as a PPS. It might look bad to the public that he is to be dismissed for promoting a decent cause, but he has usurped the role of government, and we now have no negotiating leverage to get reciprocal rights for UK citizens in each of the EU27.

Jeremy is precise when he says (as we all know) that we have a simple ask of the EU Commission – we need enough from them to get the Attorney General to change his advice to the Government on the Northern Ireland backstop, which says it may in practice prove more inflexible than intended. The EU can now focus on this. The Foreign Secretary thinks the EU will give us something before 12 March.

Good chat with Hamish Cowell in Muscat. We are as good as there with the Comprehensive Agreement. They have composed a Declaration to be signed there by the Foreign Secretary on Friday, but its content is itself more than half of the text of the broader agreement. We decide to be relaxed about it and settle for both in succession. Don't see it as duplication: see it as binding in all parts of the Omani system.

I brief Jeremy on the character and history of the Sultan. I think he takes it all in. I talk him through the agreement and the Iran issue. I also alert him to a looming problem with the Home Office who want to abolish all domestic worker visas. They have not consulted anybody, and accepting their proposal would destroy our Gulf Strategy and cause maximum offence to any senior Arab who wanted to visit the UK with his family and staff. It's nuts. No Home secretary has ever got to grips with the issue of visas.

Kashmir has been simmering away for the last two days on the edge of conflict. An Indian pilot has been captured in Pakistan after his fighter jet was shot down. It is one of the world's most dangerous flashpoints. We of course get the blame for it, as the former colonial power. The partition between India and Pakistan saw a Muslim population in Kashmir remain part of India because the Maharajah was a Hindu … and so it's gone on. It is insoluble.

Today was due to be the dramatic day of Brexit votes, but after yesterday the mood has settled. We vote as planned, but the majorities are all fine for the government. All eyes are now on 12 March.

Friday 1 March – Rutland
JH is in Oman … Pictures emerge of him crossing his legs during the audience, which I specifically briefed him not to do, as it is very bad manners in the Arab world. It is like slouching or picking your nose. A couple of my Omani friends text me the snaps with a ring around the crossed legs, as it has provoked a bit of social media criticism. But the pictures of his lunch with the Sultan looked excellent.

Monday 4 March – London
Hideous night's sleep, or rather not. I woke up every twenty minutes with a sharp cough, so for the first time in a decade take a day off to recover.

Stay in bed till lunchtime. The news is just so depressing – knife killings, the sex abuse inquiry, appalling police conduct while infiltrating animal rights activists, etc – that I can't bear to listen to the radio. It just makes Britain seem so grotty.

I'm feeling a lot better by the time James arrives and cooks a lovely salmon pasta.

Wednesday 6 March – London
Gavin Barwell briefing for junior ministers in the Grimond Room. All a bit facile. But he confirms that, in the event of a motion that blocks a 29 March No Deal exit, we will not be whipped to vote against it.

Thursday 7 March – London

Attorney General Geoffrey Cox is in Brussels to try to thrash things out, but next week's votes are looking grim.

Interesting snippets from a senior Cabinet Office official: Mark Sedwill has pulled out of the running to be the next Ambassador to Washington because he feels obliged to stay put as Cabinet Secretary/NSA to navigate the government through its turmoil. Typically dutiful and noble of him to volunteer for the short straw.

Sunday 10 March – Austria

A nice skiing weekend.

A crucial Brexit week is looming, with meaningful vote set for Tuesday. But there is a sense of despair, and the ERG idiots are flexing their muscles.

Bump into John Kerry in the ski shop. He was wearing a US Air Force bomber jacket, looking very *Top Gun*.

Monday 11 March – London

There's a deep mood of pessimism, with the BBC reporting first thing that Brexit talks have stalled. All morning journalists are phoning to speculate whether the motion on Tuesday will be tabled, and quite what it will be. Might it be one which says that the House supports the Deal, but only if the backstop is amended? Will the PM table it at all? It's bewilderment rather than frenzy. Then there is a rumour that her plane is on standby to go to Strasbourg. The underlying assumption is that we are still heading for a thumping defeat tomorrow.

Baroness [Cathy] Ashton comes in to discuss the Balkans. She is great, and a former EU High Representative. My straightforward debate in Westminster Hall last week about Kosovo has been seized on as evidence that the UK supports the Kosovan PM against both his own President, Thaçi, and the Serbs. It's all nonsense, as all I said (or was told to say) was that we don't favour land swaps as part of any discussions between Kosovo and Serbia. But then it's the Balkans, so nothing is wholly subject to reason.

Putin is trying to make Russia–UK relations appear normal by inviting a small delegation of UK businesses to see him in the

Kremlin. It might comprise Bob Dudley of BP, someone from Glencore, Ian [Taylor] from Vitol, and Charles Hendry in his capacity as Chair of the UK–Russia Chamber of Commerce. We will just have to go along with it, and I can't see it will do any damage. The fact that Charles is part of it should give us confidence that the event and subsequent comments are in safe hands.

Then from about 4pm there's a definite buzz, as the PM flies off to Strasbourg amid a growing mood of optimism that a deal is afoot. DUP non-Commons leader Arlene Foster is spotted in the Commons and may have been in to see the Chief.

Have a drink in the Smoking Room with Andrew Bowie, Ed Argar, Seema Kennedy, Victoria Atkins, Oliver Heald. Andrew is suitably discreet, but is ready to be on duty for a David Lidington statement to the Commons at 10pm. The buzz is truly buzzing. I look Andrew in the eye for a serious moment and say that if this is indeed the moment, and the DUP say they are with us, then we should press the nuclear button and threaten anyone on our side who fails to support the Deal with the withdrawal of the whip.

Dinner with Argar, Kennedy, Atkins, Heald, Menzies. Chat with Nigel Dodds at the DUP table who is clearly hopeful that the breakthrough is real. The DUP are absolutely the key. If we have them, we have a chance. If we don't, we don't.

David Lidington makes his statement at 10pm, but starts by saying that talks are still going on, so not quite making a definitive and conclusive announcement. He nonetheless says they have secured legally binding changes to the backstop and the Withdrawal Agreement, thus dangling in front of the House the hint of substantive progress. But will Nigel Dodds say that it is enough?

Tuesday 12 March – London
On the way into the FCO I first bump into Richard Harrington, who says he has just had breakfast with Arlene Foster and he feels the DUP might come on board today. It's far from definite that they will. I then encounter Arlene herself on the pavement of Storey's Gate with Laura Kuenssberg of the Beeb. After a warm embrace we each do an interview. I urge all to vote for the Deal tonight.

I text the Chief to say that if we get the DUP on board we should turn the thumbscrews on the ERG and state they will have the whip withdrawn if they fail to support the government tonight. It's the only way to win, and if any defy the whip they become self-disqualifying and a Party split would put them outside the Party and hence not a threat to it thereafter.

The Chief calls back, but focusses on asking me to trawl the tea rooms to rustle up support. I will do my best.

The morning's optimism doesn't last. At about 11am, Geoffrey Cox's advice turns out to be a disaster. His last paragraph 19 says the legal position has not changed, when he could have used much more judicious language – for example, he could have said that, although most of the underlying legal assumptions remain, the political context in which they are being applied is much more helpful. But he has blown it. We have lost the DUP, and the ERG in the course of the day reassert their stand against the PM and her Deal.

Discuss with Andrew Bowie, and later Graham Brady, the prospect of making the vote a de facto matter of confidence, but the whole option soon evaporates as it becomes increasingly clear that the DUP will not support the Deal. Brady thinks that the Gauke–Clark–Rudd trio are equally deserving of being expelled for threatening to vote against No Deal whatever: which shows how mad everyone's judgement has become.

The PM launches the debate, but has almost no voice. I feel for her. She may be boring, but she is a million times more worthy than all those around her.

Meaningful vote. Ayes 242, Noes 391, defeat by 149. Twenty or so ERG types have come round to support the PM, but most of them are still against. Damn the lot of them – Mogg, Johnson and Baker above all.

Texted Nicky Morgan to chastise her for calling for Theresa to go. She is unrepentant, saying it's all May's fault for setting all her red lines. I text back that they're all the fault of the ERG, and she's hitting the wrong target. She is not up to much: promoted too quickly, then binned, now bitter, with poor judgement and behaving self-indulgently.

What a crap day for the country.

Wednesday 13 March – London

Nice bunch around the breakfast table: Dominic Grieve, Neil O'Brien, Antoinette Sandbach. Quite a hint of gallows humour after last night, and then we discovered that given a chance we'd all now like to vote to revoke Article 50. It became heretics corner. But more cheerful as a result. From what I've been told, all it would take is a short bill to authorise revocation and the repeal of the Withdrawal Act.

The ministerial meeting with Hunt, Burt, Baldwin, Field and Freer. We are all unable to work out what happens next. I strongly put my case for making the Deal a matter of confidence as soon as the DUP come on board. If she hadn't called the disastrous election of 2017 we'd have been able to do that already, but the arithmetic of a minority government has put us at the mercy of everything else.

Head to the Commons to vote in the deferred divisions [you just sign a bit of paper for minor issues] and chat with Whip Alister Jack. He is very canny, and the list of MPs in his flock is full of ERG bolshies. Vicky Ford has just come from a meeting of the moderate ministers, and is convinced some of them are on the edge of resignation and/or rebellion for tonight's votes.

Ecuador Ambassador Jaime Marchán. He is determined to get Assange out of his embassy, but President Moreno requires a final push in order to be persuaded to press the button.

And then the rout starts. The government motion states that we are not to leave on 29 March without a Deal, but that No Deal remains the default position in law. As a sort of OK motion, we can all live with it, as it rules out No Deal at least for the short term. The Spelman amendment rules out No Deal completely, which we know is the view of the House, but it is against government policy. Spelman withdraws her amendment, but it is pressed by co-signatory Yvette Cooper. The government loses by just four, 312 to 308. The next amendment, moved by Damian Green and backed by the ERG, is a completely undeliverable version of the 'Malthouse compromise' under which we would leave in May, pay a fee and uphold certain undefined standstill agreements. It's rubbish and is rejected 164 to 374 on a free vote. I abstain.

But then the place explodes. The government motion, now amended to become a wholesale anti-No Deal motion, is to be whipped against, but there's a revolt. The group I sometimes attend have met downstairs and are not prepared to be whipped against it. It's quite a list: Gauke, Clark, Rudd, Mundell – all from the Cabinet, plus Perry, who attends it. Also Burt, Ellwood, James, Buckland, [Steve] Brine, Harrington, [Sarah] Newton. They all insist on abstaining. The Whips are in meltdown. Andrew Bowie brushes past the front bench. I tell him there's a revolt whirring on the WhatsApp group. He says he knows, and that they are being told they can go home but not vote in favour of the amended motion. In an outburst of uncontrolled frenzy, discipline collapses. The government tries but fails to whip against the motion, and collective responsibility goes down the plughole. The No Deal motion, as amended, passes 321–278. It is total, utter meltdown.

The PM makes a statement reasserting her position. But her authority has vanished. Needless to say, the shits in the ERG say that the ministers who abstained should be sacked. Sarah Newton resigns as a DWP minister. The whole pack of cards is collapsing. It is exactly what I said would happen when I wrote to Mogg last July telling him to back off or else risk sinking the ship. It is all the fault of the ERG. TV coverage has gone haywire. It could not be worse. It has reached the point where it may prove impossible to piece together any vestige of credible government.

Thursday 14 March – London/Rutland

Lord (David) Triesman comes in, an ex-foreign minister himself, to talk about Cuba. He is in despair about the Labour Party, even saying he would not feel safe as a Jewish person living in the UK if Corbyn became Prime Minister. That strikes me as a little over-fearful, but it's a sure sign of what people are beginning to think.

Friday 15 March – Rutland

There has been a hideous attack in Christchurch, New Zealand, in which a gunman moved from one mosque to another and shot fifty people dead.

The Deal might come back on Tuesday. We must get the DUP on board or it's over. Talks are due over the weekend.

As if the week in Parliament has not been bad enough, my Annual General Meeting in the constituency turns out even worse. Its timing could not be more unfortunate.

In my speech, I do not hold back. I say that the government is trying to honour the referendum but leave in a responsible way. Those who are constantly voting against the Prime Minister are forcing a choice between No Deal and No Brexit. I slam the ERG and those on our own side who have been so rebellious. My key paragraph left them in no doubt where I stood: 'If there is anyone in this room who would rather support this bunch of rebels instead of the government we are here to support, then please – just get up, and get out.' Stunned silence.

Monday 18 March – London

My survey of all embassies is beginning to throw up some indisputable evidence of how our visa regime is detrimental to our national interests. So many countries despise us for the way we treat them. The charges are exorbitant, the terms and conditions offensive, and we often send one country's passports off to another for processing, which so gets up their nose. With modern technology, why can't all of this be done without passports physically moving from one capital to another?

An explosive statement from the Speaker. Without formally being asked by anybody, he unilaterally rules that we cannot bring back the same motion to the House on the Withdrawal Agreement. This completely fossilises the deadlock. No doubt in the Speaker's mind he hopes it will instead open up options to block Withdrawal altogether. There's a lot about me which in my heart just wishes that we could bring an end to this process by pressing the reset button and concluding that exit won't work, so we'll just stay in. But I feel even more strongly that Parliament must be allowed to function as it chooses, and that a Commons victory counts for nothing if it is won on the back of the Speaker's bias. I would far rather lose honourably than win deceitfully. I'm sure we will find an ingenious way of getting around the Speaker's ruling.

So there we have it: last week the Speaker declined to call an amendment tabled by Chris Bryant on the convention about bringing back the same motion within the same session, and today he single-handedly ruled that it will not be permitted. It potentially prohibits the PM from bringing the meaningful vote back again. We all think he did so against the advice of the Clerks, and has pre-emptively ruled on it when the issue had not yet properly arisen. He is thus bypassing his obligation to allow the Commons to test its will. A friend texts me: 'I thought we fought a civil war to stop Parliament and the country from being governed by one man.'

Wednesday 20 March – London

Total gloom. Nobody knows what is going to happen. The PM is due to write to Donald Tusk to request a delay, but nobody knows quite what she is going to say. Long, short, what for?

Ministerial team meeting. Hunt just doesn't exude enough purpose or authority. Lots of rational thinking, but not enough grit. The Speaker's ruling at least stopped us having a vote this week: we didn't have the DUP on board anyway. The EU might allow an extension, or maybe it won't. Later on Tusk says we can't have a short extension unless we have passed the Deal vote: implying but not saying that we can only have a very long one. What a muddle and mess.

A senior government figure gave me some candid thoughts: the PM has no grip; the people around her are awful; she has no personality; her relations with other EU leaders are awful. It's not exactly an indiscretion – it confirms what everyone else thinks.

The Speaker allows DExEU Shadow Keir Starmer an immediate emergency debate on delay and all its consequences. It's little more than an opportunity for anyone and everyone to give the government a kicking.

I spend most of the day pacing up and down the office trying to work out what on earth might happen next.

The PM's performance at PMQs was construed as an attack on Parliament for its failure to reach a decision. It went down like a bag of cold sick. She is there because replacing her would prove so chaotic, but in truth she has only grudging support and there is no affection for her. She is on her own. She's like a single flaking old pit prop: everyone knows it will collapse, but dares not touch it to wedge in a replacement in case the roof falls in first.

So useless and cack-handed is Number 10 that when asking the Opposition to come and see her, they put Corbyn and the TIGs [The Independent Group] together, so on seeing Labour defector Chuka Umunna in the same room, Jeremy Corbyn walked out. All revealed by Vince Cable in a Sky interview. Cable has turned seventy but looks eighty, and has announced he will stand down as Liberal Leader in May.

The Sensibles meet in Anne Milton's office at 6.30pm. I chat with David Gauke and Richard Harrington outside the door beforehand, but don't stay for the meeting itself. I'll get a read-out from Vicky Ford, but the mood is funereal. The PM has no authority left; we all hate the ERG; we fear we are closer to No Deal; we want to block or delay, but feel powerless. It is hopeless.

The PM's much heralded statement in Downing Street slips a bit beyond 8.15pm. It turns out to be an utterly robotic damp squib. All it does is restate the obvious. It's what we know already with nothing new or significant. Conor Burns tweets rather acidly, 'What was the point of that?' Indeed, what was the point of it? It was excruciating. It clumsily noted that Parliament had proved incapable of reaching agreement, which, although true, will again be seen as an attack on MPs personally.

What a crappy day. We are in meltdown and seem to be on an unstoppable journey to national humiliation and decline. Fuck-a-doodle-doo!

Thursday 21 March – London
Mum's eighty-eighth birthday. She is in crackingly good nick.

The PM has headed off to Brussels again. Out of my office window I saw her leave with Gavin Barwell at the back of Number 10 at about 11am. Her statement last night was a disaster. MPs think she was blaming them and so have erupted in (fake?) indignation. She looks beleaguered in Brussels. The latest is that if we pass the Deal we can extend until 22 May, but if we don't we can extend only until 12 April.

The charming President Trump has unilaterally recognised Israel's 1967 annexation of the Golan Heights from Syria, even though they are not his to give away.

A petition to Parliament calling on the government to revoke Article 50 has gathered over 1 million signatures in little more than twenty-four hours.

Yet another vexed issue which has arisen, reflecting the Cabinet sub-committee I was attending, is whether data can be exchanged across borders when we leave. To be legal the UK requires data adequacy assessments: if we don't have them in place with the EU it could impede everything from Interpol to insurance.

Saturday 23 March – Rutland

A gloomy mood of deadlock and decay. The PM suggested last night that she would not bring the Deal to the House next week if she thought she couldn't get it through, and has written to all MPs to say that her door is open. Er …

The DUP have said that they will not support it. So indicative votes are on the way, but with nobody in charge. This is a series of votes which are designed to express the opinion of the House, but they won't lead to anything conclusive. Lidington is being peddled as a possible caretaker, but nobody at all in the Cabinet has any authority: too many are linked to leadership ambition (although not Lidders), and the prospect of the PM going and a leadership contest starting is alarming. Steve Baker says the process (I guess he means the Brexit negotiation process) has been taken over by the wrong sort of Conservative.

I text George Osborne to commend his interview on the *Today* programme, in which he argued for a long delay to Brexit and possibly even a second referendum. I see no chance of the latter ever happening, and say that a leadership contest would create utter carnage, albeit we could just revoke and withstand a few weeks of rioting!

Perhaps a million have joined the People's Vote march in London.

My regard for Jeremy Hunt has dipped somewhat. In the last couple of days he has failed to condemn Trump for saying that the Golan Heights now belong to Israel; he wanted to cancel the Prince of Wales' trip to Cuba because of US disapproval; he declined to issue a statement after Nursultan Nazarbayev said he would stand down in Kazakhstan; and he made the UK vote against a motion in the UN criticising Israel's human rights record – even though they killed 180 in Gaza, including children.

Sunday 24 March – Rutland/London

Tim Shipman has done his usual 'ship-stirring' in the *Sunday Times* about a Cabinet coup, although for once there's probably something in it.

I speak to Matt Chorley of *The Times*. We agree there is no easy way for them to get rid of the PM, and no easy way of replacing her. The turd Steve Baker – definitely the wrong sort of Conservative – is at it again. He really is a militant entryist with messianic self-belief.

The Sensibles WhatsApp is very anxious. Richard Harrington says he will resign if ministers are not allowed to vote for the Letwin–Cooper–Boles amendment.

Meanwhile, a selection have been invited to Chequers: Boris Johnson, Jacob Rees-Mogg, David Davis, Alistair Burt, Brandon Lewis, the Chief, Dominic Raab, Damian Green, Steve Barclay, Michael Gove, David Lidington, Steve Baker, Iain Duncan Smith. Two or three are decent loyalists, but the others have been given significance, status and a platform which they don't deserve. IDS turns up in an open-top Morgan, while Rees-Mogg takes his son along. I'm not sure which of the two is the greater throwback.

Monday 25 March – London

Briefing for Privy Counsellors on the impact of No Deal. We gather in Conference Room A in 70 Whitehall. The meeting is really designed for the Opposition front bench. Hilary Benn, Ed Miliband and the graceless Emily Thornberry attend.

Andrew Bridgen says that May should go; only a Leaver PM can deliver Brexit; and let's have a general election. He excels at being both nasty and stupid. I berated Tom Tugendhat, who should know better, for his lack of diplomatic good manners in openly criticising the Prince of Wales' visit to Cuba while it was under way. He was totally unrepentant. Cocky little tosser. Manners, Tom Tug, manners. One day you will be above being a thrusting riser (or rising thruster?) and will not want awkward old moments to haunt you. Learn from me!

At our meeting just before lunch with like-minded colleagues in Anne Milton's office our meeting with the PM was confirmed for 6.30pm. We are all rather in the dark about what will happen next in the Commons. Which votes will be when? The third meaningful vote and the indicative votes will take place when? Will they be whipped?

Lunch in the Terrace Cafeteria with Vicky Atkins, Vicky Ford and Simon Hoare.

6.45pm meeting with the PM in her Commons room, alongside a few fellow ministers. She is quite serene. Alistair Burt kicks off with a logical take on the situation: we are all loyal but cannot stomach leaving with No Deal, and at some stage soon will have to put our foot down. Richard Harrington explains his own position in a calm and principled manner, saying directly to the PM that despite knowing her for forty years and acting as the Treasurer of her leadership campaign, he will have no choice but to resign in order to support the Letwin amendment. He says it is the only way to plot a path to a workable alternative to a No Deal exit, should the PM's Deal fail once again to win majority support.

Anne Milton says all the indicative votes must be free and unwhipped, as it's not clear that Letwin will go through tonight without resignations.

I say to the PM that she faces a dilemma we can all see: whether to try to force through her Deal or to try to get the numbers by working cross-party. If we get the DUP on board, then we should put on the thumbscrews and make it an issue of confidence: anyone who then votes against should lose the whip and be expelled from the Party. The ERG are unpersuadable, and 'are out to get you. You need to be prepared to play your nuclear card.'

Everyone is lost and bewildered. It's so easy to have a go at the PM, but what the hell is the alternative?

So to the votes at 10pm. The Letwin amendment passes 329–302. Harrington, Burt and Brine all vote for it and resign. As we awaited the count and heard the result, I sat with the PM on the front bench. She was more chatty than ever and totally relaxed. It was almost as if it wasn't happening.

Tuesday 26 March – London

All-staff meeting on Brexit in the Locarno Room with PUS McDonald and Lindsay Appleby. McDonald doesn't realise that his ingratiating manner just puts people off. He recites his memorised script with impressive intelligence, but then ruins it with a manner which is formulaic and so oozes over-studied sincerity that it makes everyone wince.

I was sitting in the front row, but had to leave during the questions. As I was walking out, the fourth question was 'Is Brexit the most serious constitutional crisis since the civil war?' I was in full view of them all. I nodded agreement visibly to general laughter, and then loudly proclaimed 'YES' as I kept walking.

Saw JH after the staff meeting. He explained that Mark Field will assume all Alistair's Middle East role. He acknowledged that it should be me, but explained that it was because at the moment Mark is an unpaid minister, and this is a way to establish his right to be paid. It is probably true, but I detect the hand of McDonald keeping me away from the Gulf. Who cares? It is only temporary, and Mark is a good guy who will not be tetchy and defensive like Burt, as whose successor I had suggested Philip Dunne or Richard Benyon.

Bob Dudley of BP came to brief me on his recent Moscow visit and his meeting with President Putin.

I bollocked Graham Brady, Chairman of the 1922, for it being reported that he had told the PM her time was up. I told him that we now have rules, and she had won a vote of confidence in December, and that the days of the men in grey suits signing a Leader's death warrant had long since passed. I said he should not forget that we could always have a vote of confidence in him.

Chat with Ed Miliband in the corridor and went through the logic, or lack of it, of having a second referendum. For a former Party leader, he is extraordinarily naive about the complexity of doing so.

On the off-chance, I texted Matt Hancock to see if he could make dinner. He said yes. Took him to Franco's. Amusingly, Kwasi Kwarteng and Alex Burghart were there. It's normally an MP-free zone. I've come to like Matt, having rather resented his progress as Osborne's pet. I told him he'd made a great journey from pushy little shit – and that I should know about that – to becoming a contender who was gaining ground on the inside track. I told him he'd be a certainty if we were suddenly in opposition, but that it was probably too crowded and complicated for him to succeed now. He has a normal human touch which is missing in most of the others who think they should be Prime Minister. He is annoyed that Michael Fallon is supporting Tom Tugendhat: the mere notion is absurd, and shows poor judgement by both of them. I say he should consider buddying up with Jeremy Hunt, and that there are plenty around who would do anything and everything to stop BoJo getting even halfway up the Mall. He thinks Steve Baker turned up to the Chequers meeting without being invited.

Wednesday 27 March – London

It turns out to be a packed and highly charged day. Ministerial team meeting, dominated as usual by the parliamentary process on Brexit. We will tonight have a whole series of indicative votes, but the way they will be conducted remains a bit of a mystery. It feels as though the realistic options that might emerge are a deal, a customs union or a longer deferral. JH thinks that Cameron, had he been in charge, would have orchestrated lots of choices on a free vote in order to pre-empt and avoid the Letwin process taking over. Will it lead to a third meaningful vote on Friday? He also observes that the DUP are obstinate because they are driven by hatred of Irish Taoiseach Leo Varadkar.

Charles Hendry swings by to give his account of his Moscow visit to see Putin. So I have now heard the account of three who attended: Ian Taylor, Bob Dudley and Charles.

Then the Speaker once again as good as says that a meaningful vote cannot be resubmitted because it is not acceptable to keep tabling the same motion again and again. He really is over-asserting himself.

The PM comes to the 1922 Committee at 5pm. The rumours had been flying around all day that she might promise to go, and she sort of did. She said she would stand down once the Deal is through. In other words, vote for me then you can get rid of me. It will diminish her and is a further step in the unstoppable weakening of her authority. Once you go down a slope like this it will make her enemies just push her even harder. They can kill off the Deal, they can kill her off too, but the question they cannot answer is what then? What next? What follows?

I am very anxious about the Speaker's aggressive intervention on procedural matters, which is deliberately picking a fight with the government. He thinks it's a badge of honour: I think it amounts to serious constitutional conflict, not to say abuse of his office. At 8.42pm I went up to him in the Speaker's Chair: 'May I cash in on knowing you for thirty years and have five minutes with you tomorrow? I'm worried about the relationship between the Speaker and Parliament exploding.' He adopts a sour expression and astonishingly retorts, 'That sounds like a threat.'

It's very odd. I could not have been less threatening, and it was a perfectly legitimate request from a Member to the Speaker, but he defaulted to a defensive reaction. I said, 'No, it's not a threat at all – it's a concern about our constitutional plight.' He is neither reasonable nor impartial. He is an angst-ridden oddball on a mission to somewhere, at a time when we need a steady, dignified, authoritative figure in the Speaker's Chair. So I'll back off and not see him.

Bercow selected eight motions, on which we were not whipped: John Baron's in favour of No Deal – I voted No. Nick Boles' common market 2 – Abstained. Corbyn's in favour of a customs union/single market – No. Joanna Cherry's for revocation of Article 50 in the event of No Deal being rejected and the Deal not passing – Aye. Peter Kyle's confirmatory public vote – No. Marcus Fysh's Malthouse Plan B managed No Deal – No. And so on. By 9.30pm none of the eight options wins a majority. Apparently Steve Baker then makes an emotional, ranting, tear-filled speech to the ERG. He is very odd.

A day of frenzy which has achieved nothing.

Thursday 28 March – London

There's a little bit of blowback locally that I 'voted to revoke Article 50'. The precise details are lost on my Association members, but I'm past caring. They are all stuck in a rut and are not open to any informed explanation or persuasion. At least the front page of the *Rutland Times* has a pro-me splash on my road-signs campaign. Something's going right.

A small moment of humour in the Tea Room about Michael Fabricant's infamous hair: 'It's so woven, Axminster has met Westminster.'

FCO stuff. I think I am nearly there with Ecuador to get Julian Assange out of their London embassy. It's taken months of delicate negotiations, but nearly, nearly …

Regular meeting with Simon McDonald. He tries to rebuke me for being so tough in my instructions to ambassadors about responding to my survey on visas. If a minister circulates a requirement to send two pages with their thoughts on the visa system then they should do it without fail. It's why I told them in my instructions to 'do it without fail'. He said some of them complained that the language was too tough. He should have told them to get on with it. Instead he complained to me. I took none of his nonsense and sent him away firmly rebuffed. I was astonished and disappointed by his hopeless management style and attitude.

It now looks as though the PM will bring back half of the Deal, i.e. the Withdrawal Agreement in terms sufficient to extend our exit until 22 May. It is tabled for tomorrow. It won't get through, so we risk an even more intense meltdown.

Friday 29 March – Rutland
Meet Ecuador Ambassador Jaime Marchán. We are so nearly there in getting Assange chucked out of the embassy.

Head to the Commons for the meaningful vote which is due at 2.30pm. Encounter Mark Sedwill at the back of the Speaker's Chair. I say if we don't get this through we will be sliding downhill faster and faster. I show Mark someone's tweet: 'The ERG are only getting behind her today so they can stab her in the back.' We lose by 286–344. The ERG are destroying everything. So it will now go to the Letwin process on Monday. In other words, the government's control over Commons business will be ceded to the backbenches.

Mike Freer at the door of the Aye lobby is welling up and clearly on the edge of tears. He says his life's work in politics is about to be shredded if there's an election.

So 29 March has ended up as 'Not Quite Exit Day'.

Sunday 31 March – Rutland/London
My sixty-second birthday. A lovely day with just James. He gives me a beautiful Beretta photo frame which seems to be begging for a photo of the two of us. We need to print that favourite black and white pic of us in black tie.

Monday 1 April – London
Erdoğan has taken a bashing in the local elections in Turkey, which reflects popular reaction to his authoritarian behaviour.

Foreign Secretary addresses all the FCO staff in the Durbar Court. It is not as echoey as it used to be before the new sound system was put in, but we still couldn't hear a thing because there is a fan or extractor noise whirring away which nobody had thought to switch off. It's the usual stuff about how wonderful everyone is in the FCO, but the mantra about supporting the rules-based international order is becoming rather trite and, given that we are inconsistent in applying it, also untrue.

Nice chat with Jeremy's SpAd Ed Jones afterwards. Philip Dunne is in charge of Jeremy's putative leadership campaign. He is charming and genuine, but is he effective? It needs a high degree of parliamentary knowledge and application with colleagues, and he is probably too gentlemanly.

Awful sad news: MI6 Chief Alex Younger's son has been killed in a Land Rover accident in Scotland. Nothing in life is worse. I weep for him and his wife and everybody. Forget life: death is not fair.

A packed FCO day on Turkey etc. But the day is building up to the further set of indicative votes on Brexit which arise out of the Letwin amendment. People think that 'Norway 2.0' might get through, which would lead to a run-off between the PM's Deal and a trading relationship based on the one Norway has with the EU.

I bump into Mark Sedwill by the Red Lion and afterwards DfID Permanent Secretary Matthew Rycroft in New Palace Yard.

The Speaker selects four of the eight amendments tabled, which are a sort of variation on the indicative votes we had before. Ken Clarke on a customs union; one on a 'Common Market 2' which is an agri-food provision designed to get the DUP on board; the Kyle/Wilson proposal for a confirmatory public vote; and a complicated SNP amendment involving four stages to extend, vote on No Deal, if no to No Deal then revoke, then consult on a referendum. All four are defeated, so we are straight back into deadlock.

As the votes were by recorded division I'd gone home by then and so saw it on TV, but at 10.15pm after the votes Nick Boles, in an emotionally charged moment in the Chamber, resigns the whip. It has been another day of decay.

Tuesday 2 April – London

FCO Orals. Speak to Philip Dunne. He is approaching lots of colleagues quietly, but during leadership elections people become very untrustworthy, and those you recruit early can peel off later unless there is a really firm grip on every minute of their lives.

Drink with Angela Browning in the Peers' Guest Room. She is Chair of the Advisory Committee on Business Appointments which vets new jobs for former ministers under the Cabinet Office rules. I intend to finish as a minister in the summer and return to the private sector. I suspect the government will collapse then anyway, but I am prepared, *in extremis*, to cause a by-election and quietly go. This is no longer a party I feel happy in. Half of my fellow MPs are intolerant ideologues and we just don't share the same principles. They are throwbacks and nationalists; they have no proper sense of international influence and relationships. Their actions will diminish Britain.

A Cabinet meeting has been going on all day. It's a lock-in.

Then finally, after 6pm, and following a seven-and-a-half-hour Cabinet meeting without officials, the PM makes a statement in Number 10 saying she will ask for a short further extension (implicitly to a date between 12 April and 22 May) in order to agree a deal with the Opposition. The approach, it seems, is to reject No Deal and shift to a variation on the Deal towards something much softer. She added that if she cannot agree something with the Opposition then she will put binding options to the House in order to define a route to an outcome. It sort of also pushes the DUP to the sidelines – let's see how that plays out once it dawns on people.

I am rather run down and cannot shake off a chesty cough. Hail and rain. James is in Marrakech, our recess week having been cancelled. But with the House finishing at 5pm, it's nice to have a quiet cosy night at home with Noodle. I've boosted the heating.

Boris slates the PM's announcement in an extensive interview, trying to appear much more serious in tone and parading his new slimness and haircut. It's put him on the back foot, and maybe he fears running out of time in his bid to take over. Meanwhile Ed calls to say the reaction in the Tea Room was viciously anti the PM, with seemingly moderate colleagues turning on her. I don't quite see why, but then everyone is exhausted and ratty. The recess would have started on Thursday, but it has been cancelled and we will sit all through next week.

The next few days are – once again – maybe make or break. But this time it really feels like it. Our divisions and collapse of purpose as a party are paving the way for Corbyn, and then no doubt fairly quickly the more sinister McDonnell. As if the self-harm of Brexit were not enough, the wreckers now want to inflict annihilation on our own Party.

Wednesday 3 April – London

So here we go again. Another day of Brexit votes which probably won't get us anywhere.

Rees-Mogg lost it on *Today*, refusing to condemn the far-right Alternative für Deutschland, and then attacking its presenter Mishal Husain for bias. His faux politeness disguises a streak of arrogant snobbishness.

Our ministerial team meeting. Then constituency stuff to try to piece together financing for the Melton bypass, by arbitrating between Melton Borough Council and Leicestershire County Council, who are in a spat over how to commit enough money to the project out of forecast housing receipts.

The MPs' WhatsApp group is slating the PM for saying she will reach out to Corbyn to seek any cross-party solution that might exist. The thickos are accusing her of 'dealing with a Marxist', and all such crap. Are they so stupid? Yes. Enter stage right that champion dumbo Maria Caulfield. The country and the government are having a nervous breakdown.

Nigel Adams resigns as junior Welsh Minister and Whip. In the Tea Room at lunch I am forced to listen to the lazy certainty of John Redwood's vacuous opinions. 'Oh, the PM's view has already cost us x per cent in the polls.' Very tiresome.

All the Brexit fantasy options have come to be known as unicorns. As a word and emoji symbol in texts, there are unicorns everywhere. The rare sighting of this solitary beast has turned into a stampeding herd.

Have a coffee with Ken Clarke, who is about the only sensible person left. Charming Alex Chalk says we are surrounded by fruit-cakes, loonies and closet racists. We are indeed turning into a mutant UKIP.

Then Chris Heaton-Harris resigns as DExEU minister.

In the corner of the Tea Room, conspiring, are Baker, IDS, Fysh and Paterson, trying to bring down the PM, and hence everything else too.

The 5pm division on the Letwin–Cooper vote will see if his Bill gets through. The division takes ages, and there are rumours of a tie. The two Chief Whips are seen conferring, probably verifying the numbers and comparing pairing lists. We need to defeat the business motion. It is a tie: 310–310. The Speaker rules based on precedent, so the Noes have it. So the main motion is not amended. Then the Letwin amendment gets through 312–311.

The main Raab campaign team looks like Hugo Swire, Robert Syms, Geoffrey Clifton-Brown and Helen Grant.

Dinner with Mark Lancaster and Caroline Dinenage. Great gossip – much of it about Tobias Ellwood and best forgotten!

So, all in all, another shitty day in the hideous Brexit odyssey.

Thursday 4 April – London

Meeting with French Ambassador Jean-Pierre Jouyet and his very canny political adviser François-Joseph Schichan. I am very frank with them about the horrors of the Brexit process and our political plight.

My private office come in smiling. They want me to approve a Cariforum deal, which is a sort of Caribbean trade continuity agreement. It concerns bananas, sugar and rum – thus protecting, as they see it, the ingredients of the perfect punch.

Minor reshuffle. Simon Hoare is very upset not to be made a Whip. But what's the point of being a deckchair on the *Titanic* for only a few months?

Friday 5 April – London/Rutland

Three days on, the talks with Corbyn do not appear to be getting anywhere. But it will probably all get strung out and still achieve nothing. The PM has written to Donald Tusk asking for an extension to 30 June, but still wanting to leave before 22 May. Meanwhile our fortunes have not yet collapsed, as we have come a good second in the Newport West by-election to replace the late Paul Flynn.

WikiLeaks have been putting out statements saying that Assange will soon be pushed out of the embassy. We haven't quite got there yet, but they have probably picked up something from those around President Moreno. If they are hoping to whip up a frenzy to stop it they have another think coming, although it is a little annoying to have lost the element of surprise.

It is a bad time for LGBT rights. Brunei has introduced the harshest version of sharia law and could now stone gay men to death, while President Bolsonaro in Brazil has made one of his first acts the removal of any legal protection for them. What does going backwards like this achieve for anybody?

Saturday 6 April – Rutland
In Uppingham High Street, some nice people stop me to say how complicated and difficult Brexit must be.

Tend the garden. Watch Tiger Roll win the Grand National for the second time in a row.

Rory Stewart wants me to sign a letter of support to the PM. I say yes. I don't mind helping him suck up to her.

Sunday 7 April – Rutland/London
I am so bored and dismayed by Brexit. Everything is turning to dust. I am in mourning for the country. The MPs' WhatsApp group is a cacophony of puerile judgement. 'How dare she try to do a deal with that Marxist Corbyn?' 'If she does a deal with him we are finished.' 'How dare she give him credibility?', etc. They are all attacking her with fabricated accusations based on Brexit mania.

Rees-Mogg tweets, 'If a long extension leaves us stuck in the EU we should be as difficult as possible. We could veto any increase in the budget, obstruct the putative EU army and block Mr Macron's integrationist schemes.' This man is a national, and now international, disgrace. I retweet him with my own comment – 'Threats of this sort are not just unhelpful: they are diplomatically offensive. The UK has acted in good faith with the EU and will continue to do so. This kind of belligerent talk is not the way we behave @Tusk, Juncker,

Commission.' He is a cheap nationalist with faux manners, and an ego the size of a planet.

Monday 8 April – Luxembourg/London

To Luxembourg with JH on the plane from Northolt. I robustly told him that Boris is stealing a march on him, and that if he doesn't rev up his leadership efforts now he'll never catch up.

At the foreign ministers' meeting, pretty much all of them were irked and offended by JRM's tweet about 'making it difficult for them'.

On the plane back, it became clear that high-level advice to JH is not to make a stand on the Israelis' annexation of the West Bank, because our relations with the US matter more than the principles we ought to defend. It's the end of us having a credible foreign policy, and it's the end of the rules-based international order. Everything we believe in is ultimately subordinated to our not wanting to clash with the US. There must surely come a point where in order to be honest, we should just say, 'The game's up – Israel is going to take the land and we're not going to do anything to stop it.'

Tuesday 9 April – London

PM in Berlin and Paris ahead of tomorrow's EU Council meeting.

Breakfast with Fabian Picardo in the Cinnamon Club. Alastair Campbell was there and we ended up having a teasing chat. He is engagingly personable, and remains a character whose opinions spark debate.

Call with Hamish Cowell in Muscat. We're nearly there on the Comprehensive Agreement.

Wednesday 10 April – London

See Ecuador Ambassador Jaime Marchán. We are also nearly there with Assange. We have as good as been given a date for pushing him out.

If the EU offer us a one-year extension, some are now saying it opens up a window for a People's Vote, i.e. a second referendum. If in a general election Corbyn offers it, he could win. Conservatives have not yet erupted at the suggestion, but we are like a bubbling volcano. Meanwhile the PM is in Brussels, robot-like.

Mark Francois says the EU will face 'perfidious Albion', i.e. deceitful, treacherous Britain, if we delay Brexit. So Airhead Waddlebottom is now Perfidious Francois.

Thursday 11 April – London

Overnight, in Brussels, a delay to our EU exit has been agreed until 31 October. This is a very dangerous hiatus, which sets the scene for no end of danger to the PM. Technically she's protected against another leadership challenge, but events, dear boy, events …

Suddenly it's game on: I'm told that Assange will be sprung from the embassy today. So I drop everything and head to the Operations Room at the top of the Foreign Office. Operation Pelican is go – suitably assisted by one official wearing a pelican-motif tie.

We watch a live feed which ironically was available on the web from Russia Today. Fortunately, the protesters who had been camped outside seemed to have disappeared when, bang on 10am, two or three plainclothes policemen, by arrangement, enter the embassy. We were expecting Assange to be brought out very soon after their arrival, but texts to the Ops Room revealed that he had caused a bit of a commotion and had been screaming and bawling while edging towards the Ambassador's office – at which point he was forcibly restrained. Then, with military precision, six police officers marched up to line each side of the entrance steps, to form a protective corridor through which Assange was bundled out at about 10.20am.

By this time Russia Today had twigged that something was afoot and had cut the live feed. But within less than a minute the police vans were gone. So, job done at last – and we take a commemorative photo of Team Pelican.

It had taken many months of patient diplomatic negotiation, and in the end it went off without a hitch. I do millions of interviews, trying to keep the smirk off my face.

Saturday 13 April – Rutland

I had put Simon Walters in touch with Ambassador Marchán, thus giving the *Daily Mail* their scoop about the 'fetid' Assange hovel. The pictures of his living conditions were beyond repulsive.

See by chance on Sky that the Ukrainian embassy in London had their parked car rammed, and the police had fired ten shots at someone. Nobody in the FCO tells either me or my private office. I just do what ought to be done and phone their Ambassador Natalia Galibarenko, unfortunately reaching her just after she had spoken to her PM. Better staff work in the FCO would have had me in touch with her earlier.

Monday 15 April – London/Tashkent

We are at last into our delayed recess. An unusual aura of calm has descended on our politics.

The Assange issue – should he be extradited, and if so where to? – leads the news, and Brexit has for once taken second, if not third place. JH is in Japan, where he has in Japanese given an English lesson to students. It is him at his shirt-sleeved best. His interview on *Today* is so much more sparky and characterful than usual; I text him to say so.

Flight to Tashkent with Laura Thorne from my private office via the absurdly enormous new Istanbul airport. I must have walked a mile between the two connecting flights. Next time I'll develop a limp and ask for a buggy.

We land to the news that Notre Dame is engulfed in flames and faces total destruction.

Tuesday 16 April – Tashkent

It is good to make a return visit to Uzbekistan, where I am known as the first Western foreign minister to visit following their recent regime change. Good meeting with President Shavkat Mirziyoyev, with whom I have built a good personal relationship.

At dinner with Foreign Minister Abdulaziz Kamilov and Senate Chairman Sodiq Safoyev, the vodka flowed rather too freely!

Thursday 18 April – Nur-Sultan/Yorkshire

Did the rounds in Kazakhstan, with an unfortunate moment when I met the Speaker of the Majlis, Nurlan Nigmatulin. As we sat down, I drew the large chair forwards and jammed my thumbs between the chair arms and the edge of the tabletop – ouch! Indeed very ouch! I managed to retain a modicum of diplomatic nonchalance, while cursing under my breath.

The MPs' WhatsApp group remains despondent and mutinous. The daily contributions from Maria Caulfield, Nadine Dorries and Zac Goldsmith are especially tiresome. And Farage is leading the polls for the elections to the European Parliament.

Friday 19 April – Yorkshire

Good Friday.

The climate-change demonstration by the group calling them-selves Extinction Rebellion has been going on for three days so far. They have blocked Waterloo Bridge, Parliament Square, Oxford Circus and Marble Arch. God knows where they all come from, and quite who they are trying to persuade to do what, but they are a bloody nuisance and are threatening to close down Heathrow Airport over Easter.

The police have arrested over 600 protesters so far, but have only charged a handful. They seem overwhelmed.

Saturday 20 April – Yorkshire

The papers are full of reports of constituency associations determined to replace the PM. Their naivety is staggering, as they seem incapable of thinking beyond the next consequential step. A leadership election would be carnage, and instead of uniting the Party around an alter-native, it would divide us further and probably lead to the collapse of the government. Until and unless Brexit is behind us, any new leader would almost certainly provoke a few departures from the Party whip, and possibly Party membership itself, such that they would lose the numbers to be able to govern.

I have carefully studied the Fixed-Term Parliaments Act. If on our picking a new leader Corbyn were to table a motion of no confidence in the government under the Act, the government would probably win; but if a different sort of motion were tabled, the outcome might strike new constitutional ground and not be carried. For instance, if the Speaker were to allow a motion which expressed no confidence in (say) Boris Johnson as the new leader becoming PM, he might never make it up the Mall. In order to keep the Queen out of politics, we should surely be permitted and obliged to test the Commons first. If the Commons expresses its confidence in the new leader, then it would make sense for the Queen to invite him to the Palace, but if it did not, then the Conservative Party would either have to find a different leader who could attract sufficient support to stay in government, or there would almost inevitably have to be a general election during which Theresa May would remain as PM until the election outcome was clear. It is thus possible that Boris Johnson could be leader for a month but never Prime Minister.

To Sandsend near Whitby for quite the most fabulous fish dinner in a gem of a restaurant.

Sunday 21 April – Yorkshire
Easter Sunday, and it's the Queen's ninety-third birthday.

Awful beyond measure – suicide bombers in Sri Lanka have blown themselves up in churches and top hotels. The death toll is going to be something like 200. Ghastly. It is just hideous. It is reprehensible, pointless and repulsive.

Tuesday 23 April – London
The number killed in Sri Lanka is 310. Some of the UK casualties are heartbreaking.

HMA Muscat Hamish Cowell. There are two small clauses which need to be ironed out in the Comprehensive Agreement. The first is a reference to the 1800 agreement about supporting Muscat. It is a short paragraph in wonderful flowery language about support being *unshook* to the end of time, an archaic and poetic variation on the word *unshaken*. It is a lovely historic preamble to the CA, but is in fact a codicil to the original agreement of 1798, which is largely about fending off the French. Purists are arguing for a reference to the original agreement, not the codicil, but the only purpose is to include a romantic historic reference, so 1800 should be fine. The second is at the end, when the FCO lawyers want to say that the CA is not a treaty. But there is no point in inserting a negative clause, when it is obviously not a treaty, and the CA text includes termination and review clauses which make any reference to a treaty entirely redundant. So I am pro 1800 and anti the treaty clause. So is Hamish. I just need to square the Omanis.

Lunch with Sayd Badr. He is in full agreement with me on the two clauses, so I just need to bash the FCO lawyers on the treaty clause. He is rightly very concerned about the parlous state of the Oman economy. The national debt is rocketing, and over the last four years has gone from 20 per cent to 50 per cent of GDP. The current oil price is $75, up a bit from recent levels.

Good meeting with Hugo Shorter, our Americas Director. He is a proper person, a real ace. We are both still basking in the successful release of Julian Assange. A State Visit in June for Trump has just been announced. There is so much going on with Brexit and climate change that it has caused hardly a ripple. It will coincide with the seventy-fifth anniversary of D-Day, and the main controversy is whether Speaker Hobbit will permit him to make an address to the joint Commons and Lords. The Lord Speaker Norman Fowler is goading him to concede.

Nigel Evans, Secretary of the 1922, is openly calling for the PM to go, or for the rules to be changed so the Party can chuck her out. He is completely abusing his position. I'm furious. But he is being put up to it, no doubt.

James arrives in London with a beautifully trimmed Noodle, and having watered a very dry garden in Rutland.

Wednesday 24 April – London
Straight into a Westminster Hall debate on Crimea. It is five years since the Russians annexed it. We hold a firm line that it is illegal and that it belongs to Ukraine, but history tells a rather different story. Our judgement about right and wrong is rather simplistic. Chris

Bryant quite rightly draws the comparison between our stand against the Russians' annexation of Crimea and our pusillanimous disregard for the illegality of the Israelis' annexation of the Palestinian West Bank.

I am suddenly called up to answer an Urgent Question from Sir Vince Cable about the Saudis' execution of thirty-seven men yesterday. It is not my ministerial responsibility, and I am required to defend the indefensible. But I somehow manage.

Ed Argar drops by for a drink. One of the stories leading the news is the PM's supposed decision to allow the Chinese firm Huawei to participate in the building of the UK's 5G mobile network against the view of some who were at yesterday's NSC meeting. The decision is bound to be more complicated than the reports suggest, but it is being spun as a bad decision by the PM. Ed says there is a ferocious leak inquiry. I think they need to look at Gavin Williamson's phone. It is bound to be him, and Mark Sedwill should not miss the opportunity to destroy him. The over-opinionated Nadine Dorries says on the WhatsApp group, 'How many examples are there of a PM who takes a decision against the advice of the most senior cabinet ministers on an issue of such importance? I imagine none.' WTF does she know about anything like this?

Rather more edifying is the moving funeral in Belfast of Lyra McKee, a 29-year-old lesbian journalist, who was shot accidentally by the New IRA while observing rioting in the Creggan area of Derry.

Friday 26 April – Rutland

Call Erik. Amazingly he calls back and we speak for the first time in two months. It means he has restored some of his faculties, as I am told he suffered a fall. He seems broadly OK. We discuss Brexit. I tell him about the Comprehensive Agreement, to which he says, 'Never forget that the Sultan's father upset his own people by signing a friendship agreement with Julian Amery.' I don't think that can be strictly true, as the Sultan was overthrown in 1970, and Amery was only a foreign minister from 1972 to 1974. It's one of Erik's embellishments.

Hammond is in China … doing Belt and Road suck-up stuff? Simon McDonald is still globetrotting – it seems he wants to visit every FCO embassy.

Mark Lancaster calls at 8pm. He says Gavin Williamson is sweating! A full-scale leak inquiry is under way, and ministers who attended the NSC have been asked to show their mobile phones. Ooh, ooh, ooh.

Tuesday 30 April – London

Meeting with Alastair King-Smith, the FCO's Stonewall on Stilts, to discuss Uzbekistan's role at the looming Media Freedom Conference. I say firmly we should fete them and not shun them. They are moving in the right direction and should be encouraged for their future, not castigated for their past.

Catch-up with the adorable and bubbly Caroline Wilson.

Catch-up with the PUS. We covered: Falklands, Chile, visa survey, Assange, Central Asia, the Antarctic, next steps for us with Russia and sanctions regulations. And then the real issue – FCO email signatures! Throughout the FCO there is no consistency in the style and composition of the embedded signature template that pops up at the end of anyone's email. The phone numbers are randomly typeset, the job descriptions are arbitrary, and some have slogans or messages added such as 'Support the FCO in its work for diversity'. Ugh! There is a correct format for expressing UK and mobile phone numbers, and I am insisting that nothing that is incorrect should be tolerated. I want everyone to be told to adopt a single FCO house style. It's so simple, but McDonald says that such an instruction would be thought offensive. Offensive!?!? He is there to tell people what to do and maintain standards. His management standards leave a lot to be desired. You simply would not believe the resistance he puts up to a simple instruction.

Call to Roberto Ampuero, Foreign Minister of Chile, about the not-quite military coup in Venezuela. We are worried it might all backfire and boost Maduro.

Bump into Michael Portillo by Westminster Abbey, who comes home for a drink. He is writing a history of the

Conservative Party on/in Europe from Churchill to May. He voted Leave.

Wednesday 1 May – London

Breakfast with David Cameron, which is always a pleasure. He is always full of life, and ready with an amusing take on things. He got to the top early and will spend half his life being a former Prime Minister. It's a pity he's not still in the Commons, but I know he felt if he were still there it would cause too much tension. But then, that is what the place is for. He clearly feels to just sit in Parliament would be too painful after the referendum result and is so glad not to be in the middle of everything that is going on there at the moment. He has a very straightforward opinion about Boris – 'He ruined my bloody career.'

There are fizzing rumours that a ministerial sacking is imminent. Tim Shipman tweets gratuitous abuse against Mark Sedwill, accusing him of abusing his position, which is surely only because if Gavin Williamson is chopped he loses his best source. In conducting a leak inquiry, Sedwill is doing his job, and quite rightly doing it with firm authority in the national interest.

And then it happens. Williamson is summarily sacked. Penny Mordaunt goes to Defence; Rory Stewart to DfID. Dead men's shoes are great for unexpected promotion: all part of the snakes and ladders of political fortune, something which is based 90 per cent on luck and 10 per cent on talent. It is a toss-up in Parliament who is the more hated Williamson, Chris on Labour's side or Gavin on ours. One's an unprincipled leftie, the other is a scheming leaker.

Thursday 2 May – Rutland

Local elections today in the metropolitan boroughs, districts and unitary authorities.

To Bringhurst School, where James is Chairman, to address the kids. I take a bag full of House of Commons rulers for them, and Noodle!

Williamson is proving ferociously defiant after his sacking, protesting innocence. But he had refused to hand over his phone, and when he did he had deleted all his texts, which was self-incriminating. Even if he was innocent, he had it coming.

Friday 3 May – Rutland/Scotland
Gavin Williamson is tweeting brazenly, pictured with his dog. His brass neck sets a new bar.

Drive to Scotland to stay with Charles and Sallie Hendry. He's the best Energy Minister we've ever had, and a poor reflection on David Cameron that Charles was removed in order to replace him with the ridiculous John Hayes.

Local election results – dire for us. Indeed they couldn't really have been worse.

Saturday 4 May – Scotland
The fallout from local election results continues, and the 1922 Committee is reported to be ganging up against the PM. I text the Chairman, Graham Brady:

> Graham. Just to let you know that I, and I think more others than you realise, are increasingly angered by reports that you/the 1922 have been demanding that she 'name the date', or might seek a change in the rules. The 22 seems out of control. A contest now would cause further division, total carnage, and would probably cause the Govt to collapse. We'd be out at a Gen El, and probably for ages … even for ever. This is reckless talk. If however I am being unfair on you, and it's all coming from Nigel Evans, then please slap him down in public, because some are on the edge of turning on you. It is harming your good reputation which is so critical at this time. We are all in despair, but we need to be in despair together!!! Alan

He replies, very reasonably:

> Alan, we stopped a rule change the week before last but voted to ask for clarity on her plans for her departure. I agreed with her that a response before the locals would be damaging … but we

are awaiting a response. Incidentally, The Times knew that I am meeting her on Tuesday before I did. My office doesn't leak so someone at no. 10 did (as happened when the December confidence vote was about to be triggered). I agree we need calm but the party is almost evenly split – as is the '22 Executive. Best, Graham.

More Williamson tweets. David Davis and the intellectually challenged Andrea Jenkyns declare for Dominic Raab.

Monday 6 May – Rutland
Bank Holiday. Dull day. Byron Rhodes and Ken Bool brief me on yesterday's meeting at Belvoir Lodge, convened by Frances Rutland. It's the usual culprits: Her Lack-of-Grace, Chris Emmett and Geoffrey Pointon, all trying to persuade people to sign a letter demanding that a special Party meeting get rid of Theresa. Whereas I suppose I only support her out of judgement rather than affection, none of these simpleton grumps can see beyond the end of their nose to the inevitable consequences of binning her and having a leadership contest.

Twenty-minute phone call with Jeremy H – we took stock of the Brexit situation and despaired at the conduct of various colleagues. I told him about my text exchange with Brady and was pretty firm and direct about him needing to toughen up his image.

Tuesday 7 May – Germany
To Brize Norton for the start of the Royal Visit to Germany. The Duchess of Cornwall arrives ahead of HRH, who pulls up at the wheel of his classic blue Aston Martin.

Nice chat with him on the plane. I say that I thought the local election results were a protest against leaving the EU and were in large part a Remain fightback.

Arrive in Berlin for a heavy schedule. Chancellery for meeting with Angela Merkel; Schloss Bellevue for meeting with President Frank-Walter Steinmeier; Berlin Airlift wreath; Brandenburg Gate; Hotel Adlon. Queen's Birthday Party at the Ambassador's residence. Charming Health Minister Jens Spahn and his husband Daniel.

We will contest the EU Parliament elections on the 23rd, even though the MEPs won't be there for long. The results will be on Sunday 26th.

Wednesday 8 May – Germany
Breakfast with Ambassador Sebastian Wood, then train to Leipzig. Walkabout – I retrieve an enormous teddy bear from HRH the Duchess, who was given it for Prince Harry's new baby. Visit St Thomas Church. Then later St Nicholas Church.

Wörlitz Gardens. While in the main house there, we hear of the official announcement that Prince Harry and Meghan have named their son Archie Harrison Mountbatten-Windsor.

Back in Berlin, dinner at Soho House with TRH's team, and then a drink with them all at the Adlon.

The PM has seen the Executive of the 1922 Committee and is under pressure to stand down.

Thursday 9 May – Germany
Young musicians at the Barenboim–Said Akademie. Daniel Barenboim is rehearsing nearby but doesn't interrupt to greet HRH, which is excessively prima-donna-ish.

Fly from Berlin to Munich. Amazing Bavarian reception in the Max-Joseph-Platz.

Visit the Hofbräuhaus, and then the Siemens HQ.

Some minor ministerial appointments in the evening, which are more a sort of rolling reshuffle after so many resignations …

Saturday 11 May – Rutland
James and I, by post, both vote in the European elections. People are going to desert the Conservatives, and to a lesser degree Labour too. They will switch to the Brexit Party, while Remainers will vote Lib Dem as the only countervailing option.

Sunday 12 May – Rutland/London
Lovely sunny day after all the rain, but politics in contrast has storm clouds everywhere. It could not be worse. I don't care about the Party

so much as the country. Yesterday's news reported that the Brexit Party is way out ahead for the European elections on the 23rd and is now ahead of the Conservatives for people's voting intention if there were a general election. The latter is absurd, but at the very least it illustrates how Brexit (UKIP as was) will take votes off us, and so it returns us to exactly what made Cameron promise a referendum in the first place. The MPs' WhatsApp group, or at least its usual opinionated idiots, are blaming May, when it is their antics and stupidity which have led to this dire outcome. Meanwhile the turd Williamson has written an excoriating article in the *Mail* criticising May's talks with Labour, prompting Rees-Mogg gleefully to tweet, 'Sow the wind, and reap the whirlwind.' He is simply over the top about all matters Brexit. Moggy affects authority and propriety, but in practice behaves rather badly.

The garden looks lovely. Inside the house, I seem to spend half my time sorting suitcases. I unpack and pack so much, from skiing, Yorkshire, Scotland, Germany ... and then repack for Spain next weekend. The laundry will be busy.

Tuesday 14 May – London

FCO Orals. Emily Thornberry surprisingly good on Israel/Palestine, pointing out that Netanyahu's proposed legislation would allow him to overrule the country's Supreme Court.

Everyone is now openly limbering up for a leadership contest. So who's in whose camp so far? Gove: Stride. Raab: Syms, Clifton-Brown, Swire, and claiming to have twenty on the campaign committee. Oh yeah! McVey: Davis, [Gary] Streeter, [Ben] Bradley ... well that won't go anywhere. Johnson: Rees-Mogg, [Jack] Lopresti, [Jake] Berry ... but lots more in the wings I suspect. Hancock: [Tracey] Crouch. Javid: Glen. Hunt: Dunne, Brine.

Vicente calls to say that the Cypriots have gone ballistic about my reply to a question this morning about the Turks drilling for oil off Cyprus. As usual the strained and strange Theresa Villiers during Orals had lobbed a very unhelpful supplementary question into one which was on a completely different topic. Although I replied faithfully to the FCO script, the Cypriots have confected massive indignation and the President and Foreign Minister (for no justifiable reason) have condemned me in public. They have elections looming, but it is no excuse for being so offensive.

Wednesday 15 May – London

Video conference call with our High Commissioner in Cyprus Stephen Lillie, and senior official Jill Gallard. They both think that my chosen words were perfectly accurate, and that the explosive Cypriot reaction is unjustified. I insist that we should not stand for it.

Their High Commissioner Euripides Evriviades, at my request, has been summoned to the FCO. I bawl him out, making it quite clear that we can handle any disagreement between us but will not tolerate rude public attacks which go against basic diplomatic good manners. He asks if he can explain, but I say he cannot – and chuck him out after two minutes.

Speak at the opening of Liechtenstein's honorary consulate in St James's Market, and have dinner with Jack Mably from my private office. I call Euripides to say, 'Nothing personal, love you really, but they needed to know they cannot push us around so rudely – or indeed at all.'

Thursday 16 May – London

Damian Green comes to the FCO. General political chat; friendly but somewhat pointless.

I have been landed with the debate on the International Day against Homophobia, Biphobia and Transphobia (IDAHOBIT). Smile and just do it …

Nice post-Assange thank-you dinner at Wilton's with Jaime Marchán and his deputy Leopoldo Rovayo, joined by Nigel Baker, Director of our Latin America Dept.

The PM has said she will announce a timetable to go after the EU elections and the fourth meaningful vote. Her talks with Labour on trying to reach some sort of cross-party accommodation are on the point of collapse.

Friday 17 May – London/Madrid

All the talks with Labour have petered out. Lots of people are now saying they will stand for the leadership: Boris, Rory, McVey, Raab … even Truss!!

We are still facing friction with Cyprus – they must learn to be less tetchy.

Monday 20 May – Ireland

Head early to City Airport. Bump into NI Secretary Karen Bradley at the airport, with Lord (Jonathan) Caine, who for over twenty-five years in the Conservative Party has been all things Northern Ireland.

A fabulous day in Ireland with the Prince of Wales and the Duchess of Cornwall. He has visited every year for ages, and intends eventually to visit every county. It has earned him deep respect and affection, and of course purged the bitterness of Mountbatten's assassination in 1979.

Dinner at our Ambassador's residence, Glencairn. One of the guests is the mimic Oliver Callan, Ireland's answer to Rory Bremner. Over drinks after what was quite a small dinner of about twenty, he plays out an hilarious Donald Trump skit in front of the Duchess and two or three of us. As he finishes to universal laughter, HRH fixes me with a stare and a grin, and says, 'Alan – I understand you do a very good impression of my husband!'

So … where have events left us? Boris has dominated the weekend coverage as the runaway favourite, but the analysis of what he might do to navigate a solution to Brexit is extremely skimpy. His main strength is name recognition, support among activists and the perhaps questionable assumption that only he can beat Corbyn. Corbyn has zero appeal, but could win an election by default should we split between the Brexit Party and the Lib Dems. Jeremy Hunt is nowhere, and is hardly mentioned in the list of contenders.

In the lists are BoJo, Raab, Javid, McVey, Gove, Stewart, Hunt, Truss, Hancock and Leadsom. In this Grand National of runners, surely Cleverly, Tugendhat and Ellwood won't even get out of the gates. There is no Remain candidate at all, although Hunt and Stewart are the most sympathetic. What is the timetable going to be?

What are the constitutional implications under the Fixed-Term Parliaments Act and for the Queen, in the event a leader is chosen who clearly has no majority in Parliament?

Speak to Philip Dunne on the phone. I tell him that Jeremy Hunt's personality projection is non-existent and that his tacking to the right is losing him MP support. Philip says he feels constrained by being in the Cabinet. I say that the same sense of duty doesn't appear to bother Javid, Leadsom or Gove.

Tuesday 21 May – Ireland

Kilmacurragh Botanic Gardens. Glendalough North Lake.

I take my leave of TRH and visit the Dáil. Get a wave to the gallery from the Chamber below from Leo Varadkar and Simon Coveney, followed by a chat with Simon in the corridor. Fly back to City Airport.

Wednesday 22 May – London

Breakfast at the Goring with Sir Peter Westmacott. He is such a gem. He thinks that pressure is building in Turkey on Erdoğan, what with banking anxiety and looming party splits.

Then … my diplomatic triumph. In anticipation of the inevitable succession in Oman, and using Qaboos' near fifty years as Sultan, I have been urging the FCO to launch an initiative, which is something rare in the building as all they normally do is react to events. I have driven and shaped a new Comprehensive Agreement between the two of us which is designed to signal our enduring commitment to the country, and our determination to help them across all issues, such as health, education and commerce, and not just defence and security.

Today is its formal signing ceremony: Jeremy Hunt and Yousef bin Alawi. I wanted it to be in Number 10, but that was stopped by unimaginative idiots who said that, as it was not a treaty as such, its status could not be dignified by a signature in Number 10. So we had to dress up the Ambassadors' Waiting Room for the occasion.

As the afternoon goes on, it feels doomed for Theresa May. The 1922 are contemplating the rules which currently forbid a new confidence motion within a year of the last one. But the die is cast anyway. She will have to go after the EU results, whatever.

The 1922 Committee weekly meeting at 5pm attracted a medium attendance, despite all the feverish skulduggery. On the bench, left to right, Charles Walker, Geoffrey Clifton-Brown, Graham Brady, Cheryl Gillan, Nigel Evans, Bob Blackman. Not much said, except that the Executive will meet the Chief Whip at 5.30, and will announce anything after that, reconvening at 6pm.

Andrea Leadsom resigns at 7.45pm. The dribbling coup of a pathetic Cabinet has failed somewhat, and is ill-judged. The '22, it is clear, wants to see the PM off and change the rules. But it has done neither. She will limp on, but is already dead. We are in an extraordinary state of animated stasis.

Thursday 23 May – London/Rutland

Mel Stride becomes Leader of the House, and Jesse Norman Paymaster General. They'll be there for little more than a month.

Bump into journo John Rentoul in Millbank, then former Home Secretary Lord [Kenneth] Baker. Anyone and everyone just shakes their head in disbelief and bewilderment.

Some wag says, 'The Prime Minister has put the sofa up against the door.' But the reality is she could not possibly have resigned before today's European elections, which continue in the rest of Europe until Sunday. She will get enough blame as it is, without adding to it by compounding the crisis as people head off to vote. So she will probably do so tomorrow at the earliest, or more likely Tuesday, after the inevitably awful results.

Meanwhile ... BoJo got us into this deep dark hole, and now thinks he is the one to get us out of it. Something in me says that history might vindicate his confident ambition.

Friday 24 May – Rutland

A beautiful morning in Rutland, as storm clouds are set to break over Number 10. Graham Brady was due to see her there at 9am. We all know he's in there, but he must have gone in the back door. The UK has voted in the farcical elections to the European Parliament, but the results cannot be counted until the rest of the EU has finished voting on Sunday.

Rees-Mogg on Sky as good as says that he is supporting Boris so that we can leave at the end of October without fail, in other words leave without a deal. His line is that without Boris, and without a No Deal exit, you get Corbyn. In fact, No Deal is their real agenda, and they should all stop pretending they want anything other than that.

I text Beth Rigby of Sky telling her to stop indulging those who are not yet out of nappies – such as Cleverly, Tugendhat and Mercer – by saying they are possible leadership candidates. The very thought is risible. It would be better if the rules required the support of 10 per cent of the parliamentary Party for a valid nomination.

Reporters keep talking about 'the key to the door of Number 10'. It's annoying. It has no key. It only has bolts on the inside. At the moment they are being used to the full.

It looks certain that the PM will announce today that she will quit once a successor has been chosen. We return on Tuesday 4 June from the short Whitsun Recess. I guess it will be nominations in by Thursday 6th and ballots the following week on the Tuesday and Thursday.

A colleague calls. He had just received a call from Gavin Williamson urging him to back Boris. Not a chance, but the leaking slimeball issued veiled threats about his future if he didn't. That won't wash. He was asking him to join the Boris team, and left the impression that they are short of active troops. Boris has Private Pike, Conor Burns and one or two others, but no effective operators. His numbers do not match the noise. He is doing very well for now by remaining invisible and not opening his mouth.

Larry the cat is taken in, and the lectern comes out at 9.45am. It has the Government crest on it. Is resigning as Party Leader and giving notice she will resign as PM once a successor is chosen a party or a government matter? The proper process is for her to remain as PM until the very end. Unless someone has died or is ill, or somehow incapacitated, the UK system doesn't readily allow for a caretaker, so it would be destabilising to have David Lidington as a temporary PM. I'm sure she will remain as PM during the leadership contest.

10am. Boing, boing, boing. Except with Big Ben silenced behind the scaffolding, there are no boings. Or is it bong, bong, bong?

Officials, and Philip, gather in Downing Street. She emerges at 10.04.

She will resign as Conservative Party Leader on 7 June, and serve as PM until the end of the leadership contest. So there we are. That's that. More or less the timetable I expected.

Her six minutes was an elegant apologia, a dignified justification, a genuine statement of belief. It was her usual solid but stilted self until the last sentence – she was on the verge of tears, as the emotion was bursting through. Would she hold it to the end? She did – just. But she was breaking into tears during the final few words. It was deeply moving and emotional. James and I both had tears rolling down our faces. It was a remarkable moment. I just thought, Well done you, and sod the ERG.

I really must go for an urgent sanity check-up. Is it them or is it possibly me? Jason Groves' tweet illustrates the manic delusion of colleagues, in this case the potty messianic Steve Baker – 'Self-styled "Brexit hardman" Steve Baker ... "There is no shying away from it – I have had a level of support in the country I could never have foreseen. I now have to take on the challenge of deciding whether to run myself."' The nutjob should be taken away by the men in white coats and certified as clinically insane.

Elsewhere on Twitter there is an outpouring of gushing insincerity from the pygmy army who are the PM's poisonous enemies.

Speak to Jason Groves at the *Mail* to express astonishment at the Baker comment. He says it's true: he said it on the BBC, volunteering it in a way that forced his comment into the interview. As if credulity has not already been stretched to its limits, he says that Graham Brady has told Theresa that he will stand down as Chairman of the 1922 in order to put himself forward as a leadership candidate. It is bonkers beyond utter bonkers. Apart from the deceit of overseeing her removal only to stand himself, he has no qualifications that equip him for the role. It is an abuse. The Chairman of the 1922 should remain unimpeachably impartial, and be above ministerial ambition of any sort. His stock will now plummet.

So – Johnson, Hunt, Javid, Gove, Raab, Leadsom, Stewart, Hancock, McVey, Truss, Mordaunt, Brady, Baker, Cleverly. Any more takers? Larry the cat? This is collapsing into absurdity. It's a national farce. This is not the behaviour and profile of a credible party.

Brendan Carlin of the *Mail on Sunday* calls. He is aghast at the madness of Steve Baker, and then asks if I had heard that Trump might visit the Commons during the State Visit. I suppose, as it's recess, he could just do Westminster Hall and the Commons Chamber without too much security difficulty. But I've heard nothing. Meanwhile the repulsive Arron Banks and Julia Hartley-Brewer, Leave.EU maniacs, tweet vile things about Theresa, saying good riddance. And Airhead Waddlebottom, aka Mark Francois, gives the most mean-minded interview, gloating that the 'Dancing Queen has met her Waterloo'. Ha ha, an ABBA gag. Not funny, you horrid little man.

The phone doesn't stop ringing. All the journos: who can stop Boris? Does this mean that No Deal is inevitable? Who will I support? Will there be an early general election? Etc.

My constituency Executive Committee meeting in Melton was mercifully free of the animosity of a few weeks ago. Today's resignation has lanced the boil somewhat, and it left me free to give them my considered analysis. I paid proper tribute to Theresa. Surprisingly, the mood was rather anti-Boris, but not pro anyone else in particular. I dwelt on the need for the candidates to lay out their stall clearly, of course on Brexit, but also on wider policy. I said only three or four are serious candidates and all the others should get real and stop posturing. I was excoriating about Graham Brady stepping down as Chairman of the 1922 in order to contemplate standing himself. They applauded loudly when I said the contest must be taken to the wider membership and not just be stitched up by MPs. I was on a roll. They all left thoughtful rather than angry.

Once home, my phone started pinging. *Newsnight* had tweeted a little clip of me from the profile of Theresa I interviewed for a few weeks ago. I caught the programme just as it was airing. They had edited it very well, and I liked the bits they used, such as 'she was an unlucky general, but any of the others would have been a disaster; she fought an election based on a cult of personality, when she didn't really have a personality; at Oxford it was as if she didn't say certain things for fear of being seen to step out of line' etc.

Former Party Treasurer Lord (James) Lupton texted charmingly from Mallorca saying I should stand for the top job, that he would offer his house round the corner for an HQ and would raise the money for a campaign. Too late, sadly. Probably too unrealistic by any measure, but very kind and generous-spirited of him.

Saturday 25 May – Rutland

Boris Johnson, Jeremy Hunt and Esther McVey have already declared. Truss will probably not. Then two more this morning on the *Today* programme: Rory Stewart and Matt Hancock. Rory says he could not serve under Boris or support anyone who favoured No Deal. Matt broadened his comments to policy other than just Brexit: he has an attractive natural manner.

To Uppingham Speech Day. Perhaps as many as 2,000 people gathered in a massive marquee. Instead of a series of formal speeches in addition to the inevitable prize-giving there is a jazz band, a brilliant clarinet soloist, Carl Ross and his group, and a scene out of *Legally Blonde*. It was an amazing display of talent, culminating in the entire marquee singing Verdi's 'Chorus of the Hebrew Slaves'. It was deeply moving and of enormous credit to the school.

Meanwhile the line-up of absurdity grows further. Raab and Leadsom are set to declare overnight.

I called James Lupton. His foot is in bandages and a brace after a post-operative infection. He still thinks I should stand, but I put him right. If Boris wins he will resign the Party whip, despite having become more Brexit than he used to be.

Sunday 26 May – Rutland

Gove has declared. Truss says she won't. Patel says she might …
aaargh! Damian Green declares for Hancock. There will now be a
flood of declarations of support, and candidate interviews designed
to trap and trip up. People will switch off and tire of it within two or
three days.

It's all very odd, the modern world. Both Raab and Stewart solicit
my support by WhatsApp. It is just extraordinary that the candidates
themselves, or one of their closest campaign colleagues, don't call
personally. I will not respond to any of them.

Jeremy might have done a big interview in the *Sunday Times* and
think that it puts him on the map, but so far his campaign is pretty
moribund. He was supposed to call yesterday for a chat, but all I'm
getting is the occasional text from Philip Dunne with links to press
reports. I have a note in my pocket of three things to tell Jeremy very
forcibly. Sort your image – the shirtsleeves and startled eyes must be
changed. Stop tacking to the right – every time you suck up to Leave,
you trash your own brand; this is not about the fine details of policy,
because more than anything else it will be a contest about character,
charisma and competence, and hence not being Boris. Sort your
campaign – you cannot run it via SpAds and WhatsApp; it must be
organised around a buzzing core of zealous colleagues, and involve
personal MP-to-MP engagement.

Jeremy calls while I am tipping our rusty old barbecue into the
local recycling site. I tell him all these things, and he is charmingly
receptive. He says he won't pretend to be something he is not, but
knows he can be too cerebral. On tacking to the right, he reminds
me that he had always urged Theresa to hold out for certain things
more strongly during the negotiations – which is perfectly true – and
on the importance of it being an MP exercise, not one directed by
SpAds, he took it straight on board as a serious point. There is nothing MPs hate more in a leadership fight than being directed or
contacted by non-MPs. Self-importance hits the stratosphere during
any contest.

Jeremy Corbyn is seventy today. It's not his age that matters nearly
as much as his evident stupidity.

From 10pm the results of the European Parliament elections start pouring in. The overall picture is as bad as forecast: Brexit way out front with over 30 per cent, Lib Dems second with about 20 per cent, Greens overtaking us as we collapse to about 10 per cent.

Monday 27 May – Rutland
Bank Holiday.

We have been trounced. When converted into MEP seats, it's Brexit 29, Lib Dems 16, Labour 10, Green 7, Conservatives 4, SNP 3, Plaid Cymru 1, Change UK (the former Independent Group) 0 and UKIP 0. Arguably, the combined Remain vote (Lib Dem, ChUK, SNP) exceeded the Leave vote. Conservatives are the main massive losers, but Labour will also be riven with recrimination, facing growing pressure to support a second referendum. Theresa going has given us a short breather, but the leadership race will now divide us further. I think an eventual split is inevitable, and the prospect of a general election has probably risen significantly.

Speak to Philip May, who was out for a walk with Theresa. Nice friendly chat, in which he expressed appreciation for all my support. It's rather illustrative that even now that she has shaken off all the pressure that was resting on her she just doesn't have the inclination to grab the phone and say hi. But the four of us will have dinner some time. I said she should use the remaining time to have a few thank-you drinks.

Potato Head Bridgen gives another 'oh it's all so easy and straightforward, just get on with it' interview. Similar attitude to Mark Francois. It's hard to know whether Potato Head or Airhead Waddlebottom will go pop first.

Speak to Lord Chief Justice Ian Burnett. He was at Chequers for dinner on Saturday, along with the Goves and two financier couples. He says she was relaxed, almost serene.

Sajid Javid has joined the leadership race – the ninth to do so. I'm not sure his video message on Twitter is quite going to cut it.

Michael Gove texts to ask if I might have time for a chat. I say, sure – whenever he wants. Just a few minutes later we have a really cheerful discussion. He has a nice engaging sense of humour. I said

I was for Jeremy. I told him straight that he has good unifying qual-ifications but that his public image is a bit freaky. In emergency I was happy to set aside his execrable foreign policy views! We agreed to speak every now and then to compare notes. I startled him a little by asking how the Chequers dinner went, saying that I have my spies everywhere.

Nigel Farage is milking it on TV, saying he'll now make the Brexit Party a main challenger at the next general election. Much as I'd love to think he's peaked and should sod off, we are in turmoil. I've been saying for ages that we risk the complete disintegration of the post-Victorian party and parliamentary model, and that's now what might be happening. The fragmentation may not be reversible. It's a revolution without guns.

I call Cheryl Gillan. She and Charles Walker are running the 1922 now that Brady has recused himself from the process after expressing an interest in running for the leadership. I told her that I consider his behaviour unacceptable. Apart from the absurdity of him think-ing he is qualified, it is just so improper of him to be in a trusted position and then step into the fray in his own interest. He cannot be half in, half out. He should resign completely from the chairman-ship, never to return. Second, I said it was essential for the contest to conclude a good few days before we rise for the summer recess. I didn't say why, or what I had in mind. The timetable has to be agreed between the 1922 and the Party – I guess the Board, but certainly with the Chairman, Brandon Lewis. It looks as though it will be that TM will stand down on 7 June; nominations and hustings soon to follow; parliamentary stage over by 24 June; three weeks for the Party membership campaign, hustings and ballot; complete by maybe Thursday 18 July, with the House rising the following week. I think that there ought to be a confirmatory vote in Parliament before the new Leader goes up the Mall to see the Queen.

Cheryl's new puppy, Jimmy, is yapping in the background. We exchange doggy pics. Little Jimmy is ten weeks old and adorable.

I'm beginning to think that the only way out of this without destroying democratic politics more widely is to have a second referendum. I'd rather Parliament just revoked, but …

Ed calls. He says that although Sajid has launched, it is all being done by SpAds. Classic error. He has Ed, Simon Hoare, Rob Halfon and a couple of others, but he will fizzle. Ed reiterates the reasons for him and Oliver Dowden not supporting Jeremy: called by SpAds, no return call from Jeremy or even an MP, told by James Cartlidge that he was not inner core. Hopeless. To lose Ed and Oliver, the two most astute and acute members of their intake is nothing short of a crime.

So lunatic is the process that Jesse Norman is suggesting he might stand. He was insignificant as a PUSS, and has been a minister of state for four days. He is the ultimate stuffpot, with no parliamentary clubbiness. He sets out his apologia/credo in nineteen consecutive tweets. Blooming 'eck.

Mark Francois is at Hay-on-Wye. A bit odd when he isn't capable of reading a book. But Barry Gardiner crashes in the same TV interview when he refuses to be clear about whether Labour is now pro-Remain or not. And then we get more Francois. Groan, groan, groan.

Soames calls. He is declaring for Rory tomorrow in an article in the *Mail*. Having a fabulous hinterland is not the same as being able to motivate colleagues, present a credible persona and rev up the wider world. A few years on the front line facing political hardship, and then he'd begin to qualify. They all think it's just a matter of getting there, and then it'll all be plain sailing. None of the candidates is combat-trained except, ironically, Boris. And also because of his seven years in Health, Jeremy.

Tuesday 28 May – Rutland

Oh dear, oh dear. The freak show widens. Kit Malthouse, Housing Minister, has thrown his hat in the ring. Why oh why do these insignificant figures think so much of themselves? So now we have ten: Johnson, Hunt, Gove, Javid, Raab, McVey, Leadsom, Hancock, Stewart, Malthouse. Any more takers?

Jeremy has written in the *Telegraph* and has been interviewed in the 8.10 slot on *Today*. It was just so complicated, I fear he will be slammed. In essence he suggested that he would take representatives of all strands of opinion to Brussels so that anything agreed might be thought to have adequate support. So, he'll go there with Steve Baker?! It just doesn't wash. The EU is not going to change its view just because we have a new leader. Steve Baker and Jeremy Hunt both agree that it would be lunacy and suicidal to have an election before Brexit is resolved, but the difference is that Baker wants No Deal but Jeremy (and anyone sensible) does not.

Tony Blair on Sky offers the most intelligent and perceptive analysis of Brexit, including the observation that Brexit is a matching of unlikely bedfellows, the hard nationalist right and the dejected working-class left. But Alastair Campbell, his erstwhile communications director, has been expelled from the Labour Party for voting Lib Dem. At least they're falling to bits too.

It is almost unbelievable: James Cleverly is understood to be thinking of declaring. This is risible. Bonkers. Nuts.

Rory is getting some good coverage, and coming over pretty well. But his idea for a citizens' jury to decide on Brexit is tacky. It's a British version of an Afghan *loya jirga*.

Wednesday 29 May – Rutland/London

John Bercow has said, while in Washington, that he intends to stay as Speaker until the Brexit process is over. So … it could be for a further decade, but certainly won't be this summer as planned.

James 'not so' Cleverly has declared. So the addition of this shameless neophyte takes the list to eleven. There will definitely be TV hustings for the final two candidates, and possibly somewhere at the start for the whole line-up (oh yippee – that'll be riveting). Although maybe an unexpected star will emerge and make a mess of expectations. Apparently Steve Baker, Jesse Norman and Priti Patel are all limbering up. Crazy people for crazy times.

A few hours in the FCO. I record a video message for an energy conference in Brazil; receive a brief on who might get the top jobs in Europe such as President of the Commission; speak at a UK–France joint diplomats training session for recent intakes; and meet Norbert Röttgen, the Chair of the Bundestag Foreign Affairs Committee. We share our mutual despair at the widespread harm, not least to ourselves, which the UK's departure will inflict.

Have a few minutes in his room with Jeremy. I told him straight that his idea of taking others to Brussels with him to negotiate was too clever by half. It's just too complicated and had backfired. I said that in the end it will be a run-off based on character and dependability, and he needs to project himself more convincingly. The campaign among MPs needs urgent buzz and fizz. Have a drink at home later with Philip Dunne to go through all the MP lists.

Amusingly, Boris has been summonsed to attend a court hearing of a private prosecution against him for misconduct in public office, on the grounds that he lied during the referendum campaign. He did lie. But this is no way to go about it, and it will only boost his support.

Thursday 30 May – London/Rutland

IDS speaks some sense for the first time in ages. He says that the 1922 should consider adjusting the rules to require perhaps ten nominees in order to get on to the ballot paper. It would kill off the silly publicity-seekers, and so make it a contest between bigger beasts only.

Memorial service for Toby Jessel, the former MP for Twickenham. He was a total eccentric, and among many qualities was a brilliant pianist. We used to go on the annual parliamentary ski week to Davos. The Mogg gives a charming tribute, skilfully crafting a structure around Toby's campaign successes. Fighting hopeless Hull, he shamed Barbara Castle into building the Humber Bridge. After the death of his daughter he fought for the introduction of seat belts, seeing off the formidable Enoch Powell. He saved the military school of music, thus beating Margaret Thatcher who wanted to close it. 'I don't know what campaign he has now embraced in Heaven, but it's only a matter of time before God relents.'

Trump in an interview praises Farage and Boris. It would be rude of him to see either during the State Visit, but it looks as though he might try.

Twitter tells us that a poll tomorrow will have Lib Dem 24 per cent, Brexit Party 22 per cent, Lab 19 per cent, Con 19 per cent. Zac Goldsmith WhatsApps, 'Colleagues, you know what you need to

do!' The insinuation is that we should vote for Boris and leave immediately with No Deal. He has never mixed with any of us so long as
he's been an MP. He saunters in wearing corduroy trousers, holding
a leather zip folder and a phone glued to his ear. He never talks to
anyone. He presses some environmental causes through Boris, and
peddles an extreme anti-EU view which echoes his late father, Sir
Jimmy Goldsmith of the Referendum Party, and then buggers off.
The thought of Boris favouring Rees-Mogg and Zac Goldsmith in
an Old Etonian clique is just too much to swallow. Zac should realise how unpopular he is as one of those who has got us into this mess.
It is not passing the May Deal which has fragmented our politics and
led to our collapse in support; it is those who opposed it who are to
blame.

The leadership farce is turning into pantomime. Yes, it has
happened. Mark Harper has announced his candidacy. He is the
twelfth. Has he no judgement? Can he not see how stupid he looks?
It is a cry for attention, and a bid to return to a ministerial position,
but why the hell does he think it justifies a move like this? He might
be a former Chief Whip, although heaven knows why he was ever
Chief in the first place; and he is widely thought to be a lightweight
who has occasional flashes of substance. So now Harper: surely not
Brady next?

Saturday 1 June – Rutland

Tom Newton Dunn of the *Sun* has distinguished himself with a
pre-visit interview with President Trump. He has extracted an
endorsement of Boris. Trump is also nice about Jeremy Hunt, but
not Gove who had said something about Iran he didn't like.

I do the 8.30am interview on *Today*. The Trump endorsement
doesn't really matter; we need to thin the list; candidates should
impose a voluntary threshold of ten nominees, without which they
should pull out; we need to focus on deepening the discussion of
Brexit and extend it to considering leadership qualities, etc. When it
was suggested that as Boris's deputy I often had to clear up after him,
I introduced some levity by relating how one foreign minister had
asked me, 'What is it like to be Boris Johnson's pooper scooper?'

I didn't say it on air, but the thing is, Boris is going to win. But then what?

Sunday 2 June – Rutland/London

To the Rutland Show, which included thirty or more Shire and Suffolk Punch horses, the biggest such display at any county show in the UK. Good for little Rutland.

Back in the unreal world, Sam Gyimah has become the thirteenth colleague to declare for the leadership, which is no more than a platform for him to call for a second referendum. This really is getting silly. David Gauke and Ken Clarke declare for Rory.

Monday 3 June – London

Air Force One arrives at Stansted at 9am. So we're off. The State Visit has begun. Great weather. Jeremy has a friendly-looking chat with the President at the foot of the steps. I text him to say it looked as though the President was going to kiss him. As he lands, Trump tweets an extraordinarily aggressive attack on Sadiq Khan, the Mayor of London. It's a tetchy response to Khan's recent attacks on the President. It's rather undignified, but it is Trump, and it certainly made his point. More tweets to come? We are becoming a vulgar country, with senior figures losing their manners. Speaker Bercow is boycotting the State Banquet, and most of the Labour front bench are joining the protest rallies tomorrow. Marine One takes the President to Winfield House, the US Ambassador's residence.

Head to the FCO, bumping into Nigel Evans. The 1922 will decide tomorrow on the final rules for the leadership race. It will probably ask for ten nominees, but will fall short of insisting. Two candidates will go forward, with no provision for the second to drop out: in other words it will definitely go to a ballot of Party members. James Brokenshire has been on the news saying precisely what I said on Saturday, that the stragglers should drop out now. It looks as though Number 10 are pushing for this in order to have clarity of succession well before we rise for the summer.

The official welcome on the lawn of Buckingham Palace was meticulous. A forty-one-gun salute. The band of the

Grenadier Guards, the Queen in beautiful green. All immaculate and elegant.

The lunch with the Royals looked perfect, and was followed by an hermetically sealed visit to Westminster Abbey for Trump to lay a wreath on the Tomb of the Unknown Warrior.

A nice personal gathering hosted at the InterContinental Hotel by Kim Darroch ahead of the State Banquet. Hagues etc. The Banquet itself is my idea of heaven: the Royals, dignitaries, dressing up, flunkies, bagpipes, intense diplomacy. Before it in Buckingham Palace I was in a small circle with Alex Younger, Kim Darroch, Mark Sedwill, all of us with similar medals dangling from a blue and red ribbon, when the charming Sir Ken Olisa joined us. Quick as a flash I said, 'How's the phone business going?' Deep hilarity. He is the UK CEO of Huawei, who are at the centre of Trump–China–UK hot talk about whether the company should be allowed anywhere near our infrastructure. Sedwill said, 'The thing about you, Alan, is that you always go straight to the point!'

Everyone was on tenterhooks as you never know quite what Trump will do. On this occasion he was on his best behaviour and only went off-piste in his speech for a very brief moment, adding to his script an impromptu after mentioning the Queen – 'Great woman, beautiful woman'. The Duchess of Cornwall, sitting next to him, maintained admirable composure, while I suspect pinching herself to stifle a giggle.

Tuesday 4 June – London
The House returns, but is moribund.

It's the end of Ramadan, which is somewhat more cheerful. *Eid Mubarak.*

There are some great photos of the banquet in the *Daily Telegraph*, in which James and I are both clearly visible.

James Cleverly pulls out of the leadership race. Hardly surprising. He has spent a year promoting himself, and now he has crashed. I think part of it is that Twitter infects the judgement of these younger MPs, and seeing themselves on their iPhones convinces them they have mass support. They have lost their bearings, if they ever had any.

From the FCO window I watch Trump arriving at Number 10, and take a photo from above of the Trumps and Mays on the doorstep. I ping it to Philip by text.

Trump press conference in the Durbar Court. I have a nice chat with the President's younger daughter Tiffany Trump.

Chat with Sam Gyimah on the steps of the Millbank TV studios. He says he will remain in the race because he will get more than eight backers, and his block of supporters will have a well-defined Remain policy.

It's all happening. First, the 1922 and Party Board have changed the rules for the leadership contest. A candidate will require eight nominees (proposer and seconder + 6) in order to stand, and anyone with fewer than sixteen votes in the first ballot (Thursday 13 June) will go out, or without thirty-two in the second ballot. Nominations next Monday. Ballots over the following two weeks. Kit Malthouse drops out. Berk – so he should. He was silly ever to have put his name forward. Mark Harper and Esther McVey should now do the same.

Farage sees Trump in Winfield House. Brexiteers Iain Duncan Smith and Owen Paterson see him too. Oh dear … And Boris has had a phone call. Gove and Hunt will have meetings face to face. They are falling over each other to beat a path to his door, but the only three who matter are Johnson, Hunt and Gove.

And then the self-styled Change UK announce a schism. Six of them leave: Chuka Umunna, Luciana Berger, Heidi Allen, Sarah Wollaston, Gavin Shuker, Angela Smith. Those who remain in this short-lived not-quite party are Anna Soubry (now its leader), Chris Leslie, Joan Ryan, Mike Gapes and Ann Coffey. So the great splinter from the two major parties has itself splintered, having won no seats in the EU election, and having been massively overshadowed by the Lib Dem revival. They have lasted a matter of weeks and have failed to cut through into any measure of public consciousness.

The State Visit has really gone well. In the face of the worrying risk of it all going horribly wrong, it has (so far) been a triumph.

Wednesday 5 June – London

Hunt leadership team meeting in PCH.

See Clerk of the House, Dr John Benger. I'm concerned that we're rushing headlong into a constitutional crisis. Almost always when a leader, and hence Prime Minister, has changed within a parliament he or she has done so with a working Commons majority. Taking the basic Party arithmetic, let alone with its Brexit divisions, it is far from clear that anyone who succeeds Theresa May will actually then be able to govern. They might have the job, but they might not have the numbers to make it work. When a government is formed, it needs to prove that it has a majority in the Commons, so when a prime minister switches, it can't automatically be assumed that they inherit the previous government's support. So my question for the Clerk is whether it is fair to ask the Queen to summon a new party leader before it is clear that he or she can actually govern. Should the Commons endorse the new leader and prove their majority before going to the Palace, and if so, how would it be possible?

It is conceivable that the government could just limp along without ever voting on anything, or quickly collapse. Even worse, because of the FTPA [Fixed-Term Parliaments Act], it might not be able either to govern or call an election. If the Queen summons the new leader of a minority government, there is a danger that some might accuse her of making a political decision. These constitutional matters are seen by some as nitpicking, but as with the FTPA itself the details really do matter.

Great pageantry in Portsmouth for the D-Day commemorations. HM the Queen, President Trump, Macron, Merkel and other world leaders all gathered. The Queen, resplendent in cerise amid a sea of grey suits, spoke movingly of the resilience of 'my generation' seventy-five years ago, while US Ambassador Woody Johnson, immediately behind her, seemed to be videoing it on his iPhone.

Vote at 3.15pm. Speak to Boris in the lobby. Perfectly friendly and smiling. I told him directly that as long as he was the sole Brexiteers' champion in the final ballot, he would easily win, but that I was nevertheless for Hunt.

481

Thursday 6 June – London

Dominic Raab has shown how bonkers he is by saying that he favours the prorogation of Parliament so that by not sitting they cannot block the UK leaving on 31 October. So there we have it: a would-be prime minister, who says that leaving the EU is all about taking back control and restoring self-government, supports the closure of the Commons so as to disempower MPs from exercising the authority granted to them by a democratic national election. I'm not sure he is sufficiently imbued with the spirit of democracy we are there to protect.

Identify the 'never to Boris' list of colleagues: Roger Gale, Jeremy Lefroy, Bob Neill, Phillip Lee, Guto Bebb, Sam Gyimah, Dominic Grieve.

Friday 7 June – Rutland

Phew! Farage's Brexit Party has failed to win the Peterborough by-election, which will halt its seemingly unstoppable bandwagon and so reduce the incessant focus on him. Labour won by 683 votes, and we came third. Better a Labour hold than a Brexit win.

Amusing phone call with the ultra-bright and charming Andrew Bowie. I set up a call with him and Jeremy, as he will support Matt Hancock in the first round but then will need a new home.

Saturday 8 June – Rutland

Trooping the Colour. Grenadiers looking fab. HMTQ is ninety-three. The Duke of Edinburgh will be ninety-eight on Monday.

The *Mail* is serialising a book about Gove. I don't imagine it will be a bestseller, but their headline reveals that he took cocaine twenty years ago. These days, it doesn't matter a damn, except perhaps in a leadership contest, but his reaction is a little awkward. It will run or not depending on how he now handles it.

Sam Gyimah calls. He is one name short of the eight he needs. He has Bebb, Lee, Grieve, etc, but is scouting around for one more. He knows he will only be able to survive the first round, but wants to make the point. He raises the prospect of us lending him a person so that he can nominate, in return for which he would declare for Jeremy after round one. Cunning, but it could be messy.

Lovely profile of my friend Ian Taylor in *The Times* supplement. He is going to give millions to the NHS for proton-beam cancer treatment.

Sunday 9 June – Rutland/London

Hunt on Sky, Gove on *Marr*. Gove admits the cocaine story head-on, but is in trouble with the issue of honesty with the US authorities about his visa application. He will have lied in order to travel; and if he is honest in the future, will his visa be declined? That is indeed awkward. Snortgate might remain a problem for him.

James Cleverly declares for Boris; my James calls him James Dimly. Cabinet ministers Alun Cairns, Chris Grayling and James Brokenshire all declare for Boris. Bloody hell – Graything yes, but surely not the other two.

Wednesday 12 June – London

Liz Truss suffers a car-crash interview on *Today*. She sounded ridiculous in repeatedly claiming that Boris was one of the best foreign secretaries ever.

Esther McVey in an LBC interview claimed foreign aid had been spent on an airport that didn't work. When Iain Dale asked, 'Where has that happened?', she replied, 'It's … in one of the continents … abroad …'

I tweeted, 'Total rubbish. The runway in question is in St Helena. I was the DfID Minister who built it – completed early, under budget, and despite difficult wind conditions, it operates well. It fulfils our legal obligations to a UK overseas territory, so is not "foreign aid".'

Boris has launched his campaign, saying, 'I won't definitely go for No Deal, but we will definitely leave on 31 October.' Er, work that one out.

I am beginning to think that applying for an emergency debate under Standing Order 24 is the only way of establishing that Boris has sufficient authority to go up the Mall after he wins the leadership.

Strict three-line whip from 1.30pm for a vote that only comes at 4.15pm on Cooper–Letwin Mark 2. The government fends it off by 309–198.

Drink with Kim Darroch. He was relieved the State Visit went smoothly – it had taken an enormous amount of preparatory work.

It's the first ballot tomorrow. It's really a fight for second place. Gove has probably suffered a setback since Snortgate, and Boris has the declared support of about eighty. He will get more than that, but I hope it'll be under 100. The trouble is that the second layer is bound to be in a tight cluster, and we need Jeremy to be comfortably at the front of the pack.

Thursday 13 June – London/Rutland

Two tankers in the Gulf of Oman holed by suspected limpet mines.

In the first ballot, Boris tops the poll. Johnson 114, Hunt 43, Gove 37, Raab 27, Javid 23, Hancock 20, Stewart 19, Leadsom 11, Harper 10, McVey 9. So the bottom three drop out as they failed to secure the sixteen (5 per cent) threshold.

Meanwhile, Chuka Umunna has joined the Lib Dems – his third party in as many months.

Friday 14 June – Rutland

Jeremy does well on the *Today* programme, but Hancock is probably going to pull out.

Saturday 15 June – Rutland

To Tusmore for Wafic and Rosemary Saïd's fiftieth wedding anniversary lunch. It couldn't be more sumptuous. Tusmore, the house and the park, are manicured to perfection, and the 300 guests are a star-studded array of royalty, elegance and Syrian–Lebanese chic. Prince Michael of Kent, Prince Pavlos of Greece, former Canadian PM Brian Mulroney, politicians, ambassadors and a fabulous display of grandes dames. Outside the marquee it was chucking it down, but it didn't matter.

Back to Rutland. Ed Jones tells me Hancock is due to declare for Boris. I just can't believe that he has suddenly switched from striking out on his own to taking the Boris shilling, no doubt in exchange for the promise of a job. It smacks of George Osborne in the background, pulling his strings and scheming for that future moment when Boris explodes and the Hancock time arrives. But I am deeply disappointed. I text him rather ferociously, 'What a pity. You built up a fantastic reputation and you've just destroyed it. Your value was in not being biddable. In my book you have just gone from hero to zero. Sorry.' And so it has. Horse-trading for 'jobs' just sucks.

Boris is refusing to participate in tomorrow's TV debate with the other candidates. He is under a gagging order imposed by his minders. They just know that if he opens his mouth it could all go horribly wrong.

Sunday 16 June – Rutland/London
Catch-up day.

It's the first TV hustings, Channel 4 from 6.30pm to 9.00. An empty podium for Boris, but with Gove, Hunt, Javid, Raab and Stewart. All five were polite to each other, and they were far too kind about the absence of Boris. Jeremy won on authority and command, and Raab was the loser. Rory probably a zany second, and Gove and Sajid decent types in the middle.

Barrister friend Jeremy Brier texts, and I call him. He says my post-debate tweet saying the C4 debate was a credit to the Party was right, but that Rory is like an enthusiastic schoolboy whose ideas wouldn't withstand the toughness of reality.

Rory himself then calls me. We have a lively chat, and I told him straight that I would not desert Jeremy. I admired his progress, but I consider him a man for the future. Perfectly reasonably he says he is the only one who can beat Boris. True, perhaps, but he's not going to break through. Being interesting and original is one thing: stepping into Number 10 in the middle of all this shit is quite another.

I then call Matt Hancock. I said I'm sorry I was so tough on him in my text last night: I have been feeling guilty. He was adorably appreciative of the call. I think he'd been hurt. He had been agonising and had 'been walking today in the park with Rory Stewart' to talk it over. He will declare for Boris. I said it's just not needed. He must be his own man and not be bought. He objects to the reports that he is being handled by George Osborne, but feels he needs to row in behind the inevitable Johnson victory. He says all the remaining candidates have been promising people jobs. How squalid and disappointing. Shitty horse-trading ... bald men being promised a comb etc.

Monday 17 June – London

One of those days when I dart between a million different issues.

Andrew Bowie in the Tea Room. Alex Burghart also there. I tried to flush out of Andrew whether he has already committed to Boris. He was a little cryptic, but probably not deliberately. I didn't want to quiz him in front of Alex, but he said that he had texted all the candidates in last night's debate to say he would vote for someone else. So I said, 'Oh so you're for Boris.' He then suggested that he had not texted Gove. While getting a cup of tea I texted to say that I hoped he wasn't about to declare for Boris. An hour later, contrary to the Tea Room chat, he replied that he would. All over the bloody place.

The leadership campaign continues. Boris is in hiding, declining all media contact, even boycotting the hustings with lobby journalists, while Lidington backs Rory, which is a pity. Jeremy needs momentum, but the cluster to remain in the race and try for second place is very tight. Hunt, Gove, Stewart, Javid, Raab ... I think in that order.

Midday Hunt leadership meeting. We go through the list of names we need, but it's a tad amateurish. We need Bob Stewart, Bim Afolami, Tracey Crouch, Stephen Hammond, Alex Chalk, Mark Lancaster and Paul Scully ... among others.

See Dr Benger, the Commons Clerk. He will help me draft an appropriate SO24 motion to test confidence in the prospective PM, who we assume will be Boris. I am mulling in my mind the speech I will make if my plan works.

Mohamed Morsi, the 67-year-old former President of Egypt, has collapsed and died in court in Cairo. Better than in a jail, but a dismal advertisement for the country, and will inevitably give rise to suspicion and conspiracy theories.

Host a reception in the Locarno Room for the visiting Colombia delegation around President Duque. Lovely atmosphere. Jack Mably, my Assistant Private Secretary, in cracking form, handling the room brilliantly.

My mind is whirring about two things: do I write a thumping valedictory DipTel, and what do I say if I succeed in making a speech on SO24?

James arrives with Noodle at 11pm.

Tuesday 18 June – London

The US have sent another 1,000 troops to the Gulf, as the temperature with Iran rises. Meanwhile Netanyahu has unveiled a sign saying 'Trump Heights' in the occupied Golan Heights. It is a gimmick, but it is an outrageous one.

Useful briefing from officials about the attacks on some oil tankers off Fujairah. It was limpet mines, and a US helicopter has clear footage of the IRGC in a speedboat removing one that had not exploded. It doesn't prove that they put it there in the first place, but who can doubt they did?

Straight to Committee Room 14 to vote for Jeremy in the second ballot, followed by another of many regular contributions to Patrick Forbes' Channel 4 documentary on Brexit.

I have to respond at the end of a one-hour debate in Westminster Hall on the Colombia peace process, and then go straight to drinks in my office for all the Operation Pelican team, those who worked on the removal of Julian Assange from the Ecuador embassy. I gave them each a signed photo which we took in the Ops Room on the day, with a caption saying 'Julian Assange's Special Brexit Team 11th April 2019'.

Soon after I arrive, the ballot result leads the 6pm news. Johnson 126, Hunt 46, Gove 41, Stewart 37, Raab 30, Javid 33. So Dominic Raab is out. The third ballot will be tomorrow. Boris remains well ahead, but his success occurs while he hides away and says nothing. Indeed the entire ERG have maintained total radio silence. We haven't heard a squeak from Mogg, Francois or Baker. What joy.

Dinner in Lancaster House for President Duque. Warm mood, and am joined by Mark Lancaster, Thérèse Coffey and Mark Menzies. The President so liked the discipline created by the butler's gavel that at the conclusion I gave it to him as a present.

Attending the dinner meant that I missed the BBC TV candidates' debate. It was the remaining five on bar stools, chaired by Emily Maitlis. Nobody afterwards had a good word to say about the format, and the loser was the BBC, even more than Boris.

Wednesday 19 June – London

Last night's debate is being widely ridiculed as is Rory Stewart, who took off his tie while on stage and writhed oddly between peculiar contorted postures. As someone said about his tie, 'It's a leadership debate, not *The Full Monty*!'

Coffee with my prep school headmaster Alan Mould, who is now ninety-one.

Cast vote in third ballot.

Host drinks to celebrate the signing of the Oman Comprehensive Agreement.

Third ballot results. Johnson 143, Hunt 54, Gove 51, Javid 38, Stewart 27. With ten votes fewer than last time, Rory Stewart is furious that his numbers may have been inflated and then deflated by surreptitious transfers, but his performance and shameless self-appreciation had begun to attract ridicule.

Thursday 20 June – London/Rutland

It looks as though, without the knowledge of the MPs themselves, Gavin Williamson may have used their proxy votes intended for Boris to instead boost Stewart in the earlier ballots and then throw him into reverse to rob him of momentum. Just the kind of Machiavellian plot Williamson loves. Even if he didn't do it, nobody thinks he wouldn't.

Fourth ballot.

Result. Johnson 157, Hunt 59, Gove 61, Javid 34. Nooo! Hunt is two behind Gove. Two MPs have spoilt their ballot paper.

Cast vote in ballot number five.

Do BBC *PM* prog in the Central Lobby before the result comes out at 6pm.

Result: Johnson 160, Hunt 77, Gove 75. So it's Hunt vs Johnson, with 160 for Johnson vs combined 152 against. Hunt through by a whisker … just 2!

To the National Army Museum in Royal Hospital Road for a ceremonial event marking twenty years since the end of the conflict in Kosovo. Mark Lancaster there. He actually served in Kosovo at the time as an army bomb disposal officer.

Saturday 22 June – Rutland

Well, that didn't take long. Boris is all over every front page. The police were called to [his now girlfriend] Carrie Symonds' flat late on Thursday night after what is reported as a noisy screaming match accompanied by the sound of smashing glass. The neighbours are said to have recorded it and called the police, having heard shouts of 'get off me', 'you just don't care about money', 'you are so spoilt' and 'you've covered the sofa in red wine'. So the first grenade went off within hours of him topping the Members' ballot.

Ben Wallace has issued and then deleted a tweet which said that it's just nasty leftie neighbours out to get him, but it sits in stark contrast to the brutal suspension yesterday of Mark Field, for restraining a woman protester at the Mansion House dinner while Philip Hammond was speaking. Maybe Number 10 knew about the Boris domestic and so deliberately over-egged the treatment of Mark. Who knows? A domestic row is on one level entirely private, but if he behaves like this when he is supposed to be on his best behaviour, then whatever next?

It's great timing for us, as today is the first public hustings. Although it's for the West Midlands, and I am in the East Midlands, there is nothing to say I cannot be in Birmingham, so I decide to up sticks and head there.

Nearly 2,000 members at the hustings, which we amusingly call the hustlings. Lots of TV interviews, and briefings to the print media, which are then immediately trolled on Twitter. Leave.EU must have an army of nasties at computer terminals churning out vitriolic shit.

Iain Dale chaired. Boris first. Video, interview, then questions from the floor. First question went straight for the jugular about the domestic row. Boris rather flunked it. As his slapdash waffling continued you could feel the hall deflating …

In contrast, Jeremy Hunt was at his very best. I'm not normally one for the old shirtsleeves stunt, but he carried it off well, and his content was so much more serious than Boris. There was a moving moment in which he told of a friend at school who came out as gay, for whom he was very supportive.

Sunday 23 June – Rutland/London

It's all Boris, Boris, Boris in the papers …

There are now a number of stories in the papers suggesting that Boris might only be PM for a day, and that there are enough Tory MPs who would rather bring down the government than have Boris as PM and/or a hard Brexit.

Monday 24 June – London

Tobias Ellwood has said that at least a dozen colleagues would rather bring down the government than allow an EU exit without a deal. It all indicates that the government could collapse in September, or even that Boris would be PM only for a day. There is no obvious path through the political thicket.

Jeremy gives an excellent interview on *Today*, ramming home that Boris is hiding from any public debate, which is precisely what he is doing. Silly Zac Goldsmith tweets against JH: 'I'm disappointed to see Jeremy Hunt making personal attacks on Boris. It's hard to believe Party members will be impressed either.' Hunt replies, 'Au contraire. I've made clear I have no interest in his personal life, but I do have a real problem with him avoiding public scrutiny.'

Priti Unspeakable does *Today* a bit later. She is simply ghastly. Shameless crap, refusing to admit that the Boris plan for leaving on WTO terms cannot be delivered, as without a Withdrawal Agreement there can be no Implementation Period within which it can be agreed.

At last. At long last!! There is progress on smartening up the Foreign Office signs around the rising bollards and inspection point underneath the arches on the entrance into King Charles Street from Whitehall. It has taken me two years during which they put in some repulsive asymmetrical vulgar red ones. The admirable Keith Cook, who is an in-house designer in FCO Services, has come up with a scheme which is elegant and appropriate. Simple graphics on a cosmetic iron railing with a crest in the middle, which can sit just below the ledge of the stone pedestal at the foot of the arch. Never mind wars and pestilence: this will be my lasting legacy!

A nice chat with the PM and then Jeremy Corbyn behind the Speaker's Chair ahead of the 3.30pm PM statement on last week's European Council. I tell Corbyn that Hunt is on the rise, but that Boris will probably still win.

Boris has released an unconvincing saccharine photo of him and Carrie Symonds at a table in a meadow. It's just so ridiculous. Feed the media monster with no footage and no comment. Just a photo. He is hiding.

Interview on the Green with CNN, but when I was asked about Boris and the police I rather tartly said to the interviewer that it's none of her business and it's none of mine. She was rather taken aback, but we moved on.

Vote at 7pm about whether we agree to the summer recess, rising on 25 July, and returning on 3 September. We were voting Aye, and the Scot Nats No. Although Labour were abstaining, their phone message instructions came through late by which time half the Labour Party were at the door of the lobby being told to go away. One of them was Corbyn. So I explained to him that he was abstaining, and then told him the details of the planned recess, all of which he should have known about already. But I took him into a corner and told him that by rising on Thursday the 25th he could move a motion of no confidence in Boris on that very day, on his first day as PM. His look suggested that that was what he was intending to do. But more importantly it happily threw him off any thought of doing anything earlier. So far my plan is safe. Not even the Cabinet Secretary knows about the SO24 option. My pre-emptive strike still has mileage.

Tuesday 25 June – London

Boris has given an interview to the BBC. His handlers are desperate to maintain a degree of exposure, but without subjecting him to debate against Jeremy. He is too much of a liability and is being kept in his kennel except for the occasional permitted bark.

FCO Orals. Probably my last ever questions as a minister. I had the first question on the rules-based international order, and turned it into a cheerful exchange with MPs on both sides. I used it to promote Jeremy's candidacy in an amusing way. The hour went well, but the House was very thin. Yet another illustration of the collapse of the Commons into dysfunctionality.

As I walk back to the FCO Erik calls. I bump into Richard Graham. He says that Daniel Kawczynski had a serious car crash yesterday. I said, 'Oh God, I hope he's OK.' He replied, 'Well he is: it wasn't on a road – it was a disastrous radio interview defending Boris.'

Meeting with Philip Hammond in his Commons room with like-minded colleagues opposed to leaving with No Deal. Philip has 'something that is going to arise', and Oliver Letwin also has a plan. Obstruction last time was the freelance action of Chris Pincher the Deputy Whip, and was not sanctioned by Julian Smith, the Chief. It's not quite clear what the Hammond plan would involve, but he seems quite determined. He says that if he is deselected he will stand as an Independent Conservative, and so hand his seat to the Lib Dems. Those attending: Hammond (both Philip and Stephen), Gauke, [Jonathan] Djanogly, Harrington, Gyimah, Brine, [Victoria] Prentis, Neill, Newton, [Paul] Masterton, James, Sandbach. Supportive types not there: Clark, Rudd. Lee, Grieve and Clarke might vote for a no-confidence motion, but others would not, at least not so early.

Wednesday 26 June – London

The Johnson campaign has tried to reboot itself. IDS is now the campaign Chairman, Hancock and Williamson are in charge of transition, and Liz Truss is in charge of policy. There are rumours that George Osborne wants to come back into politics: I wonder if

Johnson might put him in the Lords and stick him in somewhere. Williamson seems to think that he (i.e. WmSon) should be Deputy Prime Minister. It is the ultimate horror show.

Dentist. An hour in the chair cheers me up!

To Albert Embankment to meet constituents who have come to London as part of a massive climate-change campaign day. Some nice young people, but mainly a group of crackpot angst-ridden vegan women, who just repeat slogans and can't offer a deeper argument. Their cause is right, and I agree with them, but they can't do anything other than complain and attack, whereas they could instead be building a big broad harmonious coalition.

Bump into Ben Wallace, who says we're all doomed. He began to blame May, and I defended her against all her ERG assailants. We then both agreed that whoever wins is doomed. Then we further agreed that the origin of all of it was Cameron 'feeding the fucking crocodile'.

Drink on the Terrace with Mike Freer. It wasn't quite clear what he was fishing for, but he said he was just personally intrigued to know how I saw my future. Hmm. I equivocated suitably, but said I had no particular wish to be in the Lords, as it has become something of a dustbin. Andrew Bowie came over for a chat, casually dressed and looking his usual boyish self.

Bump into Ed Jones, JH SpAd, on the way home. He comes for a drink and stays for dinner. Good thing, nice guy, like him.

Friday 28 June – Rutland
Daily Mail headline on Boris and turds. When filming for the FCO documentary he referred to the French as turds, and the FCO had to negotiate with the BBC to have it edited out of the broadcast. As it happens, I know this to be true, as I recall seeing the press office note about it.

I am booked to do an interview on the *Today* programme and confirm the story is true, and that it marks the serious difference between Boris and Hunt: 'You can have a circus act or a really serious person who does do detail and is respected in other countries and will be taken seriously in discussions.'

The 'circus act' line gets picked up a bit in the coverage throughout the day.

Monday 1 July – London

The day gets off to a nauseating start with a *Today* programme interview with Matt Hancock, who has become an enthusiastic schoolboy in support of Boris. For the sake of his own promotion, on which he has no doubt done some sort of deal, he has become a crazed apologist for him, stating things he simply doesn't believe.

Overnight, Association Chairman Byron Rhodes has forwarded a series of emails, two from members we have never heard of, calling for me to be deselected for saying that Boris isn't fit to be PM. It's once again the bloody *Telegraph*, putting in its headline that I called Boris 'unfit to govern' when I have said no such thing. I said in my Friday interview that Boris was a circus act and Jeremy is serious. But what is astonishing is how people become furiously indignant about the smallest of things and get everything out of all proportion. They are all Leave.EU maniacs.

The repulsive Geoffrey Pointon demanded at Friday's Executive Meeting that I should be asked if I would support the government in a no-confidence motion. I replied that in twenty-seven years as an MP I have never once voted against the whip, and that perhaps the Executive might contrast my unblemished record of loyalty with the conduct of those members who voted for the Brexit Party in the recent EU elections. How much longer do I have to put up with these people?

To Policy Exchange think tank for Jeremy's speech on how he would handle a No Deal exit. It was a pitch about how much more realistic he would be in handling the prospect.

No Boris on Sky TV's planned debate, so Jeremy gets an hour on his own with the snippy Kay Burley. He handled himself really well.

Tuesday 2 July – London

Team leadership meeting. I am suspicious about the Boris campaign. I think they are up to dirty tricks. Lots of people are reporting that they are being approached by their campaign by phone or email when they have no idea how they got their details. I think they are using historic lists from previous campaigns run by either the Party or referendum groups. If they are, they are doing so totally illegally, but will secure their victory before any investigation catches up with them.

See Dr John Benger, the Clerk of the Commons. He is so lucid and straightforward. If the leadership result is announced in the morning of Tuesday 23rd, then my plan is in with a chance. I can apply for an SO24 debate on Monday morning, argue for it on Monday afternoon, have it granted for Tuesday afternoon, and then the Speaker can pick the time it will happen. It would become a not-quite confidence motion in Boris immediately after he is announced as the new Leader, but before he might go up the Mall to see the Queen on Wednesday. I would need forty MPs to stand up in the Chamber on Monday after my three-minute pitch for the motion to be heard, or if there are between ten and forty there would have to be a division. I will propose he become the new PM, but not before I have said some pretty tough things. My purpose is not so much to stop Boris as to establish that he has the majority to govern. It's a fundamental constitutional principle.

Mark Field remains needlessly suspended as a minister following his Mansion House action, so I have to take a UQ on the protests in Hong Kong.

It's a duty day. A quick lunch, then into Westminster Hall for a ninety-minute debate on the Polish Contribution to the War Effort in the Second World War. It's odd we debate it, but Daniel Kawczynski is irrepressible. It ended up as a powerful and emotional occasion. Stephen Pound as good as gave an authoritative lecture, Daniel K himself was fine, and not his usual mad self, and I threw away my FCO speech and cited the Thomas Gray-inspired poem which refers to both flight and air victory. I wanted it used in the RAF Centenary Service last year, and have now used it to pay tribute to Polish airmen. I have therefore successfully read into the record of the House the poem that Squadron Leader Robert Grant-Ferris would have read had he found it before moving the Loyal Address after the Battle of Britain in 1940.

To Number 10 for their Pride reception. A nice do, although the PM was detained in Brussels, and Penny Mordaunt had to step in to read her speech.

Top-level EU appointments emerge after three days: Commission President – Ursula von der Leyen, German Defence Minister; President of the Council – Charles Michel, Belgian PM; ECB President – Christine Lagarde of the IMF; External Action Service – Josep Borrell, FM of Spain.

Sunday 7 July – London

A rare Sunday in London. Sadly Arman Kirakossian, the Armenian Ambassador to London, has died. He has been in hospital for a few weeks, and it was not unexpected, but it is important to extend the proper condolences. The Marshal of the Diplomatic Corps, Alistair Harrison, will issue a formal statement, and I make a call to their Foreign Minister Zohrab Mnatsakanyan to offer condolences. In the course of the call, the FM says how stupendous John Major was on the BBC's *Hardtalk*, which indeed he was. John had slammed Boris Johnson, and once again called for the revocation of Article 50. He interviews with a commanding authority. I wrote to him to say how good he was.

The *Mail on Sunday* splash headline is: 'Our man in US says Trump is "inept"'. Someone has leaked a whole raft of diplomatic telegrams over many months in which our Washington embassy dissects all the weaknesses of Trump. They all go out in the name of the Ambassador, so Kim Darroch is in the firing line. I call him straightaway to express solidarity. Kim says the President hasn't said anything yet, but he is braced for a furious tweet.

Monday 8 July – London

Oh, here we go. Trump has gone off on one. In the course of the day his tweets become more obnoxious and he states that he will no longer deal with Darroch. Needless to say, the tosser Farage lays into Kim, who he considers pro-EU, and the civil service more widely. I am then suddenly faced with an Urgent Question in the Commons from Tom Tugendhat.

The mood of the House is quite easy to catch, but powerfully united against the leak and in support of Kim. For Labour, Emily Thornberry is, for once, measured and sensible, and there were many other supportive comments. I strongly backed Kim as a man of integrity, stressing how vital it is that our ambassadors can express themselves with candour. Bill Cash made a stupid intervention backing the Farage line about Darroch being too pro-EU. It was utterly unworthy, and I said so.

Back to the FCO. I told my office a month ago that I intended to leave, and it feels as though they are slightly slipping into woeful valedictory mode.

Tuesday 9 July – London

William Hague, as usual, is a voice of sanity on *Today*. He strikes the right balance between supporting Darroch and disapproving of Trump's behaviour. Chat with John Glen in the street; much as I like him and consider him sensible, he says we should stick Farage into Washington just to get rid of him. I gently chide him for even thinking it, explaining that an ambassador has to do much more than ingratiate himself with the President. I say while we're at it why don't we appoint Jeremy Corbyn as the government envoy for international disarmament! And then around the corner I encounter Michael Gove. An amusing chat in which he at least concedes that Trump is a spoilt child.

To the Commons to pick up Hansard from yesterday. Saw Oliver Letwin at the Vote Office window – he has tabled another motion on the Order Paper, so I quip, 'You're giving us another busy day.' 'Well, it's more Dominic on this one,' he replied, which is true. I said I liked his tie. It was Hermès. I said I call it the airport tax because I can never go through one without spending another £100 on a tie like his. 'But I think Salvatore Ferragamo have the edge.' He emitted a high-pitched Letwin giggle and said, 'I suppose you've got hundreds: nobody can beat the Duncan wardrobe.'

The Grieve amendment is designed to stop a prorogation being used to block Brexit debate, by requiring fortnightly statements to the House on Northern Ireland so as to keep business going. The division takes ages, and then there's a flurry. It looks like the vote is tied. But then it turns out that a government whip, Jo Churchill, went into the lobby after the Deputy Speaker had shouted 'lock the doors'. So 294–294 becomes 294–293. Grieve wins by one.

Nice chat with the PM on the front bench, but she was sitting near the Speaker's Chair. Whips Iain Stewart and Mark Spencer were too shy to ask her to budge up a bit, so they asked me to ask her. So I said with a smile, 'Oi, Prime Minister, you're blocking the bench.' Slightly startled, and with a hesitant smile, she moves.

Trump has gone apeshit, tweeting that Darroch is dumb and stupid, not a good man, etc. Then news breaks out of tonight's Hunt–Johnson hustings that Boris has been less than lukewarm in defence of Darroch, clearly preferring to suck up to Trump, which is pretty shameful.

Wednesday 10 July – London
To the Paintworks in Canada Water for the Media Freedom Conference.

My office says Darroch is set to resign at midday, just as the PM stands up for PMQs.

Rush back to Whitehall. Boris' failure to support Darroch is running hard. FCO SpAd Tim Smith suggests I do an interview saying that Boris has thrown Kim under the bus. I do a full media round in Central Lobby, ferociously defending Kim and attacking Boris, who you'd think as a former Foreign Secretary would be keen to support a top ambassador. *BBC News*, *World at One*, Sky, LBC, etc. I link up with Steve Swinford to give him all my quotes. The mood is rather feverish. 'Thrown under the bus' catches on in all the reports.

An Iranian tanker is being held by Gibraltar under suspicion of breaking international sanctions. My recommendation is to release it if they will turn it around and sail out of the Med, especially as there will be tit-for-tat retaliation in the Gulf where Iranian patrol boats are now hailing a BP ship.

Thursday 11 July – London

I respond to a UQ on the Darroch resignation, tabled by Labour MP Pat McFadden. Another triumph. All except the idiot Peter Bone support Darroch. And 90 per cent of the Chamber is anti-Boris.

Chat with the Speaker in the Chair afterwards. I buttered him up by saying that our embassy in Washington is grateful for his support from the Chair. I said I will resign on Monday 22nd and may say some brutal things. I said I may need to talk to him then. So I've planted the idea that I'm up to something without quite saying what.

Friday 12 July – London

See the Clerk of the House. I tell him I am definitely going to go for my SO24 application on Monday week, and that I have teed up the Speaker by telling him that I am going to resign that day.

Speak to 2,000 at the Bastille Day celebrations in the garden of the French embassy. I deliver half my speech in French, and heap praise on French Ambassador Jean-Pierre Jouyet, with an adapted quote from Charles de Gaulle: 'Toute ma vie, je me suis fait une certaine idée de Jean-Pierre Jouyet'!

Lovely party at the home of Karen Pierce and Charles Roxburgh. Enormous fun, attended by most of those who really run the country, half of Whitehall's permanent secretaries among them. Karen is a real star – the way things are going she'll soon end up in Washington.

HMS *Duncan* is being sent to the Gulf.

Saturday 13 July – London/Madrid

The Cabinet Office have stated that the DipTels leak inquiry is now considered a criminal matter. Commander Neil Basu of the Met has said that any newspaper which chooses to publish further leaks might be committing a criminal offence and has asked anyone in possession of government documents to hand them back. This might explode! It could turn into a classic spat between government secrecy and press freedom.

Needless to say, one of the first to condemn this is Tim Shipman, who declares it a full-frontal attack on press freedom. Jeremy tweets sensibly – he deplores leaks, defends the rights of a free press, but states that anyone who has broken the Official Secrets Act should be punished. The odious big-heads soon go tweet-crazy. George Osborne, as editor of the *Evening Standard*, attacks Basu directly for stupidity and more besides, and calls on Commissioner Cressida Dick to distance herself from him. Hancock, probably coordinated with Osborne, also condemns the Basu action.

The indignees rather seem to have missed the point. By and large, the press always have a defence of last resort which is that they can claim to have acted in the public interest. That is not the same, however, as having published something that happens to have been of interest to the public. In most cases they can get away with it by claiming the former even when everyone knows it is the latter, but there is no such public interest defence in the Official Secrets Act. If you have broken it, then you have broken the law. All of these journalists think that they have the right to publish absolutely anything under cover of the public interest defence, even when it has been stolen, or when they have colluded in the theft. Actual classified documents, however, enjoy a different status and quite rightly are, and should be, subject to exceptional legal force. That is the issue with the leaked DipTels. We are only a few years on from the hacking scandal in which journalists went to prison, the *News of the World* closed down and the illegality of the media was seen to be legion. Now today, George Osborne and Tim Shipman seem to think they are above the law. I suspect we could be heading for a confrontation between the government establishment and the press which risks going on and on. The best way to break this and halt it is to terminate our fetid political stasis and bring in a new era. If only.

To Heathrow for the 3pm flight to Madrid. Rather touchingly, our Ambassador Simon Manley meets me at the airport. It's Saturday, and I'm merely in transit overnight, but he said he wanted to come to convey a special thank-you, both personally and from 'just so many others', for my defence of Kim and all diplomats. I was really rather moved by the gesture.

On arrival there's a bit of a Gibraltar crisis. Jeremy Hunt has tweeted that he's spoken to the Iranians and wants to resolve the case of the detained ship. But this has thrown Fabian Picardo into a state of fury because it cuts across the strict legal process he is obliged to follow in Gibraltar. It is precisely what I briefed Jeremy's office and SpAd Ed Jones he must not do. I text JH urging him to phone Fabian immediately. To his credit he does, and they agree a remedial statement.

Sunday 14 July – Madrid/Ecuador
The *Sunday Times* reveals that Richard Tice, Chair of the Brexit Party, is dating journalist Isabel Oakeshott, both having recently separated. It's the ultimate Brexit union, but spawns no end of conspiracies about the DipTel leak flow, as she was the journalist who broke the story, so who knew what when? There most definitely is a deep Brexit link to the leaks. Meanwhile the odious Arron Banks is trolling me, adding my Twitter handle to every abusive tweet he and Leave.EU send out. I don't quite know why he always goes for me, but such is life. He's not one of life's more attractive people.

Midday flight to Quito in Ecuador, and our wonderful Ambassador Cathy Ward is there to greet us. A couple of beers with the embassy team. Light supper and to bed. With the six-hour time difference it's 2am UK.

Monday 15 July – Ecuador
Wake at 3am local. There's just no point in trying to sleep on, but it's going to be a long day.

David Davis is on another civil liberties/free press kick, calling for Commander Neil Basu to be moved from any involvement in the DipTel leak. He overplays his role as a breast-beating crusader who wants to appear as a moral champion. In my view, if they find the leaker they should throw the book at them, and prosecute Isabel Oakeshott too.

Meeting with President Lenín Moreno. He's been in a wheelchair for twenty years since being shot in a robbery attempt. Visiting him to say thank you is an essential conclusion to the Assange episode, and he exudes goodwill and warmth. He loves the UK, and I gave him a beautiful porcelain plate from the Buckingham Palace gift shop. Job done.

Tuesday 16 July – Ecuador/Bogotá/London

Fly home overnight via Bogotá.

Tomorrow's papers, which I can see in Bogotá as it's 4am in the UK, are full of presumptuous hubris about Boris's first seventy-two hours, his wish to demolish Corbyn in an election as soon as he has delivered Brexit, and who his appointments will be. But he doesn't have a bloody majority and he clearly thinks it will all come to him on a plate.

Thursday 18 July – London

Really sad news – I learn that Ian [Taylor] has had a stroke, which explains his recent absence.

FCO. Philip Hammond calls to persuade me to abstain on this afternoon's vote. I agree to do so. The government loses the two votes: 315–274 and 315–273 on prorogation. There's then one on gay marriage and abortion in Northern Ireland. As he walked past the front bench, the DUP's Sammy Wilson said, 'I think we're comprehensively beaten on that one.' I said, 'Indeed you are, Sammy, you great poof!'

Then reply to the backbench business motion on the Bishop of Truro's Report on the Persecution of Christians Abroad. Jim Shannon, the MP for Strangford, who is himself very religious, was overcome with emotion and burst into tears. We all intervened on him so as to allow him time to compose himself.

Valedictory open-house party in my FCO office. Totally pissed!

Friday 19 July – London/Rutland

Commons Clerk to go through my SO24 application. Then to the Commons Library.

Farewells to my private office, and then off to Rutland.

Turn down attending Jeremy Hunt's party at Chevening for his leadership team. I'd rather get home to Rutland to see James again on his return from Scotland.

Saturday 20 July – Rutland

Oakham. Quiet day. Thunderstorm. So nice of Noodle to bring yet another field mouse into the TV room.

The Iranians have seized the *Stena Impero*. They think they're clever, but it's a British flag on a Swedish ship with a foreign crew and someone else owns the cargo. So not really much UK equity in that.

Sunday 21 July – Rutland/London
The big issue is the seizure of the tanker by Iran.

To London.

Speak to Jeremy Hunt … I tell him I intend to resign tomorrow, ahead of Tuesday's formal declaration of the vote of members. He is very nice about it. He says he doesn't blame me for a second – he's enjoyed working with me but guessed it was about to come to an end anyway.

Check my paperwork for tomorrow. Early night.

Monday 22 July – London
Up early. To HofC with my letters. Make a load of copies of them. Take my SO24 application letter straight to the Speaker's Secretary along with my covering explanation. Based on the Clerk's advice it seems inconceivable that he will not grant it.

Andrew Bowie and Keith Simpson in the Tea Room. Give Andrew my resignation letter, because as Theresa's PPS he can walk it over to Number 10 for me. His parting comment is 'But we don't even know that Boris can command a majority.' I say, 'Precisely.'

To the FCO. See Simon McDonald and Vicente and the private office to tell them I'm about to resign.

Back to HofC. Tell Steven Swinford he can tweet that a minister is about to resign.

Interview with Patrick Forbes. Allow SS to tweet at 10.30am that I have resigned. Phone goes bonkers.

12.00 Brief SS and Dominic Grieve of my SO24 plan.

Wait for Speaker's verdict. Astonishingly, he turns it down!! So that's that. This peculiar man makes all sorts of rulings when they fit in with his personal wishes, but when it comes to an issue of potential significance as a constitutional precedent, he doesn't give it a moment's thought. It will be interesting to learn one day what influenced his thinking, but it certainly was not the professional advice of the Clerk. He's a moody little creature, and it's quite possible that he gave it no thought and just woke up in a foul temper, and so was not minded to do anything he hadn't thought of himself.

Phone just goes totally red hot.

Agree in the end to release my SO24 application and covering letter.

Do BBC, Sky, ITV, Forbes. No radio.

Millions of texts, emails, messages, etc.

The vile Pointon and Emmett have already emailed Byron to say that the Association should get rid of me.

Attend the Commons for Jeremy Hunt's statement on Iran. Once again, after three years I've returned to the backbenches. Nice tributes as I sit there from Fabian Hamilton, Jeremy, Steve Gethins, etc.

As I walk through Members' Lobby afterwards one of the messengers calls my name and hands me a letter from the board – it is a charming appreciative letter from the Prime Minister in reply to my resignation. No doubt it was accelerated by efficient PPS work from Andrew Bowie.

Tuesday 23 July – London

BoJo will win today, probably by about 2–1.

As I walk around Westminster for various chores and shopping I am regularly stopped by people to say 'Can I shake your hand?', 'You have acted with principle,' 'Can I have a selfie?' Very interesting positive reaction which I wasn't quite expecting.

Watch result from home. It is indeed 2–1. Boris 92,153, Hunt 46,656.

Jeremy Hunt throws a party for his campaign team and supporters on the rooftop of the Trafalgar Hotel. It is typically generous and a good reflection on him that you just feel the room is full of nice people. After a couple of lunchtime beers I go home for a rare afternoon snooze.

I text James Lupton to remind him that I have a text from him saying he would resign the Party whip if Boris were to win. He said, 'I just did, 10 minutes ago.'

Wednesday 24 July – London

Our eleventh wedding anniversary. We have known each other since 14 December 2006, twelve and a half years, and we have never had an argument. Very very hot day.

It's soon to be day one of the BoJo reign. There is talk of Patel etc all coming into government. Ugh! Although Mark Spencer will be Chief Whip, which is fine.

Natter with Lindsay Hoyle in the corridor. He says it was the Speaker who said no to my SO24. He says the Clerks admitted that a clear constitutional principle was at stake. It sounds more to me as if Bercow just dismissed it on a whim.

I text BoJo to say well done, but also to beware of appointing Williamson or Patel to anything, as some are minded to walk if he does.

Theresa May's last PMQs take an hour. Bit flat. We stand and applaud when she leaves, but SNP and Labour just sit there. What a churlish lot – just compare that with our (albeit reluctant) applause when Blair left.

Hammond, Gauke, Stewart and Lidington all resign. Technically, with the appointment of a new PM all ministers are deemed to have resigned anyway, but no one pays enough attention to constitutional detail these days.

With nothing to stop him going up the Mall, once Theresa May has been to the Palace to tender her resignation, Boris arrives and kisses hands at around 3pm. So it is that the Crackpot Government begins …

Then the resignations and sackings come through … Hammond, Gauke, Lidington, Stewart, Mordaunt, Hinds, Grayling, Fox, Clark, Brokenshire, Bradley, Stride.

Javid going into Number 10. Mundell, then Hunt – both out! Patel to Home Sec. Raab to Foreign Sec and First Sec of State. Barclay to Brexit. Wright out. Wallace in. Villiers and Williamson in. It's a massacre, replacing the Sensibles with the Despicables. It seems anyone who was not pro-Brexit has been culled. That's no basis on which to form a competent and united government.

Dinner with James in Franco's. While walking home, spot

Jeremy Hunt and his immediate team all finishing dinner in a nearby restaurant on St James's Street and we drop in to join them for a bit.

Thursday 25 July – London/Rutland
Absolutely baking day. Possibly the hottest on record. The House rises for the summer, one day after Boris becomes Prime Minister without a vote of any sort in the Commons or him having come to the dispatch box in his new role.

James goes to Salma Shah's party, which is attended by Sajid Javid, to whom she was SpAd at the Home Office. Sajid tells a funny story about how Salma used occasionally to slip into Punjabi, usually just to say to him, 'Shut the fuck up.' People would look on a little bewildered, but no more than that. Then Sajid on another occasion thought he'd try the same and so threw some similar Punjabi at Salma. But this time those listening were aghast and shocked. The problem was he had forgotten he was in Delhi!

Friday 26 July – Rutland/Wales
As further ministerial appointments come through, it appears I have been replaced by Chris Pincher. Captain Peacock, as we call him, struts around in a perfectly nice way. I'm not aware of any international experience that qualifies him – it looks to me like more of a reward for being in the Whips' Office. The trouble is, in foreign affairs you do need a feel for the wider world and its complicated issues and personalities.

Boozy dinner chez the Hagues in Wales.

Saturday 27 July – Wales
Walk the ever expanding Hague estate, with its pools, newt ponds and ginkgo trees.

Half-hour call with Pincher while on my long walk. I wish him well and give him a rapid teach-in of the issues I left behind and some of the personalities in the FCO.

Wednesday 31 July – Rutland

End of week one of the BoJo era. No sooner has he taken office than Parliament shuts for the summer. This will give him a bit of a breather, which he needs to use carefully to plan what to do. The composition of the Cabinet does not augur well for unity and good policy-making. It smacks more of an unthinking Brexiteer rump of people who have done nothing other than ride the Brexit wave. As Theresa knew, it was all about the detail. Now he's at the top, Boris will either grasp the realities of government, or crumble.

Friday 2 August – London

We have lost the Brecon and Radnor by-election to the Lib Dems by about 1,400 votes. It was caused by the recall of Chris Davies, who pleaded guilty to expenses fraud, but it doesn't seem to herald a national turn against us.

Wednesday 28 August – France

It's the end of Boris week five, and he drops a bombshell – Parliament is to be prorogued for five weeks from mid-September, not returning until 14 October. Jacob Rees-Mogg (Leader of the House) and a handful of ministers flew to Balmoral for a Privy Council today, so it's a done deal. It's not as outrageous as it first appears, given we would have been in recess for much of the time anyway for the party conferences. But their argument, that they need to do it in order to get a new Queen's Speech for vital legislation, is transparent nonsense. It's clearly being done to avoid rebels taking control of the Order Paper again, and all hell has broken loose with Labour and others decrying it as a coup, with Boris cast as a dictator having 'suspended Parliament'. Few people seem to realise that prorogation happens every year, though admittedly not for this long. It's a provocative step, and might very well backfire.

Philip Hammond has emerged as an unlikely leader of the counter-attack, and is calling on MPs to seize control next week to stop a No Deal exit.

Sunday 1 September – Rutland/London

Back in London after a nice August in Marbella and the south of France. I texted Boris from the beach suggesting we have a chat, and to his credit he called me today. We had a nice chat for twenty minutes. We agreed I would retain my links with Oman and I assured him that, although I had clear views, I've never been a difficult rebel of any sort. My instinct is to support prime ministers, and will do so in the future as I have in the past. He dangled the prospect of the Lords, but not in an explicit way – oblique references to 'Putting you to work in another capacity' and the like, but I said it was up to him and I wasn't particularly bothered. It certainly didn't amount to a clear offer or commitment, nor on my part was it a request. More important was to have connected in a friendly personable way, now that he's Prime Minister.

Monday 2 September – London

Text Jeremy Hunt, to catch up, and to tell him I am staying well away from the Hammond antics, which he agrees is a wise move. Although the runner-up to Boris, Jeremy seems to be the forgotten person already. Nobody mentions him, which is a pity as he deserves better.

Lunch with Ümit Yalçin, the Turkish Ambassador. He just wants to make sense of what on earth is going to happen in the UK. I told him everything I know – which is that nobody knows!

Reception in the garden of Number 10 for Tory MPs ahead of the Commons resuming tomorrow. We could tell something was afoot, as there was an enormous flat-screen TV on a raised platform. After mingling with colleagues, the PM gives a speech in which he bullishly declares that we need to 'get Brexit done' and overcome the obstruction of Parliament. While he says he doesn't want an election, there is a thinly veiled threat that if we don't back him, he'll call one in October. He then walks out of the garden, only to reappear on the TV screen outside the front door of Number 10 to say much the same thing to the cameras.

Tuesday 3 September – London

An absolutely feverish day in the Commons. Hammond is busy rallying troops in support of the Letwin motion, and there is a feeling of apprehension and drama in the air.

Against this backdrop, Boris makes his first performance at the dispatch box as PM – a statement on the G7. He flunks it. Instead of making a sober statement he treats it like a second reading debate, being far too knockabout, which on a day when he needs maximum authority only served to undermine it.

His notional parliamentary majority then disappeared before our eyes, as Phillip Lee ostentatiously crossed the floor of the House to sit with the Liberal Democrats. With that, before having had a vote to test it, Boris became Prime Minister of a minority government.

It was one of those days when every room in Parliament was buzzing and fizzing with scheming and speculation. Oliver Letwin introduces his emergency motion under Standing Order 24, setting out the timetable to pass the Benn Bill tomorrow, which would take control of the Commons Order Paper from the government. It's really quite wrong for the Speaker to allow a substantive business motion to be tagged on to an SO24 application, or to allow a backbencher to move a business motion at all, which is rightly the preserve of the government. But Speaker Hobbit has long since abandoned any pretence at impartiality or precedent in such matters, and is content to bend the rules whenever he sees fit.

The debate goes on until nearly 10pm and, when the division is called, everyone knows the government will lose – the question is by how much, and how many on our side have abstained or backed Letwin. I hold my nose and dutifully troop through the government lobby. The result is announced – the government loses by 27: Ayes 328, Noes 301. We soon learn that twenty-one Conservatives have rebelled.

Afterwards I bump into Philip and Theresa May in the corridor – she shrugs her shoulders as if to say 'I told you so'. Her air of resignation (as it were) was completely justified.

All of the twenty-one who voted for the motion – including Letwin himself, Ken Clarke, Philip Hammond, David Gauke, Nick

Soames, Dominic Grieve and Justine Greening – are summarily stripped of the Conservative whip. It is brutal.

Wednesday 4 September – London

The first day of the Letwin–Benn government! The success of Letwin's motion last night to take control of the Order Paper means the government has effectively ceded control of the House, and the day is spent debating the Benn Bill, which would delay Brexit until 31 January unless the government passes a deal or gets a majority for No Deal.

The Bill passes all its stages, with a majority of twenty-eight at third reading. The government is now completely at the mercy of the Commons. As if to prove the point, PM Johnson then proposes another motion for an early election and is again defeated. He personifies the definition of being trapped in office but not in power.

End of week six.

Friday 6 September – Rutland

Robert Mugabe has died. All who lamented the end of Rhodesia and the start of Zimbabwe in 1980 were vilified as nasty colonial diehards, but just look at what this hideous man did to a once prosperous country.

My constitutional point about Boris becoming Prime Minister but not having the majority needed to justify him being asked to govern has been proved correct. The record so far: he has lost all four votes held in the Commons since he became PM; he has lost his majority in the Commons; he has failed to call the snap election he wanted; he has lost formal control of Commons business; a bill which cuts through his flagship policy, which he branded the 'Surrender Bill', has been passed; he has expelled twenty-one of his own MPs; he has lost another Conservative to the Lib Dems; his brother Jo has resigned as a minister and will not stand again; the Party's leader in Scotland, Ruth Davidson, has resigned. In fact all of that has been in the last week. Soames, Burt, Spelman, [Nick] Hurd, Fallon and Simpson have all said this week they will not stand again. And then Claire Perry too. It's not really going very well.

He may have seized the crown, but he's so far unable to rule. Indeed, after expelling twenty-one of his own, he has even less legitimacy than when he formed his government.

Then in Yorkshire he spoke at a podium in front of a stage-managed parade of police officers, and one of them behind him fainted, with Boris failing to seize the significance of the situation by helping her out.

He's off to Balmoral tomorrow ... with Carrie Symonds ... prompting some cynic to call it 'Balimmoral'.

Canvass for a Rutland Council by-election. The reception was surprisingly favourable, at least for me and our candidate, if not for the PM personally or Westminster in general.

One bit of good news for the government is that the High Court has today ruled that the decision to ask the Queen to prorogue Parliament was lawful, and so dismissed the case brought by Gina Miller that it was not. Quite right. You can object to using it as a political tactic, but it's perfectly within the Prime Minister's power.

Saturday 7 September – Rutland

The Benn Bill, delaying Brexit until the end of January, has passed the Lords and will be given Royal Assent. Boris is under fire: the idiotic *Daily Telegraph* says he will not obey the law. What has happened to this once great newspaper? It has gone totally bonkers. The PM and Carrie Symonds will have a curtailed visit to Balmoral.

To Uppingham, and then an impromptu visit to the Burghley Horse Trials a mere fifteen minutes away. While we were tucking into our pheasant and boar burgers the bloke next to us introduced himself as Ken Clarke's Association Chairman. I said I hoped that as Chairman he'd told Number 10 to shove it, and that locally the Association would just ignore the removal of the Party whip and let Ken stand again as their candidate.

A quiet evening in Rutland at the end of a cool fresh September day. James mows the paddocks on his tractor.

Amber Rudd resigns from the Cabinet and from the Party, accusing the PM of a breach of faith and of not being serious about negotiating a deal.

Monday 9 September – London

The government are trying for the second time to trigger an early election – either seriously or to call Labour's bluff. They have therefore tabled another motion under the Fixed-Term Parliaments Act for debate today. Suddenly we are caught by surprise as the Speaker announces that he will stand down, either today if an election is called or otherwise on 31 October. Typically, he allows this short statement to run on into lengthy puke-making tributes from Members to his wonderfulness. It was real finger-down-the-throat stuff.

With characteristic tosspottery, he then grants two SO24 applications: the first to release all communications from ministerial advisers in respect of the decision to prorogue, and to publish all 'Yellowhammer' documents, on the No Deal contingency planning. This breaks all precedent by demanding the publication of confidential advice to ministers. And then a second motion to say that the PM must obey the rule of law, which of course he must – so what's the point?

Then we move on to the motion to hold an early general election. I decide to give a speech after all and make three points: firstly that the Fixed-Term Parliaments Act is a disaster; secondly that a verdict on Brexit would not mix well with a general election; and finally that no Association chairman should be told to deselect their MP by a SpAd in Number 10.

The FTPA motion fails to meet the required two-thirds threshold, because Labour again abstained. Which means Boris has now lost six out of the seven votes held since he became PM. Not quite the record he wanted to break.

Richard Benyon is to stand down. So is Mark Prisk. I just feel that lots of other good people will follow.

Tuesday 10 September – London/Muscat

Up at 4.30 after sleeping for an hour at most. Oman Air to Muscat. I went home last night at half past midnight and so skipped the prorogation ceremony, in which the Commons would normally traipse to the House of Lords to shut up shop. When Black Rod arrived in the Commons Chamber to summon them, the Speaker sulkily declared it an inexcusable act of fiat, and some Labour MPs held up little placards saying 'silenced' and, once he'd left, put one in the Speaker's Chair. They have a point, but it is exaggerated. Normally one session ends, we stop for a few days, and then return for the Queen's Speech and four days' debate on it. And then Parliament gets into its stride. Apart from the length of a dissolution for an election campaign, the five weeks of this prorogation are indeed long, but have not added much to the time we would have taken off anyway for the conferences. But we will have risen on 9 September, returned on 14 October and debated the Queen's Speech up to and through the crucial European Council on the 17th.

Whatever happens then in Brussels, it is clear for all to see that the last ten days of October are going to be the most critical in our postwar history. Deal or No Deal, it will be humungous crisis time. If there's No Deal, the new legislation kicks in, obliging the PM to seek an extension to January. If there is a deal, it needs to be convincing enough to be seen as such, but it's quite possible that the worms in the ERG would reject it.

Having watched us stew for a couple of months, I would expect Labour to table a motion of no confidence in the government in the last week of October, and win it. There will then be a few days within the permitted fortnight under the FTPA during which people on both sides will scrabble around to try to form a government of national unity. But I just don't see how the arithmetic will stack up enough to get a majority, unless most Labour MPs back someone instead of Corbyn. I just don't see that many Conservatives would do so. Just to add to the chaos and complexity, we could find it all happening at the same time as the election for a new Speaker. Hello mayhem.

Theresa's resignation honours have been published. Nothing for Ian. The newcomers seem to count for more. It's good and bad overall. Peerage for Gavin Barwell. KCMG for George Hollingbery, KCB for Lidington, CH for McLoughlin. Knighthoods for Robbie Gibb in Number 10 and Charles Walker of the 1922. CBEs for the brutish Fiona Hill and Nick Timothy, but also for properly worthy civil servants, and Julian Smith. A knighthood for the oppressed Brexit negotiator Olly Robbins as he heads off to Goldman Sachs, and a peerage for Kim Darroch, which is fitting compensation for his inexcusable ejection from Washington.

I like daytime flights, but it's really annoying when they darken the windows. I want the daylight.

My phone suddenly connects to the plane's wifi, and ten messages approving of my speech last night download at once – Nicholas Soames, Greg Clark, Helen Goodman, Paul Williams, etc, and James sends a link to a good mention on Radio 5 Live.

As I arrive John Bolton resigns as NSA to Trump. Or at least he says he's resigned, and Trump says he's been sacked as 'his services are no longer needed'. Bolton is hawkish on Iran, North Korea and Venezuela, but then how do we know whether Trump is too? It'll be his fourth NSA. It's just nuts. Meanwhile Netanyahu says that if he is re-elected he will annex parts of the Jordan Valley in the occupied West Bank. Election ploy or not, he cannot be allowed to get away with the comment, let alone the deed. He has already, with Trump's backing, illegally claimed ownership of the Golan Heights. The world order is in tatters, and the UK has become a puny submissive lackey of the United States. I doubt we'll get a squeak out of Raab, let alone a resounding condemnation.

Ed calls. In the post-Amber Rudd reshuffle he has been made Minister of State at Health. As Hancock's de facto number two this is a significant promotion, and to think that five weeks ago he was anxious about even staying in Justice as a PUSS; he should be well pleased.

Wednesday 11 September – Muscat

It is eighteen years since 9/11, when two planes flew into the twin towers in New York, killing 3,000. Scotland's Court of Session has ruled that Johnson's prorogation was unlawful, it seems on the grounds that he was not truthful about his motives and reasons. I am astounded that the Court thinks it can rule on anything other than process. His motives are inevitably political, and that is not a matter for the Court, as the High Court in London ruled last week. Appeals against both judgments will now go to the Supreme Court, who will surely rule that you cannot second-guess the PM's advice to the Queen. We will see.

The Chief Whip has written to the whipless twenty-one about the appeal process for being reinstated. It contains an absurd sentence about those who have serially voted against the government. It's so unfair, when those now in government are some of the worst offenders, and most of the twenty-one are among the most reliable and loyal. It's all upside down.

End of week seven.

Thursday 12 September – Muscat
Catch up on the headlines from the UK … Labour wants the recall of Parliament. On the publication of Yellowhammer stuff, the PM refuses to release aides' emails and texts. The fallout from the loss of the Scottish court case is that the PM is accused of lying to the Queen. It is toxic, but all a little silly.

Friday 13 September – Muscat
Netanyahu has said he will annex the Jordan Valley, amounting to a third of the West Bank and the northern Dead Sea if he wins Tuesday's election. He is pandering to the Orthodox far right, and to parties which are even banned in the US.

Hugo Swire joins the growing number who will stand down.

Saturday 14 September – Muscat
David Cameron dominates the news with the serialisation of his autobiography in *The Times*. He guns hard for Boris and Gove. We exchange emails. I say, 'You're having fun!' and he replies, 'Not sure it's fun – necessary and painful – and glad when it's over.'

The Lib Dem conference is starting. They are positioning themselves clearly to be the 'Remain Whatever' party, which could possibly attract wider support. Sam Gyimah has joined them, in a dribble rather than a shower of publicity.

Sunday 15 September – Muscat
The Houthis in Yemen have made a drone strike on the Saudi oil installations at Abqaiq and Khurais. This could reduce their export production by 50 per cent, although they might make good the shortfall for a month or so by drawing on their strategic reserves. What will the oil price do tomorrow? Up $5? Or remain unperturbed?

Monday 16 September – Muscat
Boris has been humiliated in Luxembourg, after being booed by a large crowd and then pulling out of a joint press conference with Prime Minister Xavier Bettel, who went ahead with it anyway, leaving the podium next to him comically empty and mocking him in his absence. I exchange text messages with my good friend Jean Asselborn, their Foreign Minister: 'It looks to me as if my PM rather pissed off your PM. Well done your PM!' He replies, 'Yes, what a circus.'

Thursday 19 September – London
John Humphrys has retired from the *Today* programme. His final broadcast was very moving. He is a genius of intonation and expression and, despite his critics, has been the best inquisitor for years on the BBC. Unlike some of his female equivalents, he is never angular or snippy. His career has set a standard others are unlikely to meet.

Tom Bower interviews me for a book he is writing on Boris Johnson. I cut it short and won't do another one, as all he wants are black and white answers, invariably of condemnation, which are not what I wish to say about Boris.

The cases challenging the prorogation of Parliament have reached the Supreme Court. All eleven judges have been sitting since Tuesday.

Friday 20 September – London/Rutland
Cameron has sparked some controversy. In the documentary accompanying his memoirs he rather injudiciously revealed that his office had had a word with Buckingham Palace to prompt the Queen's 'think very carefully' comment during the Scottish referendum in 2014.

The Supreme Court case concludes. Judgment will be on Tuesday. My former parliamentary colleague Edward (now Lord) Garnier has been there in his role as a QC, representing Sir John Major, who was submitting evidence as a former Prime Minister!

Monday 23 September – Rutland
Lots of admin.

Travel firm Thomas Cook has collapsed after days of it teetering on the edge; Netanyahu is struggling to form a government in Israel; Corbyn is facing woes at Labour's Conference; Swedish climate campaigner Greta Thunberg is at the UN and gives an angst-ridden temper-tantrum speech, which is just uncomfortably bizarre.

Tuesday 24 September – London
Total bombshell: we get the Supreme Court judgment. The government has lost!!

Its rather batty President, Baroness Hale, rules that prorogation was unlawful because it was intended to obstruct the right of Parliament to sit and do its work. In other words, they have taken a view on motive rather than process. It is an extraordinary judgment which feels deeply political, and which overrides the authority of the government under the Crown. Indeed, the court has second-guessed the Queen.

It rather saves the day for Corbyn at his Conference in Brighton, allowing him to make a speech to claw back his command over the Party.

Wednesday 25 September – London
Parliament reconvenes. Lots of boring statements. We weren't allowed to prorogue, and now we're not allowed to do anything in Parliament now it's sitting. But as Boris is now back from his trip to the UN in New York, anything could happen.

End of week nine.

Wednesday 2 October – London

Eighteen weeks of protests in Hong Kong. Yesterday a teenager was shot at point-blank range in the chest. He's alive, but it's probably a turning point.

It's Boris' main Conference speech today, amid reports of an offer we will make to Brussels on the Irish backstop.

His speech started with a tribute to Theresa May. His delivery was initially rather ramshackle, but then he listed lots of things he's doing. He gave thanks also to Ruth Davidson, who has just stood down as leader of the Party in Scotland. And then he got into his stride. He is not a grandiloquent orator, but instead was an unpompous jaunty character who connected well with the audience. It was a human performance, which retained the rapt attention of Conference-goers, and so contrasted starkly with Theresa's lack of personality or empathy. He did well.

He has dispatched David Frost to Brussels to deliver his solution to the Irish backstop. There seems to be just the tiniest chink of light in the distance, but I wouldn't hold my breath.

Meanwhile the fanatical Steve Baker, now Chairman of the ERG, continues to issue judgements from on high in the same vein as trade union leaders in the 1970s.

The failure to prorogue has had us sitting this week, but with no votes. It's a one-line whip tomorrow, and it is thought the government will once again try to prorogue on Tuesday, ahead of the State Opening on Monday 14th. That'll probably work. And so the timetable unfolds.

We will therefore have the Queen's Speech on the Monday, the Brussels summit on Thursday 17th, the extension deadline in the event of No Deal on 21st and hence a likely vote of no confidence and the grand finale in the final ten days of October. How can there not be an election before Christmas? It just feels as though there has to be.

End of week ten.

Thursday 3 October – London

The Irish border proposal has been trashed by everyone except the DUP. The suspicion in Brussels and Ireland seems to be that it is not even meant to be realistic but is a fake offer, a charade, which goes through the motions while knowing it holds no chance of success. It is difficult to know if BoJo genuinely believes that his game of brinkmanship stands a chance, or whether he knows in his heart that it is bound to be rejected, so pulling the No Deal trigger. Or maybe it is indeed undoubted fantasy, and he genuinely believes it isn't.

In the Commons, however, the picture appears slightly better. The ERG (ugh!) are broadly welcoming, and some Labour MPs are nibbling at it. It'll need another twenty to twenty-five from somewhere to bank it. But if Brussels won't play ball, there's nothing to bank. Whereas we previously had a deal which the EU accepted but Parliament did not, we now perhaps have a (proposed) deal which Parliament would back but the EU will not.

I go in for the PM's 11.30 statement. In the lobby of 1 Parliament Street, Airhead Waddlebottom walks past and throws a sentence of gratuitous abuse at me, seemingly in response to the Brexit documentary. He so needs counselling.

More congenial are [James] Heappey and Burghart, the two PPSs, who Argar has christened Hinge and Brackett. I told them that I am their easiest customer.

Theresa is dressed in bright grotto blue. I bought her a coffee in the Tea Room. She is relaxed and cheerful, but evokes no frisson when she walks into the room.

Boris adopts a much more serious and emollient tone, in contrast to last week's combative mistake. I have a nice chat with him in the Tea Room afterwards. His conference gag about the kangaroo's testicle has provoked copycat quips. He had said that if Parliament were a TV game show like *I'm a Celebrity … Get Me Out of Here!*, MPs would have been voted out of the jungle, but 'at least we could have watched the Speaker being forced to eat a kangaroo testicle'. Bercow has now lost his voice and is croaking awkwardly, with some suggesting he might indeed have swallowed one.

I text the Chief, who asks me in to see him a mere fifteen minutes later. He wants to support my going to the Lords and will fix a meeting with the PM asap. Frankly I'm in two minds about whether I want ever to end up there. It's nice to be able to dine with your mates, but it has become a political dustbin.

Friday 4 October – London/Rutland

The Boris backstop proposal is being excoriated throughout Europe, especially of course in Brussels and Dublin. It just doesn't look as though it'll get anywhere. We're in the endgame for the government for certain, and the Brexit process possibly, but it is impossible to forecast precisely how.

And then another little bombshell. Rory Stewart has announced that he is resigning from the Conservative Party and will not stand at the next election. We might not have split, in the classical sense, but we are disintegrating with good people being pushed out or peeling off. By not standing again I might yet be seen as one of them. Rory's move becomes clear when George Osborne tweets that he is to stand for the Mayoralty of London as an independent. Front page of the *Standard* coming soon no doubt. More Osborne scheming which gloats over Boris. But BoJo might yet have the last laugh. The Mayoral election is next May. Rory standing will probably do for Shaun Bailey and guarantee the re-election of Sadiq Khan.

I've been pondering. What happens if the Queen's Speech is voted down?

Baroness Hale is revelling in her post-judgment publicity and is politically naive. At a literary festival she said 'let's hear it for the girly swots', thus echoing Boris's controversial language and in effect taking a swipe at him. She answers to no one, not even the Lord Chief Justice. She has gone rogue.

Sunday 6 October – Rutland

To the government's credit, the last of the stranded Thomas Cook customers have been repatriated. It has gone so well it has hardly made any news since the collapse.

Monday 7 October – London

Key landmarks in London, such as Trafalgar Square, Westminster Bridge and Parliament Square have been brought to a halt by a mere 2,000 Extinction Rebellion protesters. They are blocking junctions, cuffing themselves to steering wheels and being very tiresome. It is a bizarre mixture of pensioner campaigners and self-righteous, gobby twenty-somethings. Old hippies don't grow old, they merely change their banners ... and their teeth. As soon as the issue is climate change, these activists adopt a sneering manner which accuses everyone else of being a planet destroyer, while only they are right and all-knowing.

Sir Richard Henriques, a retired High Court judge, has published an article in the *Mail* explaining his damning report on the police investigation into Operation Midland and the so-called VIP paedophile ring. In my view the Met owes Harvey Proctor millions. The police have disgraced themselves.

Macron says the EU will decide by the end of the week whether there is anything in the UK backstop offer. There almost certainly isn't. So it's probably No Deal, delay and an election. But amazingly we are 15 points ahead of Labour in the polls (Con 38, Lab 23, Lib Dem 22, etc) so will the turkeys vote for one?

Dinner with Patrick McLoughlin, Ed Argar and Kit Malthouse. In the Smoking Room Iain Duncan Smith was incandescent about the Supreme Court. We are all irked by the conduct of Baroness Hale, but Iain says they are all lecturers and are of a quality far below that of proper experienced judges. For once I agree with him.

Tuesday 8 October – London

The smellies of XR (Extinction Rebellion) are becoming very annoying. Marsham Street and Great Peter Street are blocked by their pop-up tents and their gazebos serving coffee. They are all complete weirdos who walk around with zany smiles and wide vacant eyes. And the wretched helicopter is hovering above me all the time.

Heidi Allen has joined the Lib Dems – well, there's a surprise.

Meanwhile the world seems to be falling to bits. Trump says he'll withdraw from Syria, and the danger of allowing Turkey to invade and decimate the Kurds in north-east Syria has provoked ferocious objection in the US across both parties.

Boris has spoken to Merkel. The briefing is vicious. Apparently she has said there is no basis for a deal, or at least that one is 'overwhelmingly unlikely'. We are heading for No Deal and the triggering of the Benn Act to delay exit till the end of January. But the briefing is probably from Number 10 because No Deal is precisely what they want.

Then to the FCO for a courtesy meeting with Chris Pincher in my old office. He is enjoying it, but he doesn't yet know what he doesn't know.

Bump into David Dimbleby on the Green, on his way to interview David Davis about Brexit. I told him that it might not prove as fruitful as he hopes.

Wednesday 9 October – London

St James's Park is a hippy encampment.

It has been announced that we will sit on Saturday week, the 19th.

Boris' exchanges with the EU, especially Leo Varadkar in Ireland, have turned deeply sour. As soon as he has any discussions, someone in Downing Street – manic SpAd Dominic Cummings? – tells a stooge journalist how badly it's all gone, because the gradual collapse of any serious negotiation is exactly what they want.

We're all doomed.

End of week eleven.

Thursday 10 October – Rutland

The Turks have launched their offensive in north-east Syria. Trump is backpedalling manically.

BoJo and Leo Varadkar have met in the Wirral. Three hours alone. Better mood music. Someone has caved a little. Probably Boris. There is definitely some movement.

Monday 14 October – London

The beginning of a momentous political week. There will now be a Budget on Wednesday 6 November.

It starts with the State Opening and a Queen's Speech, the sixty-fifth of HM's reign. Corbyn in his speech on the Address called the whole thing a farce, given that the government has no majority and wants an election in a matter of weeks. Probably the common view.

There is no bill in it to prevent the prosecution of historic criminal cases against soldiers, especially in respect of Northern Ireland, Iraq and Afghanistan. Johnny Mercer, now the relevant minister in Defence, pledged his career on it, threatened to resign the whip, went on strike, etc, and yet no bill. Some colleagues are determined to mob him up by telling him he should resign. On one level he should, but that's not modern politics.

Drink later with Patrick McLoughlin and Lord Chancellor Robert Buckland … now dubbed Bobby Backtracker, for not following the tradition of walking three steps backwards from the throne after handing HM the speech during the ceremony.

A deal is on/off/on/off … who the hell knows?

Wednesday 16 October – London

The 1922 Committee meets at 4.30pm. Boris sweeps in to make a brief appearance. With a mood of growing optimism, he was nonetheless cautious. It feels as though most of our lot would be OK to support him, but it needs both the Irish and the DUP to be on board for there to be any prospect whatsoever of enough support in the Commons.

End of week twelve.

Thursday 17 October – London

A big blow. The DUP have issued a statement to say that at the moment they cannot support a deal. For them, it seems to hang on the process of consent. Anything to do with customs and the Deal more broadly in their view must have the consent of both communities in Northern Ireland.

The summit in Brussels starts at 2pm our time. We probably won't have anything substantive to vote for on Saturday other than extension.

Then at 10.45 sudden news that BoJo has a deal, which Barnier and Juncker soon confirm. We will vote on it on Saturday. Although the motion to allow us to sit on Saturday is passed, it is qualified by a further vote to allow amendments to anything brought forward then.

Michael Gove, now running the Cabinet Office, addresses Conservative MPs in Westminster Hall to rally support for the Deal. I bump into Mark Sedwill in New Palace Yard and tell him I'm giving the Darrochs dinner tonight. He drops in for a drink with us all beforehand. I sense that the Deal was very touch and go, and that if it hadn't happened there was even a chance that Boris would have resigned.

Saturday 19 October – London/Rutland
The Saturday sitting.

At the start of business, the Speaker's Chaplain Rose Hudson-Wilkin (soon to be a bishop) begins prayers with 'Do not be anxious about anything ...' The dignity of prayers collapses into laughter. After a few seconds of guffawing, it erupts again when someone says 'Amen'.

At 9.30 the sitting begins. First time we've sat on a Sat for thirty-seven years – the last occasion was when the Falklands were invaded. Twelve more days of Bercow. We eagerly await 'Berexit'. He selects the Letwin amendment which suspends formal approval of the Deal until the legislation to implement it is enacted.

Before the main debate, we start with a statement on the European Council. BoJo makes it more of a full debate speech than the conventional factual statement. But good tone and thesis.

Then the motion itself, opened by Steve Barclay who shows his inexperience and weakness as a speaker. I did not get called. Pity, as I had a good supportive speech ready.

When we get to the votes, the Letwin amendment passes 322–306. As this withholds approval for the Deal, it in effect triggers the Benn Act and requires the PM to write to the EU requesting an extension. In a defiant intervention after the vote, the PM declares that despite this he still won't negotiate an extension and says the law doesn't require him to. He maintains that we can pass the legislation needed next week and get Brexit done by 31 October. Nobody believes him, or thinks he believes it either. The whole day has gathered us all together only to run into yet another brick wall.

Monday 21 October – Rutland/London
Contrary to the government's intentions, the Speaker rules at 3.30pm that he will *not* allow a vote today on the principle of the Deal. He says the motion has not changed in substance, and the circumstances have not changed, so the government cannot bring it back again. Another wasted day.

Tuesday 22 October – London
The second reading of the EU Withdrawal Bill. Having been forbidden to vote on the principle of the Deal yesterday, we now find ourselves considering instead the legislation needed to enact it. It is topsy-turvy, because you can only be sure the Bill will get through if you know the House has approved the principle of the Deal. Once again it is all about parliamentary procedure and arithmetic.

The Bill passes its second reading at 7pm by 329–299 (+30). But every bill requires a programme motion to go with it, which has been the case ever since the Blair government introduced timetabling in 1997. The programme motion to go straight to committee tonight and complete all stages in the Commons by Thursday night is defeated by 308–322 (–14). This stops the Bill in its tracks. It means some have supported the Bill in principle then thwarted it in practice.

The Opposition and press ignorantly attack Boris for 'pausing' the passage of the Bill, but he hasn't. Quite simply, it can go no further without a programme motion. So tomorrow and Thursday will see us complete the Queen's Speech debate while they redesign the programme motion for the Bill, probably by negotiating with Labour.

But one thing it does mean is that we will not leave on 31 October, and the EU will have to grant an extension. Indeed Donald Tusk quickly indicates that he will accept the UK request to extend under the Benn Act. Nor are we now likely to have an election before Christmas, unless contrary to all expectations Labour suddenly plays the no-confidence card or simply caves in to having one. The Speaker must stick to his own departure date of the 31st. And so it goes on, and on, and on.

Wednesday 23 October – London

Nobody knows what on earth is going to happen today. We are drifting, heading nowhere, powerless, impotent. We can't proceed with the Bill or call an election. It is total stasis. We will have to wait until Friday to know what the EU decides on an extension.

Ian Blackford in the corridor says that the PM is in with Corbyn. Let's see if they agree a timetable for the Bill. Nice chat with Boris in the Tea Room after PMQs. He is very bullish and gung-ho and in typical 'Come on, let's get on with it!' mode. He seems to think that all he needs to deliver this is his own enthusiasm.

Meeting of the 1922 Committee. I asked the Whip if there will be tributes to the Speaker next Thursday. His evasive reply suggested that there won't be. Oh, what a pity. Committee hustings for the nine speakership candidates: Edward Leigh, Chris Bryant, Harriet Harman, Henry Bellingham, Shailesh Vara, Lindsay Hoyle, Eleanor Laing, Meg Hillier and Rosie Winterton.

Lindsay Hoyle was by far the most robust, informed and purposeful. Bryant was probably second and, amazingly, Bellingham third. Laing was too scripted, Vara surprisingly convincing, Hillier characterless. Winterton had too fixed a smile, but was thoughtful about the balance between the executive and the Commons.

Great steps forward this week – but unfortunately they're just round and round in a circle.

End of week thirteen.

Thursday 24 October – London/Rutland

Apparently we will table a motion on Monday calling for a general election on 12 December, as soon as the EU say our exit is delayed until 31 January.

To St Pancras. A charming couple from Rutland waiting for the same train stop me to say some lovely appreciative things about my being their MP. It makes a change!

Monday 28 October – London

The EU has granted a 'flextension' – an exit delay until 31 January, or earlier should we pass a withdrawal bill. The Lib Dems and SNP have tabled a bill to amend the Fixed-Term Parliaments Act as a procedural way of calling an election on Monday 9 December, but for it to happen only if the UK and EU agree not to leave before 31 January. It is thought we might do our own similar Bill tomorrow, but where's the catch? The SNP and Lib Dems want it on Monday 9th because they say that prevents the government having time to bring back their Deal, and they're concerned about students having broken up for Christmas any later than that, but it all seems mostly to be posturing.

At 7pm the government's third attempt at calling an early election passes by 299–70, but in the absence of two-thirds of the House voting for it, caused by Labour abstentions, no election is triggered. So we are still beached and going nowhere.

Nice dinner with Ed Argar, Andrew Bowie, Steve Double and then later Alex Chalk.

And then wow! In a business statement at 10pm it is announced that we will bring forward a short bill tomorrow, similar to the Lib Dem/SNP bill to set a date for an election on 12 December, but will not bring back the Withdrawal Bill. It's a little confusing, and maybe politically we have just proposed the 12th in order not to be seen to give in, but Jacob Rees-Mogg gives a good technical reason for rejecting the 9th in favour of the 12th: there would be no time for dissolution if it's the 9th, and crucial Northern Irish legislation would be lost.

Tuesday 29 October – London

At 11am Corbyn says he will support an early election. This looks like the decider. If we can secure two-thirds of the House, then it's game on. It seems he has at last crumbled after relentless pressure, and the obvious inconsistency of Labour demanding an election and then not voting for one.

Nice chat with Chief Whip Mark Spencer. We have fun batting about a list of possible peers: Patrick McLoughlin, Cheryl Gillan,

Liam Fox, David Lidington, Michael Fallon? But Gillan and Fox will probably stand again. Ken Clarke must get one, and surely Nicholas Soames too. Mark is caustic about the SNP and their sheer duplicity, but he thinks our Bill to hold the election will get through. Their attempt to put a wrecking amendment on the voting age and the rights of EU citizens has been ruled out of scope, so it's only the date that can be amended.

Ten of the whipless twenty-one have it restored, the distinction being that those who voted against the programme motion last week have not.

Rees-Mogg moves the business of the House motion very well, whereas Helen Goodman for Labour was an utter dimwit.

I had a long chat at the Chair with the Speaker about whether he should stay on for a couple of days, although I think the timetable for his departure and replacement is now firmly fixed. Chris Bryant, in an elegant pitch for his own prospects, used a point of order to suggest the new Speaker should be chosen by a new Parliament, and not the final moment of a previous one.

Second reading passes overwhelmingly at 5.45pm. We win on not changing the date from the 12th to the 9th by 315–295. So that's it: there will be a general election on 12 December.

Wednesday 30 October – London
I have decided to stand down and call my constituency Chairman Byron Rhodes to tell him. He knew I might, but wasn't sure that I would, and he could absolutely see why being an MP for any longer was not especially attractive.

My last PMQs. The number of those leaving is suddenly growing. It's all the moderates.

End of week fourteen. And of me.

Thursday 31 October – London/Rutland
Draw up a press statement about not contesting Rutland and Melton again, which I give to journalists.

Today would have been Brexit Day, but that will now be 31 January. But it is exit day for Mr Speaker. I pay a tiny tribute to him, quipping that someone once asked me what was the rudest thing anyone had ever said to me in politics, to which I replied, 'It's when they came up to me in the street and said, "Good morning, Mr Bercow".' I also confess that I sometimes refer to him as Mr Speaker Hobbit, for which I hoped he would absolve me.

Standing in the Chamber, I feel rather emotional – the end is nigh, so I just head up to Rutland.

Friday 1 November – Rutland

Some lovely emails and messages. Corbyn has already launched his general election campaign. Nigel Farage has interviewed Trump on his LBC radio programme, and says he will field candidates in 500 seats unless BoJo drops the Withdrawal Deal.

As my last act of service to my constituency, I am able to pass on confirmation that I have secured two massive infrastructure grants: £19 million for the Melton bypass and £30 million for the development of St George's Barracks. Not a bad announcement on which to leave.

Sunday 3 November – Rutland/London

Rishi Sunak, Chief Secretary to the Treasury, gives a good interview on *Marr*. I text him a herogram: 'Well done, that was an excellent Marr interview. You couldn't have handled it better. It's good to know there's some proper quality in the top mix. Onwards … while I put my feet up! And thanks again for the grants. They are a nice parting gift to my patch.'

He sends a nice appreciative reply, saying that he still has the photo of him and Ed Argar which I naughtily took in the Chamber on his first day in the Commons. He says I will be missed, and suggests we have a farewell lunch when things calm down.

Speak to William Hague, who says that life after politics is much better than you'd imagine, and I'll soon wonder why I didn't do it earlier.

Call with Richard Tice, who dismisses the rumour that he might stand in Rutland and Melton to replace me, and says that Dominic

Cummings is refusing to talk to anybody, by which I guess he means him and Farage.

To London. I'm told that James Cleverly as Chairman is being totally dwarfed by co-Chairman Ben Elliot who has taken over candidates, honours and donors. I can't see what Cleverly has left other than the occasional TV interview.

Monday 4 November – London
Chat to John Benger, the Clerk, in the corridor. He said he was mystified by Bercow's decision not to allow my motion to ratify BoJo as PM ahead of him going to the Palace. He thought it was wholly in order, and perfectly logical in the circumstances.

I have an awful cold and struggle through speaking at an EU-focussed lunch at the Oxford and Cambridge Club to a dozen former ambassadors.

Election of the Speaker. I vote for Lindsay Hoyle, who wins comfortably on the fourth ballot. I have no objection to it being another Labour MP despite Bercow's hostility to Conservatives and reliance on the Labour benches. Lindsay will be fair, decent and authoritative – in all respects a welcome contrast to the Hobbit.

I had reserved my seat for the day by putting a card in for prayers. As business was concluding I bid farewell to Boris, who was on the front bench. He signed my final prayer card as a memento. 'I've not forgotten,' he said cheerily.

Farewell drinks in the Smoking Room.

Tuesday 5 November – London/Rutland
The final day of the 2017 Parliament before Dissolution tonight. Remember, remember the fifth of November – my last day in Parliament after twenty-seven years. It hasn't been a bad run – politics is little more than a game of chance, and it's been going downhill steeply over the last ten to fifteen years. Now that our politics is driven by the 24-hour news cycle, by social media and by the appeal of novelty over experience, I'm not sure it's serving the country's needs as it should. But I've done my best and tried to be conscientious rather than self-seeking. Looking around at all the youngsters

who are so shamelessly pushy, I sometimes think I should have been more so.

I attend the valedictory speeches in the Chamber. I was ready to make one myself, but in the event I just couldn't. It was too emotional and I was welling up just sitting there. Instead I leave and head back to Rutland, never to sit on the green benches again.

Wednesday 6 November – Rutland

The first day of the rest of my life.

Official launch of the Conservative campaign, much heralded on the front page of the *Daily Boris*. The overconfident Lib Dem leader Jo Swinson is beginning to irritate with her shrill voice and banal simplicities.

Meanwhile the constituency is to be given three names by Central Office for the rapid selection of my successor.

Philip Hammond and Nick Herbert announce they will not fight their seats again, as does Deputy Labour Leader Tom Watson. In a bizarre twist, Alun Cairns resigns as Secretary of State for Wales after his former SpAd caused the collapse of a rape trial.

Thursday 7 November – Rutland

Clear out my Melton office.

Labour MPs Ian Austin and John Woodcock say vote for Boris. The election seems already to have become an auction of billions in spending promises.

Friday 8 November – Rutland

To Melton for the selection of my successor, ahead of which I make a short farewell speech. The process is a far cry from 1990, when I was chosen from 301 applicants. Three names were given to the Association on Wednesday – one dropped out yesterday and one was rejected by the Association, so two replacements have been added at half a day's notice. It is not exactly democracy at its best. The selection meeting chooses Alicia Kearns.

Sunday 10 November – Rutland/London

Remembrance Sunday. I attend the Melton service in the morning and Oakham in the afternoon, all togged up for my final public appearance as the MP.

The Melton sermon was pretty dire. At one point after dragging on for ages about the horrors of war, the vicar said, 'Nobody has ever tried to shoot me.' I nearly shouted, 'They might soon.'

In a week of poignant endings, I learn that Brian Mawhinney has died at the age of seventy-nine. When he was Chairman of the Party I was his PPS, and in 1995 I conducted a citizen's arrest when protesters covered him in orange paint on College Green. As one wag put it, 'He was overcome with emulsion.' He was a decent, earthy man from Belfast who was very much part of John Major's set. Although sometimes a bit ponderous, he was a bigger beast than many of them today.

Monday 11 November – London

As a final indignity which stretched my patience, I had to spend half an hour in Parliament with an HR jobsworth telling me what I needed to do to wind up my Commons office. She ignored any question I asked and just carried on with her script. No doubt if I'd complained she would have complained about me. I'm so glad to be leaving it all behind.

Farage will not contest the 317 seats which the Conservatives won in 2017.

Alicia Kearns comes in for a drink at home. She is nothing if not enthusiastic.

Tuesday 12 November – London

We have a 14-point lead over Labour following the mass Brexit candidate withdrawal yesterday, but the methodology is not uniform. In half the country's seats you can express a preference for the Brexit Party, but obviously not in the other half. So voting intention falls into two distinct categories. What the overall picture is remains unpredictable.

Lots of SpAds are being selected for safe seats: the Party and our politics are becoming ever more incestuous.

Monday 18 November – London

It is Sultan Qaboos' forty-ninth National Day. He is limping towards his fiftieth year.

Bercow is to take part in Sky TV's election night coverage, which is shameless and inappropriate. And thus entirely in character.

To the Savoy for the Carlton dinner courtesy of Rosso. Everyone is in excellent spirits, and Boris wows them all with a jovial, rumbustious, tub-thumping call to arms. I still think we will have a working majority, but perhaps only of around thirty.

Trump has declared that he considers all Israeli settlements *not* to be contrary to international law. So he alone is now the Supreme Court of the entire world.

Wednesday 20 November – London/Bahrain

Take the day flight to Bahrain.

I didn't watch the Johnson–Corbyn TV debate last night, but the widespread view is that it was a marginal win for Boris, with no knock-out blow. There was lots of superficial stuff about the NHS, Brexit and personal trust. Yawn.

Dinner in the hotel with Sir Geoffrey Tantum and General Sir Tom Beckett, joined later by Dr John Chipman, the Director of IISS.

Friday 22 November – Bahrain

Manama Dialogue. The rest of the rather reduced UK team arrive: just Alistair Burt and Colonel Bob Stewart. Alistair is not fighting his seat again, but Bob is, and says there is quite a lot of anti-Boris feeling on the doorstep in Beckenham. But I still think that overall we are comfortably ahead.

At a session on Iran the IISS present their recent research. The firm conclusion is that Iran has, through its many accessory agents and activities, definitely shifted the balance of power in the region. That is not as obvious a judgement as one might think, given their steep economic decline and unsettled populace. But when will their neighbours snap?

I sit on a panel for young Arab leaders with GCC Secretary

General Abdullatif al Zayani, who I worked with on Yemen when I was in DfID, and Peter Berkowitz from the US State Department. Our exam question was to ask when to use coercion and when to use diplomacy, and to draw on our own experience. So I drew briefly on Yemen, Palestine, Argentina/Falklands and Ecuador. But then Berkowitz focussed only on Palestine and offered a puke-making apologia for Trump's so-called peace initiatives for Israel–Palestine. I curtly put it to him that giving the Golan Heights, East Jerusalem and illegal West Bank settlements to Israel was despicable and they were not Trump's to give.

Quite a few comments that Dominic Raab is proving a bit of a disaster in the FCO. He thinks he knows it all because he used to be an FCO lawyer, he is quick to lose his temper with officials, he refuses to meet UK ambassadors when they are back in London ('I don't need to see ambassadors') and is widely disliked.

Saturday 23 November – Bahrain

Mark Sedwill arrived last night. Have a good chat with him before he sits on the panel with foreign ministers Al Jubair of Saudi and Gargash of the UAE. His words on the panel had to be, and were, judiciously chosen as he sat there as the public face of the UK in such a delicate setting.

We agree that BoJo will secure a comfortable majority, and that the TV debates are not changing anything. I said Boris had actually achieved three critical successes: the Withdrawal Deal with the EU, getting around the FTPA to call an election and orchestrating the withdrawal of the Brexit Party from Conservative-held seats. These have laid the foundations for a strong showing against a puncturing of the Lib Dem surge, and Labour stalling at under 30 per cent.

I told him it looked like I had lined up a job with Vitol and was going through the process of having the appointment approved by the Cabinet Office under the rules for ex-ministers.

During dinner with King Hamad we learn that the Conservatives have a 19 per cent poll lead over Labour. That'll do!

Sunday 24 November – Bahrain

Rather silly *Sunday Times* story saying that hardline Leavers such as Raab, Redwood, Goldsmith, Baker and Davis might each lose their seat. Zac Goldsmith will, but not the others. Raab's 23,000 majority is not going to be overturned in Esher by a Remain alliance, amusing though that would be. They're already calling him the Advent Calendar – because his days are numbered.

Back on the overnight flight.

Wednesday 27 November – London

Catastrophic reaction to Corbyn's interview with Andrew Neil last night, in which he was completely skewered on a whole series of issues ranging from anti-Semitism, paying for his promises to pensioners and whether he would support a Brexit deal negotiated by his own government. It was so bad it was wonderful.

An independent candidate for Rutland and Melton has sadly died. Had it been one from a major party, the contest would have had to be cancelled and rerun after the election.

To the Palace Theatre to be interviewed before a live audience by Matt Forde for his 'Political Party' show, which he also releases as a podcast. He says it's the best performance by anyone he's had on the show – and here I am leaving the political stage!

Friday 29 November – Rutland

To my great delight, Harvey Proctor has been awarded £900,000 by the courts, of which £500,000 will go to him and the rest in costs. The Met should have paid him three times as much, as they have behaved disgracefully in pursuing him over baseless allegations made by an obvious nutter, which anyone with a brain could have seen from the very start.

Someone has gone bonkers outside the Fishmongers Hall and stabbed people on London Bridge. The assailant was shot, but two Cambridge graduates are dead. It later transpires that the attacker was out on licence from prison, and was a known Islamic extremist.

Saturday 7 December – Rutland

John Major and Chris Patten have both called on voters to support the ex-Tory independents David Gauke and Dominic Grieve. David and Dominic are both highly decent and principled guys, but will become lost in the wash and lose.

HM the Sultan has been flown to Leuven for further treatment. This is deeply concerning. He saw the Duke of Cambridge for dinner earlier this week and was thought to be struggling somewhat. So alarm bells are ringing. I alert Boris by text, as we may all have to fly there at very short notice.

Tuesday 10 December – London

The Democrats have tabled the formal impeachment charges against President Trump.

To Clarence House for a lovely dinner given by the Prince of Wales in honour of Wafic Saïd and his charitable work, and to mark his eightieth birthday. He is a very special man who has done amazing things for Syria, the Saïd Business School and numerous other good causes. He and Rosemary looked after Margaret Thatcher in her final years, giving her the run of a lovely country house in Oxfordshire. It really upsets me that so many who have taken no risks in life rise up the ladder and are honoured when someone like Wafic and indeed Rosemary have done so much for so many and the system always finds a reason not to.

The Swires were there too, and Sasha was rather silly. I knew from Hugo that she has a publishing deal for her diaries, and when he asked me if I do, I accurately answered 'No'. She then asked me the same question, and got the same answer. She then went to ask James separately. Always ahead of the game, he gave her quite a bollocking for being so underhand, and then asked her why she was always so vitriolic on the (anonymous) MPWife Twitter account. 'How did you know that?' she asked. He'd got her! Her lapse was a total inadvertent admission that 'MPWife' is Sasha Swire.

Two days until the general election. A big poll puts last week's forecast majority of sixty-eight down to twenty-eight. That's pretty well what it feels like to me.

Thursday 12 December – London

General election day. It is the first time in thirty-two years that I haven't been a parliamentary candidate. What a relief.

The wonderful Michael Spencer and his wife Sarah had taken over the whole of Scott's for a lavish election results dinner. Everybody who's anybody was there, and Michael's generosity is exceptional. Then at 10pm the whole place erupts ecstatically when the screens broadcast the exit poll forecasting a Tory majority of eighty-six.

They forecast large SNP gains, which will be because Boris is less than popular in Scotland, they are pro-Remain and they (although not all who will have voted SNP) want an independent Scotland. The poll suggests Con 368, Lab 191, SNP 55, Lib Dem 13, Green 1. Which is +50, −71, +20, +1 … Majority = 86.

Do a quick reaction interview on the pavement outside for Patrick Forbes' documentary, saying 'I am happily gobsmacked.'

To the BBC to join their studio coverage from 2–3am alongside Jon Lansman, the founder of Momentum, who is in total denial about the failure of Labour. I say that I think he has become my new best friend because he has done so much to destroy the Labour Party and make it unelectable for years to come.

Tim Shipman issues a typically clever-clogs caustic tweet mocking my acknowledgement on the BBC of Boris's success. He's just so out of date and doesn't understand the way personal relationships work in politics. But who cares?

Friday 13 December – London/Rutland

The Sultan is back home. But it feels like time is running out.

The exit poll was pretty damned good. It forecast a majority of eighty-six, and the final result is a majority of eighty. It really is an amazing outcome. Although we hoped for it, we underestimated the salience Brexit and Corbyn had among working-class voters in the North.

They want Brexit done, and they despise Corbyn for his London Marxism and lack of patriotism. The Boris campaign just touched a nerve and delivered. Labour is smashed. So are the Lib Dems. But the SNP have made gains and will prove a serious nuisance. The authority of the government and the UK on the world stage is enhanced by the size of the majority, but a major challenge will be the need to deliver for those in the Midlands and North who transferred their confidence.

Monday 16 December – London
Labour are in total denial and disarray. There's not much calibre among those touted as their next leader.

As my own political career concludes, I reflect on the victory photo taken in Westminster Hall today of the 100 new Conservative MPs. Maybe I've achieved something in that twenty-four of them are LGBT – and probably none of them realise what it took to make that a positive news story instead of cause for resignation.

Wednesday 18 December – Tashkent
A flying visit to Uzbekistan to endorse their attempts to hold a free and fair election.

It looks as if Boris will put DfID into the FCO, but let's see. It's far more complicated than people think, because you'd have to change the law on spending 0.7 per cent of GDP on development, in order to spend its budget on other things. All radical SpAd-inspired simple stuff, but driven from a base of zero experience or knowledge. But it could happen. I'm glad I'm out of it – I'd find the process too maddening – Number 10 kiddies telling Parliament what to do. The purpose and culture of DfID is so very different from that of the FCO.

Friday 20 December – Tashkent/Rutland
Lunchtime flight back to London.

The new Parliament has its first vote, and the knife-edge of the past is replaced by a majority of 124. By 358 to 234, the Withdrawal Bill is finally voted through.

Extensive exchanges with the FCO and Number 10 as it becomes clear that the Sultan will not live much longer.

Head home to Rutland for Christmas.

2020

[I spent New Year in Oman, where anxiety about the Sultan's health was increasing. Having been closely involved with the UK's relations with the Sultanate for decades, I was playing a key role in keeping the UK government updated, and ensuring they were ready with the long-planned diplomatic show of respect when the crucial moment came. I returned to the UK on 4 January, but knew I was sadly likely to be back in Muscat soon.]

Friday 10 January – Rutland
General Stanford, the UK's Senior Loan Service Officer in Oman, texts me to say that the Omani armed forces are on 'red alert' which could be because of regional tensions, but is more likely because HM is near the end. A bit later he texts, 'It is confirmed that he is in a very critical condition.' More than ever before it feels like this is it.

Learn at 9pm that there is a summons, to whom is not totally clear, to attend the Majlis Oman tomorrow. This could be to the Oman Royal Family, for the endorsement of a successor. It sounds as though an announcement is imminent.

Saturday 11 January – Rutland
General Stanford texts me just before 1am. Sultan Qaboos has died. I watch Al Jazeera for an hour, which is wall-to-wall Qaboos footage. I tweet immediately my two prepared tweets, including a photo of me and the Sultan from 1994. I could only do so because Harriet,

who has sole possession of my tweet code, was awake and primed for action. God bless her calm sense of duty. She is a cool operator.

After a few hours' not-quite sleep I watch TV again. A modest and slightly scrappy funeral is concluding in the Grand Mosque. Very swiftly Sayd Haitham bin Tarik al Said is declared Sultan.

[There now swung into action the long-prepared plans for the UK to send a high-level delegation to pay official condolences. This would be led by the Prince of Wales, and include the Prime Minister, Defence Secretary and Chief of the Defence Staff. Despite my no longer holding office, it had been agreed I would accompany the delegation to help make introductions and smooth the process. I caught a commercial flight the following morning for this sombre epilogue to my ministerial career.]

Sunday 12 January – Oman/London

Arrive at 7.30am, go to the hotel, then later to the residence. The UK has spatchcocked together the various flights. It has been a scrabble to charter privately and use crappy RAF planes, whereas all other countries have their own jet or two. We are one of the largest economies in the world, and we don't have a satisfactory Royal or government plane … or fleet of planes. Many companies do, but HMG does not. The UK looks puny.

The condolences are at the Al Alam Palace, the early Indian-style design with a scooped edge and flat top. Built early in the reign of Qaboos, it has long since been surpassed by more majestic edifices. In the grand hall, the new Sultan sits in the middle of the top row, surrounded by ministers and grandees. In the body of the hall are perhaps 600–700 beautifully attired Omanis, although all men. The UK tribute is way ahead of any other country. HRH goes in at 1pm and has a short audience in full view, sitting beside the new Sultan; Ben Wallace, along with CDS and me in attendance, has a similar few minutes; and the PM is due at 4pm.

When I shake hands, Sultan Haitham breaks into a smile and says very pointedly, 'Hello, my friend.' It was a subtle personal courtesy, and very touching.

So we banked it: HRH, SoS Def and CDS, and then the PM. Three mini-audiences, unlike anybody else. The Duke of Cambridge was the last official visitor to see Sultan Qaboos, and the Prince of Wales was one of the very first to see Sultan Haitham. Well done, UK. We got there.

Monday 20 January – London
Boris wants to move the House of Lords to York. Just when he is sensibly looking like the serious Prime Minister we want, he backs this batshit-crazy idea.

Call from Tony Blair wanting to pick my brains on Oman. I talk him through the succession, condolences and prospects. He wants to convey a message to the new Sultan, which I suggest he does through Abdulaziz in London.

Wednesday 22 January – London
Encounter Stephen Dorrell in Smith Square. His long hair makes him appear a little deranged. He always over-articulates when speaking in interviews and so loses impact. Unsurprisingly he has recently left the Conservatives and joined the Liberal Democrats, probably in the hope of a peerage. I say, 'I can see the orange glow around you.' We agreed that having a majority of eighty is a massive opportunity for political achievement, but were both unsure whether Boris will apply adequate intellectual and philosophical direction, both of which, with discipline, he is fully capable of. Stephen then walks into 32 Smith Square, the liaison office for the EU. To think that it used to be Conservative Central Office until Michael Howard mortgaged it to its chimney pots and sold it off. How depressing it's no longer ours. Its EU flag near my front door is Michael Howard's deeply ironic legacy.

The Withdrawal Agreement Bill has passed all its parliamentary stages and is heading for Royal Assent in time for our departure on Friday week, the 31st. Ho-hum.

Thursday 30 January – London/Rutland

The World Health Organisation has declared the coronavirus a global public health emergency.

Friday 31 January – Rutland

Brexit Day! Instead of allowing a dignified conclusion to our decades of EU membership, the UKIP/Brexit Party MEPs stage a rude and churlish performance in Brussels that just makes us all look petty and ridiculous. Ann Widdecombe (of all people) makes a toe-curling little speech alongside a scrappy huddle of departing deadbeats as they leave the Parliament building, bizarrely accompanied by a kilted piper. So the brave new dawn of the UK on the world stage begins with a pathetic band of Little Englanders being screeched at by a cranky old bat as they depart into obscurity. Just about sums it up.

Back home, I attend the Rutland Civic Reception, at which its chairman Ken Bool makes a charming speech, saying, 'When they ask, "Where were you on Brexit Day?" you can say, "I was at the Rutland Civic Reception."'

We leave the EU at 11pm. Number 10 is lit up with images of Big Ben and accompanied by broadcast bongs. I'm just not interested.

Meanwhile, two cases of the coronavirus have been reported in the UK.

APPENDIX

Why This Lifelong Eurosceptic Is Now Voting to Stay In

Alan Duncan

TELEGRAPH, 23 MARCH 2016

Since voting 'No' in the 1975 referendum I have spent 40 years wishing we had never joined the EU. Nobody in the UK likes being told what to do by others. The wish to restore the power to govern ourselves is a perfectly respectable argument, and the rise of Ukip and the undimmable forces within the Conservative Party who want to leave are testament to the enduring irritation many feel. For decades, we have suffered from a post-imperial feeling of hurt pride.

I am one of those who many expected in the referendum campaign to be a fervent advocate of leaving. Until recently I also expected it of myself – even going so far as to speak to the Leave organisers at their HQ.

Most MPs have planted their flag on one side or the other, but I chose to hold back, and have been one of the few undeclared. The reason for doing so is genuine. Many voters are undecided and are yearning for enough information on which to base their decision. Many politicians are similarly agonising over where the national interest lies.

Today's world is markedly different from 40 years ago. Markets are more global and sophisticated, communism has collapsed, technological advance is staggering, and countries across the globe are more linked and interdependent than ever before. This means that turmoil in any one country has consequences for others.

The lure of Brexit is that it would deliver for the UK a tidy alternative to EU membership, and that restored self-government would empower our economic prospects and help insulate the UK from global difficulties. Our democracy would be purified, our border controls would solve the problem of immigration, and we would prosper as an economy untrammelled by others' rules. The trouble is: I don't think this is true.

Brexiteers have yet to offer a convincing picture of what a post-EU United Kingdom would look like. Statistics about the volume of trade we conduct with others are used to argue that business would continue unimpaired. Massive costs are attributed to the burden of EU regulation, and all would be better, if only we had the courage to leave. But I believe this logic is flawed.

It is a fundamental tenet of Conservative thought that we are realists who take the world as we find it – and that we reject utopian philosophies which offer a path towards perfection. Some say that leaving the EU is no different to resigning from the local cricket club and that we can simply return the UK to the status quo ante. The language of this theoretical paradise has become the Marxism of the Right. It is unwise, and is fraught with danger.

Disengaging from the EU, and dismantling its current agreements, would be massively complicated. The assurance that a new raft of trade agreements could quickly be whisked up looks like a fanciful pretence. We are being offered a promised land, with little promise.

Massive irritation surrounds the enforcement of EU directives. Large companies can readily lobby in Brussels: small ones less so. Having no say whatsoever on the EU rules, while still being subject to them, would, however, be a backward step for all of them. The over-implementation of directives is a home-grown problem, and ministers should more often tell civil servants what to do, rather than the other way round.

In terms of our broader national interest, we have our own currency, and we are not subject to the same loose borders as others within the EU. Immigration is far more complicated than many have admitted. The rules of asylum are governed by international treaties and not the EU; millions of UK citizens enjoy free movement and legal rights across the rest of the EU; and even the most ardent Eurosceptic will have benefited from the work of immigrants. Some, it would seem, are wholly against Polish workers in the UK, unless they are having their own taps fixed.

For me, however, the most compelling arguments are political. Our withdrawal from the EU would do nothing to help arrest the rise of the far right in Germany, prevent worrying developments in Turkey, or address economic pressures in Greece, Italy and Spain. We are all facing massive danger from the shores of the Mediterranean, with utter anarchy in Syria, fragile authority in Egypt, and a vacuum of power in Libya. Only politics can adequately address the deep challenges of the region.

Leaving the EU would weaken our influence over these massive issues, and pulling up the drawbridge would protect us less from regional threats. This is no time to withdraw from, and hence weaken, such an important multilateral structure as the EU. Whereas I used to think that our membership of the EU signified a loss of confidence in ourselves, I now think that leaving it would be an unforgivable expression of no confidence in our ability to affect the course of Europe's future. We cannot shape that vision by looking in history's rear-view mirror and opting to retrench.

Sir Alan Duncan is the MP for Rutland and Melton

ACKNOWLEDGEMENTS

There are many people who deserve thanks for helping me get these diaries into a publishable form, and for supporting me through the process of editing my account of these turbulent years.

First in this literary Oscars speech, I would like to thank my agent, Martin Redfern at Northbank, who after a chance meeting in 2019 suggested I should consider publishing a book on my time in government and was suitably excited when he learned I had kept a diary. He has been an enthusiastic champion for this project ever since, not just developing the pitch and securing a publisher, but offering his own wise comments on the most interesting themes of the text.

To help pull together the manuscript from the original source material I was fortunate to have the assistance of the historian Dr Nigel Fletcher, who I have known since his days as a Conservative political adviser when we were in opposition. He set about the task of rifling through my personal archive to locate original diary notes, appointment cards and correspondence, then cross-referenced these with what I had written to add extra detail and context. He has been a great help with assembling the full text, but would no doubt wish to dissociate himself from the more trenchant views it contains!

As we entered the publication process, I am of course hugely indebted to Arabella Pike and her team at HarperCollins for their work in turning my lengthy manuscript into the finished book. I now know why Arabella is considered the best in the business, and she has brought not just ruthless professionalism and experience, but also a huge amount of fun and mischievous laughter.

Peter James has been a diligent copy-editor, with the sort of commendable attention to detail (and punctuation) that I always wished to see in my civil servants. Iain Hunt has likewise proved a matchless organiser of the proofs as they graduated from start to finish. Jo Thompson has sorted through and helped select the photographs, while also navigating the minefields of legal and other clearances. As a former minister, I was required to submit the text to the Cabinet Office for comment, and to abide by the principles of the Radcliffe Report of 1976. This process necessarily involved a degree of negotiation about what should and should not be disclosed, and took up much time on both sides. I am grateful to the team at HarperCollins and their counterparts in the Cabinet Office who navigated this tricky territory.

I am very grateful to the friends and former colleagues who commented on the finished text, and all who offered kind words of encouragement.

My final and most profound thanks, however, go to James, who I suspect was pleased I had so much to keep me busy.

ABBREVIATIONS

BDS – boycott, disinvestment (or divestment) and sanctions (Israel)
BIOT – British Indian Overseas Territories
BVI – British Virgin Islands
CAABU – Council for Arab–British Understanding
CCHQ – Conservative Campaign Headquarters
CDS – Chief of the Defence Staff
CEPA – Comprehensive Enhanced Partnership Agreement
CFI – Conservative Friends of Israel
CHOGM – Commonwealth Heads of Government Meeting
CMEC – Conservative Middle East Council
DC – David Cameron
DCMS – Department for Digital, Culture, Media and Sports
DD – David Davis
DEFRA – Department for Environment, Food and Rural Affairs
DfID – Department for International Development
DT – Daily Telegraph
DipTel – Diplomatic Telegram
DUP – Democratic Unionist Party
DWP – Department for Work and Pensions
ERG – European Research Group
FAC – Foreign Affairs Committee
FCO – Foreign and Commonwealth Office
FM – Foreign Minister
FT – Financial Times
FTPA – Fixed-Term Parliaments Act

GCC – Gulf Cooperation Council
GCHQ – Government Communications Headquarters
HMA – HM Ambassador
HMG – HM Government
HMTQ – Her Majesty the Queen
HofC – House of Commons
IDS – Iain Duncan Smith
IISS – International Institute for Strategic Studies
IRGC – Iranian Revolutionary Guard Corps
ISC – Intelligence and Security Committee
KSA – Kingdom of Saudi Arabia
JCPOA – Joint Comprehensive Plan of Action (Iran nuclear deal)
JH – Jeremy Hunt
MbS – Mohammed bin Salman
MEP – Member of the European Parliament
MFA – Ministry of Foreign Affairs
MLA – Member of the Legislative Assembly (Falkland Islands)
MoD – Ministry of Defence
NICs – national insurance contributions
NSA – National Security Adviser (UK), National Security Advisor
   (US)
NSC – National Security Council
OCHA – Office for the Coordination of Humanitarian Affairs (UN)
ODA – Official Development Assistance
OFSTED – Office for Standards in Education
OPCW – Organisation for the Prohibition of Chemical Weapons
OTs – Overseas Territories
PCH – Portcullis House
PMQs – Prime Minister's Questions
PPS – Parliamentary Private Secretary
PS – Private Secretary
PUS – Permanent Under-Secretary
PUSS – Parliamentary Under-Secretary of State
R&M – Rutland and Melton
RIP – Regulation of Investigatory Powers (Bill/Act)
RUSI – Royal United Services Institute

SIS – Secret Intelligence Service (MI6)
SO24 – Standing Order 24 (emergency debate)
SofS – Secretary of State
SpAd – Special Adviser
TM – Theresa May
TRH – Their Royal Highnesses
UKIP – United Kingdom Independence Party
UKREP – UK Representation to the EU
UNSCR – UN Security Council Resolution
UNWRA – UN Work and Relief Agency
UQ – Urgent Question
WTO – World Trade Organisation

ILLUSTRATIONS

James and Noodle (*author's collection*)
Alan with the Vote Remain sign (*author's collection*)
MPs in the Commons Chamber (*author's collection*)
Boris Johnson reclining at his desk (*author's collection*)
Alan Duncan in his office at the FCO (*Patrick Tsui/Crown Copyright*)
Theresa May wins the Conservative Leadership election (*Carl Court/ Getty Images*)
Alan and Theresa May on plane (*author's collection*)
Alan with Angela Merkel (*Leon Neal/Getty Images*)
Alan with President Tusk, Prime Minister May and Sir Tim Barrow (*Thierry Monasse/Getty Images*)
Alan with Federica Mogherini (*Matthew Mirabelli/AFP via Getty Images*)
Blenheim Palace, awaiting the arrival of President Trump (*Dan Kitwood/Getty Images*)
Trump State Dinner at Buckingham Palace (*Dominic Lipinski/WPA Pool/Getty Images*)
The Queen of England and King of Bahrain (*author's collection*)
Signature of the UK/Oman Comprehensive Agreement (*author's collection*)
Alan at the Gibraltar National Day rally (*Photo by Matt Cardy/Getty Images*)
Alan on the steps of Number 10 (*Mark Kerrison/Alamy Live News*)
Alan with Prince Charles (*author's collection*)
Alan with Johnson on the day Article 50 was triggered (*Jack Taylor/ Getty Images*)

Alan with Johnson and Jean-Claude Juncker (*author's collection*)

Alan with Mike Pompeo (*Atilgan Ozdil/Anadolu Agency/Getty Images*)

Alan speaking at the UN Security Council (*Atilgan Ozdil/Anadolu Agency/Getty Images*)

Alan arriving at the OSCE summit (*Alexander Koerner/Getty Images*)

Preparing Johnson's first party conference speech (*author's collection*)

Alan with Sir Nicholas Soames (*author's collection*)

Priti Patel (*Ben Pruchnie/Getty Images*)

John Bercow (*House of Commons/PA Archive/PA Images*)

Listening to news coverage of the leadership contest with Team TM (*author's collection*)

Theresa with Philip May in her room at the House of Commons awaiting the result of the second ballot (*author's collection*)

Theresa May and other MPs in the Smoking Room (*author's collection*)

With Johnson and António Guterres (*Pierre Albouy/AFP via Getty Images*)

At the presentation of a dispatch box to outgoing US Secretary of State John Kerry (*author's collection*)

With HM Sultan Qaboos of Oman (*author's collection*)

The Sultan's Privy Council (*author's collection*)

Alan and James at Royal Ascot (*Max Mumby/Indigo/Getty Images*)

Signage outside the FCO (*author's collection*)

INDEX